Suzanne Pritchard
(310) 455-3524

Senior Editor: Virginia C. Lanigan
Editorial Assistant: Kris Lamarre
Senior Marketing Manager: Kathy Hunter
Production Administrator: Deborah Brown
Editorial-Production Service: Susan McNally
Text Design and Electronic Composition: Denise Hoffman
Composition Buyer: Linda Cox
Manufacturing Buyer: Suzanne Lareau
Cover Administrator: Linda Knowles
Copy Editor: Susanna Brougham
Photo Director: Susan Duane

Copyright © 1998 by Allyn and Bacon
A Viacom Company
160 Gould Street
Needham Heights, MA 02194

Internet: www.abacon.com
America Online: keyword: College Online

Library of Congress Cataloging-in-Publication Data

Graves, Michael F.
    Teaching reading in the 21st century / Michael F. Graves, Connie
Juel, Bonnie B. Graves.
       p.   cm.
    ISBN 0–205–26367–4
    1. Reading (Elementary)   I. Juel, Connie.   II. Graves, Bonnie B.
III. Title
LB1573.G656   1997
372.4—dc21   97–44674
                                                 CIP

Printed in the United States of America
10 9 8 7 6 5 4 3 2 1 RRD 04 03 02 01 00 99 98 97

Text Credits: p. 111 from *Too Many Tamales* by Gary Soto, text copyright © 1993 by Gary Soto. Reprinted by permission of G. P. Putnam's Sons. p. 111 from *Teeny Tiny* retold by Jill Bennett, text copyright © 1986 by Jill Bennett. Reprinted with permission of G. P. Putnam's Sons. p. 150 from *Spin a Soft Black* Poem by Nikki Giovanni. Copyright © 1971, 1985 by Nikki Giovanni. Reprinted by permission of Farrar, Strauss, & Giroux, Inc.

Photo Credits: Will Faller: pp. xx, 7, 38, 76, 134, 144, 157, 184, 247, 301, 317, 344, 361, 401, 432, 505, 509, 538; Brian Smith: pp. 22, 84, 377, 387, 532, 536, 557, 562; Will Hart: pp. 43, 71, 90, 192, 226, 233, 252, 254, 338, 354, 384, 456, 476, 495, 555; Stephen Marks: pp. 123, 173; Library of Congress: p. 437; Corbis/Bettmann: p. 462; Jim Pickerell: p. 535; Supplied by authors: pp. 281, 567, 574.

Illustrations on pages 41, 75, 101, 118, 156, 175, 188, 209, 315, 319, 395, 422, 576 by Nathan Cherry; other illustrations and technical art by Blue Moon Studio.

Teaching Reading

in the 21st Century

Michael F. Graves

Connie Juel

Bonnie B. Graves

Allyn and Bacon

Boston ■ London ■ Toronto ■ Sydney ■ Tokyo ■ Singapore

*To Susan Jones, who, in her 25 years of teaching,
has led nearly 1,000 second-graders toward critical literacy—
and to the more than 2 million other elementary and middle-grade
teachers, who each day nurture nearly 40 million students
toward this same goal*

contents

chapter three

Emergent Literacy   84

chapter four

Word Recognition   134

chapter seven

Guiding Students Toward Independence in Reading   290

chapter eight

Teaching for Understanding in Content Areas   338

chapter nine

Writing and Reading   384

chapter twelve

Classroom Portraits   532

additional features

in the classroom

In the Classroom offers examples of classroom interaction.

bibliographies

Annotated Bibliographies of Children's Literature are useful in teaching literacy skills and topics.

preface

The past three decades have been tremendously exciting and productive ones in reading education. Theoreticians, teachers, and researchers representing a variety of perspectives have broadened and enriched our conception of reading and readers. Cognitive psychologists have made great strides in revealing the mental processes underlying skilled reading and learning to read. Constructivists have appropriately emphasized the active, constructive nature of reading and the frequent subjectivity of our interpretations. Whole-language theorists have made clear the importance of providing children with intact and authentic texts, recognizing children's strengths and building on those strengths, and treating each child with the dignity he or she deserves. Advocates of literature-based instruction have shown us the beauty and power of quality literature and have forcefully argued for making quality literature a cornerstone of the reading program. Educators representing each of these perspectives and many others have come to recognize the strength of diversity and discovered powerful ways of capitalizing on the diversity of today's classrooms. And teachers and researchers representing various theoretical perspectives and research orientations have collaborated to help us really understand classrooms and discover ways in which we can assist all children in reaching their full potential as readers and as caring and productive members of society.

Over these same three decades, we have learned a tremendous amount about how to provide instruction and environments that support and nurture children's growing literacy. We have learned to build on young children's emergent literacy, capitalizing on the knowledge and skills that every child brings to the classroom. We now understand the importance of fostering children's phonemic awareness and their competence in using our alphabetic writing system, and we have validated powerful ways of strengthening children's skills in these areas. We know a lot about how to assist children in putting the right amount of emphasis on the text and appropriately using their prior knowledge in constructing meaning. We have discovered rich, powerful, and exciting ways of teaching vocabulary; and we realize how important it is for students to become adept at learning words on their own and to develop an interest in words. We have developed and validated a number of procedures for assisting students in comprehending and learning from what they read. We have also validated procedures for teaching children to be self-reliant, strategic readers, who exercise their metacognitive skills as they read. We recognize the importance of students' internalizing a deep and thorough understanding of what they read, and we have developed powerful ways of fostering this deep understanding. We have discovered a wealth of multicultural literature that we can use in the classroom to recognize and affirm all students' cultural heritage. And we have developed a variety of authentic ways of assessing students' growing literacy—ways that provide teachers with the insights they need to make instructional decisions.

Paralleling our increased understanding of the reading process and our growing ability to design effective instruction, there has been a significant shift in reading education practices in schools—a shift toward more open, more holistic, and more student-centered practices. Along with this shift has come a growing realization that there is no single road to literacy. To reach his or her full potential as a reader, each child will follow a somewhat different path, but all children will require a variety of experiences and skills. Neither phonemic awareness, nor phonics, nor a wealth of quality literature, nor a nurturing environment is by itself sufficient to lead most children to literacy. Children need a multifaceted and balanced literacy curriculum.

Along with this shift to a more holistic orientation has come also the growing realization of the importance of fostering students' deep and lasting understanding of what they read. Today, schools must go beyond simply presenting students with information. They must ensure that students retain important information, understand topics deeply, and actively use the knowledge they gain. A major goal of any reading program must be critical literacy—the use of language for thinking, problem solving, and communicating. For that reason, critical literacy is the major goal of the curriculum and instruction we elaborate on throughout this book.

On the flyleaf of Alberto Manguel's *A History of Reading* (1996) appears this poetic description of learning to read:

> *At one magical instant in your early childhood, the page of a book—that string of confused, alien ciphers—shivered into meaning. Words spoke to you, gave up their secrets; at that moment, whole universes opened. You became, irrevocably, a reader.*

Assisting each and every child in becoming "irrevocably a reader" is a goal we all share. So too is assisting each and every child in reaching the challenging goal of critical literacy. Of course, these goals will not be achieved in a "magical instant." They will be achieved over time—beginning before children enter school and continuing throughout the elementary grades and beyond. They will be achieved because a succession of competent and caring teachers immerse children in a balanced curriculum, provide them with powerful instruction, and instill in them the desire to read. *Teaching Reading in the 21st Century* is our very best effort to give teachers the knowledge and skills they need to lead all children to become lifelong readers and to attain the critical literacy necessary in today's, and tomorrow's, world.

THE ORGANIZATION AND FEATURES OF THIS BOOK

This book is divided into twelve chapters. Chapters 1 and 2—Reading and Learning to Read and Reading Instruction—deal with general concepts and principles that are applied throughout the book. These include theories of the reading process, a description of the critical literacy curriculum, instructional principles, and descriptions of current approaches to reading instruction. Chapters 3 and 4—Emergent Literacy and Word Recognition—deal with topics that are particularly important in the primary grades. These include the importance of being read to, instruction that fosters emerging literacy, the importance of recognizing printed words, and word recognition instruction.

Chapters 5–8 discuss topics that are crucial at all grade levels. Chapter 5—Vocabulary Development—describes four approaches to building students' vocabularies: wide reading, teaching individual words, teaching word-learning strategies, and fostering word consciousness. Chapter 6—Scaffolding Students' Comprehension of Text: Teacher-Directed Approaches—describes pre-, during, and postreading activities that teachers can use to help students understand and learn from what they read. Chapter 7—Guiding Students Toward Independence in Reading—details ways of teaching students comprehension strategies and ways of encouraging independent reading. And Chapter 8—Teaching for Understanding in Content Areas—discusses three approaches to helping students develop deep and lasting understanding of what they read.

Chapters 9–11 deal with three topics of special importance. Chapter 9—Writing and Reading—discusses the reading-writing relationship and ways to use writing to foster students' literacy development. In Chapter 10—Literacy Instruction for Non-Native Speakers of English—Elizabeth Bernhardt and Michael Kamil discuss what it means to read a second language and describe instructional techniques to help students whose first language is not English become confident and competent in reading English. In Chapter 11—Classroom Assessment—Robert Calfee describes test-based and teacher-based approaches to assessment, emphasizing the sorts of classroom assessment that teachers can readily use in making instructional decisions.

Finally, Chapter 12—Classroom Portraits—presents in-depth scenarios of reading instruction at three grade levels, illustrating how the principles and methods discussed throughout this book can be applied in real classrooms.

We have designed each chapter to make reading and learning as interesting, effective, and efficient as possible. Most chapters have the same components and the same organization.

Chapters begin with a brief personal statement or scenario to spark interest in the topic of the chapter and suggest one or more of its major themes. Next comes a chapter overview, a visual layout of the major sections of the chapter. Following the overview is the body of the chapter, usually consisting of two to four main sections and a number of subsections. After this comes a section titled Special Needs and Special Talents. Here, we look back at the chapter and ask if there is more that can be done to ensure that all students—those who move more quickly than their peers, those who move less quickly, and those whose experiences and schemata differ from those of many of their peers—achieve success in the areas covered in the chapter. Finally, the last regular section in the chapter is titled Concluding Remarks and includes a summary and a few comments on the chapter.

In addition to these regular sections, chapters include a number of additional features. Samples of children's work illustrate their growth toward critical literacy. Books boxes provide annotated lists of children's trade literature useful in teaching particular literacy skills and topics. Frequent interjection of teachers' "voices" creates a feel for the classroom. In the Classroom features offer a variety of examples of classroom interactions—student–teacher dialogues, vignettes, and sample lessons—designed to nurture students toward critical literacy. Engaging quotations appear in the margins to highlight vital ideas. And Reflection and Application features, which follow major sections of the text, give readers opportunities to review and try out some of the central ideas presented.

Chapters end with three standard features. The first one, Extending Learning, invites readers to apply and elaborate on some of the chapter's major ideas by observing classrooms, talking with parents and teachers, or further investigating a particular topic. Following this, briefly annotated References suggest sources that support, explain, or extend ideas presented in the chapter. Finally, a section titled Children's Literature provides citations and brief annotations of the selections mentioned in the chapter and other sources of children's literature.

ACKNOWLEDGMENTS

Of course, no project of this magnitude is ever begun, sustained, or completed without the help, encouragement, good ideas, and wise counsel of many individuals.

We are greatly indebted to

- our editor, Virginia Lanigan, who had the faith in our initial vision to take this project on, as well as Denise Hoffman, Susan McNally, Susanna Brougham, Kris Lamarre, and Nihad Farooq for their assistance in the development and production of this book.
- all the individuals who granted us permission to cite their work and reproduce their materials in this text.

- the reviewers who read the manuscript and gave us invaluable feedback: Peter Hasselriss, University of Missouri-Columbia; Timothy Rasinski, Kent State University; Susan Tancock, Ball State University; Peter Afflerbach, University of Maryland; Judythe Patberg, The University of Toledo/Sylvania Schools; Maureen Prenn, Mankato State University; Gail Singleton Taylor, Old Dominion University; and Penny Freppon, University of Cincinnati.

- the teachers, researchers, and teacher educators whose names you will see mentioned on nearly every page of this text, especially David Carberry, who contributed an extended portrait of his class, and Mark Aulls, Ann Beecher, Barbara Brunetti, Jerry Brunetti, Susan Jones, Stephen Koziol, Judy Peacock, Lynn Richards, Randall Ryder, Wayne Slater, Margo Sorenson, Kelly Spies, and Diann Stone. Each lent her or his time and very special talents to this project.

- our colleagues at the University of Minnesota and the University of Virginia, with special thanks to Richard Beach, Peter DeWitz, Felipe Golez, Simon Hooper, Dianne Monson, Margaret Phinney, Diane Tedick, and Susan Watts, whose scholarship and dedication to the profession are without equal.

- our colleagues at Stanford University—Robert Calfee for his outstanding chapter on assessment and Elizabeth Bernhardt and Michael Kamil for their outstanding chapter on reading in a second language.

- our students and teachers from kindergarten through graduate school, who over the years have inspired our thinking and contributed significantly to the ideas you will read about in this text.

- friends and family, who listened, encouraged, and sustained us throughout this lengthy, and at times exhausting, endeavor, especially Julie Graves, a molecular-biologist/artist who helped design some of the drawings, and Erin Graves, a psychology major at Stanford who never made us feel guilty of parental neglect while completing this project.

- to you, our reader, without whom this work would have neither meaning nor life, for the meaning and the purpose of this whole endeavor lies in the transaction that takes place between you and the words on the pages of this text. It is our sincere hope that the ideas we present here will equip and inspire you to create and nurture lifelong readers.

chapter one

Reading and Learning to Read

*L*auren, a college sophomore, picks up a novel from the kitchen table and begins reading it. She pours herself a cup of coffee and moves to a chair in the living room. Once seated, she continues to read, occasionally sipping coffee and from time to time adjusting her position in the chair. To an observer, her reading appears effortless, the words and their meanings seem to pass automatically from the text to her mind.

But is the observer's perception correct? Is accomplished reading an effortless and rather passive activity? The answer is a very definite no. To be sure, a skilled reader such as Lauren has automated some aspects of reading—she scans left to right, moves her eyes down the page, and, most importantly, recognizes the vast majority of words she encounters without conscious attention.

But, reading is, in many ways, very demanding. Meaning does not rise effortlessly from the page to the reader's mind but is, instead, actively constructed by the reader based on prior knowledge and experience and various sorts of perceptual and cognitive processing. Interpreting sentences, combining the meanings of sentences to construct meaning for paragraphs and larger units, making the numerous inferences that even the

CHAPTER OVERVIEW

most straightforward text requires, and remedying comprehension problems when they occur all require active mental processing. If Lauren is not actively involved in this constructive process—if Lauren's mind wanders or her thoughts turn to other matters—she will find herself having read several pages of text and having understood nothing—a phenomenon all of us have experienced.

The misleading picture of reading as a passive activity that Lauren presents is accentuated by the fact that she is reading a novel, a narrative, probably simply to enjoy it. Once Lauren turns to reading informational material, exposition, to learn new information, even as an accomplished reader, she will probably show more active behavior—take notes, underline a critical phrase, or pause to mull over and make sense of a perplexing concept.

As the developing reader proceeds through school and eventually attains the competence Lauren has, the reader will find that active processing is essential for both sorts of reading, but is particularly crucial for learning from expository material.

THE READING PROCESS

Why should you care about the reading process? Why is it vital to develop a deep understanding of it? The answer is straightforward. Regardless of what you learn about the specifics of teaching reading from this text, your university courses, and in-service sessions, conferences, and discussions with other teachers, much of what you do in the classroom will result from your personal understanding of the reading process. The number of teaching options you have is so great, the needs of different students so diverse, and the specifics of a particular teaching situation so unique, that it is impossible to anticipate the many decisions about literacy instruction that you will make each day. But understanding the mental processes involved as a mature or budding reader actually reads can prepare you to make wise choices. Though not a simple task, developing an understanding of the reading process is vital to becoming an effective reading teacher and well worth the time and effort you will spend on it.

Over the past 30 years, a widely accepted, richly elaborated, and strongly supported view of the reading process has emerged: the cognitive–constructivist view of reading. This construct forms the foundation of the approach to reading presented in this book. In the following section, we give an overview of this concept. In the section following that one, we explain several theories that elaborate, complement, and supplement it.

Everything should be as simple as it can be but no simpler.

—*Albert Einstein*

The Cognitive–Constructivist View of Reading

The cognitive–constructivist view of reading emphasizes that reading is a process in which the reader actively searches for meaning in what she reads. This search for meaning depends very heavily on the reader's having an existing store of knowledge, or schemata, that she draws on in that search for meaning, and the active contribution of the reader is significant enough to justify the assertion that she actually constructs the meaning she arrives at in reading.

For example, as Lauren reads the sentence "Cynthia swung the bottle against the bow, and the smiling crowd cheered enthusiastically" in her novel, her background knowledge and active processing of the text enable her to construct a meaning much fuller than this single sentence might seem to convey. She is quite certain that the text describes a ship-christening scene. Additionally, she can infer that the bottle contains champagne (because that's what is used to christen things), that the boat or ship being christened is somehow important (because there is a large crowd gathered), and that the weather is not cold and wet (because the crowd is smiling and enthusiastic). All this, and much more, can come from that single sentence, when combined with Lauren's background knowledge and active processing. Notice how teacher Jeffrey Frazer highlights this use of background knowledge and encourages active processing with his second-graders:

IN THE CLASSROOM
Using Background Knowledge

Jeffrey Frazer wrote the first sentence from Juanita Havill's *Jamaica and Brianna* on the board:

> *"Do I have to wear Ossie's boots?" Jamaica asked her mother.*

He read the sentence aloud to his second-graders and then said, "Let's think about what this sentence says. Can you tell me what it means?"

Angelica: Jamaica doesn't want to wear Ossie's boots.

Mr. Frazer: What makes you think she doesn't want to wear them?

Angelica: 'Cause that's what I say to my mom if I don't want to do something. "Do I have to?" (Angelica says this in a whiny voice, and the kids laugh.)

Mr. Frazer: Who do you think Ossie is?

Paul: Her brother.

Mr. Frazer: Why her brother?

Ramond: Ossie doesn't sound like a girl's name to me!

Mr. Frazer: Good point! Why would Jamaica's mom tell her she had to wear her brother's boots?

Tanya: Probably she lost her own boots.

Ramond: Or maybe her feet got too big!

Mr. Frazer: Very good thinking. So tell me, what do you know about this story just from this one sentence?

Angelica: Jamaica doesn't have any boots and she doesn't want to wear her brother's old boots, but her mom wants her to!

As the preceding dialogue illustrates, Mr. Frazer is helping his students realize that readers actively search for meaning in what they read, and that the meaning they construct from a text depends on their own knowledge about the world and its conventions.

The Cognitive Orientation

The earliest and strongest influence behind this view comes from cognitive psychology, the psychological orientation that became the main point of view of American psychology beginning in the 1960s (Gardner, 1985). Cognitive psychology can perhaps be best understood in comparison to behaviorism, which was the dominant psychological orientation in the United States from about 1930 to about 1970 and that had a huge effect on the reading instruction of that period and continues to have some influence today. Behaviorist psychologists viewed people as rather passive respondents to their environment and gave little attention to the mind and its role in learning. In fact, behaviorists denied the concept of mind, and attempts to discover "what goes on under the skin were made cautiously, if at all" (Anderson, Sprio, & Montegue, 1977, p. ix). In the behaviorist view, reading was a rather passive process in which the information on a page of text was somehow absorbed by the reader as her eyes scanned the page.

Beginning in the 1960s, behaviorism began to be replaced by the cognitive orientation. Cognitive psychologists view the mind as central to learning and the study of learners' thought processes as a central focus of their work. They also view learners as active participants, who act on, rather than simply respond to, their external environment as they learn. In the cognitive view, reading is very much an active process in which the meaning the reader gleans from a text is heavily influenced by the cognitive work that she puts into the reading process. Both the beginning reader—who we might observe carefully sounding out words as she reads orally, and the accomplished reader such as Lauren, who appears to be effortlessly absorbing the contents of the novel she is reading—are in fact actively engaged in making meaning from the text. The major differences between the cognitive and behaviorist orientations are summarized in Figure 1.1.

Schema

The concept of schema, the second influence on the view of the reading process we are describing, is closely related to the cognitive orientation. In fact, schema theory is one of the central concepts of cognitive psychology. Schema theory is concerned with knowledge, particularly with the way knowledge is represented in our minds and the importance of prior knowledge to learning something new. According to the theory, knowledge is packaged in organized structures termed schemata. David Rumelhart (1980) states that schemata constitute our knowledge about "objects, situations, events, sequences of events, actions, and sequences of actions" (p. 34). We have schemata for objects such as a house, for situations such as being in a class, for events such as going to a football game, and for sequences of events

If I were to reduce the whole of educational psychology to a single statement, it would be this: Ascertain what the child knows, and teach him accordingly.

—David Ausabel
Educational Psychologist

Cognitive Psychology	Behaviorism
The mind is an appropriate object of study, and studying its internal workings can yield useful insights.	Psychology should be concerned solely with overt behavior.
Reading and learning are active processes that demand an active learner.	Reading and learning are passive processes.
The meaning one gleans from a text involves the interaction of the knowledge and skills of the reader and the message conveyed by the text.	The meaning of a text is largely contained in the text itself, and the reader passively absorbs it.

FIGURE 1.1 *Some Major Differences Between Cognitive Psychology and Behaviorism*

such as getting up, eating, showering, and going to work. We interpret our experiences—whether direct encounters with the world or vicarious experiences gained through reading—by comparing and, in most cases, matching those experiences to existing schemata. In other words, we make sense of what we read and of our experiences more generally by a tacit process that in essence tells us "Ah ha. This is an instance of such and such."

Figure 1.2 suggests the wealth of knowledge that Maggie, and every human being, internalizes. But it only *suggests* that wealth. We could fill pages, perhaps a book, with a list of Maggie's schemata. However, while our figure and list suggest the huge number of schemata Maggie has internalized, they do not capture another crucial feature of schemata. Our schemata are related to each other and constitute a vast and elaborate network of interrelationships. To give just a very brief sample of the legion of interrelationships that exist, Maggie's schema for *house* is related to her schema for *neighborhood*, in that her house is part of her neighborhood; and it is also related to her schema for *family*, in that her family lives in her house; at the same time, her schema for *house* is related to her schema for *tepee* because both houses and tepees are dwellings.

One very important consequence of readers having these rich, internalized networks of schemata is that, once a particular schema is evoked, a huge store of knowledge becomes instantly available. Suppose a student is reading a story and comes across the sentence "Mark stopped at McDonald's on the way home." Immediately, her schema for fast-food restaurants provides her with a wealth of information: Mark ordered and picked up his food at the counter; he ordered something like a burger or fries or a malt—not steak or lobster; he had to pay for his food, but not too much; he seated himself in the restaurant or perhaps took his food somewhere else to eat it; and he

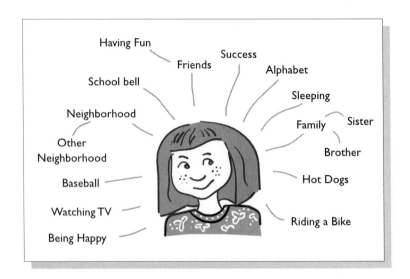

FIGURE 1.2 *A Few of Maggie's Schemata*

probably ate it fairly rapidly. Information such as this, and often richer bundles of information, become available to us as soon as we evoke a schema for something we are reading or hearing or viewing.

Right now, you are building a schema for schemata; and the more you learn about schemata, the easier it will be for you to learn even more about them. Both what we learn and the ease or difficulty of learning it are heavily influenced by our schemata. The more we know about something, the easier it will be to deal with that topic and learn more about it. Schemata assist the reader in initially making sense of what she reads, relating newly acquired information to prior knowledge, determining the relative importance of information in a text, making inferences, and remembering (Anderson & Pearson, 1984).

Three sorts of schemata that children possess to varying degrees are particularly important to reading instruction—knowledge of the world and its conventions, knowledge about the way different types of texts are organized, and knowledge of subject matter content (Adams & Bruce, 1982).

Knowledge of the World and Its Conventions. Each of us—and this includes young children just learning to read—has internalized a huge store of knowledge about the makeup of families, about daily events such as children going to and returning from school and adults going to and returning from work, about institutions such as churches and the government, about holidays such as Memorial Day and Martin Luther King's Birthday, about places such as zoos and the beach, and about a multitude of other events, places, institutions, objects, and patterns of behavior. Children acquire a good deal of this knowledge simply through life experience. This knowledge generally

> Without prior knowledge, a complex object such as a text is not just difficult to interpret; strictly speaking, it is meaningless.
>
> —Marilyn Adams and Bertrand Bruce Educational Researchers

serves students well in understanding narratives—stories, plays, and narrative nonfiction such as biographies and novels—because narratives mirror many facets of everyday experience. However, if children have grown up in a culture different from that depicted in the narrative, then the conventions familiar to them may not help them understand its content. They will need some help developing appropriate schemata.

Of course, the diversity represented in most of today's classrooms and in our society makes it critical to provide children with a broad array of reading selections that represent the diversity of our society and of the world beyond our borders. Also, if your classroom includes students representing several cultural backgrounds, you will want to take into account students' cultural backgrounds when you choose reading selections and deliberately choose selections particularly appropriate for each of the cultural groups represented in the class. This approach will build new clusters of schemata for all students, while enhancing each student's appreciation of her own traditions as well as those of other people.

Knowledge About the Way Different Types of Text are Organized. Knowledge about the way different types of text are organized is neither as equally distributed across students nor as fully developed in young children as is general knowledge of the world. Most children have fairly well developed schemata for the organization of narratives because most narratives mirror the temporal order of the world they live in and most narratives have a similar structure. They have a beginning, a middle, and an ending; most have characters and a plot that includes some sort of complication; and most end by resolving the complication. Moreover, children who have had the rich experience of being read to and having discussed books and stories with their parents or others enter school with rich narrative schemata. And most students further develop such schemata during the primary grades because they listen to and read a lot of narratives in school.

However, the situation is quite different with expository text—the informational material students encounter in social studies, math, science, health, and the like. Unfortunately, most young children do not have well developed schemata for the structure of expository material. This is true because children often have not had much experience with expository material, because expository material can have a

Most children have fairly well-developed schemata for the organization of narratives, but not for the structure of expository texts.

number of different structures, and because a good deal of the expository material children read is not very well structured. Students will benefit from additional help in dealing with these texts.

Knowledge About the Content of Specific Subjects.   The third sort of schemata that children possess to varying degrees are schemata for the content of various subjects—science, history, geography, and so on. Most of this knowledge does not come from life experience; it comes from formal schooling. Each year, schools build students' knowledge in these areas. But because students often lack both content schemata and schemata for the expository forms in which most content information is conveyed, they will often need assistance in reading informational material.

Georgia Duncan, a teacher in a combination second- and third-grade class, finds it helpful to provide her students with a graphic organizer such as that shown in Figure 1.3 before they read certain informational texts.

I have found that my second- and third-graders, even the most adept readers among them, profit from using graphic organizers before they read informational books. I look at how the information is organized in a text, for instance, Gail Gibbons's book *Whales*. Then I develop a graphic organizer presenting that information and put it on either a white board or a transparency. Using the graphic organizer as a guide, we talk about the information and how it's organized. For example, Gibbons begins and ends the book by giving general information about whales—where they are found, what they look like, the past and future of whales. In between she divides whales into two types—toothed and non-toothed—and lists and describes the whales within these two major categories. Giving students information on the topics and structure of the text puts schemata in place for both the concepts presented in the chapter and the organization of the chapter.

Georgia Duncan, Second- and Third-Grade Teacher

Constructivism

Constructivism, the third influence on the view of the reading process we are describing here, has many roots and many branches (Phillips, 1995), being in fact a philosophical (von Glaserfeld, 1995), political (Searle, 1993), and social (Gergen, 1985) construct as well as a psychological one. Here, we use the term in its psychological sense. Used in this sense, constructivism serves to emphasize a point already made and to introduce an additional point. Constructivism emphasizes the fact that comprehending a text is very much an active, constructive process.

Consider this metaphor: The author of a text, like the architect who draws a blueprint, has created a representation of her ideas. The reader, like the builder, must take this representation and construct something based on

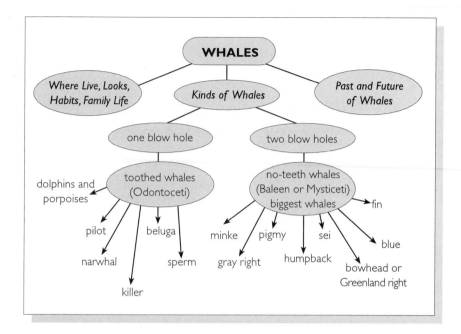

it. Much like the builder must construct a house, the reader must construct meaning. Constructivists often use the phrase "making meaning" to emphasize the reader's active role in comprehending texts. Students cannot just passively absorb meaning from texts. A truly passive reading would leave the reader simply having turned the pages. Instead, readers must actively engage with the text, consider what they are reading, and link the information they are gleaning from the text with ideas, topics, and events they are already familiar with. Moreover, the more difficult a text becomes for students—the more new and challenging information it presents—the more actively engaged readers must be.

In addition to emphasizing the active nature of reading, constructivism holds that the meaning one constructs from a text is subjective—the result of one particular reader's processing of the text. Just as no two builders will construct exactly the same house from a blueprint, so no two readers will construct exactly the same meaning from a text. Each reader is influenced by the sum total of her experience as well as by her unique intellectual makeup. Because of this, each reader constructs a somewhat different interpretation of the text, the text as she conceptualizes it (von Glaserfeld, 1984). The three student journal entries listed here illustrate this concept. All three students were given the same prompt for the picture book *Mama Bear* by Chyng Feng Sun. The story tells of a girl who bakes and sells almond cookies in order to earn enough money to buy a large, expensive stuffed bear for

But who shall be the master? The writer or the reader?

—*Denis Diderot*
Philosopher, Writer,
and Critic

Christmas because she thinks it will help keep her and her mother warm. The students were asked to respond to this question: "What did Mei-Mei want most for Christmas?" Each answer is, of course, correct, yet points up a different perspective on the story.

Kaiya: **Mei-Mei wanted a bear for Christmas.**

Lawrence: *Mei-Mei wanted her mother to be happy.*

Ali: *Mei-Mei wanted to be warm most of all*

Having noted that constructivism emphasizes the subjectivity of meaning, we want to also note that different texts differ dramatically in how much they constrain it (Stanovich, 1994). An abstract poem may prompt many appropriate interpretations, but a manual on how to install new software should prompt only one. Returning to our blueprint metaphor, we might describe the abstract poem as a sketch the author has drawn, while the computer manual presents a very detailed plan. In between these two extremes lies a range of texts that invite various degrees of individual interpretation. However, when reading straightforward stories and a good deal of informational material, most readers will construct quite similar meanings for what they read.

As we noted in beginning this section, constructivism is a social construct as well as a psychological one. Most constructivists emphasize that the social world in which we live heavily influences the meaning that we derive from our experiences, including our experiences with text. Thus, constructivism strongly supports the inclusion of a variety of sorts of discussion and group work as part of reading and learning (Calfee & Patrick, 1995).

All in all, the cognitive–constructivist view of the reading process conceives of the reader as an actively engaged participant who uses a variety of sorts of prior knowledge in constructing meaning for what she reads. Neither the meaning of the novel Lauren is reading nor the meaning of any other text simply springs into the reader's head.

> Reading is, at all stages, a form of problem solving in which readers adapt to their environment (as per Piaget) through the processes of assimilation and accomodation.
>
> —*Jean Chall*
> *Educational Researcher*

Reflection AND Application

As we have just explained, a central tenet of the view of the reading process that underlies this book is that comprehension is an active, constructive process. What that means is that, if you are to really understand the ideas we present, remember them, and use them in your teaching, you must mentally manipulate them in some way. To help you do this, we include Reflection and Application sections periodically throughout the text. Ideally, as constructivist principles suggest, you will discuss your responses with others—a study group, your class, or your course instructor.

1. Suppose that one teacher taught the word *relax* by simply saying, "*Relax* means to loosen up," while another taught it by having students view several pictures of people relaxing, having them assume relaxing positions themselves, and then having them talk about situations in which they have felt comfortable and relaxed. Explain how one teacher is demonstrating a behaviorist perspective and the other a cognitive perspective.

2. Identify a schema that both inner-city students and suburban students are likely to have, one that inner-city students are likely to have but suburban students might lack, and one that suburban students are likely to have but inner-city students might lack. Why do certain groups of students share some schemata but not others?

3. Name a text for which students are likely to construct very similar meanings, a text for which they are likely to construct quite different meanings, and a text for which they are likely to construct meanings that have both similarities and differences. What characteristics of these texts produce the similar or dissimilar meanings?

Concepts That Elaborate and Complement the Cognitive–Constructivist View

Here, we consider three concepts that extend this view of the reading process and that underlie the instructional procedures we will present throughout the text. These are the interactive model of reading, automaticity, and metacognition

The Interactive Model of Reading

Schema theory emphasizes the importance of the reader's knowledge in understanding a text. The interactive model of reading, on the other hand, reminds us that both the reader and the text play important roles in reading. Interactive models can perhaps be best understood when contrasted to what have been called "bottom-up" and "top-down" models, a contrast illustrated in Figure 1.4. Bottom-up models assume that the text is singularly important and that the reader processes text by first recognizing lower-level units and then repeatedly synthesizing lower-level units into more complex units. In this view, the reader might first perceive letters, then synthesize several let-

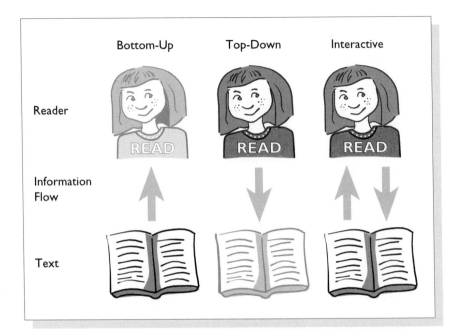

FIGURE 1.4 *Bottom-Up, Top-Down, and Interactive Models of Reading*

ters to form words, then synthesize several words to form a phrase, and so on. Processing operates in a single direction—from the text to the reader.

Top-down models are just the opposite of bottom-up models. Top-down models assume that the reader is singularly important and processes text by first hypothesizing about the content of the text and then selectively sampling the text to confirm or refute her hypothesis. In this view, the reading process begins with the highest-level unit possible—meaning in the mind of the reader—and deals with lower-level units, for example words, only to a limited extent. Again, processing operates in a single direction—but in the top-down perspective that view is from the reader to the text.

As described by Rumelhart's (1977) interactive model (which is consistent with the view of the reading process presented here), processing is neither exclusively top-down nor exclusively bottom-up. Instead, the reader arrives at her understanding of a text by simultaneously synthesizing information from a variety of sources. These include word-level knowledge, syntactic knowledge, and various sorts of schemata she has internalized.

Good readers simultaneously rely on the text and on their background knowledge as they construct meaning. We as teachers need to provide them with the sorts of texts and tasks that promote this interplay of text and background knowledge. For example, giving students a selection that deals with a largely unfamiliar topic and that includes a lot of difficult vocabulary may force them to give undue attention to the individual words and to neglect summoning up their prior knowledge to bear on their understanding of the text. More seriously, having students do a lot of oral reading, emphasizing their being one hundred percent correct in their oral reading, and putting them in a position where they face a penalty for being incorrect will almost certainly force them to give undue attention to the text and focus on words and letters rather than sentences, paragraphs, and ideas. For example, when less-able students read orally in front of their peers without adequate preparation, they will tend to focus on correctly pronouncing individual words and thus give little attention to meaning.

Conversely, having children read only silently and providing no follow-up to what they read, or having them repeatedly engage in postreading discussions that are only vaguely related to what they read may encourage students to give too little attention to the specific details of the text itself. In such situations, some students may largely ignore the words and sentences on the page, guess at the meaning of what they are reading, and make little use of the text in confirming their guesses. For example, giving students a steady diet of individualized reading may not provide them with sufficient opportunities to check their understanding of what they have read with you or with other students, and without such checks they may fall into a habit of guessing.

Figure 1.5 depicts situations that encourage too much or too little attention to the text. Again, an appropriate balance of attention to the text itself and to prior knowledge is the goal.

Situation	Result
Selection with an unfamiliar topic and difficult vocabulary	The reader will give too much attention to individual words and neglect to use prior knowledge to help in understanding the text.
Too much oral reading with an emphasis on being correct and a penalty for being incorrect	The reader will focus on individual words and letters, rather than on sentences, paragraphs, and ideas.
A less-able student reading orally in front of peers	The reader will focus attention on correctly pronouncing individual words and give little attention to meaning.
Only silent reading with no postreading follow-up discussion	The reader will pay too little attention to the ideas in the text and guess at the meaning with little use of the text to confirm guesses.

FIGURE 1.5 *Situations that Encourage Too Much or Too Little Attention to the Text*

At this point, we would like to make a qualification regarding the interactive model. It has to do with what has been called "modular processing." In somewhat the same way that conceiving of reading as an interactive process acts as a caution against overemphasizing the role of schema-driven or top-down processing in reading, the concept of modularity acts as a caution against overgeneralizing the extent to which reading is an interactive process (Fodor, 1983). As noted by Keith Stanovich (1994), elements that are processed as modules are processed by themselves. In perceiving a cardinal, for example, we typically attend to the bird itself, without considering the context that surrounds the bird—the limb that it is perched on, the kind of tree in which it chose to land, or the area of the country we are in. It's not that these surrounding factors couldn't help us identify the bird; they could. But we don't need them; we need only to attend to the bird itself—a single perceptual module. In fact, using the context surrounding the bird to help us identify it would be inefficient.

In mature reading, words function as modules (separate units of meaning, rather than a collection of letters), and word recognition proceeds without the reader's making much use of context (the words and sentences surrounding the word the reader is focusing on) or prior knowledge. For the mature reader, recognition of individual words has become so automatic and effortless that using context or prior knowledge to help identify words is both unnecessary and inefficient. In fact, beginning readers actually use context more than mature readers do to identify words because beginning readers have not yet learned words fully enough that they function as modules.

One goal of early instruction in reading is to rapidly move beginning readers to the point at which the majority of words they meet in reading are modules that are processed automatically, without the reader's needing to use context or prior knowledge. How this is best accomplished is one of the central topics of Chapters 3 and 4.

Automaticity

The concept of automaticity is both crucial and straightforward. An automatic activity is one that we can perform instantly and with very little attention. As David LaBerge and S. Jay Samuels (1974) pointed out in their pioneering work on automaticity in reading, the mind's attentional capacity is severely limited; in fact, we can attend to only about one thing at a time. If we are faced with a task in which we are forced to attend to too many things at once, we will fail. For example, a number of people have reached a level of automaticity in driving a stick shift car. They can automatically push in the clutch, let up on the accelerator, shift gears, let out the clutch, and press on the accelerator; and they can do all this while driving in rush hour traffic. Beginning drivers cannot do all of this at once; they have not yet automated the various subprocesses, and it would be foolish and dangerous for them to attempt to drive a stick shift car in an attention-demanding situation such as rush hour traffic.

Reading includes a number of subprocesses that need to take place at the same time—processes such as recognizing words, assigning meanings to words, constructing the meanings of sentences and larger units, and relating the information gleaned from the text to information we already have. Unless some of these processes are automated, readers simply cannot do all of this at once. Specifically, readers need to perform two processes automatically: They need to recognize words automatically, and they need to assign meanings to words automatically. For example, if a student is reading and comes across the word *imperative*, she needs to automatically recognize the word and automatically—immediately and without conscious attention— know that it means "absolutely necessary." If the student needs to pause often and struggle to recognize and assign meanings to words, reading will be difficult and laborious, and the student will not understand much of what she is reading.

This problem can be particularly acute for students for whom English is a second language. In addition to going through the processes that native speakers do, non-native speakers may need to translate English words into their own language in the process of arriving at meaning. Thus, becoming automatic in processing words is extremely important for ESL students. Teacher Marla Roen understands the importance of providing students with plenty of easy reading material to help them gain automaticity:

> I make sure my classroom library is chock full of books that my third-graders can read with ease. When they select a book for pleasure reading, I tell them that if they can't instantly recognize most of the words in a book, they should choose a simpler one. Publishers of children's books have sometimes made selection easier by labeling their books by levels. However, not all publishers use the same labeling system, so I group the books in our classroom library by publisher. This helps the children in selecting books at the right comfort zone for them. Over the past several years, I have seen a great increase in the number of "chapter books" written for 7- and 8-year olds in both fiction and nonfiction titles. This has really been a boon for promoting automaticity in my students—having plenty of interesting stories and nonfiction pieces written at their level of competence. Because I have several ESL students, I make sure there are plenty of very simply written books for them, books with universal characters, such as Dr. Seuss books, Frog and Toad books by Arnold Lobel, or easy-to-read books that reflect their own culture. Luckily, these simple books with multicultural characters are becoming easier and easier to find.

> Marla Roen, Third-Grade Teacher

I used to think it was enough if kids simply knew words; now I know they need to recognize words quickly, instantly, automatically.

—*Richard Garcia*
Second-Grade Teacher

Fortunately, the road to automaticity is a very straight one. In order to become automatic at an activity, we need to practice the activity a lot in non-taxing situations. To become automatic in reading, students need to do a lot of reading in materials they find relatively easy, understandable, interesting, and enjoyable; and they need to do that reading in situations that are non-taxing, that is, in situations in which they can read for enjoyment and not be faced with difficult questions or other requirements based on the reading. In brief, you need to encourage students and give them ample opportunity to read independently in material they find interesting, enjoyable, and relatively easy. Importantly, these criteria apply to the relationship between individual students and reading material. That is, for the purpose of developing automaticity, a fourth-grader who reads at the second-grade level needs a book at her level, not a fourth-grade book. The bibliography on page 17 includes books beginning readers can use to build automaticity.

> Automaticity is based on the principle that tasks become easier, requiring less attention, through practice. When less attention is required for a task and it seems to run on its own, we say the task is automatic.
>
> —S. Jay Samuels
> Educational Psychologist

Metacognition

As defined by John Flavel (1976), "metacognition refers to one's knowledge concerning one's own cognitive processes and products or anything related to them" (p. 232). With respect to reading, metacognition refers to the reader's awareness of her comprehension of a text as she is reading it and to the reader's regulation of the processes that lead to comprehension. As suggested in Figure 1.6, metacognitive readers have the ability to mentally step outside of themselves and view themselves as learners faced with particular learning tasks.

Accomplished readers have metacognitive knowledge about themselves, the reading tasks they face, and the strategies they can employ in completing these tasks (Garner, 1987). For example, as you begin to read this section, you might realize that you have no prior knowledge about metacognition (self-knowledge), notice that the section is brief (task knowledge), and decide that the strategy of reading the section through several times would be fruitful (strategy knowledge). Thus you exhibited metacognitive knowledge prior to beginning reading.

Readers can also make use of metacognitive knowledge as they are reading; in fact, most metacognitive behavior probably takes place as one is reading. For example, if a reader comes across an unknown word

FIGURE 1.6 *The Metacognitive Reader*

Books to Help Build Automaticity in Young Readers

As we just said, to become automatic in reading, students need a lot of practice reading things they find easy, understandable, and enjoyable. For children who are just beginning to read—typically first-graders—books that include frequently repeated common words (for example, *run* and *book*) and common word parts (for example, phonograms such as *-ick* and *-ake*) are ideal. Many children's authors produce sets of easy-to-read books, and several publishers produce "little books" that are excellent for beginning readers to use to develop and cement their automaticity. Here are just a few of them:

The Cat in the Hat. Random House, 1957. Two children sitting at home on a rainy day are visited by the Cat in the Hat, who shows them some games. 61 pages.

The Cat in the Hat Comes Back. Random House, 1958. The cat leaves a big pink ring in the tub and moves it from place to place with the help of his alphabet friends. 61 pages.

Green Eggs and Ham. Random House, 1960. This book shows that things are not always what they appear to be. 62 pages.

Frog and Toad Are Friends. Harper & Row, 1970. The earliest adventures of these two best friends. 64 pages.

Frog and Toad Together. Harper & Row, 1972. Further adventures of these two good friends. 64 pages.

Frog and Toad All Year. Harper & Row, 1976. The two friends share adventures throughout the year. 64 pages.

Tales of Oliver Pig. Dial Press, 1979. The beginning adventures of Oliver Pig and his family. 64 pages. Also available in Spanish.

More Tales of Oliver Pig. Dial Press, 1981. More stories of this friendly pig and his family. 64 pages.

Oliver and Amanda's Halloween. Dial Books for Young Readers, 1992. Oliver Pig and Amanda Pig prepare for Halloween and then go trick-or-treating. 48 pages.

The Modern Curriculum Press is one of many publishers of little books. Their Ready Readers series contains over 200 titles, including these:

Ashley Dennis. *One Bee Got on the Bus.* Modern Curriculum Press, 1996. Bees, bears, bunnies, and other animals ride the bus. 8 pages.

Lucy Floyd. *Pete's Bad Day.* Modern Curriculum Press, 1996. Pete has a bad day and goes back to bed. 16 pages.

Anna Kijak. *My Monster and Me.* Modern Curriculum Press, 1996. A little girl does everything her monster does. 16 pages.

as she is reading, one very reasonable response would be to read ahead a little to see if the context suggests a meaning. If it does, she can return to processing the text as a whole. If it does not, she has the choice of continuing to read even though the meaning of the word is unclear or seeking outside help with the word—perhaps asking the teacher or a classmate, or checking the dictionary.

Readers can also make use of metacognitive knowledge after reading, as David does in the following scenario:

IN THE CLASSROOM
Using Metacognitive Knowledge

Two fifth-grade students, David and Jose, are sitting side by side, silently reading their science books. David moans. "Man, I've read this whole page, and it's like I didn't even read it! I mean, I don't know what it said. Guess I'd better read it again."

"Guess so," Jose tells him.

David buries his face in his book again. A few minutes later, he lets out a heavy sigh. "This is so lame! Why can't I get this?" He looks around for his teacher. "Mr. Green, I don't get this. Can you help me?"

> A good reader proceeds smoothly and quickly as long as his understanding of the material is complete. But as soon as he senses that he has missed an idea, that the track has been lost, he brings smooth progress to a grinding halt. Advancing more slowly, he seeks clarification in the subsequent material, examining it for the light it can throw on the earlier trouble spot.
>
> —*Arthur Whimbey*
> *Psychologist*

As this scenario illustrates, David realized that he had gotten virtually nothing from reading his science text, so he read it again. And when he learned nothing on a second reading, he realized that he needed some outside help with it and concluded that he should seek some assistance from his teacher before grappling with it again.

Active awareness of one's comprehension while reading and the ability to use effective fix-up strategies when comprehension breaks down are absolutely essential tools for becoming an effective reader, and lack of such metacognitive skills is a particularly debilitating characteristic of poor readers.

The goal is to bring as many students as possible to the point where they can and will make the effort to be as metacognitive as possible. Virtually all reading authorities agree that being metacognitive is extremely important to becoming a proficient reader.

Reflection AND Application

4. Explain in your own words how the concept of reading as an interactive process differs from the concept of reading as a bottom-up or top-down process.

5. Explain how the notion that mature readers process words as modules qualifies the notion of reading as an interactive process.

6. As we noted, a reader can be metacognitive before reading, during reading, or after reading. Now that you have read this section of the chapter, exercise your metacognitive skills by characterizing your understanding of it and noting some of the steps you could take to better understand it.

THE READING PROFICIENCY
OF U.S. STUDENTS

Criticizing students' reading ability and the schools more generally has long been an American tradition. From Rudolph Flesch's best selling *Why Johnny Can't Read* (1955) to the U.S. Department of Education's *A Nation at Risk* (1983) to contemporary newspaper and television reports with titles such as "Crisis in the Classroom" or "Our Illiterate Graduates," critics have frequently lashed out at the perceived inability of our schools to educate students as well as they once did, the poor performance of our students compared to those in other countries, and the general failure of our schools to effectively teach reading and other important subjects. As David Berliner and Bruce Biddle demonstrate in *The Manufactured Crisis* (1995), many of these claims are "myths, half-truths, and . . . outright lies" (p. 4).

Here, we respond to these critics of education and go beyond their criticism to suggest the sorts of reading skills that American students can and must develop. We begin by presenting some solid evidence to dispel the myth that American students read less well than they used to or less well than students in other countries. As a teacher, you are likely to hear these criticisms frequently, and it is important that you have a substantive answer to them. Next, we briefly characterize American students' reading proficiency. Knowing how well students are presently doing will help you understand the task you face as a teacher. Finally, we consider the sorts of reading proficiency required in today's and tomorrow's world. This, of course, is the proficiency you want to help students reach.

> Seldom in the course of policymaking in the U.S. have so many firm convictions held by so many been based on so little convincing proof.
>
> —*Clark Kerr*
> *President Emeritus,*
> *University of California*

A Response to Current Criticisms

Our main purpose in this section is to respond to the frequently-heard charge that American students' reading skills are abysmal, that they are far worse than they were in this country in the past and pathetic when compared to those of students in other nations. We base our response primarily on two sources that provide the most reliable large-scale assessments data available—the National Assessment of Educational Progress (NAEP) and the International Association for the Evaluation of Education (IEA). The NAEP was established by the federal government 25 years ago to provide a periodic report card on American students' achievements in reading and other academic areas. In other words, it was established to do exactly the job we are trying to do here—communicate about how American students are doing in school. The NAEP typically tests about every four years and reports data for 9-, 14-, and 17-year-olds. Figure 1.7 shows the results of the seven adminis-

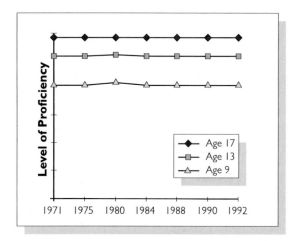

FIGURE 1.7   *U.S. Students' Reading Proficiency, 1971–1992*

trations of the NAEP reading tests for which we have comparative data (Mullis et al., 1994). The slope, or rather the lack of slope, of the trend lines for each age shows no major drop in reading ability. American students in 1992 read just about as well as American students in 1971. Comparisons with reading levels of earlier times, though difficult to make because comparable data are in short supply, show very similar results (Anderson, Hiebert, Scott, & Wilkinson, 1985).

The IEA was established in the late 1950s to conduct international studies. It is by far the most experienced body conducting such research and presents the most comprehensive and representative studies available. The most recent IEA study of reading achievement was conducted during the 1990–1991 school year in 34 countries (Elley, 1992). Figure 1.8 shows results for 9-year-olds in the United States and six other industrialized nations generally considered to have high educational standards. Although Finnish children scored slightly better than U.S. children, and Canadian and West German children fared slightly less well, for all practical purposes the data indicate that U.S. students read as well as students in other industrialized countries.

In summary, the best data we can locate indicate that U.S. students' reading proficiency has not declined in recent years and is about like that of students in other industrialized nations. However, there is still cause for

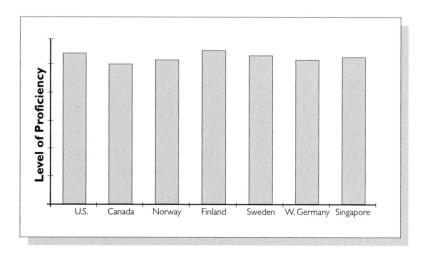

FIGURE 1.8   *Reading Achievement of 9-Year-Olds in the United States and Six Other Countries, 1990–1991*

concern. Recent NAEP data (Campbell, Donahue, Reese, & Phillips, 1996; Mullis, Campbell, & Farstrup, 1993) suggest the following pattern of performance among U.S. students: By fourth grade, the vast majority of students can read easy material and answer simple questions on it. However, once the texts become slightly more difficult—the sorts of things middle-grade students are expected to deal with—a large percentage of middle-grade students cannot read and understand the questions and neither can a sizable percentage of high school seniors. And once both texts and questions become demanding—the sorts of material one would need to read to understand political and social issues or enjoy relatively sophisticated literature—very few students, even those about to graduate from high school, can deal with them. Additionally, the data indicate that certain groups of U.S. students are not as well prepared for school as others and will need help in becoming proficient readers. Most notably, students of poverty—students whose preschool and out-of-school experiences have not prepared them for middle-class schools— are likely to need particular assistance. The reading proficiency of students attending schools in disadvantaged communities lags very significantly behind that of students attending schools in advantaged communities.

> The often heard charge, "Johnny can't read," is a little like saying "Johnny can't cook." Johnny may be able to read the directions for constructing a radio kit, but not a Henry James novel, just as Johnny may be able to fry an egg but not cook Peking duck."
>
> —Richard Beach and Deborah Appleman Teacher Educators

Critical Literacy: Literacy for Today's and Tomorrow's World

As important as it is to understand how well American students read, it is even more important to understand present-day literacy requirements and the way in which those requirements are growing. At one time, literacy was defined as the ability to sign your name. At another time, it was defined as the ability to read aloud a simple text with which you were already familiar—typically a passage from the Bible (Resnick & Resnick, 1977). Today, although there is no single definition of literacy, there is universal agreement that everyone needs a far higher level of literacy than at any time in our past, and this requirement will continue to grow. Irwin Kirsch and Ann Jungeblut (1986) define present-day literacy as "using printed and written information to function in society, to achieve one's goals, and to develop one's knowledge" (p. 3). Lauren Resnick (1987) views present-day literacy than as a "higher-order skill" and notes that it requires thinking that is complex, that yields multiple solutions, that involves multiple criteria, and that demands nuanced judgments. David Perkins's (1992) notes that contemporary education must go beyond simply presenting students with information and must ensure that students retain important information, understand topics deeply, and actively use the knowledge they gain. A truly literate person will be able to achieve these goals from reading because she consciously seeks understanding and uses for the knowledge she gains through reading. Finally,

Critical literacy requires consciously seeking to understand the ideas and information a text presents and actively using that knowledge.

Robert Calfee (Calfee & Patrick, 1995) argues that success in contemporary society demands what he calls *critical literacy*—the use of language for thinking, problem solving, and communicating. We like Calfee's term and the concept of literacy it suggests, and in the remainder of the book we will employ both the terms *critical literacy* and *literacy* to denote the high level of literacy vital in today's and tomorrow's world.

Although various authors describe the specifics of critical literacy somewhat differently, their general message is very clear and tremendously important: Critical literacy requires much more than passively absorbing what is on the printed page. It requires attaining a deep understanding of what is read, remembering important information, linking newly-learned information to existing schemata, knowing when and where to use that information, using it appropriately in varied contexts in and out of school, and communicating effectively with others. Critical literacy requires that readers be able to *do* something as a result of reading, not merely know something. Moreover, critical literacy requires that readers be able to do something with a variety of different texts—not just short stories, novels, poetry, and history texts, but also tax forms, computer manuals, complex directions for operating even more complex machines, and technical documents related to business, economics, agriculture, the military, and a huge variety of other enterprises. Many of these texts are extremely complex; and both the number of complex texts and the complexity of texts continues to grow each year.

To be sure, students do not read all of these types of complex texts in elementary school, but their early reading experiences should provide a foundation for dealing with complex material in the future. Today's elementary students must become considerably more competent, flexible, and sophisticated readers than their predecessors. Moreover, given the discrepancy between the reading proficiency of students from lower- and higher-income homes, in addition to working to improve all students' reading proficiency, we need to work especially hard to improve dramatically the proficiency of many poor children. We particularly need to improve all children's higher-level skills. We need to guide as many students as we possibly can to a level of critical literacy that enables them to read challenging material, to analyze it closely, to learn from it, to reason from it, and to problem solve; we need to nurture and encourage students to become competent readers in today's increasingly complex and demanding world.

The following glimpse into a sixth-grade classroom, which comes from *Standards for the English Language Arts* (National Council of Teachers of English and International Reading Association, 1996), exemplifies a reading experience that promotes the kind of critical literacy we are talking about.

IN THE CLASSROOM
Developing Critical Literacy in the Sixth Grade

A group of sixth-grade students are reading and studying science texts, such as primary sources, magazine articles, textbooks, and essays on scientific and environmental topics. As part of a thematic exploration of large mammals, the students read a number of magazine articles on endangered animals and work in small groups to practice using study strategies, such as underlining, annotation, and summarizing information through visual diagrams. Their teacher models study strategies in explicit class demonstrations.

One day, before reading an article on grizzly bears, the students talk about the specific ways of learning and remembering important ideas and information encountered during reading. The teacher models strategies she uses as she reads, such as underlining and note taking, "thinking aloud" for the class as she sifts through information to highlight and organize important points. She shows students a way in which to transform key ideas and details that support them into a learning web on grizzly bears that helps show the relationships among key concepts.

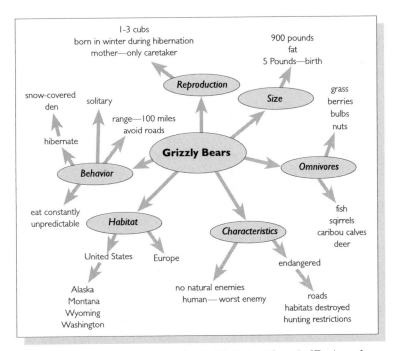

From *Standards for the English Language Arts* (p. 56), National Council of Teachers of English and International Reading Association. (1996). Urbana, IL.

The students gather in small groups to read articles about large animals. Working together, they decide which points are important enough to underline or annotate. Each group then organizes the information it has found, using a learning web. Each group displays its diagram to the class as an overhead transparency, explaining the process they used to produce it.

The next day, the students write summaries of the articles they have read and work together to prepare for an oral presentation to their class, using their notes and diagrams to help them plan.

Reflection AND Application

7. Suppose you are sitting with a small group of parents at a school open house when one woman abruptly demands to know why today's students read so poorly compared to those in her day. A man picks up her prompt and with similar abruptness wants to know why American kids can't read as well as those in other countries. Compose a response in which you cite data to reassure these parents that American students are certainly holding their own.

8. The concept of critical literacy is a complex one. At this point, describe your understanding of the concept of critical literacy in a paragraph or two. Keep your description, and add to it as you gain a broader knowledge of this concept in later chapters.

A CRITICAL LITERACY CURRICULUM

More than ever before in the recent history of this nation, educators are compelled to confront the biases that have shaped teaching practices in our society and to create new ways of knowing different strategies for the sharing of knowledge.

—*bell hooks*
Social Critic

We now turn to a description of the components of a program to lead students to critical literacy.

Before continuing, we should point out that the focus in this book is reading, and therefore some aspects of a critical literacy curriculum will not be discussed in depth. These topics include spelling and handwriting. Although we consider writing as it relates to reading, we do not present a comprehensive writing program. Finally, we do not present curricula for specific subjects such as history, science, and the like. But because knowledge of these areas is a crucial part of critical literacy, our whole approach assumes that students are developing rich knowledge bases in a variety of subjects.

To promote critical literacy, teachers must assist students in developing three types of knowledge about each of seven components of literacy.

Three Types of Knowledge

Declarative knowledge, procedural knowledge, and attitudes and inclinations constitute the three types of knowledge students need to acquire. They are illustrated in Figure 1.9. It is often best to use different modes of instruction to foster each type of knowledge.

Declarative Knowledge

Declarative knowledge is often described as "knowledge that" or "knowledge about." It includes knowledge of facts, concepts, and generalizations. The student who knows that Disneyland is an amusement park has declarative knowledge. So too does the student who knows what an exoskeleton is and the student who realizes that different societies tend to have different concepts of beauty. As these examples indicate, declarative knowledge can be concrete or abstract, simple or difficult.

Procedural Knowledge

Procedural knowledge is often described as "knowledge how." It involves the ability to do something. The student who rides a bike, plays a game of chess, or operates a computer is demonstrating procedural knowledge. So too is the student who writes an effective essay or runs a successful campaign to get her friend elected class president. Like declarative knowledge, procedural knowl-

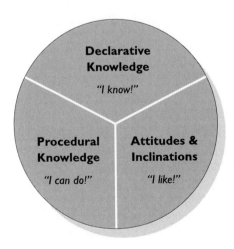

FIGURE 1.9 *Types of Knowledge*

edge can be easy or complex and can deal with concrete actions or more abstract procedures.

Procedural knowledge can be applied automatically, as it usually is in riding a bicycle, or with conscious attention, as it usually is in running a political campaign. This distinction between automatic and deliberate procedural knowledge is important in teaching: students need to learn to apply some procedures automatically and others consciously. We will refer to the automatic procedures as *skills* and the conscious ones as *strategies*.

Attitudes and Inclinations

The development of students who both can and will read should be the ultimate goal of any reading program.

—*Dixie Lee Spiegel*
Teacher Educator

Attitudes and inclinations are just what the words indicate—feelings toward various matters and propensities to engage in various activities. Attitudes and inclinations are, of course, just as important as knowledge. It does a student little good to know how to read and write if she doesn't like either of these activities or is not inclined to engage in them. In fact, it has been said that U.S. students are not so much *illiterate* as *aliterate*; that is, although most students can read, many seldom choose to do so. NAEP data collected in 1992, for example, showed that while only 37% of 13-year-olds reported reading for fun daily, 67% of this age group reported watching three or more hours of television daily (Mullis et al., 1994).

Seven Components of the Curriculum

Now we turn to the seven components of the critical literacy curriculum. These are shown in Figure 1.10. We will describe each component and give an example of the declarative and procedural knowledge and some of the attitudes that we hope to foster for each.

Knowledge About Print

As part of learning to read, students need to internalize a substantial body of knowledge about print and about the relationship between print and speech. A good deal of this knowledge is declarative, such as recognizing that the written language they are just beginning to learn about is in many ways similar to the oral language they are already quite proficient at, or recognizing that words are closely grouped sets of letters with white space at either end of them. But knowledge about print also includes procedural knowledge, such as tracking from left to right and from the top of the page to the

FIGURE 1.10 *Components of Critical Literacy*

bottom. And it includes attitudes and inclinations—the most important of which are probably realizing that reading can be a lot of fun and wanting to read.

Decoding

We will use the term *decoding* in a fairly narrow sense here, to refer to the process children use to sound out written words they do not immediately recognize. If an adept reader comes to the word *bike* and doesn't immediately recognize it, she can follow a series of steps like these to arrive at its pronunciation:

- Identify the sound of *b* as /b/.
- Identify the sound of *k* as /k/.
- Identify the sound of *i* as /ī/ (using her knowledge that the *e* at the end of the word signals the long-vowel sound).
- Blend these sounds to arrive at the pronunciation /bīk/.
- Realize that the word is *bike*, a word she knows perfectly well once she hears it.

Decoding helps children become independent readers. It certainly requires some declarative knowledge, for example, knowledge of the sounds typically represented by various letters and groups of letters, or recognizing that an *e* at the end of a word can signal a long-vowel sound. However, a great deal of the task of learning decoding involves mastering procedural knowledge. More than knowing about decoding, the student needs to become adept at doing it. Decoding also involves some important attitudes and inclinations. For example, the student needs to have some confidence in her decoding skills and be willing to slow down and take the time and effort to decode a word when understanding the word is important to comprehending what she is reading.

Vocabulary

A huge amount of research has been conducted on students' vocabulary knowledge, and reliable estimates indicate that many students have acquired reading vocabularies of something like 5,000 words by the end of the first grade and reading vocabularies in the neighborhood of 50,000 by the time they graduate from high school (Graves, 1992). Obviously, vocabulary learning represents a significant task throughout children's years in school. Much of the vocabulary knowledge children acquire is declarative knowledge, knowledge of the meanings of thousands of words. However, vocabulary learning also requires procedural knowledge, for example, the ability to use the context surrounding an unknown word to infer its meaning. And truly effective vocabulary learning also involves students' attitudes toward words; students who develop large and precise vocabularies show a keen interest in words and how they are used.

Comprehending Narratives

As we have already noted, most children enter school with relatively well developed, although tacit, understanding of narratives. If they have been fortunate, children have had many narratives read to them, and virtually all children have seen a number of narratives on television. All in all, students do quite well in comprehending simple narratives, and because of this simple narratives are used extensively in early reading instruction. But children still have a great deal to learn about narratives in school. The declarative knowledge they will learn includes understanding what narratives are and how they differ from exposition—a crucial distinction that we very briefly discuss in the next section and will discuss at more length later in the book. The procedural knowledge necessary to understanding narratives includes being able to recognize the theme in a story and explain how an author illustrates this theme. And the attitudes and inclinations that we hope to cultivate include the desire to read narratives as a leisure activity.

Comprehending and Learning from Exposition

The term *exposition* refers to informational writing—text that typically is not temporally organized, that does not tell a story with a beginning, a middle, and an end. This book and virtually all of the texts you have used in college (except novels, short stories, poetry, and narrative nonfiction) are expository in nature. Most children do not enter school with much understanding of exposition or much experience with it. And in many elementary schools, students do not get much instruction in reading expository material or even much exposure to it. This is extremely unfortunate because much of the information students need to learn appears in expository material. One important piece of declarative knowledge students need to learn about exposition is that many expository texts present new information to be learned and learning that information requires purposeful effort on their part. One very important sort of procedural knowledge students need to learn about exposition is how to recognize what is important in an expository text. And one attitude we hope to develop in students is confidence in their ability to learn from informational texts.

Reading and Writing

Reading and writing are natural companions, two activities that both build on and reinforce each other. In school, they ought frequently to be taught and practiced together, and teaching them in tandem will often be both more effective and more efficient than teaching them separately. One sort of declarative knowledge that students should gain about writing is that writing can be both an effective way to communicate with others and a way to examine one's own thoughts. As is the case with decoding, much of the knowledge students need to gain about writing is procedural knowledge; specifically, students need to learn how to write in a variety of ways for a variety of purposes. Among the many attitudes about writing we would hope to develop, students' belief in their competence as writers may be the most important. Far too many students—and far too many adults—view themselves as poor writers.

> Language is learned not because we want to talk or read or write about language, but because we want to talk and read and write about the world.
>
> —*Courtney Cazden*
> *Linguist and Teacher Educator*

Building Connections

The final component of the critical literacy curriculum cuts across all of the others. Building connections—establishing links among the vast array of schemata that students internalize—is important whether students are involved in decoding, in writing, or in the other components of the curriculum.

Students need to build connections in several directions. First, we want students to realize that what they bring to school—the wealth of out-of-school experiences that they bring when they enter first grade and that are constantly enriched each year—are relevant to what they are learning in school. For example, the pride they felt when they were first allowed to go to the grocery store alone can provide insight into a story character's feelings when she successfully meets a challenge. Second, we want students to realize that the various subjects they study in school are interrelated in many ways. For example, the understanding of the Revolutionary period they gained in social studies can help them understand the motives of Johnny in Esther Forbes's *Johnny Tremain*. Third, we want students to realize that ideas and concepts learned in school are relevant to their lives outside of school. For example, a character's discovery that persistence paid off in meeting her goal may suggest to a student that similar persistence may lead to success as she tries to help a younger brother develop the habit of putting his toys away neatly.

In concluding this section on critical literacy, we should perhaps answer a question that some of you might have: "Why are knowledge about print and decoding—seemingly preliminary and low-level skills—included in the critical literacy curriculum?" The answer is simple. These preliminary, low-level skills are absolutely essential for mastering the higher-level competencies that make up the remainder of the critical literacy curriculum. Knowledge about print is a prerequisite for learning decoding skills. Decoding skills, in turn, are absolutely necessary for students to become independent readers—readers who can learn independently the tens of thousands of words that all good readers learn.

All components of the critical literacy curriculum work together, enabling students to comprehend narratives, learn from expository material, use reading and writing as tools for learning and communicating, and build connections between the various subjects they study in school and between what they study in school and the world outside of school.

Reflection AND Application

9. Discuss or write about several examples of the declarative knowledge you possess and several examples of the procedural knowledge that you have internalized.

10. List the seven components of the critical literacy curriculum on a sheet of paper. Then, for each component, jot down one example of declarative knowledge, one example of procedural knowledge, and one attitude or inclination you would like to impart to students. Try not to use examples given in this text.

AN OVERVIEW OF THIS BOOK

Here, we first briefly note the contents of each chapter. Then, we explain the common components and organization of the chapters. Internalizing the organization of the book will be a great aid in understanding and remembering what you learn.

Chapter-by-Chapter Overview

This book is divided into twelve chapters. Chapters 1 and 2—Reading and Learning to Read and Reading Instruction—deal with general concepts and principles that are applied throughout the book. Chapters 3 and 4—Emergent Literacy and Word Recognition—deal with topics that are particularly important in the primary grades. Chapters 5 through 8—Vocabulary Development, Scaffolding Students' Comprehension of Text: Teacher-Directed Approaches, Guiding Students Toward Independence in Reading, and Teaching for Understanding in Content Areas—discuss topics that are crucial at all grade levels. Chapters 9 through 11 deal with the special topics of Writing and Reading, Literacy Instruction for Non-Native Speakers of English, and Classroom Assessment. Chapter 12—Classroom Portraits—presents in-depth scenarios of reading instruction at three grade levels.

The Components and Organization of the Chapter

We have designed each chapter to facilitate your reading and learning as effectively and efficiently as possible, and most chapters have the same components and the same organization.

Chapters begin with a brief personal statement or scenario in which we convey our interest in the topic of the chapter and suggest one or more of the major themes of the chapter. Next comes a chapter overview, a visual layout of the major sections of the chapter. Following the overview is the body of the chapter, usually consisting of two to four main sections and a number of subsections. After this comes a section titled Special Needs and Special Talents. Here, we look back at the chapter and ask if there is more that can be done to ensure that all students—those who move more quickly than their peers, those who move less quickly than their peers, and those whose experiences and schemata differ from those of many of their peers—achieve in the area covered in the chapter. Finally, the last regular section in the chapter is titled Concluding Remarks and includes a summary and a few comments on the chapter.

In addition to these regular sections, chapters include a number of additonal features. Samples of children's work illustrate their growth toward critical literacy. Strategically placed "Books" boxes provide annotated lists of children's trade literature useful in teaching particular literacy skills and topics. Frequent interjection of teachers' "voices" give you a feel for the classroom. "In the Classroom" features offer a variety of examples of classroom interaction—student-teacher dialogues, vignettes, and sample lessons—designed to nurture students toward critical literacy. Insightful quotes appear in the margins to highlight vital ideas. And "Reflection and Application" sections are embedded at the ends of major sections to give you an opportunity to review and try out some of the central ideas presented.

Chapters end with three standard features. A section titled Extending Learning invites you to apply and elaborate on some of the major ideas presented by observing classrooms, talking with parents and teachers, or investigating a particular topic further. Following this, briefly annotated references lead you to sources that support, explain, or extend ideas presented in the chapter. Finally, a section titled Children's Literature provides citations and brief annotations of the selections mentioned in the chapter and occasionally citations to other sources of children's literature.

Special Needs and Special Talents

In this section of each chapter, we ask if there is more that can be done to ensure that all students—those for whom school is easy and those for whom it's a challenge—achieve at their highest potential. Because this chapter does not deal directly with pedagogy, there is not a lot to be said here. We will, however, emphasize three points.

Different children will arrive at kindergarten, first grade, and every other grade with dramatically different schemata—varied knowledge about the world, about different types of text, about the content of specific subjects, and about school and how it functions. For example, many children who come from the East Coast will have little knowledge of the desert Southwest, children who come from other cultures may lack the American cultural knowledge assumed by some narratives, and children from affluent suburbs may have little understanding of inner-city issues. If all children are to succeed, we must take advantage of the varied schemata that different students do have, accommodate students' differing schemata, and do everything possible to make school relevant to the lives of all children.

Today, many less-advantaged students lack the reading proficiency of their advantaged counterparts. The country cannot survive this discrepancy; we must close that gap. Moreover, we must set the high standard of critical literacy as a goal for all students; we cannot afford to make critical literacy a goal for only some students.

All students at all grade levels need and deserve the opportunity to participate in all components of the critical literacy curriculum that they have not yet mastered—to have rich and varied literacy activities. This means that all students should be involved with learning vocabulary, comprehending narratives, comprehending and learning from exposition, reading and writing, and building connections. It will not do, for example, to have some beginning readers—those who are not achieving as rapidly as their peers—spend virtually all of their time on decoding and wait forever for the "good stuff."

> The first and most essential goal of formal learning must be to ensure that all children read with comprehension, write with clarity, and effectively speak and listen.
>
> *—Ernest Boyer*
> *Former Secretary of Education*

CONCLUDING REMARKS

In this chapter, we have done four things. First, we described the concept of the reading process underlying this book—the cognitive–constructivist view. We also described three theories that elaborate and complement this view—the interactive model of reading, automaticity, and metacognition. Second, we briefly characterized American students' proficiency in reading, contrasted their proficiency today to what it was in the past and to the proficiency of students in other industrialized countries, and described the sort of literacy necessary in today's and tomorrow's world—critical literacy. Third, we listed seven components of the critical literacy curriculum that serve as the foundation for the book. Fourth, we gave a brief chapter by chapter overview and explained the common organization that all chapters share.

The topics in this chapter are particularly important to internalize because they underlie the remainder of the book. As we have said several times, the richer your background knowledge relevant to the book—the more you know about the view of the reading process that informs it, the level of critical literacy it is designed to help you achieve for your students, the components of the curriculum, and the organization of the book and each chapter—the easier it will be for you to learn, remember, and use the information and procedures presented. We therefore strongly encourage you to review the chapter, take some notes, respond again to some of the prompts in the Reflection and Application sections, make use of some of our suggestions in the Extending Learning section, and perhaps search out and read some works listed in the references.

EXTENDING LEARNING

Here we suggest several activities that take you beyond this book—to schools, students, teachers, parents, libraries, and others sources of information—to help you more fully understand and appreciate your role in nurturing children toward critical literacy.

1. One way to increase your understanding of new and complex concepts is to examine several perspectives on them. The concepts about the reading process that we have discussed have all been described in a variety of other texts, and all of them are complex enough to warrant further study. Pick two or three concepts that you would like to further explore, and read more about them in either the references that we have supplied or in a general text on psychology or educational psychology.

2. Develop a set of questions about U.S. students' current level of reading proficiency, the proficiency of previous generations of U.S. students, the proficiency of students in other countries, and the proficiency needed in today's world. Then use the questions to conduct interviews with half a dozen or so adults. Solicit and record their answers to your questions, and compare their answers to the characterization of students' proficiency presented in the chapter. Write up your comparison.

3. List the seven components of the critical literacy curriculum, and interview some elementary school teachers to find out which components they deal with, which they don't, and the literacy activities they engage in that are not part of the curriculum presented in this chapter. Try to

include teachers from primary, middle-elementary, and upper-elementary grades. Once you have completed your interviews, sum up what you have discovered and comment on (1) the extent to which the teachers you interviewed employ the curriculum we have outlined and (2) any components of the literacy curriculum that are not among the seven we consider but that you probably want to include in your classroom.

REFERENCES

Adams, M., & Bruce, B. (1982). Background knowledge and reading comprehension. In J. A. Langer and T. M. Smith-Burke (Eds.), *Reader meets author: Bridging the gap* (pp. 2–25). Newark, DE: International Reading Association. This is a very readable discussion of the importance of background knowledge.

Anderson, R. C., Hiebert, E. F., Scott, J. A., & Wilkinson, I. A. G. (1985). *Becoming a nation of readers*. Washington, DC: National Institute of Education. This concise summary of what we know about reading instruction is probably the most widely circulated and influential text on reading published in the last decade.

Anderson, R. C., & Pearson, P. D. (1984). A schema-theoretic view of basic processes in reading. In P. D. Pearson (Ed.), *Handbook of reading research* (pp. 255–291). White Plains, NY: Longman. This is a challenging but extremely informative overview of schema theory and its application to reading.

Anderson, R. C., Sprio, R. J., & Montegue, W. E. (Eds.). (1977). *Schooling and the acquisition of knowledge*. Hillsdale, NJ: Erlbaum. This book offers a classic collection of applications of cognitive psychology to education.

Berliner, D., & Biddle, B. (1995). *The manufactured crisis*. Reading, MA: Addison-Wesley. This award-winning book uses hard data to debunk many of the attacks against America's public schools.

Calfee, R. C., & Patrick, C. L. (1995). *Teach our children well: Bringing K–12 education into the 21st century*. Stanford, CA: Stanford Alumni Association. This book presents one teacher–scholar's view of active, constructive elementary classrooms.

Campbell, J. R., Donahue, P. L., Reese, C. M., & Phillips, G. W. (1996). *NAEP 1994 reading report card for the nation and the states*. Washington, DC: Department of Education. Full report on the 1994 NAEP reading findings.

Educational Testing Service. (1985). *The reading report card.: Progress toward excellence in our schools*. Princeton, NJ: Author. Includes the passage presented in this chapter and other information about students' proficiency.

Elley, W. (1992). *How in the world do students read? The IEA study of reading literacy*. The Hague: International Association for Evaluation of Educational Achievement. This book gives the full report on this important study.

Flavel, J. (1976). Metacognitive aspects of problem solving. In L. B. Resnick (Ed.), *The nature of intelligence* (pp. 231–235). Hillsdale, NJ: Erlbaum. This chapter describes the role of metacognition in problem solving.

Flesch, R. (1955). *Why Johnny can't read—and what you can do about it*. New York: Harper. This best-selling book charged that students were not learning to read because they were not being taught phonics.

Fodor, J. (1983). *Modularity of mind.* Cambridge, MA: MIT Press. The author provides a technical examination of the concept of modularity.

Gardner, H. (1985). *The mind's new science.* New York: Basic Books. This is a concise history of cognitive psychology and related areas.

Garner, R. (1987). *Metacognition and reading comprehension.* Norwood, NJ: Ablex. This book is a fairly technical summary of research on metacognition.

Graves, M. F. (1992). The elementary vocabulary curriculum: What should it be? In M. J. Dreher & W. H. Slater (Eds.), *Elementary school literacy: Critical issues* (pp. 101–131). Norwood, MA: Christopher-Gordon. This is one of a number of sources noting the very large vocabularies students develop.

Kirsch, I., & Jungeblut, A. (1986). *Literacy: Profiles of America's young adults.* Princeton, NJ: National Assessment of Educational Progress, Educational Testing Service. This is a report on literacy among 21- to 25-year-olds.

LaBerge, D., & Samuels, S. J. (1974). Toward a theory of automatic information processing in reading. *Cognitive Psychology, 6,* 293–323. This is the original work on automaticity and reading.

Marzano, R. J., Paynter, D. E., Kendall, J. S., Pickering, D., & Marzano, L. (1991). *Literacy plus: An integrated approach to teaching reading, writing, vocabulary, and reasoning.* Columbus, OH: Zaner-Bloser. This teachers guide describes a number of activities for enhancing students' thinking and reasoning skills within the reading and writing workshop framework.

Mullis, I. V. S., Campbell, J., & Farstrup, A. E. (1993). *NAEP 1992 reading report card for the nation and the states.* Washington, DC: Department of Education. This is the full-length 1992 NAEP report.

Mullis, I. V. S., Dossey, J. A., Campbell, J. R., Gentile, C. A., O'Sullivan, C., & Latham, A. S. (1994). *NAEP 1992 trends in academic progress.* Washington, DC: U.S. Department of Education. This is the source of the students' reading proficiency data from 1971 to 1992.

National Council of Teachers of English and International Reading Association. (1996). *Standards for the English language arts.* Urbana, IL: Author. This describes the language arts knowledge and skills needed in today's world.

Perkins, D. (1992). *Smart schools: From training memories to educating minds.* New York: The Free Press. This extremely readable and excellent book discusses what we should be teaching and how we can teach effectively.

Resnick, D. P., & Resnick, L. B. (1977). The nature of literacy: An historical exploration. *Harvard Educational Review, 47,* 370–385. The authors present a very interesting discussion of how the standards for being considered literate have changed dramatically over time.

Resnick, L. B. (1987). *Education and learning to think.* Washington, DC: National Academy Press. This is a concise overview of what is and is not known on this topic.

Rumelhart, D. E. (1980). Schemata: The building blocks of cognition. In R. J. Spiro, B. C. Bruce, & W. F. Brewer (Eds.), *Theoretical issues in reading comprehension* (pp. 33–58). Hillsdale, NJ: Erlbaum. The original statement of concept of schemata, this article is detailed and revealing.

Stanovich, K. E. (1994). Constructivism in reading education. *The Journal of Special Education, 28,* 259–274. The author takes up the issue of when self-discovery is not the most efficacious mode of learning.

U.S. Department of Education. (1983). *A nation at risk: The imperative for educational reform.* Washington, DC: Author. This broadly circulated political document argued that the United States risked being outpaced by foreign powers because of its weak educational system.

von Glaserfeld, E. (1984). An introduction to radical constructivism. In P. Watzlawick (Ed.), *The invented reality* (pp. 17–40). New York: W. W. Norton. An introduction to and a defense of radical constructivism.

CHILDREN'S LITERATURE

Forbes, E. (1943). *Johnny Tremain*. New York: Dell. Johnny Tremain, apprentice silversmith, takes on the cause of freedom as a message carrier for the Sons of Liberty in pre-Revolution Boston. 269 pages. Audiotape available.

Havill, J. (1993). *Jamaica and Brianna*. Boston: Houghton Mifflin. Jamaica is upset when she has to wear hand-me-down boots when her friend Brianna has pink ones with fuzzy white cuffs.

Kruse, G. M. (1991). *Multicultural literature for children and young adults*. Madison, WI: University of Wisconsin Cooperative Children's Book Center. This annotated bibliography describes over 450 books with multicultural themes or topics, published between 1980 and 1990.

Lord, B. B. (1984). *In the year of the boar and Jackie Robinson*. New York: Harper and Row. In 1947, a Chinese girl comes to Brooklyn where she becomes Americanized at school, in her apartment building, and by her love for baseball. Illustrated. 169 pages.

Sun, C. F. (1994). *Mama Bear*. Boston: Houghton Mifflin. Young Mei-Mei bakes and sells cookies in order to earn enough money to buy a large and expensive stuffed bear for Christmas. Illustrated. 28 pages.

chapter two

Reading Instruction

Larry has been teaching for seven years. Over the past several years his third-grade classroom has become a busy place. Both his principal and his vice principal recommend his room when parents of potential students, members of the school committee, or other important people ask to see a class. The local university routinely sends preservice teachers to observe his classes and often also asks Larry to take a student teacher. Two other nearby universities occasionally send preservice teachers to observe him.

Walking into Larry's class, it is easy to see why it is a model classroom. The room is warm, inviting, and orderly. Desks are neatly arranged in the front of the room, oriented to Larry's desk and the chalkboard and screen behind it. Other parts of the room contain tables for small group work, and there are quiet nooks with comfortable chairs that invite readers. Several bulletin boards contain lists of class activities, rules for signing out books, and chore lists the class follows as well as progress reports on class and group projects and lots of student work.

CHAPTER OVERVIEW

But the physical arrangement is not what brings the stream of visitors. The atmosphere and the activities of the classroom are the draw. Larry always greets students at the door. The students' responses as he explains a new concept or an upcoming assignment are animated and enthusiastic. It is clear that students working in groups or alone—reading or writing—view the classroom as an interesting and rewarding place. They value their pursuit of learning. They are actively involved in learning, and, in fact, are learning.

Not every effective classroom looks like Larry's, and not all of us can create classrooms of star status. But a large and constantly increasing body of information on reading instruction exists which can help all of us create successful classrooms.

INSTRUCTIONAL PRINCIPLES

Although providing effective instruction has always been a concern of teachers, researchers, and policy makers, a huge proportion of the most productive research and theorizing on the topic has occurred in the past three decades. This chapter focuses on this body of knowledge. First, we deal with building positive attitudes and perceptions because we believe that instilling in children both the desire to learn and the confidence that they can learn is an absolute prerequisite to significant learning. Second, we consider grouping, because it is central to students' success—or failure—in school. Third, we discuss traditional instructional principles, most of which were validated in the 1960s and 1970s. In the final section, we consider constructivist perspectives, which for the most part emerged in the 1980s and 1990s and which amplify and refine earlier thinking.

> If the practices seen in the best classrooms of the best teachers in the best schools could be introduced everywhere, improvements in reading would be dramatic.
>
> —*The Commission on Reading*

Building Positive Attitudes and Perceptions

Increasingly, educators are learning that attitudes and motivation are crucial determinants of learning and therefore deserve our direct attention. In 1992, a poll conducted by John O'Flahavan and his colleagues indicated that teachers saw creating interest in reading as their number one priority; and in 1994 the International Reading Association published its first text devoted solely to affective concerns, *Fostering the Love of Reading* (Cramer & Castle, 1994).

For substantive learning to occur, students must have positive attitudes about themselves as learners, about their ability to succeed in school, and about the instructional goals that they, their teachers, and their schools set. Students' reading abilities will grow in direct proportion to the extent to which they see reading as a worthwhile and enjoyable activity that they can succeed at. In discussing ways to foster such positive attitudes, we consider the critical importance of success, attribution theory and passive failure, the importance of appropriate challenges, teacher attitudes and actions that promote positive perceptions, and characteristics of a literate environment.

The Critical Importance of Success

A dominant thought motivating not just this section of the chapter but the whole of this book is the overwhelming importance of success. Research has repeatedly verified that, if students are to learn effectively, they need to succeed at the majority of tasks they undertake (Brophy, 1986). This, of course, applies to students' reading as well as other schoolwork. Moreover, if students are to become not only proficient readers but also avid readers—children and eventually adults who voluntarily seek out reading as a road to information, enjoyment, and personal fulfillment—then successful reading experiences are even more important.

A successful reading experience includes at least three features. First, and most important, a successful reading experience is one in which the reader understands what he reads. Of course, understanding may take more than one reading, it may require the teacher's assistance or that of other students, and it will often entail the reader's active manipulation of the ideas in the text. Second, a successful reading experience is one that the reader finds enjoyable, entertaining, informative, or thought provoking. Of course, not every reading experience will yield all of these benefits, but every experience should yield at least one of them. Finally, a successful reading experience prepares the student to complete whatever task follows the reading.

To a great extent, children's success in reading is directly under your control. You can select, and encourage students to select, tasks, materials, and supporting activities that all but guarantee success. For example, suppose you have a group of third-grade students who read at a rate of about 150 words per minute and a 10-minute reading period. Giving students a selection slightly shorter than 1,500 words will ensure that they at least have time to complete it, whereas giving them a selection much longer than 1,500 words will leave them frustrated and ensure failure. Or suppose you have a group of fifth-grade students who will be reading a science chapter on the ecology of freshwater lakes but who have virtually no concept of ecology and have never even thought about the relationships between organisms and their environment. Preteaching the concept of ecology will greatly increase the likelihood that students will understand the chapter and not simply flounder in a sea of new ideas.

I have long been convinced that the central and most important goal of reading instruction is to foster the love of reading.

—*Linda Gambrell*
Teacher Educator

Attribution Theory and Passive Failure

Attribution theory helps explain and underscore the importance of success. It deals with students' perceptions of the causes of their successes and failures in learning. As Merlin Wittrock (1986) explains, in deciding why they succeed or fail in reading tasks, students can attribute their performance to ability, effort, luck, the difficulty of the reading task, or a variety of other causes. All too often, children who have repeatedly failed in reading attribute their failure to factors that are beyond their control—such as their innate ability or luck. Once this happens, children are likely to lose their motivation to learn to read and to doubt their ability to learn. From the children's perspective, there is no reason to try because there is nothing they can do about it. Moreover, as long as they do not try, they cannot fail; you cannot lose a race if you do not enter it.

As Peter Johnston and Peter Winograd (1985) have pointed out, one long-term outcome of children's repeatedly attributing failure in reading to forces that are beyond their control is passive failure syndrome. Children who exhibit passive failure in reading typically become nervous, withdrawn, and discouraged when they are faced with reading tasks. They are unlikely to actively engage in reading, to set goals and plans when they read, to monitor themselves when they are reading to see if the reading makes sense, or to check themselves after reading to see if they have accomplished their reading goal.

Obviously, we need to avoid this debilitating cycle of negative attributions and passive failure. Second-grade teacher Jerry Costello suggests four approaches:

> The first and almost certainly the most powerful way I have found to help students understand that they are in control of their learning is something I hear stressed over and over again by my colleagues and read in the literature: Make students' reading experiences successful; make them successful so frequently that students will realize that they themselves are responsible for their success, and not some outside force.
>
> Second, I tell students that their efforts *make a difference,* and when they succeed in a reading task, I talk to them about the activities they engaged in that made them successful. If, for example, after reading an informational piece about dinosaurs, students successfully answer several questions that they generated before reading, we discuss how generating those questions beforehand helped them focus their attention so that they could answer the questions as they read.
>
> Third, I avoid competitive situations in which students compare how well they read a selection to how well others read it and instead focus students' attention on what they personally gained from the selection.
>
> Finally, I try to provide a number of reading activities in which the goal is simply to *enjoy reading,* have fun, and experience something interesting and exciting, rather than offering only reading activities that are followed by answering questions or some other external accountability.

Jerry Costello, Second-Grade Teacher

The Importance of Appropriate Challenges

Although we stress the importance of success, providing appropriate challenges for children is equally essential. Saying that students should succeed at their reading tasks and that you should do everything possible to ensure success does not mean you should spoon-feed them. Unless readers under-

Reading with a friend can double reading pleasure.

take some challenging tasks, take risks, and get feedback on these efforts, little learning will take place. In order to develop as readers, children need some challenges. As Mihaly Csikszentmihalyi (1990) has learned from three decades of research on what makes people's lives happier and more meaningful, facing significant challenges and meeting them is one of the most fulfilling and rewarding experiences we can have. However, when we present students with challenges, we need to be certain that they clearly understand the goals toward which they are working, that we give them challenges appropriate to their skills, and that we provide them with whatever support they need to meet these challenges. Although true for all students, this is particularly crucial for students who have often found school to be difficult.

Teacher Attitudes and Actions
That Promote Positive Perceptions

Robert Marzano (1992) has highlighted four ways in which teachers can promote positive attitudes—instilling a feeling of acceptance in students, making the classroom a comfortable and orderly place, involving students in tasks that they value, and clarifying the tasks that students are asked to complete and the road to completing them. Additionally, teachers need to communicate to each student, with their actions as well as their words, their belief that each and every student can learn. Effective teachers create a "you can do it" attitude. Tragically, schools have frequently set different and lower reading goals for less-advantaged students and given them different instruction than that received by peers with greater advantages, with the predictable result that many less-advantaged students have seldom had an opportunity to achieve in many important areas (Allington, 1994; Pearson, 1996). Teachers need to meet students where they are and then challenge them to go further. One way to do this is to provide opportunities for students to connect literature with their lives and interests, encouraging them to select their own literature and to respond in their own unique ways. Elizabeth Bridges Smith (1995) observed the success of this approach with a fifth-grader in this urban classroom:

> It is time to reject the notion that only a few children can learn to read and write well.
>
> —*Richard Allington*
> *Teacher Educator*

IN THE CLASSROOM
Connecting Literature to Life

Michael was an academically struggling student. Qualifying for a pull-out, remedial program in math, he had low expectations for his performance in math, creating a pattern in which his attitude reinforced his academic performance, which in turn reinforced his attitude. Although his literacy skills were low average as well, Michael had scored a few percentage points above the cutoff for pull-out reading assistance. Proud of this accomplishment, Michael stated, "I don't like leavin' the room all the time. I just wanna do what everybody else be doin."

Smith noticed that Michael frequently engaged in literacy activities—reading, writing, and speaking. All of these activities bore some relation to Michael's African American heritage. He read texts with African American characters or themes; he wrote poetry with rhythms resembling rap and hip-hop; and he spoke in the cadence and patterns of the urban Black vernacular. Seldom code-switching to mainstream English, he showed these patterns in his writing as well.

After reading Ann McGovern's *Wanted Dead or Alive: The True Story of Harriet Tubman*, Michael shared this deeply personal response with Smith:

> *It just breaks my heart dat like people wanted kill other Black slaves just because they did good workings they can do. Because they tried. Cause Harriet was a good lady, she freed many slaves, she worked under hardness, she even saved one of the slaves that was runnin' away and got hit in the head with a steel metal.*

Later Michael read Eloise Greenfield's collection of poetry called *Honey, I Love and Other Poems* and combined his response to Greenfield's work with his newfound knowledge of Harriet Tubman. Proudly he came to Smith and said, "I have something to show you."

Harriet, Harriet she so good
She freed many slaves, she done real good
She smuggled them Underground
and delivered them to the North safe and sound
Harriet's fearless courage were so profound
as I learned by reading the stories regarding her now
I hope that I can grow and be
Strengthened to her humanity

Smith asked Michael about his preference for African American literature and his interest in African American history. His response was, "I just like Black history. I just wanna know a lot about my heritage." He conveyed that message to his classmates as well. Hearing students complain about a Frederick Douglass classroom project, he piped up for all to hear, "Y'all better quit. It's our heritage. We got to know this to help each other!"

A Literate Environment

The phrase "literate environment" describes the sort of classroom, school, and home environment in which literacy will be fostered and nurtured (Goodman, 1986). Probably the most important component of a literate environment is the modeling done by people whom children respect and love. In the best possible literate environment, children's teachers, principals, parents, brothers and sisters, and friends read a lot and openly display the pleasure reading gives them, the fact that reading opens up a world of information to them, the value they place in reading, and the satisfaction they gain from reading. To be most effective, of course, this modeling should occur not just once but repeatedly—all the time, really. Also, this modeling should include both repeated demonstrations—your reading along with students during a sustained silent reading period, your looking up an answer to a question children have in a book, and your sharing a favorite poem with your class—and direct testimonials: "Wow! What a story." "I never knew what fun river rafting could be until I read this article; I sure wish I'd read it sooner." "Sometimes I think the library is just about my favorite place." Third-grade teacher Mary Lou Flicker has her own testimonial to the power of modeling:

I never realized the importance of modeling the kinds of behaviors I would like my students to emulate until one rainy day in March. Normally the kids eat outdoors on picnic tables, but during this unusual California downpour we were forced inside for lunch recess. After the kids finished eating, I told them they could play games together quietly, draw on the chalkboard, read, whatever.
Instead of doing paperwork or watching the kids, I decided to read a book that a young friend had recommended, one of Barbara Park's Junie B. Jones

books, *Junie B. Jones and a Little Monkey Business*. It turned out to be an extremely funny book that I enjoyed immensely. After I finished, I looked around the room. To my amazement, there in the library corner sat Ramon, one of my least-motivated readers, a kid who hardly ever read by choice, fully absorbed in a Junie B. Jones book. Later in the day, when I told Ramon I was so pleased to see him reading, he said, "Well, you looked like you was having such a great time readin' that Junie B. Jones book, I just had to find out why!"

Mary Lou Flicker, Third-Grade Teacher

Another important component of a literate environment is the physical setting in which children read. In the best possible literate environment, the classroom is filled with books that are readily accessible for students to read in school or to take home. The walls are covered with colorful posters that advertise books and the treasures they offer. And there are several inviting places to read—a carpeted corner where children can sit on the floor and read without interruption, beanbags or other comfortable chairs that entice young readers to immerse themselves in a book, places where students can gather in groups to read to each other or discuss their reading, and some tables for students to use when reading prompts them to write.

Still another component of a literate environment is the content of the books, magazines, and other reading materials that are available to students. These texts should reflect the diversity of your classroom—the range of abilities and interests, and the cultural, linguistic, and social backgrounds of your students—as well as the diversity of the larger society. What students read must connect with their individual experiences if reading is to have meaning for them; what students read must connect them to the larger society if both students and society are to prosper. The sampling of trade books on page 47 features multicultural titles on two themes that play major roles in all cultures—food and families.

Finally, an equally important component of a literate environment is the atmosphere in which children read. In the best possible literate environment, everything that happens in the classroom sends the message that reading—learning from what you read, having personal responses to what you read, talking about what you read, and writing about what you read—is fantastic! In such a classroom, children are given plenty of time to read; they have ample opportunities to share with one another the information they learn and their responses to what they have read; they are taught to listen to and respect the ideas of others; and they learn that others will listen to and respect their ideas. In a literate atmosphere, values and ideas in books, one's own values and ideas, and other people's values and ideas are respected. Figure 2.1 shows a physical plan for a classroom designed to provide a literate environment.

Books About Food and Families in Many Cultures

Nora Dooley. *Everybody Cooks Rice*. Carolrhoda, 1991. Young Carrie gets to sample rice recipes from Barbados, Puerto Rico, Vietnam, India, and other countries when sent out to fetch her little brother at dinner time. 32 pages.

Anne Fine. *My War with Goggle-eyes*. Joy Street, 1989. In this funny story set in England, Kitty's liberal views clash with those of her mother's conservative boyfriend. 166 pages.

Kirkpatrick Hill. *Toughboy and Sister*. McElderry, 1990. In Alaska, after losing both their mother and father, two Athabascan Indian children use their wits and togetherness to survive until a villager realizes their situation. 128 pages.

Aylette Jenness. *Families: A Celebration of Diversity, Commitment, and Love*. Houghton Mifflin, 1990. Photo-essays celebrate the lives of 17 children of many cultures, races, and lifestyles. 48 pages.

Dayal Kaur Khalsa. *How Pizza Came to Queens*. Clarkson N. Potter, 1989. When Mrs. Pellegrino comes to visit May's family, she laments that there is no pizza. So May and her friends, with the help of the librarian who defines the word and finds a recipe and the ingredients, get Mrs. Pellegrino to make pizza. 24 pages.

Susan Kuklin. *How My Family Lives in America*. Bradbury, 1992. Three young children, an African American, a Chinese American, and a Hispanic American, describe their families, customs, and favorite recipes. The book includes nine recipes for rice. 32 pages.

Carmen Lomas Garza. *Family Pictures/Cuadros de Familia*. Children's Book Press, 1990. Mexican American artist Lomas Garza reminisces about the food of her childhood in a Texas border town. 32 pages.

Fran Manushkin. *Latkes and Applesauce*. Scholastic, 1990. This warm and exuberant Hanukkah story describes the Menashe family's holiday celebration, which is joyous despite a scarcity of food. 32 pages.

Patricia McMahon. *Chi-hoom: A Korean Girl*. Boyds Mills, 1993. This photo-essay depicting a week in the life of an 8-year-old girl in Seoul gives a sense of an individual's place within Korean family and culture. 48 pages.

Lensey Namioka, *Yang the Youngest and His Terrible Ear*. Little, Brown, 1992. Yang, the youngest in a musically talented Chinese immigrant family, whose heart is in baseball, not music, tries hard to live up to his family's musical expectations. 128 pages.

Barbara Ann Porte. *I Only Made Up the Roses*. Greenwillow, 1987. This book provides an engaging portrait of a multiracial family with French, Native American, and African American roots. 128 pages.

Jerry Spinelli. *Maniac Magee*. Little, Brown, 1990. In this middle-grade novel, a mixture of tall tale and realistic fiction, Jerry Magee, a homeless orphan, lives with three very different kinds of families as he goes about his mission of fighting prejudice in the town of Two Mills. 192 pages.

Sam Swope. *The Araboolies of Liberty Street*. Clarkson N. Potter, 1989. When the multiethnic, fun-loving Araboolie family moves to Liberty Street, they unsettle the drab, narrow-minded neighborhood and eliminate the tyrant General Pinch. 32 pages.

Paul Yee. *Roses Sing on New Snow: A Delicious Tale*. Macmillan, 1991. When the governor of South China visits Maylin's home, she creates a new dish in his honor, and her lazy brothers try to take all the credit. However, Maylin eventually triumphs, demonstrating that cooking, like painting, is an art. 32 pages.

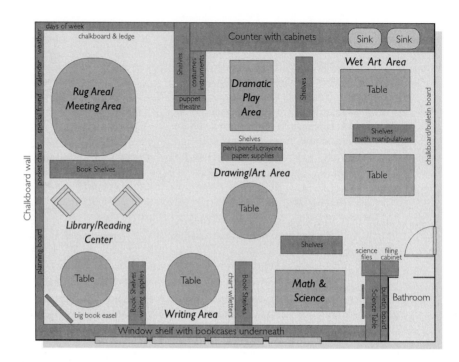

FIGURE 2.1 *Floor Plan of a Classroom That Invites Literacy*

Grouping Students for Instruction

One of the most important decisions you will make in your classroom will be how to group students. Students can be grouped in a variety ways for a variety of purposes, yet in all too many cases grouping is not used effectively and has a negative effect on many students—specifically those placed in the low-ability groups. In this section, we discuss some of the reasons for grouping, some of the problems grouping has produced, types of groups, and guidelines for grouping.

A typical class of 25 to 30 students brings with it 25 to 30 different sets of interests, abilities, attention spans, personalities, and reading skills; and it is very difficult to attend to each of these when working with the class as a whole. When teaching the entire class as a single group, teachers tend to teach to an imaginary mean; that is, they gear their instruction to what they perceive to be the middle range of interest, attention span, personality, ability, and so on. Such instruction does not meet the needs of those who are not in this range. Furthermore, in large-group situations, it is tempting for the teacher to do most of the talking, asking only an occasional question and, even then, allowing only one or two students to respond. Thus, most students play a passive role.

Dividing students into smaller groups is often helpful for a number of reasons. First, it is generally easier to keep smaller groups of students on task. Smaller groups tend to facilitate direct instructional engagement for more children and for a longer period of time. Second, smaller groups allow you to provide instruction designed to meet the needs of specific students, thus individualizing your reading program. Finally, smaller groups allow more students to be actively involved in instructional activities. In a group of five, for example, each student can respond to a question before you either run out of time or test the patience of the other students.

Given these advantages, it is not surprising that students have often been grouped for reading instruction. But unfortunately, grouping has typically been based exclusively on reading ability. During much of this century, American students have been grouped homogeneously for reading instruction, with the typical classroom having one high-, one middle-, and one low-ability group (Anderson, Hiebert, Scott, & Wilkinson, 1985). Recently, teachers and researchers have found that ability grouping results in a number of disadvantages, particularly for students in low-ability groups. Compared to students in other groups, students in low-ability groups are often given less time to read, spend more time on worksheets and less time being actively instructed, and are asked fewer higher-order questions. Additionally, students in such groups often suffer affective consequences of grouping, including lower self-esteem, lower motivation to succeed, and negative attitudes toward reading (Allington, 1983; 1994). Finally, the permanence of group membership is cause for concern; students who are placed in a low-ability group in kindergarten and first grade are all too likely to stay in the low-ability group throughout the elementary school years (Juel, 1990).

These findings have led teachers to develop a variety of grouping options, many of which deliberately create heterogeneous groups of students. Participating in a variety of groups gives children opportunities to learn how to interact with and learn from others who are in some ways different from them. Using a variety of groups also allows you to create appropriate groups to achieve the various goals you have for students. Some of the many useful types of groups include proficiency groups (short-term groups of students who share a common strength or a common instructional need), deliberately heterogeneous groups (groups specifically set up to counteract the potentially negative effect of proficiency groups), formal cooperative groups (heterogeneous groups of students specifically taught how to work together as a team), interest groups (short-term groups of students sharing a common interest), literature groups or literature circles (a particular sort of interest group in which students read the same selection and meet to discuss and respond to it), and project groups (groups designed to work together on a particular project such as making a video or preparing a dramatic presenta-

Teachers must look at what they are doing and judge the results. If groups help you to have an effective, exciting reading program for all your students, then they should be continued.

—*Cecilia E. Schrenker*
Teacher Educator

tion). The following list shows some of the most important factors to consider when deciding how to group students:

- Your general instructional objectives
- Your specific objectives for individual children
- The material your students will be reading
- Your students' individual strengths
- Students' abilities to work with others in the group
- The number and types of groups you can successfully manage
- The proviso that no student be consistently assigned to the low group

Becoming adept at grouping students is a challenge. We suggest that you first become comfortable with two or three types of grouping and then gradually add other grouping alternatives as your classroom management and grouping skills become stronger.

We do not mean to suggest that there is no place for whole-class instruction. Whole-class instruction is useful when you wish to reach all students at once. Spending five or ten minutes with the entire class before students begin working individually or in small groups allows you to touch base with all students, answer their questions, and hear their concerns. However, because lengthy whole-class instruction seldom commands students' attention throughout its duration and often invites off-task behavior, whole-class instruction should generally be kept brief and focused. The following sample lesson is based on one found in *Structuring Cooperative Learning: Lesson Plans for Teachers* (Johnson, Johnson, & Holubec, 1987):

> Whole class, small group, partnerships, and individual-child units are all effective learning groups.
>
> —*Joanne Yatvin*
> *Superintendent*

IN THE CLASSROOM

A Primary-Grade Cooperative Learning Group

The purpose of this lesson is for students to work together to find the answers to a set of story problems that require mathematical reasoning and the use of addition and subtraction.

Procedure:

- Assign three students of varying abilities to work together as a group—perhaps one high-, one medium-, and one low-achieving math student.
- Tell students you will give each group a set of ten story problems. Their job is to read each story problem, write a math sentence telling what happened in the story, and then figure out the missing number. Next, show them how they are to read and write their answers:
  1. Put a problem on the chalkboard or an overhead projector, and read it aloud. For example,

     Erika checked out 5 library books. She finished reading 2 and returned these to the library. How many books does she have left?

2. Model the mental processes you go through to arrive at the mathematical sentence: 5 - 2 = ?

3. Perform the operation: 5 - 2 = 3

- Explain to students that you want ONE set of answers from the whole group, which they all helped find and agree upon.

> I expect to see all of you helping and all of you sharing. If you don't understand or agree, ask the others in your group to explain that problem again. If you still think they are wrong, explain your answer to them and see if they agree with you. [Dramatizing, or role-playing, this situation can be helpful in getting students to understand and use this process.]

- Tell students that when they finish the ten story problems, each group member should sign his or her name to the group's paper.

> Signing your name shows me you each helped, shared, and understand. Your group should try to answer all the problems correctly. If your group gets nine or ten correct, that means you have done a super job!

- While students are working in their groups, try to interfere as little as possible. However, occasionally ask individuals to explain one of their group's answers.

- As a group finishes, quickly score the answers. Ask each member of the group if he or she participated and how he or she felt about the task. Praise groups that get nine or ten correct. Try to help groups that got a lower score discern what went wrong and what needs to be done to be more successful with similar tasks in the future.

- After the lesson has been completed, try to determine if students met the conditions you set out. Did all or most of the groups solve the story problems correctly? Do you need to teach more on story problems? Did students demonstrate understanding of the cooperative goal structure? What cooperative skills need to be taught in future lessons?

Reflection AND Application

At this point, we suggest that you pause and consciously deal with some of the ideas we have presented.

1. Describe a successful reading experience you have had and an unsuccessful one. What could you or someone else have done to make the unsuccessful one more successful?

2. Explain two or three things you might do to help a shy second-grader who tends to lack confidence in his ability to develop a more positive attitude toward himself as a learner.

3. Get together with a small group of your classmates, generate a list of positive and negative effects of grouping, and brainstorm a list of ways in which you can maximize the positive effects of grouping and minimize the negative ones.

Traditional Principles

In the period from about 1960 to about 1980, educators and researchers produced a rich body of basic information about effective instruction. Here, we briefly discuss four of the most important traditional principles established during that time. These are shown in the following list:

- Focusing on academically relevant tasks
- Active teaching and active learning
- Distinguishing instruction from practice
- Feedback

For more information on these principles, Jere Brophy and Tom Good's *Looking into Classrooms* (1997) is an excellent source.

Focusing on Academically Relevant Tasks

If you are going to get really good at something, you need to do a lot of it. You need to have a lot of what educational researchers have termed "opportunity to learn," chances to learn about and practice whatever it is you are trying to get good at (Berliner, 1979). If students are going to become proficient readers, they need to do a lot of reading in which they are truly engaged with the topic. In addition to reading itself, several subtasks are important for developing readers. If students are going to become proficient decoders— readers who can use their knowledge of letter–sound correspondences, spelling patterns, and the like to decode unfamiliar words and eventually to process them automatically—they need to be actively engaged in decoding tasks. If students are to become proficient at responding to literature orally and in writing, they need many opportunities to discuss their reading and to write about what they have read. And if students are to become critical readers and writers of informational prose, they need abundant opportunities to read and to write informational material and to make critical response to it. These are only some of the reading-related areas in which students must become proficient, but we think we have made our point: Curriculum—what students study—matters!

To be sure, students will learn many things we do not teach in school, and they will not learn everything we do teach. But if we have things we really want students to learn, it is sheer folly not to give them the opportunity to actively engage in learning them!

> Regardless of what anyone claims about student and school characteristics, opportunity to learn is the single most powerful predictor of student achievement.
>
> —*David Berliner and Bruce Biddle*
> *Educational Researchers*

Active Teaching and Active Learning

The term *active teaching* refers to a set of principles and teaching behaviors that research has shown to be particularly effective, especially in teaching basic skills. As noted by Brophy (1986), teachers who engage in active teaching are the instructional leaders of their classrooms; they are fully knowledgeable about the content and purposes of the instruction they present and about the instructional goals they wish to accomplish. Active teachers do a lot of teaching. Although they use discovery learning for some purposes, they do not generally rely on students to discover what it is they are supposed to learn, particularly when the learning deals with basic skills. Similarly, although they use a variety of materials as part of their teaching, they do not rely on the materials to do the teaching. They directly carry to students the content to be learned in short presentations, discussions, and demonstrations.

Just as it is vital that the teacher be actively involved in teaching, it is also crucial that the learner be actively involved in learning (Brophy & Good, 1997). As we explained in our discussion of the cognitive-constructivist orientation in Chapter 1, the learner must do something with the material he is studying if he is to learn much from it. Fourth-grade teacher John Fitzhugh puts it well:

> Students *must* be actively involved in order for any sort of learning to take place. That's simply a fact. But there are a number of ways this can happen. Say, for instance, a student is reading a trade book on sharks, perhaps Seymour Simon's *Sharks*. As he reads, the student can
>
> - think about the new things he is learning about sharks.
> - discuss new insights with others.
> - make outlines or sketches that depict his new knowledge.
> - write something about sharks.
> - draw relationships between the new knowledge and his existing knowledge of sharks.
> - attempt to implement the new knowledge (for example, simulate an underwater environment by making a diorama of sharks and their habitat, as one of my students did).
>
> Or the student can undertake many other activities that cause him to grapple with the new knowledge and integrate it into his existing schema. As we all know, precious little new knowledge will be absorbed passively.
>
> John Fitzhugh, Fourth-Grade Teacher

Distinguishing Instruction from Practice

Effective teaching requires both instruction and practice, but the two need to be clearly distinguished. Practice involves asking students to do something they already know how to do. Instruction involves showing or telling students how to do something that they do not yet know how to do. Simply asking students to do something does not constitute teaching them how to do it. Practice is appropriate *after* students have learned whatever it is they are to practice.

I have always spent time reflecting on my teaching. Most of this reflection is a mental playback of the day, the kind that many teachers experience. It is useful as a way of deciding how to proceed based on past events, thinking of solutions to problems and sparking new ideas.

—*Franca Fedele*
Sixth-Grade Teacher

Emphasizing this distinction, Gerry Duffy and Laura Roehler (1982) have coined the terms *proactive teaching* and *reactive teaching*. Proactive teaching consists of deliberately showing students how to do something before expecting them to do it themselves. Reactive teaching consists of first asking students to do something and then showing them how to do it only if they fail. Proactive teaching sets students up for success, whereas reactive teaching sets them up for failure. Reactive teaching is inefficient because it often leaves the teacher trying to clarify matters after the fact for students who became confused while working at something they did not know how to do; the confusion could have been avoided by providing instructions at the outset. Reactive teaching is especially demoralizing for students who repeatedly fail.

Thus, before asking students to explain the conflict in a particular story, check to see that they understand the concept of conflict as used in literature. If they do not, teach the concept before asking them to deal with it. Note that with a difficult concept such as conflict, instruction could take some time.

Feedback

Feedback is perhaps the most long-standing principle in this section on traditional principles. From the dialogues of Socrates, to the answers included in programmed instruction, to the beep our word processor makes when we key in an inappropriate command, feedback has long been a central component of instruction. In the years before school, young children get a great deal of immediate, positive feedback—fussing brings a bottle, a smile a lot of attention, saying "ball" a round object to play with. During these same years, young children also receive a good deal of immediate, negative feedback—too much fussing may bring only a closed door, a smile at the television set produces no response, and "bla" spoken in an attempt to get a round object to play with may instead bring a blanket.

Once in school, students continue to get feedback, although with one teacher working with perhaps 30 students, individual feedback is not as readily available as it was at home. But such feedback is every bit as necessary. There is no way for a learner to know whether he is on the right track unless he receives some sort of response. And this rule applies whether newly learned material is the sound represented by the letter *m*, the pronunciation of the word *rabbit*, or the identification of the central theme in a story. Sometimes feedback can be imbedded in the learning situation and does not require a response from another person; for example, when the child reads, "The rabbit really liked the carrots," his understanding of the sentence as a whole is established by his correct pronunciation of "rabbit"; the pronunciation brings the meaning to mind. At other times, other students can provide the feedback; for example, a group of fifth-graders reads a novel and agrees that the theme is the importance of friendships. But much of the time, such as in learning letter–sound correspondences, the feedback must come from the teacher. Figuring out how to provide timely, telling, and kind feedback for 30 or so students is a major task for a classroom teacher.

Reflection AND Application

4. Think back as far as you can in your schooling—to elementary school if possible, or to secondary school—and jot down a list of tasks you completed that you think were academically relevant and a list of tasks you completed that you think were not academically relevant. Then write about what does and does not constitute an academically relevant task.

5. Get together with a few classmates, review the descriptions of proactive and reactive teaching we have provided, and create and present two scenarios—one of proactive teaching and one of reactive teaching.

6. Think of a teacher you have had who has been particularly effective in his or her use of one of the traditional principles we have discussed, and describe what he or she did that was so effective.

Constructivist Perspectives on Instruction

The instructional concepts we discuss here have generally been advanced more recently than those in the previous section and are more closely related to the cognitive–constructivist orientation that underlies this book than those in the previous section. We view these concepts as absolutely vital additions to those described earlier.

Scaffolding

We believe that the term *scaffolding* was first used in its educational sense by David Wood, Jerome Bruner, and Gail Ross (1976), who used it to characterize mothers' verbal interaction when reading to their young children. In these interactions, Wood and his colleagues noted, mothers gently yet supportively guided their children toward successful literacy experiences. Thus, for example, in sharing a picture book with a child and attempting to assist the child in reading the words that label the pictures, a mother might at first simply page through the book, familiarizing the child with the pictures and the general content of the book. Then she might focus on a single picture and ask the child what it is. After this, she might point to the word below the picture, tell the child that the word names the picture, ask the child what the word is, and provide feedback on the correctness of the answer. The important point to note here is that the mother has neither simply told the child the word nor simply asked him to say it. Instead, she has built an instructional structure, a scaffold, that assists the student in learning. Scaffolding, as Wood and his colleagues have aptly put it, is "a process that enables a child or novice to solve a problem, carry out a task, or achieve a goal which would be beyond his unassisted efforts" (p. 90).

> A scaffold is a temporary and adjustable structure that allows accomplishment of a task that would be impossible without the scaffold's support.
>
> —*Linda Anderson*
> *Educational Researcher*

Scaffolding is widely used in the world outside of school, and one particular instance of out-of-school scaffolding—the use of training wheels on children's bicycles—serves as a graphic example of the procedure. Training wheels are supportive; they enable a novice bicycle-rider to do something he might not otherwise be able to do—ride a two-wheeler. Equally important, training wheels are temporary, and they can be gradually raised so that the budding cyclist increasingly assumes the task of riding with less and less support from the scaffold.

Scaffolding is also widely used in schools, as it should be. For example, a teacher is scaffolding students' learning when he sounds out part of a word for them, reads the beginning of a story aloud, or explains the organization of a difficult chapter that they are about to read. A teacher is also providing scaffolding when he models the thought processes he uses in determining what is particularly important in an informational selection students are about to read, and when he suggests a way to begin an essay they are writing. In each of these cases, the teacher is assisting students in doing something that they might not otherwise be able to do. Much of Chapter 6 describes ways to build supportive scaffolds for the many different types of reading students do.

The Zone of Proximal Development

The concept of the zone of proximal development is primarily attributed to the Russian psychologist Lev Vygotsky (1978). It emphasizes the social nature of learning and the fact that learning is very much a social phenomenon. We learn much of what we learn in our social interchanges with others. The notion is therefore very consistent with constructivist theory; in fact, it is one of the ideas that stimulated much constructivist thinking. According to Vygotsky, at any particular point in time, children have a circumscribed zone of development, a range within which they can learn. At one end of this range are learning tasks that they can complete independently; at the other end are learning tasks that they cannot complete, even with assistance. In between these two extremes is the zone most productive for learning, the range of tasks in which children can achieve *if* they are assisted by a more knowledgeable or more competent other.

If left on their own, for example, many third-graders might learn very little from a *National Geographic World* article on the formation of thunderstorms. Conversely, with your help—getting them interested in the topic, focusing their attention, preteaching some of the critical concepts such as the effects of rising heat, arranging small groups to discuss and answer questions on certain parts of the article—these same students may be able to learn a good deal from the article. However, with other topics and other texts—for example, a chapter on gravity from a high school physics text—no amount of outside help, at least no reasonable amount of outside help, will foster much learning for these third-graders. The topic of gravity and its presentation in the high school text is simply outside their zone of proximal development.

Outside of school, many people can and do serve as more knowledgeable or more competent others—parents and foster parents, brothers and sisters, relatives, friends, and clergy. As a teacher creating scaffolded reading activities, you may occasionally be able to bring in outside resources to assist students. More often, however, you will arrange reading situations so that you serve as the more knowledgeable other who assists students in successfully reading selections they could not read on their own. Additionally, in many cases students will be able to pool their resources and assist one another in dealing with reading selections that they could not successfully work with alone.

The Gradual Release of Responsibility Model

The gradual release of responsibility model depicts a progression in which students gradually assume increased responsibility for their learning. A particularly informative visual representation of the model developed by David Pearson and Margaret Gallagher (1983) is shown in Figure 2.2.

The model depicts a temporal sequence in which students gradually progress from situations in which the teacher takes responsibility for their successful completion of a reading task (in other words, does most of the work for them), then to situations in which students assume increasing responsibility for reading tasks, and finally to situations in which students take total or nearly total responsibility for reading tasks. First-grade teacher Richard Gerhardt talks about the nature of gradual release and the part that the text and students' development play in deciding on how much responsibility is appropriate for him as the teacher and how much is appropriate for students:

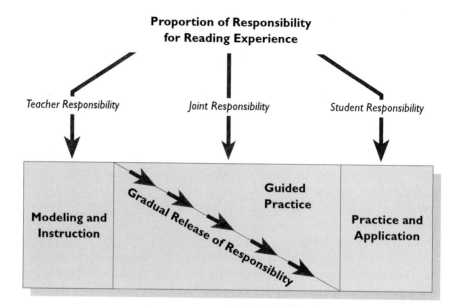

**Proportion of Responsibility
for Reading Experience**

Teacher Responsibility   *Joint Responsibility*   *Student Responsibility*

**Modeling and
Instruction**

Gradual Release of Responsiblity

**Guided
Practice**

**Practice and
Application**

FIGURE 2.2 *The
Gradual Release of
Responsibility Model*

In early October you will often find me seated in a circle with a group of children, displaying a big book. First I'll read the title aloud and talk a little bit about what it and the picture on the cover make me think of. Then I'll ask the children what the title and picture make them think of and what the book might be about. After listening to students' responses and trying to emphasize and highlight those that are likely to help them understand the story, I begin reading. Even though there are only a handful of words on each page and the story is very simple, I'll stop every two or three pages, ask students what has happened, summarize the story up to that point if children's responses suggest a summary is necessary, and perhaps ask students what they think will happen next.

After completing the story, I may ask students a few questions to see if they understood it. Or I may get some other sorts of responses from them—how they felt about one of the characters, if they have had similar experiences, or what emotions the story aroused in them. I might also share my understanding of the story and some of my personal responses to it.

Richard Gerhardt, First-Grade Teacher

Throughout this session, Mr. Gerhardt has done everything possible to ensure that each student gets something from the story and leaves the experience feeling good about it. Appropriately, because these students are just beginning to read, he took a huge portion of the responsibility for their success in "reading" the story.

Now consider Mr. Gerhardt and his class in January. Over the past four months, he has continued to take much of the responsibility for students' reading. He has done a lot of building of interest, reading to students, checking on understanding, and the like. Additionally, over this same period, he has gradually introduced children to longer and more challenging books. At this point, when students read something like the very simple picture book they read in October, he will let them handle it largely on their own. With the more challenging books, however, he will continue to scaffold activities.

At this point, you may think that the gradual release model suggests that, over the school years, teachers simply give students increased responsibility in a steady progression. But the situation is somewhat more complex than that. Over time, teachers do indeed gradually dismantle the scaffolds they have built so that students become increasingly independent readers. But as students deal with increasingly challenging texts and more complex tasks, teachers create scaffoldings for the more difficult materials even as they remove it for simpler, well-mastered tasks. At any particular point in time, learners are likely to be—and should be—dealing with some texts and tasks that are more challenging and some that are less challenging. Many fourth-graders can take full responsibility for reading an easy novel such as *Skinnybones* by Barbara Park. These same students may need a moderate amount of scafffolding to successfully deal with a somewhat challenging historical novel, such as *Pedro's Journey* by Pam Conrad; and you may need to assume most of the responsibility for their success in reading and understanding a short expository article on acid rain. Many sixth-graders, however, could deal independently with *Pedro's Journey* and would need only a little assistance from you in tackling the short acid rain article. But these same sixth-graders would need considerably more assistance from you in working through a longer and more technical article on acid rain. Thus, the scaffolding that you provide and the extent to which you release responsibility to students always depends on the particular texts and tasks that they are working with (Collins, Brown, & Holum, 1991).

Cognitive Modeling

Modeling is another very important tool to use as part of active teaching. When teachers model a task, they actually *do* something, rather than just tell students how to do it. A specific sort of modeling, cognitive modeling, is particularly useful in teaching students difficult concepts and strategies. In cognitive modeling, teachers use explicit instructional talk to reveal their thought processes as they perform the tasks that students will be asked to perform. For example, a teacher might model the mental process of determining the meaning of an unknown word in context, as shown here:

IN THE CLASSROOM
Cognitive Modeling

Teacher: Suppose I'm reading along and I come to this sentence: "It was raining heavily and water was standing in the street, so before he left for work Mr. Nelson put on his raincoat, buckled on his _____ [galoshes] over his shoes, and picked up his umbrella." Let me see—*g-a-l-o-s-h-e-s*. I don't think I know that word. Let's see. It's raining, and he picks up his raincoat and umbrella and buckles something over his shoes. *Galoshes* must be some sort of waterproof boots that go over shoes. I can't be certain of that, but it makes sense in the sentence; and I don't think I want to look it up right now.

Cognitive modeling provides a window on the teacher's mind and constitutes one of the most powerful tools for showing children how to reason as they seek to understand a text.

Responsive Elaboration

As we explained in Chapter 1, constructivism supports the position that much of a text's meaning is constructed by the individual. This is also true of the meanings students construct based on teacher presentations. As Walter Doyle (1983) has explained, students "mediate" the meaning they construct from teachers' instruction, understanding the message in their own unique ways, which sometimes differ significantly from what the teacher is attempting to convey. This happens frequently, and we as teachers need to be constantly alert to our students' understanding of our instruction. We must frequently give them an opportunity to demonstrate whether or not their interpretations are consistent with our meanings, and always be prepared to do some additional teaching when the initial instruction has not been successful.

Gerry Duffy and Laura Roehler (1987) call these follow-up instructional interactions with students "responsive elaboration." They are responsive in that teachers use evidence of students' reasoning and understanding in deciding how to further their understanding. And they are elaborations in the sense that the response is not an attempt to teach something new, but rather an elaboration and clarification of the instruction already provided. In the following example, a third-grade teacher has attempted to teach students how to identify a main idea in a paragraph, but the student's attempt to find the main idea of a particular paragraph has yielded only incomplete success. In his initial statement, the student reveals that he has taken into account only part of the information in the paragraph, and the teacher leads him to realize that the main idea must derive from all of the paragraph.

IN THE CLASSROOM
Responsive Elaboration

Teacher: What is the main idea in the paragraph?

Student: Getting new words from Indians.

Teacher: Well, let's test it. Is the first sentence talking about new words from the Indians?

Student: Yes.

Teacher: How about the next?

Student: No.

Teacher: No. It says that Indians also learned new words from the settlers, right?

Student: The Indians taught the settlers words, and the settlers taught the Indians words.

Teacher: Good. You see, you have to think about all the ideas in the paragraph to decide the main idea. (Duffy & Roehler, p. 517)

Although this brief interaction has by no means fully prepared the reader to identify the main idea in everything he reads, it is a start in that direction; and the teacher's responsive elaboration has avoided the student's beginning his learning with a misconception.

Teaching for Understanding

Seventy years ago, British philosopher Alfred North Whitehead (1929) railed against schools' fostering what he called *inert knowledge*—fragile, shallow, tip-of-the-iceberg knowledge that is usually soon forgotten and too superficial to be of much use even if remembered. Today, educators are increasingly realizing the value of teaching for understanding—dealing with fewer topics but teaching them in such a way that students not only learn the content itself thoroughly, but also appreciate the reasons for learning it and retain it in a form that makes it usable. As Harvard psychologist David Perkins (1992) puts it, teaching for understanding promotes three basic goals of education: retention of knowledge, understanding of knowledge, and active use of knowledge.

We believe that teaching for understanding is terribly important, and all of Chapter 8 is devoted to the topic. Here, we will note only that the key to teaching for understanding is teaching fewer topics but teaching them well; it also demands the sort of constructive teaching and learning advocated throughout this section of the chapter.

Cooperative Learning

David and Roger Johnson (Johnson, Johnson, & Holubec, 1994) define cooperative learning as "the instructional use of small groups so that students work together to maximize their own and each other's learning" (p. 4), and Robert Slavin (1987) defines it as "instructional methods in which students of all performance levels work together toward a group goal" (p. 8). As the Johnsons have repeatedly said, "None of us is as smart as all of us." Groups of students working together have the potential to achieve well beyond the achievement of a student working by himself. Moreover, working in cooperative groups can produce multiple benefits. Cooperative learning can improve students' achievement, their effort to succeed, their critical thinking, their attitudes toward the subjects studied, their psychological adjustment, and their self-esteem. Cooperative learning can also foster students' interpersonal relationships, improving their ability to work with others and to build relationships among diverse racial, ethnic, and social groups. Additionally, as John Seely Brown and his colleagues note (Brown, Collins, & Duguid, 1989), group learning offers learners opportunities for displaying and recognizing the multiple roles that are often required to solve real-world problems and to recognize and confront their own and others' ineffective strategies and misconceptions.

Cooperative learning is consistent with many constructivist principles that we have mentioned. It relies on the belief that the best learning is often social, gives students an opportunity to scaffold one another's work, and puts students in a position to respond to and elaborate on one another's thinking. Because of its great potential, throughout this book we frequently suggest group activities for elementary students, and many of the Reflection and Application sections suggest that you engage in group work.

Reflection AND Application

7. Each of the instructional concepts in this section is tremendously important. Define each of them in your own words. Next, check your understanding against that of a classmate, and see if you can come up with a common definition of each concept. Finally, team up with this classmate and two others, and together come up with one example of a classroom situation in which instruction is in keeping with each of these concepts and one example of a classroom situation in which instruction runs counter to these concepts.

8. Once you have completed the activities in item 7, select the concept that you think will be the most valuable for you personally, and explain your reasons, preferably in writing.

A BRIEF HISTORY OF READING INSTRUCTION IN THE UNITED STATES

The history of the United States and of U.S. schools reveals cyclical changes in which alternating political and educational stances would first dominate and in turn be criticized (Cremin, 1990; Schlesinger, 1986). To understand the development of contemporary approaches to teaching reading, the history of reading instruction in the United States can be best studied against the backdrop of tensions between these competing views. In the brief history that follows—the first parts of which rely heavily on information taken from Nila Banton Smith's *American Reading Instruction* (1965)—we focus on these tensions. In the next section of the chapter, we describe the three approaches to reading instruction that currently predominate and that continue to reflect these tensions.

The Colonial Period and the 19th Century

Much of this period—roughly the years 1600 to 1840—was relatively free of tensions over instructional approaches. The emphasis during this period was on content. The purpose of reading instruction early in the period was clearly religious, as revealed by this excerpt from the Old Deluder Act passed by the General Court of Massachusetts in 1647:

> It being one chief point of that old deluder, Satan, to keep men from the knowledge of the Scriptures. . . . It is therefore ordered that every township in this jurisdiction, after the Lord hath increased them to the number of fifty households, shall then forthwith appoint one within their town to teach allsuch children as shall resort to hime to write and read. (Smith, 1965, p. 13)

Beginning about the time of the American Revolution and continuing until about 1840, the purpose shifted, and reading series reflected what Smith has termed a "nationalistic–moralistic emphasis," as exemplified in these lines from the preface to Lyman Cobb's *The North American Reader* (1835):

> The pieces in this work are chiefly American. The English Reader so largely used in our country does not contain a single piece or paragraph written by an American citizen. Is this good policy? Is it patriotism? (Cobb, 1835, p. v)

However, regardless of whether the reading material focused on religious or patriotic content, the method of instruction throughout the period was much the same—The alphabetic-spelling method. The alphabetic-spelling method was a slow, step-by-step approach in which students first learned the alphabet, then learned to spell a large number of syllables,

I cannot live without books.

—*Thomas Jefferson*

spelled words before they read them, memorized sections of text (usually religious, moral, or patriotic in content), and read orally (Smith, 1965). Figure 2.3 shows a page from the *New England Primer*, exemplifying the tediousness of the approach.

Not surprisingly, this approach eventually came under fire, most notably by educational reformer Horace Mann, who advocated instead a focus on whole words and letter sounds. In an 1842 report to the Board of Education in Massachusetts, Mann displays his disdain for the alphabetic-spelling approach and foreshadows the controversy that, though modified, continues today.

> *Compare the above method [the more meaningful approach he favored] with that of calling up a class of abecedarians—or, what is more common, a single child—and while the teacher holds a book or card before him, with a pointer in his hand, says, a, and he echoes a; then b, and he echoes b; and so on until the vertical row of lifeless and ill-favored characters is completed, and then of remanding him to his seat, to sit still and look at vacancy.* (Mann, 1844/1965, p. 117)

New England Primer   5

EASY SYLLABLES FOR CHILDREN

Ab	eb	ib	ob	ub
ac	ec	ic	oc	uc
ad	ed	id	od	ud
af	ef	if	of	uf
ag	eg	ig	og	ug
aj	ej	ij	oj	uj
al	el	il	ol	ul
am	em	im	om	um
an	en	in	on	un
ap	ep	ip	op	up
ar	er	ir	or	ur
as	es	is	os	us
at	et	it	ot	ut
av	ev	iv	ov	uv
ax	ex	ix	ox	ux
az	ez	iz	oz	uz

FIGURE 2.3 *A Page from the* New England Primer

From Smith, N. B. (1965) *American Reading Instruction*, second edition. Newark, DE: International Reading Association.

The Heyday of Basal Readers

Although the exact dates are not important, we will define this period as running from about 1910 to about 1985. Beginning somewhat after the turn of the century, reading programs and reading instruction began to look more like those that you or your parents might have experienced. Teacher's manuals were developed, research on which words appear frequently in English resulted in carefully controlled vocabulary in basal readers, tests were increasingly used, and students were increasingly grouped by ability for reading instruction.

The basal readers themselves consisted of large collections of reading selections, worksheets, teacher's manuals, tests, and supplementary material. The books for the earliest grades employed severely controlled vocabularies, generally contained very brief narratives, and relied on pictures to convey much of their meaning. The books used in the remainder of the primary grades continued to employ controlled vocabularies and contained largely fiction, which was often rather impoverished. At about the fourth-grade level, selections became longer, vocabulary control eased, the fiction included became somewhat stronger, and some expository selections were included. Much of the instruction students received in these programs centered around directed reading lessons—which included preparation for reading, silent reading, and follow-up questions and discussion—on individual selections. These lessons were often punctuated by skills work in decoding, vocabulary, and comprehension; and students spent a good deal of time completing worksheets. Figure 2.4 shows pages from a first-grade reader in a 1950 basal series, typical of the readers of this period.

Although many controversies about reading materials and reading instruction arose during the period, the most persistent and most frequent again involved the tensions between more holistic and more segmented instruction and again centered on letters, sounds, and words. The alphabetic-spelling method had disappeared, but the whole-word method and various approaches emphasizing phonics continued to be in conflict. This conflict reached a crescendo in 1955 when Rudolf Flesch published his best-selling *Why Johnny Can't Read*. Flesch charged that American children were not learning to read because they were not taught phonics. A decade later, in 1967, Harvard University professor Jeanne Chall published a very influential review of research in which she concluded that phonics produced at least somewhat better results than the whole-word method. In that same year, the largest study of beginning reading ever conducted, the First Grade Reading Studies (Bond & Dykstra, 1967/1997), produced findings that tended to support Chall's conclusions.

Although these three publications had some effect on basals, they did not seriously affect the influence and prominence of basals in the schools. Contrary to Flesch's charge, most basals had always included some phonics

"Look, look," said Sally.
"See it go up.
See Spot run.
This is fun for Spot."

"Oh, Dick," said Jane.
"Spot can help you.
Funny little Spot can help."

12

Do What I Do
"See me jump," said Dick.
"Oh, my! This is fun.
Come and jump.
Come and do what I do.
Look, look!
Who can jump?
Who can do what I do?"

41

FIGURE 2.4 *Pages from a Typical First-Grade Basal Reader of the 1950s*

Reprinted with permission of Addison-Wesley Educational Publishers, Inc. and Scott Foresman Addison-Wesley.

instruction, and basal publishers responded to criticisms by providing somewhat more phonics. As late as 1985, the vast majority of American children continued to be taught with basal readers, and most teachers, if asked, would say that they used a basal reading approach.

The Challenge to Basal Readers

The challenge that ended the dominance of basal readers came not from the advocates of phonics, but from the advocates of more holistic approaches—most notably from the proponents of whole language, first widely popularized in the United States in the writings of Kenneth Goodman (1970) and Frank Smith (1971). We describe the whole-language approach in the next section of this chapter. Here, we will deal very briefly with the charges whole-language advocates have made against basal readers and the traditional approaches they represent.

The most basic criticism was that basal approaches artificially break up language and learning to read in a way that is unnatural, artificial, and actually makes learning to read more difficult. More specific charges were that basals included too much skills instruction, that instruction in phonics and other subskills of reading were not integrated with actual reading, that vocabulary was much too controlled, that stories were banal and not well constructed, that separating students into ability groups had dire results for less-skilled readers, and that teachers were overprogrammed and overscripted. Critics also noted that selections in basals dealt almost exclusively with white, middle-class characters, themes, and settings, and that many of the reading selections were very poor from a literary standpoint. These challenges had a marked effect on basal readers and a huge impact on the reading instruction that now takes place in American classrooms.

CURRENT APPROACHES TO READING INSTRUCTION

The majority of methods of reading instruction in American schools today can be characterized as falling along a continuum that ranges from *traditional basal* approaches to *literature-based* approaches (see Figure 2.5 for an example of such a text) to *whole-language* approaches. The traditional basal approach is becoming quite rare (Hoffman et al., 1994), but we have included

One night Bear and Little Bird were sitting outside, looking at the moon.
"You know what I wish?" said Bear. "I wish I could dance with the moon."
"Maybe she'd like to dance with you, too?" chirped Little Bird.

FIGURE 2.5 *Page from a Typical First-Grade Literature-Based Text*

From *Moondance* by Frank Asch. Published by Blue Ribbon Books, a registered trademark of Scholastic, Inc. Copyright © 1993 by Frank Asch. Reprinted by permission of Scholastic, Inc.

it here because it is still used in some schools, and it provides a contrast against which you can consider the newer approaches. Also, many of today's teachers first learned to use the basal approach, and it continues to influence both teachers and school programs.

Four factors are important to keep in mind as you consider this continuum of approaches. First, schools and districts generally either formally adopt a position or reading curriculum or adopt a de facto position or curriculum. If the teachers in your school see themselves as whole-language teachers, your attempt to use a basal reader would almost certainly be unsuccessful. At the same time, this typically does not mean that you have no choices; in most schools you will have a good deal of autonomy in your classroom as long as your approach is consistent with the general orientation of your school.

Second, these terms are abstractions; what they mean when applied to an individual teacher's instruction or to a reading program varies tremendously. If you were to examine several traditional basal reader series, you would see that they differ in a number of ways. If you were to visit a number of literature-based classrooms, you'd probably find what Richard Allington and his colleagues (1996) recently found: Some used basal series that bill themselves as literature-based exclusively, some used a combination of basals and trade books (books sold to the general public and not specifically intended for instruction in schools), and some used trade books exclusively. And if you were to ask whole-language proponent Kenneth Goodman to define whole-language, he would probably tell you that it is "a lot of things to a lot of people" and that "more than anything else, a whole-language program is an educational program conducted by whole-language teachers" (1986, p. 5). Thus, the characterizations that we give of each approach are generalizations that hold only in a broad way.

Third, there is currently a good deal of debate and controversy about how to most effectively teach reading. The general trend from more skills-oriented to more holistic approaches—which has predominated for the past 10–15 years—is currently being challenged. For example, in 1995, California—the largest consumer of textbooks in the country and therefore a very powerful influence on the content of commercial reading programs—issued a report calling for greatly increased attention to the teaching of reading skills, particularly phonics and other word-recognition skills (California Department of Education, 1995; Goodman, 1996; Honig, 1996). The direction that reading instruction will take in the next few years is far from certain.

Fourth, and perhaps most important, the approach that we are presenting and advocating in this book can best be described as a balanced approach. We belong to what David Pearson (1994) has characterized as the "radical middle." We believe strongly that most manifestations of each of the three approaches include both techniques that will help students reach high levels of critical literacy as well as some that are not likely to help. We also believe that most manifestations of each of the approaches fail to include some techniques that could help students reach high levels of critical literacy.

Figure 2.6 highlights the differences that characterize the three approaches. The figure is, of course, a simplification; in the next several pages we amplify on each of the eight aspects of the approaches shown in the figure. We also state our position on each of them.

Traditional Basal Approach	Literature-Based Approach	Whole-Language Approach
Reading Materials		
Traditional basals	Literature-based basals and trade books	Trade books only
Skills Instruction		
Typically sequenced, isolated skills work	Some skills work; may not be sequenced	No sequence of skills and no isolated skills work
Word-Recognition Instruction (Most Notably Phonics)		
Some systematic phonics instruction is likely to be used.	Some systematic phonics instruction may be used.	Any phonics instruction is imbedded in ongoing reading.
Ability Grouping		
Often three relatively fixed ability groups	Used cautiously; temporary groups	Not used
Assessment		
Standardized tests and objective tests that come with the basal	Both standardized and less formal tests	Performance-based, subjective assessment
Student-Centered Orientation		
Primarily teacher-centered	Mixture of student-centered and teacher-centered	Strongly student-centered
Active, Constructive Teaching and Learning		
Most teachers endorse these principles.		
Integrating Reading with Writing, the Other Language Arts, and the Curriculum as a Whole		
Most teachers endorse these principles.		

FIGURE 2.6 *Comparison of Basal, Literature-Based, and Whole-Language Approaches*

Reading Materials

Traditional basal programs, of course, employ traditional basal readers. Literature-based programs may use literature-based basals, trade books, or a combination of the two. Whole-language programs almost never use basals, making it a point to use trade books. However, somewhat confusingly, several companies now publish series that they refer to as whole-language series, a term that many whole-language advocates find an oxymoron.

For the most part, traditional basals use selections written by authors employed by the basal publishers and specifically intended for reading instruction. With the exception of the first-grade readers, which tend to be relatively short, these selections are packaged in large anthologies along with prereading activities, postreading activities, and skills work of various sorts. As we have noted, these selections employ carefully controlled vocabulary so that students are not introduced to many new words at once and encounter the new words that are introduced a number of times, and they are deliberately sequenced from easier to more difficult. One frequent charge made against traditional basals is that the selections lack literary merit. Since about 1993, few publishers have produced traditional basals (Hoffman et al., 1994).

Most basals published today are literature-based, using selections written by professional children's authors rather than in-house authors who write material specifically for instructional purposes. As with the traditional basals, these selections are generally packaged in anthologies, but they contain few pre- or postreading activities and little skills work. The anthologies include longer and more complete selections with more literary merit and offer much less vocabulary control. Also, these programs use selections more representative of our multicultural society, and they include somewhat more expository material. Although a literature-based first-grade reader is certainly intended for first-graders, much less attention appears to be given to sequencing the selections for difficulty. However, many of the literature-based programs include some more highly sequenced material and skills work in separate supplementary books.

Trade books, of course, include whatever content their authors chose to include, and their difficulty level is not likely to be their authors' chief concern. At the same time, children's authors write for children; they employ vocabulary, language patterns, and content appropriate for children. Additionally, some trade book publishers pay close attention to difficulty level and even use formulas to assess and sometimes govern the difficulty levels of their books. Like literature-based basals, trade books increasingly reflect cultural diversity, and more and more expository material is becoming available.

Our best judgment is that, for most teachers, a combination of graded readers and trade books provides the most manageable and most effective program.

Students enjoy and benefit from a wide variety of reading materials.

Skills Instruction

Traditional basal programs follow a scope and sequence of skill development, and teachers who take a traditional approach are very likely to follow it. Literature-based programs are less likely to map out a scope and sequence of skills, and literature-based teachers typically focus less on skills and follow a less-rigid sequence than traditional teachers. According to the whole-language position, skills are to be taught only in context and only as the need to use them presents itself. Thus, a scope and sequence of skills is seen as inappropriate, and skills are likely to receive less emphasis.

Our best judgment is that some skills are definitely prerequisite to others and should be sequenced. For example, a certain amount of phonemic awareness (recognizing the individual sounds in words) necessarily precedes learning to sound out words. We also believe that sequencing other skills and strategies can avoid gaps and redundancies for students. For example, if all the third-grade teachers in a school agree to give particular attention to the comprehension strategy of determining what content is most important, and all fourth-grade teachers agree to give particular attention to the comprehension strategy of making inferences, students would be guaranteed the opportunity to learn both strategies. Of course, this doesn't mean that teachers cannot teach or reteach a skill or strategy when a specific need for it arises in class.

Word-Recognition Instruction

Word-recognition skills—phonics, syllabication, blending, and the like—are particular types of skills, and the three approaches deal with them in very much the same way that they deal with other skills. Traditional basal programs are likely to contain a scope and sequence, and most traditional basal teachers are likely to follow it; teachers in literature-based programs are less likely to have a scope and sequence or to follow it; and whole-language programs typically teach phonics and other word-recognition skills only if they come up in the context of students' reading.

As we just said with respect to skills generally, we believe that some skills are prerequisite to others and should be sequenced. This definitely includes some word-recognition skills.

Ability Grouping

In general, traditional basal programs are likely to employ low-, middle-, and high-ability groups; literature-based programs are much less likely to do so; and whole-language programs are extremely unlikely to do so. However, information about the negative outcomes of fixed ability grouping (Juel, 1990) has been widely disseminated, and information about the advantages of short-term grouping for specific purposes (Hiebert, 1996) is beginning to be disseminated. As a result, teachers using traditional basals group by ability less frequently and go out of their way to ensure that students do not get trapped forever in a low group, and at least some literature-based and whole-language teachers use short-term ability grouping when a particular group of children can profit from work in a certain area.

Our best judgment is that fixed ability grouping has serious negative effects and should be avoided. We also believe, however, that the logistics of one teacher working with 30 or so students demands that students be grouped for instruction when they will profit from work in a particular area.

> Of all the civil rights for which the world has struggled and fought for 5,000 years, the right to learn is surely the most fundamental.
>
> —W. E. B. DuBois
> *Author and Social Critic*

Assessment

Traditional basal programs typically employ standardized tests such as the Stanford Achievement Test (1992), both objective and informal tests that come with the basal readers, and informal assessment procedures. Literature-based programs may also employ all these sorts of assessment, but they are likely to have fewer standardized and objective measures and suggest more informal procedures, such as collecting portfolios of students' work and keeping anecdotal records of their progress. Whole-language teachers are likely to eschew commercial and objective measures and exclusively use teacher-constructed informal methods such as portfolios and anecdotal records.

As we will explain in detail in Chapter 11, different types of assessment serve different purposes and different audiences, and both formal tests and various forms of informal assessment can serve useful functions.

Student-Centered Orientation

A student-centered classroom is one in which students make most of the decisions about what to study and how to study it. Almost by definition, traditional basal programs will be the least student-centered, whole-language programs the most student-centered, and literature-based programs somewhere in between.

As we said earlier, we strongly advocate a balanced approach. A combination of school and teacher decision making and student choice is likely to constitute an appropriate balance.

Active, Constructive Teaching and Learning

Despite the many differences that exist among these three approaches and their advocates, the majority of teachers, administrators, and program designers recognize that reading and learning to read are active, constructive processes, like those described in the cognitive–constructivist view of reading and the related concepts we discussed in Chapter 1; and most educators would endorse the majority of the instructional principles described earlier in this chapter.

Obviously, we endorse this view strongly. The wide acceptance of this view is terrific news for students and for those who care about their learning, because learning is indeed an active, constructive process.

Integrating Reading with Writing, the Other Language Arts, and the Curriculum as a Whole

Virtually all teachers agree on the importance of integrating reading with writing, the other language arts, and the curriculum as a whole. At the same time, there is likely to be more integration in literature-based programs than in traditional basal ones and more in whole-language programs than in literature-based ones. Moreover, despite the universal agreement that integrating reading with the rest of the curriculum is important and worthwhile, most classrooms would profit from more integration than they actually employ.

We vigorously support curricular integration, and we have made it a point to suggest possibilities for integration throughout the book.

> Only a generation of readers will spawn a generation of writers.
>
> —*Steven Spielberg*

Reflection AND Application

9. Consider the three historical periods of reading instruction outlined in this chapter—the colonial period and the 19th century, the heyday of basal readers, and the period of challenges to basal readers—and decide which period you would choose to learn to read in and why.

10. Describe the program of reading instruction you received as a youngster in terms of the eight aspects of instruction listed in Figure 2.6.

11. Identify one or two features of each of the approaches that you very much support and one or two features that you question. Share your thinking with a classmate, and discuss any of the differences the two of you have and the possibility of resolving—or simply appreciating—those differences.

Special Needs and Special Talents

As you know, students differ from one another in many ways that we as teachers need to attend to. This section will assist you in accommodating those differences and in capitalizing on the opportunities that this diversity presents. Most of the instructional principles we discuss here holds for virtually all students, and all students must participate in a rich critical literacy curriculum if they are to achieve the level of literacy needed in our society. Still, different students will profit from some different experiences. Here we consider the matters of success, differing participation structures, a diverse classroom library and time to read, and grouping.

Success

> All of the kids I work with are either at risk of failing to learn to read or are desperately below their expected reading level. For all kids, I think it's important to capitalize on what kids know and can do and to build success into every reading experience.
>
> —Mary Medo
> Reading Specialist

All children need success. But for those whose preschool experiences have not developed the proficiencies required for a smooth entry into school and for older children who have not met with much success in their first few years of school, fostering success will be both more crucial and more difficult. For these students, success may require a great deal of scaffolding on your part. Perhaps you will read a story to the child several times before he attempts to read along with you, and then you and the child will read the story together several times before he has developed the proficiency and confidence to try reading it by himself. This is particularly true for those students who have repeatedly failed in school, have come to attribute their failure to factors outside of their control, and have fallen into a syndrome of passive failure. Not only must these children be led to success; they must also be brought to realize that success is under their control, that they can do something about it.

Students whose preschool experiences prepared them for school and who handle routine school tasks competently will often succeed at typical literacy tasks without a great deal of scaffolding and will need sturdy scaffolding only for more challenging tasks. Still other students will succeed independently most of the time and will need significant scaffolding with only the most difficult tasks; providing appropriate challenges will be your main concern with these students. The youngster who comes to school already reading should not be required to wade through a word-study curriculum that he has already mastered and be limited to reading only brief, easy materials.

Differing Participation Structures

When working with learners with different cultural and linguistic backgrounds, it is important for the teacher to understand differing participation structures. Participation structures are the tacit arrangements that exist between speakers and listeners as they interact in certain social situations—in this case, in classroom conversations. As Shirley Brice Heath (1983) has pointed out, differences in the conversational patterns of middle-class teachers and of students who are not from the linguistic mainstream can be very debilitating. For example, Kathryn Au and Jana Mason (1983) explain how the mainstream instructional pattern in which teachers direct questions at individual students clashes with the participation structures familiar to native Hawaiian children. Hawaiian children are used to a participation structure in which several people talk at once, and being singled out to individually answer a question can seem uncomfortable and difficult to understand. Of course, other linguistic and cultural groups follow other participation structures, and thus teachers need to learn the cultural and linguistic patterns of interaction followed by their students.

A Diverse Classroom Library and Time to Read

Many features that constitute a literate environment are the same for all students—but not all of them. The classroom library that fosters a literate environment for a diverse set of students must include books that are easy and books that are challenging for *all* students. The library books must span a significant range of difficulty. It must also include books on topics of interest and relevance to those from various cultures and backgrounds. And the classroom must provide the opportunity for independent reading for students who can concentrate on reading for ten minutes as well as for those who can lose themselves in a book for an hour.

Grouping

I learned that I work better with a partner than in a small group. In a small group, if one person is not cooperating, then the rest don't cooperate and that is frustrating. What I enjoyed about this project was working on the play we did to show about Inca life. I Like acting a lot. I need to improve my work habits by contributing more of my ideas. This is hard for me to do in a big group.

—Megan, Sixth Grader

Flexibility, using several different sorts of grouping, will help address special needs and talents in your classroom. Thus, if it is useful to group students who have difficulty understanding the concept of plot so that you can review it with them, it is important to also include each of these students in heterogeneous groups or interest groups so that they do not stigmatize themselves or become stigmatized by others as a low group. Similarly, students should see that both low- and high-performing students are sometimes grouped for instruction and that grouping is often based on a criterion other than reading proficiency. Thus, in addition to pulling aside a group that is having problems with plot, it may be useful to assemble a group of your most proficient writers and give special attention to a concept such as audience. Or, as an example of grouping according to a different criterion, you might group students with particular skills in painting to work on scenery for a class skit.

Finally, when students are grouped heterogeneously, it is important that all believe they are spending their time usefully. In a heterogeneous group of writers, for example, the less-proficient writers should learn something and get opportunities to contribute, but the more proficient writers also should learn something. Otherwise, they may feel that they have been relegated to helping the less-competent writers and are learning nothing new themselves.

Students learn from one another as they work together in groups to solve a common problem.

In concluding, we readily admit that adjusting to differences among students presents significant challenges. There are no perfect solutions; many of the choices you make will be compromises, with advantages and disadvantages. Still, there are some general rules that overarch the specific suggestions we have made here. Remember that each student is an individual with both unique emotional strengths and weaknesses and unique cognitive strengths and weaknesses. Over time, all students need and deserve an abundance of success, appropriate challenges, work with others with similar strengths and weaknesses, and work with others with quite different strengths, weaknesses, interests, and concerns.

CONCLUDING REMARKS

In this chapter, we have discussed three topics: first, the importance of positive attitudes and perceptions and ways to foster them, considerations and options when grouping students for instruction, traditional principles of instruction, and newer constructivist perspectives on instruction; second, a brief history of reading instruction in the United States; and third, the three most widely used approaches to reading instruction—the traditional basal approach, the literature-based approach, and the whole-language approach.

It is worth summarizing several main points. Both affective and cognitive concerns are vital in teaching reading. Any learner must want to learn; believe that he is capable of learning; be introduced to and, in most cases, taught what it is he is to learn; receive appropriate scaffolding and be coached as he becomes increasingly knowledgeable of and capable of whatever he is learning; and receive both feedback on his performance and encouragement as he works toward further competence. The history of reading instruction in the United States indicates that various approaches to reading have come and gone and that tensions continue to exist between proponents of the traditional basal approach, the literature-based approach, and the whole-language approach. Each of these approaches contains both strengths and weaknesses, things that help children as they progress toward critical literacy and things that hinder them.

The most effective approach to instruction, the one most likely to lead the most children to a high level of critical literacy, takes the best from each approach and discards from each those aspects that do not promote critical literacy. The critical literacy curriculum has both elements that change over time and elements that persist. For example, most children will have mastered most of what they need to know about print and most decoding strategies by the end of second-grade, and thus these elements constitute a small part of the critical literacy curriculum after that time. Conversely, to participate fully in the critical literacy curriculum, all children should be involved in listening to and later reading narratives and expository material beginning in kindergarten, and all children should continue reading both narrative and expository texts throughout their years in school.

EXTENDING LEARNING

As we noted in Chapter 1, in these sections we suggest activities that take you beyond this book to observe and work with schools, teachers, parents, and various sources of information that can help you more fully understand and appreciate your role in fostering students' critical literacy.

1. Although we have described some of children's attitudes and perceptions about school and some of the attitudes and perceptions we want them to cultivate or overcome, the best source for getting a feeling for what students think of school is the students themselves. Identify an age group that you're interested in, and find two or three students of that age who will talk to you about school and learning. You might talk to children of friends or relatives. If that is not possible, see if you can get permission to talk to a few students in the school where you will be observing or student teaching. Whatever the source, be sure you get parents' permission to talk to their youngsters. Keep the conversation light, and stress the positive. Ask the students what parts of school and what activities they like best. Ask them what they do best. And ask them to describe something they did in school that went particularly well and that they are proud of.

2. We have named a number of different ways of grouping students—probably more than any single teacher uses—yet there are undoubtedly other forms of grouping. Get together with several classmates, consider the types of groups we have described, and make up a set of interview questions that you can ask of teachers to discover the groups they use and how they handle them. Keep the questionnaire simple—what groupings do they use, how often do they use them, what are some of their strengths and weaknesses? Then you and classmates you are working with should interview one or two teachers, pool your results, and get together to discuss what you found. If you can make tentative decisions about the types of groups you might use during your student teaching or when you first begin teaching, do so. You might write these tentative conclusions in your journal so that you will have them when you need them.

3. Identify a simple skill that you have mastered but that many of your classmates probably have not. Choose something specific that can be learned relatively easily—such as tying a square knot. Review the tradi-

tional and constructivist principles of instruction—active teaching, scaffolding, gradual release, feedback, and the like—and decide which can be incorporated into your instruction. Next, write out a specific plan for teaching your skill—a lesson plan—noting just what you are going to do and indicating which principles you are following at each point. Rehearse your instruction, with a partner if possible; then teach a small group of your classmates the skill. If possible, have a classmate who is not part of the group observe you. Finally, sit down with your classmates—both the learners and the observer—and critique your instruction, being sure to attend to how well people learned the skill, what did and did not go well, how you might improve the lesson, what instructional principles you followed, and what additional instructional principles you might incorporate to improve learning.

4. Choose whichever of the three current approaches to reading instruction you are most interested in, and examine a specific instance of that approach. Get a sample of the materials that make up the program. For a commercial reading program, this would include student materials and the teacher's manual for a particular grade. If the approach does not use a commercial program, the materials should include the trade books students read and any guidelines the teacher follows. Then, do three things: First, study the materials, and make a list of half a dozen questions about how they are used. List questions that could probably be answered by observing the program and talking to a teacher who is using it. Second, observe a teacher using the materials in class, answer as many of your questions as the observation makes possible, and jot down the most important additional questions that come up during the observation. Finally, meet with the teacher you observed, talk with him about the program, and try to answer the questions you have left.

REFERENCES

Allington, R. L. (1983). The reading instruction provided readers of different abilities. *Elementary School Journal, 83*, 548–559. The author describes how the instruction provided for less-able readers lacks many positive features of that provided for more-able readers.

Allington, R. L. (1994). The schools we have: The schools we need. *The Reading Teacher, 48*, 14–29. This article explores a variety of tensions between things as they are and things as they might be and makes suggestions for change.

Allington, R. L. , Guice, S., Michaelson, N., Baker, K., & Li, S. (1996). Literature-based curricula in high-poverty schools. In M. F. Graves, P. van den Broek, & B. M. Taylor (Eds.), *The first r: Every child's right to read.* New York: Teachers College Press (pp. 73–96). An empirical study of literature-based classrooms is presented.

Anderson, R. C., Hiebert, E. F., Scott, J. A., & Wilkinson, I. A. G. (1985). *Becoming a nation of readers.* Washington, DC: National Institute of Education. Although this book is becoming somewhat dated, it remains a concise and cogent summary of what we know about reading instruction.

Au, K. H., & Mason, J. M. (1983). Cultural congruence in classroom participation structures: Achieving a balance of rights. *Discourse Processes, 6,* 145–167. This work is the source of our example of the different participation structures of native Hawaiian children.

Berliner, D. C. (1979). Tempus educare. In P. L. Peterson & H. J. Walberg (Eds.), *Research on teaching: Concepts, findings, and implications.* Berkeley, CA: McCutchan. A leading researcher of teaching effectiveness takes a careful look at the importance of instructional time.

Bond, G. L., Dykstra, R. (1967). The cooperative reading program in first-grade reading studies. *Reading Research Quarterly, 2,* 5–141. This report of a huge study generally supports the superiority of code emphases to beginning reading instruction.

Brophy, J. (1986). Teacher influences on student achievement. *American Psychologist, 41,* 1069–1077. The author gives a cogent review of the research on teaching.

Brophy, J., & Good, T. (1997). *Looking into classrooms* (7th ed.). New York: HarperCollins. Chapters 3 and 4 provide very detailed information on the authors' views on effective instruction.

Brown, J. S., Collins, A., & Duguid, P. (1989). Situated cognition and the culture of learning. *Educational Researcher, 18*(1), 32–42. The authors present a strong argument for the importance of situated learning.

California Department of Education. (1995). *Every child a reader: The report of the California reading task force.* Sacramento, CA: Author. This state department report calls for more attention to reading skills.

Chall, J. S. (1967). *Learning to read: The great debate.* New York: McGraw-Hill. This well-known and widely read book reviews the literature and argues that a code emphasis to beginning reading instruction is superior to a meaning emphasis.

Cobb, L. (1835). *The North American reader.* New York: B. and S. Collins. This was a popular reader of its time.

Collins, A., Brown, J. S., & Holum, A. (1991). Cognitive apprenticeship: Making thinking visible. *American Educator 15*(4), 6–11, 38–46. This is an updated and expanded version of the Brown, Collins, and Duguid chapter listed above.

Cramer, E. H., & Castle, M. (Eds.) (1994). *Fostering the love of reading: The affective domain in reading education.* Newark, DE: International Reading Association. This is the first IRA book to focus exclusively on affective concerns.

Cremin, L. A. (1990). *Popular education and its discontents.* New York: Harper & Row. This brief and focused history was written by the recently deceased dean of American educational historians.

Csikszentmihalyi, M. (1990). *Flow: The psychology of optimal experience.* New York: Harper & Row. This popular book summarizes Csikszentmihalyi's 30 years of work on optimal human experiences—the joy, creativity, and total involvement he terms *flow.*

Doyle, W. (1983). Academic work. *Review of Educational Research, 53*(2), 159–199. This classic paper discusses the way classrooms function.

Duffy, G. G., & Roehler, L. R. (1982). Commentary: The illusion of instruction. *Reading Research Quarterly, 17,* 438–445. This article looks at the way in which practice is sometimes mistaken for instruction.

Duffy, G. G., & Roehler, L. R. (1987). Improving reading instruction through responsive elaboration. *The Reading Teacher, 40,* 514–520. The authors explain responsive elaboration and give actual scripts of teachers providing responsive elaboration for students.

Flesch, R. (1955). *Why Johnny can't read.* New York: Harper & Row. This best-selling book argued that schools were not teaching phonics.

Goodman, K. (1970). Behind the eye: What happens in reading. In K. S. Goodman & O. S. Niles (Eds.), *Reading: Process and program.* Urbana, IL: National Council of Teachers of English. This is one of the earliest presentations of Goodman's view of the reading process.

Goodman, K. (1986). *What's whole in whole language?* Portsmouth, NH: Heinemann. This is the most popular statement of Goodman's whole-lanuage philosophy.

Goodman, K. (1996). The report of the California reading task force: Forced choices in a non-crisis. *California English, 1*(3), 8–10. This position paper argues that the call for more attention to reading skills is ill-advised and not needed. See Honig (1996) for a contrasting position.

Heath, S. B. (1983). *Ways with words: Language, life, and work in communities and classrooms*. Cambridge, UK: Cambridge University Press. The author provides a detailed and compelling account of language and life in three very different communities, and of the implications of these differences for schooling.

Hiebert, E. H. (1996). Creating and sustaining a love of literature . . . and the ability to read it. In M. F. Graves, P. van den Broek, & B. M. Taylor (Eds.), *The first r: Every child's right to read*. New York: Teachers College Press. This is a description of programs teachers created when they discovered that not all their children were succeeding in typical literature-based classes.

Hoffman, J. V., McCarthey, S. J., Abbott, J., Christian, C., Corman, L., Curry, C., Dressman, M., Elliott, B., Matherne, D., & Stahle, D. (1994). So what's new in the new basals? A focus on first grade. *Journal of Reading Behavior, 26*, 47–73. The authors offer a very complete description of the differences between the pre-1993 and post-1993 basal reader series.

Honig, B. (1996). The role of skills in a comprehensive reading program. *California English, 1*(3), 16–20. This position paper argues that California needs to include more attention to skills in its reading program. See Goodman (1996) for a contrasting position.

Johnson, D. W., Johnson, R. T., & Holubec, E. J. (1994). *The new circles of learning: Cooperation in the classroom and school*. Alexandria, VA: Association for Supervision and Curriculum Development. This book is a very practical introduction to cooperative learning by some of its top theoreticians and practitioners.

Johnson, R. T., Johnson, D. W., & Holubec, E. J. (1987). *Structuring cooperative learning: Lesson plans for teachers*. Edina, MN: Interaction Book Company. This book describes cooperative learning and how to implement it in the classroom, along with teacher lesson plans from primary grades through high school.

Johnston, P. H., & Winograd, P. N. (1985). Passive failure in reading. *Journal of Reading Behavior, 17*, 279–301. The authors have written a powerful and important explanation of this very destructive phenomenon.

Juel, C. (1990). Effects of reading group assignment on reading development in first and second grade. *Journal of Reading Behavior, 22*, 223–254. This article points out the broad and enduring effects of grouping.

Mann, H. (1965). Method of teaching young children on their first entering school. In N. B. Smith, *American reading instruction* (2nd ed., p. 117). Newark, DE: International Reading Association. (Original work published 1844.) This work of Horace Mann is quoted in Smith's history of reading instruction.

Marzano, R. J. (1992). *A different kind of classroom: Teaching with dimensions of learning*. Washington, DC: Association for Supervision and Curriculum Development. This book outlines a comprehensive, learning-centered curriculum.

O'Flahavan, J., Gambrell, L. B., Guthrie, J., Stahl, S., Gaumann, J. F., & Alvermann, D. E. (1992, August/September). Poll of IRA members guides National Reading Research Center. *Reading Today*. This is the source of information on teachers' concern in getting students interested in reading.

Pearson, P. D. (1994, October). *Reading research and practice: Recovering our center*. Paper presented at the Guy Bond Reading Conference. Minneapolis, MN. This is the original presentation of the 1996 paper.

Pearson, P. D. (1996). Reclaiming the center. In M. F. Graves, P. van den Broek, & B. M. Taylor (Eds.), *The first r: Every child's right to read*. New York: Teachers College Press. The author analyzes current controversies in the field and how they might be resolved.

Pearson, P. D., & Gallagher, M. C. (1983). The instruction of reading comprehension. *Contemporary Educational Psychology, 8*, 317–344. This older article is still a useful summary of the research on teaching reading comprehension.

Perkins, D. N. (1992). *Smart schools: From training memories to educating minds*. New York: The Free Press. This book takes an in-depth look at thoughtful approaches to teaching and learning and is the source of much of our thinking in Chapter 8.

Sampson, M. B., Sampson, M. R., & Linek, W. (1994/1995). Circle of questions. *The Reading Teacher, 48*(4), 364–365. This article describes a strategy for engaging groups of students in brainstorming, predicting, generating questions about text, categorizing, and interacting with text to answer questions.

Schlesinger, A. M., Jr. (1986). *The cycles of American history*. Boston: Houghton Mifflin. This is a wide-ranging view of American history by a major historian.

Slavin, R. E. (1987). *Cooperative learning: Student teams* (2nd ed.). Washington, DC: National Education Association. This book is a brief overview of several of Slavin's approaches to cooperative learning.

Smith, E. B. (1995). Anchored in our literature: Students responding to African American Literature. *Language Arts, 72,* 571–574. Smith describes her experience in a fifth-grade classroom, underscoring the importance of connecting literature to the lives and interests of the children we teach.

Smith, F. (1971). *Understanding reading: A psycholinguistic analysis of reading and learning to read.* New York: Holt, Rinehart & Winston. This is Smith's original description of his view of the reading process.

Smith, N. B. (1965). *American reading instruction* (2nd ed.). Newark, DE: International Reading Association. This is one of very few available histories of reading instruction in the United States.

Stanford Achievement Test, 8th ed. (1992). New York: Psychological Corporation. This is one of the most frequently used standardized tests.

Vygotsky, L. S. (1978). *Mind in society*. Cambridge, MA: Harvard University Press. This is one of Vygotsky's classic texts, probably best known for its description of the zone of proximal development.

Whitehead, A. N. (1929). *The aims of education and other essays*. New York: Macmillan. These thought-provoking essays are still very relevant some 70 years after they were written.

Wittrock, M. C. (1986). Students' thought processes. In M. C. Wittrock (Ed.), *Handbook of research on teaching* (3rd ed., pp. 297–314). New York: Macmillan. This authoritative review explores the effects of teachers and instruction on various aspects of students' perceptions, motivation, and understanding.

Wood, D. J., Bruner, J. S., & Ross, G. (1976). The role of tutoring in problem solving. *Journal of Child Psychology and Psychiatry, 17*(2), 89–100. This article introduces the concept of scaffolding and provides an insightful examination of parent–child interactions.

CHILDREN'S LITERATURE

Barrett, J. (1978). *Cloudy with a chance of meatballs.* Illustrated by Ron Barrett. New York: Atheneum. Life is delicious in the town of Chewandswallow, where it rains soup and juice, snows mashed potatoes, and the like—until the weather takes a turn for the worse. 32 pages.

Carle, E. (1984). *The mixed-up chameleon.* New York: Crowell. A bored chameleon wishes he could be more like others. Illustrated. Unpaged. Videotape available.

Conrad, P. (1991). *Pedro's journal: A voyage with Christopher Columbus, August 3, 1492–February 14, 1493.* Honesdale, PA: Boyds Mills. A cabin boy keeps a diary which records his experiences as he sails with Columbus. Illustrated. 80 pages.

DePaola, T. (1975). *Strega Nona.* Englewood Cliffs, NJ: Prentice Hall. In this folktale, when Strega Nona leaves Big Anthony alone with her magic pasta pot, he is determined to show the townspeople he knows how it works. Illustrated. Unpaged. Audiotape and videotape available.

Dygard, T. J. (1995). *Infield hit.* New York: Morrow Junior Books. After transferring to a new high school during his junior year, Hal tries to make friends, gain a starting position on the baseball team, and hide the fact that his dad is a famous ex–major leaguer. 149 pages.

Forbes, E. (1943). *Johnny Tremain*. New York: Dell. Johnny Tremain, apprentice silversmith, takes on the cause of freedom as a message carrier for the Sons of Liberty in pre-Revolution Boston. 269 pages. Audiotape available.

Fritz, J. (1985). *China homecoming*. New York: Putnam. Noted author Jean Fritz describes her return to China, the country where she was born and grew up. This is both a touching and very informative book. Photographs. 143 pages.

Golenbock, T. (1990). *Teammates*. New York: Harcourt Brace Jovanovich. This book describes the racial prejudice experienced by Jackie Robinson when he joined the Brooklyn Dodgers and became the first Black player in major league baseball. It also depicts the acceptance and support he received from his white teammate Pee Wee Reese. Illustrated. Unpaged.

Greenfield, E. (1978). *Honey, I love and other poems*. New York: Harper. This collection of poems explores a variety of childhood experiences and feelings. 48 pages.

Holabird, K. (1983). *Angelina ballerina*. Illustrated by Helen Craig. New York: Clarkson N. Potter. This is the story of a little mouse who wants to become a ballerina. 24 pages.

Lord, B. B. (1984). *In the year of the boar and Jackie Robinson*. New York: Harper & Row. In 1947, a Chinese girl comes to Brooklyn, where she becomes Americanized at school, in her apartment building, and by her love for baseball. Illustrated. 169 pages.

Kellogg, S. (1986). *Best friends*. New York: Dial. Kathy feels lonely and betrayed when her best friend goes away for the summer and has a wonderful time. Unpaged.

MacLachlan, P. (1980). *Arthur for the very first time*. New York: Harper & Row. Arthur spends a summer with his unconventional aunt and uncle and begins to look at life, his family, and himself differently. Illustrated. 117 pages.

MacLachlan, P. (1985). *Sarah, plain and tall*. New York: Harper & Row. When their father invites a mail-order bride to come live with them in their prairie home, Caleb and Anna are captivated by their new mother and hope that she will stay. 58 pages. Audiotape and videotape available.

McGovern, A. (1965). *Wanted dead or alive: The true story of Harriet Tubman*. New York: Scholastic. This dramatic account describes Harriet Tubman's flight for freedom and the Underground Railroad. 64 pages.

National Geographic World. National Geographic Society. Richly illustrated, monthly periodical for intermediate-grade students.

Park, B. (1982). *Skinnybones*. New York: Knopf. Alex's sense of humor helps him get by in a hectic world. 112 pages.

Park, B. (1993). *Junie B. Jones and a little monkey business*. New York: Random House. Misinterpreting what her grandmother says, Junie thinks her new baby brother is really a baby monkey and reports this astounding news to her kindergarten class. 68 pages.

Paterson, K. (1977). *Bridge to Terabithia*. New York: Crowell. Jess's life expands when he becomes friends with Leslie, a girl from the city who opens doors to culture and imaginative play. But then tragedy strikes. Illustrated. 128 pages. Audiotape and videotape available.

Simon, S. (1995). *Sharks*. New York: HarperCollins. With full-color photos and engaging text that describes fascinating details about 350 different kinds of sharks, Simon demystifies this greatly feared predatory fish. Unpaged.

Soto, G. (1990). Talent show. In G. Soto, *Baseball and other stories*. San Diego, CA: Harcourt Brace Jovanovich. Manuel suffers pre–curtain time jitters before the talent show.

Steig, W. (1969). *Sylvester and the magic pebble*. New York: Simon & Schuster. In a moment of fright, Sylvester the donkey looks to his magic pebble for help. 32 pages. Audiotape available.

Szilagyi, M. (1985). *Thunderstorm*. New York: Macmillan. A little girl is comforted by her mother during a thunderstorm. 32 pages.

Viorst, J. (1972). *Alexander and the terrible, horrible, no good, very bad day*. Illustrated by Ray Cruz. New York: Atheneum. On a day when everything goes wrong for him, Alexander is consoled by the thought that other people have bad days too. 32 pages. Audiotape available. Spanish text and audiotape also available.

chapter three

Emergent Literacy

*L*ee *opens her eyes. She awakes to find her favorite stuffed animal lying next to her—a teddy bear named Pooh after the character in* Winnie the Pooh. *Lee grabs Pooh and takes him down to breakfast. At the table, her mother asks her if she can read the letters on the cereal box to Pooh. After breakfast, Lee scurries off to watch* Sesame Street *on television. She names all the letters she sees on the screen to Pooh. Later that morning, Lee goes to the grocery store with her mom. Lee shows off her letter knowledge by naming printed letters as they wheel around the store. She also helps her mom check off items on her shopping list.*

On the way home, Lee is dropped off at afternoon kindergarten. She puts her gear in a cubby that has her name above it. She sees her name on the list of helpers for the day. After settling in, the children gather around to hear their teacher read a long-popular Ukrainian folktale, The Mitten *by Alvin Tresselt (1964). When the teacher finishes the story, she asks the children to recall as many characters as they can. As the teacher names each character, she puts a cardboard picture of the animal on a feltboard. She then has the children help her retell the story. She puts up the animals as they appear in the story. When necessary, she prompts children with questions like,*

CHAPTER OVERVIEW

"Then who came along?" If they aren't sure, she opens up the book and asks them to check. After several retellings, the teacher hands out small posters shaped like mittens with line drawings of the animals that are in The Mitten. She asks students to color the pictures and then take the mittens home to share.

At home again, Lee is eager to retell The Mitten using her paper mitten and animal pictures. First, she tells it to her older sister and then to her mom and dad.

As she snuggles into bed with Pooh, Lee eagerly waits for her dad, who will read one of her favorite stories. Her dad throws an arm around his daughter as he begins reading from James Marshall's retelling of The Three Little Pigs.

> Once upon a time
>
> an old sow sent her three little pigs
>
> out into the world to seek their fortune.
>
> "Now be sure to write," she said.
>
> "And remember that I love you."

ON BEING READ TO AS A VERY YOUNG CHILD

To establish the link between a letter and a sound, the learner must first establish a clear image of each.

—*Marilyn Adams*
Psychologist

Books form the heart and soul of reading. What is read to young children is often a reflection of their parents', other caregivers', and teachers' tastes and beliefs about the books children should be exposed to. Books that are reread to young children become the ones they respond to with enthusiasm and an absolute insistence that they be read over and over to them.

Children learn about the world from books. Values, beliefs, traditions, knowledge, and language shared by cultures are transmitted through books. A bedtime reading ritual like that of Lee and her father communicates the importance and love of reading. Children can also learn something about how to read from hearing books read to them. As Lee's father begins to read *The Three Little Pigs*, Lee remarks that there was also a wolf in *The Mitten*. Her knowledge of how stories are put together and the role of characters is growing. Her father points to the *L* in *Little* and asks Lee if she knows anyone with a name that starts with that letter. Lee's knowledge of the mechanics of reading is expanding. She asks her father to point to the word *love* and exclaims, "It starts with an *L!*" Lee's vocabulary grows as she asks her father about the meanings of words such as *sow* and *fortune*. As they get into the story, father and daughter both chuckle over the silly illustrations. Lee associates reading with enjoyment and love. Children who are frequently read to have encountered interesting vocabulary, imaginative scenes, and the sounds of written language.

Children who have been read to in the years before formal schooling enter classrooms with considerably more ideas about how print works, more understanding of how stories work, and more knowledge of literary language and structure than children who lack this advantage. They are also more likely to understand the types of questions about books that teachers will ask of them. When we asked Lee's father, Philip, if he asked her questions about the stories they read together, this is what he said:

Yes, many times I will ask Lee questions. She seems to like it. It keeps her interested and involved in the story, and it's also fun for me to see how her mind works, what she knows, and what she thinks about. For example, if we're reading *The Three Little Pigs*, I might ask, "What is the first pig's house made of? What happens now? Where is the letter in your name in this word? What is a sow? Is the wolf here like the one in *The Mitten?*" Of course, she likes to hear the same stories over and over again, so I have to change the questions!

Philip Treisdale, Father

Lee's father is preparing her for the types of questions she will be asked in school—even the compare-and-contrast questions that will form the heart of learning and school assignments. Lee will be more likely to correctly answer the questions asked of her, and also she will be much more comfortable with the form these questions take—for example, "What is _____?"—than the child who lacks extensive preschool book experience (Heath, 1983). Lee's father is gently scaffolding her reading of favorite storybooks—each rereading requires a bit more of Lee in terms of her recall of characters, plot, and even words. This idea of scaffolding a child's learning is extremely important, and we revisit it throughout the book.

Most of all, children who have been read to already belong to the world of books. Books have a place in their lives and are recognized as important. Their imaginations have been piqued. They know that infinite varieties of meaning can be created through the written word.

CHILDREN'S GROWING KNOWLEDGE ABOUT READING

Emergent readers are children who are in the process of learning what reading and writing are for and how to read and write. Children enter school with wide differences in both their exposure to text and what they know about text. Many kindergartners begin school knowing the letters of the alphabet; some even know the sounds those letters make, can reproduce those letters, and can write a few words. But some children cannot. Although some children entering first grade are already readers, most are not. Most children in kindergarten and first-grade classrooms will need considerable help from you to become increasingly competent and independent readers.

In this part of the chapter, we begin by examining some of the text-level and word-level understandings that facilitate learning to read and write. Next, we consider the development of alphabet recognition—a simple and straightforward matter—and the development of phonemic awareness—a more complex matter that is crucial to learning to read. We then describe two stages most students go through in learning to recognize words. Finally, we examine the differences between learning to speak and learning to read. There are in fact many differences between the two tasks, and it is important that teachers understand these thoroughly and teach accordingly. The primary goal of preschool and kindergarten teachers is to foster a love of books, words, and ideas. To achieve that goal, we must foster text- and word-level understandings.

Learning to read, whatever else it is, is a question of *learning*. And what is learned is the workings of a writing system and a specific orthography.

—*Charles Perfetti*
Psychologist

Emerging Knowledge About Text Structures

The more prior knowledge you have about a topic, the easier it is to comprehend a text about it. This holds true for knowledge of text structures. When you read a recipe, for example, it will help if you are familiar with the format recipes usually follow. You can anticipate that a list of the ingredients will appear at the start. You know that the directions for the recipe will then proceed in a step-by-step fashion. You also know that it might be wise to read the whole set of steps before you begin cooking, because an overly time-consuming step might require that you change your plans if you are on a tight schedule. You have a schema for how recipes are put together. It not only provides an overall outline that will aid your comprehension, but it also allows you to write a recipe that could be followed by others.

Children who have been read to have probably developed a schema for how written stories, like the ones they will encounter in school, are put together. Although they may not be able to articulate this structure, they can demonstrate their knowledge if asked to tell a story. In the basic story or narrative structure that they intuitively know, a central character or characters typically try to overcome a problem. The resolution of the problem generally develops through a chronological sequence of events. We provide a more complete look at narrative structure in Chapter 9; for now, you might consider the narrative structure of *The Three Little Pigs*. The main characters are the three pigs and a wolf. The problem is that the wolf is hungry, but the three pigs are unwilling to be the target meal. As the sequence of events unfolds, the wolf moves from the first to the second to the third house of the three pigs. For this particular story, the resolution differs depending on the author rendering it. Sometimes the wolf succeeds; sometimes one or more pigs survive.

Children who have been read to a lot may have encountered the different versions of the basic story of the three little pigs. They may have intuitively learned how a basic story structure allows the writer options to vary the narrative. They may also have discussed the story with an adult and have been encouraged to see the story through either the eyes of the pigs or the eyes of the wolf. Depending on whose perspective is taken, a different character can be seen as having a problem (for example, the wolf's problem is hunger; the pigs' problem is survival). Seeing the world through another's eyes is something humans try to do throughout their lives. Taking the perspective of different characters in a fictional world is a safe place to begin.

But whether or not children have been read to before they arrive at school, experiences designed to help them understand the structure of texts will greatly increase their chances of becoming proficient readers. Wordless picture books, in which the story is told through illustrations, are good vehicles for this endeavor. In the following scenario, Mrs. Willey shows how this can be done.

IN THE CLASSROOM
Using Wordless Picture Books in a Kindergarten Classroom

Seated in a chair, with her kindergartners gathered comfortably around her on the carpeted floor, Mrs. Willey displays a copy of the mostly wordless picture book *Have You Seen My Duckling?* by Nancy Tafuri. Mrs. Willey tells the children that they are going to help make up a story about a mother duck who has lost her ducklings.

Mrs. Willey asks the children to close their eyes. "Think about the baby duck, a duckling we call it, that you just saw. Try to imagine what it feels like to be a duckling, to be so new, so small. What do you see? "Now, open your eyes. Tell me. What did you see?"

"Grass!"

"Bugs!"

The children take turns suggesting what the world might look like from the perspective of a baby duck.

Next, Mrs. Willey has the children point to the mother duck on the cover illustration and count her ducklings. She opens the book and has them notice what happens on the opening page.

"There are eight ducklings in a nest. But one of them is climbing out!" Tamara volunteers.

Mrs. Willey smiles and turns the page. "Early one morning . . . ," she begins, and then stops and asks, "What happens?"

Jason replies, "Early one morning eight baby ducks got up."

"Ducklings!" Tamara corrects him.

"Well, okay, ducklings," Jason says. "They saw a butterfly and one duckling got into the water and tried to swim after it."

"Then what happens?" asks Mrs. Willey, as she flips the page to uncover new illustrations.

Mrs. Willey continues to call on different children who add to the story by considering the upcoming illustrations, their own imaginations, and their knowledge of stories, mothers, children, and ducks.

After Mrs. Willey and her kindergartners complete making up a story for *Have You Seen My Duckling?*, the children go to three classroom centers. In one center the children have a few additional copies of the book. Here they each get a chance to retell the story to a buddy.

In the art center there are some black and white drawings of a duck and eight ducklings. The children cut out the drawings, color them in, and paste each one on a tongue depressor to serve as a puppet. Then they retell the story to each other, using their puppets to act it out.

In the library center are several wordless picture books. The children take turns making up stories and telling them to each other as they turn the pages.

Making up stories for wordless picture books helps young children understand the structure of text.

Whether you find that the children you teach have been read to a lot or that they have had little exposure to books, reading to children pays great dividends—*at all grade levels*. As you read to young children, you can draw their attention to elements of story structure, vocabulary, ideas, imaginative notions, and language. You can foster thinking and engagement with the world through books such as those listed on pages 92–93.

Emerging Knowledge About Word Structures

If you asked a typical class of children at the beginning of first grade what they expect to learn during the year, most would reply that they will learn to read. However, despite their high motivation and expectations, some children will experience considerable difficulty, frustration, and an early loss of self-esteem in learning to read.

Let's look closer at a classroom of first-grade children at the beginning of the school year and see if we can predict who in the class will learn to read with relative ease, and who will not. The following list of factors can predict children's success in reading (Share, Jorm, Maclean, & Matthews, 1984). Try to rank these predictors from strongest to weakest.

- Phoneme segmentation ability (for example, the ability to tell you the first sound in the spoken word *sun*)
- Letter names (for example, knowledge of the alphabet)
- Kindergarten teacher's predictions of reading success
- Performance on Peabody Picture Vocabulary Test (a measure of oral English vocabulary)
- Parent's occupational status (jobs such as bank executive or assembly-line worker that typically reflect socioeconomic status)
- Library membership (whether the child already has a library card)
- Number of books the child owns
- Amount that parents read to their child
- Gender
- Amount that parents read in their spare time
- Whether or not the child attended preschool

You may be surprised to learn that these traits are listed in the exact order in which they predicted the end-of-year reading ability of more than 500 first-grade Australian children. In fact, the top two predictors (phonemic segmentation and letter-name knowledge) were by far the strongest. Most people are surprised that parents' reading to their child is not the most predictive factor. Certainly, from what you have read so far, you know how much children learn from being read to. But learning to read requires that a child *independently* identify many printed words so she can read on her own.

First-grade teacher Glenna Schwarze expresses her view on this sort of empowerment. She knows that reading independence means making sure her students get instruction in decoding skills.

> I am sure any first-grade teacher will tell you the same thing: At the heart of first-grade reading instruction is ensuring that children learn to decode words. Of course, we want children to be able to instantly recognize as many words as possible, but we also need to be sure they are equipped with strategies and skills to use when they don't instantly know a word. The beginning reader, of course, cannot instantly recognize many words. As teachers, however, we can help children identify words they don't know by helping them recognize the letters in the words and how to translate those letters into the sounds they represent.
>
> Glenna Schwarze, First-Grade Teacher

Children who have been read to have frequently heard the sounds in spoken words linked to printed words and letters. They may, for example, have laughed at the silly phrases such as "a wocket in my pocket" and at-

Books to Foster Emergent Literacy

Big Books

Big books are enlarged copies of standard size books. Big books might be as tall as some children! They can be used with large groups of children because the print is big enough for them to see it clearly and follow along. At first, they will realize that what you are saying is what is printed on the page, then that each individual word you say is represented by an individual word on the printed page (you must point out the words), and finally that they can literally follow the words as you read. An annotated bibliography of selected big books appears later in the chapter.

Repetitious Stories, Predictable Books, and Pattern Books

In these books, a phrase or word is repeated throughout the story, thus making a predictable pattern. After the first few pages, children can "read" along because they know the pattern.

Picture Books

This large category includes books with illustrations on all or most of the pages. The illustrations entertain children and help them follow the story.

Wordless Storybooks

Some picture books tell a story without using words. The precise story line is developed by the reader. Thus, these books give children the opportunity to tell stories themselves, which most children really enjoy.

Touch-and-Feel Books

These books employ textures that can be felt with the fingers, to help children to learn the meanings of words and to distinguish textures.

Concept Books

These books are designed to teach spatial and directional concepts or concepts related to particular school subjects. They help students learn "school language"—words that are typically used in instruction.

Alphabet Books

These books focus on the correspondence between letters of the alphabet and the sounds they represent. Each page is usually devoted to one letter and a picture of something that illustrates that letter's sound. Of course, many letters in the English language represent more than one sound, so alphabet books are usually used as a prelude to, rather than a vehicle for, teaching letter–sound correspondence.

Number Books

The numeric counterpart to alphabet books, these books focus on teaching numbers. Usually, each page presents one number, and an illustration shows the corresponding number of items.

> The primary objective of early reading instruction is to enable children to process written discourse in the same manner as oral discourse, applying the same powerful inferential process that they apply to understand oral language discourse.
>
> —*Carl H. Frederiksen*
> *Educational Researcher*

tended to the sounds in the rhymes of Dr. Seuss's *There's a Wocket in My Pocket*. To make *basket* into *wasket* requires the deletion of the /b/ (the initial sound in *basket*, called a phoneme) and its replacement with a new speech sound (phoneme), a /w/. The segmentation, deletion, and replacement needed to recognize this switch fosters awareness of the sounds in words, the phonemes.

Alliteration—the repetition of initial consonant sounds—also focuses attention on phonemes. Nursery rhymes such as "Peter Piper picked a peck of pickled peppers" or the frequently occurring phrase "teeny tiny" in Jill Bennett's *Teeny Tiny* are likely to draw a child's attention to sounds in words. This attention will also be fostered by reading rhyme-filled texts such as Dr.

Shape Books

These books deal with shapes such as circles, squares, triangles, and rectangles, as well as other geometric concepts, such as straight lines and curves. They help prepare students for reading because letters are made up of shapes that must be recognized.

Nursery Rhymes

These books represent many old favorites. Because these stories and verses employ rhyme, they are easy to remember and follow.

Caption Books

These books provide labels for items pictured on the page. They do not tell a story. Because there is little print in these books and the pictured items are familiar, they can help children develop print awareness.

Fairy Tales, Fables, Myths, and Folktales

These traditional stories, which often involve imaginative settings and plots, are enjoyed and often memorized by children. Because their format is often similar, they provide useful illustrations of the structure of stories.

Poetry Books

Short poems are easy to enjoy in relatively brief time periods—perhaps a few free minutes just before lunch—in addition to being a regular part of the literature experience.

Series Books

Providing a series of books in which one or more characters face new situations and adventures encourages children to read other books by the same author and offers a sense of continuity.

Multicultural Books

These books represent various cultures and employ diverse writing styles, stories and characters from particular cultures, illustrations depicting a variety of locales and peoples, and authors of various cultural origins. Because children are excited to see aspects of their lives reflected in their reading, it is important to offer a significant store of books related to the cultural groups represented in your classroom.

Books Written by the Teacher, the Class, or a Child

Books written about events, places, and people in a child's life are most meaningful. Children particularly appreciate books about themselves. Such books can be created as joint projects, read repeatedly, shared with others, and displayed for class visitors.

Seuss's *Cat in the Hat* and nursery rhymes such as "Jack and Jill went up the hill" aloud. Words that rhyme share component sounds, like *Jill* and *hill*. To recognize rhyme is to begin to be aware of words as sequences of sounds—sounds that reoccur in different words.

As parents or teachers read to their children, they often point out letters. A mother, for example, might tell her daughter that her name, Anna, begins with the letter *A*, just like that of her favorite storybook character, Angelina, whom she knows well from Katherine Holabird's series of Angelina Ballerina books. Anna's mother might also mention that there are two *a*s and two *n*s in both names and then ask Anna to find them. Of course, as a teacher of emergent readers, you will want to provide many opportunities to link what the children already know about letters to new experiences with the printed word. In the following scenario, Robert Felton helps his kindergartners make such connections. See if you can pick them out.

IN THE CLASSROOM
Kindergartners and the *P* Words

Mr. Felton's kindergartners, sitting in a semicircle on the floor, look quizzically at a large chart he has put on a stand. It is a poem that he has printed in large letters with a black felt pen.

"This is a poem, boys and girls," he tells them. "It's from a favorite book of mine called *Whiskers and Rhymes* by Arnold Lobel." He holds up his copy of the book.

"The poem is about a cat named George, who brushes his teeth!"

The children giggle.

"But guess what George uses for toothpaste? Pickle paste!"

The children roar with laughter as they consider toothpaste made from pickles.

Mr. Felton invites the children to come up and take a look at the book and the three pictures that accompany this poem. First, George squeezes a toothpaste tube labeled "Pickle Paste" onto his toothbrush. Second, he brushes his teeth, and green foam emerges from his mouth. Third, George smiles a big green-teeth smile. When the children sit back down, Mr. Felton reads the poem from the chart, pointing to each word as he reads.

Then, Mr. Felton asks the children to find the letter *p* in the words. A child comes up and points to the *p* in *pickle,* and another child points to the *p* in *paste.*

Mr. Felton asks, "Which letter in *pickle* makes it say /p/?"

The children respond, "*P.*"

He asks, "Which letter in *paste* makes it say /p/?"

The children respond, "*P.*"

Mr. Felton says, "The letter *p* says /p/," emphasizing the /p/ as he says "pickle paste."

The children can't help giggling as they say "pickle paste" over and over.

Next, Mr. Felton show the children a large tube of toothpaste cut out of construction paper—just like the one George had. It has "Pickle Paste" printed on the tube.

Mr. Felton asks the children if they can spot some other *p* words in the room to write on the tube. The children glance around at the books on the chalkboard ledge, most of which Mr. Felton has read to them. They find the *p*s in the title of Dr. Seuss's *Hop on Pop*, James Marshall's *The Three Little Pigs*, and Eve Rice's *Peter's Pockets.*

Mr. Felton carefully prints the following words on the tube as he emphasizes and underlines the letter *p*: *pig, Peter, pocket, hop, pop.* He then tells the children he is going to name some colors, and they should say "pickle" if they hear a /p/. He emphasizes putting his lips together as he pronounces the /p/ in this list of words: pink, red, green, purple. Following some discussion, Mr. Felton adds *pink* and *purple* to the tube. He tacks the tube to the wall for future reference and the addition of new words.

Mr. Felton has been emphasizing phonemic segmentation and alphabet knowledge—*the very things that early on predict so well learning to read in first grade, are, in fact, most likely to have their origins in having been read to as a young child!* Since awareness of words as sequences of sounds and knowledge of letters are directly linked to initially learning to read words, they have substantial predictive value. However, a major source of this understanding and knowledge about word forms is likely to have come from interacting with books. British researchers Morag Maclean and her colleagues (MacLean, Bryant, & Bradley, 1988) followed a group of children from the age of about 3 until they were nearly 5. They found that children's knowledge of nursery rhymes at age 3 was closely related to their ability to perceive and produce rhyme and alliteration, as well as to recognize letters and some simple words, 15 months later. In other words, children who at an early age had experienced a lot of nursery rhymes were better equipped with the knowledge and understanding that enhance learning to read in school.

Children who have been read to are likely to come from "literacy-rich" homes, in which they have played with magnetic letters on the refrigerator, played oral language games such as the "backward game" (as one young child did when she called one of us "Johnny Cool"), or been encouraged to write their own messages. Children who have been read to may even have focused on the two things that tend to be most useful in identifying words—letters and sounds. It is entirely possible that what is learned about sounds and letters from being read to is the strongest factor affecting reading acquisition in first grade (and it will also have considerable influence in later grades).

The Australian study we just mentioned is not unique in finding that phonemic awareness is one of the best predictors of early reading and writing ability. Ingvar Lundberg (1984), in an in-depth study of children learning to read in Sweden, found that phonemic awareness in first grade was very strongly related to reading achievement in sixth grade. And in a longitudinal study of learning to read and write in an elementary school in Austin, Texas, one of us found that development of phonemic awareness early in first grade was critical to children's successfully learning to read and write in first grade (Juel, 1988; Juel, 1994; Juel, Griffith, & Gough, 1986).

Phonemic Awareness and Alphabet Recognition

Of the two competencies we discuss here, alphabet recognition is the simpler matter and relatively easy for students to learn. Students need to recognize letters and their distinguishing features in order to work effectively with print; learning the names of letters is also very useful. We discuss fostering alphabet recognition later in this chapter and in Chapter 4.

Phonemic awareness is a more complex matter. Although it is a competency that you mastered long ago, it is probably not a concept that you are familiar with. Because phonemic awareness can be a challenging competency for children to acquire, we consider it at some length.

What Is Phonemic Awareness?

Phonemic awareness is the knowledge that spoken words are composed of somewhat separable sounds. You can play with these sounds (there's a wasket in my basket; dilly dilly, silly Willy), rearrange them (Johnny Cool), rhyme them (pig, jig, fig), alliterate them (teeny tiny Tina), and even make up words with them (as done in Pig Latin). Phonemic awareness is not equivalent to phonics. It is *not* knowledge about which letters represent particular sounds. Rather, it is an insight about speech itself. Phonemic awareness requires attention to the sounds (phonemes) that reside within words. Phonemes do roughly correspond to letters, but only roughly. For example, there are three phonemes in *cap*, but there are also three phonemes in *cape*, and three in *shake*. Perceiving words as sequences of phonemes is important in learning to read and write because the link between phonemes and letters is the basis for alphabetic writing systems such as English. However, keep in mind that a child can have achieved phonemic awareness and still not recognize a single letter of the alphabet. Phonemic awareness is an awareness of the *sounds* of language.

> Only by understanding that spoken words contain phonemes can one learn the relationships between letters and sounds.
>
> *—Steven Stahl*
> *Teacher Educator*

Unfortunately, phonemic awareness does not come naturally. Achieving it demands that a child attend to the form, rather than the meaning, of speech. This is difficult because our natural inclination is to attend to meaning. Thus even those children who arrive at school with well-developed oral language may not have developed phonemic awareness. Phonemic awareness is not necessary for speaking or for listening, but it is vital to reading.

Understanding phonemes is complicated by the fact that we rarely say them separately; instead, they run together. In speech, we actually begin forming our mouths to pronounce the upcoming phoneme as we are still saying the previous one. For example, in saying *cat*, we begin saying the /ă/ before we finish the /k/. It is almost impossible to say some phonemes in isolation. That is, it is almost impossible to say either the /k/ or /t/ in *cat* without adding a vowel sound, such as /ə/.

Teaching phonemic awareness is thus sometimes quite difficult. Some children will need a good deal of assistance in gaining this understanding.

Why Do Phonemic Awareness and Alphabet Recognition so Strongly Predict Success in Reading?

Phonemic awareness and alphabet recognition are highly predictive of success in beginning reading because learning to pronounce words is a primary task for the beginning reader. Children must unlock the relationships between the sounds they use to say words and the letters they use in reading and writing words. A child trying to spell *dog*, for example, tries to connect the phonemes she perceives to the actual letters. Initially, *dog* may be represented by just *D*, since the initial consonant is often the easiest for a child to attend to and attach to a letter. Later, this child may spell it *DG* because she feels these two consonants in her mouth as she says the word. Still later she may spell it *DAG*. These early spellings are called invented spelling and are perfectly natural for young children. Invented spelling plays an important role in Kay Hollenbeck's first-grade classroom:

> Having the freedom to use invented spelling is essential for my first-graders. It allows them to be writers from day one. We call it "sound spelling," because they write words the way they think they sound, using the letters they know. This is a big accomplishment for them and they are proud that they can "write" any word they can say.
>
> For example, yesterday Mara wrote *Tuda iz mi brda i m 6*. When I read the words back to her—"Today is my birthday; I am six"—her face beamed, delighted that I could actually read what she had intended to say. I knew what she had written, both because she had chosen letters that approximated the sounds in the words she intended and also because I was able to use context clues. I knew it was her birthday, and the picture she had drawn was a give-away, too—a girl and a birthday cake with six candles! Although Mara was thrilled that I knew her exact words, she also was concerned that she hadn't "spelled the words right." So she asked me to "write them the *right* way." Which I did, of course, in her "word book"—a little booklet of pages stapled together that students keep on hand for me to write words they request. There is one page for each letter of the alphabet.
>
> Kay Hollenbeck, First-Grade Teacher

Eventually, of course, children like Mara will need to understand the connections between the approximately 40 phonemes of spoken English and the 26 letters that we use to represent them. This is one of the key tasks of learning to read, and it is not easy. As we all know, the English writing system does not reflect a consistent one-to-one relationship between letters and sounds. Letter–sound correspondences in English have their quirks. However—and this is a key point—words contain enough predictable correspondences to at least aid in identification or spelling. In identifying the "irregular" word *come*, for example, the letters *c, m,* and the silent *e* reliably represent certain sounds. A child who can figure out which sounds these letters are likely to represent has a powerful tool for recognizing words, while the child who cannot figure out letter–sound correspondences will often be stumped when she comes to a word she has not previously learned to read.

Reflection AND Application

1. At the beginning of this part of the chapter, we noted that having a schema for the structure of narrative texts is very important to children's success in reading. It is also important that *you* understand it. Take a few minutes to jot down that structure in your own words.

2. In her comment about empowering students to become independent readers, first-grade teacher Glenna Schwarze emphasizes that students need both decoding skills and the ability to instantly recognize many words. In your own words, explain why both of these skills are necessary.

3. Suppose you were reading a simple storybook to a kindergarten student and wanted to help her develop phonemic awareness. Describe three things you could do. (You can learn more from this activity if you focus on a particular storybook and give specific examples of things you might point out and questions you might ask.)

Two Stages in Learning to Identify Words

As children learn to identify words both by figuring things out for themselves and receiving assistance and instruction from teachers and other knowledgeable adults, they generally pass through two broad stages—one in which they use visual–selective cues in their reading and writing, and one in which they become spelling–sound readers and writers.

The Visual–Selective Cue Stage

Initially, children begin to read and write before they can identify or write all the letters of the alphabet and before they have phonemic awareness. Often, the first word children learn is their own name. Diane, for example, was 4-years old when her mother, a student in one of our university classes, came in during office hours. To keep Diane busy while she talked, her mom handed her daughter her notebook. Diane slowly and laboriously wrote her name and then wrote the message shown in Figure 3.1.

When Diane was finished, her mother asked her to tell what the message said and to also say the letters in her name. She easily told the message. It was about what she and her mom were going to do after they left the office—though she did not look at her paper as she "read" the message. However, Diane was unable to name any but the first letter, the *D*, in her name.

Diane treated her name as a visual unit, without distinguishing and naming individual letters as components. Quite frequently, the first letters

Diane

[handwritten letterlike forms]

FIGURE 3.1   *Diane's Note*

children learn are those in their own names. Certainly writing your name is an important step in declaring your identity (Bloodgood, 1996). It is also clear that Diane knew a lot about print: She knew that it moves left to right across the page, and there were clearly letterlike forms in her writing. Still, it was real work for her to write her name because she had to remember its visual form without fully understanding that it is composed of individual letters with particular shapes and names.

Fairly frequently, children begin reading by writing. People are natural message makers; we want to leave our mark. Young children re-create nature or events in their earliest symbolic play with building blocks, Legos, and drawings. Diane's message is called invented writing. Invented writing represents an important level of understanding for a child who is learning to read—that lifeless-looking squiggles can convey real messages.

As children learn letterlike forms, these forms frequently start to creep onto the pages of their drawings. In Figure 3.2 another emergent reader, 5-year-old Jake, has drawn himself doing karate.

> The only sure way to prevent a child from learning to read is to preclude all opportunity to make appropriate associations between written letters and the sounds they represent.
>
> —*Barbara Bateman*
> *Educational Researcher*

FIGURE 3.2   *Jake's Drawing*

Jake's reversal of letters in his name does not indicate a problem; it simply illustrates that Jake perceives his name as a single visual unit. At this stage of development, Jake does not experience directionality as a relevant characteristic of his world. Until children begin working with print, virtually each thing they experience and learn to name retains the same name, regardless of the way it might be facing. Jake is still Jake whether he stands on his head or his feet. His dog is a dog whether he is coming or going. A table may look funny turned upside down, but it is still named a table.

Only in writing is this principle violated. Jake will catch on to the importance of directionality in writing as he writes and reads more. Also, once Jake learns the names of the letters, his task will become easier. When he knows that his name is made of the letter sequence *J, a, k, e,* he will find the spelling of his name easier to recall and to write.

Another interesting feature of Jake's writing is that it shows an initial understanding that letters can represent sounds. The speech bubble coming out of Jake's mouth contains the letters *a* and *e,* which he says make the sounds he makes as he does a karate chop. Here, he shows some fairly advanced understanding of letters and sounds.

At this point, is it appropriate to say that Diane or Jake can read? In a sense, they can, and in a sense, they cannot. Jake can tell what came out of his mouth in his drawing, though he seems to change it a bit each time he is asked. Diane can read her message, though she does change it somewhat every time she is asked to reread it.

During a visit one of us made to Diane's house, her mother pointed to a copy of Margaret Brown's *Goodnight Moon* and said that this was Diane's favorite bedtime story and that she could read it. With a little prompting, Diane agreed to do so. As she started to read the first page, it was clear she was scanning the picture and not the print. The story begins, "In the great green room there was a telephone." But Diane began, "The bunny has a big room, and it's green and there's a phone" (said as she pointed to the phone). Her meaning and that of the text were quite close, to be sure. But she wasn't really reading the book. Instead, she remembered some of what her mother read to her, prompted by the pictures and perhaps a bit by the text.

At one point, Diane's mother asked her to point to the word *moon* on the cover of the book. With some hesitation and an unwillingness to keep her finger in place, Diane waved her finger in the right direction. Her mother then asked her to point to the word *moon* on the first page of the story. Diane pointed to the word *room.* Diane's mother pointed to the word *green* and asked her what it was. Diane shrugged; then she pointed to the word *balloon* and happily shouted "moon." Diane appears to have noticed something about the word *moon*—perhaps the two distinctive circles and the *n*—and she saw similar circles and an *n* in *balloon.*

Diane's approach to word recognition is typical of an emergent reader. She uses the visual cue of distinctive letter shapes. But she also uses this cue selectively—that is, she uses some letter shapes but not others. In fact, her use of some distinctive letter shapes and her failure to attend to others prompt her to call both *room* and *balloon, moon.* Children who use visual–selective cues to remember words often recall cues such as word length, the first letter of the word, and the place on the page where the word occurs (Ehri & Robbins, 1992; Gough & Hillinger, 1980; Juel, 1991). They use these characteristics, in conjunction with the clues provided by illustrations, to identify words. Thus children who use visual–selective cues can correctly identify words one day but then fail to do so the next day. Visual–selective cues are arbitrary and easily forgotten. Yet use of these cues is normal for most children, a stage that they pass through on their way to becoming competent readers. With appropriate practice, feedback, and instruction, children will move beyond this stage and become increasingly competent at correctly and consistently identifying words in print.

An activity that will give your emerging readers such practice and feedback is described here:

IN THE CLASSROOM
Letter Puppets

Purpose: To give students practice and feedback in recognizing the initial sound in a word and the letter that represents that sound.

Procedure: Purchase or make a set of puppets with alliterative names such as Pink Pig, Red Rooster, Bobby Banana, Nice Nora, Mad Mike, and so on.

- Put on one of the hand puppets, such as Pink Pig, and introduce the children to it, saying "Pink Pig only likes things that start with a /p/, like her name, Pink Pig." Emphasize the /p/ as you talk.

- Walk around the room and ask the children what Pink Pig likes as the puppet touches the object. For example, "Does Pink Pig like pencils? Does Pink Pig like Peter? Does Pink Pig like Paula? Does Pink Pig like red?" and so on.

- After you have touched several objects and the children have responded, ask, "What do you think is Pink Pig's favorite letter of the alphabet?"

- Students can take turns wearing the puppet and asking the same questions, and other puppets can be used to give practice with additional letters.

The Spelling–Sound Stage

Once children learn letter names and possess some degree of phonemic awareness, they frequently use the names of letters to help them recall and spell words. They may be particularly dependent on the names of initial consonants for word recall. The name of the letter *b* is the sound of the word *bee*, and the name of the letter *j* is part of the sound of the word *Jake*, for example, and this overlap may help children identify these words when they see them in a text (Ehri & Robbins, 1992).

In writing words, children often use letters whose names represent the sounds that they perceive in the words. As we have already noted, at first, they may represent only the initial consonant or the most distinctive sound (for example, *b* written for *bee* or *l* for *elephant*). Even this level of processing represents a remarkable advance in understanding. To do this, children need both some phonemic awareness—to perceive the sounds represented by *b* or *l*—and knowledge of the alphabet. When children use this knowledge to spell, the result is invented spelling. This term describes young children's attempts to spell words using their limited knowledge about letters and sounds. In the previous section, Diane engaged in invented writing, as do children who write entirely random strings of letters (for example, *czfdyxsy* for *this is my blue umbrella*). Invented spelling is a more sophisticated accomplishment.

It is quite interesting that children seem to progress in invented spelling in a very predictable fashion (Henderson, 1990). Also, as we will discuss in Chapter 4, the analysis of a child's invented spelling is a useful diagnostic tool in planning appropriate phonics instruction for the child.

The easiest units of sound for children to perceive in single-syllable words are the onset and the rime. The onset is the initial consonant or consonants in the word—for example, the /k/ in *cat*, the /f/ in *fish*, and the /st/ in *Stan*. The rime is the vowel unit that follows the onset—for example, the /ăt/ in *cat*, the /ĭsh/ in *fish*, and the /ăn/ in *Stan* (Treiman, 1992). In the rime unit, the more distinctive phoneme is often the consonant. That is, as you slowly say "cat," you are probably most able to feel in your mouth, or perceive, the /k/ and the /t/. As we have noted, as they start to spell, children often first represent the initial consonant, for example, writing *cat* as *K*.

Children next tend to write the consonant they perceive in the rime unit. So *cat* is written as *KT*. Later, vowels begin to creep in. Long vowels are often represented before short ones, partly because long vowels are the familiar names of the letters. Short vowels can be troublesome to perceive. For example, whereas the long *a* in *Kate* is fairly obvious, the short *a* in *cat* tends to be masked by the /t/.

Children's writing and the way it becomes increasingly accurate in representing sounds are very important because children frequently develop conscious awareness of the phonemes in words as they try to write them. In the following dialogue, 5-year-old Paul illustrates his phonemic awareness in questions addressed to his mother, Glenda Bissex (1980).

Paul: *What makes the /ch/ in* teach?
Mother: CH.
Paul: *What makes the /∂/ sound?*
Mother: *In what word?*
Paul: Mumps.
Mother: U.

Perceiving that there is a /ch/ in *teach* and a /∂/ in *mumps* is an instance of phonemic awareness. Connecting these phonemes to letters constitutes discovering the code of printed English. Not surprisingly, silent letters are not represented in a child's spelling early on—for example, if Paul were to write the word *teach*, he would probably spell it *TECH*.

The invented spelling of 5-year-old Jordan displayed in Figure 3.3 shows how much this emergent reader has already learned about the code of written English. Jordan has encountered some common words frequently enough to have memorized their correct spelling (for example, *Jordan, and, in,* and *is*). He uses the sounds conveyed in the letter names in his spellings (for example, *mi*). He more frequently represents consonants than vowels (for example, *kindrgrdin* and *grd*). He is actively working to link the phonemes he perceives to actual letters. For example, on one occasion he writes *grade* as *GRD*, whereas on another he writes it as *GROB*, adding a letter representing a vowel sound and reversing the *D*. Again, he will on occasion reverse a letter or number and, as with Jake, this is not a concern.

Do you think Jordan would be able to read the word *grade* if he came across it in a text? Probably not. He is not yet consistently writing silent let-

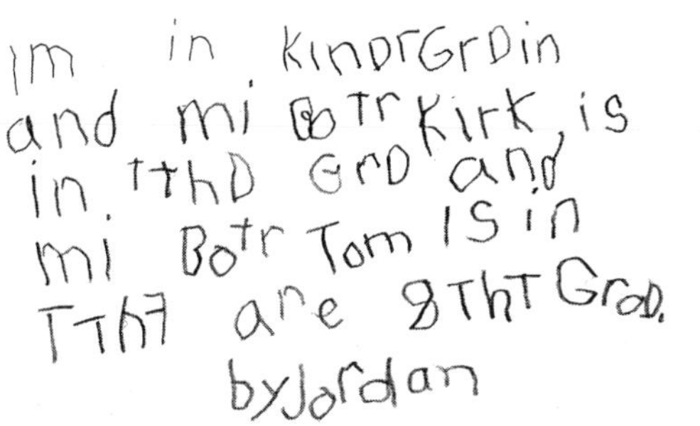

FIGURE 3.3   *Jordan's Writing*

ters. To do so requires considerable knowledge of within-word spelling patterns (Henderson, 1990). To acquire such knowledge, a child must have engaged in rather extensive reading. Silent letters must be noticed to be learned. One of the most common within-word spelling patterns is the silent *e* marker, as in *grade*. Another common spelling pattern is *ea*, representing a long *e* (the sound heard in *teach*). As Jordan reads more, he will start to notice these patterns. Thus, Jordan is likely to progress from *GRD* to *GRAD* to *GRADE* in writing *grade*. Jordan is also likely to overgeneralize patterns as he is first learning them, as we will discuss in the next section. Thus, he may move from *TECH* to *TECHE* and even *TEACHE* in writing *teach*.

Notice also that Jordan spells the last syllable in *kindergarten* with *IN*. Jordan is from Texas, where *en* is pronounced /ĭn/. In many regions of the United States, both *em* and *en* receive short *i* pronunciations. That is, words like *pin* and *pen*, *ten* and *tin*, and *Jim* and *gem* have identical pronunciations. Sensitivity to dialect is important as we evaluate children's speech and invented spellings to plan instruction. Unfortunately, sometimes teachers use the word *hen* to represent a short *e* sound when both the teacher and her students pronounce this word as /hĭn/.

Figure 3.4 summarizes our discussion about the visual–selective cue stage and the spelling–sound stage that most children pass through on their way to becoming proficient readers.

Reflection AND Application

4. One of us (Juel, Griffith, & Gough, 1985) once asked some first-grade children to read the word *rain*. Here are the replies of 14 children: "ring," "in," "runs," "with," "ride," "art," "are," "on," "reds," "running," "why," "ran," "ran," "ran." We also asked these 14 children to spell the word *rain*, and here are their spellings: *rach, in, yes, uan, ramt, fen rur, Rambl, wetn, wnishire,* one drawing of rain drops, *Rup, ran, ran.* Do you think these children were mainly visual–selective cue readers and writers or spelling–sound readers and writers? Explain your answer. Which spelling might be that of a budding letter-name speller?

   Two first-grade children correctly read the word, but one spelled it *raine* and another spelled it *rane*. What can you say about these two children's understanding of the code of printed English?

5. Explain the progress in perceiving words as sequences of sounds and connecting those sounds to letters, as well as learning common spelling patterns, that a child is making as her spelling of *rain* moves from *R* to *RAN* to *RANE* to *RAIN*.

Stage	Understandings Needed to Advance to This Stage	Possible Readings of "Mary was on her way to school."	Sample "Spellings" of *rain*
Visual– Selective Cue	Symbols carry messages. Print carries messages. Some letter knowledge	"My kitty ran away." "____ water on hen with to is." "My on here we soon." "____ on her ____ to ____ ."	/ / / wnishire rach ramt
Spelling– Sound	Stable concept of word Alphabet knowledge Phonemic awareness Spelling–sound knowledge	"Mary was on her way to sk, aol, skol." "Mary was on her way to ____ " [I don't know that word.] "Marey was on her way to school."	ran rane raine

FIGURE 3.4   *Understandings and Reading Production at Two Stages of Learning to Identify Words*

The Relationship Between Learning to Read and Learning to Speak

Educators have sometimes stressed the similarities between learning to speak and learning to read. There are indeed some important ones. In particular, children try to figure out both oral and written language by trying them out (babbling sounds and using invented writing or invented spelling for words) and actively forming hypotheses about how the systems work. But there is also a very important difference between learning to read and learning to speak: Learning to read is much, much harder!

Just as in learning to speak, children learn to read and write partly by observing and listening to others and then forming hypotheses about how they are doing it. Invented writing and spelling can indicate a child's emerging hypotheses about how print works.

Also, different children's invented spellings progress through a remarkably similar sequence (Henderson, 1990). This parallels the process of children's oral language development. As they speak, and as their speech reflects their understanding of how spoken English works, their tacit understanding of how language works solidifies. In fact, parents who try to explicitly teach their children correct forms at this stage are usually ineffective. In oral language development, children may initially use correctly the past-tense form of commonly heard words, for example, saying *broke* as the past tense of *break*. But as they learn about *-ed* endings, they will overgeneralize them and use *breaked* or *broked* as the past tense of *break*. To the casual observer, it might appear that the child has regressed, but she is actually learning and implementing the rules as she understands them. In the writing of young children, we see the same type of overgeneralizations about rules that appear in oral language (Juel, 1994; Juel, Griffith, & Gough, 1985).

> Literacy is a cultural convention. It is far from universal.
>
> —Charles Perfetti
> Psychologist

Although learning to speak and learning to read and write share tasks of hypothesis making, children have a harder go at it with print. Learning to read and write requires more explicit instruction because successful hypothesis formation is more difficult.

Unlike acquiring oral language, acquiring written language is not a biologically driven process (Liberman & Liberman, 1992). Many human cultures exist without written language; but no civilizations, communities, tribes, or bands of humans who lack an oral language have ever been discovered. Written language evolved as a fairly recent development in human history—about 3,000 years ago. Humans have produced oral language for a much, much longer period of time. Writing systems are cultural inventions; speaking appears to be a universal biological feature of human beings.

Infants begin to utter strings of sounds from the crib and seem to delight in uttering them; they do so when no other human is present. Except when a child is deprived of human contact or has serious physical or mental differences, it is virtually inevitable that the child will learn to speak.

On the other hand, if we were to provide vast quantities of print to a child, there is no guarantee that that child would learn to read. Reading requires more knowledge about the mechanics of the system (such as conscious awareness of phonemes) than does the biologically driven process of learning to speak (Gough & Hillinger, 1980; Liberman & Liberman, 1992). Children also need to be consciously aware of the form of printed words—of how phonemes relate to letters—and the directionality of text (that it runs from left to right).

When children approach print, it may surprise adults that many are not aware of individual words. In speech, we run one word into another—"Howyadoing?" It is not until children encounter the white spaces between words in print that words stand out so clearly to them. The even more abstract concept of the phoneme poses a still greater challenge.

Learning to read is indeed much more difficult than learning to speak! Most children need instruction, guidance, and support to master this task.

> Given all that we have said, we might well expect young children to have difficulty in becoming aware of the phonological structure and, in fact, they do.
>
> —Isabelle Liberman and
> Donald Shankweiler
> Psychologists

Reflection AND Application

6. To more fully appreciate the fact that learning to read is more difficult than learning to speak, consider the huge number of adults who have not learned to read. Use the library, the Internet, or the help of a librarian to answer these questions: How many adults in the United States have not learned to read? How many adults in other industrialized countries (for example, Germany) have not learned to read? How many adults in developing countries (for example, Bangladesh) have not learned to read? Then write a brief statement comparing the universality of speech to the universality of reading.

INSTRUCTION THAT FACILITATES CHILDREN'S GROWING LITERACY

We began this chapter by emphasizing the value of being read to as a very young child and then discussed children's growing knowledge about reading and the similarities and differences between learning to speak and learning to read. We talked about how children learn about the structure of text and the structure of words, develop phonemic awareness, move through the two stages of learning to identify words, and pursue the challenging task of learning to read and write.

In this part of the chapter, we discuss emergent literacy instruction, beginning with setting up a literate environment—something we stress throughout this book. Next, we suggest ways to foster literacy growth using the four modes of language—reading, writing, listening, and speaking. Finally, we take you into a kindergarten classroom to see a master teacher at work, guiding and nurturing her children's emerging literacy.

The Environment

The starting point in fostering children's emerging literacy is to make your classroom a language-rich environment that immerses students in print. As we explained in Chapter 2, a language-rich environment abounds with things to read, write, listen to, and talk about, and provides a host of opportunities to read, write, listen, and talk. Therefore, your classroom walls should be covered with posters, signs, labels, and student work. The room should have a reading center that includes a library chock full of books. It also might contain comfortable chairs, pillows, stuffed animals, a rug, and anything else that will make it an enticing and secure spot for young children.

In addition to a classroom reading center, there should be a special area of the room designated for writing. This area should contain paper of various sizes, textures, and colors, as well as a variety of pencils, pens, markers, crayons, alphabet strips, and the like.

In addition to having the materials needed to read and write, children need *time* to read and to write. You need to continually show children that reading and writing are valuable and enjoyable. The best way to do this is to model the activities you want children to value and engage in. Read and write yourself, and share information with your students about what you are reading and writing as well as your reactions to what you read and write.

Your activities with children on the threshold of literacy should focus on reading for enjoyment and reading for meaning. The fact that print conveys meaning is the central concept to develop, and not all students will have already grasped it. Of course, offering many opportunities for children to talk

> A stimulating environment is required to enable natural curiosity, intelligence, and creativity to develop, and to enable our biological capacities to unfold.
>
> —Noam Chomsky
> Linguist

Early literacy activities should engage the interests of young children and convey the idea that print conveys meaning.

and to listen will enhance skills in reading and writing. As you read the following sections, you will see that literacy activities, like the four modes of language, are highly interrelated. You will also see that opportunities to create worthwhile, interesting, and motivating activities are endless.

Reading Opportunities

Authentic opportunities for children to read in the classroom are almost limitless. Here we present some ideas you can try out and expand on in your classroom.

The Morning Meeting

The beginning of each school day is a wonderful time to gather your students in a comfortable place and meet with them as a community of learners. You want them to know that school is a safe and exciting place to be. The morning meeting can develop and nurture this sense of belonging, community, and purpose, as well as engage students in a variety of literacy experiences. The amount of time you spend, whether it is 10 minutes or 20, will depend on how long your students are able to focus without becoming restless. This time may be relatively short at the beginning of the year and increase as the year progresses.

During this meeting, many activities can take place. This is an opportunity to prepare students for the day as well as to allow them to explore valuable concepts such as time, weather, the days of the week, and the months of the year. The meeting usually begins with an attendance count. As students become more adept with print, attendance might be taken by showing name cards and having students respond to their names in print.

The morning meeting is a good time to write the day and date on the board with students, reminding them of what day came just before and what day will come after (simultaneously teaching and reinforcing children's knowledge of the days of the week and the concepts of *before* and *after*). You can also talk with students about the weather, teaching words such as *sunny*, *rainy*, *cold*, and *warm*. In addition, it is an excellent time to catch up on the latest news. Students always enjoy sharing the events of their lives, and the morning meeting is perfect for such sharing; students might take turns (depending on how much time you wish to spend on this) so that several students can share each day. Certainly, you will have information that you wish to share as well, and one way to do this is to write messages to your class. In Chapter 9, we show how one first-grade teacher uses the morning meeting to create a classroom newspaper as a shared writing experience (a topic we cover in more detail later).

> Typically, the first words learned are their [kindergartner's] own names and those of classmates. Why learning these words early is typical is no mystery. The fact that the names are meaningful, constantly available, and named often makes them memorable.
>
> —*Dolores Durkin*
> *Teacher Educator*

The Morning Message and the Daily Schedule

We recommend writing a short message to your class each day so that when they arrive they know that they will be "reading" a note from you. This message serves two major purposes. First, it reinforces the notion that print conveys meaning. Second, it provides children with practice in tracking print as you read aloud. In fact, it is often worthwhile reading the message several times. At this time, you might also ask students whether they recognize any of the letters or words, and have them come up and circle those they recognize. Along with the morning message, a daily schedule is particularly helpful. Going over it at the beginning of the day gives students a sense of what the day holds and, equally important, illustrates another use of print. As the day progresses, you can refer back to the schedule from time to time.

"Read the Room"

All classrooms, but especially kindergarten and first-grade classrooms, should be language-rich. One of the easiest and most effective ways to fill your room with print is to label objects in the room, a task that children may be able to help with. Labels can be attached to objects such as your desk, your chair, the bulletin board, the clock, the coatrack, the windows, and so on. Labels illustrate the point that words represent things that exist in the world, some of which are concrete objects. Of course, abstract concepts can be labeled too. You could label a bulletin board filled with pictures of your smiling students with the word *happy*. During the morning meeting, or at some other time during the day, you can offer your students the opportunity to "read the room." That is, students can look around and read any labels that they wish to. At first, they will not really be reading the labels; they will take their cue from the labeled objects. However, they will be learning that the words they are looking at stand for something, a very important message. With time, they will begin to associate specific labels with the objects they name.

Free Reading

Each day, students should have several opportunities to read books of their own choosing in any way they like. Some children might wish to share a book with a friend. They might do this by telling a favorite story that they have committed to memory, using the pictures as cues for turning the pages; if you model this activity for them, they will likely find it inviting. Others will silently look at books. Still others will want to be read to or listen to a book that has been tape-recorded. Whatever their choice, children will be getting experience with books. These sessions need not be long, since the attention spans of young children tend to be relatively short, but opportunities for such engagement with books should occur throughout the day.

Environmental Print

In addition to books, children can "read" several other things. These include posters, greeting cards, cereal boxes, bumper stickers, names of toys, letters, charts, magazines, coloring books, and milk cartons. By having children read text on objects that exist in their environment, you will reach most all of your students. Although not all children in your classroom will live in homes with rich stores of books, most will be surrounded by other forms of print that can reinforce the notion that print carries meaning, thus enhancing their literacy development.

Selecting Books for Specific Purposes

At the beginning of this chapter, we talked about books as the heart and soul of reading. They also serve a host of specific literacy-development purposes. Here, we consider three of them.

Books That Motivate Children to Enter the World of Print. As a teacher of young children, you will want to select books that develop their vocabularies, expand their knowledge of the world, connect to their lives, increase their knowledge of story structures, and increase their desire to read. Such texts can be well-known children's favorites, such as James Marshall's *The Three Little Pigs* (1989), or newer ones, such as Gary Soto's *Too Many Tamales* (1992). Imagine how children will identify with the characters and situation and expand their knowledge of the world by listening to *Too Many Tamales*, excerpted here:

> Snow drifted through the streets and now that it was dusk, Christmas trees glittered in the windows.
> Maria moved her nose off the glass and came back to the counter. She was acting very grown-up now, helping her mother make tamales. Their hands were sticky with masa.
> "That's very good," her mother said.
> Maria happily kneaded the masa. She felt grown-up, wearing her mother's apron. Her mom had even let her wear lipstick and perfume. If only I could wear Mom's ring, she thought to herself.

Books That Highlight the Sounds of Language. Since emergent readers need to attend to the form of words, it is important to read texts in which the structure of words is particularly transparent, highlighting the sounds of words in order to foster phonemic awareness. You can choose texts with features such as word play, rhyme, and alliteration to accomplish this goal. One example is Jill Bennett's rendition of *Teeny Tiny* (1986).

> Once upon a time there was a
> teeny tiny woman who lived
> in a teeny tiny house
> in a teeny tiny village.
> One day this teeny tiny woman
> put on her teeny tiny hat
> and went out of her
> teeny tiny house
> to take a teeny tiny walk.

More systematic phonemic awareness and letter activities can follow, as kindergarten teacher Jeff Baptista explains:

I use books such as *Teeny Tiny* with my first-graders to help them develop phonemic awareness. After we have enjoyed the story, I will ask them, "What letter in *teeny* makes it say /t/? What letter in *tiny* makes it say /t/? Can you think of other words that start with /t/, like *teeny tiny?*"

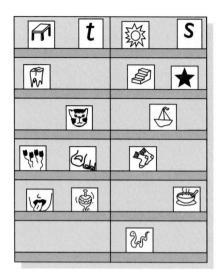

Then we might sort pictures or objects that start with /t/ into one column on a pocket chart, and those that start with /s/, like Silly Sally, in another. I will cut pictures from a magazine or create simple line drawings. These pictures can be easily sorted, based on the initial sound of the concept or object they depict. Those that start with a /t/ sound (for example, *table, tail, tiger*) are placed together, while all the /s/ pictures (for example, *sun, salad, soup*) are placed together. Sometimes I will have the children work in pairs or small groups to decide in which column pictures should go. I have also cut a teeny-tiny-woman shape out of construction paper and printed the children's favorite *t* words on it. A word wall works well, too—a large sheet of butcher paper that the children and I fill with *t* words, or whatever letter we are currently focusing on.

Jeff Baptista, Kindergarten Teacher

In Chapter 4 we describe in greater detail such letter–sound activities.

Word-level instruction begins with a focus on a meaningful text. Then, words in that text are highlighted, just as Jeff Baptista did in working with *Teeny Tiny*. The links between meaning, words, and word parts should always be clear.

Books That Children Can Learn to Read on Their Own. The books with predictable patterns that we described earlier in the chapter are purposely written so that children can remember them after hearing them a few times. The overall structure of the books is repetitive, and the picture clues are rich and informative. All in all, these books can make children "instant readers" after only a few readings by the teacher. In Chapter 4, we include a bibliography of these books.

Brian Wildsmith's *Cat on the Mat* exemplifies this repetitive structure and strong picture support. In this tale, various animals join a cat on the mat:

> *The cat sat on the mat.*
> *The dog sat on the mat.*
> *The goat sat on the mat.*

As the child rereads the text and points to the lines and words after hearing it read several times, she can begin to gain insight into the conventions of print, such as the directionality of print going from left to right. After rereading many predictable texts, a child may learn the printed form of some high-frequency words, such as *the*, and some high-interest words, such as *dog*; she may even begin to associate some letters with sounds.

You can encourage such understanding by using big books, which are large enough for the whole class or a group of students to see as you read. They allow you to replicate activities that parents or other caregivers do as they read to their children at home: point to the print, track the print as children speak it, and highlight words. Predictable text in big books or on charts can encourage children to follow along, echoing or chorally reading as you point to individual words.

To highlight words, letters, or text, you can frame words in a big book with your hand or cover a page with an acetate sheet on which you underline words, word parts, or letters. You can also ask questions or make comments about specific elements in the text; a few suggestions are listed here:

- Point to where it said "goat."
- Where does it say "cat"?
- Can you find a word that starts like Devon's name?
- I see some words that end with *at*. What are they?
- Here are some books that we have read before. Can you find *at* in the titles? [The books might include Carle's *Have You Seen My Cat?*, the Berenstains' *Old Hat, New Hat*, and Dr. Seuss's *The Cat in the Hat*.]

As a teacher of emergent readers, you will want to model how to use initial consonant sounds to help identify unknown words in text. Mary Caruba talks about how she models using initial consonant sounds to help her kindergartners identify unknown words:

> Sometimes when I'm reading to my children from a big book, I will pause before reading a word that begins with a consonant sound that we have talked about. I model how to identify the unknown word by combining what makes sense, picture and context cues, and initial consonant knowledge. For example, in the sentence "A cat sat on the mat," I might pause before the word *cat* and ask, "Do you think this says 'cat' or 'dog'?" Children will suggest one or the other, based on pictures or initial consonants. Or I might have the children listen as I say "cat" and "dog," with an emphasis on the initial sound. I then ask the children to recall which letters represent each beginning sound, /c/ and /d/, and to notice the first letter in the unknown word *cat*.
>
> Mary Caruba, Kindergarten Teacher

In the book lists that we include throughout this text, we annotate a number of children's books suitable for reading aloud to emergent readers. A number of these titles are available in a big book format. The following list provides a small sampling of big books.

The best way to get children to refine and extend their knowledge of letter–sound correspondence is through repeated opportunities to read.

—*The Commission on Reading*

Big Books

Lydia Marie Child. *Over the River and Through the Woods*. Morrow/Mulberry, 1994. This book is a lovely rendition of a Thanksgiving classic. 32 pages.

Lois Ehlert. *Eating the Alphabet*. Harcourt Brace, 1994. Beginning with apricot and artichoke, this big book takes readers on an alphabetical tour of the world of fruits and vegetables. 32 pages.

Muriel Feelings. *Moja Means One: Swahili Counting Book*. Puffin, 1994. This counting book, which portrays the language and customs of Swahili East Africa, is beautifully illustrated by Tom Feelings. 32 pages.

Myra Cohn Livingston. *Space Songs*. Scholastic, 1994. This collection of poetry contemplating space is accompanied by bold illustrations. 32 pages.

Gerald McDermott. *Zomo the Rabbit*. Scholastic, 1996. Zomo may not be big or strong, but he is clever enough to do three impossible tasks to earn wisdom from Sky God. 32 pages.

Bruce McMillan. *Time to . . .* Scholastic, 1996. This story follows a kindergartner through his day as he learns to tell time. 32 pages.

Ann Morris. *Loving*. Scholastic, 1996. This book about families around the world is richly illustrated in color photos. 32 pages.

David Schwartz. *How Much Is a Million?* Morrow/Mulberry, 1994. Marvelosissimo the Magician uses his magic to help explain the concepts of million, billion, and trillion. 32 pages.

Kate Waters and Madeline Slovenz-Low. *Lion Dancer: Ernie Wan's Chinese New Year*. Scholastic, 1995. In this story 6-year-old Ernie prepares for his first Lion Dance during Chinese New Year. 32 pages.

Audrey Wood. *Silly Sally*. Harcourt, 1994. Sally, the power walker, turns a stroll to the city into a rollicking adventure in this rhyming text. 32 pages.

Especially for young students, writing offers students an opportunity to discover the cipher, the map between letters and sounds. When students are encouraged to write using invented spellings, when teachers respond to a request to spell a word by encouraging students to spell it as best they can, they are forced to confront the principles that govern the way speech sounds are mapped onto letters.

—*P. David Pearson*
Teacher Educator

Writing Opportunities

In order to become increasingly competent readers, children need to become message-makers and authors themselves. For this to happen you need to create authentic writing opportunities for them. Here we describe some tried-and-true approaches.

Journals

When children write, they begin to internalize the notion that ideas can be represented symbolically. We know several kindergarten and first-grade teachers who have students keep journals, beginning on the first day of school. The journal need not be elaborate—several sheets of paper folded over to make a little book is quite sufficient. In the journal, students are encouraged to express themselves in whatever way they choose. They can be given ideas to write about, or they can be allowed to write without prompts.

Like most emergent literacy activities, journal writing should be modeled for children; modeling should show children many ways to express themselves in writing: drawing pictures, making squiggles, writing letters, and combining several forms of expression. Thus, children can "write" even if they do not yet know the letters of the alphabet. They can then read back what they have written, which is easiest if they can do so right away. Another way for young children to write is to dictate a sentence or two that you or a classroom aide writes down. As children experiment with writing, they should be encouraged to get their ideas down in print even if they do not know some letters or spellings; urge them to use invented spelling.

First-grade teacher Sid Burns invites each child to work with a special word each day:

> As children are busy illustrating their "word," I circulate around the room and take down dictations. Each child has his or her own journal, made of blank pages stapled between a construction-paper or wallpaper cover. Each student tells me a word that is "on her mind" or special to her that day. (For example, *love* and *heart* were big last week—Valentine's Day fell on Friday.) I write the dictated word in the child's journal. She can then trace or copy it. Sometimes children discuss the word with me or with other children, draw a picture that illustrates the word, and dictate a sentence or two for me to write down regarding the picture. For example, Marta asked me to write, "I love my dog. Her name is Asta." As I wrote the sentences, I used the opportunity to comment on the form of print in a way that was appropriate for Marta. I pointed to the word *dog* and said to her, "dog," emphasizing the initial sound, /d/. "What letter makes that /d/?" Then I asked her to reread the two sentences and point to the words.
>
> My first-graders enjoy having an audience for their work and appreciate sharing their journal entries with one another as well as with me.
>
> Sid Burns, First-Grade Teacher

Inviting children to read and write what they dictate (whether that dictation be taken by a teacher, a parent helper, or an older student) is only one of the many reading–writing experiences you will want your emergent readers to be engaged in.

Language-Experience Activities

Copying down children's dictation and then having them read their own words, as Sid Burns does, has been termed the *language-experience approach*. Using this approach, an adult or older student writes down the words of a story spoken by a student or group of students, using the students' language. When the story is read, students can readily read along. Its vocabulary is familiar, since students generated it, and they have prior knowledge related to its content because it is based on their experiences. Since this approach is entirely student-centered, it is particularly useful for meeting the needs of students who vary in ethnic background, English language competence, and educational needs. In fact, as we point out in Chapter 10, it is an extremely valuable procedure to use with students whose first language is not English.

Shared Reading and Writing Experience

Another opportunity that encourages writing is the shared reading and writing experience, which we discuss again in Chapters 9 and 10. In the following scenario, a first-grade teacher, Connie Martinez, combines reading instruction with an opportunity for students to compose a rhyme together. Although the children are not *physically* writing the words, they are participating in the act of composing; their teacher provides a sturdy instructional scaffold.

IN THE CLASSROOM
Reading and Writing Rhymes

Sitting in a large rocking chair, Ms. Martinez holds a big book of Mother Goose nursery rhymes. The children gathered around her can see the words on the first two pages as she begins singing the rhyme.

> *Lavender's blue, dilly, dilly,*
> *lavender's green;*
> *when I am king, dilly, dilly,*
> *you shall be Queen;*

Ms. Martinez has the children take turns pointing to the color words they know. She helps them with *lavender* and has them tell each other what color this is close to (for example, purple). "Is anyone wearing lavender or blue or green today?" she asks.

Next, she asks them which word in the verse rhymes with *green*.

"Queen!" they chime in unison.

Ms. Martinez stands up and writes *green* and *Queen* directly underneath each other on the portable chalkboard next to her. She asks the children to name the letters in each word and which ones they share.

"E-E-N!" a couple of children answer.

Then, Ms. Martinez remarks, "*Dilly* is a silly word!"

And one child declares, "They rhyme!"

So she writes *dilly* on the board, with *silly* right underneath it. She asks them if they can think of some names of boys that rhyme with *dilly* and *silly*. She helps by saying, "dilly, silly, Billy?"

They shout, "Yes." Then she says , "Dilly, silly, James," and they shout, "No."

Ms. Martinez tells the children they are going to write their own rhyme. She puts a large chart pad on a stand. The chart has part of a rhyme already printed on it . The children will suggest words or letters to complete it, and Ms. Martinez will print them on the lines. She begins by asking the children if they want to write about "Silly Billy" or "Silly Willy." They opt for Willy. Ms. Martinez prints *Willy* in the blank on the chart. The children alternate rereading the rhyme, as Ms. Martinez points to each word, and adding a word in the blank.

Here is the poem they wrote, showing how they filled in the blanks:

Silly _____ ,

Silly, silly, _____ ,

Silly, silly, m____ ,

I fell down and scratched

my _____ .

I stood up and shook my head.

I stood up and this is what I said:

Silly, silly, _____ ,

Silly, silly, m____ ,

I fell down and hurt my head.

I think I should just go

to _____ .

Silly ___Willy___ ,

Silly, silly, ___Willy___ ,

Silly, silly, m**e**___ ,

I fell down and scratched

my ___knee___ .

I stood up and shook my head.

I stood up and this is what I said:

Silly, silly, ___Willy___ ,

Silly, silly, m**e**___ ,

I fell down and hurt my head.

I think I should just go

to ___bed___ .

Every so often during the week the children recite this rhyme either as a class or in partner reading, always pointing to the words as they say them.

At the end of our week in Ms. Martinez's class, we were surprised and delighted to hear some of the children on the playground reciting the poem as they jumped rope. *Silly Willy* made a perfect jump-rope jingle. We wouldn't be surprised if the children thought up new verses to add over the days and weeks to come!

Making Books

Children can be encouraged to take their language-experience stories or perhaps write their own stories and make them into small books with illustrations. In fact, making and illustrating books is a wonderful way to actively involve children in writing and reading. Bookmaking can be as elaborate or as simple as you wish. Books can be laminated and bound with a plastic spiral or hand-sewn binding or simply stapled together. We recommend saving the more elaborate bindings for class books that can be saved and read over and over again.

Mailboxes

A classroom mailbox system in which students can post one letter a day and have pen pals to correspond with reinforces print awareness and gives students motivation for writing and for reading their own writing (since, early on, they will probably be the only ones who can read their messages).

Play Centers

Many kindergarten teachers include play centers in their classrooms. In these centers, children act out real or imagined situations and events. They might act out what happens at a restaurant or events in a story they have just heard. Literacy activities can easily be included in such play centers. In playing restaurant, for example, a simple pad of paper can be provided for a waitress or waiter to write down orders, or a chart of recipes can be printed for the cook to follow. Similarly, in planning to act out a story, you and the children might together block out the sequence of the story, illustrating it with simple pictures and a few words and phrases. Let your imagination soar as you consider ways to incorporate meaningful literacy activities in your classroom every day.

Listening and Speaking Opportunities

Of course, listening and speaking are normal parts of the kindergarten and first-grade school day. Here, we briefly mention some specific activities that enhance skills in these areas and, as you know by now, promote skills in reading and writing as well.

Reading Aloud

We cannot overemphasize the importance of reading aloud to all children, but it is especially important for emergent readers and doubly so for students who have not had the benefit of being read to at home. When you read to your class, you give students a chance to hear fluent reading and to develop the critical skill of listening comprehension. You also give them the pleasure of hearing a good story and sharing your enjoyment and enthusiasm for it. To create an effective read-aloud experience, it is helpful to keep four hints in mind:

1. Select a story that interests you as well as your students.
2. Practice the story so that you use the most effective intonation and show the pictures effectively. Also, pick good stopping points for elaborating on the information presented in the story and making sure that students understand the action.
3. Pay attention to students as you read the story so that you can respond if they appear to grow restless or confused. Encourage active participation by stopping at appropriate points to ask questions and responding to them. You might, for example, ask whether students have any idea what will happen next or whether they have ever experienced something similar to what the main character is going through.
4. Whenever possible, invite students to join in! If a word or a phrase is repeated, or if you are reading a story students have heard before, encourage them to read along with you. Also, some stories lend themselves to gestures and simple movement.

For more ideas on reading aloud and a host of suggestions on specific books to read aloud, we strongly suggest Jim Trelease's *The New Read-Aloud Handbook* (1995). This insightful and interesting text has inspired thousands of teachers and parents to read aloud to their children.

> Reading aloud is seen as the single most influential factor in young children's success in learning to read.
>
> —*Regie Routman*
> *Teacher and*
> *Teacher Educator*

Choral Reading

Choral reading simply refers to having children read passages aloud in unison. The passage may be as short as a phrase or as long as a poem or story, but it should definitely be something that is fun to read. Choral reading gives children an opportunity to experience the cadence of oral language, the structure of various forms of text, and the correspondence between print and talk. It also allows them to read aloud in a nonthreatening environment, wherein their voice is one among many. Children enjoy choral reading, and it is a particularly good technique for students whose first language is not English (see Chapter 10).

Tape Recordings

Tape-recording stories yourself or having a classroom aide or older student do so can provide you with an inexpensive and useful resource. Of course, commercially prepared tapes are also available for many popular trade books, and we have indicated those books that we know are available on tape recordings in the Children's Literature sections at the end of each chapter. With tape recordings, a number of children can listen to stories at any time during the day, and you are freed to give attention to other students.

Sing-Alongs

Singing with students encourages listening and speaking development because lyrics are, of course, words. Whenever possible, lyrics should be posted on the wall or put on an overhead projector during singing so that children can follow along.

A Kindergarten Scenario

To show you how a very skillful teacher engages her students in the meaningful literacy experiences we have just described, here we give you a glimpse into a typical day in Ellen Hawkins's afternoon kindergarten class. The location is suburban Virginia. It is February, and the types of literacy activities you will see here have been going on all year.

11:25 A.M.

Twenty-five children enter the afternoon kindergarten class, shortly after 23 children have left the morning class. The new arrivals put their gear in their cubbies or go straight to a wall chart of library pockets—like those found in library books—one for each child, with the name printed on it. As the children file by, they remove the checkout card that they had put in the pocket the day before. The card is from the book they checked out and took home. After they remove the card and put it back in the book, they return the book to the class library.

11:40 A.M.

All the children gather by the class calendar in a front corner of the classroom. Ms. Hawkins asks, "What kind of day is it—lamb or lion?" She has developed this literary vocabulary throughout the course of the year. Voices declare that this roaring, windy day is a "lion" day.

One child mentions that they should add the words *lamb* and *lion* to the L wall chart that they have been making. Ms. Hawkins is happy to oblige and adds these two words to the list, which already includes *lock, list,* and *library.*

Ms. Hawkins asks for any news. One child says her tooth came out. After she smiles to show the space and the class responds, the child is told to add this news to the class news record on the chalkboard. As she goes to write her message (in invented spelling), Ms. Hawkins turns to the rest of the class and continues with the calendar. She asks more questions: "How many days have we been in school so far? [They have been keeping track.] How many days are left? What day is it?" As the response of "Thursday" is given, she points to each letter of the word and names it. She remarks that when she says the *th* sound, her tongue is placed between her teeth. The children giggle as they try saying "Thursday" and discover this.

Ms. Hawkins then turns her attention to the child who has written her news on the board. The child reads the information. Next, Ms. Hawkins reads her news about what they will do this day. She points to the words, which are clearly printed in neat large print on the board, as she says:

Good morning
boys and girls!

We get to go to P.E. today.

We can read our books.

Do you see signs of spring?

Some children chime in as she reads. Ms. Hawkins asks the children to keep a record in their journals of the signs of spring they see. One child volunteers that she saw a robin. This begins a discussion of what other children have seen and will write in their journals. On a page in an oversized journal, Ms. Hawkins writes, "I saw a _____." She will leave this journal on an easel with this page open to serve as a model for students.

11:50 A.M.

Ms. Hawkins turns to a wall chart that has two columns of words. One is the list of words beginning with *l* and the other is a list of words that include an *l* somewhere:

leprechaun	yell
list	Emily
Lara	Carlos
library	Melissa
lion	Philip
Lee	Alex
Laura	Michele
love	sell
letter	seal
lost	table
like	
leopard	

Ms. Hawkins asks the children what is the same and what is different about the two lists. The children puzzle over this and start to talk. Most children easily determine that the first column contains words that start with *l*.

There is lots of discussion about the second list. Some children recognize names, some capital letters; some see that the letter *l* appears in the words. They realize that all the words in the second list have *ls* in them. Ms. Hawkins points out that many of the words came from the morning kindergarten class. She asks if they can contribute more words. They add:

```
Lee            Alyssa
Laura          Ronald
Lars           Angela
               yellow
```

Children continue to volunteer words, and Ms. Hawkins says they will add these later. One child says that *later* has an *l*, and Ms. Hawkins adds it to the list—even though she had declared that they were done for now, she can't pass up such a wonderful connection.

12:00 Noon

Ms. Hawkins asks the class to stand up and put their hands under their chins, over their heads, and under and over other places. She then asks them to sit down. She says she did that because she is going to read *Over, Under, and Through* by Tana Hoban (a concept book). She reminds the children that they have seen other books with photos by this author, such as the book *Look*, and a child gleefully notes that *look* starts with *l*, so it is added to the list. As Ms. Hawkins points to pictures in the book, she asks if the child in the photo is over, under, or through the object pictured.

The children discuss a photo that shows a girl standing in the middle of a circle drawn on the ground. The circle is under the girl, but there is some debate about this. In addition, Ryan says, "It's not a circle, it's an oval, and oval has an *l* in it!"

As Ms. Hawkins continues through the book of photos illustrating the concepts of beside, below, against, and behind. The children carefully note which concept each photo represents.

Most kindergartners are eager to learn and to share their own knowledge about print.

12:05 P.M.

Ms. Hawkins asks the children to stand and make their bodies into bridges. Then she says:

> Go over the water (the children giggle as they collapse).
> Lie down on your back.
> Make your feet go over your body.
> Sit back down and face the other way.
> Make rain go over your head.

After the children settle down, she gives them directions for the project of the day. Each child will get a large sheet of white construction paper. Across the bottom is printed *over and under*. At each table in the room, there are strips of colored paper that children can glue to make over-and-under patterns. Ms. Hawkins reminds them to use only a raindrop of glue and demonstrates how to do this. She demonstrates how to work with the strips of paper, twisting them over and under each other in imaginative ways.

The children go to their seats to make their own over-and-under projects. Tomorrow, Ms. Hawkins will give them an opportunity to use their creations when they read Jim Cowley's *Dan the Flying Man*.

12:25 *P.M.*

Ms. Hawkins asks the children to finish their projects and put them in the hallway to dry.

12:30 *P.M.*

Almost all the children have finished their work, put their projects in the hallway, and returned to their seats.

Children then select books from the classroom library. There are many books that they can choose, including copies of *Over, Under, and Through* that Ms. Hawkins just read to the class as well as trade books, books individual children have written, and books the class has written. Some children read together, and some read alone. While the children read, Ms. Hawkins has two children read to her the journals they have been working on. She often does this, and it gives her a chance to focus on individual children. In some journals, she finds rather accomplished writing. Others display much less sophisticated work—some drawings, a few letters, perhaps some invented spelling. Ms. Hawkins knows her individual students' emerging capabilities and is able to praise them or give them a nudge based on where they are in their journey to becoming readers and writers.

12:40 *P.M.*

Ms. Hawkins asks the children to finish reading and join the class in the front of the room to share some of their writing. The children bring their personal journals and books. A few children read stories that they have written or dictated to Ms. Hawkins on previous days. Most of the narratives are takeoffs of Ezra Jack Keats's *The Snowy Day*. Ms. Hawkins had read this story aloud the day before. The children had been encouraged to think of another type of "weather" day and what they like to do on such a day. Some had been illustrating and writing their books over the past few days and are now ready to share the finished product. Mostly their books consist of statements that they dictated to Ms. Hawkins and that she neatly printed. The children look very proud as they read their books and show their illustrations.

As you will see in the examples, each book includes a page about the author. This gives students more practice in writing, and it personalizes their books. Here is what Jack reads:

<u>The Warm Day</u>
by Jack
I like to play baseball at the park.
I like to rollerblade at the park.
I like to ride my bike down the street.

<u>About the Author</u>
Hi! I'm Jack Hooper.
I'm 6 years old.
I live in Minnesota.
I like the Gophers.

And here is what Sarah reads:

<u>The Sunny Day</u>
by Sarah R.
I would like to jump rope.
I would like to go swimming.
I go in the pool.
I run around the tree.

<u>About the Author</u>
I am 5.
My name is Sarah R.
I am a girl.
I like to swim.

After Jack and Sarah have read, several other children read what they have written.

12:55 P.M.

Snack.

1:05 P.M.

Ms. Hawkins points back to the day's morning message and says it is time for P.E.

Now that's emergent literacy in the classroom! The children in Ms. Hawkins's classroom have listened to and discussed books. They have selected books for themselves, and they have heard books read that were chosen to develop their conceptual knowledge. They have been message-makers, recording their thoughts, news, and stories. They have shared their writing with others. They have had experiences specifically aimed at developing their knowledge of the letters and sounds in words. Multiply these types of experiences over a school year—including different types of texts—and you can tell how well these children are being guided toward becoming proficient readers and writers who will be prepared to enter first grade.

Reflection AND Application

7. Suppose you knew a preschool-age youngster who was beginning to take interest in environmental print, and you wanted to take her to a nearby town or city to nurture that interest. Where might you take her on your outing, and what examples of environmental print would you point out? Think of an actual place, and give specific examples of the environmental print you could find.

8. Ellen Hawkins is an outstanding teacher, and she does a terrific job nurturing her kindergartners' emerging literacy. Nevertheless, a kindergarten classroom offers almost innumerable options for assisting young learners in their progress toward becoming readers, and it is worthwhile to explore other ways. Go back to two or three of the time slots we have shown, and describe optional or additional activities that you might use.

Special Needs and Special Talents

Learning to read and write involves gaining control of the written form of words and text. To comprehend text and to create interesting writing requires imaginative thought and knowledge of the world. Young children may have very different backgrounds. Some children enter our classrooms with considerable experience with print, message making, books, and exposure to the different places and creatures of our world. These children may need less help learning the form of words and the content in books.

For children who come to school with less exposure to print and books or having primarily used a language other than English, one-to-one assistance from older students can be particularly helpful and is also economically and logistically feasible. The task that is easiest to orchestrate is simply having the older students read appropriate books to or with the younger students—predictable books, concept books, alphabet books, and the other ones that foster emergent literacy. As the older students read, they can answer questions the younger students have and talk to the younger students about what they liked about the book, what they would like to read next, and other matters related to fostering their interest in reading.

Older readers do not, of course, have to be students. Parents, senior citizens, or any other readers can be a great asset to emergent readers, particularly to those who need a little extra help and who will profit from the one-to-one relationships that volunteers can offer. Additionally, as we emphasize in Chapter 10, for children whose primary language is not English, bilingual volunteers who speak the children's first language as well as English can be of tremendous help.

Also, although reading to or with children is likely to be the most frequent activity assigned to older children or volunteers from outside the school, they can make other contributions as well. They can take dictation from children, print out the dictation, and then let the children read back their own stories. Such language experience stories offer tremendous advantages. Children are very interested in their own stories; they of course have the background knowledge to understand them, and they know a lot about the specifics of the stories.

Although different children will need different amounts of help, all of them will profit from receiving some help. As you plan instruction and activities, it is helpful to consider both form and content—letters and words themselves and the meanings they represent—and to deliberately devise ways that children can respond and grow in their reading competence despite initial differences in knowledge and experiences. In Ms. Hawkins's classroom, there were ample opportunities for children who were reading at different levels to select different books to take home. But all children were

> Educators are recognizing that the family is the key to successful literacy development for both children and their parents. . . . Literacy programs in school will only be successful if they have home support: therefore family literacy programs are crucial for literacy development.
>
> —Lesley Mandel Morrow
> *Teacher Educator*

involved in the stimulating conceptual discussions involving the book *Over, Under, and Through*. Similarly, all children were involved in writing, but each could respond successfully through her knowledge of print conventions, and the writing the class did was considerably varied.

Quite a few children will have trouble with hearing words as sequences of sounds—in gaining phonemic awareness. Some children will need considerable help in this area, and additional ideas for developing this understanding will be presented in the next chapter. We should take care, however, not to lose sight of the forest for the trees. That is, the pieces of language and print, such as knowledge of the alphabet and phonemic awareness, are only building blocks. Their importance lies in what can be accomplished with them—*reading* and *writing*. As you plan instruction on the form of print, be sure that children see the relation of the form to the content, the meaning, of a text. The letter *t* and the phoneme /t/ are meaningless by themselves; but when they are appear in a story such as *Teeny Tiny* or in a Halloween card a child has written to her mother, they gain meaning, importance, and relevance to things children care about.

CONCLUDING REMARKS

In this chapter, we discussed how very young children develop as readers and writers. Our job as teachers of young children is to provide the literary experiences that ensure for all children the strongest possible literacy footing on which to build lifelong reading and writing skills and a lifelong love of reading.

We discussed the specific text-level and word-level experiences that children need to develop in order to read and write. The knowledge and competencies that children need to gain as developing readers include knowledge of stories, phonemic awareness, alphabet knowledge, and a beginning understanding of how letters and sounds relate to make printed words. We highlighted the instructional experiences that can promote these understandings.

We described the two broad stages that children pass through in learning to read: First comes a visual–selective cue stage in which distinctive visual cues such as word length, initial or distinctive letters, and reliance upon illustrations form the primary way in which children access printed meaning. Next comes a spelling–sound stage in which children add knowledge of how letters correspond to speech sounds as a means to recognize words. We discussed that moving into the second stage is often difficult because it requires an understanding of the rather abstract concept of phonemes. And we emphasized that learning to read is much harder than learning to speak precisely because learning to read requires a *conscious* awareness of phonemes that is not needed in learning to speak.

In the latter part of the chapter, we included a number of instructional ideas for facilitating and nurturing children's growing literacy in the four modes of language—reading, writing, speaking, and listening. We gave examples of literacy experiences that can take place during the classroom morning meeting, and use of a morning message and daily schedule. We talked about the value of engaging students in activities such as "read-the-room," free reading, and reading environmental print. We also talked about engaging students in experiences with books and providing opportunities for writing, listening, and speaking activities that can foster knowledge of how printed language works.

The chapter concluded with a glimpse into a kindergarten classroom in which a master teacher involves children in literacy activities that are appropriate for each child, no matter where she is on her journey toward literacy. In Chapter 4, we will consider and describe more advanced literacy activities.

Since much of this chapter concerns words, letters, and sounds, in concluding the chapter we want to remind you that this book's overarching theme is the development of critical literacy. We want to help students be active thinkers both when they read and when they write. Such a stance begins right from the start. We can encourage children to compare how characters (such as a wolf) are portrayed in different books and how they can be seen from different perspectives within the same book. We can encourage children to select their own books and to write their own messages. We can let children know that *we* know that they have important things to say, to write, and to read. And we can show children that we value their efforts and are there to provide help.

EXTENDING LEARNING

1. Find an adult who reads to a young child at home or in a day care center. Carefully watch and listen to their storybook interactions. How does the adult keep the child's attention? What appears to interest the child? What does the child wonder about in the story? What does the child ask about? What is the child learning about the form or content of books and print in this interaction?

2. Observe a preschool or kindergarten classroom. Make a list of the kinds of literacy activities you see. Then explain how each of these activities helps children learn about books and print. Alternatively or in addition, observe a preschool or kindergarten child outside of school, and make a list of the literacy activities the child is involved in.

3. In the latter part of the chapter, we mentioned using books with children for three different purposes—to motivate children to expand their knowledge of the world and their imaginations by reading, to highlight the sounds of language in words, and to engage students in reading right from the start by using books with predictable text and helpful illustrations. Go to a library, perhaps a public library, that has a good collection of children's books. Begin an annotated list of books that you think will motivate children to read and to expand their knowledge of the world, books that highlight the sounds of language in words, and books that contain predictable text and helpful illustrations that allow reading right from the start. Include five to ten books in each of these three categories.

4. Go to a kindergarten or first-grade class to observe children's writing activities. Jot down the different kinds of activities you see them engaged in. Write a paragraph or so describing which of the four writing opportunities presented in this chapter you would most like to try in your own classroom, and why.

REFERENCES

Adams, M. J. (1990). *Beginning to read: Thinking and learning about print*. Cambridge, MA: MIT Press. This monumental book provides a comprehensive summary of how children learn to read, how the skilled reader reads, and what research says about the role phonics plays in the process.

Bissex, G. L. (1980). *Gnys at Wrk*. Cambridge, MA: Harvard University Press. The author describes, in careful detail, the reading and writing development of her son.

Bloodgood, J. R. (1996). *What's in a name? The role of name writing in children's literacy acquisition*. Dissertation, University of Virginia. This research study explores the role a child's name plays in literacy growth.

Ehri, L. C., & Robbins, C. (1992). Beginners need some decoding skill to read words by analogy. *Reading Research Quarterly, 27*, 13–26. This research study suggests that some decoding skill is needed before a child can read an unknown word by reference to a known word.

Gough, P. B., & Hillinger, M. L. (1980). Learning to read: An unnatural act. *Bulletin of the Orton Society*, *30*, 179–196. In a discussion of what is required in learning to read, the authors describe why learning to read is a considerably more difficult task than learning to speak.

Heath, S. B. (1983). *Ways with words*. Cambridge, UK: Cambridge University Press. This widely acclaimed ethnographic study examines how children from three different communities learn at home and at school.

Henderson, E. H. (1990). *Teaching spelling* (2nd ed.). Boston: Houghton Mifflin. This very useful book discusses how to develop spelling at each grade level.

Juel, C. (1988). Learning to read and write: A longitudinal study of fifty-four children from first through fourth grade. *Journal of Educational Psychology*, *80*, 437–447. This four-year longitudinal study tracks the literacy development of children from one elementary school as they go from first through fourth grade.

Juel, C. (1991). Beginning reading. In R. Barr, M. L. Kamil, P. Mosenthal, & P. D. Pearson (Eds.), *Handbook of reading research* (Vol. 2, pp. 759–788). New York: Longman. This extensive literature review includes a discussion of different views on how children learn to read.

Juel, C. (1994). *Learning to read and write in one elementary school*. New York: Springer-Verlag. This extended discussion of Juel's 1988 study includes detailed case studies of individual children.

Juel, C. (1994). The role of phonics in the integrated language arts. In L. M. Morrow, J. K. Smith, & L. C. Wilkinson (Eds.), *The integrated language arts: Controversy to consensus* (pp. 133–154). Boston: Allyn & Bacon. This article disscuses the role of phonics in an integrated language arts classroom.

Juel, C., Griffith, P. L., & Gough, P. B. (1986). Acquisition of literacy: A longitudinal study of children in first and second grade. *Journal of Educational Psychology*, *78*, 243–255. This research study begins with a model of reading and writing development. The model is then evaluated through a two-year study of children in first and second grade.

Liberman, I. Y., & Liberman, A. M. (1992). Whole language versus code emphasis: Underlying assumptions and their implications for reading instruction. In P. B. Gough, L. C. Ehri, & R. Treiman (Eds.), *Reading acquisition* (pp. 343–366). Hillsdale, NJ: Erlbaum. This important discussion of the linguistic nature of learning to read clarifies many issues.

Lundberg, I. (1984, August). Learning to read. *School Research Newsletter*. National Board of Education in Sweden. This report gives results of a longitudinal study of learning to read and describes the importance of phonemic awareness in that process.

Maclean, M., Bryant, P., & Bradley, L. (1988). Rhymes, nursery rhymes, and reading in early childhood. In K. E. Stanovich (Ed.), *Children's reading and the development of phonological awareness* (pp. 11–37). Detroit: Wayne State University Press. This study suggests that an important source of phonemic awareness is knowlege of nursery rhymes in preschool.

Pinker, S. (1994). *The language instinct*. New York: Harper Perennial. This is a must-read book for those interested in how language develops and how language works.

Share, D. L., Jorm, A. F., Maclean, R., & Matthews, R. (1984). Sources of individual differences in reading achievement. *Journal of Educational Psychology*, *76*, 1309–1324. This longitudinal study examines many child, school, and home factors involved in learning to read.

Treiman, R. (1992). The role of intrasyllabic units in learning to read and spell. In P. B. Gough, L. C. Ehri, & R. Treiman (Eds.), *Reading acquisition* (pp. 65–106). Hillsdale, NJ: Erlbaum. This article reviews research on the role of phonograms and analogies in learning to read.

Trelease, J. (1995). *The new read-aloud handbook* (4th ed.). New York: Penguin. This best-seller contains a wealth of insight for both teachers and parents.

CHILDREN'S LITERATURE

Archambault, J., & Martin, B. Jr. (1994). *A beautiful feast for a big king cat*. New York: Harper-Collins. This rhyming story is about a little mouse who habitually teases a cat and must use its wits to avoid being eaten. 32 pages.

Bennett, J. (1985). *Teeny tiny*. New York: Putnam. A very small woman finds a very small bone and puts it away in her cupboard before she goes to bed. Illustrated. Also available in Spanish. 32 pages.

Berenstain, S., & Berenstain, J. (1970). *Old hat, new hat*. New York: Random House. This rhyming text poses the question of whether a new hat can really replace a perfect old one. 32 pages.

Brown, M. W. (1947). *Goodnight moon*. New York: Harper. A good night is said to each one of the objects in the great green room in this classic bedtime story. French and Spanish texts and audiotape available. 32 pages.

Carle, E. (1987). *Have you seen my cat?* Natick, MA: Picture Book Studio. A boy encounters cats of all sorts while searching for his own lost cat. 25 pages.

Cowley, J. (1990). *Dan the flying man*. Bothell, WA: The Wright Group. This book about a flying man is designed for group reading.

Galdone, P. (1973). *The three billy goats gruff*. New York: Seabury Press. The classic Norwegian folktale about the three billy goats who outsmart the old troll who lives under the bridge. 32 pages.

Hoban, T. (1973). *Over, under, and through, and other spatial concepts*. New York: Macmillan. Spatial concepts are illustrated with text and photos. 32 pages.

Holabird, K. (1983). *Angelina ballerina*. New York: Crown. A little mouse wants to become a ballerina more than anything else in the world. 24 pages.

Holabird, K. (1985). *Angelina at the fair*. New York: Crown. Angelina is annoyed when she has to take her little cousin to the fair, but after a day of adventurous fun, the two become friends. 25 pages.

Keats, E. J. (1962). *The snowy day*. New York: Viking. A young city boy enjoys adventures in the snow. Spanish text and audiotape available. 32 pages.

Lobel, A. (1985). *Whiskers and rhymes*. New York: Scholastic. This book presents a collection of short, humorous rhymes in the nursery rhyme tradition. 48 pages.

Marshall, J. (1989). *The three little pigs*. New York: Dial. In this version of the familiar tale, one of the three pigs survives encountering the wolf by using its head. 32 pages.

Martin, B., Jr., (1983). *Brown bear, brown bear*. New York: Holt. Different animals in different colors are depicted in very predictable sentence structure. 24 pages.

Rice, E. (1989). *Peter's pockets*. New York: Greenwillow. Peter's new pants don't have any pockets, so Uncle Nick lets Peter use his until Peter's mother solves the problem in a clever way. 32 pages.

Seuss, Dr. (1957). *The cat in the hat*. New York: Random House. Two children sitting at home on a rainy day are visited by a cat who shows them some tricks and games. Audiotape available. 61 pages.

Seuss, Dr. (1963). *Hop on pop*. New York: Random House. Pairs of rhyming words are introduced and used in simple sentences. Audiotape and videotape available. 64 pages.

Seuss, Dr. (1977). *There's a wocket in my pocket*. New York: Random House. In this silly tale filled with rhyme, unusual household creatures help beginning readers identify common household words. Audiotape available.

Soto, G. (1992). *Too many tamales*. New York: Putnam. Maria tries on her mother's wedding ring while helping make Christmas tamales and later discovers that it's missing. Spanish text available. 32 pages.

Tafuri, N. (1984). *Have you seen my duckling?* New York: Greenwillow. A mother duck leads her brood around the pond as she searches for one missing duckling. 32 pages.

Tresselt, A. (1964). *The mitten*. New York: Lothrop. An old Ukrainian folktale about animals sleeping snuggly in a lost mitten until the bear sneezes. 32 pages.

Wildsmith, B. (1982). *Cat on the mat*. Oxford, UK: Oxford University Press. This cat liked to sit on the mat until the other animals wanted to sit on it too. 16 pages.

chapter four

Word Recognition

Six-year-old Anthony tries to read a page from the popular children's book, Rosie's Walk, by Pat Hutchins (1968). He sits in a circle with other children around his first grade teacher Ms. Sullivan. Yesterday, following along with Ms. Sullivan, the children read the story aloud together. The story is about a hen named Rosie, who takes a walk around a farmyard, blissfully ignorant of the fox who follows her. Along her way, Rosie walks:

> across the yard
> around the pond
> over the haystack
> past the mill

Ms. Sullivan has all the children point to the words as they read. Some children are more able to do this than others. Ms. Sullivan either has the entire class read a line aloud, or calls on a few children to read, or calls on one child to read. She has just called on Anthony. He points to "around" and slowly says, "around the . . . ," stops, and looks up. Ms. Sullivan suggests that he look at the picture.

CHAPTER OVERVIEW

Anthony looks at the page and asks, "Tree?"

"Well," says Ms. Sullivan, "it does look as if she might walk around that tree, but what is the tree in front of? What is all this (as she points to the pond)?"

Anthony smiles and says, "Water."

"Yes," agrees Ms Sullivan. "It is water. Remember, though, it is a special kind of water. Look at the word. What letter does it start with?"

"P," replies Anthony.

"P, puh—does water start with a puh?" asks Ms. Sullivan.

"No."

"So, it can't be water. What starts with a puh and is a type of water?"

"Puddle!"

"Yes, puddle does start with a p. But this is more water. Remember? Pointing to the letters, she slowly says, "It's a puhon."

"Pond," declares Anthony.

THE IMPORTANCE OF RECOGNIZING PRINTED WORDS

To young children like Anthony, who are just beginning to read on their own, recognizing printed words is *the* big stumbling block to reading. Anthony is a typical 6-year-old. He entered first grade with a command of spoken English that is nearly complete in terms of its structure (its underlying grammar and phonological development). He already has a vocabulary and a command of spoken English that would be the envy of any non-native English speaker who, as an adult, is trying to learn English. Nonetheless, Anthony, like most first-grade children, will work very hard at acquiring even a basic reading vocabulary. Also, like most young children, Anthony will depend upon his classroom teacher to help him acquire this reading skill.

Clearly, both spoken and printed English involve the same language. But the reason Anthony can't read, although he is already quite competent at speaking and comprehending oral English, is that *he does not yet know how to translate the printed word into the spoken word*. The printed word forms a barrier between him and the meaning of the text. He needs to learn how to get meaning from this printed form of language. To do this, he must, in a sense, get his eyes to do what his ears currently do for him. When he can do this, the ultimate human language comprehender, the mind, will be able to make sense of printed language.

The goal of both listening and reading is the same—to construct meaning, to understand. But the listener finds the task easier than the reader for several reasons. We will briefly look at five of these reasons and why Anthony's task as a reader is harder than his task as a listener.

Reading is partly about print. A reader can translate scribbles on a printed page into meaningful messages

—*Robert Calfee*
Educational Psychologist

Why Listening Is Easier Than Reading

In Chapter 3, we talked about the four language modes—reading, writing, listening, and speaking. Each involves an act of communication, and each has its own distinct features. When we look at the features of spoken language that help speakers communicate, we see things that are not as likely to be present in written language.

Shared Background Knowledge

Conversational partners typically share *background information* about a topic. When you get together with a friend to chat, you most likely share a history of people, places, and events. This means that you as a speaker probably know which words, concepts, and topics are going to be easily comprehended by your friend and which are likely to be difficult. A shared history is much less likely, of course, to exist between an author and a reader. Pat Hutchins, who wrote *Rosie's Walk*, does not know if Anthony has ever seen a pond.

Immediate Feedback

When you are listening to what a friend is saying and don't understand what he says, you can simply tell him so—"Wait a minute. What do you mean when you say to 'caramelize' the onions before I put them in the stew? How do I caramelize them?" On the other hand, when Anthony is reading *Rosie's Walk* and doesn't understand something, he certainly can't ask Pat Hutchins what she meant. And in many cases he can't ask the teacher either, because the teacher is often busy with other students.

Visual Cues from the Speaker

A listener can see the speaker's features. Lips move as they shape sounds, providing an additional clue to the speech sound being uttered—an especially useful clue in a noisy environment. Additionally, speakers can enhance their message by exaggerating or adding intonation, facial expressions, vocal emphasis, tone of voice, repetition, and gesture. "Body language" can even override the speaker's words and send a different message than the words do.

More Common Words

We generally converse using words more common than those we employ in writing. In a conversation with a friend, for instance, you might say, "Last night I just talked on and on about . . . " In penning your autobiography, however, you might write, "All evening, I chattered incessantly about . . . " The reader, unlike the listener, is likely to encounter less-common words—such as *chattered, incessantly, beehive, mill, pond*—and less-common words are, of course, less likely to be familiar.

No Translation Needed

Most important, the modality of input in listening is primarily aural, whereas the modality of input in reading is visual. Language underlies both listening and reading, of course. But to get to that language in the medium of print requires additional translation: The reader must be able to translate the rather dead-looking printed word into the speech he already knows. Once the text is translated, the reader has access to meaning just as he would in speech. So the child's basic problem in learning to read is learning to translate the printed words into the speech he already understands.

Skilled Readers Automatically Recognize Words

Perhaps the single most striking characteristic of skillful readers is the speed and effortlessness with which they can breeze through text. In particular they appear to recognize whole words at a glance, gleaning their appropriate meaning at once.

—*Steven Stahl, Jean Osborne, and Fran Lehr, Teacher Educators*

Although the context of what a person is reading occasionally suggests what upcoming words may be, the skilled reader can identify words so quickly that he doesn't need to consider the surrounding context (Adams, 1990; McConkie & Zola, 1981; Stanovich, 1991a, 1991b, 1992). That is, if you are reading "Kevin was walking his . . . " and then come to the word *dog*, you automatically—instantaneously and without conscious attention—process the letters in *dog*, even though in this case the word is fairly predictable. This seemingly obsessive and unnecessary processing of the letters actually makes word recognition faster than trying to predict upcoming words based on context, such as guessing what type of animal Kevin might be walking. Instantaneous word recognition is especially desirable, too, because in many instances context is not that helpful and can even be misleading.

The words that tend to be the most predictable in text are the *function words*, which express primarily grammatical relationships. They include articles (such as *a* and *the*), prepositions (such as *of* and *in*), and conjunctions (such as *and* and *but*). There are relatively few function words, and the same ones reoccur frequently—this makes them predictable. The child who is not a good reader can therefore make a good guess about the identity of a function word based on its length and a letter or two. A good guess for a three-letter word that starts with *th* is *the*. In addition, the child's knowledge of grammar helps him identify function words. He knows that a sentence often begins with the word *the*, and that long sentences frequently contain the word *and*.

On the other hand, the *content words*, which carry much of the specific meaning of what we are reading, are often not very predictable. This is because there is an enormous number of content words—nouns, verbs, adjectives, and adverbs—in English.

Because young children cannot quickly recognize many words, we encourage beginning readers to use what they already know about language and the world, as well as the context of the story and its illustrations, to supplement their fledgling skill in word identification. *However, as a child is taught specific ways in which letters relate to sounds, these letter–sound cues to word identification should take precedence over contextual and picture cues. Ultimately, letter–sound cues provide much more reliable information and a more efficient means to word recognition than do contextual cues or illustrations.*

The efficient skilled reader is able to (and while studying must) spend time thinking about the meaning of what is being read. Efficient word recognition allows the reader to attain this level of reflection and thinking. Your ability to think about, enjoy, and learn from what you read depends upon thinking about the content, not thinking about word recognition. Still, efficient word recognition does not ensure good comprehension: A reader may lack the prior knowledge, conceptual knowledge, interest, analytic skill, wit, and other factors required to understand a particular text. Good comprehension, however, is rarely achieved without efficient word recognition.

Although we do believe that learning to recognize words involves learning to respond instantly to common spelling patterns such as *at, and, ig,* and *ack,* we do not believe that early reading instruction should focus on these parts of words without first placing them in the context of whole words and whole texts. The challenge you will face as a teacher of young children is to help them learn to recognize words without losing sight of the goal of reading—getting meaning. Children must learn how to rapidly pronounce *pond,* but they must also know the meaning of it. Swift and accurate word recognition is the quickest route to finding a text's meaning. Attention to and instruction based on these letter–sound patterns and relationships will be helpful for most children.

Finally, learning to read in the first grade, which very definitely means learning to recognize words, is extremely important because the child who flounders at this tender age will have difficulty catching up. Studies in several countries, with different curricula and languages, have found this to be the case (Clay, 1979; Juel, 1994; Lundberg, 1984). It is absolutely critical, then, that teachers of young children be thoroughly competent in teaching beginning reading. To attain this competence, you will need to understand the structure of spoken and written English, the strengths and weakness of various approaches to beginning reading instruction, and specific procedures for teaching beginning readers to recognize words. These topics form the remaining parts of this chapter.

THE STRUCTURE OF SPOKEN AND PRINTED WORDS

Say your name out loud. You just created speech, using your vocal system to modify the flow of air as you exhaled from your lungs. There are a limited number of things you can do to this exhalation in your throat. You can modify it with your tongue and with your lips, and you can change the direction in which the outgoing breaths are channeled and the length of time it takes the air to pass through the vocal system. Making a speech sound requires several simultaneous manipulations. You can build a puff of air behind your closed lips and let it suddenly burst out to make a /p/ sound; or, as you do so, you can move your tongue up to touch the ridge behind your upper front teeth and make it a /t/ sound.

Teachers need substantial knowledge about the way in which language is structured, particularly with respect to its orthographic and phonological features. They must be able to teach their students about phonemes and how phonemes are represented in writing and about morphemes (the smallest meaningful units in words) and their spelling patterns.

—*Joanna Williams*
Educational Researcher

The Makeup of Spoken and Written English

The speech sounds that are used to distinguish one word from another in a particular language are called *phonemes*. In English, /p/ and /b/ are phonemes. Phonemes represent a rather abstract level of language analysis, and what is perceived as a phoneme differs from one language to another. English employs approximately 40 phonemes, which is about the average number. As you learn to speak a foreign language, you are likely to pronounce the phonemes in that language with the sound patterns of your native language, leading the native speaker to say you have a foreign accent. Thus, the native English speaker will tend not to trill *r*s when speaking Spanish (as would a native speaker of Spanish) but instead pronounce them as English phonemes. The native speaker of Japanese pronounces the *l* in English as an *r* because in Japanese these two sounds are not distinctive phonemes. As we will note in Chapter 10, you can expect that children who are not native English speakers may need particular help in perceiving and pronouncing the phonemes in English that are dissimilar from those in their first language.

Vowels and Consonants

Phonemes are divided into vowel and consonant sounds. *Vowel* sounds are made when the air leaving your lungs is vibrated in the voice box (the larynx or Adam's apple) but then has a clear passage from the voice box to outside your mouth. Different vowel sounds occur depending on how you hold your tongue as the air passes by. *Consonants*, on the other hand, are speech sounds that occur when the airflow is obstructed in some way in your mouth. The consonant sound /p/, for example, is made by letting air build behind the lips before it is released from your mouth.

Syllables, Onsets, and Rimes

In all languages, the basic phonological unit of speech is the *syllable*. At a minimum, a syllable contains a vowel, and most basic syllables contain an onset and rime. The *onset* is the initial consonant, and the *rime* is the vowel and any consonants that follow it. In *sat*, the onset is *s* and the rime is *at*. In *smack*, the onset is *sm* and the rime is *ack*.

In the speech stream, the syllable unit is most noticeable. It is no coincidence that nursery rhymes and Dr. Seuss books are filled with wordplay involving the onsets and rimes of syllables. Onsets and rimes are naturally compelling sound units, and playing with them typically delights young children. They are likely to repeat lines such as "Jack and Jill went up the hill" literally hundreds of times, just for the fun of it.

A syllable contains one vowel sound. Different languages have different rules about what sounds can precede and follow that core. In English, an onset can be made up of a single consonant or a cluster of up to three consonants, and although most English syllables do have an onset, they do not have to. A rime in English must contain a vowel, and a rime usually ends with a consonant or a consonant cluster. In English, the most common syllable structure is consonant–vowel–consonant, or CVC, as in *dog, cat,* or *pig.* CVC syllable units can be strung together to create multisyllabic words, such as *market* or *napkin.* English also allows several modifications of this CVC unit. For instance, two or three consonant sounds can occur together, as in *flat, split, blast,* or *splash.*

Word Families and Phonograms

Unfortunately, quite a few terms are used in discussing word study, and they are not always used consistently. Current teacher materials are likely to refer to onsets and rimes. But another term commonly used for rimes that have the same spellings is *phonogram,* and you will sometimes see these two terms used interchangeably. Words that share phonograms are called a *word family.* Thus *cat, bat, hat, flat,* and *mat* share the *at* phonogram and belong to the *at* word family. Similarly, *same, game, tame, blame, fame, flame,* and *same* share the *ame* phonogram and belong to the *ame* word family.

Morphemes

All languages use *morphemes* to represent the meaning level of speech. Morphemes are the smallest meaning units into which a word can be divided, and both words and parts of words can be morphemes. *Dog* is a morpheme, and the *-s* in *dogs* is also a morpheme; the *-s* has meaning in that it indicates that the word is plural. Figure 4.1 shows various ways of segmenting words.

Any word can be described at both the morphemic level and the phonological level. *Dog* is a one-syllable word with one morpheme. Its

Words	planet			cat			
Morpheme	planet			cat	s		
Syllables	plan	et		kats			
Onsets and Rimes	pl	an	∂t	k	ats		
Phonemes	p l	a n	∂ t	k	a t	s	

FIGURE 4.1 *Various Ways of Segmenting Words*

phonological structure is the common CVC syllable pattern: *D* is the onset and *og* is the rime. *Dog* is also called a *root word* or *root* because it can both stand alone and be combined with other roots to form new words. *Doghouse* is a *compound word* containing two root words, *dog* and *house*. *House* consists of the onset *h* and the rime *ouse*.

Affixes: Prefixes and Suffixes

Morphemes that cannot stand alone to form meaningful words are called *affixes*. There are two types of affixes. The first is called a prefix. A *prefix* is placed before a root to form a word with a meaning different from that of the root. Prefixes cannot stand by themselves as words; they must be attached to roots. The three most frequently occurring prefixes are *un-* as in *unhappy*, *re-* as in *redo*, and *in-* as in *insufficient*.

The second type of affix is called a suffix. A *suffix* is placed after a root to form a word with a different meaning or a different grammatical function. Like prefixes, suffixes cannot occur by themselves; they must be attached to roots. The common suffixes that change a root to suit the grammatical form of the sentence include *-s* as in *dogs*, *-ed* as is *snowed*, *-ing* as in *snowing*, and *-er* as in *teacher*.

You need to be familiar with all of these units—phonemes, syllables, onsets, rimes, morphemes, roots, and affixes—in order to best help children as they learn to identify words. In the following classroom scene, Mr. Alvaro, a veteran kindergarten teacher, works with his kindergartners while a group of university students who are planning to be teachers observe. Mr. Alvaro is assisting students in learning to track print by focusing on consonants. As you will see, he is very familiar with the makeup of English words.

IN THE CLASSROOM
Tracking Print During Shared Reading

It is January. Mr. Alvaro's twenty 5-year-old children are having a snack. Mr. Alvaro takes the opportunity to briefly chat with the university students. He explains that they will be seeing him develop print knowledge with the children by having the children track the print on a chart. The print is a nursery rhyme that the children now know by heart because they have recited it many times.

> To market, to market, to buy a fat pig.
> Home again, home again, jiggety, jig.

The children finish their snack and gather around Mr. Alvaro. They sit on the floor in front of the chart. Mr. Alvaro reads the rhyme aloud, pointing to each word as he says it. He

encourages the children to chime in, and most do so. He then asks for volunteers to come up and point to the words as they read the poem. Several children volunteer. All can easily recite the rhyme, but many have difficulty pointing to the words as they say them. Some children just sweep their hand across the line of print. One boy says one word for each letter, and he finishes the poem while still pointing at the first few words. Most children get off track with the multisyllabic words. Anna is typical. She easily recites the poem, but when she says the second syllable in *market, ket*, she is already pointing to the second *to* on the chart.

Mr. Alvaro congratulates Anna on how well she has memorized this rhyme. He then asks her to point to the word *market*. Anna does this. He asks her what letter *market* starts with. She says, *"M."*

Mr. Alvaro agrees. He says, "*M* makes an *mmmmm* sound." He then slowly says *market* and points to each letter as he says the phoneme associated with it. He especially emphasizes the *k* in *market*. He asks for volunteers to come up and recite the part of the poem that says, "To market." Several children, including Anna, can now easily track *to market* and its repetition. He asks the children how they located the two *markets*. Most mention looking for the two *ms*; a few indicate other letters as well. Finally, Mr. Alvaro asks for volunteers to find various words, such as *pig*. As the children point to the word, he asks how they knew that word. Most spontaneously mention the first letter and what sound it makes. Mr. Alvaro seems pleased. He has been teaching consonant sounds and has encouraged the children to use these to track print.

Back at the university, the students discuss what they saw. Sharon remarks that, even though she had read about the prominence of syllables in speech perception, she was still amazed at how words aren't as clear. Trina reminds everyone that in speech there are no white spaces between words; we don't pause between most words as we speak them. Trina gives the example of her daughter asking her, when she returned from a trip, "Whadjagitme?" Jaimie suggests that when children learn to connect some sounds to letters, this knowledge "acts like a radar device to help children accurately track print." Kara summarizes by saying how wonderfully Mr. Alvaro models, instructs, and actively involves all his children in learning the process of reading.

The Alphabetic Principle

According to the alphabetic principle (the basic principle underlying English writing), the distinctive speech sounds of a particular spoken language, the phonemes, are represented by symbols called letters. The three letters in *mad*, for example, correspond to the three phonemes /m/, /a/, /d/. Of course, as you know, the correspondence between letters and sounds in English is not perfect. In spoken English there are about 40 phonemes, but we use an alphabet with only 26 letters. Many letters represent more than one sound—for example, *e* represents /ĕ/ in *pet* but /ē/ in *beat*. Two or more letters sometimes represent a single sound—for example, *ea* represents /ĕ/ in *head*. And many sounds can be represented by more than one letter—for example /o͞o/ is represented by *oo* in *booth* and by *ew* in *threw*. As you know,

This kindergartner is having fun naming the letters of the alphabet. Little does he realize that alphabetic writing systems are considered to be one of the most important human inventions.

the vowels are the most troublesome in this regard, but some consonants also represent more than one sound—for example, *c* can represent both /s/ and /k/.

Another difficulty with alphabetic writing systems is that phonemes don't exist as nice, neat, cleanly divisible units. As you say the word *mad*, you actually begin forming your mouth to say the *a* while you are still saying the *m;* likewise you begin to pronounce the *d* while finishing the *a*. This process is called coarticulation. It allows rapid and seamless speech, but it also makes phonemes less accessible and perceivable in spoken words. Some phonemes are even impossible to say in isolation without adding a vowel sound. If you had to tell a child what sound (phoneme) the letters *d* or *p* stand for, for instance, you would probably say something like "duh" or "puh." But there is no *duh* in *dad* and no *puh* in *pat*.

Since phonemes don't leap out at listeners, devising the notational system to link letters and phonemes required considerable insight and abstraction, and it appears that an alphabetic writing system was not invented until sometime between 1000 and 700 B.C., that is, relatively recently. Alphabetic writing systems are often considered to be among the most important human inventions. Their abstract nature is also part of the reason that children have difficulty learning them: Being able to attend to the less-than-concrete phoneme in a spoken word, isolate it, and attach it to a letter is quite a mental feat. Anna, in Mr. Alvaro's class, easily perceives syllables in the speech stream. But in order to track those units in printed words, she has to perceive at least some of the phonemes in words.

The Structure of Printed Words: The Good News

We are thus faced with the fact that the English writing system presents some considerable challenges to children learning to read. The good news, though, is that the words with the strangest spellings tend to be the ones we see most frequently in print. Because of this, we have many opportunities to memorize them. The even better news is that *despite glaring exceptions, there is a lot of predictability in English spelling.* Even words with strange spellings include some letters that provide useful sound cues to their identity. Usually, the most reliable letters are the consonants.

Through years of reading, you have learned a lot about the structure of printed words, even though you may not be able to articulate what you know. You know intuitively, for example, that some letter sequences are much more likely to occur than others. For instance, you know that words are more likely to start with *pr* or *br* than with *rb* or *rp*—while just the opposite is true at the end of words. You have this tacit knowledge because for years you have carefully looked at individual words as you read. Even as very skilled readers, we do look at almost every word in the text we are reading (Carpenter & Just, 1983). Indeed, we look at the individual letters in most words we encounter (Adams, 1990).

Even multisyllabic words, though they are admittedly difficult, yield to analysis. Multisyllabic words are simply strings of syllables, which themselves are composed of onsets and rimes. Though not perfectly consistent, there is a tendency in English to "chunk" words into syllables by placing at a syllabic division letter sequences that are less likely to occur next to each other within a syllable. In the word *haystack*, for example, we have several clues as to where to divide the word. First, there are two morphemes, *hay* and *stack*. Second, each syllable is a common variant of CVC units and contains common onsets—*h* and *st*—and common rimes—*ay* and *ack*. Third, the letter combination *ys* is not likely to begin a syllable. Double consonants are also a common signal of a syllabic division. Only one consonant is actually pronounced, as you can see in *dinner* or *rabbit*.

A big part of what makes you an efficient recognizer of words is having read a lot. There is a lesson in this for you as a teacher: *Wide reading in and of itself is going to teach children a lot that will speed their word recognition.*

Skilled readers can read many different words because they know a great deal about the structure of printed English words. They have learned the pronunciation of many common words, such as the function words *the* and *that*, and other common words, such as *mom* and *red*. Skilled readers have also learned to respond instantly with the pronunciations of many within-word spelling patterns, such as the onsets *p* and *st* and rimes such as *ick, and,* and *at*. Adults can even read nonsense words that contain common spelling patterns and common affixes almost as fast as they can read their own names.

Reflection AND Application

1. Identify the onsets and rimes in *hen, past, back, mill,* and *time*. Now make a list of other words that share one of these rimes and thus belong to the same word family.

2. Identify the function words and the content words in the sentence *Rosie the hen went for a walk across the yard.*

3. What are the morphemes, roots, and affixes in the words *haystack*, *dinner*, and *beehives*? What are some clues as to how to divide the words into syllables?

4. We just noted that skilled adults can read nonsense words almost as quickly as they can read their own name. See how quickly you can read these nonsense words—*zat*, *mig*, *unplick*, *kip*, *cleef*, *fand*, and *bufwixable*. To the extent that you read them quickly, you are proof of the incredible sophistication skilled readers have in analyzing words and coming up with their pronunciations.

THE INFLUENCE OF THE STRUCTURE OF SPOKEN AND WRITTEN ENGLISH ON READING INSTRUCTION

You have just read about some of the challenges that beginning readers face because of the structure of spoken and written English. How have reading educators and publishers of reading materials responded to these challenges? In Chapter 2, we mentioned some of the responses when we talked about the history of reading instruction and described the most prominent current approaches. Now, we very briefly describe three approaches to dealing with word-recognition skills. Having some knowledge of these will help inform the decisions you will soon be making about reading instruction in your classroom.

High-Frequency Word Approaches in Basal Readers

In the most popular basal readers published between about 1910 and 1985, words for beginning books were chosen primarily on the basis of their frequency rather than their consistent letter–sound correspondences. Initially, students were presented with very few different words, but they saw these words again and again, and of course eventually learned them.

The most famous of the basal readers with controlled vocabulary was the series that featured a brother and sister, Dick and Jane. The first book for use in first grade in the 1946–1947 edition starts out with a drawing of a young boy, with his name, Dick, printed underneath him. On the second page, Dick is shown clowning around in some fall leaves. The text underneath reads: "Look, look." On the next page, Dick is shown accidentally tipping over a basket of raked leaves, and the text reads: "Oh, oh, oh." The story ends with a picture of Dick with the basket on top of him, and the text repeats two of the three words introduced thus far, as shown in Figure 4.2. The

Look, look.

Oh, oh, oh.

FIGURE 4.2 *A High-Frequency Word Approach in a 1940's Basal Reader*

Reprinted with permission of Addison-Wesley Educational Publishers, Inc. and Scott Foresman Addison-Wesley.

text continues in much the same fashion, very slowly introducing new vocabulary and frequently repeating it.

In addition to containing very few words and selecting words on the basis of frequency rather than consistency of letter–sound correspondences, these series featured white, middle-class characters and were heavily stereotyped. Dick and Jane, for example, came from a suburban family. They had a father who went to work, a mother who stayed home, a baby sister named Sally, and a dog named Spot. In general, everyone was happy, and all was right with the world.

Because of the tightly controlled vocabulary and because the publishers also tried to keep the sentences short, the language of these series had a stilted and unnatural structure. Also, the stories were generally much less than riveting, particularly to an adult. (In fairness to the publishers of basal readers, we should point out that although the stories were often vacuous and we certainly do not recommend them as a steady diet for young readers, a number of children pursue them with great delight, their excitement over mastering the written word overcoming the banality of what they read.)

Phonics Approaches

As we just said, one criticism of the high-frequency word approach employed in many of the basals was that it did not give enough attention to teaching students to deal with letter–sound correspondences. In other words, the charge was that these basals did not have enough phonics. *Phonics* is the area of reading instruction that deals with the relationship between letters and sounds—between the phonemes of oral English and how writing systems represent them, for example, how the letter *m* stands for /m/. Phonics instruction attempts to call a child's attention to the alphabetic principle and to which letters represent which phonemes.

One response to the call for more emphasis on the structure of words and more phonics is shown in the following text, which is taken from a phonics-oriented series of the early 1980s.

> *A red bug is in the sand.*
> *Gus digs in the sand.*
> *Gus digs up the rug.*
>
> *Dot tugs at Gus.*
> *Dot and Gus tug on the rug.*
>
> *Gus drags the rug to the grass.*
> *Dot did not get the rug.*
> (Walcutt & McCracken, 1981)

As you can see, the text has a tongue-twisty feel and certainly does not demonstrate a natural use of language. Although it employs lots of words exemplifying letter–sound correspondences and spelling patterns, thus giving students an opportunity to learn them, the approach seriously constrains the content and the story.

Additionally, although you cannot see it from this example, traditional phonics approaches were often flawed in the way they taught phonics. As we discussed earlier in this chapter, the relationship between letters and phonemes is rather abstract, and each letter does not conveniently correspond to a single sound. Yet some of these programs taught letter–sound correspondences as if the system was quite regular.

Many traditional phonics programs emphasized rules that specified how a single letter or two would sound under any circumstances. Some of these rules were very reliable, especially for consonants. The letter *c*, for example, when followed by the letter *o* or the letter *a*, corresponds to /k/ 100% of the time. But other rules were not very dependable. You might recall being taught the rule "When two vowels go walking, the first does the talking." When there are two vowels together, however, the first one is long and the second is silent only about 45% of the time (Clymer, 1963/1996). In fact, most of the phonics rules taught, particularly those involving vowels, were found to be disturbingly inaccurate. Many of the less-reliable rules, however, are reliable when applied to specific spelling patterns. The vowel combination *oa*, for example, does comply with the "two vowels" generalization 97% of the time.

Earlier in this chapter, we discussed onsets and rimes. When the spelling unit of a rime is considered, generalizations can be made with more accuracy (Stahl, 1992). Within a syllable, if a vowel is considered *in relation to the following consonant*, the sound of the vowel is frequently very predictable. In almost all *ea* rimes, for example, the first vowel is long and the second is silent, as in *beat, seat, heat, meat, neat, wheat, cheat,* and *treat*.

Literature-Based and Whole-Language Approaches

As we pointed out in Chapter 2, advocates of literature-based approaches may or may not recommend using a reading series and advocates of a whole-language approach are not likely to recommend using a series. But whether or not they recommend using a reading series, advocates of literature-based and whole-language approaches take exception to much content of both high-frequency word basal approaches and phonics approaches. One complaint against both approaches is that the selections in most series are banal and uninteresting. Another related complaint is that high-frequency word basal readers and phonics series employ unnatural and uninteresting language. And a third complaint against them is that they give inadequate attention to minority characters and settings and the diversity of modern life. Finally, phonics approaches are criticized for giving too much attention to phonics, thereby distracting students from gaining meaning, the major goal of reading.

In place of high-frequency word basal readers and phonics series, advocates of literature-based and whole-language approaches recommend that students learn to read with trade books, which are written simply to be read rather than to be used in teaching children to read. Word-recognition skills are then introduced by the teachers in the context of students' reading if the need for teaching a skill becomes apparent. In the words of one reading educator, David Pearson (1996), advocates of literature-based and whole-language approaches believe that "skills are better caught than taught."

As it turns out, publishers of today's basal readers have responded to many of these complaints, and most current basals are in fact literature-based. That is, as we pointed out in Chapter 2, today's basals include, for the most part, reproductions of trade books. Such books often employ varied vocabulary, do not typically use artificially short sentences, and all in all present realistic and natural-sounding language. Trade books also represent the diversity of today's world and are in many cases socially conscious. Thousands of trade books are published each year, and they are written by authors who themselves represent the diversity of the contemporary United States. Moreover,

two friends

lydia and shirley have
two pierced ears and
two bare ones
five pigtails
two pairs of sneakers
two berets
two smiles
one necklace
one bracelet
lots of stripes and
one good friendship

by Nikki Giovanni

41

FIGURE 4.3 *Selection from a Contemporary First-Grade Reading Series*

From *Collection III* of *Literature Works* Reading Program. Copyright © 1996 Silver Burdett Ginn Inc. and by permission of the author.

publishers of today's basals take great pains to choose selections that represent the diversity and multicultural nature of today's society. Public opinion and adoption committees demand that they do so. A sample page from a contemporary first-grade basal is shown in Figure 4.3.

All in all, contemporary basals and trade books carefully chosen to represent the diversity of today's society are a tremendous improvement over many of the materials used to teach reading in the past. At the same time, these materials, like those that came before them, are open to some criticism. The most notable ones relevant to word-recognition instruction are these: Current basals and trade books sometimes include such varied vocabulary that children do not encounter the same words frequently enough to learn them fully. They may employ such varied vocabulary that letter–sound correspondences and basic spelling patterns are difficult for children to recognize. They may use varied and sophisticated vocabulary that is simply too difficult for some students. And they may provide or encourage very little systematic phonics instruction.

Quite a few publishers of contemporary basals have recognized these potential problems, and a number of them now publish supplementary "little books," short books with controlled vocabulary. Also, several publishers of contemporary basals now publish supplementary word-study programs, which provide more systematic word-recognition instruction than the series proper does.

Our Position on Phonics Instruction and Related Matters

We believe that learning the relationship between letters and sounds—the way in which the written language represents the spoken language, is absolutely crucial to becoming an accomplished and lifelong reader. We further believe that, although a small percentage of children learn this relationship on their own without formal instruction, most children stand the best chance of learning it through direct teaching. This position is consistent with the findings of Jeanne Chall, a Harvard professor who reviewed the research on beginning reading instruction in a landmark book titled *Learning to Read: The Great Debate* (1967), and with most interpretations of Guy Bond and Robert Dykstra's *First Grade Study* (1967/1997), the most ambitious study of beginning reading conducted in this country. The position is also consistent both with the findings of Marilyn Adams's *Beginning to Read: Thinking and Learning About Print* (1990), the most comprehensive review and analysis of beginning reading ever done, and with the position expressed in a special issue of the American Federation of Teachers journal *The American Educator*, which was titled *Learning to Read: Schooling's First Mission* (1995). Finally, the position is consistent with the majority of research on beginning reading and with common sense. We are the enormously fortunate inheritors of an alphabetic writing system; we need to teach our children how to take advantage of that fact.

Some children need less phonics instruction than others, and phonics instruction must always be kept in proper perspective—as a means to an end. Constructing meaning is the main goal of reading; and reading, writing, speaking, listening, and being read to must form the heart of the literacy curriculum. But for readers who have not yet mastered the code of written English, word-recognition instruction—which includes phonics—plays an essential role. How to provide that instruction is the topic of the next and final part of this chapter.

> Obviously, young children cannot read or write without encountering the use of phonics, grammar, spelling, and other conventions of written language.
>
> —*Dorothy Strickland*
> *Teacher Educator*

Reflection AND *Application*

5. Discuss the pluses and minuses of the two types of traditional reading series we described—high-frequency word basal readers and traditional phonics series. What do you think was beneficial about the type of texts that were used in the "Dick and Jane" readers? What lessons might we draw from this? What do you think was beneficial about the type of texts used in traditional phonics readers? What lessons might we draw from this?

6. Discuss some of the characteristics you think that ideal beginning reading texts should have. Would you want lots of repetition of high-frequency but irregularly spelled words? Would you want lots of repetition of the same spelling patterns? What sorts of stories would you like to see? What sorts of setting and characters would you like to see in the stories? Would you like to see expository writing as well as narratives included in the earliest readers?

WORD-STUDY INSTRUCTION

Word study refers to instruction about words. And, as you are well aware by now, any sort of word-study instruction is a means to an end—comprehension of text. We want to empower children with the knowledge and skills to unlock the meaning of the printed word. Word-study instruction can include a focus on the spelling patterns in words (phonics), attention to high-frequency words, and attention to the meaning elements in words (for example, affixes such as -ed and root words such as play). Word-study instruction requires active teaching and active learning as represented by the following examples, which we illustrate with concrete illustrations throughout the remainder of this chapter.

- Teachers provide explicit instruction concerning which letters represent which onsets, rimes, and phonemes.
- Children sort picture cards on the basis of the onsets, rimes, or phonemes contained in the pictured words.
- Teachers model how to segment words into their constituent sounds and link those sounds to letters.
- Children sort word cards on the basis of common spelling patterns.
- Children read text with repetitions of both high-frequency words and different words with common spelling patterns.
- Children create word-study journals to record words that share common features of spelling such as phonemes, phonograms, or features of meaning such as prefixes, suffixes, and root words.
- Children write dictated words and sentences that contain target spelling patterns or high-frequency words.

Five General Principles of Word-Study Instruction

The word-study instruction we recommend follows the five basic principles outlined here:

1. Start where the child is.
2. Make word study an active, decision-making process in which children classify words according to the similarity of their sounds and spelling patterns.
3. Base word study on contrasting words with different sounds or spelling patterns.
4. Help children understand how the writing system works.
5. Keep comprehension as the goal.

First, effective word-study instruction is based on the child's current understandings about words. *Start where the child is*, with the concepts about words the child already understands and the words the child can read. If a child doesn't know many letters, but can recognize his name, then learning the names of the letters in his first and last name is a good starting place. Or, if the child writes words primarily as initial consonants (onsets) such as *pig* as a *p*, *dig* as a *d*, and *big* as a *b*, but stops there, then it is time to teach the child rimes such as *ig*.

Second, word study is based on the premise that *learning occurs as an active process of classification*. Children learn about words as active decision makers who analyze and classify spoken and written words on the basis of whether or not they share certain features. Words are classified on the basis of features such as whether they have the same or a different onset, rime, spelling pattern, affix, or root word.

Third, *effective word-study instruction is based on contrasts*. That is, a child learns to perceive the *ig* in words by contrasting *ig* words with words that have another rime, such as *ug* or *ad*. All else being equal, a child will better learn the spelling of the phonogram *ig*—which letters correspond to the *ig* sound in a word such as *pig*—by contrasting words that have the *ig* phonogram with words that have a different phonogram. By contrasting *pig*, *dig*, *wig*, *fig*, *jig*, and *big* with *pit*, *sit*, *hit*, *fit*, *bit*, and *bug*, *dug*, *hug*, *rug*, and *mug*, the child can more readily perceive which letters are responsible for which pronunciations. By comparing words that have contrasting patterns, children can focus on which features make which differences.

Words can be contrasted in different ways. Sorting picture cards is one effective way to highlight contrasts. A picture card is simply what its name suggests—a card with a picture on it, a picture of a pig, rug, wig, or hug, for example. Picture sorting for particular phonemes or rimes is an excellent activity for developing phonemic awareness. It does not require drill or memorization; rather, it requires critical thinking skills to make categorical judgments (Bear, Invernizzi, Templeton, & Johnston, 1995).

Fourth, *children need to understand how the writing system works*. In learning to read and write, children need to understand how speech is written down. They need to perceive units of speech, such as phonemes and rimes. They need to learn which speech units are represented with which letters. As a teacher of emergent readers, you will want to model how to segment spoken words into speech units and how to connect these units to letters. You will also want to help students perceive the units of speech that are represented in writing—words, syllables, and phonemes. And, finally, you will want to help children learn how to represent these units in their own writing. As children learn to write, they are learning the ways words are constructed. As they learn the ways to write, or encode, a word, they are learning what they will need to know to decode a printed word in reading.

Teach phonics as one more tool in a kit students need for rendering texts sensible. . . . The point is to help students learn that phonics—along with contextual analysis, structural analysis, and attention to meaning—can help them decipher unknown words and bring meaning to otherwise confusing text.

—*P. David Pearson*
Teacher Educator

Fifth, *children need to understand that word study is a means to an end—comprehension.* "We are learning what letters make these sounds, so very soon you will be able to read all these wonderful stories yourself! In fact, after what we learn today, you will be able to read this book to a friend!" The goal is for students to learn to decode words until words become automatically identifiable for them. Students must be given many opportunities to read and reread stories so that words can be learned to the point of automaticity. We want to as quickly as possible get students to that point so all of their attention can be focused on comprehension. The rest of the chapter presents ways to achieve that goal.

We encourage you to keep the five principles in mind as you plan word-study instruction. These principles will apply whether you are working with initial consonants, phonograms, short vowels, or affixes. They apply to children of any age. And, as we discuss specific word-study activities, we urge you to also keep in mind that word study is but a piece of reading instruction. Children's understanding of how our writing system works depends both on understanding that *writing is for communication* and that *speech is related to writing.*

Teaching Children to Recognize Words

So where do you begin? Picture a first-grade classroom. The door opens, and suddenly the room fills with an assortment of bright-eyed children eager to learn. However, these hopeful, energetic children may or may not be able to recognize or produce the letters of the alphabet, may or may not accurately track speech to print by finger-pointing to memorized text, may only be able to scribble letters or intersperse letters and scribbles in their writing, and may not be able to read any words. The emergent readers who enter your classroom are just beginning to understand what reading and writing are for and how they work. Your job will be to help these children

- recognize and produce letters.
- gain phonemic awareness of initial consonant sounds.
- learn which letters represent initial consonant sounds.
- begin to track speech to print.
- gain phonemic awareness of rimes.
- learn which letters form common rimes.
- learn to instantly recognize some high-frequency words.
- begin to communicate in conventional writing.

We start by discussing sight-word learning, the language-experience approach, and the importance of wide reading. Then, in the next section, we move into word study that involves teaching children letter–sound correspondences—phonics.

Sight Words and Word Banks

Words that children can recognize instantly are often referred to as *sight words*. As we mentioned earlier, there is a small set of words that children encounter frequently in text. These are *high-frequency words*. They are the most common words in printed English and include function words such as *as, the, and,* and *of,* and common content words such as *girl, blue,* and *little.* High-frequency words appear often in text, and it is difficult to read very much without knowing them.

Many lists of high-frequency words are available, and most reading series that you might use in your classrooms will identify the high-frequency words that appear in their materials. Certainly you will want to help your emergent readers quickly learn a body of high-frequency words. This will be useful for them in beginning to read straight away. Instantaneous word recognition is often referred to as sight-word recognition.

Sight words also serve as examples of how students approach words in word study. It is easier for a child to focus on the parts of a word he knows; familiar letters or patterns may help him recall the whole word. When a child can immediately recognize the word *cat*, it frees him to really focus on which letters relate to the /k/ or the /ăt/. He can then compare less-known words, such as other *at* words (*sat, fat, hat*), to this anchor word. Proceeding from the known to the unknown, our first principle is always the best direction. You will see this principle at work later in this chapter and throughout the book.

Thus, a good way to teach sight words is to start with words the child already knows. Most children entering first grade can read their names and a few words they learned in kindergarten, such as color words, names of family members, and household pets. A quick individual assessment of the words each child knows might be helpful. Your school, or the materials you teach with, may provide such an assessment. In any case, you can easily create a quick assessment by clearly printing a selected set of words on a list or on individual index cards (Figure 4.4). Then, make a duplicate copy of the "test" for recording what a child says as you ask him to read the list. As you record what a child says, note not only which words he can easily read, but what he does when he can't read a word. Does the child try to use an initial consonant? What does he already know about words that you can build on? Recording this information on a chart is helpful.

the	dog	big	cat	run	is
at	like	see	can	to	dog
he	my	yellow	and	red	get
up	go	she	girl	bus	was

FIGURE 4.4 *A List to Use for a Quick Check on Words Children Know*

The word list in Figure 4.4 includes both high-frequency function words and common content words. You can modify it by adding words that you are planning to have the child read in books, on charts, around your room, or at home.

Words that a child already knows can be the initial words to place in *word banks*. A word bank is a child's personal collection of words that he knows well enough to recognize in isolation. The words are printed on small cards and kept in a small plastic bag or other container. It is best if you, rather than the child, print the words, unless the child is a good printer, since most emergent readers are still learning how to accurately form letters. New words will be added to the word bank each day. Words can be reviewed in a variety of ways, as well as sorted according to their letter–sound features.

Start a word bank by printing a child's first name on a small card. Then, add words the child can already read, such as those he could read on the list in Figure 4.4. Next, you might personalize the word bank by asking the child what other words he can read, writing those on cards, and adding them to the collection. You might also add a few words that the child volunteers he would like to learn. These might include a favorite food, the name of his dog, the name of a favorite friend, a favorite activity, or any other word. Figure 4.5 shows the word bank of Marcos, a first-grader. It includes the words he could read from the list in Figure 4.4, as well as the words his teacher added because Marcos wanted to learn to read them.

A child's word bank should continue to grow until it has about 100 words. At that point, a word bank becomes unwieldy, and a child should have developed enough knowledge about decoding to be able to read more on his own. Words are added to the word bank as they are encountered in books and as they are needed in a child's individual writing. Selection of words to put in the word bank is done by both the child and the teacher. In particular, high-frequency and high-interest words that a teacher knows the child will encounter in books are good word-bank candidates.

FIGURE 4.5 *Marcos's Beginning First-Grade Word Bank*

Marcos
   cat
   the   soccer
   and   pizza
   red   Luis

Word banks, collections of words children can identify by sight, help children continue to recognize previously learned words as new ones are added.

Reviewing word-bank words and frequently encountering them in materials they are reading (perhaps by following along in a big book) will help children continue to recognize the previously learned words as new ones are added. Emergent readers use visual cues selectively. As we described in Chapter 3, they frequently have incomplete knowledge of all the letters in a word. They might recognize a word by its initial consonant or by its length. So it is not surprising that as new words are added to the word bank, old words may be "forgotten." Thus, recalling the word *cat* because it starts with the letter *c* fails when the word *can* is introduced. The more times children look at the word-bank words and compare them, the more likely they are to gain full mastery of them. First-grade teacher Gordon Scholander told us how he uses word banks with his emergent readers:

> My young scholars frequently enjoy sharing their word banks. They will sometimes read their word-bank cards to each other or with a buddy sort their cards into categories—such as animals or words that start or end with a particular letter. Sometimes I'll have them spread out ten or so of their individual word-bank cards on their desks, or work with a buddy, to try variants of a "pick-up" game. Here are some prompts I give them for the game:

Teachers will be most effective, particularly with struggling readers, if they see their role as one of helping children discover the writing system as opposed to simply teaching children about the writing system. Children must be actively involved in this process.

—*Barbara M. Taylor*
Teacher Educator

- Pick up all your animal words. Read your words to a buddy. Do you and your buddy have any of the same animals?
- Pick up all your color words. Hold up the card with your favorite color on it.
- Pick up all your words that start with /sssss/. Read them to a buddy.
- Pick up all your words that start with the letter s. Read your s words to a buddy.
- Pick up words that rhyme with *cat*. What do you have?
- Pick up all your words that have three letters. Read them to a buddy.
- Pick up your longest word and share it with a buddy.

Gordon Scholander, First-Grade Teacher

Language Experience

Our focus thus far has been on developing a core set of high-frequency words—words likely to be encountered in many different books—that children can readily identify. Later we show how to help children gain confidence and ability in identifying unknown words by using letter–sound correspondence strategies. But as we discussed in Chapter 3, children can learn much about how speech and print relate by noting how *their own speech* is linked to letters. Teachers can help children see how speech is written down and develop a more solid concept of words by taking dictation as a child talks. As the teacher writes the child's words, he can explain something about what is being printed. For example, if a child says "sun," the teacher can emphasize the /s/ while printing an *s*. As we mentioned in Chapter 3, this method of instruction has been termed *language experience*: The text is based on the language and experience of the child. Language experience can take various forms. We talked briefly about some of these in Chapter 3. Here we describe a few more:

- Each child has a special book. This can be created with a construction paper cover and filled with plain paper or paper that is plain on top and lined on the bottom. Each day a child can think about a special word. As children draw pictures of their words, the teacher walks around the class and takes dictation. The teacher carefully prints each child's word while talking about its features, such as saying its letters while printing them. The child can copy the word. Some children may dictate more than a single word, and some children might add additional writing to the page.

- Children dictate a group description or story to the teacher, who writes it down on a large pad of lined chart paper. A description might be called "How to Feed Our Fish." A different version of a familiar story might be recorded, such as a version of *Brown Bear, Brown Bear, What*

Do You See? by Bill Martin, Jr., titled "Brown Dog, Brown Dog." In Chapter 9, we will show how a first-grade teacher uses the language-experience approach to create a classroom newspaper; the students report on what is going on in their lives, and the teacher writes down their ideas on a large sheet of paper.

■ A large sheet of plain paper (about 6 feet long) can form a bulletin board, pinned to the wall in the classroom or hallway. Children can dictate various phrases or words for the teacher to write. The teacher begins by writing each child's name, then adds children's comments. Children can easily find their names to read back their comments. Words that an individual child dictates are good candidates for addition to that child's word bank.

Read, Read, Read

In this chapter, we look at specific instructional ideas for increasing children's knowledge about how words work and how they are constructed. We emphasize developing phonemic awareness through sorting picture cards, writing for sounds, classifying and contrasting spelling patterns, and having children discover spelling patterns. We don't want to lose sight of the fact, however, that we can never teach every spelling pattern that children will encounter. The word-study instruction we talk about helps give children insights on how words work. But much of what they learn will come from wide reading.

> Exemplary phonics instruction focuses on reading words, not learning rules.
>
> —*Steven Stahl*
> *Teacher Educator*

We want to stress the importance of *applying word-study skills in the context of actual text reading* (Juel & Roper/Schneider, 1985). As a teacher of emergent readers, you will want to make sure children have practice reading words with the common spelling patterns that you teach them in real text. For most teachers we know, this is routine. Georgia Woods talks about one of the books she uses in conjunction with teaching long *a* spelling patterns:

I like to begin and follow up activities on spelling patterns for long *a* with reading books such as *Who Has a Tail?* (1996) by Fay Robinson. This text has actual photographs of animals, and many of the words show spelling patterns for long *a*. For example, here are the lines from pages 3 and 4:

Who has a tail that shakes like a rattle?

The snake does.

When this snake shakes its tail, the tail rattles. That way, other animals hear it. They stay away.

As you can see, this book gives students the opportunity to practice reading long *a* word patterns in words such as *tail*, *shake*, *stay*, and *away*.

Georgia Woods, First-Grade Teacher

In the section on long and short vowels later in the chapter, you will find a bibliography that lists several appropriate titles for students working on those letter–sound correspondences. As we have said previously, *predictable texts* are also excellent sources of practice for emergent readers.

If it becomes difficult to find enough books to provide sufficient practice with particular spelling patterns or books that contrast the particular spelling patterns under study, "leveled" books may provide the solution. These books are leveled according to phonics elements and are currently available commercially. Leveled books are useful for providing children with the reading practice they need. Emergent readers need to see common spelling patterns repeated numerous times in many different words. Some leveled readers are listed in the Books to Build Automaticity bibliography in Chapter 1. Sets of leveled readers, such as *Ready Readers* (1996) from Modern Curriculum Press, often include hundreds of little books. This series, like others, includes several copies of each title as well as big books. Many current reading series, such as *Literature Works* (1996) from Silver Burdett Ginn, include leveled readers in addition to anthologies of children's literature.

The main point to keep in mind is that the more texts the children can read successfully on their own, the more skilled they will become at reading. And the more skilled they become at reading, the more they will read on their own.

Teaching Children About Letter-Sound Correspondences

Begin teaching children about letter–sound correspondences by following the first principle of word-study instruction: Start where the child is! We start in Phase 1 with learning the alphabet and recognizing letters—prerequisites to learning letter–sound correspondences—and end with teaching multisyllabic words in Phase 3. Figure 4.6 presents some general guidelines for moving from Phase 1 to Phase 3. But remember that these are general guidelines, not a lockstep progression of what you must do.

Intensive, explicit phonics instruction is a valuable component of beginning reading programs.

—Marilyn Adams
Educational Psychologist

Phase I	Phase 2	Phase 3
Alphabet recognition and production	Consonant blends	Short vowels
Beginning word study: onsets, rimes, and blends	Consonant digraphs	Long-vowel patterns
		Multisyllabic words

FIGURE 4.6 *Three Phases of Word-Study Instruction*

Phase 1: Learning the Alphabet and Beginning Word Study

Phase 1 begins with pre-phonics—ideas for helping students recognize and reproduce letters in the alphabet. Next, we move to beginning word study—ideas for introducing the basic speech unit, the onset and rime, and how to blend words.

Alphabet Recognition and Production.   It is difficult to track print and to attend to printed words as sequences of letters (let alone as onsets and rimes) until letters are recognized. Letter recognition can be taught both directly and indirectly. If you discover that some of your students are weak in letter recognition, you can involve them in incidental alphabet activities throughout the day, as well as provide them with direct alphabet instruction during their word-study time.

You can create incidental alphabet activities as opportunities arise. Keeping a chart of letters that children know is useful for tailoring alphabet work to fit individual students. You can talk about the letters students know when you run across them in your readings. For example, you might say something like this: "Look at the title of this book. Can you find the letter *m* in two places?"

Or you might say, "I want you to point to all the *p*s on this page."

As you or a child writes, focus on problem letters by using statements such as this one: "You'll need a lowercase *b* to write the word *boy*. Here it is on the alphabet strip [located on the children's desks]."

It is also helpful to keep in mind the letters that are problematic for particular children in your classroom.

You will want to engage your students in direct alphabet activities if a child or a group of children have very incomplete alphabet knowledge. In the following list, we suggest some activities that will help students learn the letters in the alphabet:

IN THE CLASSROOM
Alphabet Activities

Start with the Children's Names and Their Favorite Things

A good starting place for children who do not know many letters is to work on the letters in their names. Names are particularly meaningful to children. When they know the letters in their first names, work on last names or friends' names or the names of their favorite foods, colors, pets, and so forth. Write each letter on a separate card. Lay the cards out in order, and name them as you spell the words. You might use capitals in one row and ask the children to match lowercase letters to them in another row below. Scramble the letter cards and have the children reassemble them, naming them as they point to them. This activity works particularly well when partners team up to name the letters in their names and those of classmates.

Arrange the Letters in Order

When students know about half of the letters or more, they can work on putting a set of letters in alphabetical order from *a* to *z*. Use a set of alphabet flash cards or letter tiles. Use either capital or lowercase letters. You might have children work in pairs and have one child put the capitals in order while another child works to match the lowercase letters right below. Let the children refer to alphabet strips. You might teach children to sing the ABC song. If you do, be sure to have them touch the letters (on their own alphabet strips) as well as sing them.

Aa Bb Cc Dd Ee Ff Gg Hh Ii Jj Kk Ll Mm
Nn Oo Pp Qq Rr Ss Tt Uu Vv Ww Xx Yy Zz

Use Alphabet Trade Books and Personal Alphabet Books

Have children look up the letter they are studying in an alphabet book or picture dictionary to find things that begin with that letter. Create an alphabet book for each child by stapling together blank sheets of paper and assigning a letter to each page. This book can be used in a number of ways for children who need to learn letters:

- Encourage students to practice writing upper- and lowercase forms of the letter.
- Decide on a key picture that is spelled beginning with that letter (*M m* and a picture of a moon). You or the child can draw the key picture and paste it on the page. Key pictures for alphabet books can also be computer-generated.
- Write other words that begin with the letter. Look them up in an ABC book or picture dictionary.
- As children begin to acquire word banks, these words can be added to the alphabet book to create a dictionary of known words.

Beginning Word Study: Onsets, Rimes, and Blending. After students have a good grasp of the letters in the alphabet and can recognize some high-frequency words, they are ready to begin learning how our alphabetic writing system works. Word-study instruction on letter sounds, or phonics, starts with the sounds of beginning consonants (the onsets) and moves to the sounds of rimes (phonograms).

As we discussed earlier in this chapter, the syllable is the basic speech unit, and the common syllable unit in English is consonant–vowel–consonant (CVC)—or an onset and a rime—as in the word *cat*. There is considerable evidence that children more readily perceive the sounds in syllables as onsets (the beginning consonant units) and rimes (the vowel and what follows) than as sequences of phonemes. Awareness of these intrasyllabic units is easier to develop and occurs before a child is able to attend to the individual phonemes that make up a rime or a complex onset (Treiman, 1992). Thus, a child perceives the onset *k* and the rime *ăt* in *cat* more readily than he perceives *cat* as containing the three phonemes /k/, /ă/, and /t/.

Using predictable text to foster knowledge of high-frequency words and initial consonants is a good way to begin phonics instruction. In predictable text, there is repetition of structure, rhythm, or some other pattern that, when combined with lots of illustrations, supports the fledgling reader. In the very popular predictable text *Brown Bear, Brown Bear, What Do You See?* by Bill Martin, Jr., (1983) colored drawings of animals and a repetitive structure support the emergent reader:

> "Brown Bear,
> Brown Bear,
> What do you see?"
> "I see a redbird
> looking at me."
> "Redbird,
> redbird,
> What do you see?"
> "I see a . . . "

The scaffolding provided by predictable text ensures that children will be readers from the start. As we noted in Chapter 3, children can often become instant readers after hearing an adult read predictable text just once or twice. Emergent readers can then enjoy, understand, and read text on their own. After your children have enjoyed hearing a predictable story, you can then focus on certain words to study. They might include high-frequency words or words with specific onsets that are being studied in class. These words will make sense to the children, as they have already seen them function in a meaningful text.

The downside, however, of predictable text is that once the text is memorized, children need not look at the words to "read" the text. They can recite the text from memory, getting any help they need from the pictures. So although predictable text can be extremely helpful in early reading instruction, you will gradually need to phase it out. Also, you can maximize the impact of your instruction by including simple procedures such as the one Harriet O'Dell uses with her first-graders:

> One method I have found effective in helping children focus on *all* the letters in words is to have them match their word cards to the words in the predictable text. For example, if a child has read *Brown Bear, Brown Bear, What Do You See?*, I can be very certain he will have a word card with *brown* written on it in his stack of word cards. He can check that it is *brown* by putting the word card underneath the word in the memorized text that he knows is *brown*. In trying to match the word on the card to the word on the text, that child has to compare all the letters. Children can also use the text to identify a word they aren't certain of on a word card. I use large zip-lock bags containing a predictable text and some word cards in school and to send home.
>
> Harriet O'Dell, First-Grade Teacher

You can decide which words in a text will be particularly useful for children as they read future texts and put these on word cards. There are two ways you can make word cards. One way is to create large word cards (about 4 by 8 inches) on which you have printed key words with a large black felt-tipped pen. These cards are particularly useful when you are working with your whole class or a group of children. You can also create smaller individual word cards. Words can be preprinted (access to a computer will help), photocopied on heavy stock paper, and cut apart by the children. For *Brown Bear, Brown Bear, What Do You See?*, useful word cards might highlight color words or animal words.

The following scenario will help build your schema for helping emergent readers learn onsets. Ms. Campbell and her first-graders have completed the language-experience portion of a lesson:

IN THE CLASSROOM
Beginning Work with Onsets

After Ms. Campbell's entire class has listened to and discussed the story *What Do You Like?*, she says, "It's center time." Ms. Campbell tells each child which center to go to. She reminds them that they will spend about 20 minutes in each center and that today they will each rotate through all the centers. About a third of the children go to the classroom library center. There they can read with a buddy or read alone a book of their choosing. She has added a copy of *What Do You Like?* to the center. Another third of the children go to the writing center. There they will write and illustrate their "I like" books. And the other third will work at the word center.

Ms. Campbell calls the first seven children to the word center. Here she meets with groups of children who will profit from similar word and phonics instruction. The seven children she sees in this rotation need to review initial consonants. They bring their word banks to the center. Ms. Campbell has seven copies of *What Do You Like?* They each take one. She first has them chorally read the text together as they point to the words. Then she passes out small word cards to each child. The words on the cards are *rainbow, like, love,* and *play.* Three of these words are common, and *rainbow* is one that Ms. Campbell knows they would like to learn. She tells them to find the page in their book that has *rainbow* on it. They easily do this. She then says, "Find the word card that says *rainbow* . Check it to see if it is a match by putting it under the word *rainbow."* She asks the children how they know the word is *rainbow.* Most say because it is long and starts with the letter *r.* Sara mentions that she can also hear an / ā / in it. Since they have already covered the sound /b/, Ms. Campbell has them point to where it starts saying *bow.*

She next has them put *rainbow* as the heading on their desk and search their word banks for other *r* words. They each line up their *r* words under *rainbow.* Ms. Campbell asks them to read their list to the person sitting next to them. She includes herself, for an even number of participants. Ms. Campbell repeats this procedure with the words *like, love,* and *play.*

The final word center activity is called Writing for Sounds. Ms. Campbell gives the children pencils and blank sheets of paper, and each writes his or her name on the paper. She has them write the letters *p, l,* and *r* across the top of the paper. She then calls out words that start with one of these letters. When she calls out "play," she expects children to write it under the letter *p.* She doesn't expect them to be able to write all of its letters but encourages them to write as many as they can. She emphasizes the initial consonant as she says the word, as this is the phonics element the group has been working on. She will look at these papers later to check on how each child is progressing. Right now, she simply collects them as it is time to rotate the children to another center in the room.

We suggest you take a moment now to see how Ms. Campbell's instruction in word study met each of the five principles listed previously. You might also want to compare her teaching to the goals outlined for emergent readers at the beginning of the section on word-study instruction.

We turn now from onsets to rimes. As we discussed earlier in this chapter, the basic syllable is composed of an onset and a rime. Rimes with the same spellings are called phonograms. Words that share a phonogram form word families, such as *hat, mat, cat, sat, chat,* and *fat.* We have already talked about how to develop children's knowledge of onsets, as well as a corpus of high-frequency words. Once some initial consonants are known, we can expand children's reading vocabularies by teaching them rimes.

As you may recall from earlier in this chapter, the pronunciation of vowels by themselves is hard to predict. But there are many common phonograms whose pronunciations are quite dependable. Richard Wylie and Donald Durrell (1970) developed a list of rimes that are stable and occur in nearly 500 primary-level words. These are in listed Figure 4.7.

Obviously, word-study instruction should focus on these 37 rimes. Children can make analogies based on these syllable units that will help them read and write new words (Goswami & Bryant, 1992; Goswami & Mead, 1992). That is, once a phonogram such as *at* is known, a child can use his knowledge of initial consonants and the rime to write or read a never-before-seen word, perhaps *rat* or *hat.*

ack	ail	ain	ake	ale	ame	an
ank	ap	ash	at	ate	aw	ay
eat	ell	est	ice	ick	ide	ight
ill	in	ine	ing	ink	ip	ir
ock	oke	op	ore	or	uck	ug
ump	unk					

FIGURE 4.7 *37 Rimes That Occur in Nearly 500 Primary-Level Words*

At, in fact, is a good phonogram with which to begin rime work because it is fairly easy to perceive and it appears in a lot of words, such as *at, bat, cat, fat, hat, mat, flat, sat, scat,* and *rat*. In the following outline, we suggest one procedure for studying the rime *at*:

IN THE CLASSROOM
A Procedure for Working with the Rime *at*

- Locate a story with lots of *at* words, such as Alice Cameron's *The Cat Sat on the Mat*.
- Read the story aloud to students, and then have students read it chorally.
- Have students locate the *at* words in the story, making sure they finger-point to the words as they read them.
- Print the *at* words on an outline drawing of a cat, and post it on a wall. This word wall poster will be a good reference for children to refer to as they decode and encode words. As other stories are read with *at* words, these words can be added to the word wall.
- Additionally, invite children to take the known word *cat* from their word bank or another source and find the *at* in it.

The early emergent reader also needs to learn to blend the sounds together in a word. As rimes are introduced, show children how to blend the sounds of the onset and rime together. You can model holding the sound of the onset until you add the rime. As much as possible, it is important to not stop saying the onset until the rime is added. There will be less distortion of the initial consonant. In other words, rather than pauseing after the /k/ in *cat* and thus adding an *uh* sound to it, go straight into the *at*, as in /kkkkăăăătttt/. *Children have problems with blending, and teachers should take every opportunity to model this process.* Here's an example of what you might say about a word printed on the chalkboard:

> If I don't know what a word is right away, here's how I figure it out. First, I look at the word and I find any parts I know. So, let's pretend I don't know this word, *mat.*

> I know it starts with a /mmmm/ [said as you point to *m*] and then I recognize *at* [said as you point to *at*]. So, I say /mmmmăăăătttt/ [said as you finger-point to each letter as it is pronounced]. *Mat*—that makes sense.

Phase 2: Consonant Blends and Consonant Digraphs

As the name implies, a consonant blend refers to the combined sounds of two or three consonants. *Pl* in *play* and *spr* in *spring* are examples of blends. A consonant digraph, on the other hand, is a combination of consonants that makes a unique sound, unlike the sound made by any of the individual letters within the digraph. Examples include *ph* as in *phone* and *sh* as in *share* and *fish.*

Consonant Blends.   After single consonants are known, children's competence with words can be greatly expanded by helping them blend together the phonemes represented by consonant blends. The study of blends can be interwoven with the study of rimes by including blends with short-vowel phonograms. For example, the *at* family, such as *sat*, *mat*, *cat*, and so forth, can be expanded to include *flat*, *scat*, and *brat*.

Again, start with the known. Find the *at* rime in a word like *flat*. Then help children blend together the phonemes represented by the initial consonants. Your modeling of the process might sound like this:

Here's how I would figure out a word I don't know right off. First, I look at the word and I find any parts I know. So, let's pretend I don't know the word *flat*. I know it starts with a /ffff/ [said as you point to *f*] and then I put that together with the letter *l*, so I have /ffffllll/. I recognize *at* [said as you point to *at*]. So, I say /ffffllllăăăătttt/ [said as you finger-point to each letter as it is pronounced]. *Flat*—that makes sense.

To help children develop phonemic awareness of consonant blends in words, sorting picture cards is again useful. Words with different consonant blends can be easily contrasted and classified based on their sounds. For example, pictures with words that start with the phoneme /s/ may be contrasted with pictures starting with the consonant blends *sc, sk, sl, sm, sn, sp,* or *sw. S* blends are probably the easiest of the blends (because /s/ is easier to isolate and elongate) and make a good starting point. *R* blends (*br, cr, dr, fr, gr,* and *tr*) and *l* blends (*bl, cl, fl, gl,* and *sl*) are more difficult. Like all picture sorts, each column should be headed by a card with the letters being taught (*s* juxtaposed with *st,* for example). Having children write the words that were just sorted with the picture cards will provide practice and serve as a good diagnostic tool to see if children understand blends.

The following description shows how word-study instruction on *r* blends such as *br, cr,* and *dr* might take place:

IN THE CLASSROOM
Word-Study Instruction on Blends

- Ask children to find *br, cr,* and *dr* words among their word-bank words. Write these words on the board. Or, start by having students locate some of these words in a book.

- Illustrate the difference between a consonant–vowel–consonant (CVC) word and a consonant–consonant–vowel–consonant (CCVC) word by writing a word such as *brat* on the board and asking the children which letter you need to erase to make *bat.* Or, ask which letter do you need to add to *bake* to make *brake.* Or, ask how to make *light* into *bright.*

- To further develop phonemic awareness of blends, have children sort picture cards by the consonant blend and its component phonemes. For example, they could write three headings on a sheet of paper (*b, r,* and *br*) like this:

b	r	br

- Have children work with a buddy or in small groups to sort appropriate pictures, such as those depicting *bat, bed, bell, rat, room, ring, brick, bread, bridge, broom, bride,* and *brat* under the correct heading. The children might enjoy mixing up the picture cards and re-sorting them to see if they can get faster. Similarly, they can work with a buddy or in small groups to sort the pictures under the correct heading (*s* or *st* for *six, sun, saw, star, stick,* and *stairs,* for example). Or, under the headings *d* and *dr,* the following picture cards can be sorted: *dog, duck, dime, dress, drive, drum, drip, dream, dragon.* Or instead of small cards, you could do similar activities with a group of students or the whole class by using large picture cards, modeling how to place them in columns on a pocket chart.

- After the children are comfortable sorting picture cards by sounds, you can turn to connecting these sounds to letters. Have the children write *br, cr,* and *dr* on cards. As you call out a word, ask children to hold up the card with its first two letters. Or, they could write down the first two letters in words you call out. Emphasize the first two sounds in words such as *drip, drive, drop, crab, crib, bring, drain,* and *brat.*

- Show children how to blend consonants, using initial blends and known short vowel phonograms (*dr + ip = drip*). Do this with several words, pointing out that each word begins with a consonant blend (such as *br, cr,* or *dr*) and is followed by a rime.

- Now have the children write some words. Tell them that some will have the *r* and some won't. Try words such as *rag, drag, dip, drip, rat, brat, rib, crib, cab, crab, top, crop.*

- Include some sentence dictations with words that contain the onsets, rimes, and high-frequency words you have taught. (*Drip, drip, went the drops of rain.*) Say the sentence. Slowly pronounce each word in the sentence and encourage children to write the words. Emphasize the sounds in the words.

- For extra blend practice, give children word parts on cards to blend together and make into words. You could also give them a card with a blend, such as *br,* and several rimes, such as *at, ag, im, ap,* and *it.* Have them work individually or in groups to make all of the words they can by combining the two parts.

Consonant Digraphs.   Unlike blends, consonant digraphs (which are really a combination of two phonemes) behave like single consonants in that they represent one sound. Examples of consonant digraphs are *ph, ch, th, sh,* and *ng.* The study of initial consonant digraphs can be interwoven with rime study, much like that of consonant blends. The most common initial consonant digraphs are *sh, th, wh,* and *ch.* As previously described, picture sorting can be very useful in drawing attention to these units. In particular, it is helpful to have children compare single initial consonants to corresponding digraphs by using picture cards. For example, we might compare pictures of *sun, sail,* or *sink* with pictures of *shoe, ship,* or *shirt.* Of course, you would head each category with the corresponding letters *s* or *sh.*

Some consonant digraphs occur at the end of the rime unit. The most common of the ending digraphs are *sh, ght, ng,* and *ck.* These ending digraphs will probably be learned as part of a high-frequency word family rather than in isolation. The *ight* word family, for example, includes *light, might, fight, sight, night, right,* and *slight.*

Learning the first few short-vowel rhyming families, or the first few consonant blends, may go slowly. Fortunately, most children will begin to need much less reinforcement with later families or phonics elements as they transfer their learning to new vowels and spelling patterns. However, since the first understanding of any new principle is always the hardest, you will want to provide plenty of opportunities for practice on these initial families. Once the basic alphabetic idea is understood, learning tends to progress at a much faster rate.

On the other hand, if a child is not catching on, it generally does not work to just plow ahead. Taking the time to review and reteach until a word family is mastered is generally better than marching on with children not fully prepared to study the next word family. You are seeking to help your children understand the rather abstract and elusive nature of how letters and sounds relate. This understanding isn't going to emerge after just one introduction to a word family. It takes plenty of opportunities to see you model reading words, to engage in their own hands-on sorting of words by sound and spelling patterns, to practice writing words with target patterns, and to read text that contains words exemplifying the spelling patterns to reach mastery. Simply telling a child that *at* says /ăt/ doesn't mean he will get it. Teaching isn't just telling; it involves providing experiences that will foster true understanding.

In the following scenario, you will see how a teacher combines study of onsets and rimes. Mr. Andersen is working with a group of children who have solid knowledge of initial consonants, consonant blends, and some consonant digraphs. The children have also been introduced to *at* and *an* rimes, and *op* and *og* rimes. In this lesson, Mr. Andersen is introducing *ig* rimes. He has chosen to have the children read *Stop That!* by Maryanne Dobeck because it has a lot of the target rimes.

> The research adds up to a clear principle of reading instruction: Help the child acquire the reading codes. Help the reader, that is, discover the alphabetical principle and the specific relations that it holds in his or her writing system. Let's put this a bit stronger, since this is not something to leave to chance. Make sure the child discovers the codes. Make sure the child learns that the letter *t* associates with the first speech segment in "Tom," and the final speech segment in "ate" and in "met."
>
> —*Charles A Perfetti*
> *Educational Researcher*

IN THE CLASSROOM

Practicing Onsets and Rimes with Students Who Know Consonant Blends and Some Digraphs

It is October. Mr. Andersen is working with a group of children in his first-grade class. Each of the six children has a copy of *Stop That!* Mr. Andersen begins by having them read the title. He has them point to the letters in *stop* that make it say /ŏp/ and the letters in *that* that make it say /ăt/.

The cover page shows a very bossy-looking cat with her hands on her hips, scolding two scared-looking pigs. Mr. Andersen suggests that the children put their hands on their hips and say, "Stop that," as the cat is doing. He then has them predict why she might be scolding the pigs. The text contains lines with a repetitive structure:

> Two little pigs did a jig.
> "Stop that!" said the cat.
> Two little pigs put on wigs.
> "Stop that!" said the cat.

Mr. Andersen reads the book to the children. He encourages them to echo his reading and finger-point to the words while he says them. After reading through the text, the children check to see if any of their predictions on why the cat was angry were correct. Then Mr. Andersen asks the children to reread the book with partners. He encourages them to sound really bossy when they read the cat's part.

After the children have had fun mimicking the bossy cat, Mr. Andersen turns to phonics instruction. He passes out some picture cards with *ig* and *at* pictures. He has each child find the picture of the pig and the cat. They will be placed in two columns, with *ig* words under *pig* and *at* words under *cat*. After they do this, he has each child "read" his or her column of pictures and make any corrections needed. Then he hands out word cards to be matched to each picture. Finally, he collects the picture cards and has the children work with partners to sort the word cards into *at* and *ig* columns. They read the columns to each other as fast as they can, then scramble the cards, re-sort them, and reread them. The children then add the new *ig* words to their word banks.

Mr. Andersen brings out a construction-paper pig shape. The children help him spell *ig* words, which he writes on the pig cutout. He tacks it up on the word wall.

Mr. Andersen concludes this word-study session by handing each child a piece of lined paper and dictating some sentences for them to write. He will study these later to see which children might need some additional help on the onsets and rimes, as well as the high-frequency words, that he has covered. The sentences are:

> The cat said, "Stop that."
> The little pigs said, "Scat, cat."
> That big cat scat.

Notice how Mr. Anderson began with reading for meaning and enjoyment, then proceeded to a lesson on phonics, and concluded by having the children write what they had learned. This is an excellent sequence.

Phase 3: Short Vowels, Long Vowels, and Multisyllabic Words

When children are showing substantial facility with rhyming word families and consonant blends and digraphs, they are ready to use word sorting to compare short vowels in nonrhyming words, work with the sounds and spellings of long vowels in words, and work with multisyllabic words. The following list gives a sequence for phonics instruction:

1. Initial consonants
2. Common rimes
3. Consonant blends and digraphs
4. Short vowels
5. Long vowels
6. Multisyllabic words

Notice that alphabet recognition is not included because being able to recognize letters and name them is not part of phonics instruction, but a prerequisite to it. We caution again that this series of steps is merely a guideline. You will revisit each of these steps many times as you help students learn about words and how they operate.

Short Vowels. In order to draw attention to the short-vowel sounds in nonrhyming words, we once again find picture cards useful. A good vowel to begin with is short *a*, contrasted with either short *o* or *i*. Contrasting short *a* with short *e* and contrasting short *e* with short *i* will be the tasks children find the most challenging and should be dealt with later. We list our suggested sequence for short-vowel contrasts here:

1. Short *a* contrasted with short *i*
2. Short *i* contrasted with short *u*
3. Short *i* contrasted with short *u* and short *a*
4. Short *e* contrasted with short *o*
5. Review of all short vowels

The general plan for teaching short vowels in nonrhyming families is to first sort pictures by short-vowel sounds and then sort known words. For example, a teacher can gather large picture cards of short *a* and short *i* words for use on a pocket chart. The teacher begins by putting a picture of a cat under a card with the letter *a* and says, "Cat, at, /ă/—this sound is a short *a*." The teacher repeats this with a picture of a pig, saying, "Pig, ig, /ĭ/—this sound is a short *i*." The teacher continues modeling with several more pictures and then hands the children pictures to add to the pocket chart. After this group sorting activity, smaller picture cards are handed to the children to use in sorting short *a* and short *i* words with a buddy.

Now that children are concentrating on the phoneme level, another good activity is to have them use *letter cards* to make words. Blending can easily be emphasized as letter cards are put together to form words. Letter cards can be made into words on a pocket chart. As the teacher pronounces a letter, a volunteer can come up and add the letter card. For example, the

Reviewing letter sounds one-on-one provides an excellent opportunity for a teacher to note those letters and sounds the student still needs to master.

teacher might say, "What letter does *big* start with?" A child would put up the letter *b*. Then the teacher might say, "What do we add to make it say /bĭĭĭĭ/?" The child would add the letter *i*. Finally, the teacher might say, "How do we make it say *big*?" The child would add the letter *g*.

IN THE CLASSROOM
Short-Vowel Work in the First Grade

It is December. Mrs. Kee is working with a group of early readers who are ready to focus on short vowels. They are going to practice spelling short *i* and short *a* words. The children sit around a large table. Mrs. Kee gives them each a set of letter cards and a holder for them. The holders for the letter cards are individual pocket charts. Mrs. Kee made the charts by folding a small piece of construction paper into 3 to 5 sections and stapling the bottom up to form pockets. She asks the children to spread out the letter cards in front of the holders on the table.

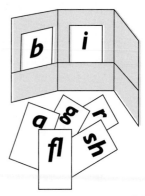

Mrs. Kee asks the children to spell *big* with their letter cards. Once the word is spelled, she says, "Show me." The children hold up their individual pocket charts. Mrs. Kee has her own pocket chart, and she shares her spelling with the children. She prompts the children to correct any misspellings by repeating the word, elongating or emphasizing the misspelled phoneme.

Once all the children have spelled *big* on their pocket charts, Mrs. Kee calls out other words to spell. These words include *bag, bat, bit, fit, fat, flat, flash,* and *fish.* She lets the children work together, as needed. The hands-on work keeps their attention. As they manipulate the letters, they really see the influence of particular letters and letter combinations.

Word hunts are another useful activity for developing word knowledge, especially for the early reader who has outgrown the use of a word bank. Word hunts are literally hunts for words with specific spelling patterns. Children can hunt for words independently or in teams. They might, for example, look for short *a* and short *i* words in stories they have read or are reading. They might write lists together and meet as a class to share the lists, adding words to the word wall, other group charts, or records of favorite words in individual word-study notebooks.

When children read with partners, they assume roles that can give teachers insight into how they view the reading process and their own reading abilities.

—Laurie MacGillivay
Teacher Educator

Long-Vowel Patterns. Long vowels are deceptive. They are easier to perceive in words than short vowels are (compare *mad* and *made*), but they are represented by a considerable number of spelling patterns (for example, *made* and *maid*). Learning which particular long-vowel patterns are represented by which letters in which words involves a considerable amount of practice and memorization. The following scenario gives several examples of ways to contrast short- and long-vowel patterns.

IN THE CLASSROOM
Contrasting Short- and Long-Vowel Patterns

After you and your children have read and enjoyed a story or stories that contain examples of long and short *a* sounds, there are many ways to help them master short- and long-vowel patterns. Here are some examples:

- Write the words *mad* and *made* on the board. Invite a child to point to the letter in *mad* that says /ă/. Remind the children that the letter *a* often says /ă/.

  Have the children write *a* as a heading on a sheet of a paper. Now have them focus on the word *made*. Invite a child to point to the letter in *made* that makes the long *a* sound. Ask the children to tell you the difference between *mad* and *made*. The letter *a* often has a long *a* sound when the letter *e* follows it.

  Have the children write *a_e* as the second heading. Now call out various long and short *a* words, and have the children write them under the correct heading. The words might include *cape, cap, ape, make, map, skate,* and *date*.

- Have the children sort some short *a* and long *a* pictures. Have them work with a buddy or in small groups. The pictures might depict words such as *gate, cat, hat, sad, shade, game, cake, lake,* and *shake*. The children might enjoy mixing up the picture cards and re-sorting them to see if they can get faster.

- Have the children make words with pocket charts and letter cards. For example, you can have children spell *can* and then they can:
  - add *e* to make *cane.*
  - make it say "cape," "cap," "man," mane," take," "wake."
  - continue replacing initial and final letters to make new words.

- Read another book with lots of short *a* and long *a* (CVCE) words. Have children go on a word hunt to find these words and record them on a word wall or on an individual word-study notebook page.

- Choose sentences to dictate such as *The brave man had on a cape and a cap.* Dictate the entire sentence. Then slowly say each word in the sentence, and encourage children to write each word. Emphasize the sounds in the words.

- Encourage children to figure out "rules." Have the children work in small groups to sort word cards under the headings "short *a*" and "long *a*." They can help each other pronounce the words, decide if the word contains a short or a long *a*, and then try to come up with some spelling "rules." The sorting would look something like this:

Short *a*	Long *a*		
bat	rain	cane	hay
cat	train	cake	tray
flat	sail	plane	t
van	pail	plate	ja
pan	jail	ape	c
trash	nail	cape	p
cash	tail	grape	s
map	snail	vase	N
rash	nail	gate	
mask	hail	skate	
strap	quail	blaze	
trap	pain	lake	
wrap	brain	snake	

Of course, there are other ways children could sort these words. You can encourage them to think of other ways and to verbalize why they sorted the words as they did. They might, for example, put all the words with the spelling pattern *ack* together, or the words with *ail,* or the words with *ate,* or even the words that start with *s* blends.

Every time children sort words based on spelling patterns, they are attending to the fact that such patterns exist, and they are more likely to recall and use these spelling patterns to recognize and spell words. A helpful source for word families lists is *Phonics Patterns: Onset and Rhyme Word Lists* (1997) by Edward Fry. In the following bibliography, we include titles suitable for word study on the long and short *a* sounds.

Books Featuring Short and Long *a* Vowel Sounds

Many engaging books with interesting characters and plots and with lively language give children opportunities to practice different vowel sounds. Here is a brief list of titles. For a more complete listing of books featuring the other four vowel sounds, see Phyllis Trachtenburg's (1990) list.

Short a

Marjorie Flack. *Angus and the Cat*. Doubleday, 1931. Angus, a Scottie dog, spends three days chasing the family's new cat. But when the cat disappears, Angus misses it. 32 pages.

Helen Griffith. *Alex and the Cat*. Greenwillow, 1982. Three easy-to-read stories are about Alex, who wants to be treated like the family cat, wants to live in the wild like a wolf, and then restores a baby bird to a robin's nest. 63 pages.

Bernard Most. *There's an Ant in Anthony*. Morrow, 1980. After discovering *ant* in his name, Anthony searches for the word *ant* in other words. 32 pages.

Joan L. Nodset. *Who Took the Farmer's Hat?* Harper & Row, 1963. The wind blows away a farmer's hat and he finds it being used in a most surprising way. 31 pages.

Dr. Seuss. *The Cat in the Hat*. Random House, 1957. Two children sitting at home on a rainy day are visited by a cat who shows them some tricks and games. 61 pages.

Long a

Verna Aardema. *Bringing the Rain to Kapiti Plain*. Dial, 1981. A cumulative rhyme relates how Ki-pat brought rain to the drought-stricken Kapiti Plain. 30 pages.

Molly Bang. *The Paper Crane*. Greenwillow, 1985. A mysterious man enters a restaurant and pays for his dinner with a paper crane that magically comes to life and dances. 32 pages.

Judy Blume. *The Pain and the Great One*. Bradbury, 1974. In this contemporary tale of sibling rivalry, a 6-year-old (the Pain) and his 8-year-old sister (the Great One) envy each other's position in the family. 32 pages.

Kevin Henkes. *Sheila Rae, the Brave*. Greenwillow, 1987. When brave Sheila Rae, who usually looks out for her sister Louise, becomes lost and scared one day, Louise comes to the rescue. 32 pages.

Anna Grossnickle Hines. *Taste the Raindrops*. Greenwillow, 1983. Despite a mother's initial objections, a child is delighted to walk in the rain, feeling and tasting the raindrops. 23 pages.

Short a and Long a

Esphyr Slobodkina. *Caps for Sale*. Scholastic, 1987. A band of mischievous monkeys steals all of a peddler's caps while he naps under a tree. 42 pages.

Multisyllabic Words. As we discussed earlier in this chapter, the basic unit in speech is the syllable. All words have either one syllable or more than one syllable. As students move into more advanced reading with the demands of multisyllabic words, we want to help them realize that such words are simply strings of syllables that contain the spelling patterns they already know. They need to examine long words to find familiar "chunks." As we have discussed, these chunks can be onsets, rimes, affixes, and root words.

Children tend to be intimidated by long words. You need to model how to approach them—how to recognize the chunks within them that children already know. Put words on the board, and think aloud as you break them into chunks. Then, after ample modeling on your part, invite children to point out the onsets, rimes, morphemes, and even vowel patterns or consonant digraphs that they spot in words. Ms. Kenney uses this technique with her second-graders in the following scenario:

IN THE CLASSROOM
Multisyllabic Words

Because of her constant modeling of how to identify multisyllabic words, Ms. Kenney's second-grade children enjoy being word detectives. Each day, Ms. Kenney writes a multisyllabic word on the board, talks about any clues to its identity that she can find, and lists these clues on the board. Then, she writes another multisyllabic word on the board and asks the children to find clues to its identity. Here are some of the words she and the children have worked with and some of the observations of different children that helped the class figure out the words:

- *chipmunk*
  Karl noticed the common rime *ip*.
  Marty said she got *unk* because she knew the word *skunk*.
  Tasha volunteered the pronunciation of the consonant digraph *ch*.

- *shameful*
  Katy said she instantly saw the affix *-ful* meaning "full of."
  Ming said he knew the *ame* rime by heart.
  Tasha volunteered the pronunciation of the consonant digraph *sh*.

- *transit*
  Lily said she knew how to chunk it because she saw the familiar *an* and *it* units.
  Kyle added that another clue was that the letter combination *ns* doesn't start a syllable.
  Tasha volunteered the pronunciation of the consonant blend *tr*.

We hope that the ideas we have presented for word-study instruction will give you a good foundation on which to begin planning instruction for your emergent readers. Remember, base any word-study instruction you design on the five principles we presented at the outset. Use your imagination, summon up your creativity, and have fun. Your enthusiasm will be contagious.

As one progresses in mastering the relationship between print and spoken language, he is cracking the code. . . . One must "crack the code" to gain independence in reading.

—*Arthur Heilman*
Teacher Educator

Reflection and Application

7. As you have noticed, much word-study instruction begins by sorting picture cards for sounds, and following that activity by sorting word cards based on their spelling patterns. Explain the rationale for this basic two-step process.

8. Discuss how the following word cards might be sorted under the three headings: *frog, toad, porch*. What might children learn by sorting the following words under these three vowel-pattern categories? If any of the words don't fit under the headers, consider adding an "odd-ball" category: *home, flock, morning, broke, storm, hope, boat, know, on, pond, rock, corn, wore, acorn, forlorn, lost, hot, wrote, note, snow, ghost, most, post, old, coast, told, gold, cold, hold, nose, rose, cove, croak, soak-ing, road, coach, boat, toast, float, vote, hose, smoke, block, sock, roast, stove, torch, short, spot, sport, worn, store, fork, thorn, fort, snoring, blow-ing, growing, snowing, blown, Joan, foam, grove, note, moaning*

9. Now, consider how these same words could be sorted to reveal spelling patterns, and jot down the words you would put in several of the groupings you identify.

Special Needs and Special Talents

Many children readily succeed at word study and become accomplished readers quite quickly. Others struggle and will need additional instruction and encouragement. The most typical problem that children will have in learning to read words is perceiving them as sequences of sounds, that is, ac-quiring phonemic awareness. To determine how readily children can do this, carefully observe them to see whether or not they can sort pictures based on onsets (*s* versus *b* versus *m* pictures), rimes (*at* versus *ig* versus *an*), or more difficult medial vowels (short *i* versus short *a*). To help children better per-ceive onsets and rimes, you can read nursery rhymes and stories that employ alliteration, such as Jill Bennett's *Teeny Tiny* or Dr. Seuss's *There's a Wocket in My Pocket*. You can pronounce words to emphasize, elongate, and seg-ment them into their component sounds for children. And you can help them link speech segments to writing by modeling how to do this and pro-viding abundant writing and reading experiences for them.

You can also get a good understanding of how children are perceiving sound sequences in words, as well as their ability to link those sounds to let-ters, by examining their spelling. A child who consistently and accurately uses initial (or other) consonants in his or her writing—such as spelling *rain* as *r* or *dog* as *dg*—signals a readiness to learn specific word families or rimes.

A child who spells *rain* as *b* and *dog* as *x* may need instruction about onsets. A child who spells *rain* as *rane* might benefit from sorting words with *ain*, *ane*, and other long *a* patterns.

Additionally, you can determine your students' needs by looking at what they do when they don't instantly recognize a word in print. First, if children are stumbling over many words, the text is probably too difficult. Children need to be able to read most of the words (say 95%) of the text they work with. At this recognition rate, they can both read for meaning and enjoy reading. Their approach to the words they can't identify provides information for planning instruction. Do they guess randomly or focus on the pictures to the exclusion of the print? Do they look at initial letters? Do they look for patterns they recognize within words? Our job as teachers is to look at what our children know and plan appropriate activities to expand their word knowledge.

For children who are really struggling in first grade, there are a number of special programs available. The best-known is a one-to-one tutoring program titled Reading Recovery. This program was originally developed in New Zealand by Marie Clay (1979, 1992) and adapted for use in the United States by Gay Sue Pinnell (Pinnell, Fried, & Eustice, 1990). Although it has recently come under some criticism (Barnes, 1996/1997; Hiebert, 1994), if you have struggling first-graders you may want to look at it. A somewhat similar program, but less expensive because it uses small groups rather than individualized instruction, is titled Early Intervention Reading. This program was developed and successfully implemented by Barbara Taylor and her colleagues (Taylor, Short, Frye, & Shearer, 1992). Additionally, a recent study (Invernizzi, Juel, & Rosemary, 1996/1997) explores the use of a tutoring program in which community volunteers tutor first- and second-graders who need help in beginning reading skills.

If you find yourself teaching students beyond the first-grade level who still need to develop basic word-study skills, Elfrieda Hiebert (1996) has developed a program for third-grade children, and Taylor and her colleagues a program for second- and fourth-grade children (Taylor, Hansen, Swanson, & Watts, in press). Additionally, Hiebert and Taylor's *Getting Reading Right from the Start* (1994) describes a number of programs designed to help early readers who are struggling.

Although most children do not have reading skills when they enter school, we must recognize that some children do. As much as possible, we want to provide these children with books that will challenge and expand their knowledge. In other words, we will need a considerable range of reading levels in the books we stock in our classrooms. In a typical first- or second-grade classroom, we might need to stock some reading materials that extend to the upper grade levels.

"I've got a secret!" Anyone reading this sentence knows something hidden to many U.S. citizens. "Cracking the code" is tied to schooling, but also to privilege, class, culture, and language status. Although correlated with social indicators, failure in this rudimentary skill often means failure of the individual.

—*Robert Calfee*
Educational Psychologist

We also need to plan many activities to which all children can respond—regardless of their current reading level. In writing words, for example, some children may successfully spell only the features that we have taught (and after all, we can hold children accountable only for that), yet others may be able to go well beyond this and represent fuller spellings. Both groups, however, are being successful and should receive our praise, encouragement, and the next level of instruction to expand their knowledge.

CONCLUDING REMARKS

This chapter has emphasized the importance of word recognition and focused on how to help children learn to read and write words. We began by discussing why it is so important for children to learn to recognize words early on. Then we discussed the structure of spoken and written words. In the third section, we examined how the structure of both spoken and written English has influenced how reading has been taught. In the last part of the chapter, we described specific instructional techniques for teaching the emergent and early reader.

The topics in this chapter are particularly important to understand thoroughly because without the ability to read words, children will have difficulty with nearly everything else at school. Our goal is the development of critical literacy. Reading, writing, being read to, discussing what is read, and thinking about what is read are all crucial to attaining critical literacy; and word study must never replace these activities. However, without competence in word recognition, attaining critical literacy is extremely unlikely.

EXTENDING LEARNING

1. Observe a first-grade classroom, or better yet, several first-grade classrooms at different times during the year. What kind of word-study instruction do you see? What kinds of texts are the children reading? How are the children progressing?

2. Meet individually with several kindergarten and first-grade children, and have them spell some words for you. Here are some possibilities: *cat, run, jump, name, goat, van, arm, stripe, little, coat, rope, back, smash,* and *light*. What can you tell from the child's spelling about what he or she knows about words? What might you plan for word-study instruction to help the child grow?

3. Meet individually with several kindergarten or first-grade children, and ask if they have a book they would like to read to you. Notice what happens as each child reads. Does the child look at the words? What happens when the child forgets a word? What insights do you have about what the children know about words? What might you do to build on their current knowledge?

REFERENCES

Adams, M. J. (1990). *Beginning to read: Thinking and learning about print.* Cambridge, MA: MIT Press. This monumental review of the literature relevant to beginning reading instruction has had a huge influence on the field.

American Educator. (1995, Summer). Learning to read: Schooling's first mission [Special issue]. Washington, DC: American Federation of Teachers. This issue of a widely read magazine for teachers and school personnel focuses on how to teach children to read. It stresses the need for decoding instruction.

Barnes, B. L. (1996/1997). But teacher you went right on: A perspective on Reading Recovery. *The Reading Teacher, 50,* 284–292. A Reading Recovery teacher discusses some of her uneasy feelings about the program.

Bear, D., Invernizzi, M., Templeton, S., & Johnston, F. (1995). *Words their way: A developmental approach to phonics, spelling, and vocabulary instruction.* Columbus, OH: Merrill/Macmillan. This is an excellent source book for teachers on how to develop word recognition and spelling in children. It includes specific instructional activities and materials.

Bond, G. L., & Dykstra, R. (1967/1997). The cooperative research program in first-grade-reading instruction. *Reading Research Quarterly, 2(4),* 1–142. (Reprinted in *Reading Research Quarterly, 31.*) This is the most ambitious comparison of methods of beginning reading instruction ever attempted.

Carpenter, P. A., & Just, M. A. (1983). What your eyes do while your mind is reading. In K. Rayner (Ed.), *Eye movements in reading. Perceptual and language processes.* New York: Academic Press. The authors present a very graphic account of just what the mind does as we read.

Chall, J. S. (1967). *Learning to read: The great debate.* New York: McGraw-Hill. This is a classic examination and summary of research on the effectiveness of different instructional approaches to teaching children to read.

Clay, M. M. (1979). *The early detection of reading difficulties.* Portsmouth, NH: Heinemann. This is an early description of Clay's thinking and the Reading Recovery Program.

Clay, M. M. (1992). *Reading Recovery: A guidebook for teachers in training.* Portsmouth, NH: Heinemann. This book provides a recent description of Reading Recovery training.

Clymer, T. (1963/1996). The utility of phonic generalizations in the primary grades. *The Reading Teacher, 16,* 252–258/50, 182–187. If you ever wanted to know the utility of specific phonic generalizations, this is the article for you.

Fry, E. F. (1997). *Phonics patterns: Onset and rhyme word lists* (3rd ed.). Laguna Beach, CA: Laguna Beach Educational Books. Useful lists of common phonograms are given.

Goswami, U., & Bryant, P. (1992). Rhyme, analogy, and children's reading. In P. B. Gough, L. C. Ehri, & R. Treiman (Eds.), *Reading acquisition* (pp. 49–63). Hillsdale, NJ: Erlbaum. This study describes how children use analogies as they learn to read.

Goswami, U., & Mead, F. (1992). Onset and rime awareness and analogies in reading. *Reading Research Quarterly, 27,* 153–162. A research study explores the roles of onsets, phonograms, and analogies in developing word recognition.

Hiebert, E. H. (1994). Reading Recovery in the United States: What difference does it make to an age cohort? *Educational Researcher, 23*(9), 15–25. This article reviews research critically examining the effects of the Reading Recovery program.

Hiebert, E. H. (1996). Creating and sustaining a love of literature . . . and the ability to read it. In M. F. Graves, P. van den Broek, & B. M. Taylor (Eds.), *The first R: A right of all children.* New York: Teachers College Press. This article describes a program for helping struggling third-grade readers.

Hiebert, E. H., & Taylor, B. M. (1994). *Getting reading right from the start: Effective early literacy interventions.* Boston: Allyn & Bacon. This collection of articles describes a number of early intervention approaches.

Invernizzi, M., Juel, C., & Rosemary, C. A. (1996/1997). A community volunteer tutorial that works. *The Reading Teacher, 50,* 304–311. A successful ongoing volunteer tutoring program for first- and second-grade struggling readers is depicted.

Juel, C. (1994). *Learning to read and write in one elementary school.* New York: Springer-Verlag. This book describes the literacy development of a group of children as they go from first through fourth grades.

Juel, C., & Roper/Schneider, D. (1985). The influence of basal readers on first-grade reading. *Reading Research Quarterly, 18,* 306–327. This study examines the effects of two different reading series: one with a phonics emphasis and one without.

Lundberg, I. (1984, August). Learning to read. *School Research Newsletter.* Swedish National Board of Education. This issue reports on a longitudinal study of learning to read and the importance of phonemic awareness in that process.

McConkie, G. W., & Zola, D. (1981). Language constraints and the functional stimulus in reading. In A. M. Lesgold & C. A. Perfetti (Eds.), *Interactive processes in reading* (pp. 155–175). Hillsdale, NJ: Erlbaum. This article reviews what eye-movement studies tell us about the reading process.

Pearson, P. D. (1996). Reclaiming the center. In M. F. Graves, P. van den Broek, & B. M. Taylor (Eds.), *The first R: Every child's right to read* (pp. 259–274). New York: Teachers College Press. This article gives Pearson's perspective on the core principle of an effective reading program.

Pinnell, G. S., Fried, M. D., & Eustice, R. M. (1990). Reading Recovery: Learning how to make a difference. *The Reading Teacher, 43,* 282–295. A brief description of this widely used program for struggling early readers is presented here.

Stahl, S. A. (1992). Saying the "p" word: Nine guidelines for exemplary phonics instruction. *The Reading Teacher, 45,* 618–625. This is an excellent review for teachers who wish to improve their phonics instruction.

Stanovich, K. E. (1991a). Changing models of reading and reading acquisition. In L. Rieben & C. A. Perfetti (Eds.), *Learning to read.* (pp. 19–31). Hillsdale, NJ: Erlbaum. A distinguished psychologist reviews reading models.

Stanovich, K. E. (1991b). Word recognition: Changing perspectives. In R. Barr, M. L. Kamil, P. B. Mosenthal, & P. D. Pearson (Eds.), *Handbook of reading research* (Vol. 2, pp. 418–452). New York: Longman. This provides an extensive review of the literature on word recognition.

Stanovich, K. E. (1992). Speculations on the causes and consequences of individual differences in early reading acquisition. In P. B. Gough, L. C. Ehri, & R. Treiman (Eds.), *Reading acquisition* (pp. 307–342). Hillsdale, NJ: Erlbaum. This study offers some research-based explanations of why some children have particular difficulty learning to read.

Taylor, B. M., Hanson, B., Swanson, K., & Watts, S. (in press). Helping struggling readers in grades two and four: Linking small-group intervention with cross-age tutoring. *The Reading Teacher.* The authors describe a successful program in which older struggling readers help younger ones.

Taylor, B. M., Short, R. A., Frye, B. J., & Shearer, B. A. (1992). Classroom teachers prevent reading failure among low-achieving first-grade children. *The Reading Teacher, 45,* 592–597. This is a description of a successful program to help first-grade struggling readers.

Trachtenburg, P. (1990). Using children's literature to enhance phonics instruction. *The Reading Teacher, 43,* 648–654. This article provides a list of literature appropriate for the development of various letter–sound correspondences as well as guidelines for the use of literature in conjunction with phonics instruction.

Treiman, R. (1992). The role of intrasyllabic units in learning to read and spell. In P. B. Gough, L. C. Ehri, & R. Treiman (Eds.), *Reading acquisition* (pp. 65–106). Hillsdale, NJ: Erlbaum. This chapter gives a technical description of intersyllabic units.

Walcott, C. C., & McCracken, G. (1981). *Starting out.* New York: Lippincott. This book typifies phonics-oriented series of the early 1980s.

Wylie, R. E., & Durrell, D. D. (1970). Teaching vowels through phonograms. *Elementary English, 47,* 787–791. This article presents research on which phonograms are especially useful to teach and why.

CHILDREN'S LITERATURE

Bennett, J. (1985). *Teeny tiny.* New York: Putnam. A very small woman finds a very small bone and puts it away in her cupboard before she goes to bed. Illustrated. Also available in Spanish. 32 pages.

Cameron, A. (1994). *The cat sat on the mat.* Boston: Houghton Mifflin. This story teaches simple vocabulary by following the activities of a cat. 32 pages.

Dobeck, J. (1996). *Stop that!* Parsippany, NJ: Silver Burdett Ginn/Parsippany, NJ: Modern Curriculum Press. This predictable text repeats *ig* and *at* phonograms.

Grejniec, M. (1992). *What do you like?* New York: North-South Books. Children discover they can like the same things and still be different. 32 pages.

Hutchins, P. (1968). *Rosie's walk.* New York: Macmillan. A hen unwittingly leads a fox into one disaster after another before arriving safely home from her walk. 32 pages.

Martin, B. Jr. (1983). *Brown bear, brown bear, what do you see?.* New York: Holt. Different animals in different colors are depicted in very predictable sentence structure. 24 pages.

Robinson, F. (1996). *Who has a tail?* Parsippany, NJ: Silver Burdett Ginn/ Parsippany, NJ: Modern Curriculum Press. This predictable text repeats *ay, ai,* and *ae* patterns.

Seuss, Dr. (1957). *The cat in the hat.* New York: Random House. Two children sitting at home on a rainy day are visited by a cat who shows them some tricks and games. Audiotape available. 61 pages.

Tafuri, N. (1984). *Have you seen my duckling?* New York: Greenwillow. A mother duck leads her brood around the pond as she searches for one missing duckling. 32 pages.

chapter five

Vocabulary Development

At about the time of your first birthday, you probably spoke your first word. It is likely to have been a consonant sound followed by a vowel sound—something like ma, or perhaps a repetitive mama. You are likely to have followed the first utterance by an additional fifty or so words over the next few months. After that, your vocabulary grew impressively. In fact, you began school probably with an oral vocabulary of several thousand words. Then, after beginning school, you started acquiring a reading vocabulary, and soon both your reading vocabulary and your oral vocabulary grew impressively.

That growth continues for most of us throughout the elementary school years—and well beyond the elementary school years. To be sure, a large part of your vocabulary grew outside of school and would have grown whether or not you attended school. Nevertheless, your vocabulary certainly would not be what it is today if you had not gone to school and had teachers who both taught vocabulary and nurtured your interest in words.

You have the opportunity to have a similar, positive effect on the vocabularies of the students you teach, something certainly worthwhile. Teaching vocabulary can improve students' reading comprehension Teaching vocabulary can improve students' writing. Teaching vocabulary can improve students' speaking. A person's vocabulary strongly influences other people's judgments about ability, education, and overall competence. Is it any wonder that vocabulary instruction occupies a prominent place in schools?

THE VOCABULARY-LEARNING TASK

Estimates of vocabulary size vary considerably, depending primarily on what counts as a distinct word. Most people would agree that *talk, talks,* and *talked* should be counted as one word. But what about *business* and *busy?* And what about idioms such as *take someone under your wing* or proper words such as *Missouri* and *Germanic?* As Richard Anderson and William Nagy (1992) point out, decisions such as these have very large effects on estimates of vocabulary size. However—and this is the major point—regardless of such decisions, children come to school with very large vocabularies, and their vocabularies grow markedly throughout the school years and beyond. Based on the work of Jeremy Anglin (1993), Anderson and Nagy (1992), Nagy and Anderson (1984), and Thomas White and his colleagues (White, Graves, & Slater, 1990), we can make these very conservative generalizations: Most students enter school with relatively large oral vocabularies (perhaps 5,000 words) and quite small reading vocabularies (perhaps numbering only a few words). Ahead of them lies a very sizable task. The materials used by children in grades 3–9 contain about 90,000 words, and the average sixth-grade student has a vocabulary of something like 20,000 words that she can both read and understand. By the time they enter second grade, children are likely to have reading vocabularies ranging between 2,000 and 5,000 words, and their reading vocabularies are likely to grow by something like 3,000 to 4,000 words each year. Even these conservative estimates show that the vocabulary-learning task students face is huge.

Quite obviously, each year students learn many more words than we can teach directly. This represents a tremendous learning achievement, yet it is partially explained by the fact that students lack deep and rich meanings for many of the words they know. Instead, they often possess partial and incomplete meanings, which hinder full comprehension of reading materials that contain the words and students' confidence in using them in their speaking or writing. Isabel Beck and her colleagues (Beck, McKeown, & Omanson, 1987) have distinguished three levels of word knowledge—the *unknown, acquainted,* and *established* levels. A word at the unknown level is, as the name indicates, completely unfamiliar. The word *repel* is likely to be unknown to most third-graders. A word at the acquainted level is one whose basic meaning is recognized, but only after the student gives it some deliberate attention. The word *resident* would probably be understood by most fifth-graders, but would require a moment's thought. A word at the established level is easily, rapidly, and automatically recognized. For most second-graders, the word *house* would be at the established level.

Of course, students do not need to know *all* the words they encounter in reading at the established level. They do, however, need to know most of the words they encounter at the established level because, as we noted in

Although a considerable amount of vocabulary learning is associated with primary language in the early years, the acquisition of most of the vocabulary characteristic of an educated adult occurs during the years of schooling, and in fact one of the primary tasks of the school, as far as language learning is concerned, is to teach vocabulary.

—John Carroll
Psychologist

Chapter 1, words that are not recognized automatically will thwart the process of comprehending text. Moreover, as we just mentioned, unless words are understood at the established level, students are not likely to use them in speaking and writing.

A comprehensive vocabulary program must reflect these facts about children's word knowledge and how it grows, and the one we describe here does so. The program has four major thrusts. First, it emphasizes the importance of wide reading because students learn much of their vocabulary from reading. Second, it includes instruction on individual words because such instruction can assist students in learning some words, improve comprehension of selections from which the words are taken, and show students the value you place in words. Third, it provides instruction in learning words independently because students must learn much of their vocabulary on their own. Finally, it promotes activities leading to word consciousness because only if students are interested in words, value them, and find them intriguing are they likely to develop full and rich vocabularies.

THE IMPORTANCE OF WIDE READING

By wide reading we mean extensive reading—reading a lot in a variety of materials. If you consider that students learn to read something like 3,000 to 4,000 words each year, it quickly becomes clear that most of the words students learn are not taught directly. With a 180-day school year, teaching 3,000 to 4,000 words would require teaching approximately 20 words each and every school day. Obviously, this does not happen. Instead, as we have already noted and as Richard Anderson (1996) has explained in some detail, students learn many words from their own reading. Thus, if you can substantially increase the amount of reading students do, you can markedly increase their vocabularies. In fact, Linda Fielding and her colleagues (Fielding, Wilson, & Anderson, 1986) found that the amount of time children spend reading books is among the best predictors of their vocabulary size. Moreover, wide reading will foster automaticity and provide knowledge about "sentence structure, text structure, literary forms, and topics ranging from the Bible to current events" (Anderson, Hiebert, Scott, & Wilkinson, 1985, p. 77). Thus, wide reading is both tremendously important and powerful for vocabulary development and for reaching a number of other goals.

Unfortunately, many students do very little reading. For example, Fielding and her colleagues found that on an average day, fifth-graders spent only about 10 minutes of their out-of-school time reading books. Clearly, children need to be encouraged to do more reading. Here, we offer several suggestions.

The importance of vocabulary is demonstrated daily in schools and out. In the classroom, the achieving students possess the most adequate vocabularies. . . . After schooling has ended, adequacy of vocabulary is almost equally essential for achievement in vocations and society.

—*Walter Petty, Curtis Herold, and Earline Stoll
Teacher Educators*

As a starting point, we encourage you to learn about as many interesting and engaging books for your students as you possibly can. *Book Links*, a bimonthly magazine from the American Library Association, features annotated bibliographies, essays, reviews, and recommendations for using literature with children from preschool through eighth grade. Sources such as *The Reading Teacher*'s annual "Children's Choices" and "Teachers' Choices," *Social Education*'s "Notable Trade Books in the Field of Social Studies," *Children and Science*'s "Outstanding Science Trade Books for Children," and compilations such as *More Kids' Favorite Books* (International Reading Association, 1995) offer a way of doing this. Additionally, *The Reading Teacher, Language Arts*, and state reading and English journals frequently have articles on children's literature, and children's literature is an increasingly popular topic at reading and English education conferences.

As we noted in Chapter 2 regarding a literate environment, we suggest having a host of books readily available in your classroom and making the classroom a place where books are regularly discussed and exchanged. Of course, the books available should be diverse, both in the cultures they reflect and in their reading levels. For students experiencing difficulty in learning to read and for second-language learners, wide reading is especially critical for building both word knowledge and world knowledge. Walter Elley (1996), for example, has conducted a number of studies showing that *book floods*—deliberate attempts to immerse students in appealing books—produce large benefits for students learning English as a second language. Thus, it is particu-

> This book [*The Read-Aloud Handbook*] is about more than reading aloud. It's about time that parents, teachers, and children spend together in a loving, sharing way.
>
> —The *Washington Post*

larly important to have interesting and readable books available for these students. Sustained silent reading—extended time periods during which students read books of their own choosing (McCracken, 1971)—should be a frequent activity. Add to this effort frequently reading to students, modeling your enthusiasm for reading, getting parents involved in securing good reading materials, reading to their children, and generally promoting reading at home. Jim Trelease's *The Read Aloud Handbook* (1995) provides a host of insights about reading aloud and a rich bibliography of materials to be read, and the book is equally valuable to parents and to teachers.

Taken together, approaches such as these and those you develop out of your classroom experience will indeed promote wide reading, and wide reading will in turn promote vocabulary development.

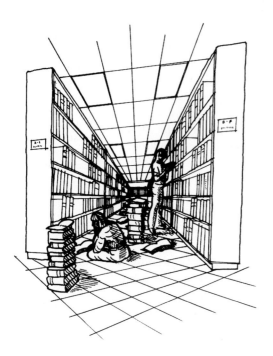

Reflection AND *Application*

1. Based on the growth rates we suggest, give some estimates of the size of students' reading vocabularies at the end of grades 2, 3, 4, 5, and 6. Note that because we give a range for vocabulary size at the end of first grade and a range of growth rates, a range of answers will be correct.

2. Identify one word that is likely to be at the unknown level, one at the acquainted level, and one at the established level for second-graders; then think of one word that is likely to be at each of these levels for fifth-graders.

3. Suppose that two concerned parents come to you and say that they really want to help their daughter build her reading vocabulary but don't know just how to do that. Assuming that you do not want to suggest they do direct teaching of words, what might you suggest they do to help their daughter build her vocabulary?

TEACHING INDIVIDUAL WORDS

Here, we first discuss the various word-learning tasks students face and ways of identifying words to teach. Then we consider teaching procedures for each of these word-learning tasks.

Word-Learning Tasks

All word-learning tasks are not the same. They differ depending on matters such as how much students already know about the words to be taught, how well you want them to learn the words, and what you want them to be able to do with the words afterward. Here, we consider four tasks students face in learning words. Note that the type of learning required and the difficulty of the learning differ from task to task.

Learning to Read Known Words

Learning to read words that are already in their oral vocabularies is the major word-learning task of beginning readers. Words such as *surprise, stretch*, and *amaze* are ones that students might be taught to read during their first three years of school. By third or fourth grade, good readers will have learned to read virtually all the words in their oral vocabularies. However, this task will remain incomplete for many less-able readers and for some second-language learners.

Learning New Words That Represent Known Concepts

A second word-learning task students face is learning to read words that are in neither their oral nor their reading vocabularies but for which they have an available concept. For example, the word *pant* would be unknown to a number of third-graders, but almost all students have seen dogs panting and know what it is like to be out of breath. All students continue to learn words of this sort throughout their years in school, and this is one of the major word-learning tasks for intermediate-grade students. It is also a major learning task for second-language learners, who of course have a great number of concepts for which they do not have English words.

Learning New Words That Represent New Concepts

Another word-learning task students face, and a very demanding one, is learning to read words that are in neither their oral nor their reading vocabulary and for which they do not have an available concept. Learning the full meanings of words such as *equation, impeach*, and *mammal* is likely to require most elementary students to develop new concepts. All students continue to learn words of this sort throughout their years in school and beyond. Once again, learning new concepts will be particularly important for second-language learners. Also, students whose backgrounds differ from that of the majority culture will have internalized a set of concepts that is at least somewhat different than the set internalized by students in the majority culture. Thus, words that represent known concepts for some groups of students will represent unknown concepts for other groups.

Clarifying and Enriching the Meanings of Known Words

The last word-learning task we consider here is that of clarifying and enriching the meanings of already known words. The meanings students originally attach to words are often imprecise and become fully specified only over time (Carey, 1978). For example, students initially might not recognize any difference between *brief* and *concise*, what distinguishes *cabin* from *shed*, or that the term *virtuoso* is most frequently applied to musicians. Although students will expand and enrich the meanings of the words they know as they repeatedly meet them in new and slightly different contexts, direct approaches to teaching meanings are definitely warranted.

Identifying and Selecting Vocabulary to Teach

Once you have considered the levels of word knowledge that you want your students to achieve and the word-learning tasks students face, you still need to select specific words to teach. In this section of the chapter, we recommend a two-step process in which you first identify words likely to be unknown to your students and then follow several criteria to select the words. Later in the chapter we will suggest an approach that students can use in selecting words to learn on their own.

Identifying Unknown Words

The most useful source of information about what words students know is the students themselves. You can identify words in upcoming selections that you think will be difficult for students and build multiple-choice or matching tests to confirm your judgment. Of course, constructing such tests is time consuming and not necessary for every selection. However, several experiences of identifying words that you think will be difficult and then checking students' performance against your expectations will sharpen your general perceptions of which words are and are not likely to cause problems for your students.

In addition to testing students on potentially difficult words using these traditional types of tests, you can simply ask students which words they know. An easy way to do this is to list words on the board, point to them one by one, and have students raise their hands if they do not know a word. This approach is quick, easy, and risk-free for students; it also gives students some responsibility for their word learning. Moreover, research (White, Slater, & Graves, 1989) indicates that students can be quite accurate in identifying words that they do and do not know.

Selecting Words to Teach

Once potentially difficult vocabulary is identified, criteria for identifying the most important words to teach need to be established. The answers to the four questions listed here should be helpful:

1. *Is understanding the word important to understanding the selection in which it appears?* If the answer is no, then other words are probably more important to teach.
2. *Are students able to use context or structural analysis skills to discover the word's meaning?* If they can use these skills, then they should be

An effective way to identify potentially difficult words is to list them on the board, point to them one by one, and have students raise their hands if they don't know a word.

allowed to practice them. Doing so will both help them consolidate these skills and reduce the number of words you need to teach.

3. *Can working with this word be useful in furthering students' context, structural analysis, or dictionary skills?* If the answer is yes, then your working with the word can serve two purposes. It can aid students in learning the word, and it can help them acquire a strategy they can use in learning other words. You might, for example, decide to teach the word *regenerate* because students needed to master the prefix *re-*.

4. *How useful is this word outside of the current reading selection?* The more frequently a word appears in material students read, the more important it is for them to know the word. Additionally, the more frequently a word is used, the greater the chances that students will retain the word once you teach it.

These four questions do not function independently. In fact, the answer to one question may suggest that a word should be taught, whereas the answer to another suggests that it should not. In such cases, you will need to use your best judgment about which words to teach.

Methods of Teaching Individual Words

How might you go about providing instruction for each of the four word-learning tasks described? As you will see, the instruction needed for some word-learning tasks is much more complex than that for others. Note too that some of these instructional methods will promote deeper levels of word knowledge than others.

Learning to Read Known Words

In learning to read known words, the basic task for the student is to associate what is unknown, the written word, with what is already known, the spoken word. To establish the association between the written and spoken forms of a word, the student needs to see the word at the same time that it is pronounced; once this association is established, it needs to be rehearsed and strengthened so that the relationship becomes automatic. We have listed these steps to emphasize just how straightforward the process is:

1. Look at the word.
2. Listen to the word while looking at it.
3. Rehearse that association again and again.

Each of these three steps can be accomplished in a number of ways. Students can see the word on the board, on a computer screen, or in a book that they are reading or that you are reading to them. They can hear the word when you say it, when another student says it, or when a voice simulator on a computer says it. And they can rehearse the association by seeing the word and pronouncing it a number of times, writing it, and playing games that require them to recognize printed versions of it. However, wide reading in materials that contain many repetitions of the words and that are enjoyable and easily read is by far the best way to empower students to automatically and effortlessly recognize these words whenever they see them.

Finally, one very important point to remember when teaching these words is that there is no need to teach their meanings. By definition, these are words students already know and understand when they hear them; they simply cannot read them. Time spent "teaching" students the meaning of words they already know is time wasted.

Learning New Words That Represent Known Concepts

We have found three particularly-useful approaches for teaching students new words that represent known concepts. In the following section we describe them. As you will see, each requires different amounts of the teacher's

> The creation of effective vocabulary instruction calls for careful crafting of experiences in consideration of specific learning goals, the words being taught, and the characteristics of the learners.
>
> —Isabel Beck,
> Margaret McKeown,
> and Richard Omanson
> Educational Researchers

time, class time, and the students' time and effort; and they are likely to yield different results. Each, however, is very appropriate for introducing a small number of potentially challenging words from a selection the class is about to read.

IN THE CLASSROOM
Three Ways to Introduce New Words Representing Known Concepts

Context Plus Use of the Dictionary

This requires little teacher preparation time, but a fair amount of students' time.

Purpose: To provide students with a basic understanding of a word's meaning and give them practice in using the dictionary.

Procedure:

- In a handout, on a computer file, or on the chalkboard, give students a word in context. For example, for the word *excel* you could use this sentence: *To get into the Olympics, a person must really excel at an Olympic sport.*

- Have students read the word and the context-rich sentence and then look up the meaning of the word in a dictionary.

Definition Plus Rich Context

This requires a fair amount of teacher preparation time, but very little class time.

Purpose: To provide students with a basic understanding of a word's meaning and give them practice in reading dictionary entries.

Procedure:

- Provide students with both a definition of a word and a rich context. For example,

    vital (VI tle)— extremely important, perhaps even necessary

    In areas where water is very scarce, it is *vital* that everyone takes extra care to ensure that no water is wasted.

- Have students read the definition and context-rich sentence.

Context-Relationship Procedure

This approach (developed by Graves & Slater, 1996) requires quite a bit of teacher preparation. However, presenting words in this way takes only about a minute per word, and we have repeatedly found that students remember quite rich meanings for words taught in this fashion.

Purpose: To provide students with both a basic understanding of a word's meaning and practice in using context to determine a word's meaning.

Procedure: Create a brief paragraph that uses the target word three or four times. Then, follow the paragraph with a multiple-choice item that checks students' understanding of the word. A sample paragraph and multiple-choice item and the steps for presenting each word are shown here:

> *conveying*
>
> The luncheon speaker was successful in *conveying* his main ideas to the audience. They all understood what he said, and most agreed with him. *Conveying* has a more specific meaning than *talking*. *Conveying* indicates that a person is getting his or her ideas across accurately.
>
> *Conveying* means
>
> _____ A. putting parts together.
> _____ B. communicating a message.
> _____ C. hiding important information.

1. Explain the purpose of the procedure.
2. Pronounce the word to be taught.
3. Read the paragraph in which the word appears.
4. Read the possible definitions, and ask students to choose the best one.
5. Pause to give students time to check a definition, give them the correct answer, and answer any questions students have.
6. Read the word and its definition a final time.

Learning New Words That Represent New Concepts

As we have noted, learning new words that represent new concepts is often a challenging task. The following approach based on a method developed by Dorothy Frayer (Frayer, Frederick, & Klausmeier, 1969), illustrates one very effective method to help students gain knowledge of new words that represent new concepts. Although the example is for second- graders, the procedure is appropriate for all grade levels.

IN THE CLASSROOM
Introducing New Words That Represent New Concepts

Purpose: To introduce second-grade students to the new word *globe* and the concept of globe.

Procedure:

- Define the new concept, giving its specific attributes. For example, *A globe is a spherical (ball-like) representation of a planet.* When possible, show a model or a picture illustrating the concept.

- Distinguish between the new concept and similar but different concepts with which it might be confused. It may be appropriate to identify accidental attributes that might falsely be considered definitive attributes of the new concept. For example, *A globe is different from a map because a map is flat. A globe is different from a contour map, a map in which mountains and other high points are raised above the general level of the map, because a contour map is not spherical.*

- Give examples of the concept, and explain what makes them good examples: *The most common globe is a globe of the earth. Globes of the earth are spherical (display a sphere or spheres such as a ball or an orange) and come in various sizes and colors. A much less common globe is a globe of another planet. A museum might have a spherical representation of Saturn.*

- Give nonexamples of the concept, such as a map of California or a map of how to get to a friend's house, and explain why they are not examples of the concept at hand.

- Present students with examples and nonexamples of the concept, and ask them to distinguish between the two. You might include an aerial photograph of New York (nonexample), a red sphere representing Mars (example), a walking map of St. Louis (nonexample), and a ball-shaped model of the moon (example).

- Have students present examples and nonexamples of the concept, and explain what makes them examples or nonexamples. Give them feedback on their examples and explanations.

Teaching concepts using the Frayer method will take a good deal of your time and a good deal of students' time. The method also will require considerable thought from both you and your students. However, for important concepts, the fruits of the labor will be well worth the effort, for with this method students can gain a new idea, another lens through which they can interpret the world. The two methods discussed in the next section—semantic mapping and semantic feature analysis—can also be used for teaching new concepts. Although they are generally not as powerful as the Frayer method and require that learners have some background information about the new concepts, they often take considerably less time than the Frayer method.

Clarifying and Enriching the Meanings of Known Words

People with well-developed vocabulary possess rich, interconnecting networks of concepts.

—*Jana Mason, Patricia Herman, and Kathryn Au*
Teacher Educators

Semantic mapping and semantic feature analysis, which are illustrated in the next section, are two methods of clarifying and enriching the meanings of known words. These methods, both developed by Dale Johnson (Heimlich & Pittelman, 1986; Johnson & Pearson, 1984; Pittelman, Heimlich, Berglund, & French, 1991), are also useful in preteaching unknown words to improve students' comprehension of a selection, one of the most important purposes of vocabulary instruction. They work particularly well because they focus not only on the words being taught but also on related words and on the part the words play in the selection. As we just mentioned, these two methods can also be used to teach *new* concepts—if the concepts are not too difficult and if students already have at least some information related to them.

IN THE CLASSROOM
Semantic Mapping and Semantic Feature Analysis

Semantic Mapping

Sometimes called semantic webbing, semantic mapping makes use of a graphic organizer that looks something like a spider web. Lines connect a central concept to a variety of related ideas and events. Shown here is a semantic map for the word *tenement*. You and your students might create a map such as this before or after reading a social studies chapter on urban housing.

Purpose: To enrich and clarify students' existing knowledge of a concept by having them identify categories of ideas and events that relate to that concept.

Procedure:

- Put a word representing a central concept, such as *tenement*, on the chalkboard.
- Have students form groups, brainstorming as many words as they can think of related to the central concept.
- Write students' words on the chalkboard, grouped in broad categories.
- Have students name the categories and perhaps suggest additional ones.
- Discuss with students the central concept, the other words, the categories, and their inter-relationships.

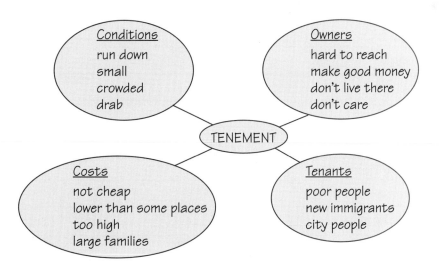

Semantic Feature Analysis

This procedure employs a grid, such as the sample grid on vehicles shown here, which is modeled on one provided by Pittelman and her colleagues (Pittelman, et al., 1991).

Purpose: To enrich and clarify students' existing knowledge of a concept by having them identify words that belong to a category, list the features of the words they have identified, and compare and contrast them using a grid.

Procedure:

• Select a category, for example, *vehicles.*

• With students' help, list words that fall into this category.

• With students' help, list the features of the items you have identified. For example, some of the features of vehicles might be two wheels, four wheels, motor, gasoline, and so on.

• Determine which items possess and do not possess each feature. Use plus and minus signs to indicate this. Discuss these distinctions with students.

• Add more words and features. Work with students to extend the grid, particularly when making distinctions that require adding features. For example, a feature such as "operates on water" would be needed to distinguish rowboats from iceboats.

• Have students complete the grid. They can do this independently, in groups, or with your help.

VEHICLES	two wheels	four wheels	more than four wheels	motor	diesel fuel	gasoline
car	–	+	–	+	–	+
bicycle	+	–	–	–	–	–
motorcycle	+	–	–	+	–	+
truck	–	+	+	+	+	–
train	–	–	+	+	+	–
skateboard	–	+	–	–	–	–
sailboat	–	–	–	–	–	–
iceboat	–	–	–	–	–	–

- Examine and discuss the completed grid. This discussion is often the most interesting and revealing activity. For example, you would want to acknowledge that a few cars do use diesel and many small trucks use gasoline.

As with many instructional activities, follow the gradual release of responsibility model in working with semantic feature analysis. Initially, you may need to do much of the work. Later, students can be given grids with some terms and some attributes and asked to add to both the list of related words and the list of attributes and then to fill in the pluses and minuses. Still later, after becoming proficient in working with partially completed grids that you supply, students can create grids for sets of related words that they themselves suggest.

Another level of challenge and interest can be added by including the designator S, meaning "sometimes," in addition to the pluses and minuses. For example, S might be used in the vehicle grid in the "car" row under the headings "diesel fuel" and "gasoline," since some cars do use diesel fuel. In all cases—whether or not S is used—there should be a good deal of discussion, for the essence of semantic feature analysis lies in the discussion.

In this part of the chapter, we have listed seven approaches to teaching individual words. Although these are certainly enough approaches to begin your work in teaching individual words, you may eventually want to add others. One source of additional approaches that we particularly recommend is William Nagy's *Teaching Vocabulary to Improve Reading Comprehension* (1988).

Reflection and Application

4. Consider each of the four word-learning tasks we have listed, and explain how each of them requires a different sort of learning. It would be useful to work with a classmate in doing this, but after you have discussed your response, write it. Writing your response will force you to really think it through, and it will give you a response on paper that you can examine and evaluate.

5. Identify a group of students. Select one word that is likely to be in their oral vocabularies but that they probably don't recognize in print, one that is a new label for a known concept, one that represents a new concept, and one that they probably know but for which you would like to give them a fuller understanding. Choose an instructional procedure described in the chapter for teaching each word, create the materials you would need, and then explain how you would go about teaching each of them. If you have a few classmates available who could serve as "students," role-playing the teaching rather than explaining how you would do it would be an excellent idea.

TEACHING WORD-LEARNING STRATEGIES

As we noted at the beginning of the chapter, students learn something like 3,000–4,000 words each year, many more than could be directly taught. Thus, even when instruction in individual words is as frequent and rich as possible, students still need to learn much of their vocabulary independently. In this section of the chapter, we consider three strategies that students need to become independent word learners: using context, using word parts, and using the dictionary.

Using Context Cues

Most vocabulary is learned from context. During the course of one's lifespan, one is exposed to innumerable words through seemingly countless sources— textbooks, lectures, newspapers, magazines, friends, enemies, parents, movies, and so on. Even if one learned only a small proportion of the words thus encountered in the contexts in which they are presented, one could plausibly develop a vocabulary of tens of thousands of words.

—*Robert Sternberg*
Psychologist

It is almost certainly the case that we learn most of the words we know from meeting them in context (Anderson & Nagy, 1992; Sternberg, 1987). No other explanation can account for students' learning 3,000–4,000 words each year. At the same time, gleaning a word's meaning from most contexts is not an easy task. However, wide reading exposes students to a huge number of unknown words; and, given a typical amount of reading over a year's time, students with average skills in learning words from context might acquire over 1,000 words from meeting them in the context of their reading. Additionally, students learn a large number of words from oral contexts—conversations, lectures, films, and even television. Of course, students who have better-than-average skills in learning words from context will acquire more words from context than students with only average skills.

In this section of the chapter, we discuss teaching students to use context cues—the words, phrases, and sentences that surround an unknown word and provide clues to its meaning—to learn word meanings. The instruction we suggest includes two steps: first, a well-planned unit on context cues; second, ongoing reminders of the value of using context to learn word meanings, encouragement to use context, and opportunities for students to get feedback on their efforts.

Step 1: An Introductory Unit on Using Context Cues

We would begin work on context with a three- or four-day unit. This concentrated effort seems necessary to get students off to a solid start. As with most strategy instruction, begin by telling students what you are going to be working on, why the strategy is important, and when and where they should use it. Also, if students are likely to have had previous experience working with context, acknowledge that. Your introduction might look something like the following example, although you would of course modify what you say to fit your class and your style of talking with children:

> Today, we're going to begin working with using context cues to figure out the meanings of words we don't know or aren't sure of. Context cues are cues and hints that the words and sentences surrounding an unknown word give us about the meaning of the unknown word.
>
> Learning to use context cues is important because much of the time when we read we will come upon at least some words we don't know. And learning words we don't know is important because knowing the words in something we're reading helps us understand it. Also, learning more words and using them helps us speak and write clearly.

At this time, put several sentences containing unknown words or nonsense words and some fairly rich context on the board or the overhead projector, and talk through the cues that context provides to the words' meanings. It is important to include some nonsense words so you can be certain students deal with at least some unfamiliar words.

> *The buttery and salty odor of the* **zeemee** *filled the theater lobby, and Sara's mouth began to water.*

> Let's see. *Zeemee* has an odor, it smells buttery and salty, you get it in a theater, and smelling it makes Sara's mouth water. That's easy. It's popcorn.

> *Rusty* **scowled** *angrily at Mary and then stamped out of the room. "I'm never coming back!" he shouted as he left.*

> Hmm. *Scowled* is something Rusty did at Mary. He was angry, and he did this *scowling* just before he stamped out of the room, and then he shouted at Mary. I'm not sure what *scowled* means, but it must have something to do with expressing anger. Maybe it means the same thing as shouted, or maybe it means *sticking out your tongue,* or maybe it means *giving a mean look.* I'm still not sure what *scowled* means, but I think it's related to anger, that it's a way of showing anger.

After discussing several examples, continue your introductory remarks.

Using context cues to figure out the meanings of unknown words is something you'll do often. In fact, if you're reading along and come across an unknown word, and if that word seems important to understanding what you're reading, checking the context to see if it will give you a clue to the word's meaning is usually the first thing to do.

Now I know that some of you have worked with context cues before, and that's good. Why don't you tell me some of the things you've learned about context cues, and then we'll go on to see if there isn't more to know that would be useful in figuring out unknown words.

At this point, let students volunteer what they know about context cues, being as accepting as you can with their answers but at the same time clearing up misconceptions. The most likely misconceptions are that context always yields a word's meaning, that it yields exact meanings, and that the important thing to know about context cues is the names of the various cues.

Following this discussion, say something positive about students' existing knowledge of context cues, but then say that there is more to be learned, that you are going to be taking a slightly different approach with context cues, and that learning to use context cues, like learning to play a musical instrument, requires repeated practice.

Next, introduce the basic facts students need to know about context cues. These could be initially presented on an overhead projector or the board, but they should also be put on a chart to be displayed and referred to occasionally over a period of a few weeks.

- Most words are learned from context. Therefore, it is really important to learn to use context well.
- Sometimes context clearly tells a word's meaning. More often, however, it only hints at a word's meaning.
- Context cues include words, phrases, and sentences that tell something about the unknown word.
- Cues can occur both before the unknown word and after it, and often more than one cue relates to a particular unknown word.
- The most useful cues are usually close to the unknown word, generally in the same sentence. However, sometimes cues occur in other sentences and even other paragraphs.

Don't have students memorize these points, but do discuss them, clear up any confusion there seems to be, and give examples where appropriate. Also, tell students that eventually you do want them to learn these facts about context, and that you will bring them up from time to time in discussions about how context provides cues to unknown words they come across. This concludes the first day of the context unit.

On the following day, present students with the procedure for using context shown in the following list. Again, outline the procedure on an overhead projector or the board, and also put the steps on a chart for easy reference. Do ask students to memorize the steps of the procedure at this time, and call on several students to state the steps before going on with the lesson.

- Identify the unknown word.
- List the words or phrases that tell something about its meaning.
- Start at the beginning of the sentence containing the unknown word, and list all the cues in that sentence. Then, if you think you need more cues, look at other sentences before and after the one containing the word.
- Guess the unknown word's meaning, based on what you have found in the context.

Now comes a crucial part of the instruction—modeling the procedure and then gradually transferring the task to students, so that in time students can use the procedure independently. This gradual release of responsibility was discussed in Chapter 2; as noted there, it is broadly applicable to teaching strategies. In modeling the procedure, you are attempting to reveal to students the mental processes that you employ when using context to figure out word meanings. Prompted by your modeling, students will begin to use similar processing.

Your first attempt at modeling should resemble your treatment of the examples you used to introduce the concept of context cues. However, slow down a bit here to emphasize the steps. Begin by putting a sentence containing an unknown word and some rich context on the board. Then, model the procedure, asking students to follow along and record the cues on paper as you put them on the board.

> *As Byron stood in the valley, the snow began falling thickly, quickly covering the ground and **obliterating** the view of the mountain that he had seen clearly only moments before.*

First, I find the word I don't know. It's *obliterating*.

Second, I look for cues to its meaning in the sentence. It's snow that does the *obliterating*. And it's thickly falling snow. And it's the view of the mountains that got *obliterated*. And Byron could see the mountain clearly before the snow began.

Once the cues have been listed, synthesize them to get the unknown word's meaning.

Third, I try to add it all up and get a meaning for *obliterating*.

Let's see. Thickly falling snow *obliterates* the view that Byron could see before. *Obliterating* must mean something like *covering up*.

One good word is worth a thousand pictures.

—*Eric Sevareid*
Journalist

203

And, fourth, I'll try my meaning in the sentence to see how it works. "As Byron stood in the valley, the snow began falling thickly, quickly covering the ground and *covering up* the view of the mountain that he had seen clearly only moments before." That makes sense, so for now at least I'll assume that *obliterating* means "covering up."

In order to transfer responsibility for this task to students so that they internalize the procedure and repeat its steps independently, use it with additional sentences, gradually letting students do more and more of the task. With the next sentence, for example, volunteer some cues and let students supply others. Then let students locate some of the cues and try to put the cues together to arrive at a meaning for the unknown word. Next, still working at the board, have students volunteer all of the cues and attempt to add them up to get a meaning.

Finally, give students some sentences as seatwork or homework. At first, have students work in pairs; later, they can work independently. In both cases, review the work as a group activity, praising students when their responses are correct, trying to figure out what went wrong and how it can be avoided in the future when their responses are incorrect, and reteaching as necessary.

The process of modeling, getting responses from student volunteers as you work at the board, having students practice using context in pairs and independently, and discussing their work and reteaching as necessary should continue over several days. Conclude this concentrated instruction once you think students have internalized the basic procedure, typically in three or four days.

Step 2: Further Work with Context

After the introductory unit, most work with context should take place when students need to figure out unknown words in their reading. As we noted before, further work should include reminders of the value of using context to learn word meanings, encouragement to use context, and opportunities for students to use context and get feedback on their work. Of course, you might later teach another unit on context, either as a review or as an extension activity working with longer and more difficult contexts. Whether or not you teach another extended unit on context, further work with context is vital. Only your nurturing of students' proficiency with context, periodic incidental instruction in context, and some additional instruction can ensure that students maintain and extend their ability to use context.

Third-grade teacher Gloria Fleming provides one example of how she gives her class practice in using context:

I am always on the lookout for specific books that offer particularly rich opportunities to practice certain reading skills and strategies. Arthur Dorros's *Abuela* provides an excellent opportunity for my students to hone their skills in gleaning word meanings from context. Since I have a number of students who speak Spanish as their first language, many of whom are still in the process of learning English, it is a particularly good choice. This very colorfully illustrated book tells the fanciful story of Rosalba and her grandmother, her *abuela,* as they fly over Manhattan, turning somersaults in the air, gliding low over the water to race sailboats, or circling around the Statue of Liberty.

The basic English text is spiced with Spanish phrases, which are then defined in context, as in the following excerpt:

> Today we're going to the park.
> *"El parque es lindo,"* says Abuela.
> I know what she means.
> I think the park is beautiful.

This happy combination of English and Spanish provides a triple bonus. It gives all my students a very pleasant opportunity to practice their use of context. It gives English-speaking students an opportunity to learn some Spanish. And it gives Spanish-speaking students some extra support and an opportunity to shine by reading and translating the Spanish phrases.

—Gloria Fleming, Third-Grade Teacher

Using Word Parts

Frequently, context is not the only aid that students can call on when they encounter an unknown word. Often, they can also use structural analysis. Here, we discuss teaching students to use prefixes and Greek and Latin roots in learning word meanings. We do not suggest teaching students to use suffixes to learn word meanings because most suffixes have grammatical meanings tacitly understood by students or abstract meanings that are very difficult to teach.

As Anglin's (1993) study of elementary students' vocabularies indicates, learning to use word parts in dealing with word meanings can be extremely valuable to students. In fact, as both Anglin and Nagy and his colleagues (Nagy, Winsor, Osborn, & O'Flahavan, 1994) point out, about half of the "new words" that students meet in their reading are related to familiar words and can be understood if students see these relationships. In addition to being useful in learning word meanings, word parts can help students remember meanings and spellings.

The instruction we suggest for teaching students to use word parts includes three steps. First, you identify the specific word parts to teach. Second, you provide an introductory session or sessions on using word parts to learn

Attention must be given to affixes, context clues, awareness of words and their meanings, and motivation to learn them. But any attention to increase incidental learning substantially must include an increase in the opportunity to learn new words, and this will occur primarily through regular, sustained reading.

—William Nagy
and Patricia Herman
Vocabulary Researchers

word meanings. Third, over time, you repeatedly remind students of the value of using word parts, review how to use them, give them opportunities to use them and get feedback on their efforts, and teach additional word parts.

Step 1: Identifying Word Parts to Teach

It is useful to divide meaningful word parts into two groups: (1) frequently occurring prefixes and (2) less-common Greek and Latin roots and prefixes. English includes a small number of prefixes particularly worth teaching because of their extremely frequent occurrence. Figure 5.1, based on the work of White and his colleagues (White, Sowell, & Yanagihara, 1989), shows the most frequently occurring prefixes and the number of words in written school English that contain each. These prefixes are used in over 2,500 different words, and the four most common prefixes—what White and his colleagues call "the big four"—account for about 65% of these words.

These particular prefixes are the meaningful word parts students should learn first, and one very reasonable approach is to teach the list systematically over a year or two, beginning with most frequently occurring prefixes and working toward the less-common ones. Because prefixes become common in students' reading material only at about grade 4, that's when prefix instruction should generally begin. Other attributes that make prefixes good choices for instruction are the fact that most have a clear meaning, most are attached to the root in a fairly straightforward way, they tend to be

Prefix	Number of Words with the Prefix
un-	782
re-	401
in-, im-, ir-, il- (not)	313
dis-	216
en-, em-	132
non-	126
in-, im- (in or into)	105
over- (too much)	98
mis-	83
sub-	80
pre-	79
inter-	77
fore-	76
de-	71
trans-	47
TOTAL	2,686

FIGURE 5.1 *Frequently Occurring Prefixes*

consistently spelled, and they occur at the beginning of words. All of these factors make them relatively easy for students to recognize and learn.

The other group of meaningful word parts—less-common Greek and Latin prefixes and roots such as *tele-* and *spectare*—represent a very different situation. Since there are a great many of these relatively infrequently occurring elements, there is no convenient brief list of them to teach. Additionally, many of them—particularly the roots—are variously spelled, and the relationships between the original Greek or Latin meanings and their meanings in English words are not always clear. For all of these reasons, less-common elements should generally be taught only after students have gained facility with most of the frequently occurring prefixes and should be selected from the material students are reading. Choose those that are likely to occur again in their texts. The Greek prefix *tele-*, for example, might be used several times in a chapter on communications, and it might also come up in related supplementary reading. It would therefore make good sense to teach it as students are reading the chapter.

Step 2: An Introductory Session on Meaningful Word Parts

As with instruction in using context cues and most strategy instruction, begin by explaining to students what they will be working on, why the strategy is important, and when and where they should use it. Here, we describe introductory work with frequently occurring prefixes. You could slightly modify the instruction for teaching other meaningful word parts.

We have found the following procedure, based on the work of Judith Irvin (1990) to be very effective:

1. Write two familiar words containing the prefix on the board or overhead projector, and have students define them.
2. Underline the prefix and note its spelling. Then point out the meaning of the prefix, or have students supply it.
3. Write a novel word that contains the prefix in a sentence on the board or overhead projector, and model the process you would use in figuring out its meaning. You might write the word *disapprove* in a sentence such as *Certainly, most people disapprove of cooking too much food and then throwing it away*. Then think aloud as you work with the prefix and the root to arrive at the word's meaning.

   "Let me think. I see that the word begins with *dis-*, which can be a prefix, and I know that the prefix *dis-* means 'not.' If I take *dis-* away from *disapprove*, I'm left with the word *approve*, which I know. It means 'to agree with' or 'to think well of.' Therefore, disapprove must mean 'to not approve' or 'to not think well of.' Now, I'll try the meaning in the sentence. Yes, 'not approving' makes sense in the sentence. Many people would not approve of cooking too much food and then throwing some of it away."

4. After you have modeled the procedure once or twice, give students an opportunity to try it. Let them work with a few other prefixed words employing the prefix *dis-*, following the same procedures you used with *disapprove. Dishonest* and *distrust* could be used. Support students as necessary here, joining in when necessary. At the same time, try not to provide too much support because your goal is for students to become competent with the procedure.

5. Give an example of a word students know in which the letter group just taught does not represent the meaning taught, and caution them that letter groups that look like prefixes are sometimes just groups of letters. For example, the letter group *dis* does not have the meaning "not" in *distant;* the letter string *tant* is not a word, and the idea "not tant" makes no sense.

In order to further students' proficiency with prefixes, over the next several days have them look for examples of the prefix *dis-* in material they are reading and bring the examples to class, together with the sentences in which they occur. Ask students to explain how they used the meaning of the prefix and the root word to arrive at the word's meaning and how they checked the meaning against the context in which the word occurred. You should in turn give them feedback on their explanations and provide additional modeling and support as necessary. As the students look for the prefix *dis-*, they should also find instances of the letter string *dis* when it is not a functioning as a prefix and discuss these examples as well. Of course, if students bring in a word with a false prefix as an example of a prefixed word, explain to them that it is a false prefix, and again remind them that not all letter strings that look like prefixes will be prefixes.

Step 3: Further Work with Meaningful Word Parts

Further work with meaningful word parts varies, depending on whether you are dealing with frequently occurring prefixes or less-common elements. After teaching a unit on the four most frequently occurring prefixes (*un-, re-, in-,* and *dis-*), it makes sense to teach a similar unit on the next five or six most common ones (*en-* through *sub-*) later in the school year, and then a unit on the remaining five (*pre-* through *trans-*) during the following school year. You can provide instruction with less frequently occurring elements (for example, *anti-, tele-,* and *gram*) when they appear often in students' reading material. Of course, once students understand how to use meaningful word parts, subsequent instruction can be simplified.

Beyond formal instructional sessions, most work with word parts should take place when students need to figure out unknown words in their reading. Like working with context, ongoing work with structural analysis is

Words give kids power, power to express who they really are.

—Margo Sorenson
Teacher and
Children's Author

vital. Most students need many varied experiences, frequent reminders, and a good deal of feedback if they are to make structural analysis a tool that they can and do use.

Using the Dictionary

As George Miller and Patricia Gildea (1987) have convincingly demonstrated, elementary students frequently have difficulty using the dictionary to find definitions of unknown words. For example, after finding the phrase "eat out" in the definition of *erode*, one student showed her confusion in using the definition by composing the sentence *Our family erodes a lot.* Another student showed similar confusion after looking up the meaning of *meticulous* and finding the phrase "very careful" in its definition. Her sentence employing the new word read *I was meticulous about falling off the cliff.* Obviously, these students found at least some dictionary definitions considerably less than helpful. Perhaps this should not be surprising. Students' experience in working with dictionaries is often limited to instruction in alphabetical order, using guide words, and understanding pronunciation keys. Thus many students don't learn to work effectively with a tool that they will use throughout their schooling and that many adults use almost daily after completing school.

To provide students with help in learning to use the dictionary effectively, an explanation of the task, specific guidelines, modeling, and the gradual release of responsibility together provide a powerful approach. Begin by telling students that you are going to work on using the dictionary to define words, and tell them that the activity is worthwhile because using the dictionary sometimes isn't as simple as it seems. Then, put some guidelines, such as those shown in Figure 5.2, on a bulletin board, and leave them up over the coming weeks. In the figure, we have phrased the guidelines to suit fifth- or sixth-graders; for third- or fourth-graders, they could be phrased more simply.

Don't have students memorize these guidelines, but talk through them, amplifying on them as necessary. For example, you should probably add to the third guideline by telling students that if they find that they still know nothing about an important word after considering context, looking for word parts, and checking the dictionary, they will probably want to ask someone about its meaning.

The remainder of the procedure continues to parallel that used with context and structural analysis. Do some modeling; demonstrate how you would look up the meaning of an unknown word.

Think aloud, sharing your thinking with students as you come across the un-known word in a text. Show students how you look through the dictionary and find the word, locate the definition that seems to fit, consider all of that definition, and then mentally check to see if the meaning you choose makes sense in context. Then, gradually, let students take over the procedure and

Rule #1   **Dictionary Man and The Two Stooges**

Dictionary Man Says:

Many words have several meanings. When you look up a word's meaning, you need to choose a meaning that makes sense in the context in which the word occurred. You can't just take the first definition listed!

foul (foul) 1) very dirty; nasty: *We opened the windows to let out the foul air.* 2) make dirty: become dirty: Mud fouls things. 3) very wicked; vile: *That murder was a foul crime.* 4) unfair; against the rules. 5) in football, basketball, etc., an unfair play. 6) a baseball hit so that it falls outside the base lines.

Rule #2

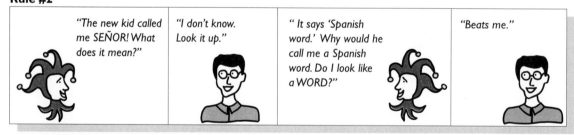

Dictionary Man Says:

When considering a definition, we need to consider the full definition given and not just part of it.

Señor (sà nyor') a Spanish word meaning: 1) Mr. or sir. 2) a gentleman.

FIGURE 5.2 *Guidelines for Looking Up Definitions in the Dictionary*

210

model it for you and for each other. Finally, encourage students to use the procedure when they come across unknown or vaguely known words in context, and from time to time give them opportunities to model their thinking as they use the dictionary so that you can check their proficiency and give them feedback and further instruction as needed.

Rule #3

"It says here that the whale was a PILOT"	*"Look up PILOT."*	*(Looks up PILOT in the dictionary.)*	*"I don't think the author knew what she was talking about. How can a whale fly an airplane or steer a ship?!"*

Dictionary Man Says:

Even though we are careful to consider all of a definition and to choose a definition that makes sense in the context in which we found the word, dictionary definitions help us only if we already know something about the word.

Rule #4

"I want to say the monster was VILE. Does that sound right?"	*"Look it up."*	*(Looks up VILE in the dictionary.)*	*"Perfect!"*

Dictionary Man Says:

Often, the dictionary works best when we have some idea of a word's meaning but aren't certain about it. This makes the dictionary useful when we want to use a word in our writing but aren't certain of its meaning.

In addition to learning this general approach to using a dictionary, students need to learn some things about the particular dictionary they use—what the entries for individual words contain and how they are arranged, what aids to its use the dictionary provides, and what features beyond the basic word list the dictionary includes. Much important information appears in the front matter of the dictionaries themselves, but it is very seldom read, and simply asking students to read it is hardly sufficient instruction. Thus, explicit instruction in how to use specific dictionaries is usually useful.

Finally, as teacher educator Judythe Patberg suggests, it's definitely a good idea to teach children one of the most common uses that adults make of dictionaries:

> One thing I particularly recommend to teachers is to teach children that one excellent use of the dictionary is to use it as adults do much of the time—to confirm, clarify, or refute the meaning they have arrived at using context or a meaning they are only somewhat confident in. I think this is the most common thing I use the dictionary for. I've got an idea about what the word means, but I'm not certain. Maybe I want to use the word in something I'm writing, or maybe I just want to be darn sure I have its meaning down pat. In either case, I frequently turn to the dictionary, and a quick check oftens gives me a good clear answer.
>
> Judythe Patberg, Teacher Educator

Reflection AND *Application*

6. In order to get a feeling for the extent to which context reveals word meanings, team up with a classmate. Each of you should independently select and photocopy a few passages of college-level material. Next read, identify, and "white out" some difficult words in each passage. Then get together and discuss how and to what extent you can infer the deleted words' meanings from context.

7. Identify a grade level and a subject that you will be teaching, select a text appropriate for that grade level and subject, and search the text for prefixes or Greek and Latin roots that might be worth teaching. Then jot down a note on what you found and your preliminary thoughts on the frequency of prefixes and Greek and Latin roots in student reading material. Also, a list of Greek and Latin roots from which you might select some to teach is provided by Edward Fry and his colleagues (Fry, Kress, & Fountoukidis, 1993).

8. Stop by the curriculum materials library at your university or a local public library, and examine the different levels of dictionaries that they have. Note, for example, how dictionaries for younger students have fewer words, define words more simply, and are generally easier to use and therefore more appropriate for younger readers.

FOSTERING WORD CONSCIOUSNESS

Thus far, we have described three approaches to vocabulary development—wide reading, teaching individual words, and teaching word-learning strategies. Here we describe a fourth approach—fostering word consciousness. As defined by its most prominent advocates (Anderson & Nagy, 1992; Beck, McKeown, & Omanson, 1987; Scott et al., 1994), word consciousness is a disposition toward words that is both cognitive and affective. The word-conscious student knows a lot of words, and she knows them well. Equally important, she is interested in words, and she gains enjoyment and satisfaction from using them well and from seeing or hearing them used well by others. She finds words intriguing, recognizes adroit word usage when she encounters it, uses words skillfully herself, is on the lookout for new and precise words, and is responsive to the nuances of word meanings. She is also well aware of the power of words and realizes that they can be used to foster clarity and understanding or to obscure and obfuscate matters.

> **Words are all we have.**
> —*Samuel Beckett*
> *Playwright and Novelist*

Fostering such attitudes is something to achieve across the elementary school years—and, of course, in the years beyond the elementary grades—and there are a myriad of ways to develop and nurture such positive attitudes. These include modeling and encouraging adept diction, promoting wordplay such as the use of rhymes and puns, using wordplay books and playing word games, and providing intensive and expressive instruction in vocabulary. On the following page, we list a few word books and word games. In the remainder of this section, we consider some ways of modeling and encouraging adept diction, and discuss approaches to intensive and expressive instruction.

Modeling and Encouraging Adept Diction

The starting point, we believe, in encouraging and nurturing word consciousness lies in our own attitude toward words and how we project it to students. We want children to feel that adept diction—the skillful use of words in speech and writing—is worth striving for. We want them to see that, by using the right word themselves and recognizing the adept word choices authors make, they can both communicate more effectively and more fully appreciate an author's message. Several conscious efforts promote skillful diction. One is to model adept word usage in your classroom talk, deliberately using and perhaps explaining words that at least some of your students might not yet know. Thus, in describing how you were startled by a low-flying jet on the way to school, you might tell your fourth-graders that the jet made a *thunderous* noise and point out that *thunderous* is an excellent word for describing a really loud noise because it reminds us of the great booming sound of thunder.

Books About Words and Word Games

Books About Words

Linda Bourke. *Eye Spy: A Mysterious Alphabet.* Chronicle Books, 1994. In this exquisitely illustrated alphabet book, each letter appears with three vividly colored panels depicting a word beginning with that letter and a fourth panel that depicts a homonym or homograph beginning with that letter and cues the word used to represent the next letter.

Fred Gwynne. *A Little Pigeon Toed.* Simon & Schuster, 1988. A marvelous collection of ambiguous phrases and amusing illustrations depicting the wrong interpretations of those phrases. Other similar books by Fred Gwynne include *Chocolate Moose for Dinner* (Windmill Books, 1976) and *The King Who Rained* (Simon & Schuster, 1970).

Norton Juster. *The Phantom Tollbooth.* Random House, 1961. In this story, a young boy named Milo makes a fantastic journey through Dictionopolis, a city where words of all kinds live.

Peggy Parish. *Thank You, Amelia Bedelia.* Harper-Collins, 1964. Amelia has a recurring problem with homophones and often confuses literal and figurative meanings. Asked to make a jelly roll, for example, she scoops a jar full of jelly onto the floor and tries her best to roll it around. Other books in the Amelia Bedelia series include *Play Ball, Amelia Bedelia!* (Harper, 1972) and *Come Back, Amelia Bedelia* (Harper, 1971).

Word Games

Articulation. Word Origins, 1993. In this commercial board game, players move toward the finish line and victory by rolling the dice, drawing cards, and answering questions about slang, jargon, and word origins. One slang card, for example, asks if a *clay pigeon* is an escaped convict, a substitute teacher, or a fool. With the cards provided, Articulation is most appropriate for students in grades 5 and above. However, with the game board and rules in hand, it is easy for you to make alternative slang, jargon, and word origin cards—creating a game appropriate for your students.

Fictionary. (Also sold commercially as Balderdash, Gameworks Creations, 1984). Playing Fictionary is a great way for students to develop their sense of what characterizes a dictionary definition. One student (the leader) thumbs through the dictionary looking for a word that is sure to be unknown to the rest of the group. She then writes the word on a card, says it to the group, and spells it for the group. Each person writes the word and a made-up definition for it on a card, and the leader writes the real definition on her card. Then the leader collects the cards, mixes them up, and reads each definition. After trying to figure out which definition is the real one, the students vote for the one they believe to be correct; the leader earns one point for each player who does not select her correct definition, while each player earns one point for each player who selects his or her incorrect definition. Leadership then rotates to the next person in the group until each person has had a chance to lead.

Taboo. Milton Bradley, 1989. Based on the long-running television show *The $10,000 Pyramid*, Taboo requires players to describe a mystery word or concept succinctly so that a partner can guess it before time runs out. An added challenge comes from the fact that obvious prompts are listed as "taboo" and cannot be used. This works particularly well when adapted for team play because it encourages students to talk about words and their meanings.

A simple, widely used, and very effective way of focusing students' attention on words is to include a word-of-the-day activity in daily plans. Appropriate for all ages, word-of-the-day activities can take a number of forms. In a first-grade classroom, word meaning can be linked to word recognition and general language facility by sharing with students a particular word of interest and paying special attention to the way it sounds, the way it looks, and what it means. The words of the day can be added to a bulletin board each day until, at the end of the month, the entire board is filled. Words of the day can also be acted out, used in a game of charades, or drawn. They can also be made part of a song, riddle, pun, poem, or some other form of artistic expression.

In a fourth-grade classroom, the teacher might designate a period of five minutes every day to introduce a new and interesting word. At the beginning of the year, she could choose the word and present it to the class by telling what it means, explaining why she selected it, and giving one or two examples of how it relates to either her life or that of her students. Students often have questions and comments, so this period of time is spent thinking deeply about one particular word. After the first month of school, students take the responsibility for selecting a word and introducing it to the class, either individually or in pairs.

Here, fifth-grade, special education teacher Bette Rochman explains how she uses word-of-the-day activities in her class:

> I teach fifth-grade youngsters with learning disabilities, and one vocabulary activity I have found to be quite successful is to pair up students to be responsible for coming up with a word of the day. After our morning announcements, the student pair responsible for that day's word writes it on the board and explains to the class what it means, why they selected it, and how to use it in a sentence. Sometimes the pair selects words they aren't too sure about and say something like, "We're not sure exactly how you use this word but when we find out, we'll let you know!" I let the students know that such partial knowledge of the word is certainly okay, as long as students set their sights on gaining fuller knowledge. Of course, students always enjoy stumping me by presenting words that are new to me as well as to their fellow students!

Bette Rochman, Fifth-Grade, Special Education

Students can select words from any number of sources—books, newspapers, another classroom, their parents, and teachers, to name a few. Teachers can also suggest that students find their special words in particular sources in order to complement certain classroom activities. For example, during a unit on the newspaper, the teacher might suggest that students find words in the newspaper; and during a unit on weather, he or she might suggest that students choose "weather words." More often, however, it is worth-

Words are not only tools; they are also weapons. . . . But if words are weapons, they are also toys. Words are fun to play with.

—Peter Bowler
Author

Imagine a world without words.

—Daniel Lavoy
Sixth-Grade Teacher

A word-of-the day-recorded on a word wall not only spurs interest in words but helps build students' vocabulary.

while to let students find their words wherever they wish. Then they tend to view the words as their own, take greater pride in sharing them, and more readily see learning new words as an enjoyable experience.

Another occasion for focusing attention on words comes when children are reading, as sixth-grade teacher Terry Cronemeyer suggests:

> I personally love words and take every opportunity I can to point out wonderful word choices. This opportunity most often arises in conjunction with the literature children are reading. Since good authors employ appropriate and often colorful words, I will often point out to my sixth-graders particularly felicitous or interesting word choices. For example, I was sitting in on a literature circle with a group of students who were reading and discussing Russell Freedman's *Eleanor Roosevelt: A Life of Discovery*. When one of the students chose to read these lines aloud, "Franklin remembered Eleanor as a skinny girl in a hopeless party dress. Now she was wearing a stylish outfit from Paris," I decided I could not resist butting in. "How could a party dress be *hopeless?*" I asked. A lively discussion then ensued that uncovered the ripples of meaning that Freedman was able to achieve by using that particular word.

Terry Cronemeyer, Sixth-Grade Teacher

Still another opportunity for recognizing and promoting adroit word usage comes from children's own writing. Thus, you might compliment a third-grader for describing banana slugs as *gigantic* and give a little recognition to a sixth-grader who noted that the odds of winning the lottery are *astronomically small*. During writing conferences, you might also encourage students to rethink word choices in an effort to make their writing more colorful and precise.

Providing Intensive and Expressive Instruction

Some very interesting and highly effective activities that can foster word consciousness have been developed and carefully researched by Isabel Beck and Margaret McKeown (1983) and by Ann Duin (Duin & Graves, 1988). The activities are quite similar, except that Beck and McKeown's goal was full and deep understanding of words, while Duin's goal was full and deep understanding of words coupled with children's using the words in writing. Developing and presenting these activities involves several steps. The first step is to select a small set of words that are semantically related. For example, a set used by Beck and McKeown—*rival, hermit, novice, virtuoso, accomplice, miser, tyrant,* and *philanthropist*—contained words that refer to people; a set used by Duin—*advocate, capability, configuration, criteria, disarray, envision, feasible, habitable, module, quest, retrieve,* and *tether*—contained words that can be used in talking about space exploration.

The next step, the central part of the instruction, is to have students work extensively and intensively with the words, spending perhaps half an hour a day over a period of a week with them, and engaging in a dozen or so diverse activities with them—really getting to know them, discovering their shades of meaning and the various ways in which they can be used, and realizing what interesting companions words can be. Beck and McKeown's activities, for example, included defining the words, asking students to use them in sentences, and asking students to respond to words such as *virtuoso* and *miser* with thumbs up or thumbs down to signify approval or disapproval. Their activities also included asking which of three actions an *accomplice* would be most likely to engage in—robbing a bank by him- or herself, stealing some candy, or driving a getaway car; and asked questions such as "Could a *virtuoso* be a *rival*? Could a *virtuoso* be a *novice*? and Could a *philanthropist* be a *miser*?"

Duin's activities also began with defining the words and asking students to use them in sentences. Her other activities included asking students to discuss how *feasible* space travel might soon be, asking them how a space station could *accommodate* persons with disabilities, and asking them to write brief essays called "Space Shorts" in which they used the words in dealing with topics such as the foods that might be available in space. Reports from teachers who have used these activities indicate that students really got involved in them and did indeed become more word conscious.

The third step, which is used only if the goal includes students' using the words in their writing, is to have students write more extensive essays—using as many of the taught words as possible, playing with them, and exploring their possibilities. Students appear to really enjoy this activity. As one teacher observed, "Students who were asked to write often and to use the words in written classwork showed great involvement in their writing."

Finally, we conclude with a fourth step—directly discussing with students the word choices they make, why they make those choices, and how adroit use of words makes speech and writing more precise, more memorable, and more interesting.

Duin found that students were very successful in using the words in their writing, as this seventh-grader's essay—in which the taught words are italicized—demonstrates:

> I think the space program would be more *feasible* if we sent more than just astronauts and satellites into space. We need to send tourists and change the whole *configuration* of the space shuttle so that it could *accommodate* more people. While the tourists are in space, they could fly some of the manned-maneuvering units and *retrieve* stuff from space. They could maybe even see if our planets are *habitable* now. When the tourists would come back, they would have the *capability* of doing anything in space. They truly would be *advocates* of space. But, in order to make these special missions happen, we will need to add more *modules* onto our space station, so that we can store more equipment, supplies, food, and people!
>
> After about ten years or so we would perhaps go back to the same old thing with astronauts and satellites until we found another new idea for the space program.
>
> My *quest*, someday, is to reach the stars. I hope to be not just an engineer, but a space engineer. We have to get more people interested since the crash. We have to try harder than ever.

Seventh-Grade Space Exploration Fan

Obviously, this student enjoyed the instruction, learned from it, and tried to do his best—he managed to get 9 of the 13 words that were taught in the unit in his essay. To be sure, some of the usage is a bit forced, but at this point in the student's writing career that is probably just fine. He is interested in words and in using new and different words in his writing, and with practice, feedback, and encouragement from thoughtful respondents to his writing—his teachers and his peers, for the most part—we expect him to become a skilled and precise word user.

We believe that vocabulary learning will endure when it has personal meaning for a child. Our job, as teachers, is to help children become thoughtful about the words they choose. We believe that attention to word choice will occur when they value their writing and want to communicate well with others. Words are the tools which make this possible.

—Judith Scott and
her Teacher Colleagues

Reflection AND Application

9. Review a recent paper you wrote, looking for the word choices you made and asking yourself if you used appropriate, powerful, and perhaps even colorful word choices. If you did, consider how these helped make the paper strong and effective. If you didn't, try going through the paper and changing some of the vocabulary to make it more appropriate, powerful, and perhaps colorful. Then look at your changes and consider how they affect the paper.

10. Get together with a classmate, identify a group of students, and brainstorm a set of brief and upbeat activities you might employ over a semester to foster their word consciousness.

Special Needs and Special Talents

At this point in the chapter, we look back and ask if there is more to be done to ensure that all students achieve their greatest potential—in this case, that all students develop full and rich vocabularies, learn approaches to learning words on their own, and develop an interest in words. Here we will consider the particular needs in vocabulary instruction for four groups—gifted learners, special students, children who had little exposure to books and reading before they came to school, and students who speak English as a second language.

Before we consider these groups individually, however, we want to emphasize the importance of wide reading in enjoyable and relatively easy material for children in all of these groups. Note that this means different books for different students. The book that a gifted student finds relatively easy may of course be a challenge for special students and will be virtually impossible to read for a student who speaks almost no English. Your task is to learn about your students and learn about books so that you can get the right book into the right student's hands. Beyond the obvious need of getting to know each of your students as an individual—her likes, her dislikes, her fears, her aspirations, areas in which she is quite knowledgeable, and areas in which she lacks knowledge—we have three recommendations.

First, take advantage of the bibliographies that appear annually in periodicals. There is a list of them at the end of this chapter. Tastes and interests change over time, and these periodic bibliographies can alert you to some of the very best books being published at a particular point in time. Second, also take advantage of book-length bibliographies. Though not as timely as bibliographies that appear annually, they can be tremendously valuable in helping you match a student with a book because they provide specific information. For example, *More Exciting, Funny, Scary, Short, Different, and Sad Books Kids Like About Animals, Science, Sports, Families, Songs, and Other*

Things (Carroll & Meacham, 1992) provides annotations on over 500 books that librarians have found to interest children, emphasizing titles for grades 2 to 5. Sections such as "I want to be really scared" and "Where are the animal books?" can help you find just the right book for each student. Third, establish the best-possible classroom library, and be sure that it includes books appropriate for all of your students. As Richard Allington (Allington et al., 1996) has recently noted, even in up-to-date classrooms with otherwise well-stocked libraries, often there are very few books for less-proficient readers. Finally, as Irene Gaskins (1994) recommends, get to know the difficulty level and content of the books in your classroom library very well—perhaps make up cards for yourself that describe a book's topic and include the designation easy, about average, or challenging—so that you can quickly grab the right book for a particular student.

Beyond making the right book for each student readily available, we have several recommendations for particular groups of students. With gifted students, be leery of teaching a new vocabulary-learning strategy when the student already has a perfectly good one. If a student already has a strategy for learning words from context that works well for her, there is no reason to teach her a new strategy.

With special students, be patient, and be sure they get the opportunity to work with higher-level tasks as well as less-challenging ones. Specifically, teaching special students vocabulary-learning strategies will take time and effort, and it may be tempting to avoid or minimize such attempts and simply teach them individual words. But don't give in to these temptations. Special students need vocabulary-learning strategies even more than more able students.

Be patient too with students who have not had rich experiences with books and reading outside of school. These students do not begin school with the same literacy skills or probably the same love of reading that many children with richer out-of-school literacy experiences do. They need time, nurturing, opportunities, and instruction. These students particularly need frequent experiences in reading appropriate books, something we discussed earlier. They also need and deserve to be taught strategies, to have fun with words, and to develop word awareness.

Finally, there is the special case of building the vocabularies for students for whom English is a second language, particularly those ESL students who have very small English vocabularies. We have four suggestions. First, pair each ESL student with a native English speaker. Have each pair frequently read together, do writing and other schoolwork together, and perhaps even do homework together. Encourage out-of-class activities among the pairs.

Second, obtain reading materials specifically for your ESL students. For those with meager English vocabularies, locate short and simple selections,

selections in students' native language, and, when possible, materials that have both a version in students' native language and an English version. Like all learners, ESL students need a lot of easy reading, and some of this reading can be in their native language. Thus, books that present the text in English and one or more other languages can be particularly useful. Fred Burstein's *The Dancer/La Bailarina*, a good example of such books, describes the sights and sounds a father and his daughter encounter as he accompanies her to her ballet lesson—a horse, a flower, a fish, and more—and gives these sights and sounds in English, Spanish, and Japanese.

Third, contact students' parents and enlist their aid. In most cases, parents' assistance will be largely in encouraging their children and ensuring that they have a time and place to do their homework and that they do it. Let parents know about books or homework you send home, and keep in touch with them on their children's progress.

Finally, for those with meager vocabularies, consider some sort of systematic word study that takes place both in and out of school. I. S. P. Nation (1990) offers a number of suggestions for such study.

CONCLUDING REMARKS

In this chapter, we have described the vocabulary-learning task students face, noted the importance of wide reading, described four word-learning tasks and ways of selecting vocabulary to teach, and presented teaching procedures appropriate for each of the four word-learning tasks. We have also suggested approaches to teaching students to use context and prefixes to unlock word meaning and ways of teaching them to use the dictionary. Finally, we have described methods of promoting word consciousness.

Summed up in this way, the task of teaching vocabulary appears to be a large one. However, no single teacher is expected to accomplish all of the various tasks of vocabulary instruction. You can choose which word-learning task is most important at a particular point in your class, which level of word knowledge you expect students to achieve with particular words, which teaching procedure or procedures will be most appropriate for the words in a particular selection your students are reading, and what specific words you wish to teach. Moreover, as we suggested earlier, not every teacher needs to take major responsibility for teaching students to use context, use word parts, and the like. You and the other teachers in your school can work together to decide who is responsible for these various teaching tasks. We believe that the discussion and teaching procedures presented here will help you make appropriate decisions that will help your students gain rich and powerful vocabularies.

As a firm believer in the credo that one lives in his head or not at all, I view a knowledge of words as a means to this end and as a *sine qua non* of life.

—*Garrard Beck*
High School Teacher

Rich and powerful vocabularies are of course an important part of critical literacy. Students who have achieved critical literacy have vocabularies that enable them to be precise and even colorful in their own speech and writing, to recognize and appreciate the skillful use of words in the literary selections they read, and to understand the sometimes subtle and often crucial meanings of words in the informational reading they do.

EXTENDING LEARNING

1. Throughout the chapter, we have emphasized the importance of wide reading for developing vocabulary. Your ability to promote wide reading among your students will depend heavily on getting the right books into children's hands. As one step toward becoming more skilled in selecting books for children, imagine a particular grade level and group of students and brainstorm possible topics that would interest this group. Then, using bibliographies, library card catalogs, electronic databases, and the advice of a librarian, select half a dozen books on this topic that are likely to be of interest to your students. If the group of students you are considering includes less-skilled readers or ESL students, be sure to include some books appropriate for these children.

2. Identify a grade level and group of students to whom you might teach vocabulary. If at all possible, this should be an actual group of students whom you can really teach. If you are able to work with elementary students, talk to their teacher and ask her to select half a dozen or so words that she would like her students to learn. If not, select a set of words yourself. Next, identify one of the procedures presented in the chapter that is appropriate for teaching these words, develop whatever materials you need, and prepare to do the teaching. If you haven't taught much before, it would be a good idea to rehearse with a classmate. Finally, teach the vocabulary, and then afterwards talk to students to get their reaction to your instruction. If it isn't possible to work with a real class, simulate this experience using your classmates as students.

3. Look back at the procedure for teaching context cues, and assume that you have already presented the initial day of instruction and the second day of instruction, much as they are described in the chapter. Assume further that you did some modeling of your using context cues, and that students seemed to be picking up on the technique, but you think some further modeling would be useful. Select two sentences containing difficult words and some cues to the words' meanings, much like the sentence we used with *obliterating*. Then, create a lesson plan for modeling your use of context to puzzle out the words' meanings. Be-

cause this is your first attempt with this procedure, actually write out the script of what you would say, just as we did. Finally, teach your excerpt from a unit on context cues with some of your classmates playing the role of students.

REFERENCES

Allington, R., Guice, S., Michaelson, N., Baker, K., & Li, S. (1996). Literature-based curricula in high-poverty schools. In M. F. Graves, P. van den Broek, & B. M. Taylor (Eds.), *The first R: A right of all children* (pp. 73–96). New York: Teachers College Press. The authors provide an overview of instruction in literature-based classrooms.

Anderson, R. C. (1996). Research foundations to support wide reading. In V. Greaney (Ed.), *Promoting reading in developing countries*. New York: International Reading Association. This article presents a very powerful argument and marshaling of evidence for the value of wide reading.

Anderson, R. C., Hiebert, E. H., Scott, J. A., & Wilkinson, A. G. (1985). *Becoming a nation of readers*. Washington, DC: National Institute of Education. A concise summary of what we know about reading instruction is given in this book.

Anderson, R. C., & Nagy, W. E. (1992, winter). The vocabulary conundrum. *American Educator*, pp. 14–18, 44–47. The authors examine the instructional implications of the fact that children's vocabularies are very large and grow very rapidly.

Anglin, J. M. (1993). Vocabulary development: A morphological analysis. *Monographs of the Society for Research in Child Development*, 58(10, Serial No. 238). This extremely well done but technical report details the growth of children's vocabularies.

Beck, I. L., & McKeown, M. G. (1983). Learning words well: A program to enhance vocabulary and comprehension. *The Reading Teacher, 36*, 622–625. This article describes a program for developing rich and deep word meanings and inspired the Duin and Graves program discussed in the chapter.

Beck, I. L, McKeown, M. G., & Omanson, R. C. (1987). The effects and uses of diverse vocabulary instructional techniques. In M. G. McKeown & M. E. Curtis (Eds.), *The nature of vocabulary acquisition* (pp. 147–163). Hillsdale, NJ: Erlbaum. The authors describe various sorts of useful vocabulary instruction.

Carey, S. (1978). Child as word learner. In M. Halle, J. Bresnan, & G. Miller (Eds.), *Linguistic theory and psychological reality* (pp. 347–389). Cambridge, UK: Cambridge University Press. This article delineates the concept that children first learn rather imprecise word meanings and then refine them.

Duin, A. H., & Graves, M. F. (1988). Teaching vocabulary as a writing prompt. *Journal of Reading, 22*, 204–212. This interesting and effective program builds students' expressive vocabulary and their interest in words.

Elley, W. B. (1996). Using book floods to raise literacy levels in developing countries. In V. Greaney (Ed.), *Promoting reading in developing countries*. New York: International Reading Association. Evidence for the effectiveness of book floods is marshaled from Fiji, Singapore, Israel, England, Canada, and the United States.

Fielding, L. G., Wilson, P. D., & Anderson, R. C. (1986). A new focus on free reading: The role of trade books in reading instruction. In T. E. Raphael (Ed.), *The contexts of school-based literacy*. New York: Random House. Research and theory on the importance of free reading is discussed here.

Frayer, D. A., Frederick, W. D., & Klausmeier, H. J. (1969). *A schema for testing the level of concept mastery* (Working Paper No. 16). Madison: Wisconsin Research and Development Center for Cognitive Learning. This report gives a detailed presentation of a powerful approach to teaching concepts.

Fry, E. B., Kress, J. E., & Fountoukidis, D. (1993). *The reading teacher's book of lists* (3rd ed.). Englewood Cliffs, NJ: Prentice Hall. This text provides extremely useful lists of words, spelling patterns, phonics elements, and the like.

Gaskins, I. W. (1994). Creating optimum learning environments: Is membership in the whole language community necessary? In F. Lehr & J. Osborn (Eds.), *Reading, language, and literacy: Instruction for the twenty-first century* (pp. 115–130). Hillsdale, NJ: Erlbaum. The author discusses the values of whole language and other approaches to literacy instruction.

Graves, M. F., & Slater, W. H. (1996). Vocabulary instruction in content areas. In D. Lapp, J. Flood, & N. Farnan (Eds.), *Content area reading and learning: Instructional strategies* (2nd ed.). Boston: Allyn & Bacon. This text presents procedures for teaching vocabulary in the middle and secondary grades.

Heimlich, J. E., & Pittelman, S. D. (1986). *Semantic mapping: Classroom applications.* Newark, DE: International Reading Association. This extremely informative and practical booklet will help anyone wanting to use semantic mapping extensively.

International Reading Association. (1995). *More kids' Favorite Books.* Newark, DE: Author. This is a collection of the Children's Choices annotated bibliographies printed in The Reading Teacher from 1992 to 1994.

Johnson, D. D., & Pearson, P. D. (1984). *Teaching reading vocabulary* (2nd ed.). New York: Holt, Rinehart and Winston. This book discusses techniques for vocabulary instruction and other word-level instructional techniques.

McCracken, R. A. (1971). Initiating sustained silent reading. *Journal of Reading, 14,* 521–524, 582–583. This article suggests six rules to follow when implementing sustained silent reading in the classroom.

Miller, G. A., & Gildea, P. M. (1987). How children learn words. *Scientific American, 257*(3), 94–99. The section on the problems caused by dictionary definitions is particularly illuminating.

Nagy, W. E. (1988). *Teaching vocabulary to improve reading comprehension.* Newark, DE: International Reading Association. Principles and techniques for teaching vocabulary specifically to improve comprehension are discussed.

Nagy, W. E., & Anderson, R. C. (1984). How many words are there in printed school English? *Reading Research Quarterly, 19,* 304–330. This revealing study shows the number of words in materials students read.

Nagy, W. E., Winsor, P., Osborn, J., & O'Flahavan, J. (1994). Structural analysis: Some guidelines for instruction. In F. Lehr & J. Osborn (Eds.), *Reading, language, and literacy* (pp. 45–58). Hillsdale, NJ: Erlbaum. The authors give excellent and very practical guidelines for structural analysis instruction.

Nation, I. S. P. (1990). *Teaching and learning vocabulary.* Boston: Heinle & Heinle. The entire book deals specifically with teaching English vocabulary to ESL students.

Pittelman, S. D., Heimlich, J. E., Berglund, R. L., & French, M. P. (1991). *Semantic feature analysis: Classroom applications.* Newark, DE: International Reading Association. This extremely informative and practical booklet will inspire anyone wanting to use semantic feature analysis.

Scott, J. A., Jones, A., Blackstone, T., Cross, S., Skobel, B., & Hayes, T. (1994). The gift of words: Creating a context for rich language use. Manuscript prepared for a microworkshop presented at the meeting of the International Reading Association, Toronto, Canada. This exciting set of teacher-developed ideas encourages students to use rich and colorful words in their writing.

Sternberg, R. J. (1987). Most vocabulary is learned from context. In M. G. McKeown & M. E. Curtis (Eds.), *The nature of vocabulary acquisition* (pp. 89–105). Hillsdale, NJ: Erlbaum. This powerful essay stresses the importance of learning from context.

White, T. G., Graves, M. F., & Slater, W. H. (1990). Growth of reading vocabulary in diverse elementary schools: Decoding and word meaning. *Journal of Educational Psychology, 82*(2), 281–290. This article offers details on the size of first- through fourth-grade students' vocabularies.

White, T. G., Slater, W. H., & Graves, M. F. (1989). Yes/No method of vocabulary assessment: Valid for whom and useful for what? *Cognitive* and social perspectives for literacy research and instruction. Chicago: National Reading Conference. Clear evidence of students' ability to indicate which words they do and do not know is presented.

White, T. G., Sowell, J., & Yanagihara, A. (1989). Teaching elementary students to use word-part clues. *The Reading Teacher, 42,* 302–308. This article discusses which word parts to teach and how to teach them.

CHILDREN'S LITERATURE

Books

Burstein, F. (1993). *The Dancer/La Bailarina.* New York: Bradbury. A little girl and her father walk to her ballet class. The brief text is in English, Spanish, and Japanese. Illustrated by J. Auclair. 32 pages.

Dorros, A. (1991). *Abuela.* New York: Dutton Children's Books. In this fanciful story, Rosalba and her grandmother, her *abuela,* fly over Manhattan, turning somersaults in the air, gliding low over the water to race sailboats, or circling around the Statue of Liberty. It includes a glossary of Spanish words and phrases. Illustrated by E. Kleven. 40 pages.

Freedman, R. (1993). *Eleanor Roosevelt: A life of discovery.* New York: Scholastic. This is a rich and insightful photobiography of an admirable and courageous woman. Photographs. 198 pages.

Bibliographies

Book Links (bimonthly from the American Library Association, 50 E. Huron St., Chicago, IL 60611). This glossy magazine features annotated bibliographies, essays, reviews, and recommendations for using literature with children from preschool through eighth grade.

Carroll, F. L., & Meacham, M. (1992). *More exciting, funny, scary, short, different, and sad books kids like about animals, science, sports, families, songs, and other things.* Chicago: American Library Association. This text provides descriptions of books in each of these categories.

CCBC Choices. (annually, in spring). Cooperative Children's Book Center. This annotated list of recommended children's trade books is selected by a committee of the Cooperative Children's Book Center, P.O. Box 5288, Madison, WI 53705-0288.

Children's Choices. (annually, in October). *The Reading Teacher.* These fiction and nonfiction books have been identified as favorites by children in elementary and middle school.

New Books for Young Readers. (annually, in May). Edited by Dianne Monson, College of Education, University of Minnesota. This annotated list cites new trade books that have been selected for their appeal and appropriateness for children from preschool to young adult. Department of Curriculum and Instruction, 159 Pillsbury Drive S.E., Minneapolis, MN 55455.

Notable Children's Books. (annually, in March). *School Library Journal* and *Booklist.* This nonannotated list of recommended children's trade books is compiled during the American Library Association's winter meeting. Copies are available from ALA.

Notable Children's Trade Books in the Field of Social Studies. (annually, in April/May). *Social Education.* Short reviews of notable social studies trade books for kindergarten through eighth-grade children are given.

Outstanding Science Trade Books for Children. (annually, in March). *Children and Science.* This publication offers short reviews of outstanding science trade books for prekindergarten through eighth-grade children.

Teacher's Choices. (annually, in November). *The Reading Teacher.* This lists fiction and nonfiction books teachers have identified as among their favorites for kindergarten and elementary-age students.

Trelease, J. (1995). *The read aloud handbook* (4th ed.). New York: Penguin Books. This rich source provides information on predictable books, wordless books, reference resources, picture books, short novels, novels, poetry, and anthologies.

chapter six

Scaffolding Students' Comprehension of Text: Teacher-Directed Approaches

Alex, a fourth-grader in Mark Schroeder's suburban classroom, slammed his social studies book shut, and complained to his teacher. "I just don't get this. It's boring. Why can't I just read comic books?"

Mr. Schroeder, a first-year teacher, didn't know how to respond to Alex's frustration. This wasn't the first time one of his students complained about reading. What was he doing wrong? Why weren't they motivated to read? He had always loved to read. Why didn't his students?

CHAPTER OVERVIEW

Obviously, there are no simple answers to Mr. Schroeder's questions. The world in which Alex and the other students in Mr. Schroeder's class live is, in many ways, vastly different and more complex than the one in which Mark Schroeder grew up. But there are some things teachers can do to help ensure that their students' reading experiences are successful ones, that they are continually learning and relearning that reading is purposeful and enjoyable. In this chapter, we will discuss a number of approaches.

THE ROLES OF PURPOSE, SELECTION, AND READER IN PLANNING A SUCCESSFUL READING EXPERIENCE

The purpose, the text, and the reader are essential and interrelated components in the reading transaction.

—Mara Esbensen
Reading Specialist

When we look carefully at what it means to comprehend text, three factors are always involved—the purpose or purposes for reading, the selection, and the reader—the *why*, the *what*, and the *who*. We cannot overstate the importance and interconnectedness of these three components in planning any classroom reading experience. These critical factors will be at the forefront of your thinking whenever your students are about to read.

The Role of Purpose

Can you imagine reading something without a purpose for doing so? You may not articulate your purpose or even be conscious of it, but it is there nevertheless. Why do you pick up the evening newspaper? Why do you read that mystery novel before you go to bed? Why are you reading this text now? Purpose is what motivates us, helps focus our attention, or gives us a goal, something tangible to work toward. As literate adults, we have internalized the truism that reading is purposeful. This is the message we want students to get from day one and to similarly internalize. We read because somewhere in those combinations of symbols is something we need or want—information, escape, excitement, knowledge, or whatever our purpose might be.

The Function of Purposes

Purposes serve a variety of functions in reading. First, they motivate or give a reason for reading. Such motivation is missing when a teacher merely states, "Open your science text and read chapter 5." "Why?" a student might ask. And rightly so. In order to create a purpose for reading, the teacher might instead say, "What are three things you'd like to find out about earthquakes? Write those down, and then read chapter 5 to see if the author answers those questions for you. Later we will talk about what you learned." In addition to giving a reason for reading, purposes also determine *how* a selection is to be read—quickly in order to get the gist of the text, or slowly in order to really understand the material. Your students might read the description of an experiment quickly to see what materials they will need, but to fully absorb the steps in photosynthesis will take a slow and careful reading.

Having clear purposes aids comprehension. Purposes can serve as a cue for activating a reader's background knowledge before reading a text, suggest a plan for the reader to use while reading, and help him sort out relevant from irrelevant information while reading. Since there are numerous purposes for reading, choosing and using the ones that will assist comprehension is the key.

Guidelines for Establishing Reading Purposes

The following list provides guidelines for establishing reading purposes, some of which were suggested by William Blanton and his colleagues (Blanton, Wood, & Moorman, 1990) and some of which are our own:

- *Students should have a purpose for reading.* Students should understand why they are reading a selection, be able to articulate their reading purposes, and embrace these purposes as their own, knowing that achieving them will give a measure of satisfaction.

- *Students should be encouraged to develop their own reading purposes.* As we stress throughout this book, one of our goals as teachers is to develop students' independence. Students need to be continually nudged and encouraged to take responsibility for their own learning, to realize what it is they need to know and how to achieve their personal goals.

- *Purposes should be appropriate for the text.* After studying theme, an appropriate purpose for a group of third-graders reading the stories in Arnold Lobel's *Days with Frog and Toad* might be to discover each story's theme. On the other hand, since these characters are anthropomorphic, an *inappropriate* purpose would be to read the book to find out the characteristics of amphibians.

- *Purposes should be appropriate for the reader.* You wouldn't ask a group of beginning readers who had no experience with theme to read *Days with Frog and Toad* to discover the book's themes. You could, however, ask that same group of students to find the problem in a story and how it was solved. Also, it is always appropriate to encourage readers, no matter what their age, to respond personally to what they read. You might prompt them with questions: What did you get from this? How did you approach reading it? Purposes reflect the nature of the reading selection and the background knowledge, needs, interests, and desires of the reader.

- *Purposes should have significance, value, and importance to the reader.* For example, if students need to update their knowledge about fire safety, an appropriate purpose for reading an article on the subject would be to add new information to what they already know. They could make a chart to reflect their old and new knowledge, which they could then share with a wider audience.

Different purposes for reading require different sets of strategies, and different ways to attain these strategies. Achievement of these different purposes relies on a set of common processes, including decoding and basic comprehension processes.

—*Steven Stahl*
Teacher Educator

229

- *Single purposes are often preferable to multiple ones.* As teachers, we don't want to overload our students with so many reading purposes that they either fail at them all or are only somewhat successful at each. We'd rather have them achieve success with just a few.

So, you see, we might take purpose for granted as adults—something that we have internalized so completely that we don't consciously think about it as we read. However, it is an all-important factor to consider if we want our students to succeed in the reading they do in our classrooms.

The Role of the Selection

As you may have noticed in the previous section, the selection being read was either named, described, or implied in discussing purpose. That is because the type of text being read is inextricably intertwined with purpose. For example, if your purpose is to be entertained, you probably wouldn't choose to read your computer user's guide or the telephone book. And, although you might look to the comic pages of the newspaper to learn about current world events, it's not likely to be your primary purpose in doing so.

Obviously, your students will be reading a variety of texts for a variety of purposes. Your goal, as well as theirs, is for them to read each one successfully. They need to understand what the author is trying to communicate and to build meaning so that they can achieve their reading goals. After a successful reading of a text, students will have developed their own understanding of the facts, issues, themes, settings, and characters that the author has presented.

Types of Selections

Ideally, your students will be reading a wide range of materials, representing a broad spectrum of cultures, genres, and ability and interest levels. Of course, the ones that they will actually read in your classroom will depend not only on the choices you and your students make, but also on your school's curriculum and the grade level you will be teaching. As Elaine Bieger (1996) reminds us, when left on their own, children "generally choose literature that is familiar and that reflects their own interests and culture. Therefore it is important for teachers to expose children to literature that reflects many cultures, themes, and views" (p. 309). Figure 6.1 provides a short list of authors who create books about parallel cultures.

In addition to exposing students to a variety of cultures, they need to be encouraged to read in different genres—narratives and exposition across a broad range of categories.

Alma Flor Ada	Virginia Hamilton	Jerry Pinkney
Joseph Bruchac	Minfong Ho	Faith Ringgold
Ashley Bryan	Angela Johnson	Allen Say
Floyd Cooper	Barbara Knutson	Virginia Driving Hawk
David Diaz	Jeanne M. Lee	Sneve
Leo and Diane Dillon	Julius Lester	Gary Soto
Michael Dorris	Sharon Bell Mathis	Mildred Taylor
Arthur Dorros	Patricia McKissack	Joyce Carol Thomas
Tom Feelings	Walter Dean Myers	Yoshiko Uchida
Jean Craighead George	Lensey Namioka	Mildred Pitts Walters
Paul Goble	Ifeoma Onyefulu	Lawrence Yep
Eloise Greenfield	Brian Pinkney	Ed Young

FIGURE 6.1 *Authors Who Create Books About Parallel Cultures*

Narratives. Narratives, as we have discussed previously, are stories that typically recount events in chronological order, whereas expository texts provide information organized in a variety of ways. Although many variations exist within each of these categories, most of what your students read will fall into one of these two broad types. Each has a unique structure and purpose, and being aware of these can help you create appropriate reading experiences. Although these two types of texts are organized very differently (Drum, 1984), they both provide cues that help readers construct meaning (Calfee & Patrick, 1995). Typical narratives reflect the temporal order of real-life events in which motives, actions, results, and reactions occur in sequence, and episodes in the main character's life are integrated by goals and subgoals. Time frame thus provides a natural structure for remembering episodic information.

Exposition. Exposition is another matter. Expository text can be organized in a variety of ways, and different authors have categorized these organizational patterns differently. Richard Anderson and Bonnie Armbruster (1984), for example, list description, temporal sequences, explanation, compare/contrast, definition/examples, and problem/solution as typical organizational patterns. Robert Calfee and Marilyn Chambliss (1988), on the other hand, identify description and sequence as the two major rhetorical patterns and then further subdivide each of these categories. Moreover, since there is no single prototypic structure for exposition, previous reading of exposition—even well-written exposition—does not provide clues to the structure of upcoming expository texts in the way that previous reading of narratives prepares readers to understand upcoming narratives. In other words, most students will have a schema in place for understanding narratives, but not one for exposition. For that reason, preparing and guiding students in their reading of expository texts is often the best prescription for success.

Text Difficulty

When we discussed the teacher's role in helping students comprehend texts, we noted how important it is to make sure not to assign texts that are far too difficult. Here, we list the factors to consider when deciding whether or not a particular selection is a good match for the potential reader:

- Familiarity of content
- Required background knowledge
- Organization
- Unity of the writing
- Quality and verve of writing
- Interestingness
- Sentence complexity
- Vocabulary
- Length

Matching Texts with Students and Purposes

Here are a few guidelines for matching selections with purposes and readers:

- Students should be encouraged to select their own texts whenever possible. Self-selection helps ensure a good match between text and reader, since youngsters tend to choose what interests them and what they think they can read successfully.

- The teacher should read and become familiar with any selection that students are asked to read, paying particular attention to the background knowledge the selection requires; its organization; sentence complexity, unfamiliar vocabulary, or other stumbling blocks; and the opportunities it presents for instruction for the student or group of students who will be reading it.

- The selection should be appropriate for the student. Although *The Wizard of Oz* might be a wonderful read-aloud for a group of third-graders, few would be able to read it successfully on their own. The texts students read should be commensurate with their abilities and interests. To quickly check this student–text match, have students read a page from the text orally. If they can read fewer than 100 words per minute, or make more than five or so errors, the text is probably not a good choice for them.

- The selection and reading purpose should match. If the reading purpose is to gain practice in fluency, *The Adventures of Huckleberry Finn* by Mark Twain would probably be an inappropriate choice for most elementary-age students, since it is filled with dialect and challenging vocabulary.

- The selection will dictate how students should approach it and what students will gain from it. Math story problems, for instance, will require a different kind of reading than a poem. Thus, the activities you set up to prepare, guide, and enrich the reading experience will be quite different for each.

The Role of the Reader

When you analyze reading material to find ways to help students successfully read it, the readers themselves obviously will be the uppermost priority in your planning. Understanding that students bring unique sets of experiences,

No two readers are the same. Each will bring a unique set of experiences, expectations, and abilities to the texts they read.

expectations, and abilities to each reading experience will help you create situations that will foster their success in their making meaning with the texts they read.

The Centrality of Background Knowledge

As a teacher, all your planning decisions should take into consideration your students' prior knowledge. What schemata do they have in place that will help them make meaning with the text? What do they know about the topics, concepts, vocabulary, theme, and structure of the selection they are going to read? Will their background knowledge allow them to make meaningful connections with the ideas in the text? Fifth-grade teacher Lamont Franklin reflects on the importance of background knowledge as it relates to the texts students read:

> I teach fifth-graders who are average-to-poor readers living in a Midwestern city. Our social studies curriculum includes a unit on Australia, and one of the reading selections is an informational piece on the Great Barrier Reef. Although most of my students have heard of Australia and seen pictures of it in the media, they haven't been there. In fact, most have never even seen an ocean. To read this article successfully, these students will need prereading experiences that provide background information to help fill the gaps in their repertoire of concepts about Australia and about oceans, reefs, and other topics central to this piece. Also, since the reading level of the article is sixth grade, and many of my students read below sixth-grade level, I'll have to do something extra to make sure they understand it. This may include preteaching potentially difficult vocabulary and providing them with a graphic organizer that shows what topics are included and how they are organized.
>
> Lamont Franklin, Fifth-Grade Teacher

It is important to realize that culture is not exclusively a result of ethnic background. Many other factors, such as religion and geographical region, are also involved.

—*Lara L. Hillard*
Kindergarten Teacher

On the other hand, if, unlike Mr. Franklin's class of Midwesterners, the class reading the selection on the Great Barrier Reef is a group of above-average readers in Hawaii or on the West Coast, the prereading activities will be quite different. These may include having students discuss what they know about the topic before reading it, perhaps even writing down what they know about Australia, reefs, and the ocean. After reading the article, the students might discuss new information or ideas they discovered from the reading, questions that arose while they read, and where they might find the answers to those questions.

Factors to Consider About the Reader

To help students successfully engage with a text, here are a few questions to consider:

- What are the readers' needs and concerns? What is it they need from a particular text? How can these needs be met in a reading selection?

- What are the readers' interests? How do these interests relate to a reading selection? How can you capitalize on these interests to make the reading experience meaningful?

- What are the readers' strengths and weaknesses as learners? How might these influence what they comprehend? How will these influence the kind of scaffolding (support to ensure a successful reading experience) that you provide?

- What schemata do students have that will help them make meaning with the text? What do they know of the text structure of the piece, its topics, concepts, vocabulary, theme? Will their background knowledge (for example, their ethnic, cultural, religious, and geographical backgrounds) allow them to make meaningful connections with the ideas in the text?

Reflection AND Application

1. Think about the different kinds of reading you do. Do you ever read something without a purpose? Explain. Do you think it's important for students to have a purpose for the reading they do? Why or why not?

2. Suppose you are teaching second grade and your students are going to read nonfiction books about different occupations. When you go to the library or school media center to select "occupation" books for your class, what questions will you ask yourself as you look through the books to make your selections? (For example, How difficult is the vocabulary?)

3. Suppose you are teaching fourth-graders who come from a variety of backgrounds. Your literature curriculum includes *Number the Stars* by Lois Lowry, an award-winning middle-grade novel set in Nazi-occupied Denmark. The story revolves around 10-year-old Annemarie, who, with the help of her family, helps her best friend's family escape to Sweden. Are all of your students likely to succeed in reading this selection without help from you? Why or why not?

THE SCAFFOLDED READING EXPERIENCE (SRE)

After reading the previous section, you are perhaps wondering how you can enhance literacy growth in classrooms populated with students with a variety of backgrounds, expectations, needs, strengths, learning styles, and intelligences as they read all sorts of different texts for many different purposes. We won't pretend that there are simple answers or that the task will always be easy. But in this section we describe an easily implemented framework that will assist you in ensuring that your students succeed with the reading they do in your class.

Background and Rationale

In Chapter 2 we discussed the notion of scaffolding. Scaffolding, you will recall, is "a process that enables a child or novice to solve a problem, carry out a task, or achieve a goal which would be beyond his unassisted efforts" (Wood, Bruner, & Moss, 1976). The scaffolded reading experience (Graves & Graves, 1994; Graves & Graves, 1995; Graves, Graves, & Bratten, 1996) is designed to do just that—to ensure a student's reading success in whatever he is reading, for whatever purpose.

> There is one thing that I've discovered over and over again: When people use language for things that count and share that language with people who count (including themselves), motivation will follow. One of our most crucial goals should be finding a way to make our classrooms places that support this important work.
>
> —*Susan Hynds*
> *Teacher Educator*

In addition to being firmly rooted in the concept of scaffolding, the scaffolded reading experience (SRE) is thoroughly consistent with all of the theories and instructional principles we discussed in detail in Chapter 1 and Chapter 2. In designing the SRE, we attempted to take the current knowledge about teaching and learning and design a flexible framework whose form fits its purpose—helping teachers help students to successfully read specific texts. In addition, the SRE was also influenced by knowledge of today's classroom—the reality of the challenges teachers face. As Brian Cambourne (1994) points out, classrooms are very complex, and this complexity is often difficult to orchestrate. The SRE provides a framework for working in such environments, making teaching and fostering students' success more manageable.

The SRE Framework

The SRE framework takes into consideration the three all-important factors we have just discussed—purpose, selection, and reader—and then illustrates how you can create learning experiences to address them. After carefully considering a purpose, a selection, and a group of readers, the teacher develops a set of prereading, during-reading, and postreading activities that support students in achieving their reading goals. Figure 6.2 provides a graphic presentation of the framework.

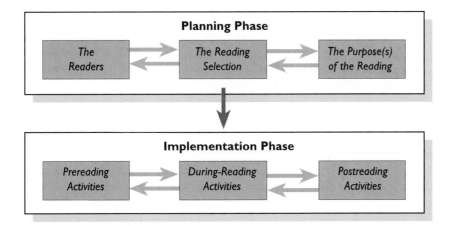

FIGURE 6.2 *The Scaffolded Reading Experience*

As the figure shows, the SRE has two phases—a planning phase and an implementation phase.

The Planning Phase: Purpose, Selection, and Reader

In the planning phase, the teacher considers

- *the purpose or purposes for reading:* What is the reader to gain from the reading experience? For what purposes is he reading?
- *the selection:* its topics and themes, the background knowledge required, its organization, difficult vocabulary or other stumbling blocks, and the opportunities it presents for instruction.
- *the reader:* his needs, concerns, interests, strengths, weaknesses, background knowledge—anything that might influence his success (or failure) in reading a particular selection.

As we have pointed out numerous times, these three factors are interrelated, and decisions made about one factor will influence and constrain the decisions that can be made about the other two. In other words, purpose is linked to text and the students who are reading it, and students' skills and interests will largely determine which selections and purposes are appropriate for them. For example, if the reading purpose for your competent secondgraders is to gain automaticity, your choice of text will reflect that purpose.

The Implementation Phase: Prereading, During-Reading, and Postreading Activities

The implementation phase of the SRE also has three components—prereading, during-reading, and postreading activities. After considering the readers, the text, and the purpose, the teacher then develops and implements the pre-, during-, and postreading activities that will lead these students to successfully understand, respond to, and apply the text ideas. We have chosen the word *activities* because it denotes action, and here we caution you that we mean *purposeful action*—not busy work or activities for their own sake—but ones that help students make meaningful connections with text.

In general, when working with less-proficient students, difficult selections, and challenging purposes, more scaffolding will be needed. A difficult expository piece might require several pre-, during-, and postreading activities. Conversely, with more proficient students, less difficult selections, and less challenging purposes, less scaffolding is needed. A straightforward short story might only require your saying, "This is a terrific story. Read and enjoy." Then you can have students read the entire story silently and afterward discuss whether they enjoyed it, and if so, why. In situations in which students are reading self-selected books for pleasure, little or no scaffolding will be required. In fact, as we stress in detail in Chapter 7, in many situations we want to deliberately nurture students' independence in reading by encouraging them to read independently on their own. But SREs suit the many occasions that call for assistance.

In the next three sections, we discuss the prereading, during-reading, and postreading phases of SREs. Then we will discuss comprehensive SREs that combine these activities.

Prereading Activities

Prereading activities get students ready to read a selection. Taking time to prepare students before they read can pay big dividends in terms of their understanding what they read and finding reading an enjoyable experience. Obviously, prereading activities take place prior to reading a selection. Not quite as obviously, they can serve multiple purposes. The following list shows some of the many uses of prereading activities:

- Motivating and setting purposes for reading
- Activating and building background knowledge
- Building text-specific knowledge
- Relating the reading to students' lives
- Preteaching vocabulary and concepts
- Prequestioning, predicting, and direction setting
- Suggesting comprehension strategies

This list, though not exhaustive, can serve as a guide in planning prereading activities. In this section, we discuss and give examples of each of these types of prereading activities. A number of them overlap. For instance, an activity that builds background knowledge can also motivate. Similarly, an activity primarily designed to motivate students may also activate prior knowledge, introduce a new concept, and relate the reading to the students' lives. Several kinds of endeavors can be useful as you prepare students to read—these types of activities are not meant to suggest an elaborate system of mutually exclusive categories.

Motivating and Setting Purposes for Reading

As you well know, most of the time we need to be motivated to do something—reading is no exception. Think about yourself and the reading you are doing right now. What is motivating you to read this? In an ideal world, our motivation would be intrinsic, stemming from an internal need or desire that is fulfilled when we read. This is the ideal we strive to develop in the students we teach.

Motivational activities incite enthusiasm, an eagerness to discover what the written word has to offer. In general, motivational activities will draw on the interests and concerns of the particular group doing the reading. Puppets and puppies might be part of a motivating activity for first- and second-graders, a rap song or challenging puzzle for fourth-, fifth-, and sixth-graders.

Motivational activities will often involve hands-on experiences, active student participation, drama, and intrigue:

> Feel this fabric and tell me what it makes you think of and how it makes you feel.

> Guess what's in this box?

Once students' interest is piqued, comes the next step—transferring that interest to the reading material.

> Robbie, the little boy in the story you will read today has a special blanket made of the fabrics you were feeling—flannel and satin.

> I guess my clues were good ones, and you're pretty good detectives. What was in the box is pumice, and we'll be reading about it and other kinds of igneous rocks in our science chapter today.

Motivating activities, then, are any kinds of activities that help students delve into reading material eagerly, knowing there will be a reward at the end—new knowledge, experiences, discoveries, excitement, or laughter. It is there for them if they will but read.

Motivation must be at the heart of the language arts curriculum because the quality of the content of the program matters little if it is not taught in a way that both engages and enriches students.

—*Linda Gambrel*
Teacher Educator

Activating and Building Background Knowledge

As we explained in Chapter 1, having appropriate background knowledge—schemata—is absolutely crucial to understanding text. When *activating* background knowledge, we help students draw upon information they already have on a particular subject; when *building* background knowledge, we provide students with information they need to understand the text. For example, let us say a group of third-graders is going to read an expository piece on wildfires. To activate their prior knowledge, you might have them talk or write about what they know about fire. To build their background knowledge, you might draw an illustration of the fire triangle, explaining the three elements necessary for making fire, or show a video about wildfires.

Obviously, the background knowledge students have will vary from classroom to classroom, student to student. For instance, suppose you are teaching a class of fourth-graders in southern Florida and they are going to read a story in which a blizzard plays a central part. Their background knowledge will be quite different from that of a class of third-graders in rural Minnesota. Similarly, the background knowledge that high-achieving fifth-graders bring to reading a chapter on the Constitution will differ from that of low-achieving students in that same class.

Given the vital importance of prior knowledge to comprehension and remembering what has been read, it is critical to recognize that different students bring different stores of prior knowledge into the classroom and are thus differently prepared to read some selections. Recognizing and accommodating these differences in today's culturally and linguistically diverse classrooms form one of the major challenges teachers face.

Building Text-Specific Knowledge

If you read Shakespeare's *Romeo and Juliet* in high school or college, chances are your instructor told you something about it before you began reading—either a bit about the plot or setting or thumbnail sketches of the characters. In doing so, he was building text-specific knowledge. The reason for building text-specific knowledge is similar to the reason for activating background knowledge: Having schemata for concepts in a text prior to reading it greatly facilitates comprehension.

For expository text, two frameworks are particularly helpful in building text-specific knowledge—outlines and graphic organizers. Giving students an outline or graphic organizer, showing the headings and subheadings of the material they are going to read, provides them with a conceptual framework for understanding and remembering. For example, if students are going to read a chapter on waves in their science text, you might provide them with an outline or graphic organizer like those shown in Figures 6.3 and 6.4. Giving students information on the topics and structure of the text puts a schema in place that includes both the concepts presented in the chapter and how the chapter is organized.

Another effective way to build text-specific knowledge is to give students a preview of the material they are going to read. A preview of a reading selection is similar to previews of movies and TV shows. Previews of infor-

WAVES

I. How Do Waves Transfer Energy?
II. Types of Waves
    A. Electromagnetic Waves
        1. Radio Waves
        2. Higher Frequency Waves
            a. Infrared Waves
            b. Light
            c. Ultraviolet Waves
            d. X rays and Gamma Rays
    B. Lasers

FIGURE 6.3 *Outline of Chapter on Waves*

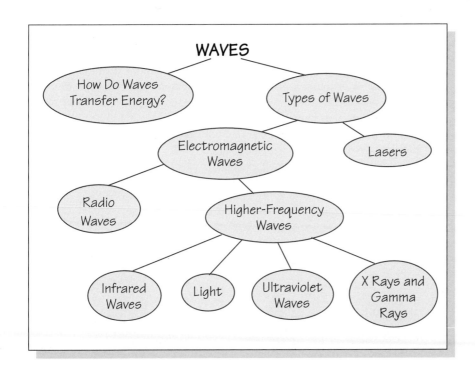

FIGURE 6.4 *Graphic Organizer of Topics in Chapter on Waves*

mational texts typically include the topics, events, people, or places covered, and unusual or difficult vocabulary. Previews for narratives typically include information on the setting, characters, and plot as we mentioned earlier in *Romeo and Juliet*.

Previews are probably the most robust prereading activity we know of for increasing comprehension. A substantial body of research (for example, Chen & Graves, 1996; Dole, Valencia, Greer, & Wardrop, 1991; Graves, Prenn, & Cooke, 1985) has shown them to be effective with students of various age and ability levels, and with ESL students as well as with native English speakers.

Relating the Reading to Students' Lives

> A book with strong characters presents us with people who are real to us, people we care about. We know how they feel about one another. And, in well-written works, we also notice how the major characters change over the period of the story.
>
> —*Diane Monson*
> *Teacher Educator*

Like activating background knowledge and building text-specific knowledge, activities that relate reading to students' lives also build on and activate prior knowledge. In this case, however, the goal is to draw students into the text by helping them recall situations in their lives that are similar to those found in the selection. Relating a reading selection to students' lives is an extremely powerful approach for getting them to commit themselves to a text, to claim ownership of it. If students can see how something relates to their lives, then they are making a personal connection. They suddenly have a vested interest in it.

Marcie Goodman, a fourth-grade teacher, shares how she helps students make personal connections with text:

I almost always do something with my students to relate what they are going to read to their lives, and I try to tie that relationship in with a theme or topic we are exploring or that I want them to think about as they read. For example, a group of my fourth-graders were planning to read biographies of Martin Luther King, Jr. Before they began reading, I had them think about and discuss times in their lives when they felt that they were not treated as well as others, when they felt they were mistreated or treated unfairly. Having my students think and talk about these experiences helped them understand better the concept of discrimination, a central theme in the biography and a topic that had recently become an issue in our community. A few of these students related stories that their parents had told them about being discriminated against in the United States, and one student who had recently moved from South Africa told about recent memories of discrimination. These discussions built in immediacy and relevancy for the biographies they would read.

Marcie Goodman, Fourth-Grade Teacher

Relating the reading to students' lives can take many forms, and all are likely to pay big dividends in both understanding and interest.

Preteaching Vocabulary and Concepts

Preteaching vocabulary and concepts also comes under the umbrella of building prior knowledge—in this case, prior knowledge of words and the concepts they represent. As we noted in Chapter 5, it is frequently useful to spend some time preteaching important words and concepts. Since we described a number of specific ways of doing so in that chapter, we will not repeat them here.

Prequestioning, Predicting, and Direction Setting

Prequestioning, predicting, and direction setting have a very similar purpose: These activities focus readers' attention on what to look for as they read, directing them to a particular aspect or several aspects of the text. With prequestioning activities, you and your students pose questions about the upcoming text that they would like to find answers to. As an example of teacher-generated prequestioning, let us say you have been studying nutrition in your sixth-grade class and one student brings in an article from the Sunday paper that includes a stir-fry dish touted as healthful. Before students read the article, you might ask them to think about the question "Is this a healthful recipe or not?" as they read, and to be prepared to defend their answers in a postreading discussion. In student-generated questioning, students ask their own questions about an upcoming selection and read to discover the answers. For example, suppose that during the nutrition unit, these same students are asked to create a puppet play to teach good eating habits to the kindergarten and first-grade classes. When they read material to prepare for their play, they will need to ask all sorts of questions in order to create an appropriate script: What are some good healthful foods that 5- and 6-year olds will like? What unhealthful foods should children avoid? What makes these foods unhealthful? The answers to questions like these will provide students with the raw material for their play.

In predicting activities, students make predictions about the text and read to find out whether their predictions are accurate. Even very young children can make predictions about narratives based on prior knowledge and what they see on a book's cover and in its illustrations. Accurate predictions about exposition depend on students' having some prior knowledge about the topic or skimming the selection to get some idea of its contents. Students' predictions will not always be accurate, but even inaccurate predictions can be useful because they prompt active reading and the search for meaning. Of course, you will want to explain to students that their predictions will not always be accurate and that their goal as active readers is to confirm or disconfirm their predictions. At least some of the time you'll want to give students feedback on more far-fetched predictions before they read, so they don't get off on the wrong track.

Direction setting comes at the end of your prereading activities. It is a final word of encouragement and guidance to readers before they begin reading, reminding them what to attend to while they read. Sometimes these will be oral instructions—"Read the story to find out if your predictions are correct." Other times you might write instructions on the chalkboard, a chart, or a handout so that students can refer to them.

Suggesting Comprehension Strategies

As you read this chapter, what are you doing to help yourself understand and recall the ideas in it? Are you relating the ideas to what you already know about the topics? Are you asking questions such as "Why would this procedure work?" or "In what situations wouldn't it work?" Are you creating pictures of classrooms and students in your imagination as you read? Do you stop and reread something when it doesn't make sense to you or when you realize your eyes have skimmed over the words but your mind was elsewhere? If you engaged in any of these, you were reading strategically, being the sort of metacognitive reader we described in Chapter 1. All good readers read strategically, and we want to teach all students to do so as well.

In the past several years, a number of reading strategies have been identified as valuable for understanding, remembering, and enjoying text (Graves, 1997). These include active processes such as using prior knowledge, asking and answering questions, creating mental images, and monitoring comprehension. We discuss strategies and procedures for teaching students these strategies in Chapter 7. Once you have taught a strategy, it is important to remind students to use it when reading material for which it is appropriate.

Prereading Activities: Summary and Guidelines

By now, you are probably aware that the possibilities for prereading activities are almost limitless. But there is a common thread to all of them—each builds a bridge from the student to the selection, connecting what students already know to what they will learn or meet in the text. Sometimes just one brief prereading activity will be sufficient. At other times you may want to support students' efforts by using several. Your prereading plans will be determined by the purposes for reading, the selection itself, and those who are reading it. You will also coordinate your prereading plans with student activities during and after reading, matters we will consider in the next two sections of the chapter.

As you plan prereading activities, ask yourself questions such as these:

- For what purpose or purposes are students reading this selection?
- How can I get this particular group of students really interested in this selection?

- What background knowledge do they have on this topic?
- What might they need to know to profit most from their reading?
- Is there anything in the material that I can relate to their lives?
- Are there any concepts or vocabulary in the selection that students might benefit from working with?
- Could they use any of their repertoire of comprehension strategies to help them better understand the material?

After answering these questions or similar ones, you can begin to plan prereading activities that will motivate and prepare students for a successful reading experience.

Reflection AND *Application*

4. In what kinds of reading situations are prereading activities likely to be unnecessary? In what situations are prereading activities essential? How might different prereading activities be appropriate for different students?

5. Do any of your college instructors engage their classes in prereading activities? If so, what are these activities? Do they help you better understand the assigned reading material? Explain.

6. What functions do prereading activities serve? Jot down as many as you can, and briefly explain how each prepares readers to comprehend and enjoy the selection they will read.

During-Reading Activities

After you have built the bridge from reader to text with prereading activities, students are ready to get into the act itself. *During-reading activities* include both things that students do themselves as they are reading and things that you do to assist them—activities that facilitate or enhance the actual reading process. The following list shows five types of during-reading activities:

- Silent reading
- Reading to students
- Oral reading by students
- Guided reading
- Modifying the text

As we discussed in Chapter 1, reading is a constructive process—that is, readers build meaning as they read, combining what they know with the author's words and coming up with meaning. One of our responsibilities as teachers is to make sure this meaning building is taking place, to foster active involvement in thinking and reasoning about the text. You have already begun this process with prereading activities, but you will have additional opportunities to support students' efforts as they interact with the text.

Silent Reading

You are probably doing silent reading right now. Particularly in the middle- and upper-elementary grades, most reading is carried out most efficiently by reading the words silently. Silent reading will be the most frequent during-reading activity done by middle- and upper-elementary students. Reading itself, obviously, is the primary activity within the scaffold: the other endeavors are designed to support and enhance it. Prereading activities prepare students for reading, other during-reading activities guide them through it, and postreading activities take them beyond it, to build and respond to the meaning they have constructed.

Reading to Students

Although students will mostly read silently, sometimes it is appropriate to read the material to them. If the text cries out to be heard, for whatever reasons—because the language is beautiful and inspiring, because students need a good send-off for a lengthy or challenging selection, or because the concepts are new and need interpretation—then hearing the words may help students grasp the material. Then, when and if they do read it on their own, it will hold more meaning, pleasure, and interest for them.

A blessed thing happened to me as a child. I had a teacher who read to me.

—Bill Martin, Jr.
Writer and Storyteller

Reading aloud to your students can make certain texts accessible, and the intonation, pitch, stress, pauses, and inflection that you use can give meaning to a text that their own silent reading might not (Horowitz & Freeman, 1995). Reading to students the first few paragraphs or pages of a challenging text is often particularly useful. And reading aloud to students acquiring English can be very effective. Yet, as Alfredo Schifini (1996) notes, literature in English that is read to ESL students must be carefully selected. Schifini suggests that while students are at the beginning stages of acquiring English, they respond well to stories that represent universal experiences or those common to newcomers; selections should not require culturally specific knowledge that is not a part of their schemata. Also, as we note in Chapter 10, nonfiction selections that deal with parts of the physical world that are much the same the world over are very appropriate for students acquiring English. These read-alouds should also involve clear visuals that will invite discussion and link prior knowledge and new concepts.

Reading to your students also provides a model for expressive reading. By reading aloud, you can show your enthusiasm for information, ideas, and language. As Jim Trelease (1989) has pointed out so powerfully in his introduction to *The New Read-Aloud Handbook*, "A large part of the educational research and practice of the last twenty years confirms conclusively that the best way to raise a reader is to read to that child—in the home and in the classroom" (p. xiv). We most emphatically agree: Reading to children builds their vocabularies, their knowledge of the world, their knowledge of books and many of the conventions employed in them, and—probably most important—their interest in reading. Reading aloud to students is one way to demonstrate the beauty and power of language, and for students who struggle with reading on their own or have had little exposure to books, it may be the most significant way.

Oral Reading by Students

Having students read orally is, of course, another option. Three popular read-aloud activities are *choral reading*, *readers' theater*, and *buddy reading*. In choral reading—by using contrasts such as high and low voices, different voice combinations and contrasts, sound effects, movements, gestures, or increasing or decreasing tempo—students together convey and interpret the meaning of a text. Usually students will work on a piece in small groups to decide how they might use their voices, movement, and gestures to express to others the meaning they have constructed from a text. Choral reading builds confidence, fluency, and automaticity as students respond creatively to a text.

Reading aloud to students is a powerful way to engage them in text and demonstrate the beauty and power of language.

Readers' theater, in which students take turns or assume roles in reading portions of text aloud, can be used effectively to interpret poetry, narratives, and even expository materials (Young & Vardell, 1993). In readers' theater, students present drama, prose, or poetry by "reading the text out loud using their voices, reading fast or slow, loudly or softly, emphasizing certain words or phrases to reading rate, intonation, and emphasis on the meaning-bearing cadences of language to make print come alive" (Hoyt, 1992, p. 582). Preparation for a readers' theater performance is similar to that of choral reading. First, a group examines a text and decides what they want to communicate from it. Then they revise the text and use their voices, movement, and sound effects or other props to convey that meaning to others. Sheri Forsythe (1995), a second-grade bilingual teacher, discusses her experience with readers' theater:

"Second-graders can write and present their own Readers Theatre." This statement by my professor, Dr. James Flood, brought me up short. Not in my class, I thought; very few of the second-graders entering my bilingual class in July are readers. But the challenge was there: Use Readers Theatre as a teaching tool. So I did. Now I'm glad I took the challenge. It worked!

Our school is on a year-round schedule, so I plan in quarters using a thematic, integrated approach. I knew the students right out of first grade were not going to sit down and write a Reader Theatre for me, so I decided to work one step at a time. . . .

There was an extreme range of abilities in the class. Several students worked with the resource specialist, but all participated in the Readers Theatre, writing and performing scripts. Our classroom routine also included writers' workshop and flexible reading groups, but the focus of the year was the Readers Theatre. Often the classroom was noisy and appeared to be in total chaos, but work was in progress. And, of course, all our work was in Spanish.

At the end of the year, all 30 students were comfortable standing before an audience and speaking into a microphone; in fact, they loved it. All my students were successful. They were proud of their accomplishments, but not nearly as proud as I was. (pp. 264–265)

Sheri Forsythe, Second-Grade Bilingual Teacher

Of course, both choral reading and readers' theater can also be used as postreading dramatic activities, which we discuss later in the chapter. And they can be used in a variety of ways, many of which are discussed in Nellie McCaslin's *Creative Drama in the Classroom and Beyond* (1996).

In buddy reading, two people read the same passage aloud together or take turns reading. This kind of oral reading is particularly useful for younger students and those who need extra support. Buddies can be two peers, cross-age students, a parent and a student, an aide and a student, or a teacher and a student.

If done in a supportive, nonthreatening way, students' read-aloud activities can enhance their interest and enjoyment of reading, improve fluency, increase vocabulary, and add to their storehouse of knowledge and concepts.

Guided Reading

Guided reading activities focus students' attention on certain ideas as they read. Much of the time, particularly with narratives, students will read the material from beginning to end without stopping to record or reflect on what they are reading. Responses might be shared after they have read, or perhaps not at all. But sometimes, particularly with exposition, it is appropriate to guide students' reading, to help them focus on, understand, and learn from certain aspects of the text. Fourth-grade teacher Robert Lopez describes how he plans such activities:

Whether or not I plan any guided reading activities depends on my students, what they are reading, and why they are reading it. For example, if they are reading a chapter in their social studies text on the establishment of missions in California and they need to recall when the missions were established in order to understand and retain the main ideas of the chapter, I provide them with a time line or have them make their own. As they read about each mission, they record on their time line its name and the date it was founded. I know from past experience that seeing a graphic display of names and dates will help them keep these straight in their minds. For other chapters, or other kinds of expository text, I might give them a guide that helps them focus on the organizational patterns the authors use, such as cause and effect or problem and solution.

Robert Lopez, Fourth-Grade Teacher

In addition to Mr. Lopez's suggestions, here are a few other options for guiding students' reading of exposition:

- Encourage critical thinking by having students note examples of fact and opinion, make inferences, draw conclusions, or predict outcomes.
- Lead students to manipulate the text in ways that will help them better understand and retain key concepts—recording main ideas and their supporting details, outlining, summarizing, and making graphic organizers.
- Have students monitor their understanding of what they read.

Although guided reading activities are most often used to help students read expository material, they can also be employed with narratives. Perhaps you feel students would understand and enjoy a story more if they focused their attention on certain aspects of character, setting, plot, or theme. Or maybe you want them to be aware of colorful or unusual language. Perhaps you want them to make personal responses to what they read, make predictions, or consider how they or the characters are feeling. These are all good reasons for designing guided reading activities for narratives.

Guided reading activities for narratives can include the following:

- Informal writing that elicits personal responses, such as journaling or writing letters
- Reading with a partner and pausing to reflect out loud
- Using reading guides, which might include answering questions or completing charts or outlines that focus on character, plot development, point of view, or aspects of language or style

Guided reading activities should get students thinking about and manipulating the ideas and concepts in the material in a way that will help them better understand, enjoy, and remember it.

In the same way that reading to children and sharing books with children who are considered to be fluent readers should continue to be essential daily activities within a balanced language program, so should guided reading. At any stage of a reader's development, guided reading allows you to make children aware of the "why and how and the knowledge that you know" of reading.

—Margaret Mooney
Reading Consultant

Modifying the Text

Have you ever read Cliff Notes, listened to a novel recorded on audiotape, or heard an instructor tell you, "Read only sections II and IV of Chapter 15"? These situations are examples of modifying the text—altering the original text or the medium of presentation. Sometimes, because of curriculum requirements or availability of texts, students will be reading selections whose length or difficulty presents too much of a challenge. In these cases, modifying or shortening the selections is a practical and powerful option. Fifth-grade teacher Deborah Reisman offers some suggestions:

> I teach fifth grade, and my school district requires that students learn the concepts presented in the state-adopted U.S. history text. While the text is written at a fifth- to sixth-grade reading level, the reading ability of the students in my class ranges from second-grade to twelfth-grade levels. To make it accessible to the students who read below fifth-grade level, something has to be done to the material. I sometimes read portions of the text orally or tape-record some sections (or have a sixth- or seventh-grade-level student record these for me). Tape recordings make it possible for these struggling readers to listen to a selection as they follow along silently. Another option is to have students read only selected portions of the chapter—the ones that I think are the most critical. This makes an otherwise impossible task quite feasible for my slower readers.
>
> Deborah Reisman, Fifth-Grade Teacher

We agree with Ms. Reisman, but of course, modifying the text is not always desirable. Reading part of a text or listening to it is not the same as reading the original. But, bearing in mind that success must be a constant goal and that some students may fail in reading some original texts, modifying the text can help ensure success. Moreover, this technique can be particularly effective with less-skilled readers or students just acquiring English.

During-Reading Activities: Summary and Guidelines

Like prereading activities, there are many different kinds of during-reading activities and many ways of varying them. All during-reading activities, however, involve students with the text as they read it in a way that best suits the students, the text, and their purposes. Here are some questions you might ask before designing during-reading activities:

- What is the student's purpose for reading this selection?
- How might the reading transaction best be accomplished—silently, orally, with a buddy, or a combination of these approaches?
- What might I do to actively involve students with the text?

- What can I do to help make this material come alive for students as they read?
- What would make this material more accessible to students?
- What might students do as they read that will make the text more understandable or memorable or enjoyable, so that they achieve their reading goals?

Reflection AND Application

7. Suppose you are teaching second grade. What kinds of during-reading activities might you engage your students in, and why?

8. Briefly discuss in writing, or with a classmate, the purpose and function of guided reading activities. Discuss your personal philosophy about guided reading activities, when they might be appropriate, and when inappropriate.

9. Identify a narrative or expository text you might use in the classroom. Answer the questions listed in the previous Summary and Guidelines section to help you design during-reading activities for that piece.

Postreading Activities

Why engage students in postreading activities? What function do these activities serve in the scaffold? Why, after reading a selection, shouldn't students just go on to something else? Generally, *postreading activities* encourage students to *do* something with the material they have just read, to think—critically, logically, and creatively—about the information and ideas that emerge from their reading, and sometimes to transform their thinking into actions. These responses can take a variety of forms—speaking, writing, drama, creative arts, or application and outreach. To determine the appropriateness and the type of response called for, we again consider the *selection*, the *reader*, and the *purpose*. Do they suggest or require postreading activities?

We have categorized seven kinds of postreading activities:

1. Questioning
2. Discussion
3. Writing
4. Drama
5. Artistic and nonverbal activities
6. Application and outreach
7. Reteaching

Some books are to be tasted, others to be swallowed, and some few to be chewed and digested.

—Francis Bacon
Essayist and Philosopher

Questioning

Postreading questioning activities encourage students to think about and react to the information and ideas in the material they have read, either orally or in writing. Thinking about or answering questions about certain aspects of the text is a natural outgrowth of what has taken place before and during reading and will serve as a final link in the comprehension and engagement chain.

Questions can promote thinking on a number of levels. They might help readers recall what they have read, show that they understand what was read, or give them an opportunity to apply, analyze, synthesize, or elaborate information and ideas. Questions might also encourage creative, interpretive, or metacognitive thinking and illustrate the various perspectives among readers.

One way to ensure that students are engaged in thinking about a text on a variety of levels is to deliberately consider three types of questions. David Pearson and Dale Johnson (1978) have termed them *text-explicit*, *text-implicit*, and *script-implicit questions*. Assume that fifth-graders are reading a biography of the Pulitzer Prize–winning Native American author N. Scott Momaday (Globe, 1993). Text-explicit questions are directly answered in the reading selection. Here is one text-explicit question for the cited selection: When did Momaday win the Pulitzer Prize? The biography specifically states that he won the Pulitzer Prize in 1969. Text-implicit questions are also answered in

No matter what text is being read, from poetry to mathematics, postreading questioning that promotes creative and analytical thinking can be an exciting activity for teachers and students alike.

the reading selection, but they require making at least one inference. Here is an example of a text-implicit question about the Momaday text: How did Momaday's winning the Pulitzer Prize influence his writing career? The biography contains a good deal of information that answers this question, but it does not directly answer it. Script-implicit questions, in contrast to text-implicit questions, require the reader to use prior knowledge in formulating answers. Here is one script-implicit question for the Momaday biography: How would you feel if, like Momaday, you often encountered situations in which your background and experiences were very different from those of others? Although this question is prompted by Momaday's biography, much of the answer must come from the reader's schemata. Students who are taught about these three sorts of questions and where to find answers to them have been found to become more adept at answering them (Raphael, 1982).

As we noted when discussing prereading questioning, questions can be generated by the teacher or by students. The questions we posed for the Momaday biography are examples of teacher-generated questions. Student-generated questions evolve from students' interests and their need or desire to know. Fourth-grade teacher Patricia Lyle reflects on the use of postreading questioning:

> I encourage my students to do a lot of questioning when they read, and that includes questions that arise *after* they have read. For example, after reading a chapter on California missions in their social studies text, I asked students to write five questions they still had about the issues or topics in the chapter. To answer the questions, they referred back to the text or looked for the answers in other sources.
>
> I also have students develop a set of questions for the books they read that other students will answer. First we talk about the different sorts of questions to ask. Often these are text-explicit, text-implicit, and script-implicit types of questions.
>
> I have found that my good readers often ask text-inspired questions without any prompting. Yet I have learned as a result of my repeated modeling and the modeling provided by students who are active questioners, readers who do not initially ask such questions begin to do so.
>
> Patricia Lyle, Fourth-Grade Teacher

Discussion

As you can imagine, a large number of classroom reading experiences will include discussion—exchanging ideas out loud. The key word here is *exchanging*—some like to use the term *dialogue* to describe the give-and-take nature of discussion. The intent of discussion is to freely explore ideas, to learn something new or gain a different perspective by pooling the information or insights that more than one person can give. Research studies show that positive

Student-led discussions encourage students to be responsible for their own learning .

effects accrue when children engage in small-group discussions about text. These discussions enhance text recall, aesthetic response to text, and reading comprehension (Gambrell, 1996).

Of course, good discussions do not just happen. As Donna Alvermann and her colleagues (1987) explain at length, good discussion requires planning and effort both on your part and on your students' part. To become proficient in discussion, students need explicit instruction, modeling, and many opportunities for practice. Students also need feedback from you and their peers on what has been learned in a discussion and on the process of the discussion itself. That is, you and your students need to talk about matters such as the need for all students to participate, for students to listen to one another and to respect one anothers' opinions, and for evaluating the group's success in dealing with the topic. Joyce Wiencek (1996) points out that with "students in first and second grades, teachers often choose to fully participate throughout the discussion. This method enables them to scaffold and support the developing abilities of young students to sustain a discussion and allows the teacher to model behaviors and strategies students may adopt" (p. 216).

Discussion groups can be led by the teacher or by students. They can involve the entire class, small groups, or pairs. Whatever format is used, these guidelines will help you implement discussions:

- Develop a clear purpose or purposes. What is the discussion meant to accomplish? Are students examining two or more sides of an issue? Are they trying to discover a book's theme? Are they solving a problem or mastering the content of a text? Discussion should not be rigidly structured—but without clear purpose or focus, it runs the risk of deteriorating into meaningless chitchat.
- Discussion leaders (as well as participants) should be supportive, noncritical, and open-minded. Leaders should encourage response from all members of the group and be sparing in their own comments and suggestions.
- Teachers need to prepare students for good discussion. Skills and behaviors such as active listening, paraphrasing, and courtesy need to be taught.

- Discussions should incorporate a number of kinds and levels of thinking. These might include recall, application, analysis, synthesis, and evaluation and interpretation of information and ideas.
- When differences of opinions arise concerning literal or recall questions, the text should be consulted in order to verify or refute such opinions.
- Group members should be encouraged to evaluate discussions. Was their purpose achieved? Did everyone get a chance to participate equally? What were strengths and weaknesses of the discussion? What might be done differently in the future?
- Discussion must always take place in an atmosphere of trust. In order for students to take risks in expressing their thoughts, they need to feel secure.

As we just noted, students should be encouraged and challenged to think about a text, not to merely cite facts and figures, but to delve more deeply into meanings and implications. Quality literature generates and communicates ideas—ideas that humans need to survive, to make strides personally and collectively (Monson, 1992).

Writing

Writing has been called the twin sister of reading—a powerful way to integrate what you already know with the information presented in a text as well as to find out what you really understand and what you don't. Writing is powerful because it requires a reader to actively manipulate information and ideas. We discuss writing at length in Chapter 9; here we focus on writing as a postreading activity. As such, writing can help a student connect information and ideas. Writing also provides opportunities for students to extend ideas, to explore new ways of thinking, doing, and seeing—to invent, evaluate, create, and ponder. Before planning postreading writing activities, ask these questions: Why are you encouraging students to write? What purpose does the writing serve as a postreading activity? For whom is the student writing—himself or herself, or someone else?

Postreading writing activities should, like all the other activities we have discusssed, relate to the initial purposes set for reading the selection, the selection itself, and the readers. If your purpose in having a group of fifth-graders read a chapter on electricity is to ensure that they understand and remember the information, then having them write a summary for each of the sections of the chapter would be a useful writing activity. If your purpose is to have primary-grade students respond personally to a poem about feelings, you might ask them to write a poem describing similar feelings they have had. Or, if your purpose is to have students synthesize information they

I don't know what I think until I see what I said.

—E. M. Forster
Novelist

Writing is my favorite type of extension. Writing is a way of showing how I feel about a book. It also helps me appreciate the author more. Because when I write I try to do what the author did. I use words that give the audience a picture in their minds. I describe what happened and who the characters are and what they're thinking and feeling.

—Pete
Fourth-Grader

have read about, you might have them write an alphabet picture book on the topic. For example, after a unit on animals, teacher Mary O'Hara had her sixth-grade students create alphabet picture books depicting an animal of their choice. Sara chose cats. Figure 6.5 shows her dedication page and the text for five of her entries.

Writing is a powerful way to help students become actively involved with what they read, since it requires that they really think about what they know. Writing gives students the opportunity to take the ideas they have gleaned from the reading and synthesize or apply them in a new way, as Sara's book on cats demonstrates.

Any well-written book can inspire written responses of various kinds, from personal responses jotted down in a journal to more formal endeavors such as stories or poems. Here we list a mere eight titles to give you a taste of the possibilities.

Books That Invite Writing

John Agard. *The Calypso Alphabet*. Holt, 1989. This colorfully illustrated text, which provides an introduction to Caribbean culture, could be used as a springboard for students of all ages to write alphabet books about their own cultures.

Caroline Feller Bauer. *Snowy Day: Stories and Poems* Lippincott, 1986. The snow poems and stories from three diverse cultures that are found in this collection are sure to inspire children to write their own snow poems and stories.

Marilee Robin Burton. *My Best Shoes*. Tambourine, 1994. In this predictable book, a young girl wears a different pair of shoes for each day of the week, including "no shoes" on Sunday. The vivid descriptions of the shoes, such as "scratched and scuffed and muffed" and "twinkling in the light shoes" can inspire young readers to write descriptions of their own clothing for each day of the week.

Wade Hudson. *Jamal's Busy Day*. Just Us Books, 1991. This picture book, in which Jamal talks about his day as busy, important, and filled with "work" like that of his architect dad and accountant mom, can motivate students to write about their own "busy" days.

Steven Kellogg. *Pecos Bill*. Morrow, 1986. Kellogg's humorous retelling of this famous tall tale, which he embellishes with wild and vivid illustrations, can spur students of all ages to invent their own contemporary tall tales.

Reeve Lindbergh. *If I'd Known Then What I Know Now*. Viking, 1994. After reading this rhyming story about an inept "handyman" dad, in a house where there are "holes in the roof, leaky plumbing, a stove that gets cold, and a refrigerator that gets warm," students might enjoy writing their own rhyming household-disaster stories.

Richard McGuire. *Night Becomes Day*. Viking, 1994. In this story, day and night come full circle, with one object folding into another—"tree becomes paper and paper becomes news." Children might enjoy writing and illustrating their own "full circle" stories.

Allen Say. *Grandfather's Journey*. Houghton Mifflin, 1993. In this picture book, an adult narrator tells of his grandfather's journey from Japan to America, which he also later takes. Students might interview grandparents or other family members who have immigrated and write their stories. Or students who have themselves moved from one country or community to another might write accounts of the journey and the emotions they felt.

Dedication: This book is dedicated to my mom for always being there for me and to my two cats who I love dearly.

A is for Abyssinian. The Abyssinian is a very slender cat, and is surprisingly one of the strongest breeds in the world.

B is for Burmese. The Burmese has a short neck and its fur is a golden brown shade. The Burmese is a very muscular cat.

C is for Cheetah. The cheetah is the fastest animal in the world. This animal is becoming extinct because people love their skin and kill them just for the skin.

D is for the Dogcat. This cat is a very unusual cat. It is sometimes mistaken for a dog because it is so big.

E is for Egyptian Mau. The Mau was first found in 1400. It's one of the oldest breeds in the world.

FIGURE 6.5 *Excerpts from Sara's Cat Book*

Dramatics

As a postreading activity, drama, like writing, encourages students to extend existing meanings they have constructed with a text and to generate new ones. In the hands of a skillful, sensitive teacher, drama can become an enjoyable and highly motivating way to involve students in all of the cognitive tasks we listed at the beginning of this section—recalling, applying, analyzing, synthesizing, evaluating, and creating.

Although classroom drama may incorporate many different activities, such as visualization, movement, pantomime, improvisation, and role-playing, to address curriculum goals, we focus on story dramatization as a postreading activity. In story dramatization, students work together, usually with some assistance from the teacher, to improvise or to plan out and enact something they have read. Dramatizations don't require an audience; they can be prepared and enacted by the children for themselves, as their own way of engaging in and making meaning from a text they have read. Dramatizations may also be shared with others—children in the same class, children from other classrooms, parents, or people beyond the school walls in places such as day care centers or nursing homes.

Because most children love to get into the act, drama presentations of all kinds—plays, skits, retelling of stories, pantomimes, and readers' theater—provide a wonderful way to actively involve students in the material they read. Multigrade teacher Harold Bolinski cites several examples of how he uses dramatizations:

> I have used dramatization with every kind of text and students of all ages. For example, I've had an entire class of second-graders pantomime Indian tigers while I read them Ted Lewin's informational picture book *Tiger Trek*. When I taught a multiage class, small groups of first- through third-graders gathered together to prepare a dramatization of their favorite poems in Jack Prelutsky's *Tyrannosaurus Was a Beast*. This year two of my fifth-graders played the parts of Gilly and Miss Ellis, Gilly's caseworker, and dramatized the opening scene from Katherine Paterson's *The Great Gilly Hopkins*. Another two students, after reading a chapter on the 1960s in their social studies text, decided to portray Martin Luther King, Jr., and Lyndon B. Johnson. They carried on a conversation posing as these two individuals. They did such a great job that we videotaped their conversation and aired it on the community cable TV station. I've even had students play blood cells and dramatize the flow of blood through the circulatory system in response to the science texts they have read! You name it, my students have dramatized it.
>
> Harold Bolinski, Multigrade Teacher

> Dramatizations are ways for children to construct and share meaning from the texts they read, and they help build a positive climate for learning in the classroom. In dramatizations, whether as enactors or observers, children are active in their learning. In very fundamental ways, dramatization activities help the teacher to "uncover" the curriculum rather than cover it.
>
> —Stephen M. Koziol
> Teacher Educator

Artistic and Nonverbal Activities

The preceding four categories—questioning, discussion, writing, and drama—have all in some way involved words. But as we have mentioned before, and according to the work of Howard Gardner (1993), we have multiple intelligences—a variety of ways to learn and express what we know. This category takes into account those modes of expression that are not predominantly verbal, including the visual arts, music, and dance. We also include response activities that involve the creation of media productions, visual displays, and representations.

Art, music, and dance each represent a specialized language that can be used in response to printed and spoken communication. Third-grade teacher Michael Henning encourages students to express themselves creatively using art, music, and dance in this scenario:

IN THE CLASSROOM
Artistic Responses to Readings About Animals

Mr. Henning's third-grade class has just finished a unit on animals. Over a four-week period, they have read numerous fiction and nonfiction trade books, and Mr. Henning has read *Dr. Doolittle* aloud to them as well. As a culminating activity, he reads William Jay Smith's book of poems, *Birds and Beasts*. Next, he divides the class into three heterogeneous groups and assigns each group one of the three nonverbal expressive languages—art, music, or dance. Each group then decides which animal it will portray in its appointed "language" and brainstorms about materials and approaches they might take. For example, the art group suggests watercolor painting, collages, scratchboards, paper sculpture, clay modeling, and papier-mâché. After the students have decided on their animal and some possibilities for depicting it visually with the resources available, they then work individually, in subgroups, and in pairs to create their animal, using whatever medium they feel will best capture its essence.

The music group's goal is to create an instrumental piece to depict their animal. During their brainstorming session, students think about the musical resources available to them as well as the characteristics of their particular animal. They consider rhythm and percussion instruments and those that produce melody. Some of their suggestions include drums, cymbals, sticks, sandpaper blocks, recorders, song flutes, xylophone, bells, piano, and electric keyboard. After they decide how they will depict this animal through music, they begin working in pairs or small groups to do so.

The dance group's goal is to depict their chosen animal through movement. During their brainstorming session, students offer suggestions about body movements that represent this animal. Their discussion involves both showing and telling, with these sorts of words describing the characteristics and movements of their chosen animal—*slow, steady, heavy, swinging, head moving, tail swishing, clomp, clomp, clomp*. Although the group decides to work together to create one dance that represents their animal, they might have chosen to work in pairs or subgroups.

After their brainstorming sessions, students spend an hour or so on each of two or three days to come up with nonverbal expressions of their chosen animals. On the fourth day they present their work; their animals come to life in visual art, in music, and in dance, and other students guess the animals that are being portrayed by each group.

Numerous children's books will help connect students with the arts—for example, *Down by the River*, a collection of Afro-Caribbean rhymes, games, and songs compiled by Grace Hallworth (1996). In her article "Music and Children's Books," Kathleen Jacobi-Karna (1996) gives an extensive list of children's books that suggest musical possibilities. On page 60, we list ten titles, many of which were recommended by Cheri Estes (1995) in her article "Musical Links, Part I."

In addition to responding to a selection through art, dance, and music, students can engage in artistic and nonverbal activities involving the creation of

- media productions—audiotapes, videos, and slide shows.
- visual displays—bulletin boards, artifacts, models, and specimens.
- visual representations of information—graphs, maps, charts, trees, maps, diagrams, and schematics.

Books That Invite Musical Connections

Jan Brett. *Berlioz the Bear*. Putnam, 1991. Berlioz the bear and his fellow musician are due to play for the town ball when their bandwagon becomes stuck in a hole in the road. A strange buzzing in Berlioz's double bass turns into a surprise that saves the day.

Claude Clement. *Musician from Darkness*. Little, Brown, 1990. In lyrical prose, Clement tells the story of an outsider from primitive society who discovers the power and magic of music.

Claude Clement. *Voice of the Wood*. Dial, 1989. A craftsman builds a cello from a well-loved tree. When an arrogant musician tries to play it, he discovers it is "only a heart in tune with the voice of the wood can make it sing."

James Lincoln Collier. *The Jazz Kid*. Holt, 1994. In this story, set in Chicago in the 1920s, 12-year-old Paulie wants to become a jazz cornetist and play the Black jazz music of Louis Armstrong, King Oliver, and the New Orleans Rhythm Kings. But his prejudiced parents are against it.

Ezra Jack Keats. *Apt 3*. Aladdin, 1986. On a rainy day, two young boys search for the source of the harmonica music they hear in their apartment building.

Robert Kraus. *Musical Max*. Simon & Schuster, 1990. Max the musical hippo drives his father and neighbors crazy with his daily practicing on every sort of instrument. One day he loses interest and stops. But the effect is not what the complainers thought it would be.

Bill Martin, Jr. *The Maestro Plays*. Holt, 1994. The subtleties of music are introduced with rhyming text as Martin describes the way a maestro plays the music, "proudly, loudly, busily, dizzily."

Metropolitan Museum of Art. *Go in and out the Window: An Illustrated Songbook for Young People*. Holt, 1987. Art and music are brought together in this handsome volume of 61 familiar songs illustrated with works from the Metropolitan Museum of Art.

Brian Pinkney. *Max Found Two Sticks*. Simon & Schuster, 1994. A would-be drummer, Max beats on different surfaces, echoing the sounds around him. He imagines church bells, a marching band, a train; then a real band marches by and a drummer tosses Max a pair of sticks.

Mildred Pitts Walter. *Ty's One-Man Band*. Four Winds, 1987. A young Black child, while playing by the pond, meets a one-legged, one-man band who brings music to the community.

Like drama activities, artistic and nonverbal activities have great potential for showing students that language can be transformed and that ideas can be seen, heard, and felt.

Application and Outreach

Books open doors. They invite us to step out, to go beyond the text to see for ourselves, to act on newfound knowledge, and to apply it in a unique way. Each of the previously mentioned categories in one way or another reflects the idea of going beyond the text to explore other realms and other applications of information and ideas. In application and outreach endeavors, readers take the ideas and information from a text and deliberately test, use, or explore them further. Students might read a story about making ice cream or an article describing several science experiments, but it's not quite as much fun as actually following the steps and eating the ice cream or doing the experiments. The logical next step after reading about something is to try it out in the real world.

Not only how-to books invite real-world applications, however. Fiction, nonfiction, and poetry can spark many different kinds of personal and social action. After reading Chris Van Allsburg's *Just a Dream*—in which a child dreams of a future wasted due to poor management of the environment—students might decide to write letters to state and local representatives encouraging them to support legislation to better the environment, or they might develop an environment-related ad campaign for their school or neighborhood. Or after reading Mem Fox's touching picture book *Wilfrid Gordon McDonald Partridge*—in which a young boy discovers a unique way to help the forgetful Miss Nancy recapture her memories—students might be inspired to share the story with residents in a nursing home or to try this memory-recapturing approach with an elderly relative or friend.

Students will not always make on their own the connections necessary to transfer ideas from the text to the real world. In fact, as David Perkins (1992) and others have noted, many students all too infrequently relate school learning to life. By providing activities that demonstrate such connections, you can drive home a critical aspect of the nature of good text—we should not be the same after we have read it. We should be a little more than we were before. Our new selves contain new information and ideas that we can now use.

Reteaching

The six types of activities that we have just discussed encourage students to make logical connections between ideas and to explore new ways of thinking and of expressing themselves. Our seventh category, reteaching, is the safety net in the reading scaffold, a way to make sure students leave a reading selection with a sense of accomplishment, of a job well done.

Reteaching is often necessary when students, after reading a selection and engaging in various activities of an SRE, have not reached their reading goals. Robert Dickenson, a fifth-grade teacher, discusses his reteaching approaches:

> I sometimes find it necessary to include reteaching activities in the scaffold I build to support my students' reading experience. This happens when my students have not reached their reading goals. These reteaching activities usually consist of a retracing of the steps of a specific activity *with* students, to see what went

wrong and where—for example, if students had difficulty completing a reading guide or answering postreading questions. In these cases my reteaching might include discussing with students the problems they had and why they had them, and then reviewing the purposes and steps involved in completing the guide or answering the questions.

Alternatively, reteaching sometimes involves creating a totally different activity. I do this when the original activity was a disaster—something that happens more times than I'd like to admit, even though I'm a seasoned teacher.

Sometimes I have students simply repeat the original activity, approaching it with their new level of understanding. I do this when students have gained quite a bit from their reading, but a second attempt could result in greater gains. My purpose in all of these approaches—discussing the problem and then modifying the activity, creating a new activity, or repeating the original one—is to do everything possible to ensure that my students have successful and fulfilling reading experiences.

Robert Dickenson, Fifth-Grade Teacher

Postreading Activities: Summary and Guidelines

> The art of educating for literacy engagement is to link students' intrinsic motivations to classroom activities.
>
> —*John T. Guthrie*
> *Educational Psychologist*

Again, postreading activities help students go beyond the text and do something with the material they have read in order to help them see the relevance of reading, how it relates to their own lives and to the wider world around them. Response activities will also help students better remember what they have read, provide them with opportunities to express themselves in a variety of ways, encourage the development of multiple intelligences, and give them opportunities to see how others interpret selections and additional opportunities to succeed.

Postreading activities involve students with ideas gleaned from text in a way that is customized to suit the text itself, the students, and their purposes. You might ask these questions when developing postreading activities:

- Will students benefit in some way from postreading activities?
- Does the activity reflect the initial reading purpose, and is it a logical outgrowth of pre- and during-reading activities?
- Will the activity further students' understanding of the ideas in the selection?
- Will the activity enhance students' critical literacy?
- Will the activity expand students' schemata for the ways of responding to text ideas?
- Is the activity doable and enjoyable?
- What response activities are generated or suggested by students themselves?

Reflection AND Application

10. What purposes do postreading activities serve? Do you think you will engage your students in postreading activities for most of the reading they do in your class? Why or why not?

11. Suppose you are teaching-fifth graders who have just finished reading biographies of prominent figures in U.S. history. What sorts of postreading activities might these students engage in and why?

    Suppose you are teaching first-graders who have just read a beginning chapter book on the theme of friendship. What sorts of postreading activities might these students engage in, and why?

12. Do you think it's important to engage students in application and outreach postreading activities? Why or why not?

Comprehensive SREs

In the previous three sections, we have focused on individual pre-, during-, and postreading activities. Now we discuss how these activities are interrelated and linked, one to the other, in response to the students, the selection, and the overall purpose for reading. A scaffolded reading experience (SRE) is built around the six key factors that we have discussed:

Purpose	Prereading Activities
Selection	During-Reading Activities
Reader	Postreading Activities

Suppose, for example, your third-graders are going to read *Too Many Tamales* by Gary Soto. Figure 6.6 outlines a sample SRE for that situation. Figure 6.7 shows another SRE for the same selection to be read by a different group of students. Figure 6.8 outlines an SRE for an entirely different selection, group of students, and purpose.

You can see from these brief examples the effect that the students, the purpose for which they are reading, and the selection have on the type and quantity of activities. Once you have (1) identified your students' needs, capabilities, and interests, (2) become familiar with the selection's topics, themes, and vocabulary, and (3) know your purpose, then you can begin selecting and planning activities.

Prereading	*During-Reading*	*Postreading*
Prepare for meaning	Build meaning	Build and respond to meaning

Before ending this section, we want to reemphasize that the purpose of the SRE is not to fill up precious reading time with a lot of activities (no matter how engaging or purposeful in their own right they might be) but rather to provide a scaffold for students to successfully build meaning from the texts that they read and to do something with their newly gained knowledge and insights.

Students	Selection	Purpose
Third-graders (3 ESL students and 1 academically challenged student)	*Too Many Tamales* by Gary Soto	To understand, enjoy, and artistically respond to a light-hearted story

Prereading Activities	During-Reading Activities	Postreading Activities
1 Motivating 1 Preteaching Vocabulary 2 Building Background Knowledge 1 Suggesting Strategy	1 Guided Reading 1 Oral Reading by Teacher 1 Silent Reading	1 Discussion 1 Drama 1 Artistic and Nonverbal 1 Reteaching (This became part of the scaffolding when it became apparent that students were having problems using the strategy suggested during prereading.)

FIGURE 6.6 *Sample SRE for Third-Graders Reading* Too Many Tamales *by Gary Soto*

Students	Selection	Purpose
Third-graders (above average and gifted)	*Too Many Tamales* by Gary Soto	To understand, enjoy, and respond to a light-hearted mystery

Prereading Activities	During-Reading Activities	Postreading Activities
1 Building Background Knowledge, which combines motivation and purpose setting	1 Silent Reading	1 Writing (creative)

FIGURE 6.7 *Alternative SRE for Third-Graders Reading* Too Many Tamales *by Gary Soto*

Students	Selection	Purpose
Fifth-graders of mixed abilities; two ESL students	Chapter on World War II Postwar Years	To understand, recall, respond to, and analyze the important topics and issues in the chapter

Prereading Activities	During-Reading Activities	Postreading Activities
l Motivational l Preteaching Concepts 2 Building Background Knowledge l Suggesting Strategies	l Guided Reading l Oral Reading by Teacher l Oral Reading by Students l Modifying the Text (for ESL students only)	l Discussion l Artistic and Nonverbal l Writing

FIGURE 6.8 *Sample SRE for Fifth-Graders Reading a Chapter on World War II*

SELECTED PROCEDURES FOR FOSTERING COMPREHENSION OF INDIVIDUAL SELECTIONS

In this section, we describe a number of additional teacher-led routines that differ from the SRE in that they were designed to achieve very specific instructional goals or to focus on a particular part of reading. Some are used prior to reading, some during reading, some after reading, and some at several points in the reading process. All of them encourage active and reflective thinking and can be modified for any elementary classroom. We have divided them into three categories:

1. Procedures for narratives
2. Procedures for expository texts
3. Procedures appropriate for all types of texts

Procedures for Narratives

As we have already noted, narratives are written primarily to entertain. Well-written stories, whether simple or complex, have a fairly similar structure, and most children have a basic schema for this structure. Teachers can help students make this understanding explicit and give them a language for talking about stories. When teachers build on this schema, students' comprehension and enjoyment of narrative literature will be enhanced, as will be their writing in this genre. Using story grammars and story maps are two ways to help students enhance their schema for stories.

Story Grammars

To identify the common elements that make up a well-developed story, several variations of story grammar have been developed (Mandler & Johnson, 1977; Thorndyke, 1977). Story grammar is similar to sentence grammar in that it attempts to explain the various components in a story and how they function. The story grammar we have found most helpful is a synthesis of those that both educational researchers and fiction writers have identified as consistent across stories. This grammar includes a *setting* with a *character* who has a problem to solve or a goal to achieve, the character's *attempts* to solve the problem or achieve the goal, the *results* of these attempts, and a *conclusion*. This conclusion illuminates the story's theme. Figure 6.9 shows these components and their relationship to one another and to the three phases of a story: beginning, development, and ending.

How might this analysis of stories aid teachers in their instruction and students in their critical literacy growth? We go back to the all-important notion of schema. Developing and refining children's schema for stories can help improve both their comprehension and writing of stories.

One way to help develop this schema is with a story frame. A story frame (Cudd & Roberts, 1987; Fowler, 1982) is a series of blanks linked by transition words that represent a line of thought. It can help build students' schema for stories and give them a language for talking about stories. The student fills in the blanks with the appropriate words or phrases as he reads. Story frames can be designed to reflect the particular story being read and to focus on selected story elements, such as main idea or plot or a comparison of characters. Gerald Fowler has developed frames that emphasize five different story features—plot, setting, character analysis, character comparison, and a story's summary. Figure 6.10 shows one type—the plot frame. The plot frame can be used in a postreading activity. For example, after a group

> Stories are marvelous means of summarizing experiences, of capturing an event and the surrounding context that seems essential. Stories are important cognitive events, for they encapsulate, into one compact package, information, knowledge, context, and emotion.
>
> —*Donald Norman*
> *Cognitive Psychologist*

FIGURE 6.9 *Representative Story Grammar*

of first-graders has read the story silently, you might put the plot frame on an overhead projector and complete it together. The students can help supply the information as you write the words on the transparency, as illustrated in Figure 6.11.

In this story, the problem begins when _____

_____ After that, _____

_____ Next, _____

_____ Then, _____

The problem is finally solved when _____

_____ The story ends _____

FIGURE 6.10 *A Plot Frame for* Amazing Grace *by Mary Hoffman*

In this story, the problem begins when _Grace wants to play Peter Pan in the class play and the kids tell her she can't because she's a black girl and Peter's a white boy._ After that, _Grace tells her mother and Nana, and they tell her she can be anything she wants to be if she puts her mind to it._ Next, _Nana takes Grace to see a ballet in which a black ballerina dances the role of Juliet._ Then, _Grace practices for the Peter Pan part._ The problem is finally solved when _Grace auditions for the part and gets it._ The story ends _with the show being a big success and Grace an amazing Peter Pan._

FIGURE 6.11 *A Completed Plot Frame for* Amazing Grace *by Mary Hoffman*

Although frames are most often used as a postreading activity, they can be useful as a prereading and during-reading activity to help focus students' attention on major parts of the story (Reutzel, 1991). To use a story frame as a prereading activity, the teacher first provides story clues by reading the story title, displaying the cover illustration, identifying the main character, and briefly discussing these. Students then use the frame as a guide to predicting story events. For primary-grade youngsters, the teacher will work with students, writing in their suggestions to complete the frame on the chalkboard or an overhead transparency. For middle- and upper-elementary students, teachers can provide copies of a frame and have students write their own predictions in pencil, revising them as they read the story or afterward.

Story Maps

Simply put, a story map is a listing of the major events and ideas in a story, beginning at the starting point and moving through the story in sequential order. Isabel Beck and Margaret McKeown (1981) recommend that teachers create a story map to help identify the major structural elements, both explicit and implicit, in a story that students will be reading in class. Based on the map, the teacher then generates a question for the students to answer related to each major event. In the worksheet illustrated in Figure 6.12, you will see that the left column gives the story event and the right column the corresponding question for students to answer. These questions, when answered, constitute the essence of the story and elicit information that is central to understanding it. To create a story map, first decide what the starting point for the story is, list briefly the major events in chronological order, and then write a question for each event. Students can discuss the questions before they read as a sort of preview, use them as they read to record their understanding of the story, or answer them after they read to assess their comprehension.

Story map questions can both improve students' existing schema for story and improve their story comprehension. As Beck and McKeown note, however, story map questions are not the only questions to ask concerning reading selections. Once students understand the essence of the story, then interpretive, analytical, and creative questions are appropriate and important to pursue. For example, you might ask, "Have you every been warned not to do something, as Katrina was? What were you warned not to do? What happened?"

Before we move on to expository texts, we want to emphasize that the procedures for teaching story structure or grammar are to be used in con-

Event	Corresponding Question
Event 1: Katrina's father warns her not to go into the woods where the witch, Baba Yaga lives.	*Why did Katrina's father warn her not to go into the woods?*
Event 2: The cruel housemaid sends Katrina into the woods to take food to a sick aunt.	*What did the cruel housemaid ask Katrina to do?*
Event 3: Katrina finds a dying dog in the woods and revives it with milk from her jug.	*What did Katrina do to help the dog she found in the woods?*
Event 4: A bit farther, Katrina stops to grease the squeaky hinges of a rusted gate.	*Why did Katrina stop to grease the gate?*
Event 5: Deep in the forest, Katrina comes upon Baba Yaga's hut, not the sick aunt's, and realizes the housemaid has betrayed her.	*Whose hut did Katrina reach deep in the woods?*
Event 6: Baba Yaga takes Katrina as a prisoner and slave.	*What did Baba Yaga do to Katrina?*
Event 7: Katrina shows kindness to Baba Yaga's cat by combing its matted fur and the cat tells her to flee from Baba Yaga at midnight.	*Why did Baba Yaga's cat tell Katrina she should escape?*
Event 8: Katrina flees with Baba Yaga pursuing her but is able to escape with the aid and magic of those she was kind to—the cat, the gate, and the dog.	*Who helped Katrina escape from Baba Yaga, and why?*
Event 9: Katrina throws the rag with which she had greased the gate at Baba Yaga; it turns into a lake, and Baba Yaga drowns.	*What happened when Katrina threw the rag at Baba Yaga?*
Event 10: Katrina returns home, and her father sends the evil housemaid packing.	*Why did Katrina's father "send the housemaid packing"?*

FIGURE 6.12 *Sample Story Map Worksheet for Baba Yaga, retold by Margaret Yatsevitch Phinney*

junction with the specific stories students are reading in class and not in an abstract, general fashion. Tying them in with a particular selection will help students understand and enjoy that selection and build their schema for stories in general.

Procedures for Expository Texts

As we have mentioned earlier, in contrast to narratives, which are written primarily to entertain, expository texts are generally written to impart some sort of information or knowledge. We typically read them to make that information and knowledge part of our own schemata, either to use or to store for future application. That purpose alone makes reading these texts a different sort of endeavor than reading a story in which places, characters, and events unfold in our imagination. As Louise Rosenblatt (1982) has suggested, readers take two different stances when reading—an aesthetic stance for narratives and an efferent stance for expository text. In aesthetic reading, the primary concern is not with what you remember about a text after you read it, but with what happens to you as you read. The primary purpose when reading aesthetically is not to gain information, but to experience the text. In reading efferently, however, your purpose is to locate or remember information. Therefore, with most expository texts, your attention will be focused primarily on what you will take from the reading—what information you will learn.

But our stances or purposes for reading aren't the only factors involved in how we comprehend texts. The structure of the texts themselves plays a major role. As we noted previously, narrative and expository texts are structured very differently, and these structural differences make the comprehension, or meaning-building, process different as well. And, as we also mentioned earlier, unlike stories, which have a grammar or predictable structure, exposition includes a variety of organizational patterns, which differ across texts and even within a single selection. For example, a trade book on earthquakes might define an earthquake by giving examples, compare and contrast several different earthquakes, list sequentially the events that take place in an earthquake, and provide cause-and-effect explanations of earthquakes as well. Successful comprehension of exposition requires skills and schemata not demanded for story reading. Expository text offers a special challenge to both teacher and student.

Here we describe two procedures that are particularly useful for helping students comprehend expository material—the K-W-L and reading or study guides.

K-W-L

K-W-L stands for *what do you Know? what do you Want to know?* and *what did you Learn?* The K-W-L procedure, developed by Donna Ogle (1986), is a three-part process designed to motivate and guide readers in acquiring information from expository texts; it is perhaps the most well known and most frequently used procedure for delving into expository texts. The following scenario illustrates how this procedure is put into practice in a California classroom with a group of fourth-graders who are reading the trade book *Earthquakes* by Seymour Simon:

IN THE CLASSROOM
Using K-W-L

After motivating students by relating the topic to their lives, fourth-grade teacher David Scott writes the title *Earthquakes* on the chalkboard. Underneath that title and to the left, he writes the heading *What Do You Know?* He then asks students to give some of the facts they know about earthquakes and jots down their responses under the heading *Earthquakes*.

EARTHQUAKES

What Do You Know?

Can cause damage
Are unpredictable
Are scary
Happen in California
Not all are the same
Shake the earth
Don't happen at night
Are getting worse

Not all of the students' responses are accurate, even though during this brainstorming session Mr. Scott had asked students questions to help them consider the correctness of their statements, such as "How did you learn that?" or "How could you prove that?" Later, during the postreading discussion, he and his students will clear up the remaining misconceptions.

After Mr. Scott's students give a variety of responses, he shows them the cover illustration of *Earthquakes* and asks them to think about the kinds of information that might be included in the book. He then writes their suggestions underneath their initial responses as illustrated here.

EARTHQUAKES

What Do You Know?

Can cause damage
Are unpredictable
Are scary
Happen in California
Not all are the same
Shake the earth
Don't happen at night
Are getting worse

Categories of Information that might be included:

How earthquakes happen • When they happen • What we can do about them • How much damage they do • Why they happen • Descriptions of some of the worst quakes

Next, Mr. Scott reminds his students that informational books such as *Earthquakes* are written to give information that we might need or want. He then asks students to think about what they would like to know about earthquakes—things they don't already know or aren't quite sure of. He records these responses in the column to the right of the *What Do You Know?* column as shown here.

EARTHQUAKES

What Do You Know?

Can cause damage
Are unpredictable
Are scary
Happen in California
Not all are the same
Shake the earth
Don't happen at night
Are getting worse

What Do You Want to Find Out?

What causes earthquakes
How earthquakes are measured
What places have earthquakes
What was the worst earthquake
When most earthquakes happen
What we can do about earthquakes

Categories of Information that might be included:

How earthquakes happen • When they happen • What we can do about them • How much damage they do • Why they happen • Descriptions of some of the worst quakes

On the chalkboard to the right of the previous two headings, Mr. Scott writes *What Did You Learn?* He explains to students that this is the last part of the K-W-L procedure—a procedure they can use when they read informational books and articles. He says, "You have already completed the first two steps—thinking about and writing down what you know about earthquakes and what you would like to know. The last step is to record what information you do learn."

At this point, Mr. Scott gives students their own K-W-L charts and tells them, "In the first column record what you *know* about earthquakes, in the second column what you *want* to know. Then as you read, write what you *learned* in the third column." He also reminds students that not all of their questions, of course, will be answered in the text. Later they will talk about where they might find answers to those questions.

The K-W-L procedure is extremely useful for dealing with informational material. The three phases of the procedure—brainstorming, establishing purposes through questioning, and finding answers to those questions—virtually guarantee that students will be actively involved in their learning. The procedure provides a scaffold to support students' own interest and inquiries. Also, as Ogle points out, K-W-L "helps students keep control of their own inquiry, extending the pursuit of knowledge beyond just one article. The teacher is making clear that learning shouldn't be formed around just what an author chooses to include, but that it involves the identification of the learner's questions and the search for authors and articles dealing with those questions" (p. 569).

Reading Guides

Reading guides are "teacher-developed devices for helping students understand instructional reading material" (Wood, Lapp, & Flood, 1992, p. 1). Although reading guides, also called study guides, are sometimes useful in working with narratives, they are most often designed to help students understand and learn from expository material. These guides consist of questions and activities related to the specific texts students are reading and their purposes for reading them. Students respond to the questions or engage in the activities as they read the text. Reading guides provide a learning scaffold for students, while at the same time giving them control over their learning. As Karen Wood and John Mateja (1983) have noted, a reading guide serves as a "tutor in print form."

Well-developed reading guides help achieve two purposes. First, they aid students in building meaning with the text; second, they guide students' thought processes toward whatever the teacher or student has deemed the goal for reading that particular text. This second purpose will determine the type of reading guide you will use for a particular text. For example, let us say your fifth-grade health text includes a chapter on nutrition, and because you are concerned with your students' eating habits and their attitudes toward food, you particularly want them to read and comprehend the section entitled How Much Should You Eat? You also know this particular group of young-sters tends to read either very laboriously or very rapidly. You want them to develop flexibility in reading rate, to learn to slow down to concentrate on the most salient information and to skip over or read quickly through less-impor-tant material. For these objectives and this text, the Guide-O-Rama devel-oped by Dick Cunningham and Scott Shablak (1975) is an appropriate read-ing guide. As shown in Figure 6.13, this reading guide helps students develop flexibility in their reading rate while learning important information about how much they should eat. You can, of course, develop similar guides for other students as they read a variety of different texts.

How Much Should You Eat?

Page 95, title
  Read the title. Briefly answer the question posed by the title.

Page 95, paragraph 1
  Paragraph 1 introduces the material. Read it quickly.

Page 95, paragraph 2
  Paragraph 2 describes what calories are and what they do. Be sure you understand calories before you go on.

Page 95, paragraph 3, 4, and 5
  As you read paragraphs 3, 4, and 5 under "Choosing the Right Amount for You," compare the number of calories (or food) needed for girls and boys; for large persons and small persons; and for active and inactive persons. (Making a chart may be helpful.)

Page 96, paragraph 1
  Skim through the section "Controlling Your Weight" to determine what is needed for maintaining a desirable weight.

FIGURE 6.13   *Sample Guide-O-Rama for a Chapter on Nutrition*

This, of course, is only one of many types of reading guides. One teacher we know provides students with questions that encourage them to make connections between themselves and the text, similar to the Application and Reflection questions you find throughout this text. Another teacher frequently gives students a handout that lists the main headings of the selection they are reading and provides space for their notes following each heading. Wood and her colleagues (1992) describe many other types of reading guides.

Procedures Appropriate for All Types of Text

Some procedures are appropriate for any type of text, if adapted to reflect the specific selection, readers, and purposes involved. Here we present a few of them: the discussion web, semantic webbing and weaving, ReQuest, and the DR-TA—activities we believe meet the criteria for engaging students with the text and developing their critical literacy. The discussion web and semantic webbing and weaving make use of graphic organizers and discussion to help students think about and organize ideas. ReQuest and the DR-TA help students actively engage with text by generating their own questions and predictions.

Discussion Web

The discussion web (Alvermann, 1991) uses a graphic aid to help students look at both sides of an issue raised in a text before they draw conclusions. Using this graphic aid as a guide, students meet in pairs and then in groups of four to reach consensus about the issue. This process is carried out in the following sample lesson:

IN THE CLASSROOM
Discussion Web for the Novel _Frozen Fire_
by James Houston

Frozen Fire is the story of Matthew Morgan and his Eskimo friend Kayak, who battle to stay alive in the harsh Canadian wilderness close to the arctic circle while attempting to rescue Matthew's father and a helicopter pilot. This story poses a number of questions worth pondering. One in particular arises from an incident in which Matthew discovers gold nuggets at a frozen waterfall. The boys have given up their search for Matthew's dad and are desperately trying to make their way back to Frobisar. Their food supply is nearly gone and death imminent if they don't reach Frobisar soon. However, overjoyed at the fortune within his grasp, Matthew loads his pockets and backpack with the precious metal against Kayak's warning that the gold will be only a hindrance to their struggle to get home. Since most students are intrigued by the idea of instant fortune, the question "Should Matthew have taken the gold nuggets?" should make for a lively discussion.

On the chalkboard, a transparency, or individual worksheets, duplicate the following chart:

Reasons

_____   _____

_____   _____

_____   _____

No   *Should Matthew have taken the gold nuggets?*   *Yes*

_____   _____

_____   _____

_____   _____

Conclusions

Pair students, and explain that they are to discuss the pros and cons of Matthew's taking the gold nuggets. Encourage them to come up with good reasons for both sides of the issue, and to write these down on a sheet of paper. Stress that the initial goal is to list all possible reasons for and against taking the gold, *not* to support one position or the other. Explain that they might want to refer to their books but need only write key words or phrases in the appropriate column. They should try to give an equal number of reasons in each column.

Some sample responses are given here:

Reasons

Didn't belong to him   Didn't belong to anybody

Were worthless in Arctic   Would make him rich

Kayak told him not to   Would have made his dad happy

No   *Should Matthew have taken the gold nuggets?*   *Yes*

Would slow Matthew down   Could buy things for Kayak's

Could cost him his life   family

                                        If took only a few, would have

                                        been a little richer

Conclusions

After the partners have had a chance to jot down their reasons, pair one set of partners with another set. Ask the new groups of four students to compare their reasons why Matthew should or shouldn't have taken the gold nuggets. Explain to students that although the goal is to work toward consensus, it is perfectly acceptable for members to disagree with that conclusion if they can justify their position. Tell them that you will have a large group discussion at the end of the period in which dissenting views will be heard.

When the groups of four have reached their conclusions, select a spokesperson for each group or have them select their own. Give each group about three minutes to choose the one reason that best supports the group's conclusion, and have the spokesperson jot it down. When each group has chosen its reason, call on the different spokespersons to report the group decisions. At this time ask each spokesperson to also give any dissenting viewpoints and the support for these positions. Finally, as a follow-up activity, you might have students write their individual answers to the question "Should Matthew have taken the gold nuggets?" and post them in the classroom for others to read.

The discussion web can be used any time students read material that raises a question that might evoke dissenting viewpoints. For example, in *In the Year of the Boar and Jackie Robinson* by Bette Bao Lord, Emily, the sixth-grade class president, is supposed to present Jackie Robinson with the key to P.S. 8, but gives the honor instead to Shirley Wong, the protagonist in the story. Students might use the discussion web to decide the answer to this question: Should Shirley have allowed Emily to give her the honor of making the presentation to Jackie Robinson?

The discussion web can be modified for use across the curriculum. Suppose students have read a selection on the Civil War that discusses Stephen A. Douglas, Abraham Lincoln, and their opposing views on slavery. As a postreading activity, you might substitute the names *Douglas* and *Lincoln* for the *Yes* and *No* columns of the discussion web, write *slavery* in the box where the question usually goes, and have students discuss the two men's differing views on the issue.

Semantic Webbing and Weaving

Semantic webbing and weaving are procedures that you and your students can use together or that students can use on their own to organize ideas and graphically show their interrelatedness. Semantic webbing, which we described as a vocabulary technique in Chapter 5, is sometimes called semantic mapping. Semantic webbing, or mapping, makes use of a graphic organizer that looks like a spider web—thus its name. The web connects a central topic to a variety of related ideas and events, as shown in the web in Figure 6.14 on sea otters (Heimlich & Pittelman, 1986).

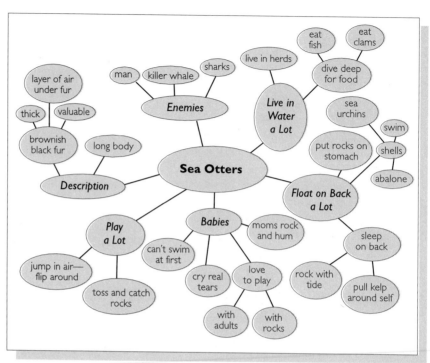

FIGURE 6.14 *Sample Semantic Web for Sea Otters*

Webbing can be used with students of any age before reading a selection, to develop and connect a key concept in that selection to their prior knowledge. The thought processes involved in organizing concepts by making connections between them prepares the reader to make similar connections when meeting the ideas in the text. This web, or visual display, illustrates graphically the interconnectedness of ideas. The concept or concepts that are webbed, should, of course, be of central importance to the reading material.

This webbing activity can be used before, during, and after reading. Students might develop their own webs as they read a selection or after they have finished reading. Webbing can be done as a teacher-led postreading activity as well. For example, after reading the stories *Swimmy* and *Frederick the Mouse*, both by Leo Lionni, a second-grade teacher used semantic webs like the one shown in Figure 6.15 to do a character study of the main characters in these two picture books (Calfee & Patrick, 1995). Students can be asked to justify their choices and note the page numbers of the passages that support their answers.

Like a web, a weave is also a graphic organizer, a visual display of information and how it is related. However, a weave, which we also described as a vocabulary technique in Chapter 5, is very similar to semantic feature analysis. It differs from a web by highlighting comparisons. Notice how the weave on the characters Swimmy and Frederick shown in Figure 6.16 (Calfee & Patrick, 1995) allows students to focus on the similarities and differences between these two characters. "Both of these stories connect with important issues," Calfee and Patrick tell us, "but it is rare for them to be brought together for comparison" (p. 79). Webbing and weaving provide the vehicle for that comparison.

Using graphic organizers such as webbing and weaving supports high-level thinking and comprehension by providing a framework for focusing on important points, rather than getting lost in myriad unimportant, unrelated details. It provides a public forum for exploring the process of understanding a text, whether narrative or expository. As Calfee and Patrick (1995) state, "Student reactions, instead of disappearing into thin air, become part of a written record. Thinking becomes external, and the class has a tool for combining individual efforts. Moreover, all students—even very young ones—can appreciate and apply high-level concepts for analysis and synthesis, for comprehension and composition" (p. 79).

ReQuest

In contrast to the graphics-supported procedures we have described so far in this section, ReQuest consists of a questioning routine that teachers use with students in small groups before, during, and after they read a selection. The ReQuest procedure, first introduced by Anthony Manzo (1969), encourages students to ask their own

FIGURE 6.15 *Sample Semantic Web Comparing the Characters Swimmy and Frederick*

	Swimmy	Frederick
scared	yes	no
brave	yes	sort of
nice	yes	yes
smart	yes	yes
thinkful	yes	sort of
lazy	never	sometimes
hungry	no	yes
poet	no	yes

FIGURE 6.16 *Sample Weave Comparing Swimmy and Frederick*

questions about the material being read. To see how this procedure works, follow Susan Jones as she works with second-graders who are reading a short chapter book, *The Best Worst Day* (Graves, 1996).

IN THE CLASSROOM
ReQuest in the Second Grade

After a motivational prereading activity and instruction on asking questions, Ms. Jones and her students read silently the first page of this short chapter book. When they have finished, Ms. Jones closes her book and the students ask questions of *her:*

Kelly: Who is the story about, Ms. Jones?

Ms. Jones: I think Lucy is the main character. But I think the story may be about Zach and Maya, too.

Lamont: Where was Lucy?

Ms. Jones: On a bus, a school bus, I imagine.

Sondra: What time of day was it?

Ms. Jones: That's a good question, Sondra. I don't think the author gave the time, so I will have to figure it out from the other things she told me. Let's see . . . Lucy's on a school bus. She could either be going to school or coming home, so I suppose it could be morning or afternoon. But she is making her plans for that day, to become best friends with the new girl, Maya, so I would have to say it was morning. Do you agree?

Next, the students close their books, and Ms. Jones asks them questions on the same material.

Ms. Jones: Hmmm. This is going to be hard. You've asked such good questions already! Let's see . . . What did Lucy draw on the window?

Erin: A heart with Maya's name!

Ms. Jones: What did she draw it with?

Lamont: Her finger. I've done that, too. On the bathroom mirror. You know how it gets cloudy when you take a shower?

Ms. Jones: Now I'm going to ask a question like the one Sondra asked me, a question that the author doesn't give the answer to, but that you have to figure out from what you know. This is called an inferential question. (Ms. Jones writes the word *inferential* on the chalkboard.) Why did Lucy draw a heart with Maya's name inside?

Several students: Because she likes Maya, and she wants her for a friend!

Did you notice how Ms. Jones was able to weave in some information about narratives (bringing in the notion that there can be more than one important character) and about types of questions (defining and illustrating an inferential question) into this brief session?

This ReQuest procedure is continued until students have finished enough reading to make predictions about the remainder of the book. Ms. Jones then asks, "What do you think the rest of the story is about? Why do you think so?" Next, the students read the book silently. After they have finished, they have a follow-up discussion.

DR-TA

Like ReQuest, the directed reading-thinking activity (DR-TA) developed by Russell Stauffer (1969) takes students through the three phases of a teacher-led reading experience—prereading, during-reading, and postreading. However, the DR-TA constitutes a much broader framework. Whereas ReQuest focuses on student-generated *questions*, the DR-TA focuses on student-generated *purposes*. The importance placed on getting students to generate purposes themselves is based

As part of the ReQuest procedure, Susan Jones' students ask her questions about the story, The Best Worst Day.

on the premise that reading is a thinking process in which the reader uses his own experiences to reconstruct the author's ideas. The teacher's role in the DR-TA is to create a situation in which this thinking process will occur.

Implementing the DR-TA for a group of students in any grade has two phases: a teacher-directed reading–thinking process and a skill-training phase. In the first phase, the teacher encourages students to make their own predictions concerning what they are about to read, read to discover how accurate their predictions were, and produce proof to verify their predictions by orally rereading the passage that yields the answer. To summarize, the teacher involves the reader in three steps: predicting (setting purpose), reading, and proving. The second phase, the skill-training phase, occurs after students have read a selection and have completed the directed-thinking phase. Here students reexamine the story, which might also involve analyzing teacher-selected words or phrases, pictures, or a diagram. Revisiting the story develops students' reading–thinking abilities and other reading-related skills. This skill training might include vocabulary work, creating semantic webs or weaves, summarizing, and other postreading activities.

Before leaving this section, we want to again note that the primary purpose for engaging students in any of the procedures we have described is to enhance their reading enjoyment, to foster understanding and learning, and to increase their competence and confidence in making meaning with texts.

Reflection AND Application

13. In this section we presented examples of the story frame and the story map. Why might either of these two procedures be helpful to use with a group of primary-grade students who are reading a folktale?

14. With what sorts of texts might the K-W-L procedure be helpful? With what sorts of texts would the K-W-L be inappropriate? These are good questions to discuss with a classmate, and your explanations of your answers are as important as the answers themselves.

15. Skim through this section, and jot down the various procedures that are described. Draw a graphic organizer or semantic web that shows which procedures are recommended for narratives, which for expository texts, and which for both types of text.

Special Needs and Special Talents

In order to move forward into a world that values all of us, both because we are human and also because of the differences that make us who we are, each of us must take individual and institutional responsibility for creating education in which all children will thrive.

—*Frances E. Kendall*
Teacher Educator

We hope by now we have made the point that successful reading experiences are created by taking into account the varying needs and talents of the individual readers in your classroom. In this section, we give some suggestions for further addressing the needs of your challenged and accelerated students.

Virtually all of the activities described in the chapter will scaffold students' reading, and thus all are appropriate for readers who might experience difficulties. Here, we highlight some that are particularly appropriate for readers who are challenged and note a few additional techniques to use with these students:

- Create a scaffolded reading experience with particularly strong supports during the prereading and during-reading phases.
- Provide tape recordings of the material students are reading, and have them read along silently as they listen.
- Have students who listen to a selection on tape tell about the selection in their own words. Type up their recollections in a booklet for them to read independently. This is particularly useful for ESL students who do not yet automatically recognize common words. It is also an opportunity for more accomplished students to pitch in and do some of the typing.
- For primary-grade students, read a selection aloud to them one or more times before asking them to read it silently.
- Have students read the material with a partner who is a more accomplished reader—a classmate, an aide, an older student, or a classroom volunteer parent or grandparent. These reading "buddies"

can take turns reading from the text or read the text in unison with the student.

- Provide a number of nonthreatening oral-reading experiences such as choral reading. If a selection employs a regular pattern or rhyme, have students sing or chant the text.
- Encourage students to read books at their reading level or below. Frequent reading of this kind of material will improve automaticity and confidence.
- Encourage students to reread material that is at their reading level or below.
- Use the reciprocal teaching strategy (Palincsar & Brown, 1985), which we describe in Chapter 8.
- When creating reading scaffolds around a particular text or texts, take into account talents other than verbal ones. Incorporate drama, art, music, movement, and other modes of expression in prereading, during-reading, and postreading endeavors.
- Show by your attitude and actions that you have total confidence that students can successfully read a selection and that you will support them in their effort.

Your classroom will also have its share of competent readers who read above grade level. You will also want to provide for their needs, challenging and inspiring them to go further in their thinking. Here are a few suggestions:

- Have additional reading material available that relates to the selection being read. For example, if the class is reading *Lincoln: A Photobiography* by Russell Freedman, have other biographies of Lincoln available or other biographies by Freedman.
- Provide more challenging selections as an addition or alternative to the text being read.
- Let students select their own additional reading materials related to a selection's theme, genre, or author.
- Invite students to engage in long-term, in-depth projects that relate to the material being read. For example, upper-grade students could research and read periodical literature dealing with the topics in their science text. This would provide them (and the rest of the class) with information more current than that provided in the text.
- Encourage students to create narratives or expository pieces that relate to the reading.

One size does *not* fit all

As we have cautioned many times, all students, regardless of their particular needs or talents, need to explore ideas and express themselves in a variety of ways—through writing, speaking, and artistic and dramatic endeavors. We need to take care to be inclusive, not exclusive, in providing a wide variety of opportunities for students. Sometimes students who struggle with the basics or lack in traditional literacy skills have been left out of enrichment activities and the growth that they can provide. We believe that all students deserve and will benefit from a range of activities and should explore as many as possible. Thus they will make connections between what they know and what they discover in texts and will apply that new knowledge in ways to make their lives more enjoyable, productive, and meaningful.

CONCLUDING REMARKS

This chapter has focused on teacher-led approaches and procedures that foster students' comprehension and enjoyment of the texts they read in the classroom, highlighting the possibility of offering a wide range of approaches and to customize activities in order to accommodate individual differences. The scaffolded reading experience, which we described in the first part of the chapter, provides a flexible framework for supporting students' reading endeavors. And time-tested procedures such as K-W-L, story maps, the discussion web, ReQuest, and the DR-TA, which we discussed in the latter half of the chapter, help engage students with the narrative texts and exposition they read.

Before moving on to the next chapter, in which we discuss teaching comprehension strategies and fostering students' independence in reading, we recommend that you review this chapter, respond to the prompts in the Reflection and Application sections if you haven't already done so, and make use of the suggestions listed in the Extending Learning section that follows. They will greatly enhance your schema for the topics covered in the chapter and thus prepare you to make informed decisions about fostering students' success with the texts they read.

EXTENDING LEARNING

1. Choose one of the topics we have covered—the scaffolded reading experience, the DR-TA, ReQuest, or another—and read more about it. Present what you learn to your instructor and classmates, emphasizing a particular aspect of it—perhaps the research and theory behind the procedure or a lesson based on it. You may want to read more about the procedure you choose, and the reference section at the end of this chapter is a good starting point for finding information.

2. Visit an elementary school classroom, and take notes on the kinds of supports the teacher provides for students as they read a selection. Using the same selection for the same group of students, design your own plan for helping them understand and enjoy the selection. Try out your lesson on your target students or share it with your classmates.

3. From the children's section of your library, select an expository text that you think would interest students at the age level you would like to teach. Create a scaffolded reading experience especially for those students and that text. Give your plan to a classmate to get his or her feedback. We recommend the following three books to help you select appropriate titles: *Essentials of Children's Literature* by Carol Lynch-Brown and Carl M. Tomlison (1994); *Collected Perspectives: Choosing and Using Books for the Classroom*, edited by Hughes Moir (1992); and *Kaleidoscope: A Multicultural Booklist for Graders K–8*, edited by Rudine Sims Bishop (1995).

REFERENCES

Alvermann, D. (1991). The discussion web: A graphic aid for learning across the curriculum. *The Reading Teacher, 45*, 92–99. This article offers a complete description of this very useful graphic aid and the teaching procedures that accompany it.

Alverman, D., Dillon, D. R., & O'Brien, D. G. (1987). *Using discussion to promote reading comprehension.* Newark, DE: International Reading Association. This monograph balances the whys and how-tos of classroom discussion in content area instruction.

Anderson, T. H., & Armbruster, B. B. (1984). Content area textbooks. In R. C. Anderson, J. Osborn, & R. J. Tierney (Eds.), *Learning to read in American schools* (pp. 193–226).Hillsdale, NJ: Erlbaum. This influential article discusses what is wrong with textbook writing and how it can be improved.

Beck, I. L., & McKeown, M. G. (1981). Developing questions that promote comprehension: The story map. *Language Arts, 58*, 913–918.The authors discuss problematic approaches to selecting and sequencing questions and offer a valuable alternative.

Bieger, E. M. (1996). Promoting multicultural education through a literature-based approach. *Reading Teacher, 49*(4), 309. This article presents a four-level hierarchical model for integrating ethnic content into the curriculum.

Bishop, R. S. (Ed.). (1994). *Kaleidoscope: A multicultural booklist for grades K–8.* Urbana, IL: National Councils of Teachers of English. This book is an annotated bibliography of selected books about or related to African Americans, Asian Americans, Hispanic Americans, and Native Americans.

Blanton, W. E., Wood, D. W., & Moorman, G. B. (1990). The role of purpose in reading instruction. *The Reading Teacher, 43*, 486–493. This article examines the role of purpose setting in facilitating understanding during reading.

Calfee, R. C., & Chambliss, M. (1988, April). *Structure in social studies textbooks: Where is the design?* Paper presented at the meeting of the American Educational Research Association. New Orleans. This analysis shows that many social studies texts are poorly designed.

Calfee, R. C., & Patrick, C. L. (1995) *Teach our children well.* Stanford, CA: Stanford Alumni Association. Recounting the collaboration between a private university and public schools, this engaging text underscores the importance of students' developing critical literacy—learning to use all forms of language for thinking, problem solving, and communication.

Cambourne, B. (1994). Compelling questions in reading education: What inquiry questions are reading educators around the world currently asking? *Reading Today*, *12*(3), 1, 10. This report details a seven-year study on the dynamics of settings that teachers are expected to create in order to teach literacy.

Chen, H.-C., & Graves, M. F. (1996). Effects of previewing and providing background knowledge on Taiwanese college students' comprehension of American short stories. *TESOL Quarterly*, *29*, 663–686. This empirical study documents the effectiveness of previews and, to some extent, building background knowledge for ESL students.

Cudd, E. T., & Roberts, L. L. (1987). Using story frames to develop reading comprehension in a first grade classroom. *The Reading Teacher*, *41*(1), 74–81. The authors discuss the use of story frames for teaching reading comprehension to first-graders.

Cunningham, D., & Shablak, S. L. (1975). Selective reading guide-o-rama: The content teacher's best friend. *Journal of Reading*, *18*, 380–382. This article describes procedure designed to help students identify key ideas, major points.

Dole, J. A., Valencia, S. W., Greer, E. A., & Wardrop, J. L. (1991). Effects of two types of prereading instruction on the comprehension of narrative and expository text. *Reading Research Quarterly*, *26*, 142–159. The positive effects of previews with both narrative and informational texts are presented here.

Drum, P. (1984). Children's understanding of passages. In J. Flood (Ed.), *Promoting reading comprehension* (pp. 61–78). Newark, DE: International Reading Association. This article provides a very lucid examination of what children understand from narrative and expository texts.

Estes, C. (1995). Musical links: Part I. *Book Links*, *4*, 48–52. The author describes a number of children's books with musical possibilities along with ideas for classroom applications.

Forsythe, S. J. (1995). It worked! Readers theatre in second grade. *Reading Teacher*, *49*(3), 264–65. This description highlights using readers' theater with bilingual students.

Fowler, G. L. (1982). Developing comprehension skills in primary students though the use of story frames. *The Reading Teacher*, *36*(2), 176–179. The author suggests using story frames to guide students' responses to comprehension questions.

Gambrell, L. B. (1996). What research reveals about discussion. In L. B. Gambrell & J. F. Almasi (Eds.), *Lively discussions!: Fostering engaged reading* (pp. 25–38). Newark, DE: International Reading Association. This article summarizes what research reveals about discussion. It is the second of 18 articles that provide strategies and techniques for using discussion to promote interpretation and comprehension of narrative and expository texts in elementary classrooms.

Gardner, H. (1993). *Multiple intelligences: The theory in practice*. New York: Basic Books. The author discusses multiple intelligences and their educational applications by looking at research projects in the schools.

Graves, M. F. (1997, March). The status of comprehension strategy instruction in the 1990s. Paper presented at the meeting of the American Educational Research Association, Chicago. This paper briefly summarizes what we know about comprehension strategy instruction.

Graves, M. F., & Graves, B. B. (1994). *The scaffolding reading experience: Designs for student success*. Norwood, MA: Christopher-Gordon. This book presents the theoretical base for the scaffolded reading experience and describes, with many concrete examples, how to implement the scaffolding framework.

Graves, M. F., & Graves, B. B. (1995). The scaffolded reading experience: A flexible framework for helping students get the most out of text. *Reading*, *29*, 29–34. This article describes the scaffolded reading framework.

Graves, M. F., Graves, B. B., & Braaten, S. (1996). Scaffolded reading experiences: Bridges to reading success. *Educational Leadership*, *53*, 14–16. The authors describe the use of SREs with special students in inclusive classrooms.

Graves, M. F., Prenn, M. C, & Cooke, C. L. (1985). The coming attraction: Previewing short stories to increase comprehension. *Journal of Reading*, *28*, 594–598. The authors give specific guidelines for writing previews and previewing and also summarize the research.

Heimlich, J. E. & Pittelman, S. D. (1986). *Semantic mapping: Classroom applications*. Newark, DE: International Reading Association. This brief text gives many practical examples of how to use semantic mapping in the classroom.

Horowitz, R., & Freeman, S. H. (1995). Robots versus spaceships: The role of discussion in kindergartners' and second-graders' preferences for science text. *The Reading Teacher, 49*, 30–40. In this article, the authors examine how discussion influences young children's preferences for science text.

Hoyt, L. (1992). Many ways of knowing: Using drama, oral interactions, and the visual arts to enhance reading comprehension. *The Reading Teacher, 45*, 580–594. This brief article accomplishes just what its title indicates.

Jacobi-Karna, K. (1996). Music and children's books. *Reading Teacher, 49*(3), 265–269. This article describes ways to connect books and music; it includes an extensive bibliography.

Mandler, J., & Johnson, N. (1977). Remembrance of things parsed: Story structure and recall. *Cognitive Psychology, 9*, 111–151. The authors analyze the underlying structure of simple stories.

Manzo, A. V. (1969). The ReQuest procedure. *Journal of Reading, 12*, 123–126. The first description of the ReQuest procedure, this article includes a rationale, procedures, and suggestions for use.

McCaslin, N. (1996). *Creative drama in the classroom and beyond* (6th ed.). New York: Longman. This comprehensive text describes what creative drama is and activities for elementary teachers to use in their classrooms.

Moir, H. (Ed.). 1992. *Collected perspectives: Choosing and using books for the classroom*. Norwood, MA: Christopher-Gordon. This annotated bibliography gives suggestions for classroom reading-related activities for approximately 1,000 children's titles.

Monson, D. L. (1992). Realistic fiction and the real world. In B. E. Cullinan (Ed.), *Invitation to read: More children's literature in the reading program* (pp. 24–39). Newark, DE: International Reading Association. Succinct and practical, this article discusses the importance of linking literature to life and ways of doing so.

Ogle, D. (1986). K-W-L: A teaching model that develops active reading of expository text. *The Reading Teacher, 39*, 564–570. This article presents the initial description of the K-W-L procedure.

Palincsar, A., & Brown, A. (1985). Reciprocal teaching: A means to a meaningful end. In J. Osborn, P.T.,Wilson, & R.C. Anderson (Eds.), *Reading education: Foundations for a literate America*, (pp. 299–310). Lexington, MA: D.C. Heath. The authors discuss the reciprocal teaching procedure and the thinking behind it.

Pearson, P. D., & Johnson, D. D. (1978). *Teaching reading comprehension*. New York: Holt, Rinehart & Winston. Probably the first text to present a view of teaching reading consistent with cognitive psychology, this book contains one of the earliest treatments of semantic mapping.

Perkins, D. (1992). *Smart schools: From training memories to education minds*. New York: The Free Press. This well-written, engaging book presents a comprehensive plan for teaching for understanding.

Raphael, T. (1982). Question-answering strategies for children. *The Reading Teacher, 36*, 186–190. This article presents a clear description of how students can be taught to use Question-Answer Relationships (QARs).

Reutzel, D. R. (1991). Understanding and using basal readers effectively. In B. L. Hayes (Ed.), *Effective strategies for teaching reading* (pp. 254–280). New York: Allyn & Bacon. The author gives practical and useful suggestions for using basal readers effectively in the elementary classroom.

Rosenblatt, L. (1982). The literary transaction: Evocation and response. *Theory into Practice, 21*, 268–277. This article discusses the importance of reading for cognitive understanding and aesthetic enjoyment.

Schifini, A. (1996). Discussion in multilingual, multicultural classrooms. In L. B. Gambrell & J. F. Almasi (Eds.), *Lively Discussions!: Fostering engaged reading* (pp. 39–49). Newark, DE: International Reading Association. This chapter provides an insightful commentary on multicultural and multilingual considerations for discussion.

Stauffer, R. G. (1969). *Directing reading maturity as a cognitive process.* New York: Harper & Row. This text gives a detailed description of the DR-TA procedure and rationale for its use.

Thorndyke, P. (1977). Cognitive structures in comprehension and memory of narrative discourse. *Cognitive Psychology, 9,* 97–110. This empirical study explores the effects of structure and content on memory and comprehension of narratives.

Trelease, J. (1989). *The new read-aloud handbook* (2nd ed.). New York: Penguin. This best-seller contains a wealth of insight for both teachers and parents.

Wiencek, E. J. (1996). Planning, initiating, and sustaining literature discussion groups: The teacher's role. In L. B. Gambrell & J. F. Almasi (Eds.), *Lively Discussions!: Fostering engaged reading* (pp. 208–223). Newark, DE: International Reading Association. This chapter provides a model for literature discussion groups, the Conversational Discussion Group (CDG), and a process for developing these groups in the classroom.

Wood, D. J., Bruner, J. S., & Ross, G. (1976). The role of tutoring in problem-solving. *Journal of Child Psychology and Psychiatry, 17*(2), 89–100. This introduction to the concept of scaffolding also includes an insightful examination of parent–child interactions.

Wood, K. D., Lapp, D. & Flood, J. (1992). *Guiding readers through text: A review of study guides.* Newark, DE: International Reading Association. This book discusses the whys and hows of study guides with detailed examples for classroom use.

Wood, K. D., & Mateja, J. A. (1983). Adapting secondary level strategies for use in elementary classrooms. *The Reading Teacher, 36,* 492–496. The authors explain how to adapt three secondary strategies for use with younger children.

Young, T. A.,& Vardell, S. (1993). Weaving readers theatre and nonfiction into the curriculum. *The Reading Teacher, 46,* 396–406. This article presents a variety of ways for using readers' theater with informational trade books.

CHILDREN'S LITERATURE

Duncan, A. F. (1995). *Willie Jerome.* New York: Macmillan. No one but Willie's sister appreciates his jazz trumpet playing until she finally gets their mama to really listen and let the music speak to her. Unpaged.

Fox, M. (1985). *Wilfred Gordon McDonald Partridge.* New York: Kane/Miller. A small boy tries to discover the meaning of memory so he can restore that of an elderly friend. 32 pages. Text available in Spanish.

Freedman, R. (1987). *Lincoln: A photobiography.* New York: Clarion. In photographs and text, this Newbery Award–winning book traces the life of Civil War president Abraham Lincoln.

Gibbons, G. (1991). *Whales.* New York: Holiday House. This picture book describes the different kinds of whales, what they look like, their habits, habitats, and how they bear their young. Unpaged.

Globe. (1994). *Native American biographies.* Paramus, NJ: Author. This collection of inspirational biographies focuses on Native Americans who have succeeded in their fields. 250 pages.

Graves, B. (1996). *The best worst day.* New York: Hyperion. In this chapter book, second-grader Lucy struggles to prove herself "best" in order to win the friendship of Maya, the new girl in class. 64 pages.

Hallworth, G. (1996). *Down by the river.* New York: Scholastic Cartwheel. This book offers a collection of Afro-Caribbean rhymes, games, and songs. 32 pages.

Hoffman, M. (1991). *Amazing Grace.* New York: Dial. With inspiration from her grandmother and determination of her own, Grace earns the role of Peter Pan in the class production. Unpaged.

Houston, J. (1977). *Frozen fire: A tale of courage*. New York: Atheneum. Determined to find his father who has been lost in a storm, a young boy and his Eskimo friend brave wind storms, starvation, and wild animals on their trek through the Canadian Arctic. 149 pages.

Lewin, T. (1990). *Tiger trek*. New York: Macmillan. This informative narrative details the preying habits of the Indian tiger and the numerous animals that live on a hunting preserve in Central India. Unpaged.

Lionni, L. (1984). *Swimmy*. New York: Pantheon. Through teamwork and cooperation, Swimmy the fish and his friends triumph over the "big" fish. 32 pages. Videocassette available.

Lionni, L. (1985). *Frederick*. New York: Pantheon. Frederick, an apparently lazy mouse, has a special surprise for the mice who thought he should have been storing up supplies for the winter. 32 pages. Videocassette available.

Lobel, A. (1970). *Frog and Toad are friends*. New York: Harper & Row. Five stories about the friendship of Frog and Toad and their adventures in the woods. 64 pages. Audiocassette and videocassette available.

Lord, B. B. (1984). *In the year of the boar and Jackie Robinson*. New York: Harper & Row. A young Chinese girl emigrates to Brooklyn in 1947 and assimilates into a strange new culture of class elections, stickball, and the Brooklyn Dodgers. 169 pages.

Lowry, L. (1989). *Number the stars*. Boston: Houghton Mifflin. Set in 1943 during the German occupation of Denmark, 10-year-old Ann Marie learns about courage when her family shelters a Jewish family from the Nazis. 137 pages. Audiocassette available.

Paterson, K. (1978). *The great Gilly Hopkins*. New York: Crowell. This novel portrays feisty 11-year-old Gilly, a foster child who, in her longing to be reunited with her birth mother, schemes against all who try to befriend her. 152 pages. Spanish text and audiocassette available.

Phinney, M. Y. (1995). *Baba Yaga: A Russian folktale*. Greenvale, NY: Mondo. In this rhymed retelling, Katrina is able to escape from the cruel witch, Baba Yaga, because of the kindnesses she showed to others. Unpaged.

Prelutsky, J. (1988). *Tyrannosaurus was a beast: Dinosaur poems*. New York: Greenwillow. Poems celebrate 14 dinosaurs in rollicking rhyme and illustration. 32 pages.

Simon, S. (1991). *Earthquakes*. New York: Morrow. With full-color photos and text, this book describes how and where earthquakes occur, how they can be predicted, and how much damage they cause. Unpaged.

Smith, W. J. (1990). *Birds and beasts*. New York: Godine. In poetry and pictures, this volume presents a fun and satisfying, if slightly off-beat, view of 29 animals. Unpaged.

Soto, G. (1992). *Too many tamales*. New York: Putnam. Maria tries on her mother's wedding ring while helping make Christmas tamales and later discovers that it's missing. Unpaged. Available in Spanish.

Twain, M. (1959). *The adventures of Huckleberry Finn*. New York: Penguin. The classic tale of the adventures of two outcasts fleeing down the Mississippi River on a raft and the metamorphosis that occurs. 279 pages.

Van Allsburg, C. (1990). *Just a dream*. Boston: Houghton Mifflin. A young boy has a dream about the environment that causes him to wake up to his indifference. Unpaged.

chapter seven

Guiding Students Toward Independence in Reading

*S*uppose you are reading a newspaper and you come to a sentence you do not under-stand. What do you do? Perhaps you read on, hoping that the next sentence or two will make the meaning clear. Or, perhaps you reread the sentence or go back to the sentences preceding it.

Or, suppose it is Saturday, and you have two tests coming up on Monday. You need to read a novel, three textbook chapters, and four journal articles. What do you do? You know you won't have time to read and study each in depth, so you must use some efficient approaches to understand and remember what you read. The novel you read quickly, skipping over lengthy descriptions and dialogue and concentrating on the basics of setting, plot, and characters. As you read, you look for recurring themes. When you finish, you might ask questions like, "Why was the protagonist so driven?" and "What were the main themes?" Before you read the chapters and articles, you might think about points your instructor emphasized. While you read, you might take notes or underline material relevant to these points; and, after your first reading, you might reread the sections that are most relevant to the course.

CHAPTER OVERVIEW

Teaching Reading Comprehension Strategies

Key Comprehension Strategies

A Validated Approach to Teaching Strategies

Encouraging Independent Reading

Independent Reading

Literature Response Groups

A Framework to Promote Reader Response

What you have done in both of these cases is to use reading strategies—deliberate plans to help you understand and recall what you read. Learning to use reading strategies is one important part of becoming an accomplished reader. But it is not all there is to being a reader.

Suppose it is now Monday evening. Your exams are over, and for tonight at least, the press of schoolwork is over. What do you do? If you're a reader, one thing you are likely to do is pick up a book—a book that you choose to read, a book that interests you, and a book on which you will not be tested. You may sit in a comfortable chair, sprawl on the couch, or even lie on your bed. You certainly will not take notes! And, in fact, you may fall asleep—which is just fine!

Fostering independent reading, nurturing children's love of reading so that they not only can but also will read, is just as important as teaching reading strategies.

TEACHING READING COMPREHENSION STRATEGIES

As defined by David Pearson and his colleagues (Pearson, Roehler, Dole, & Duffy, 1992), reading comprehension strategies are "conscious and flexible plans that readers apply and adapt to a variety of texts and tasks." Readers engage in them in order to better understand and remember what they read. One strategy, for example, is determining what information is important in a reading, that is, deciding which of the numerous concepts in any text deserve special attention. Particularly when reading informational material to gain specific knowledge on a topic, readers must determine just what they need to learn. You might identify the important information in a textbook chapter by considering which points the instructor has emphasized. Two other ways would be to read the chapter introduction and summary or to skim through the chapter's headings and subheadings. Readers adept at determining what is important in a reading selection have available these and a variety of other strategies, and they employ whichever strategies best fit each reading situation. For all students, including ESL students and students with special educational needs, using strategies leads to independence in reading.

> The strategy research on comprehension instruction conducted during the 1980s and early 1990s was ample and showed powerful effects. This was especially true when the instruction was combined with specific teaching behaviors—direct explanation, modeling, guided practice, feedback, and application.
>
> —Janice Dole
> Teacher Educator

Key Comprehension Strategies

Fortunately, there is substantial agreement on a core of key strategies that students need to master (Pearson et al., 1992; Pressley, Johnson, Symons, McGoldrick, & Kurita, 1989). These are shown in the following list and discussed in the remainder of this section.

- Using prior knowledge
- Asking and answering questions
- Making inferences
- Determining what is important
- Summarizing
- Dealing with graphic information
- Imaging
- Monitoring comprehension

Each of these strategies involves readers in actively constructing meaning as they read. Additionally, many of them help readers transform ideas from one form to another or generate relationships between ideas, activities that Merlin Wittrock (1990) and many other theorists see as crucial to comprehension and memory. For example, when readers summarize they must transform the author's text into more concise statements, and when they make inferences they must relate information in the text to information they already know.

Using Prior Knowledge

When using this strategy, readers purposely bring to consciousness information that relates to what they are going to read or what they are reading. Thus they put a set of schemata into place, establishing a framework for the new information that they will encounter in the text.

Let us say, for instance, that a second-grader is perusing the library shelf and picks up a book titled *Mistakes That Worked* by Charlotte Foltz Jones. Before the student begins reading the book, she thinks about what she knows about mistakes. As she thinks, she recalls mistakes she has made and mistakes others have made. But she really can't think of any "mistakes that worked." Thus, she begins to read the book with the realization that most mistakes don't work and that the book is going to present something different. The student is using her prior knowledge to set up expectations about what she might encounter in the text. When she reads about one of the mistakes that worked, she will be able to contrast it to her own mistakes, and making that contrast will help her both understand what she is reading and remember what she has read.

Asking and Answering Questions

Using this strategy, the reader poses questions prior to reading a selection or as she is reading the selection. Then she attempts to answer the questions while reading. Employing this strategy virtually guarantees that reading will be an active process. It also serves to focus the reader's attention. A reader who has asked a particular set of questions will be particularly attentive to the information that answers those questions.

Consider a sixth-grader preparing to read a chapter on nutrition in a health text. As the first step, she might survey the chapter and find these headings: Nutrients and the U.S. RDA, The Seven Dietary Guidelines, Shopping for Groceries, and Preventing Disease Through Proper Diet. Then, she might pose one or two questions about each heading: What are nutrients? What is the U.S. RDA? What are the seven dietary guidelines? Do I follow them in my diet? Should I follow them? How is shopping for groceries related to nutrition? Can a proper diet prevent all disease? As she reads, the student will get answers to some of her questions, find that others are not answered in the chapter, and pose and answer additional questions. As a result of this active involvement, she is likely to learn a good deal.

> Understanding requires learner generation of relations between the subject matter and one's knowledge and experience.
>
> —Merlin Wittrock
> *Educational Psychologist*

Making Inferences

When they apply this strategy, readers infer meanings by using information from the text and their existing knowledge of the world, their schemata, to fill in bits of information that are not explicitly stated in the text. No text is ever fully explicit, and thus readers must constantly make inferences to understand what they are reading. By teaching students to make inferences, you are helping them learn to use their existing knowledge along with the information in the text to build meaning.

Suppose that a fifth-grader is reading a science text and learns that woodchucks build deep burrows and huddle in them in large groups during the winter. Knowing that a fair number of animals hibernate, she might infer that woodchucks hibernate in their burrows. Then, remembering that last week her teacher explained that ground temperature remains stable and fairly warm at depths greater than three or four feet, she might further infer that woodchucks make their burrows deep in order to take advantage of this warmth.

Determining What Is Important

Making use of this strategy requires that readers understand what they have read and make judgments about what is and is not important. As Robert Marzano (1992) and others have explained, most texts contain much more information than a reader can focus on and learn. Consequently, determining what is important is a crucial and frequently required strategy. Sometimes, texts include direct cues to what is important—overviews, headings, summaries, and the like. As seventh-grade science teacher Victor Hammel notes, it is well worth teaching students to use these aids:

> At the beginning of each year, I make it a point to go through the textbooks we will be using and talk with my students about whatever learning aids the books contain. At this time, I also actually model how I would use these aids. Although some students would make good use of the aids even if I didn't discuss them and model how I use them, a lot of students wouldn't. The benefit to them, as well as the time I save by helping students learn to use the aids independently, is really substantial.
>
> In addition, I check the books to see how well the aids work. For example, I look at the headings to be sure they accurately reflect the content that follows them. Sometimes textbooks aren't that well constructed, and when that's the case I tell students. I think this is an important part of becoming a critical reader—knowing that you have to use your brain as you read and that even textbooks aren't perfect.
>
> Victor Hammel, Seventh-Grade Teacher

Give a man a fish, and you feed him for a day. Teach a man to fish, and you feed him for a lifetime.

—*Chinese Proverb*

We certainly agree with Mr. Hammel that such aids can be useful. In many cases, however, the text does not contain obvious clues to what is important, and students need to rely on their prior knowledge to infer just what is important in a particular selection.

For instance, while reading the short story "The Kite" by Arnold Lobel (1979), a first-grader might think about the most important characters and events in the story and come up with the following set of important points:

Frog is helping Toad fly a kite.

The kite doesn't fly on the first try.

Toad wants to give up, but Frog tells him to try again.

The kite doesn't fly.

Frog tells him to try a third time and still the kite won't get off the ground.

Frog tells Toad to make one more try.

This time the kite flies.

Together, these important points constitute the essence of the story.

Summarizing

Using this strategy requires students to first determine what is important and then condense it and put it in their own words. Ann Brown and Jeanne Day (1983) have suggested some basic rules for summarizing. Slightly modified, they include the following steps:

- Deleting trivial or irrelevant information
- Deleting redundant information
- Providing a superordinate term for members of a category
- Finding and using generalizations the author has made
- Creating your own generalizations when the author has not provided them

The earlier list of important ideas from "The Kite" constitutes a good summary of the story. By dropping less-important details and focusing on the most important aspects of the story, the student was able to understand what was taking place. An even briefer summary, focusing on the theme of the story, is also possible: Frog was trying to help Toad. By listening to Frog and doing what he said, and by continuing to try instead of quitting, Toad was able to get his kite into the air.

Dealing with Graphic Information

When they employ this strategy, readers give conscious attention to the visual information supplied by the author. Before youngsters learn to read, they are drawn to and fascinated by the visual material books offer. Teaching them when, how, and why to use the illustrations, graphs, maps, diagrams, and other visuals that accompany selections will enable them to make optimal use of the visual aids texts often provide.

History texts, for example, almost always contain maps that include a legend to the symbols they employ. Students need to learn that maps usually have legends, the kind of information legends normally contain, where legends are typically placed, and how to interpret them.

Imaging

Using this strategy, readers create visual representations of text, either in their minds or by reproducing them on paper or other tangible forms. One kind of imaging occurs when readers visualize people, events, and places. Another kind of imaging consists of visually organizing key ideas in text in a way that graphically displays their relationships. The former type of imaging is most frequently used with narrative material, while the latter is most frequently used with expository text. The following directions suggest how you might reinforce the imaging strategy with a group of first-graders to whom you have previously taught it:

IN THE CLASSROOM
Practicing Imaging with First-Graders

To give students practice in creating mental images of story characters, setting, and events as well as practice in sequencing story events, you can have them draw and sequence pictures. Here is how this might be done with Maurice Sendak's *Where the Wild Things Are*.

- Tell students that you are going to read one of your favorite stories to them, and as you read, you want them to create pictures in their minds. Remind them of their lesson on this important reading strategy. Tell them how creating pictures in their minds of what's happening in the story—the characters and what they look like, the place where the characters are, what the characters are doing—can help them enjoy and understand the story better. Today they are going to practice that strategy with *Where the Wild Things Are* by Maurice Sendak. Explain that you are not going to show them the pictures as you usually do when you read them a picture book, because you want them to make up the pictures in their minds. Tell them the story is about Max, a little boy with a wonderful imagination, who, because he was naughty, was sent to bed without his supper.

- Have students close their eyes, and then read the story aloud. For the first page or so, model this strategy yourself by sharing your own mental pictures. Then, as you read the rest of the story, remind students to make pictures in their minds about what they're hearing. For example, you might say, "What is Max doing here? What is Max seeing? Can you picture it in your mind?"

- After you have read the story, invite students to describe the pictures they saw.

- Tell students you are going to read the story again, and when you finish, they will get the chance to draw a picture from the story.

- After you have finished, encourage students to talk about what happened at the beginning of the story, the middle, and the end.

- Next, give each student a large sheet of drawing paper. Have students count off by threes and write their number on the back of their paper. The people who have the number one will draw a picture for the beginning of the story; those with the number two will draw something in the middle of the story; those with the number three, something that happened at the end.

- As the students are drawing, circulate around the class. Have students tell you what their picture shows and write their words on the back of their paper.

- Collect the pictures when students are finished, and sort them in stacks of ones, twos, and threes.

- Later, perhaps the following day, select one set of three pictures (labeled one, two, and three), and invite students who created them to come to the front of their class and tell about their pictures, but not give away their number. Encourage the rest of the class to sequence the pictures according to when they happened in the story. Select several more sets of three. When students become adept at sequencing, try adding more pictures.

One imaging technique appropriate for intermediate-grade students is constructing semantic maps of key concepts. As you will recall, we discussed semantic maps or webs in Chapters 5 and 6. In those chapters, however, we emphasized the use of webs by teachers or by teachers and students working together. Here, we are concerned with students learning to create their own semantic maps. For example, a student-constructed semantic map for a chapter on mountains in a geography text might look like that shown in Figure 7.1.

Monitoring Comprehension

As we explained in Chapter 1, good readers are metacognitive; that is, they monitor their comprehension. Monitoring comprehension is a more general strategy than any of those discussed thus far. In monitoring comprehension, readers keep track of what they wish to gain from a text and of their under-

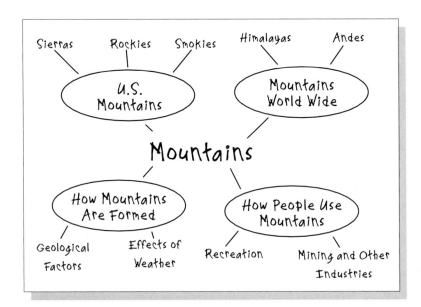

FIGURE 7.1 *Semantic Map of Mountains*

standing—or lack of understanding—of the text as they are reading. They then use whatever strategies they need to maintain or improve comprehension. You might think of monitoring comprehension as the employer and the other strategies as the employees, the workers who get the job of comprehension done.

Readers who monitor their comprehension are asking these kinds of questions: Am I understanding what the author is saying? What do I do if I don't understand something I'm reading? What could I be doing to understand better what the author is saying? Can I do something that will help me remember the material better?

Sixth-grade teacher Ron Novack makes it a point to encourage strategic reading by periodically challenging his students with questions about being strategic:

Mr. Novack: What do you do when you are reading along and suddenly realize you don't understand what you're reading?

Amad: When that happens to me, I go back and read the same words again.

Mr. Novack: You mean you reread. That's a good strategy.

Ted: If I'm reading science or social studies, or something like that, and there are words I don't know, I'll look them up or ask somebody.

Mr. Novack: You consult another source. That's a good strategy, too.

April: Sometimes it helps me to look at the pictures or maps if there are any.

Mr. Novack: You consider any graphic information. Good.

Doug: If something isn't making sense, I'll think about something I already know and see how it fits what I'm reading.

Mr. Novack: You connect what you already know with what you're reading. Excellent strategy.

Felicity: I try to picture in my mind what I'm reading, what the author's describing. I guess I'm always drawing pictures in my mind when I read.

Mr. Novack: You're imaging, and that's another very effective comprehension strategy.

Ron Novack and His Sixth-Grade Students

Mr. Novack encourages his students to do whatever is necessary to arrive at a satisfactory understanding of what they are reading. This, of course, is precisely what we want to prepare students to do.

The strategies described here—using prior knowledge, asking and answering questions, determining what is important, summarizing, making inferences, dealing with graphic information, imaging, and monitoring comprehension—will help students reach the goal of understanding and learning from what they read. In learning these strategies, students are internalizing a way of reading and thinking that is active, critical, and reflective. Having learned this mode of thinking, students will be both able and inclined to engage in a variety of reading and learning strategies to understand, appreciate, and learn from what they read. It should be noted that students will differ in the rate at which they learn the strategies that have been described. We believe it is more important for students to have a thorough understanding of a fewer number of strategies than to have a superficial understanding of a larger number of strategies. Although the ultimate goal is for students to have a repertoire of strategies to apply, what is most important is that they are able to effectively use the strategies they have.

It is also important that students get a feel for what it means to be strategic. One way to help students understand the concept of being strategic is to use children's literature that illustrates children using strategies, like those selections listed in the following books feature.

What do you do when you realize you don't understand what you're reading?

Try to picture in my mind what I'm reading.

Look at the pictures or diagrams, if there are any.

Reread.

Look up words I don't know in the dictionary, or ask someone else.

Books That Illustrate Strategic Behavior

Children's literature abounds with characters (real and imaginary) who strategically go about trying to achieve their goals or solve problems. These characters, who exhibit deliberately planned behavior that takes into account their unique situation, are among children's favorites in literature. Here is a small sampling.

Alma Flor Ada. *My Name Is Maria Isabel*. Atheneum, 1993. Renamed Mary by her teacher, Maria Isabel, recently arrived in the United States from Puerto Rico, finds a way to get back her own name *and* to fit in with her classmates. 57 pages.

Louise Erdrich. *Grandmother's Pigeon*. Hyperion, 1996. When three eggs in one of Grandmother's bird nest collection miraculously hatch a breed of passenger pigeons long thought to be extinct, Grandmother's family takes matters into their own hands when visiting scientists threaten the hatchlings' freedom. 32 pages.

John Reynolds Gardiner. *Stone Fox*. Crowell, 1980. Determined to earn the money to pay the taxes on his grandfather's farm, ten-year-old Willie enters a dogsled race against the legendary Indian, Stone Fox. 85 pages.

Jean Craighead George. *The Talking Earth*. HarperCollins, 1983. While spending three months alone in the Florida Everglades, a young Seminole girl learns about herself and her people. 151 pages.

Rosa Guy. *The Disappearance*. Delacorte, 1979. After leaving an alcoholic mother behind in Harlem, Imamu Jones finds hope for a better life with a middle-class family in Brooklyn. Once there, he becomes involved in locating his missing sister. 246 pages.

Patricia Hermes. *Mama, Let's Dance*. Little, Brown, 1991. Eleven-year-old Mary Belle learns to cope with being in charge of her brothers and sisters when her mother leaves home. 168 pages.

Phillip Hoose. *It's Our World, Too! Stories of Young People Who Are Making a Difference*. Little, Brown/Joy Street, 1993. These stories profile young people who have changed their communities and responded to social and environmental needs using nonviolent methods. 166 pages.

Mary Elizabeth Haggerty. *A Crack in the Wall*. Lee & Low, 1993. Left home by himself while his mother works, Carlos finds a way to transform their small, modest apartment into something beautiful and magical. 32 pages.

June Jordan. *Kimako's Story*. Houghton Mifflin, 1981. Left with her brother when her mother goes to work, 7-year-old Kimako learns to become independent and to fill her hours with reading and writing puzzle poems. 32 pages.

Loreen Leedy. *The Great Trash Bash*. Scholwtec, 1991. Mayor Hippo thinks the town of Beaston has too much trash, so with the help of his fellow town-animals, he finds a way to do something about it. 32 pages.

Gary Paulson. *Hatchet*. Bradbury, 1987. This gripping adventure story is about Brian Robeson's surviving 54 days alone in the northern Canadian wilderness. 195 pages.

Ann Turnbull. *Too Tired*. Harcourt Brace, 1994. In this humorous adaptation of the Flood story, Noah and the rest of the animals manage to rescue the sloths, who are "too tired" to climb aboard themselves. 32 pages.

Cynthia Voight. *Homecoming*. Atheneum, 1983. After their mother abandons them in a shopping mall parking lot, 13-year-old Dicey keeps her three younger siblings fed and out of harm's way as they journey in search of a home. 312 pages.

Reflection AND *Application*

1. Identify one of the eight strategies that you use or that is similar to one you use. Then describe two or three situations in which you have used it and why it was appropriate in those situations. It would be a good idea to do this in writing.

2. Consider the eight strategies we have discussed, and identify those that are likely to be particularly useful for second-graders, for fourth-graders, and for sixth-graders. Then compare your assessments to those of a classmate.

A Validated Approach to Teaching Strategies

So how do you go about teaching strategies? In this section, we describe an approach to teaching comprehension strategies that has been quite thoroughly researched and found to be effective by a number of researchers, including Donald Deshler and Jean Schumaker (1993), Janice Dole and her colleagues (Dole, Brown, & Trathen, 1996), and Michael Pressley and Vera Woloshyn (1995). To illustrate the approach, we first describe the components that make up the first two days of instruction. Next, we consider how instruction proceeds and changes over the course of a three- or four-week unit. After that, we discuss the ways in which good strategy instruction must be constructive in nature. Finally, we discuss the types of transfer, review, and integrating activities that are needed to make a strategy a tool that students will really use.

> The essence of the instructional procedures [for teaching strategies] is *scaffolding*. One does not direct the learner, as one can do when teaching an algorithm, but rather, one *supports* or scaffolds learners as they develop internal structures.
>
> —Barak Rosenshine
> *Educational Researcher*

Although instruction will vary somewhat with different strategies, different students, and different age groups, the general plan presented is widely applicable. However, we want to stress that what we present here is a general plan and not a script to be rigidly followed. What actually occurs in the classroom will be dictated by the interaction between you and your students. As Ann Dyson and Sara Freedman (1991) explain, "The process of teaching and learning is dynamic. The learner affects the teacher just as the teacher affects the learner, as both move to build a support structure that meets students' needs" (p. 768).

Reading strategies help students understand and learn from the texts they read.

The First Day's Instruction

The activities described in this section are those used on the first day of instruction on a new strategy. In this illustration, the students are fourth-graders, and the strategy to be taught is determining what is important. The students have had some experience with the strategy in previous grades, but this is the first time it is formally taught. Recently, they have been having difficulty sifting out less-important details and focusing on more important ideas in their science and social studies books, and so this seems to be an opportune time for instruction in this particular strategy. The first day's instruction includes six different components.

Motivation and Interest Building (About 5 Minutes). To capture students' attention and build interest, introduce the strategy by having students guess the categories represented by various sets of words you write on the board. Choose categories and words of interest to the particular group of students being taught. We have chosen fast-food restaurants, sports that use balls, and sports that don't use balls. Write the word sets on the board underneath unlabeled umbrellas—an idea suggested by James Baumann (1986) and illustrated here. Tell students that these words are examples of more general ideas, have them guess what those more general ideas are, and have them write these more general ideas in the umbrellas above the sets of examples.

What idea covers all of these?

McDonald's	tennis	swimming
Burger King	soccer	track
Wendy's	football	gymnastics
Arby's	basketball	weightlifting
Taco Bell	broomball	archery

Teacher Explanation (About 5 Minutes). After students have determined the more general ideas represented by several sets of examples, explain that identifying these ideas is part of a strategy you are going to teach them. At this point, ask students about the reading they have been doing in science and social studies, and discuss some of the challenges they have faced. One of the challenges that is likely to come up is that these books cover a lot of information, and it is hard to remember all of it. Explain that the strategy they will learn—determining what is important—will help them to better understand and remember what they read.

Next, explain that when they use this strategy, they should focus on the most important information and let the less important details fade into the background. Talk about how much of the social studies and science material they read contains a great deal of information and how concentrating on only the most important information cuts down on what they need to learn and remember. Tell students that knowing how to determine what is important can make understanding and remembering what they read much easier.

Teacher Modeling (About 5 Minutes).   Reveal more about how the strategy works by writing a sentence such as *Matthew Blaine, a fourth-grade student at Ridgeview Elementary School, won first prize in the Rotary Speech Contest with his essay titled "What Freedom Means to Me"* on the board. Read the sentence aloud, and model the thought processes you might go through in identifying the most important information in the sentence.

> Let's see, what is the main idea the author is communicating in this sentence? The topic seems to be Matthew Blaine. And what is the most important information about Matthew? Winning first prize sounds pretty important. [Circle the phrases *Matthew Blaine* and *won first prize in the Rotary Speech Contest* on the board.] The other information— that he's a fourth-grade student at Ridgeview Elementary School and the title of his essay—are interesting, but not as important. [Cross out *a student at Ridgeview Elementary School* and *with his essay titled "What Freedom Means to Me"* on the board.]

The board work used to illustrate that Matthew Blaine won the Rotary Speech Contest is the most important information in the sentence is shown here.

Matthew Blaine, a fourth-grade student at Ridgeview Elementary School, won first prize in the Rotary Speech Contest with his essay titled, 'What Freedom Means to Me.'

Once you have explained the strategy and modeled it, check to see if students were following you by asking a few students to explain the strategy and tell why it is worth knowing.

Large-Group Student Participation and Teacher Mediation (About 10 Minutes).   Put a paragraph from one of the students' social studies or science texts on the overhead, and read it aloud. The paragraph should be one in which the important information stands out. The sample paragraph used here is taken from *Scaly Babies: Reptiles Growing Up* by Ginny Johnson and Judy Cutchins:

> *For many people, the word* reptile *describes an ugly, slippery, and sometimes dangerous animal. But reptiles are not slimy, and most are not dangerous. There are nearly six thousand different kinds of these scaly-skinned animals in the world today. It is true that some are large and scary-looking and a few are venomous, but most reptiles are harmless to humans. Like many wild animals, reptiles may strike or bite to defend themselves. But they rarely bother a person who has not disturbed or startled them.* (Johnson & Cutchins, 1988, p. 1)

Ask students what the paragraph is mainly about (reptiles). Next, ask them how they determined this (everything in the paragraph is about reptiles). Have students supply the details about reptiles that are given in the paragraph and write these on the board, as shown here:

Reptiles

ugly, slippery, dangerous—some people think
not slimy and most not dangerous
scaly skinned
6,000 in world
some large and scary, a few venomous
most harmless to humans
may strike to defend themselves
rarely bother people

After you have written the details students have suggested on the board, ask them which information in the paragraph is the most important. Explain that all of these details say something about reptiles, but that one is the most general and important idea, probably the idea that the author really wants to get across. Help students determine the most important idea by asking questions such as these about each of the details: Is this the most important idea in the paragraph? Do the other ideas support this one? Do you think this is the main thing the author is trying to tell you?

After students have agreed on the most important idea, rewrite the chart on the board to show the most important idea with its supporting details underneath it, as shown here:

Although many people think reptiles
are dangerous, most are not.

not slimy and most not dangerous
a few venomous
most harmless to humans
may strike to defend themselves
rarely bother people

Thus far, this introductory session has lasted about 25 minutes. In most classrooms, it would be a good idea to move to another topic at this time and continue the strategy instruction the next day.

The Second Day's Instruction

Very briefly review the first day's lesson, again discussing what strategies in general are and what the specific strategy of determining what is important is, motivating students by reminding them how helpful the strategy will be for understanding and remembering what they read, and modeling your thought processes as you determine what is important in a short text—probably the paragraph with which you ended yesterday's lesson.

More Large-Group Student Participation and Teacher Mediation (10 to 20 Minutes). Work together with students to determine the most important idea in several additional paragraphs in the same book. Call on students to determine what is most important in each paragraph and to explain how they determined that the information they selected is the most important. On the board, create a visual display similar to the one for the first paragraph. If students seem to understand the strategy, move to the next step. If not, do some further explaining and modeling.

Cooperative Group Work (About 10 Minutes). Once large-group questioning indicates that students have a basic understanding of the strategy, they need a chance to practice it. Initially, they can practice in pairs. Remember, they are just beginning to work with the strategy, and a lot of scaffolding is appropriate. You want to ensure that students are successful and feel successful at this point. Since they have worked only with paragraph-length selections thus far, they should continue with paragraph-length selections in this practice session. Also, since the selections used thus far have been ones in which the important information stood out clearly, the practice paragraphs should also clearly reveal the important information. Two or three such paragraphs might be a good number for this part of the lesson.

Sharing Group Work and Teacher Response and Mediation (About 10 Minutes).   Once students have had an opportunity to use the strategy in pairs, they should share their work with the class. Call on pairs to present the important information they found in the passages, and discuss how they determined that this was the crucial information. Monitor their responses carefully, and provide feedback and clarification as necessary.

This would conclude the first two days of instruction and practice with the strategy. The remainder of the unit is discussed in the next section. First, however, we do want to remind you that teacher explanation, modeling, and mediation need to be carried out in a way that engages students and keeps them attentive. It is difficult to capture the flexibility and fluidity of good strategy instruction in a written text. Also, we want to note that the instructional periods will vary greatly according to the age and maturity of the students. For example, most first-graders may be able to attend to a teacher presentation for only 5 to 10 minutes, while upper-elementary students may be able to attend for 15 to 20 minutes.

Overview of a Unit

A typical unit might last for three weeks. Although instruction should continue to include a number of the features of the first day's instruction, it should gradually change as students become increasingly competent with the strategy. Here are some of the major ways in which it should change.

Subsequent Instructional Periods Become Shorter.   During the first few days of instruction, the instructional periods should be fairly lengthy, perhaps averaging 20 minutes. After the first few days, the periods of instruction get shorter, with those at the end of the unit perhaps lasting only 5–10 minutes. As students gradually assume more and more responsibility for using the strategy, it is appropriate to have less instruction and more practice.

Instruction Becomes Less Concentrated Each Week.   During the first week, students should work on the strategy nearly every day; then, with each successive week, they should work on it less frequently. For example, during the first week there might be four days of instruction; during the second week, three days; and during the third week, two days.

Students Do More of the Work.   Particularly on the first day of instruction and to a lesser extent during the first few days of instruction, the teacher bears the burden of much of the work. In other words, the teacher heavily scaffolds instruction. Teacher explanation, teacher modeling, and teacher response and feedback occupy a significant amount of the time on the first few days. Increasingly, however, the teacher should gradually release responsibility for completing the strategy to students. More and more time is spent on actual work with the strategy. Also, perhaps after the first week or so, students move from working in pairs to working independently at least some of the time.

Texts Become Longer and More Challenging.   In addition to students doing more of the work themselves, over time they need to work with increasingly lengthy and more challenging texts. On the first few days of instruction, students might work with paragraphs; next they might work with one-page texts; then, eventually, they will work with typical chapter-length texts. Similarly, on the first few days, students would work with selections in which the important information stands out prominently, that is, selections in which important information is cued by titles, headings, or topic sentences. Later, they would work with material in which the important information is less obvious, material more typical of much of what they will read.

Strategies Are Used on Authentic Tasks.   Since the purpose of learning strategies is to enable students to use the strategies as part of their normal reading experiences, they need to be given many opportunities, prompts, and encouragement to employ the strategies outside of the context of specific strategy instruction. Such opportunities can be pointed out during class time devoted to reading; during class time devoted to other subjects, such as social studies and mathematics; and when the strategies are likely to be useful for work done outside of class. For example, almost any written report requires that students determine what is important in the material they read for the report.

Students Are Encouraged to Use the Strategies Independently.   Of course, when students set out to read something or encounter a comprehension problem in what they are reading, you usually will not be there to suggest what strategy they can use to read effectively or to remedy the problem. Thus, once students reach the point at which they can routinely use the strategies when you prompt them to do so, you need to repeatedly encourage them to use the strategies on their own. For example, from time to time you can ask students which of the strategies you taught they have been using, and occasionally you can remind students of the strategies they have worked with and where they might use them in their present reading. Also, a colorful bulletin board such as that shown in Figure 7.2 can serve as a reminder to use the strategies they've learned or reviewed during the year, and as a refresher on how to use them.

FIGURE 7.2 *Strategy Bulletin Board*

The Constructive Nature of Good Strategy Instruction

As we just mentioned, conveying the constructivist, interactive, flexible nature of good strategy instruction is difficult to do in a textbook, and we want to be certain that our description of strategy instruction has not left some of you thinking of it as rather rigid and teacher-centered. Good strategy instruction is neither rigid nor teacher-centered. We emphasize this by presenting a comparison of teacher-dominated instruction to constructivist instruction in Figure 7.3.

Transfer, Review, and Integration Activities

Thus far, we have described the first two days of strategy instruction, explained how instruction changes over a three- to four-week unit on a strategy, and examined the way in which good strategy instruction must be a constructive, interactive, and flexible process. If you were to create and present a unit based on the suggestions thus far presented, students would be well on their way to becoming effective and independent strategy users. However, in order to assist students in completing their journey toward mastery of the strategies, you will need to provide additional reviews of the strategies you teach, help them transfer their use of the strategies to all appropriate areas of learning, assist them in modifying the strategies and making them truly their own, and aid them in integrating their use of newly learned strategies with other strategies. If students are to become permanent strategy users, their use of the newly learned strategy needs to be encouraged and nurtured beyond the initial unit of instruction. Several types of follow-up are important.

One- or Two-Day Formal Reviews.   By formal reviews, we mean 15- to 20-minute instructional sessions in which renewing students' understanding and competency with a strategy is the main topic of the lesson. One-shot instruction—even if it is a lengthy three-week unit—is not likely to permanently alter students' approaches to reading. Assuming that initial instruction in the strategy took place early in the school year, the first review might be given in November and the second review in February or March.

Occasional Minilessons.   In addition to the 15- to 20-minute formal reviews, occasional 5- to 10-minute minilessons should be given when the materials students are working with offer an authentic opportunity to use a strategy and a short review seems needed. It is important to conduct these minilessons using science, social studies, and other content area materials. Strategies are not to be used only during the designated reading period. In order to ensure that students actually use the strategies you have taught in

When teachers see their role as a "strategic–content" teacher as opposed to a "content" teacher, they present strategy instruction in a sustained fashion, thus ensuring that at-risk students as well as others in the class receive more consistent exposure to instruction in "how to learn" than they would during traditional instruction.

—Donald D. Deshler
and Jean B. Schumaker
Educational Researchers

309

Teacher-Dominated Instruction	Constructivist Instruction
The teacher lectures and the students listen.	The teacher and the students interact, with modeling, explanation, and discussion prominent.
Children assume the role of passive, rather than active, participants.	Children assume the role of active participants.
Instruction is given as if the knowledge the teacher has can be transmitted directly to the students; the metaphor is that of pouring information from one container (the teacher's head) to another (the student's head).	It is understood that the knowledge the teacher has cannot be transmitted directly to the students; the metaphor is that of an instructional conversation between teacher and students.
There is little discussion and argument.	There is a great deal of discussion and argument.
Teachers do very little on-the-spot diagnoses of individual students' understanding and progress.	Teachers frequently make on-the-spot diagnoses of individual students understanding and progress.
The instruction proceeds at a pre-determined rate and sequence, dictated by the curriculum employed in the classroom.	The instruction proceeds at a rate and sequence dictated by the students' needs and progress.
Teachers appear to follow a script, and students are expected to proceed at the same rate.	Lessons are not scripted. Students are expected to proceed at their own rate, with teacher and peer scaffolding facilitating progress.
Skills are emphasized at the expense of understanding.	Understanding is emphasized as strategies are developed.
Students are rarely told about why they practice the activities they do or taught how to monitor and self-regulate their use of the strategies.	Students are always informed about the purposes of the skills they are taught and help to develop monitoring and self-regulation of the strategies.

FIGURE 7.3 *Teacher-Dominated and Constructivist Strategy Instruction*

The descriptions here are modified forms of descriptions originally written by Ann Brown and Joseph Campione (1990) and Michael Pressley and his colleagues (Pressley, Harris, & Mark, 1992).

real situations of trying to understand and learn from a text, you will need to deliberately point out opportunities to use the strategies in the many content areas in which they are useful. And part of this "pointing out" will consist of minilessons on the strategies.

Finding Opportunities to Use the Strategies. Not only is it important that you find authentic opportunities to use newly taught strategies, but students too should be encouraged to find appropriate and authentic opportunities to use the strategies they are taught. After all, it is the students and not you who will need to decide when and where to use the strategy outside of your class and in the future.

Listening to Students and Providing Feedback and Responsive Elaboration. Even after a substantial unit on a strategy, many students will still harbor some confusion and uncertainty about it. Really listening to students and trying to understand their thinking is necessary in order to clear up confusion and reduce uncertainty. This means frequently employing the sort of responsive elaboration that we describe in Chapter 2.

Repeatedly Providing Motivation to Use the Strategies. Reading strategically—really understanding what you're reading, caring whether or not you're understanding it, and doing something about it if you're not—isn't easy. It's not like sitting down in front of the TV and half-attending to what's going on. If students are to put in the effort to be strategic readers, we need to constantly motivate them to read strategically. The main motivation, we believe, is showing students that reading is purposeful, that they gain something from reading, and that by reading strategically they can take control of their reading and learning.

Frequent Suggestions to Use the Strategies. Not every reminder to use a newly taught strategy needs to be some sort of lesson. As you will recall, suggesting strategies is one of the prereading activities we suggest as part of the SRE approach we describe in Chapter 6. Whenever the materials students are using lend themselves to use of a strategy that has been taught, you can give students a brief reminder that the strategy may prove useful. You can also invite students to suggest the use of a newly taught strategy to their classmates when they discover a situation suited to its use.

Giving Students the Freedom to Modify Strategies and Make Them Truly Their Own. The goal is to teach a small number of strategies over the elementary school years and have students learn the taught strategies well so that they have internalized a well-learned routine that they can employ independently. Once students have learned a strategy, however, they will begin to modify it and use it in a way that conforms to their individual strengths and needs (Garner & Gillingham, 1996). This is to be expected and encouraged. We want students to adapt the strategies so that they are truly their tools and not ones they have borrowed from us. We want students to consciously choose how, when, and where to use strategies. The bottom line of strategy use, really the ultimate strategy, is being metacognitive, knowing that there's a cognitive task to be completed and choosing an appropriate strategy to achieve it.

Reflection AND *Application*

3. Get together with half a dozen of your classmates, pick a strategy and a grade level, and design the first two days of instruction on the strategy, with each of you creating one segment of the instruction—for example, the motivation and interest-building segment. Then, actually present the instruction to another group of your classmates.

4. Consider our description of the ways in which strategy instruction changes as you progress through a unit, and see if you can come up with some other ways in which it might change as students become more and more competent and comfortable with a strategy.

5. Look over the suggestions for assisting students in integrating strategies into their day-to-day reading, and identify those that you will be most likely to use when you teach strategies. You can of course decide that you will likely use all of them. As you know (and as we will emphasize in the Writing to Learn and Understand section of Chapter 9), writing your answers will help you fully grasp the ideas you are learning and fix them in your mind for use in the classroom.

ENCOURAGING INDEPENDENT READING

Independent reading. Just what does that mean? In the first half of this chapter, we talked about reading comprehension strategies and suggested procedures for teaching students to use these strategies. Now, in this half, we describe ways that you can ensure that students have plenty of opportunities to read on their own, to explore independently the wonderful world of ideas that books have to offer. First, we discuss independent reading generally and the simplest form of independent reading, sustained silent reading. Second, we briefly discuss the reader response approach to reading literature and describe two types of response groups that encourage students to make personal responses to literature. Third, we describe the reading workshop, a framework that promotes reader response.

Independent Reading

In independent reading, as we define it here, students select their own material to read for their own purposes. These purposes may include any of a myriad reasons—pleasure, information, insight—whatever reason those who love reading so often pick up a book. If students are to become fluent and engaged readers who constantly choose to read for knowledge and pleasure, it is crucial that they be given many opportunities to do so. Some years ago, Dixie Lee Spiegel (1981) suggested several benefits of independent reading: It develops positive attitudes toward reading. It gives students a chance to expand their background knowledge. It provides practice in decoding strategies and develops automaticity. And as we mentioned in Chapter 5, it is a way for students to develop their vocabularies. Recently, Richard Anderson (1996) has summarized research that clearly demonstrates that reading accounts for up to two thirds of children's annual vocabulary growth and that the amount of reading children do is strongly related to intellectual growth generally. Anderson also points out that providing children who are learning English as a second language with a wealth of appealing and interesting books to be read and shared significantly improves their English proficiency, a topic we will discuss in Chapter 10.

Providing Time to Read

Common sense tells us that we get better at just about anything by doing more of it. Reading is no exception; and, as we just noted, research confirms this notion. In one study, for example, Anderson and his colleagues (1988) investigated fifth-graders' activities outside of school and the relationship of those activities to reading proficiency. Not surprisingly, what they found was that those students who spent time reading books made greater strides in reading in grades 2 through 5 than those who spent their time on other activities. In another very different study, Richard West and his associates (West, Stanovich, & Mitchell, 1993) approached adults who were reading as they waited in airports and adults who were not reading as they waited in airports and gave them a battery of tests. Results indicated that the readers outper-

> Independent reading can no longer be a little thing our students do while we collect milk money. It can no longer be a time for kids to settle down after recess, to get drinks of water, to unpack papers for the afternoon. Independent reading needs to be central to our reading curriculum.
>
> —*Lucy Calkins*
> *Author and Teacher*

formed the nonreaders on all of the tests given—except those that involved knowledge about television programs and personalities. These and other results led Anderson (1996) to conclude that "there is a rather strong case, a case based on hard facts, that increasing the volume of children's playful, stimulating experience with good books leads to accelerated growth in reading competence" (p. 74).

Given this overwhelming evidence, how much time then should be set aside each school day for students to read independently for pleasure in order to have "playful, stimulating experience with good books"? Based on their research, Linda Fielding and her colleagues (1986) recommend at least an hour per week. The amount of time spent in independent reading each day can vary from 5 minutes to 30 minutes and will depend on a number of factors— how often you schedule independent pleasure reading; what other opportunities for sustained reading students have in your classroom; the likelihood that students will read outside of school; and the age, interests, and maturity of students. As a rule of thumb, we recommend beginning with 5- to 10-minute periods for primary-grade children and 15- to 20-minute periods for older students, with primary students having independent reading sessions daily and older students having them perhaps three days per week. These times can of course be increased if your curriculum and students' interest and involvement allow it. All in all, the exact amount of time is not as important as making certain that there *is* a time set aside for pleasure reading on a consistent basis.

> Children need to read lots of easy stuff.
>
> —*Richard Allington and Patricia Cunningham*
> *Teacher Educators*

Providing a Rich Array of Reading Material, the Incentive to Read It, and a Place to Read It

Providing a rich array of reading material, plenty of motivation to read it, and a comfortable and inviting place to read are crucial. This is true for all students, but it is particularly true for those who do not gravitate to reading and those whose home environment does not prompt and nurture reading. Student reading material can come from a variety of sources—including their homes, their friends, the classroom library, classroom book clubs, the school library, and the public library. Types of selections can and should run the gamut—fiction, nonfiction, trade books, magazines, even textbooks—the choice is up to the student.

Although children's chosen material should vary considerably and come from a variety of sources, we have found it extremely important for the classroom teacher to make these materials readily available—in fact, virtually unavoidable. One absolute essential is a well-stocked classroom library, a feature lacking in all too many schools (Allington et al., 1996). If school funds will not support a classroom library, we suggest that you investigate the possibility of obtaining funds from parents or a local civic group. Joining a classroom book club—a commercial club that sells paperbacks at low prices and frequently sends out class sets of attractive and enticing flyers—can be an excellent way to promote books. Typically, students purchase the books with their own funds, and the classroom receives free books based on the number purchased—a wonderful way to stock the classroom library. If students and their parents cannot afford book club purchases, we again suggest you consider approaching a local civic group for support. Also, you will want to become thoroughly acquainted with your school library and local public library and the media specialists and librarians there, and you will want to introduce your students to these libraries and librarians. Regular class visits to the school library and occasional field trips to the local public library are time well spent.

Commercial book clubs make it very easy for you and your students to order books. The list of commercial book clubs on the following page gives the addresses, phone numbers, and some sample offerings from three book clubs.

Assisting Students in Selecting Material

Helping students select the right material—material that they can read, will read, will enjoy, and will profit from—is tremendously important. Moreover, this is a task that is particularly important and particularly difficult with less-able and less-avid readers, students who do not read much and are therefore less familiar with what's available and less skilled at selecting appropriate material.

> Providing choices gives students a great deal of ownership, but the freedom can also be a challenge for some.
>
> —Penny Redman
> Multiage Teacher

Here are three suggestions. First, find out what students like and don't like. Over the first few weeks of the year, talk to each student about her interests, what she has and hasn't read, what she did and didn't like and understand. Make some notes on your findings for each student (probably in the teacher log book we describe in Chapter 11), and update your notes on each student throughout the year as you learn more about your students. Second, solicit the help of others. Talk to your school librarian about what is available and what she has found particularly appropriate for students such as yours; talk to your students' previous teachers about what reading material she has found successful with them; and talk to your students about

Books from Commercial Book Clubs

The book clubs listed below are three of the best known ones. Here, we list just four of the very large number of titles available from each publisher. The annotations are ones the clubs provided in their recent brochures.

Scholastic Book Clubs, Inc.
P.O. Box 7503
Jefferson City, MO 65102-7503
(800) 724-2424

Joanna Cole. *The Magic School Bus Inside a Hurricane*. The Magic School Bus turns into a weather balloon and goes into the middle of a hurricane! 48 pages. $2.95.

Trudie Engel. *We'll Never Forget You, Roberto Clemente*. Roberto grew up poor—but hard work made him a baseball star. 80 pages. $1.95.

Ruth Stiles Gannett. *My Father's Dragon*. A delightful adventure about a young boy who sets out to free an imprisoned dragon. Newbery Honor Book. 80 pages. $.95.

Karen Berman Nagel (developed with Marilyn Burns). *The Lunch Line*. (Hello Math Series) Kim has five dimes and two quarters. What can she buy for lunch? 32 pages. $1.95.

Troll Book Clubs
100 Corporate Drive
Mahwah, NJ 07430
(800) 929-8765

Melvin Berger. *Oil Spill!* When an oil tanker crashes in the sea, sticky oil is everywhere—on the bodies of seabirds and in the gills of fish! Learn how experts clean it up, and how spills can be stopped. 32 pages. $1.95.

Paula Danzinger. *Thames Doesn't Rhyme with James*. Kendra is going to London to visit Frank! But will they spend any time together? 192 pages. $1.95.

Nick Griffiths. *Incredible Inventions*. A cool collection of mechanical marvels and their makers—from the wheel to virtual reality—are explored. 32 pages. $2.95.

Taro Yashima. *Umbrella*. Momo loves her new umbrella so much, she can't wait for a rainy day in this delightful story about the rewards of patience. ALA. 40 pages. $1.95.

The Trumpet Club
P.O. Box 6003
Columbia, MO 65205-6003
(800) 826-0110

Eve Bunting. *Flower Garden*. A flower garden in a shopping cart, on the bus, and going up the stairs? What's a garden doing in the city? Ages 4–8. 32 pages. $2.50.

Beverly Cleary. *Dear Mr. Henshaw*. Someone is stealing Leigh's lunch, his dog is missing, and his parents just separated. Leigh's got a lot to tell his favorite author. Ages 9–11. 144 pages. $2.95.

Madeleine L'Engle. *The Arm of the Starfish*. When Adam Eddington goes to Portugal to work for a scientist whose work could change mankind, he gets caught in the middle of a deadly power struggle. Whose side is he on? 240 pages. $3.50.

Gary Soto. *A Fire in My Hands*. Do you have a best friend? Have you ever had a crush? Here are 23 poems about growing up in the barrio that you'll want to read again and again. 64 pages. $1.95.

An inviting, well-stocked classroom library goes a long way in nurturing life-long readers.

books and other material they have enjoyed. Become familiar with the many guides to selecting reading material for children; in *Choosing Books for Literature Circles*, Dianne Monson (1996) describes some characteristics particularly desirable in books students will share with one another. Third, use this information in talking to students as they are selecting independent reading, and advertise the best and most enticing material you have discovered with colorful posters, pictures, reviews, and testimonials prominently displayed in your classroom. The following guidelines summarize some of these suggestions and present some additional ones for assisting students in selecting materials to read:

IN THE CLASSROOM
Helping Students Select Reading Material

To help students select material,

- give book and author talks. Occasionally introduce students to a new author and his or her works by telling a little about that author, giving previews of his or her works, and reading excerpts from them.

- read from a big book and then make multiple copies of the "little" books available.

- read a chapter from a novel or chapter book, and then make that book available.

- suggest students use the "Goldilocks Principle"—choose a book that's not too hard, not too easy, but "just right."

- invite students to give book and author talks in which they recommend books and authors they have enjoyed.

- invite students to write previews, reviews, and testimonials, and display them around the room.

- invite a guest author to read from his or her work, and then make those works available.

- Invite your school media specialist or the librarian from your public library to talk about her favorite books and authors as well as give information on the library's resources and how to locate materials.

- Invite other adults—parents, the principal, secretary, custodian, coach, nurse—to talk about their favorite books.

Establishing and Maintaining an Independent Reading Program

The special time set aside for recreational reading has been given many different names over the years. You have probably heard of and may well have been involved in one or more of them—recreational reading (RR), drop everything and read (DEAR), daily independent reading time (DIRT), sustained silent reading (SSR), and uninterrupted sustained silent reading (USSR). Although the names are different, each program's goal is the same—to provide a designated time when the teacher and all of the students in class read self-selected materials for a set amount of time and for their own purposes.

We recommend that every elementary classroom establish an independent sustained reading program and that it be established early in the school year. At the outset, discuss with your students what the activity entails and the purposes for doing it—why they are doing it and how it will help them (Spiegel, 1981). Give the activity a name, or let your students choose or create one. Here are the basic guidelines for SSR; you may wish to modify them for your class:

- Everyone reads, including the teacher.
- Choose just one selection, but have an extra close at hand in case the selection is finished before time is up.

- Decide where to sit before reading begins. There is no getting up from the reading spot once timing has started.
- The designated time for sustained silent reading is the same each day.
- Nobody is required to answer questions or give a report on what they read.

Here are some additional suggestions. Use these or modify them to fit the needs of your students:

- Put a *Do Not Disturb* sign on the outside of the classroom door.
- Use a timer to keep track of the time. This avoids having to watch the clock.
- Begin timing when the last person is ready to read.
- Have extra books available for students who forget their books.
- Provide students with bookmarks to mark their spot for the next time. Bookmarks are available through the American Library Association (ALA), or students can make their own.

You might find it helpful to make a poster of your sustained reading rules and post it in a prominent place, at least until the routine has been firmly established. Sharon Hilbert (1993) has suggested these basic rules, and we have prefaced these with one of our own:

- Always bring your independent reading material to class.
- Everyone reads.
- Everyone is quiet.
- Everyone stays seated.

By incorporating an uninterrupted reading time into your daily routine, you will not only be contributing to students' growth in reading fluency, but also you will be sending several powerful messages, including these: Reading books is important; reading is something anyone can do; reading involves communicating with an author; children are capable of sustained thought; and you believe that they can and do comprehend what they read (McCracken & McCracken, 1978).

> Too many children are growing up today without the benefit of imagination. Some live in constant contact with reminders of poverty and violence. Others are surrounded by toys and technology that do it all for them. Reading and writing give students the opportunity to dream of a better life, to be creative. They can safely test the results of different choices and then make plans for their own future.
>
> —*Susan Jones*
> *Second-Grade Teacher*

Literature Response Groups

Perhaps you recall a time when your teachers asked a series of questions about a story you read. You believed there were "right" answers to those questions, and you tried your best to deliver them. Some of those questions certainly did have "right" answers. For example, if your teacher asked you to name the two main characters in "Gone with the Wiener," and you answered Homer and Gustav when they actually were Tina and Joey, your teacher might assume (rightly) that either you read a different story, didn't comprehend the story, or hadn't read the story (certainly an unlikely eventuality!). However, other kinds of questions leave room for interpretation, for that personal transaction that takes place between the reader and the text. One such question is, How do you think Tina felt when Joey sent her roses? *You* might answer the question by saying that Tina felt happy because Joey remembered her birthday. However, another reader might decide that Tina felt nervous because roses are a symbol of love and Tina was ambivalent about her own feelings for Joey.

Reader-response theory—much of which evolved from the extended work of Louise Rosenblatt (1938, 1978)—centers on the belief that the reader is crucial to the construction of the literary experience. The reader doesn't come to the text empty, hoping to be filled, but brings meaning to the text. Reading is a transaction between the reader and the writer. Any particular reading of a text—particularly a literary text such as fiction and poetry—will produce an interpretation that reflects both the meaning intended by the author and the meaning constructed by the reader. Author Madeleine L'Engle (1980), for example, suggests that a new book is written every time someone reads a particular book: "If a reader cannot create a book along with the writer, the book will never come to life" (p. 34).

A number of the postreading activities we discussed in Chapter 6—for example, those involving writing, art, dance, music, and drama—promote reader response. As you recall, many of these encourage students' personal responses to literature and give them opportunities to use a variety of modes of expression in doing so. Here, we talk about discussion groups specifically designed to foster diverse responses and give students opportunities to share their responses.

What Are Response Groups?

A host of types of postreading discussion groups designed to foster reader response have emerged in the past several years—literature response groups (Reutzel & Cooter, 1991), literature discussion groups (Routman, 1991), reading response groups (Ruddell & Ruddell, 1995), literature circles (Short

& Klassen, 1993), and open discussion groups (Sorenson, 1993). Like the many approaches to independent silent reading, the names and some specifics of each approach vary, but at the heart of each, the purpose is much the same—eliciting personal responses from students and making these public through discussion. These discussions provide forums for exchanging ideas, for enhancing and refining those ideas, and for thinking creatively and critically about topics, ideas, and issues. Some of the common elements of reader-response groups are listed here:

- They are formed around a small group of students (usually four or five, with a maximum of seven) reading a single selection.
- Students lead the discussion; sometimes the teacher participates as a member, sometimes not.
- Students are encouraged to contribute their personal responses.
- Students are encouraged to listen to one another's responses.

Differences among these groups include the following:

- Students can gather in heterogeneous small groups, in homogeneous small groups, or as a whole class.
- The focus of discussion changes with purpose, text, and readers.
- Texts are typically selected by students but they can also be assigned.

> Literature circles are a way to bring wonderful literature into the classroom, to provide time for children to respond to literature, and to grow in their understanding and appreciation.
>
> —*Mary Medo*
> *Reading Specialist*

Establishing Response Groups—an Example

As we just mentioned, there are many types of response groups. To help you develop a schema for them, for how they are organized and how they function, we present a scenario showing how teacher David Kline in a public school in Minnesota set up response groups that he calls "literature circles" (Short & Klassen, 1993)—small groups of students who will read and discuss their responses to a particular text —in his fourth-grade class.

IN THE CLASSROOM
Literature Circles

To establish literature circles, Mr. Kline begins by having his students look through several titles of books he has preselected and ordered multiple copies of. In this particular instance, all the books are by a single author, Patricia MacLachlan. Two or three times a year, Mr. Kline selects one author whose works students read and compare. The books he has made available are *Journey*; *Baby*; *Sarah, Plain and Tall*; *The Facts and Fictions of Minna Pratt*; *Cassie Binegar*; *Arthur for the Very First Time*; *All the Places to Love*; and *Skylark*.

After students have had a chance to look through the books, Mr. Kline asks students which titles they would like to read and writes those titles on a sheet of butcher paper. He then gives a "book talk," or preview, of each of the chosen books, telling something about the setting, the main characters, and the premise of the story. Next, he asks students to write their names on the butcher paper under the titles of their first two choices.

Sarah, Plain and Tall	Baby	The Facts and Fictions of Minna Pratt	Cassie Binegar	Arthur for the Very First Time	Skylark
(1) Marit	(1) Corey	(1) Amber	(1) Cassie	(1) Miguel	(1) Ali
(2) BRENDON	(1) Blaine	(1) Paige	(1) Amy	(1) Jacob	(1) Yanfeng
(1) Rachel	(1) Michelle	(1) Garrett	(2) Marit	(1) Paul	(1) BRENDON
(1) Jay	(1) LATASHA	(1) Anna	(2) Latonia	(2) Jay	(1) David
(2) Jared	(2) Rachel	(1) Rory	(1) Lori	(1) Jared	(2) Case
(1) Latonia	(2) BRYAN	(1) Fang	(2) Michelle	(2) Blaine	(2) Anna
(2) David	(2) Garret	(2) Jenna	(2) Amber	(2) Rory	(2) Fang
(1) BRYAN	(2) Cassie	(2) LATASHA	(2) Paige	(2) Yanfeng	(2) Jacob
(1) Lori		(2) Amy			(2) Paul
(1) Case		(2) Ali			
(1) Jenna					
(2) Corey					
(2) Miguel					

Mr. Kline tries to group the children so that they can read their first or second choice. Once the groups are formed, the members of each group and Mr. Kline jointly decide how long they will spend on the book, how many pages a day they will read to reach that goal, when the group will meet (Mr. Kline meets with only one group per day), and how they will respond to their reading. At this point, Mr. Kline is very careful to remind students when the next meeting of their group will be, how many pages they will need to read, and what type of response will need to be completed before their next meeting. Since his students have decided to keep reading-response journals, he asks them to jot down this information in their journals.

As students are reading their novel, Mr. Kline meets periodically with each group—as a participant, not as a leader—while students take turns leading the discussion, which revolves around the individual responses they have recorded in their journals. When the group is close to completing the book, they discuss possible postreading activities [like those listed in the SRE framework described in Chapter 6]. After all groups have completed their books and related activities, the groups are disbanded. New groups will be formed for future response activities so that children will have the opportunity to work with other students and gain other perspectives.

Although this scenario illustrates organizing response groups based on works of literature by a single author, groups might also be organized to focus on themes and topics—including topics from content areas such as science. For example, students might select books about friendship, the Civil War, or the solar system. Whatever their focus, literature circles put a premium on preserving the element of student choice and on encouraging thoughtful discussions.

Through discussion in response groups, students share their own understanding of what they have read, test it against what others have gleaned, and come to new insights and interpretations. Through this synthesizing process, they come to a deeper understanding and appreciation of the literature they read.

To conclude this section on reader-response groups, we offer testimonials from three students:

> In literature circles, everyone has a chance to give their opinion and even if you don't agree with that person, you keep on talking because you know that you will get more ideas. You aren't trying to figure out one right answer. In reading groups, when someone gave the right answer, we were done talking. In literature circles, we keep on going. We try to come up with as many different directions as possible. (Short & Klassen, 1993, p. 84)
>
> **Chris, Third-Grade Student**

> I like it [literature study circle] because you get to communicate with the others and get to share feelings together. Like some people have different ideas and they could give you some ideas too. You could just remember what the book is about because other people are talking about it and you kind of forget what was in the book and then when you start talking it comes to you. (Samway et al., p. 203)
>
> **Melindevic, Fifth-Grade Student**

> I like discussion, because if you have only one view, others will teach you or enlighten you with different aspects. (Sorenson, 1993, p. 47)
>
> **Franklin, Sixth-Grade Student**

I love books. I spend hours reading and talking about books. My students are now recommending books to me and calling each other on the phone to talk about books. Literature circles helped spark this love of reading.

—*Anne Klein*
Multiage Teacher

323

A Framework to Promote
Reader Response

Like sustained silent reading and literature circles the approach we describe here—the reading workshop—encourages independent reading. However, it goes beyond providing opportunities for students to read and respond by offering a framework that includes specific opportunities for instruction and feedback.

The Reading Workshop

In reading workshop I expect everyone will read. I expect they'll all discover books they love, that together we'll enter the world of literature, make connections, become captivated, find satisfaction, and learn.

—Nancy Atwell
Author and Teacher

The reading workshop, first developed by Nancy Atwell (1987), structures reading time and activities to make reading the primary activity and to give students ownership of their reading. The reading workshop stresses the importance of the teacher's demonstrating and endorsing the value of reading by discussing books that she has read and what reading means to her, teaching strategies that will help students become independent readers, giving students time to read, responding to students' responses to what they read, and giving students opportunities to share their responses to what they read with others.

Since Atwell originally proposed the reading workshop, various authors (for example, Reutzel & Cooter, 1991; Swift, 1993; Tierney, Readence, & Dishner, 1995) have critiqued, tried out, and modified the procedure. Also, Susan McMahon and Taffy Raphael (McMahon & Raphael, 1997; Raphael & McMahon, 1994) have described and investigated a very promising approach, which they call the bookclub. Our suggestions been influenced by these authors and by our experiences.

The four main components of the version of reading workshop we suggest are listed here:

- Teacher sharing time (5–10 minutes)
- Minilessons (5–15 minutes)
- Self-selected reading and response (30–40 minutes)
- Students sharing time (5–10 minutes)

During the short *teacher sharing time* that begins each session, the teacher shares her own feelings about reading and some of the selections that have touched and interested her. For example, she might share the poem "Buffalo Dusk" by Carl Sandburg with her fifth-graders who are studying American history.

Next comes a short and tightly focused *minilesson*, a 5- to 15-minute period during which the teacher instructs the class as a whole. Early in the year, minilessons are likely to deal with procedural matters about conducting the reading workshop: what materials can be read, how long the reading period is, what sorts of reporting will be required, what to include in a response to a selection, what sorts of conferences will be held, and the like. Later minilessons can focus on whatever skill, strategy, convention, or general information is particularly relevant to what students are reading. You might teach a minilesson on a literary device such as foreshadowing, or you might use a minilesson to give students advice on how to choose books they're likely to enjoy. Minilessons are often motivated by student needs that the teacher has observed. For example, if quite a few students are writing summaries of what they have read and their summaries lack focus, you might review the strategy of summarizing. But minilessons can also be used to deal with topics prescribed by the school's or district's curriculum or to systematically review the comprehension strategies you have taught.

Sharing a self-selected book with a buddy underscores the fun and value of reading.

Self-selected reading and response is the core of the reading workshop. On most workshop days, most students will spend 30–40 minutes silently reading, and during some of this time the teacher is likely to be reading silently also. However, silent reading is punctuated with several other activities.

The most frequent of these other activities is journaling. As they are reading their books, students keep a dialogue journal in which they record their reactions, questions, and musings about what they are reading. These dialogue journals typically go to the teacher, who periodically gives a personal response to each student's thoughts. Dialogue journals can also be addressed to other students, so that there is student-to-student dialogue as well as teacher-to-student and student-to-teacher dialogues. The following excerpts are from dialogue journals of two of Atwell's students, Mike and Heather (Atwell, 1987, p. 191). As you will notice from Mike's last statement, answering Heather's frequent entries is taking away from his reading time, and he lets her know.

Teachers need to have literally hundreds of books in their class libraries, including books written at a range of reading levels, in order to have enough books so that every student can read during reading workshop.

—*Gail Tompkins*
Teacher Educator

325

Mike,

I have read some really good books this year. I think you should read *Haunted*. It is my favorite book. Or try *The Spectator*. Kelli said it was good.

Heath

Dear Heather,

I read *Haunted* last year. It was good. I finished it in two days. It was one of the best ones I read. Kelli told me *The Spectre* was good too. I'll probably read it soon.

I hate to be mean, but I don't have any other way to put it. DON'T WRITE BACK AGAIN THIS PERIOD!!!

Sincerely,
Mike

Another activity is teacher conferencing. Periodically, the teacher meets with each student to discuss her reading accomplishments and upcoming plans for reading, as well as any concerns the student has. Because you are likely to have 30 students and conferences take up a fair amount of time, these conferences are typically held once a quarter or so, toward the end of the quarter. However, more frequent conferences are possible if you and the students want to hold them and can find the time to do so.

Another possibility is student meetings. If several students discover that they are reading the same author, book, or genre, they may decide they have some things to discuss. Similarly, if you learn that several students have something to share—or a common need—you might schedule a small-group meeting. Whether or not you're present depends on the topic and purpose of the meeting. If there is a common need—perhaps a group of students who confuse facts and opinions when reading informational material—then it is a good opportunity for you to join the group and do some teaching. If, on the other hand, the meeting is simply an opportunity for a group of students who are reading mysteries to talk about their favorites, then students can probably meet without you.

Student sharing time is the last component in the reading workshop, a time when the class comes together to share the things they have been doing. As in the writing workshop, which we will describe in Chapter 9, not every student shares each day. Often it works best to have students sign up in advance to share, usually two to four students per session. The most common activity involves students talking about what they have been reading and sharing their experiences and suggestions for good reading. But this time can also be used for other purposes. Some students may have questions that they think the whole class could help them with. Others may be looking for partners with whom to discuss their reading. Still others may have found a great source of inexpensive paperbacks or a librarian who is particularly knowledgeable about baseball books or books about animals.

Sixth-grade teacher Kathleen Swift talks about what happens during a typical reading workshop in her classroom:

> The period begins with a 10- to 15-minute minilesson. I choose the lesson topic according to the current needs of the class. At the beginning of the school year the lessons center on the organization of the classroom: behavioral expectations, choosing books, checking out books, how to complete dialogue journals, grading, and earning extra points. I frequently introduce books and authors that I think the children will like. Once students know my expectations and organization, I devote more lessons to topics such as narrative voice, point of view, author's purpose, leads, theme, and specific reading strategies such as focusing on important words.
>
> When I finish my lesson, students begin reading. A few students choose to sit on the cushions in the reading area. One or two pull their chairs to isolated corners of the room. Students do not use the period to look for books in the library unless they happen to finish a book during class. I expect everyone to come to class ready to read. A student might leave the room to read a book with a parent volunteer. This is the strategy I have developed for those few children who need the guidance of an adult to focus their attention. The adults help students find books they want to read and read aloud with them, alternating paragraphs.
>
> From time to time students go to the shelves to get their reading dialogue journals. In them they add the title of the book they just started to a list of previously read books at the back of the journal. They then turn to the correspondence section of their journal, write the date, and begin a letter to me. Each student has to write a minimum of once every 2 weeks, telling me the title and author, sharing his or her opinion of the book, and relating the book to his or her life in some way. I respond in writing to each letter, expressing my own ideas and encouraging students to try books and authors new to them. (Swift, 1993, p. 367)

Kathleen Swift, Sixth-Grade Teacher

Perhaps the greatest value of the literature response log is that the student comes to realize that what he has to say is valid and important.

—*Regie Routman*
Teacher and
Teacher Educator

In concluding this section on the reading workshop, we want to comment on something we said at the beginning of the section: Reading is the primary activity in the reading workshop. However, as our description makes clear, it also includes the other language arts—writing, speaking, and listening. We also want to stress that various authors have written about and experimented with reading workshop (Atwell, 1987; Reutzel & Cooter, 1991; Samway et al., 1991; Swift, 1993). We recommend that you read what they have to say and consider the perspectives they offer.

In concluding the topic of independent reading, we wnat to stress again that it is vital to provide ample time and opportunity for students to read and respond to books of their choosing each day. This is especially important for struggling readers who need books to choose from that they can read easily and enjoyably on their own. Students will not become independent readers if they constantly depend on you to choose what they read.

Reflection AND Application

6. List as many advantages as you can for a simple independent reading program such as SSR. Can you think of any disadvantages? Discuss the pros and cons of SSR with a classmate or group of classmates.

7. Now list as many advantages as you can for one of the other approaches—literature circles or reader workshops. As before, think also of disadvantages to these methods, and discuss the pros and cons of these ways of organizing reading with a classmate or group of classmates.

8. Identify a grade you would particularly like to teach. Then, in writing, describe the approach or approaches you would use to foster independence in reading in that class, explaining your rationale and procedure as you might describe them to parents at your first classroom open house.

Special Needs and Special Talents

As we have repeatedly noted, the critical literacy curriculum is for all students—more accomplished readers, less-accomplished readers, students who come less prepared to school, and students who do not speak English as their native language. This also holds as true for comprehension strategies and independent reading; however, adjustments for individual needs will be important here as well.

With strategies, one danger is that capable readers who have already learned comprehension strategies might be both unreceptive to learning new strategies and actually confused by attempting to replace an already functional strategy with a new one. The solution here is to know your students and their capabilities well, find out what strategies they already have, check periodically to see if they view the new ones as useful, and not make them continue to learn a new strategy that just isn't working for them.

With less-proficient students, on the other hand, comprehension strategies are likely to be particularly welcome—if, that is, students see them as helpful; and the only way they will see them as helpful is if they are. You need to be especially careful to introduce them at a rate slow enough to prevent frustration, to give students plenty of time to apply them in class, and to deliberately structure students' work and the assessment system you use to reward their use of strategies. Over the past two decades, Donald Deshler and Jean Schumaker (1993) have conducted over a dozen studies clearly indicating that at-risk students can successfully learn to use comprehension strategies—if they are properly instructed.

When ESL students receive some instruction in their native language, it may be useful to introduce the strategies in students' native-language and use it with native language material before helping students transfer its use to English material.

For students from certain cultures, the group work involved in learning strategies may be particularly facilitative and particularly comfortable. With these students, you might let the group work continue for some time, gradually building in independent assignments and explaining to students that they will often need to use strategies in situations in which their classmates are not available, such as with work done at home.

With independent reading, one extremely crucial thing to keep in mind in making adjustments for students with different strengths, interests, and weaknesses is that students need to read material that is interesting and understandable to them. At the Benchmark School, which has been particularly successful in improving the reading performance of less-proficient readers, all of the books in the very large library are color-coded for difficulty level (Gaskins, 1994). The Benchmark School requires its students, all of whom are less-proficient readers, to read a lot of books; having color-coded books greatly simplifies the task of getting the right books to each student. Sometimes, however, students will select a book that is too challenging. What can you do then? Deciding on just the right approach is not easy, because there are likely to be "costs" to any decision you make. If you leave the student alone in order not to damage her growing confidence in her reading, she may become frustrated by her lack of understanding. If, on the other hand, you intervene and suggest an easier book, her confidence may be weakened by that suggestion. Realizing these potential costs, make your best professional judgment for the particular student in the particular situation.

When working with less-proficient readers, having well-stocked classrooms and school libraries is also critical. Though important for all students, such libraries are particularly important for less-proficient readers because many do not have much to read at home. Similarly, providing less-proficient readers with a time and place to read in school is vital because they may not have a good place to read outside of school.

> We must recognize students as individuals and then shape school experiences so students can stretch and extend their scholarship on the basis of their individual backgrounds, interests, and needs. It is often tempting to teach by covering the curriculum through a sequence of predetermined topics or aiming lessons for the middle of the class. But if all are to learn, the needs of individuals must be both recognized and met.
>
> —*Patricia L. Scharer*
> *Teacher Educator*

Finally, we want to say something about out-of-school reading—for all students. We have stressed the importance of in-school reading because that is the reading that you as a teacher have the most control over. However, anything you can do to encourage and support out-of-school reading is likely to be well worth your efforts. As we have said repeatedly, students need to read a lot if they are to get really good at it. Since students spend about 1,300 hours per year in school but nearly 8,000 per year out of school, out-of-school reading can contribute hugely to the amount of practice students get.

Getting parents involved can greatly enhance students' out-of-school reading time. One idea is to use book bags and home–school reading logs. Book bags are simply bags made of sturdy material, such as corduroy or canvas. And reading logs are small journals that fit into the bags. Students carry books to and from school in these bags. Parents and student use the logs to make any comments about the books they read. A "letter from the teacher" every month can serve as a communication tool and highlight what students and parents might jot down in the journal—interesting words they encounter, something new they learn, something funny or sad. Comments can come from either the student or the parent. Sometimes parents can be encouraged to write observations about their youngsters' reading. "Marit read this story three times to me, and then when her dad came home she wanted to read it again!" Here, Roslyn Breslouer describes an exciting parent-involvement program she calls, We Love to Read Beary Much (*Reading Today*, 1997):

> As part of the We Love to Read Beary Much program, my first-graders carry books home for their parents to read with them. Their parents sign a comment sheet, and many include notes about their reading experience. I think something as simple as sending home a book or letter on a regular basis makes a big difference. I think parents just need that personal communication.
>
> As part of the bear theme, all students have their own bear symbol on a bear bulletin board, and they get a bear sticker for every book that a parent has signed a card for. We have a big bear named Love-a-Lot that sits on a chair in the front of the classroom. Sometimes children read to Love-a-Lot or to Ted, the troll who sits on the bear's lap.
>
> One of the keys to the success of this program is a classroom library well stocked with paperbacks. Another important factor is keeping parents involved. To do this, I hold We Love to Read Beary Much parties in December, March, and June each year. These parties often draw 15–20 parents, who sometimes bring along grandparents, aunts and uncles, and students' younger siblings. Students recite poetry to the group of parents, who then spread out and read to their own children (and sometimes others as well). They like the idea that they

can read with the children and hear the children read and recite. I also hold after-school workshops twice a year to give parents advice on how to read to children.

It's especially enjoyable to me that the program gets the parents to spend quality time with their children to read and discuss books. By the end of the year, the kids love books. Books are an integral part of their lives.

Roslyn Breslouer, First-Grade Teacher

CONCLUDING REMARKS

In this chapter, we dealt with two topics: teaching reading comprehension strategies and encouraging independent reading. With respect to comprehension strategies, thus far we have

- defined comprehension strategies.
- identified eight key strategies.
- described well-researched procedures for teaching strategies.

One very important task remains—your decision on which strategies to teach. These strategies will, in some cases, be determined by your school's curriculum. More often, however, identifying strategies to teach will be left up to you. In this case, we have a definite recommendation: Teach a few strategies well, rather than many strategies less well. Comprehension strategies are complex procedures, and they need to be learned well if they are to be of real use to students. Teaching either one or two a year is a reasonable goal. In choosing them, we suggest that you teach those that your students appear ready to learn and that can be used frequently in dealing with the selections students read in your classes. Additionally, where possible, it would be a good idea to coordinate the teaching of strategies with other teachers in the school. Whatever strategy or strategies you teach, remember that learning the strategy itself is not the primary goal. As with word-recognition strategies, comprehension strategies are the means to an end—students' understanding, learning from, and enjoying what they read.

Encouraging independent reading—the second topic we explored in this chapter—is a vital addition to teaching students reading comprehension strategies. Here we discussed the importance of providing time to read independently, a rich array of reading materials, the incentive to read them, and an inviting place in which to read. We also suggested ways to help students select material for independent reading and for establishing and maintaining an independent reading program. As an adjunct to independent reading, we talked about reader-response groups, which encourage students to make personal connections with the texts they read, to express their own ideas, and to listen to those of other students. Finally, we presented the reading workshop, an instructional framework that enables you to make independent reading and student response the focal point, with instruction supporting this main endeavor.

Both of the topics we presented in this chapter are important components of a well-balanced critical literacy curriculum; both are vital to helping students meet the challenging reading demands of the 21st century.

EXTENDING LEARNING

1. Probably the best single experience you could have in order to fully understand and appreciate the nature of good comprehension strategy instruction is to observe a teacher who is doing an excellent job of it. We suggest that you attempt to locate an effective strategy instructor, observe her teaching, and afterward talk to her about it. Potential sources for locating teachers are your university instructor, your cooperating teacher, other teachers you know, and your classmates.

2. To really come to understand strategy instruction, it is useful to study quality materials used in teaching strategies. Probably the most widely available materials are those published by the Institute for Research in Learning Disabilities at the University of Kansas. Try to get one of their manuals, for example, *The Error Monitoring Strategy: Instructor's Manual* (Schumaker, Nolan, & Deshler, 1985). Study it carefully, and compare the instruction suggested there to the suggestions in this chapter. You will find a lot of similarities, but you will also find some differences. Also, you will be able to examine a number of specific examples of the concepts discussed in this chapter.

3. Imagine you are a beginning teacher in a new school, and your principal tells you that the PTA will purchase 30 books for your classroom library. Select a grade you would most like to teach. Write up a brief description of that class—ages of students, ethnic backgrounds represented, and range of reading ability. Using resources such as *Collected Perspectives: Choosing and Using Books for the Classroom* (Moir, 1992), and *Adventuring with Books* (Jensen, 1993) select 30 books for your library.

4. Select a grade you would most like to teach. If possible, arrange to visit a classroom to observe independent reading and literature discussion groups in this grade. Take notes on what you observe. What are students reading? Do they appear to be engaged in the reading? How do they respond to their reading (in a journal, through discussion, or merely privately in their minds as they read)? Plan a reading experience for these students that will include group discussion that focuses on reader response. Let them select a book, or assign one yourself. Write your plans for this reading experience from beginning to end, including how the students will be prepared for the experience, how the reading will be done, and how the discussion will be handled. Here are some questions to think about as you develop your plan: What will your role be? What will students' role be? How will the reading be handled? How will the discussion be handled? What will be discussed? Who will lead the discussion? How will it begin and end? How will you ensure student engagement, participation, and success? If possible, try out your plan on a group of students. If this isn't possible, present your ideas to your classmates for feedback.

REFERENCES

Allington, R., Guice, S., Michaelson, N., Baker, K., & Li, S. (1996). Literature-based curricula in high-poverty schools. In M. F. Graves, P. van den Broek, & B. M. Taylor (Eds.), *The first R: Every child's right to read* (pp. 73–96). Teachers College Press. This article presents a detailed look at and critique of some literature-based classrooms that differ a good deal.

Anderson, R. C. (1996). Research foundations to support wide reading. In V. Greaney (Ed.), *Promoting reading in developing countries* (pp. 55–77). Newark, DE: International Reading Association. This is a convincing, data-based argument for wide reading.

Anderson, R. C., Wilson, P. T., & Fielding, L. G. (1988). Growth in reading and how children spend their time outside of school. *Reading Research Quarterly, 23*, 285–303. This empirical study shows that the amount of reading done is a strong predictor of reading achievement.

Atwell, N. (1987). *In the middle: Writing, reading, and learning with adolescents.* Portsmouth, NH: Heinemann. The author discusses how to teach adolescents by connecting reading and writing through reading and writing workshops.

Baumann, J. F. (1986). The direct instruction of main idea comprehension ability. In J.F. Baumann (Ed.), *Teaching main idea comprehension* (pp. 133–178). Newark, DE: International Reading Association. The author describes a method of teaching a particular comprehension strategy.

Brown, A. L., & Day, J. D. (1983). Macrorules for summarizing text: The development of expertise. *Journal of Verbal Learning and Verbal Behavior, 22*, 1–14. This scholarly article describes the tacit rules summarizers use and how these develop.

Deshler, D. D., & Schumaker, J. B. (1993). Skills mastery by at-risk students: Not a simple matter. *Elementary School Journal, 94*, 153–167. This article gives a summary and discussion of a large body of the authors' work with strategy instruction for at-risk students.

Dole, J. A., Brown, K. J., & Trathen, W. (1996). The effects of strategy instruction on the comprehension performance of at-risk students. *Reading Research Quarterly, 31,* 62–88. A truly excellent example of well-planned and thoughtfully presented comprehension strategy instruction.

Dyson, A., & Freedman, S. H. (1991). Writing. In J. Flood, J. M. Jensen, D. Lapp, & J. R. Squire (Eds.), *Handbook of research on teaching the English language arts* (pp. 754–774). New York: Macmillan. This is an excellent summary of the research on writing instruction as well as a source of good ideas about teaching more generally.

Fielding, L. G., Wilson, P. T., & Anderson, R. C. (1986). A new focus for free reading: The role of trade books in reading instruction. In T. E. Raphael (Ed.), *The contexts of school-based literacy* (pp. 149–160). New York: Random House. The authors discuss the importance of reading, particularly emphasizing the value of reading books.

Garner, R., & Gillingham, M. G. (1996). *Internet communication in six classrooms: Conversations across time, space, and culture.* Mahwah, NJ: Erlbaum. This book is an interesting chronicle of teacher and student conversations over the Internet.

Gaskins, I. W. (1994). Creating optimum learning environments: Is membership in the whole language community necessary? In F. Lehr & J. Osborn (Eds.), *Reading, language, and literacy: Instruction for the twenty-first century* (pp. 115–130). Hillsdale, NJ: Erlbaum. In this volume, researchers, teacher educators, and publishers give their perspectives on the teaching of reading and how children learn to read.

Hibert, S. B. (1993). Sustained silent reading revisited. *The Reading Teacher, 46,* 354–356. This article illustrates that when SSR is managed strategically and carefully orchestrated to foster student interaction, readers of all ability levels benefit and learn to recognize the value of wide reading.

Jensen, J. (Ed.). (1993). *Adventuring with books.* Urbana, IL: National Council of Teachers of English. Published every four years, this volume contains annotations of approximately 1,500 children's trade books.

L'Engle, M. (1980). *Walking on water: Reflections on faith and art.* New York: Shaw. This book details the author's views on the creative process.

Marzano, R.J. (1992). *A different kind of classroom: Teaching with dimensions of learning.* Washington, DC: Association for Supervision and Curriculum Development. This book provides a detailed description of five types of thinking that schools should promote and ways of promoting them.

McCracken, R. A., & McCracken, M. J. (1978). Modeling is the key to sustained reading. *The Reading Teacher, 31,* 406–408. This article discusses the value of teachers serving as models during sustained silent reading periods.

McMahon, S. I., & Raphael, T. E. (Eds.). (1997). *The book club connection: Literacy learning and classroom talk.* New York: Teachers College. This book presents the theoretical and research foundations for the book club as well as reports from many researchers and teachers who have implemented book clubs in their classrooms.

Moir, H. (Ed.) (1992). *Collected perspectives: choosing and using books for the classroom* (2nd ed.). Boston: Christopher-Gordon. This book contains detailed annotations and suggestions for classroom use for approximately 1,000 trade books for children in primary grades through junior high.

Monson, D. (1996). Choosing books for literature circles. In B. C. Hill, N. J. Johnson, & K. L. S. Noe (Eds.), *Literature circles and response* (pp. 113–130). Norwood, MA: Christopher-Gordon. The author discusses the qualities to look for in choosing books from four genres—traditional literature, fantasy, realistic fiction, and informational books.

Pearson, P. D., Roehler, L. R., Dole, J. A., & Duffy, G. G. (1992). Developing expertise in reading comprehension. In S. J. Samuels & A. E. Farstrup (Eds.), *What research has to say about reading instruction* (2nd ed.), (pp. 145–199). Newark, Del.: International Reading Association. The authors present an up-to-date view of reading comprehension instruction, with particular emphasis on teaching comprehension strategies.

Pressley, M., & Woloshyn, V. (1995). *Cognitive strategy instruction that really improves children's academic performance.* Cambridge, MA: Brookline Books. This book offers a detailed summary of much of Pressley's work on strategy instruction.

Pressley, M., Harris, K. R., & Marks, M. B. (1992). But good strategy instructors are constructivists! *Educational Psychology Review, 4,* 3–31. The authors present an argument that good strategy instruction is consistent with constructivist principles.

Pressley, M., Johnson, C. J., Symons, S., McGoldrick, J. A., & Kurita, J. A. (1989). Strategies that improve children's memory and comprehension of text. *The Elementary School Journal, 90,* 3–32. The authors present an excellent examination and discussion of key comprehension strategies.

Raphael, T. E., & McMahon, S. I. (1994). Book Club: An alternative framework for reading instruction. *The Reading Teacher, 48,* 102–116. This article describes a book club program that integrates reading, writing, student-led discussion groups, whole-class discussion, and instruction.

Reading Today. (1997, February/March). Program gets parents, students to love reading "beary" much, p. 28. Newark, DE: International Reading. This article gives a brief description of a program that gets parents involved with their students' reading.

Reutzel, D. R., & Cooter, R. B. (1991). Organizing for effective instruction: The reading workshop. *The Reading Teacher, 44,* 548–554. Following Nancy Atwell's model for the reading workshop, the authors provide a rationale and succinct description for organizing classroom reading instruction.

Rosenblatt, L. (1938). *Literature as exploration.* New York: Appleton-Century. This is Rosenblatt's original presentation of her response theory.

Rosenblatt, L. (1978). *The reader, the text, the poem: The transactional theory of the literary work.* Carbondale, IL: Southern Illinois Press. Another presentation of Rosenblatt's response theory; both this and her 1938 book have had enormous influence on the teaching of literature.

Routman, R. (1991). *Invitations: Changing as teachers and learners K–12.* Portsmouth, NH: Heinemann. Written for practicing teachers, this text encourages teachers to try whole-language techniques and strategies in their classrooms.

Ruddell, R. B., & Ruddell, M. R. (1995). *Teaching children to read and write.* Boston: Allyn & Bacon. This is a methods text on teaching reading in the elementary schools.

Samway, K. D., Whang, G., Cade, C., Gamil, M., Lubandina, M. A., & Phommachanh, K. (1991). Reading the skeleton, the heart, and the brain of a book: Students' perspectives on literature study circles. *The Reading Teacher, 45,* 196–205. This article discusses the influence of literature study circles on students' reading abilities and attitudes.

Schumaker, J. B., Nolan, S. M., & Deshler, D. D. (1985). *The error monitoring strategy: Instructor's manual.* Lawrence: University of Kansas Institute for Research in Learning Disabilities. This is an example of one of the most widely used professionally prepared materials for teaching strategies.

Short, K. G., & Klassen, C. (1993). Literature circles: Hearing children's voices. In B. E. Cullinan (Ed.), *Children's voices: Talk in the classroom.* Newark, DE: International Reading Association. This chapter provides a rationale for literature circles, how they are set up, and what they can accomplish.

Sorenson, M. (1993, January). Teach each other: Connecting talking and writing. *English Journal,* pp. 42–47. This article describes the rationale behind the development of open discussion groups and how and why they work.

Spiegel, D. L. (1981). *Reading for pleasure: Guidelines.* Newark, DE: International Reading Association. This work discusses the importance of recreational reading and offers guidelines for setting up and maintaining a pleasure-reading program in the classroom.

Swift, K. (1993). Try reading workshop in your classroom. *The Reading Teacher, 46,* 366–371. A sixth-grade teacher's account of her success with the reading workshop.

Tierney, R. J. , Readence, J. E., & Dishner, E. K. (1995). *Reading strategies and practices: A compendium.* Boston: Allyn & Bacon. This broad collection of strategies for teaching reading is intended to stimulate thoughtful reflection, evaluation, and use of the instructional procedures presented.

West, R. F., Stanovich, K. E., & Mitchell, H. R. (1993). Reading in the real world and its correlates. *Reading Research Quarterly, 28,* 34–50. This clever and revealing study contrasts readers' and nonreaders' knowledge.

Wittrock, M. C. (1990). Generative processes of comprehension. *Educational Psychologist, 24,* 345–376. The author offers a convincing argument for the importance of readers generating relationships between ideas in the text and between ideas in the text and their prior knowledge.

CHILDREN'S LITERATURE

Johnson, G., & Cutchins, J. (1988). *Scaly babies: Reptiles growing up.* New York: Morrow. This informational book has four chapters of descriptive text and color photographs highlighting snakes, lizards, crocodiles, turtles, and their young. 40 pages.

Jones, C. F. (1991). *Mistakes that worked.* New York: Doubleday. Informational book describing 40 inventions—such as Silly Putty and Velcro—that were created as a result of an accident. 78 pages.

Kellogg, S. (1986). *Best friends.* New York: Dial Books for Young Readers. In this picture book, young Kathy's best friend goes away to camp, and Kathy must deal with her feelings of betrayal. Unpaged.

Lobel, A. (1979). *Days with Frog and Toad.* New York: Harper & Row. This classic beginning chapter book with five humorous stories stars best friends Frog and Toad and dramatizes universal truths about life and friendship. 64 pages. Audiotape available.

MacLachlan, P. (1980) *Arthur for the very first time.* New York: Harper & Row. This novel describes 10-year-old Arthur's summer on the farm with his eccentric aunt and uncle, and how he learns to see himself, his family, and life in general a bit differently. 117 pages.

MacLachlan, P. (1982). *Cassie Binegar.* New York: Harper & Row. One summer, fourth-grader Cassie learns to accept change and to find her own space. 120 pages.

MacLachlan, P. (1985). *Sarah, plain and tall.* New York: HarperCollins. This Newbery Award–winning novel tells the story of mail-order bride Sarah from Maine and the family who longs to have her stay with them on the prairie. 58 pages. Audio- and videotape available.

MacLachlan, P. (1988). *The facts and fictions of Minna Pratt.* New York: Harper & Row. Eleven-year-old Minna, a cellist student in New York City, learns about life, love, and music through her family, her first boyfriend, and Mozart. 136 pages. Audiotape available.

MacLachlan, P. (1991) *Journey.* New York: Delacorte. This novel explores how photographs and a grandfather's love enable young Journey to come to terms with his mother's abandonment and restore a past that he feels has been erased. 83 pages.

MacLachlan, P. (1993). *Baby.* New York: Delacorte. This exquisitely crafted short novel is about a family learning to deal with the death of their own infant son after a baby girl is left on their doorstep for them to care for. 132 pages.

MacLachlan, P. (1994). *All the places to love.* New York: HarperCollins. In this picture book, a young boy describes his favorite places on his grandparents' farm and the surrounding countryside. Unpaged.

MacLachlan, P. (1994). *Skylark*. New York: Harper-Collins. In this sequel to *Sarah, Plain and Tall*, Anna and Caleb worry that a drought on the prairie will send their new mother, Sarah, back to her home in Maine. 86 pages. Audio- and videotape available.

Martin, B. (1983). *Brown bear, brown bear, What do you see?* New York: Holt. Each page answers the call "Brown bear, brown bear, what do you see?" by revealing an animal or person, who, in turn, leads to a new verse. 32 pages.

O'Dell, S. (1960). *Island of the blue dolphins*. Boston: Houghton Mifflin. Marooned on a Pacific island for ten years, a young Indian girl uses her wits to survive. 192 pages.

Paterson, K. (1977). *Bridge to Terabithia*. New York: Crowell. Jesse's life turns upside down when he becomes friends with his new neighbor, a girl named Leslie. Tragedy strikes when she tries to reach their secret hideaway, Terabithia, during a rainstorm. 144 pages.

Raskin, E. (1966). *Nothing ever happens on my block*. New York: Atheneum. While Chester Filbert complains that nothing happens on his block, adventures occur all around him in this humorous picture book. Unpaged.

Sandburg, C. (1965). Buffalo Dusk. In *Arrow book of poetry*, selected by Ann McGovern. New York: Scholastic. This evocative poem laments a time gone by when the great buffalo herds once roamed the prairie.

Sendak, M. (1963). *Where the wild things are*. New York: Harper & Row. When Max is sent to bed without his supper, he imagines a world where he is king of the "wild things." 32 pages.

Simon, S. (1990). *Oceans*. New York: Morrow. This informational book describes the marvels of the ocean world with concise language and stunning full-color photos. Unpaged.

chapter eight

Teaching for Understanding in Content Areas

I magine, if you will, a snowball fight in space. Half a dozen astronauts emerge from each of two spaceships and arrange themselves in two parallel lines about ten yards apart. They are all in free fall, traveling at the same speed and in the same direction; and as long as they do nothing, the lines will remain parallel and about ten yards distant from each other. But these astronauts are not going to do nothing. They have been in space for several months, and today, they have decided that a snowball fight would provide some much needed recreation. Each astronaut carries a bag of snowballs, and as soon as they receive the go signal, they will begin tossing snowballs at the opposing team. What will happen?

If you are familiar with Newton's theory of motion and understand that theory, you will be able to predict the outcome of the snowball fight rather accurately. The snowball fight will be brief, and both teams will be ineffectual. As soon as the astronauts begin tossing the snowballs, they will move away from each other. The force of throwing a snowball will push each astronaut backwards. To further complicate matters, because

CHAPTER OVERVIEW

the astronauts' arms are away from their centers of gravity, the force of throwing the snowballs will start each of them spinning. The snowballs will go in the wrong direction. Even if they had gone in the right direction, the spinning "targets" would be elsewhere before the snowballs arrived. The end result is that it wouldn't be much of a snowball fight, and the astronauts would be forced to search for some other form of recreation.

This episode, paraphrased from one described by David Perkins (1993), suggests the nature of understanding. A person who understands something is able to actively use the knowledge actively that he has internalized. As Perkins, one of the most articulate and insightful authors on teaching for understanding, puts it, "Understanding a topic of study is a matter of being able to perform in a variety of thought-demanding ways." The person who understands a topic can "explain, muster evidence, find examples, generalize, apply concepts, analogize, represent in a new way, and so on" (p. 13). it is this sort of deep, lasting, and useful knowledge that is the topic of this chapter.

THE TEACHING FOR UNDERSTANDING PERSPECTIVE

Understanding, as we noted in the opening scenario, enables a person "to perform in a variety of thought-demanding ways . . . . [to] explain, muster evidence, find examples, generalize, apply concepts, analogize, represent in a new way, and so on" (Perkins, 1992, p. 13). Understanding is one of the principal goals of the critical literacy curriculum we described in Chapter 1. As we said there and as David Perkins (1992) emphasizes, to teach for understanding we must go beyond simply presenting students with information and ensure that students

- retain important information.
- understand topics deeply.
- actively use the knowledge they gain.

Among the many agendas of education, surely understanding must rank far up on the short list of high priorities.

—*David Perkins*
Educational Psychologist

The reader who has attained an understanding perspective consciously seeks understanding and uses the knowledge he gains through reading. Of course, everything we have discussed in this book thus far has understanding as an ultimate goal. But here we treat understanding as a specific goal. There is a good deal of evidence that we should do so.

As authorities such as Lauren Resnick (1987), Richard Prawat (1989), Perkins (1992), John Bruer (1994), and Isabel Beck and her colleagues (Beck, McKeown, Hamilton, & Kucan, 1997) point out, expectations of schooling and the level of knowledge and skills that our society requires have risen dramatically in recent years and will continue to rise, perhaps even more dramatically, in the future. Yet as these same authorities indicate and as empirical data such as that produced by the National Assessment of Education Progress (for example, Williams, Lazer, Reese, & Carr, 1995; Williams, Reese, Campbell, Mazzeo, & Phillips, 1995) indicates few American students are performing at the advanced levels necessary for full participation in our society. Teaching for understanding can change this.

Some Key Attributes of Teaching for Understanding

We turn now to explaining what teaching for understanding looks like, and we begin with a dramatic example of what it is not. The example, taken from an observer's field notes as he observed a fifth-grade class (Prawat,

1989), is from a mathematics lesson rather than a reading lesson, but we use it here because it is such a telling example of how instruction sometimes goes astray. Here are the observer's notes:

> *The focus of this lesson is on multiplying decimals. Prior to assigning students a series of seatwork problems, Miss Jones is working through two problems on the board. One example involves money—$32.45 × 0.5. The teacher repeats the algorithm that students are going to use in doing these problems: First, multiply as you would with whole numbers. Second, count the number of places to the right of the decimal point in the top number, then count the number of places to the right of the decimal point in the bottom number. Add these together, and place the decimal point so that the product contains this number of places. Most students seem to understand the procedure and are anxious to get started, when one little boy raises his hand. He has a perplexed look on his face. Suddenly he blurts out, "This doesn't make sense. You started with 32 dollars and 45 cents and ended up with 16 dollars and whatever cents. You multiplied by that number [0.5], how did you get less? Two other children agree that it does not make sense. At first the teacher thinks she has made a computational mistake, so she works the problem again. It soon become obvious that this is not the problem. The little boy thinks that the product should be bigger, not smaller, than the number that is multiplied. The teacher is at a loss about how to handle the question. She repeats the algorithm, explaining to the class, "I'm just teaching the computational way. What I'm looking for now is for everyone to understand where to place the decimals." The little boy shakes his head, still confused. The teacher assigns the problem set. (pp. 316–317)*

In talking to the observer after the lesson, Miss Jones noted that she moved on despite the boy's confusion because she was already a chapter behind and needed to finish the book by the end of the year—a very frequent problem teachers face and one we will address shortly. She also noted that the immediate goal was for students to get the basics, that she didn't have time for the "fancy stuff," and that "later on, at the junior high level, it'll start to make sense to them" (p. 317).

From the teaching for understanding perspective, this won't do. If at all possible, the concepts and procedures that students are learning need to make sense to them *as they are learned*. In fact, it is only when things make sense that there will be any real learning. In this particular instance, then, the teacher might have stopped, done her best to understand the little boy's (we'll call him Tom) confusion, and attempted to clarify the situation. The following scenario suggests one alternative:

IN THE CLASSROOM
Dialogue That Promotes Understanding

Miss Jones: You know, Tom, I think I see what you mean. Often, when we multiply we do get numbers that are larger. For example, if we multiply 6 × 2, we get 12. And what do we get if we multiple 6 × 3?

Tom: 18.

Miss Jones: That's right. If we multiply a number by 2 or 3 or anything larger than 1, we get a larger number. But what if we multiply by 1? What do we get then, Tom?

Tom: Let's see. If we multiply 6 × 1, we get 6; and if we multiply 12 × 1 we get 12. I think when we multiply anything by 1 we get the same number.

Miss Jones: That's right. When we multiply a number by 1, we get the same number. And when we multiple anything by a number larger than 1, we get a larger number. Now comes the tough part. What happens when we multiple a number by something smaller than 1? Say we multiply 6 by .5. What happens then, Tom?

Tom: Hmm. 5 × 6 is 30, but there's a decimal point, so it is 3.0. This time the number gets smaller. I think I see. When we multiply by a number smaller than 1, even though we are multiplying, our answer gets smaller.

Next, Miss Jones summarizes what Tom has said. She then orally gives some problems with multipliers larger than 1 and multipliers smaller than 1 to other students in the class. Finally, she repeats the generalization so that everyone understands.

Of course, even doing everything that Miss Jones did in this scenario does not guarantee that all her students will understand. However, it certainly makes understanding more likely, and it is almost certainly a better solution than simply continuing with the planned lesson even though some students are confused.

Even though our example was a math lesson rather than a reading lesson, the principle is the same. Our goal virtually always ought to be making sure that students understand whatever we are discussing. Despite the press of time, despite the need to "cover" the curriculum, despite the well-planned lesson you're aching to get on with, when students do not understand, we need to stop what we are doing and do our very best to help them understand. Third-grade teacher Robin Cazet talks about how she deals with this issue in her classroom:

As soon as I realize that my students are confused about something, I will stop trying to forge ahead with the lesson and address their confusion. Doing this, of course, takes time and means that we may not cover all the material that I had planned. But it doesn't make sense to continue with something if my students don't understand! For example, last week we were working with finding the main idea in paragraphs from the science trade books they are reading. When it became painfully obvious that my students really didn't remember what a main idea was, I decided we had better revisit that topic. What followed was a rather lengthy discussion about what is and what isn't a main idea. I took a topic with which they were familiar—our class. I wrote a number of phrases about our class on the chalkboard, and together we sorted them into what they would consider examples and nonexamples of main ideas about our class. This is what the sort looked like:

Main Idea	Not a Main Idea
28 third-graders	Have lunch at 11:15
McKnight Elementary School	Sarah was absent on Wednesday.
Learn about many interesting things	Are going to the zoo next week
Are good readers and writers	Jose is a new student in class.
Meet in room 6	The windows need washing!

Sometimes, however, if only one or two students are confused, I will continue the lesson and talk to those students later to try to clear up their confusion, rather than take the whole class's time to do this.

Robin Cazet, Third-Grade Teacher

Ms. Cazet's comments remind us of the first key attribute of teaching for understanding—it takes time. Prawat suggests three additional key attributes. These four key attributes of teaching for understanding are listed here:

- It takes time.
- It requires focus and coherence.
- It involves negotiation.
- It is highly analytic and diagnostic in nature.

We have already discussed and illustrated the first attribute of teaching for understanding, the fact that it takes time. In fact, teaching for understanding takes a good deal of time. However, the time is well spent because when we don't teach for understanding, the knowledge students acquire is fragile, inert, of little or no use in solving real problems, and soon gone.

Because teaching for understanding requires more time, it also demands focus. If we are going to spend a good deal of time on something, we had better be sure just what it is we are spending time on. Similarly, if we are going to spend a good deal of time on a topic, it needs to be coherent—to us as teachers and to students as learners. Thus, for example, if we are dealing with narratives and focusing on plot, it is important that both we and the students understand that we are focusing on plot, understand what plot is, and understand why we are focusing on plot.

In order to ensure coherence, we are frequently going to have to negotiate meaning with students. As we discussed in Chapter 1, the process of

> We must provide the time students need for mental restructuring. Hurrying on to the next lesson or the next topic does not allow for sufficient reflection on the implications of the present lesson.
>
> —James A. Minstrell
> Science Teacher

Because teaching for understanding requires negotiating meaning with students, it often takes time and a good deal of mental effort. But the reward of true understanding is worth the effort.

making meaning is a constructive one. Meaning does not simply spring from a text to the reader's head. Readers must grapple with a text, manipulate ideas, shape them, and interpret them if they are to derive significant learning from what they read. What the reader gets from reading depends heavily on the sum total of his experience and on his unique intellectual makeup. No two readers or listeners will construct exactly the same meaning from a particular text or discussion. Thus, in situations in which we want students to construct the same meaning or very similar meanings, we will often need to engage in negotiation—a give-and-take discussion in which students and their teacher talk through a topic, often rereading a text and listening to what the other is saying, attempting to understand what each person is saying, and coming to some agreement on the meaning.

This sort of negotiation is nicely shown in the following excerpt provided by Beck and her colleagues (1997), in which a teacher and several students in Pennsylvania negotiate the meaning of a fourth-grade Pennsylvania history text. The passage the group is considering describes some insights George Washington had about the willingness of the French to relinquish their holdings in Pennsylvania.

Washington gave the Governor's letter to the French leader. No one knew this, but Washington made a drawing of the fort. Washington saw that the French planned to make war on the English. At last, the French leader gave Washington a message for the governor. He said that the French would not leave Pennsylvania. (Wallower & Wholey, 1984, p. 41)

> **Teacher:** *So, what's the author's message here?*
>
> **Kalondah:** *That, um, the French aren't gonna leave Pennsylvania. And they just plan to keep it.*
>
> **Teacher:** *The French plan to keep it for themselves. What's the author say to make Kalondah think that?*
>
> **Deandre:** *They were planning to stay, and I think that they're bound to have a war.*
>
> **Teacher:** *Deandre said that they were bound to have a war. Hmm. What do you think gave Deandre that idea?*
>
> **Kristen:** *Because the governor knew that, um, the French were staying because, um, I think he knew that the French wouldn't just let the English have it without having a war.*

What is important to recognize here is how the teacher's prompts serve to focus the discussion, get several students involved, and help the students come to some consensus on the meaning of the passage.

Finally, teaching for understanding is both analytic and diagnostic. That is, the teacher needs to analyze students' responses in an effort to determine what they are thinking, decide whether or not there is a problem of understanding, and if there is a problem, diagnose its nature and come up with a solution. Suppose that the social studies passage just discussed had produced these responses:

> **Teacher:** So, what's the author's message here?
>
> **Kalondah:** That, um, Washington wants to make war on the French.
>
> **Teacher:** Now, why do you say that Kalondah?
>
> **Kalondah:** Well, because he made a map.
>
> **Teacher:** That's true. He did make a map, and he might have made it because he wants to make war on the French. But we don't really know that. Can anyone suggest another reason he might have made a map?
>
> **Deandre:** Maybe he didn't want a war. Maybe he just thought that the French might want a war, and he wanted a map just in case, in case they made war, so he could fight back.
>
> **Teacher:** Now what Deandre said is certainly possible. And what Kalondah said also make sense. The truth is, we're not sure what Washington's plans are yet. He might want a war, or he might just want to be prepared in case the French start a war, or he might have other plans. We'll have to read further and see if we can learn more.

In classrooms that emphasize teaching for understanding, the teacher must be a learner and openly negotiate knowledge with students. . . . Teachers must be in authority without being authoritarian.

—Martha Stone Wiske
Educational Technology
Specialist

Here, the teacher has tried to find out what caused Kalondah to make the inference she did, how other students are interpreting the passage, and what the passage actually does and does not reveal. And the result of his analysis and diagnosis is the very reasonable conclusion that the class will need to read further to find out more about just what is going on. We believe that many discussions of text will take a form much like this, as students and teachers delve into texts and their interpretations of them in the quest for true understanding.

A General Framework for Teaching for Understanding

Complementing Prawat's consideration of key attributes of teaching for understanding is Perkins's framework for guiding students toward deep understanding. Underlying the framework is the assumption that understanding can often be fostered by teaching in thematic units, which might last for two to four weeks and which allow students the time to reach true understanding and give them opportunities to establish links between the many concepts necessary to really understanding something. Perkins's four-part framework is shown in the following list:

- Generative topics
- Understanding goals
- Understanding performances
- Ongoing assessment

Here we define each of these parts, elaborate on each, and give an example or two of each.

Generative Topics

Generative topics are central to the subject area students are studying, accessible to students, and connectable to many other topics in the same subject and in other areas. Generative topics can be concepts, themes, procedures, historical periods, theories, ideas, and the like. For example, in the field of literature, plot is a generative topic. Plot is central to the study of literature, is an important element in many types of literature and in many individual pieces of literature, and exists outside of literature as well. Historical episodes—for example, the Civil War period—basically follow a plot, as do our lives. As another example, consider the field of history. Cause and effect is a concept central to much of history, and like the generative concept of plot, cause and effect also exists in areas outside of history. In fact, many, if not most, fields of study—science, humanities, and art, for example—deal with cause and effect. As still another example, consider the idea of beauty. Beauty is a central concept in art and literature, of course, but beauty also plays an important role in our lives and even in science. Frank Press (1984), former president of the National Academy of Sciences, once spoke of the discovery of the double helix that broke the genetic code as not only rational, but beautiful as well. Finally, consider the topic of health. Health can be considered a part of science, but it is also a subtopic of social science; there is of course psychological health as well as physical heath. Of course, health can also be related to government—as when a powerful world leader becomes ill; and it can be related to myriad other areas, including our daily lives. Some examples of generative topics for first-graders and fifth-graders are listed in Figure 8.1.

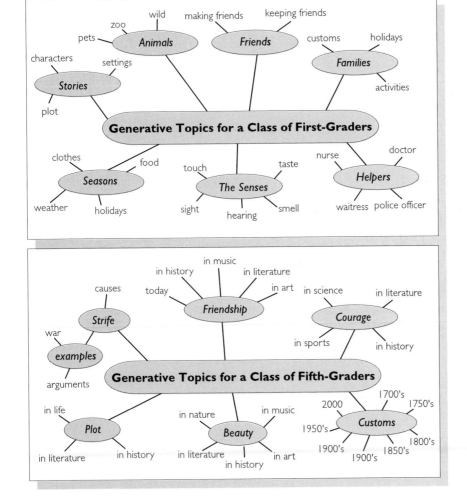

FIGURE 8.1 *Some Generative Topics for First-Graders and Fifth-Graders*

Working with highly generative topics whenever possible is important because, as we have already noted, teaching for understanding takes time. If we are going to spend a good deal of time on a topic, and that's what we do when we teach for understanding, we need to carefully choose topics that are important, that connect to many other topics, and that students can access and appreciate.

Understanding Goals

One problem with generative topics is that they are often too broad. The concept of beauty, for example, could be studied in any age, in any medium, and in almost any field. Even though understanding units may last for two to four weeks, the time available is obviously not infinite, and we almost always need to select one or several parts of broad generative topics to deal with and some specific goals to be achieved. For example, one possible understanding goal for sixth-graders studying the idea of beauty might be to understand that people's idea of physical beauty has changed over time, that the ancient Romans' idea of beauty differed from that held by Italians during the Renaissance and from that held by Italians today. Another possible understanding goal for these sixth-graders might be to grasp that the idea of what constitutes physical beauty also differs from culture to culture and even from individual to individual.

Or consider again the generative topic of health, and assume that the students we are concerned with are in first or second grade. Obviously, they will be able to deal with only some aspects of health. They could, for example, understand and profit from studying some aspects of nutrition. In this case, one goal for understanding might be to have students learn the six types of food described in a contemporary food pyramid (grains, vegetables, fruits, dairy products, proteins, and fats). Another might be to understand what foods help keep them healthy. And another might be to become more knowledgeable consumers, learning at least a little about food labels and advertising.

These goals were in fact developed by a group of first- and second-grade teachers we worked with as they designed an understanding unit on nutrition (Asfeld, Schwab, Gagliardi, & Henke, 1994), and we use their unit as an example as we discuss the remainder of Perkins's four-part format. Their understanding unit was developed for typical classes of first- or second-graders and involved children in a variety of interesting, involving, instructional, and fun activities over a period of about three weeks. An outline of the unit is shown in Figure 8.2. As the titles of the lessons suggest, the unit dealt with a variety of topics—including grains, vegetables, fruits, labels, menus, and advertising—and it involved students in a variety of activities—including listening, reading, writing, planning, and creating. This is indeed a significant set of topics and issues, and we would expect some significant learning and understanding to develop during the three-week unit.

When children build on their prior knowledge and natural curiosity, their understanding and confidence blossom.

—Paul E. Heckman
Teacher Educator

Lesson	Topic
1	Why Do We Need Nutrition?
2	Introduction to the Food Pyramid
3	Grains
4	Vegetables
5	Fruits
6	Dairy Products
7	Proteins
8	Fats, Oils, Sweets
9	How to Read a Food Label
10	Introduction to Menu Planning
11	Menu Planning
12	Looking at Food Advertising
13	Letters to Consumers
14	Designing a Commercial
15	Conclusion

FIGURE 8.2 *Lessons from a First-Grade Understanding Unit on Nutrition*

Understanding Performances

In Perkins's four-part framework, students demonstrate their learning and understanding in what he calls "understanding performances." Understanding performances are student activities that require an understanding of the content you are teaching. Thus, when students complete an understanding performance, they demonstrate that they have in fact understood. During the three-week nutrition unit we have outlined, students took part in a number of understanding performances. Fairly early in the unit, they demonstrated their understanding of the six types of food in the food pyramid by classifying products presented in commercials according to the food groups. Later in the unit, they demonstrated their understanding of how foods are labeled by discussing food labels they had located. And still later, they demonstrated a very practical understanding of nutrition by developing nutritious menus. The following list shows these and some other understanding performances students engaged in.

- Classifying projects presented in food commercials
- Journaling food intake
- Discussing food labels
- Writing letters to consumers
- Dramatizing grocery store experiences
- Making a commercial focusing on nutritional values
- Developing nutritious menus

As the list shows, these children engaged in a lot of understanding performances. Also, as we just noted, they engaged in these understanding perfor-

Teachers should
challenge students to
find alternative solutions
for problems they have
already solved.

—Irving Sigel
Psychologist

mances throughout the unit; they did not wait until the end of the unit to demonstrate their understanding. This is important; students should be engaged in understanding performances throughout the period that they are studying a topic.

Ongoing Assessment

The last part of Perkins's four-part framework, ongoing assessment, is closely related to understanding performances. Just as students should be engaged in understanding performances throughout the unit, students and teachers should be engaged in ongoing assessment throughout the unit. Of course, one of the things that teachers assess is students' understanding performances—for example, whether or not the first- or second-graders taking part in the nutrition unit can correctly classify food items in the appropriate food groups. If some of them cannot, then they need feedback and some reteaching, and they need the feedback and reteaching early on so that they do not continue through the unit with misconceptions about foods and food groups and the resulting confusion. Each of the later understanding performances—journaling about food intake, discussing labels, and so on—offers additional opportunities for ongoing assessment, and for feedback and reteaching, if needed. However, ongoing assessment is not limited to understanding performances. At all points in the unit and during all activities—individual conferences, small-group discussions, writing assignments, or other events—it is important to constantly be assessing whether or not students are understanding and to constantly be ready to assist students in reaching understanding if they are experiencing problems. As Perkins and Tina Blythe (1993) put it, "To learn for understanding, students need criteria, feedback, and opportunities for reflection from the beginning of and throughout any sequence of instruction" (p. 7).

Summary Comments on a Teaching for Understanding Perspective

Certainly all of us want to teach for understanding. We obviously would not want to teach for misunderstanding or teach with the goal of getting students to forget whatever they have learned. Yet we know that in too many cases, misunderstanding and forgetting take place. Teaching for understanding is hard. But by keeping its attributes (time, focus and coherence, negotiation, and frequent analysis and diagnosis) clearly in mind and by employing the four-part framework (generative topics, understanding goals, understanding performances, and ongoing assessment) in situations where it is appropriate, understanding is a goal we can reach. The following bibliography gives resources to help you choose and develop themes for your students.

Five Resources on Theme Teaching

Five, C. L., & Dionisio, M. (1995). *Bridging the gap: Integrating curriculum in elementary and middle schools.* Portsmouth, NH: Heinemann. This article explores a fifth-grade unit on discoveries and a middle school unit on trying on someone else's skin, in some detail.

Meinbach, A. M., Rolthlein, L., & Fredericks, A. D. (1995). *The complete guide to thematic units: Creating the integrated curriculum.* Norwood, MA: Christopher-Gordon. This very complete resource includes sections on developing and using themes, activities, assessment, and specific suggestions for themes.

Moss, J. (1994). *Using literature in the middle grades.* Norwood, MA: Christopher-Gordon. This rich source includes eight chapters on themes and specific literature to use with them. Since the themes discussed here focus on literature, we suggest supplementing them with readings in history, science, and other areas.

Walmsley, S. (1996, August). 10 ways to improve your theme teaching. *Instructor,* pp. 54–60. Ten practical, powerful, and on-target suggestions for theme teaching are offered along with some suggestions for themes for grades 1–6.

Walmsley, S. (1994). *Children exploring their world: Theme teaching in the elementary school.* Portsmouth, NH: Heinemann. The author provides steps for creating and managing themes, along with discussions of specific themes elementary teachers have found useful.

Reflection AND Application

1. One of the key attributes of teaching for understanding is that it takes time, more time than we often allot to topics in school. Take a moment to think about a fairly difficult concept that you understand quite thoroughly. Now think back and try to remember how you came to understand the concept—when you were first introduced to it, how you were first introduced to it, what you did to initially learn it, how you refined and extended your learning of it, and when and how you actually made use of the concept. Now consider the total amount of time you put into mastering this difficult concept. With a classmate, share your recollections of learning the concept and the time it took you to do so. Then let the classmate share a similar recollection with you.

2. Outline a teaching for understanding unit for a particular grade level. Choose a generative topic, state one or more understanding goals that fall under that topic, describe at least two understanding performances that students could engage in as they participate in the unit, and explain how you could provide ongoing assessment very early in the unit and periodically throughout the remainder of it. Do this in writing, and make it as specific and concrete as you can.

There is quite a debate among educators . . . some are adamant that all themes should be student-created. While I like the idea of students creating themes, I see nothing wrong with teacher-generated themes, provided that they are appropriate for kids.

—*Sean A Walmsley*
Teacher Educator

351

THREE APPROACHES TO TEACHING FOR UNDERSTANDING

There are of course many ways to teach for deep understanding. Here, we focus on three of the best of them—explaining each fully and giving examples of each.

Knowledge as Design

Knowledge as design is a simple and straightforward yet very powerful discussion framework that you and your students can use to fruitfully investigate almost any topic. It was first described by David Perkins in 1986 and has been refined and further developed since that time (Perkins, 1994). Like each of the instructional procedures discussed in this chapter, it is fully consistent with the cognitive-constructivist model of reading discussed in Chapter 1 and with the instructional principles described in Chapter 2, particularly the constructivist perspectives on instruction.

Two basic principles underlie knowledge as design. One is that considering the design of a topic—the relationship between its structure and its purpose—allows us to talk meaningfully and even insightfully about almost any topic. The other principle is that learning is a consequence of thinking. If we can get students actively thinking about a topic, then they will be learning about that topic. Knowledge as design suggests that students can productively answer the four questions about a topic or object shown in Figure 8.3. Answering these questions as a group gives students the opportunity to share what they know about the topic and come up with a rich set of information on it.

As we said, the procedure is simple and straightforward, as you will see in the following scenario. Olivia Martinez, a fifth-grade teacher, began by identifying the topic of television shows, which grew out of students' reading

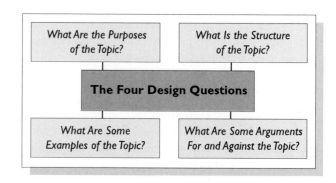

FIGURE 8.3 *Knowledge as Design Questions*

of *The TV Kid* by Betsy Byars. The class then took up the four design questions one by one, engaging in what Perkins calls a design conversation. Finally, the class worked toward some sort of closure. Here is a small sample of the many responses these fifth-graders generated in discussing the topic of television shows:

To draw students into the depth and complexity of a subject, we must look for topics that relate to students' lives.

—*Vito Perrone*
Teacher Educator

IN THE CLASSROOM
A Design Conversation About Television

Purposes of Television Programs

Ms. Martinez: What are some of the purposes of TV shows? Why do we have TV shows? Why do you watch them?

Students: They're fun. They're exciting. It's something to do. It's better than homework.

Structure of Television Programs

Ms. Martinez: How are TV shows organized? What are they like? What are the parts of them?

Students: They're different. Some are an hour, and some are half an hour. They have commercials. They're on every week. Some are on every day.

Examples of Television Programs

Ms. Martinez: What are some examples of TV shows? What are some shows that you know?

Students: Cartoons. Power Rangers. Monday Night Football. Goosebumps. Seinfeld.

Arguments For and Against Television

Ms. Martinez: What are some good things about television shows, some things you like?

Students: They're exciting. They're fun. They give you something to do. The good guys win. They let you forget your troubles—like homework.

Ms. Martinez: What are some arguments against television, maybe some things you think or maybe some things your parents think?

Students: The ads, there are too many ads. Reruns. There's a lot of shooting. They rot your brain. Sometimes the stuff's not for kids.

Quite obviously, these fifth-graders know a lot about television. Using the design conversation has enabled them to get what they know out on the table, where the whole class can think about it and see what it means.

Design conversations give students the opportunity to share what they know about a topic and come up with a rich set of information about it.

At this point, we will consider each of the three parts of a design conversation—choosing a topic, the design conversation itself, and closure—in slightly more depth.

Choosing a Topic

The first step in using knowledge as design is of course to choose a topic. Although knowledge as design can be used with virtually any topic, like each of the approaches we consider in this chapter it is most appropriately used with worthwhile topics that justify students' spending time delving into them. Additionally, in order to ensure students' success with the procedure when they are first learning to use it, it is a good idea to initially choose topics that are concrete, that students know a lot about, and that students are likely to be interested in. The topic of TV shows obviously meets these criteria. And, when you consider that American students watch an average of about four hours of television a day and that carefully considering the topic might make them more selective in their viewing—or even convince some of them to cut down their viewing—then it also meets the criterion of importance.

Once you choose a topic, it's a good idea to see if it will work as a design conversation before giving it to students. To do so, simply jot down one or two purposes, the structure of the topic, one or two examples, and some arguments for and against the topic. Figure 8.4 shows the responses we came up with when considering the topic of television shows for about one minute.

> Teachers must teach learners how to become active . . . and show students that their effort in learning will produce tangible results, that the educational system is sensitive to them and will recognize and reward their attempts to learn.
>
> —Merlin Wittrock
> *Educational Psychologist*

Television Shows

Purposes:	*entertainment*
	information
Structures:	*half-hour shows*
	hour shows
	mini-series
Examples:	*nightly news*
	football games
	Seinfeld
Arguments	
For:	*informative/engaging*
Against:	*mindless*
	addictive

FIGURE 8.4 *Responses to Considering Television Shows as a Topic for a Design Conversation*

If the topic seems to work for you, try to think of how it will work for students. Think about some of your students, what they know, and how they are likely to respond to each of the design questions. If it seems as if your students will be able to answer the design questions, then you have probably chosen a good topic.

Leading a Design Conversation

Once you have chosen the topic and are confident it will be a useful one for your students, the next step is to lead students through the four design questions. Frequently, the question—What are the purposes of the topic?—is asked first. However, this does not need to be the case. You might also begin by asking about the structure of a topic or asking students to give some examples of it. Wherever you begin, the procedure usually works best if you get as many responses as possible on one question before going on to another one. You will want to keep a record of students' responses, and that can be done on the board or on an overhead transparency with a template that provides convenient spaces for students' responses to each of the questions. Such a template, which Perkins calls a design conversation worksheet, is shown in Figure 8.5.

As you ask the questions, it is very important to do everything possible to promote an open discussion and to encourage students to volunteer answers. This means treating all students' answers with respect by acknowledg-

Purposes	Specific Examples
_____	_____
_____	_____
_____	_____
_____	_____
Structure	**Pro Arguments**
_____	_____
_____	_____
_____	_____
_____	_____
Con Arguments	**Conclusions**
_____	_____
_____	_____
_____	_____
_____	_____

FIGURE 8.5 *Design Conversation Worksheet*

ing partially correct responses and avoiding criticism. It also means being sure all students have opportunities to respond, and seeing that students treat one another with respect. In Chapter 6, we gave several guidelines for effective discussions. Many of these apply to design conversations.

Something else to consider as you conduct the design conversation is that the four categories of questions should be thought of in broad terms, not narrow or limiting ones. The purpose question, for example, can be thought of as a question about goals, objectives, functions, or aims. In asking about purposes, you are asking What is it for? What does it do? What can we accomplish with it? Similarly, the structure question can be thought of as a question about organization, features, materials, or parts. In asking about organization, you are asking How is it organized? What does it look like? What is it made of? What are its parts? How is it put together? Interpreting each of the design questions broadly allows you to use the procedure with a very broad range of topics.

Closure

The third step of knowledge as design—closure—gives students the opportunity to synthesize the information they have produced, connect it to their existing knowledge, search for insights, and draw conclusions. With most topics, closure can take a variety of directions. With the topic of television shows, for example, students might compare television shows to other forms of entertainment—radio, the movies, and live theater. They might also compare watching television to doing other activities—working on hobbies, reading, participating in sports, and completing schoolwork. Certainly, since so many American students watch so much television, you might be inclined to work toward a closure that critically evaluates the value of watching television or at least raises the possibility that watching somewhat less television might be worth considering.

Continued Work with Knowledge as Design

As we suggested, in working with knowledge as design, it is essential to choose topics that are relevant to students—what's going on in their lives, what they're reading about, what they're interested in. As students become increasingly competent with the procedure, you can introduce topics from subject areas that will further challenge students' imaginations and thinking abilities. Shown in Figure 8.6 is a design conversation worksheet illustrating the responses third-graders gave on the topic of jobs before beginning a unit on workers in the community. The bibliography on page 359 shows just a small sample of the many children's books on the topic of jobs:

Britta Olson, the third-grade teacher whose students completed the design conversation worksheet on jobs, comments on how this sort of activity helps her students:

> The students' responses, I believe, show some real understanding of the nature of jobs. And it's just this sort of understanding that will help these children appreciate the work people do in a community and how jobs serve both the worker and the community. Also, because the students arrived at their understanding in a give-and-take class conversation, it strengthens the likelihood that they will internalize what they have learned and incorporate it into what they already know about the role of jobs in a community.
>
> Britta Olson, Third-Grade Teacher

Purposes	Specific Examples
to make money	mechanic
to help people	teacher
something to do with	doctor
your time	waitress

Structure	Pro Arguments
get paid	earn money
you _do_ something	help people
work at a certain time	keep you out of trouble
have a boss	give you something to do

Con Arguments	Conclusions
not enough time to play	lets you buy things
can tire you out	helps other people
can be boring	jobs you like are fun
can stress you out	jobs you hate are bad

FIGURE 8.6 *Design Conversation Worksheet on Jobs*

As we suggested earlier, in your initial work with knowledge as design, it is a good idea to work with topics that are concrete and that students know a lot about. As students become increasing competent with the procedure, you will find that they can also use knowledge as design with more abstract and unfamiliar topics. The following scenario is an excerpt from a design conversation on voting, carried out by the sixth-grade students in Mark Pallota's class. The topic grew out of their reading about Rosa Parks, particularly Chapter 14, "Voting Rights," in *Rosa Parks* by Kai Friese. Students were asking, "What's such a big deal about voting, anyway?" This particular class had been engaging in design conversations throughout the year and knew the procedure well, so one student, Mike, suggested they have a design conversation on the topic. The scenario also illustrates an instance in which the conversation leader, Mike, begins the conversation with *examples:*

Books on the Topic of Jobs

Eve Bunting. *A Day's Work*. Clarion, 1994. A young Mexican American boy, Francisco, learns something about telling the truth when he tries to help his non-English-speaking grandfather find work. 32 pages.

Omar S. Castaneda. *Abuela's Weave*. Lee & Low, 1993. Esperanza, who is learning how to weave cloth the traditional way from her grandmother, fears their handmade wares won't be able to compete with the factory-made ones at the market. 32 pages.

Gail Gibbons. *Fire! Fire!* Crowell, 1984. This broad picture of the many aspects of firefighting shows firefighters battling forest fires, waterfront blazes, a barn fire, and a city fire. 32 pages.

Carol Greene. *I Can Be a Librarian*. Children's Press, 1988. One of the books in the I Can Be series, this entry describes what librarians do, the kinds of libraries they work in, and how to become a librarian. It includes full-color photos, a glossary, and an index. 32 pages.

Kathy Henderson. *I Can Be a Geographer*. Children's Press, 1990. Another book in the I Can Be series, this entry discusses the subjects geographers must know and the variety of occupations they might have. It includes full-color photos, a glossary, and an index. 32 pages.

Wade Hudson. *Jamal's Busy Day*. Just Us Books, 1991. After an active day at school where Jamal works all day with numbers, research, and experiments, this African American youngster learns that his architect father and accountant mother aren't the only ones who work hard in the family. 24 pages.

William Jaspersohn. *A Week in the Life of an Airline Pilot*. Little, Brown, 1991. This book traces a pilot's flight to India in a 747, with descriptions of his duties and the excitement of the job. 96 pages.

Karla Kuskin. *The Philharmonic Gets Dressed*. Harper & Row, 1982. The author gives a humorous but accurate description of the individual preparations that orchestra members make before a concert. 32 pages.

Patricia C. McKissak. *Ma Dear's Aprons*. Atheneum, 1997. The author pays tribute to domestic workers of a bygone generation. 32 pages.

Paul Sipiera. *I Can Be a Rancher*. Children's Press, 1990. Another book in the I Can Be series, this entry discusses the work ranchers do, the skills and training they need, and the kinds of animals they raise. It includes full-color photos, a glossary, and an index. 32 pages.

IN THE CLASSROOM

A Design Conversation on Voting

Examples

Mike: OK, we're going to talk about voting. What do we know about voting? Let's start with some examples. What have you voted for? What about your parents or other people—you know, adults—what are some examples of what they vote for?

Jordan: Last week we voted for what new books we wanted for our class library.

Lisbeth: Friday we'll vote for a new class president.

Honing: My parents get to vote for president, mayor, governor, people like that, in government. Also laws, in the United States when you're 18 you can vote for laws and stuff like that.

359

Purpose

Mike: *(after collecting a few more examples)* Good. OK, now let's look at these voting situations, you know, why are people voting for books, people, etc.? Marla, would you write down what people say about voting purposes?

(Marla writes student responses on the board.)

Seth: People feel good because they have a say. Like with the library books. Even if your book doesn't win, at least you had your say.

Jana: Before we vote for class president, there will be campaign speeches. Then Ms. B. will let us argue about who will be the best president. Maybe that way we'll choose the best one. If we couldn't vote, if Ms. B. just chose a president, it would be just her opinion.

Carlos: OK, you know if you're voting between two things, like this Friday when the election is just between Jena and Kari? Even if a few people are not happy with who wins, most people are—at least the ones who voted for the winner!

Structure

Mike: *(after collecting a few more purposes)* Good list of purposes, I'd say. Now, what about the structure of voting; you know, what is voting like? What are some of its important features?

Jana: Each person gets a single vote.

Paul: You vote secretly.

Seth: Someone is in charge of counting the votes.

Arguments

Mike: Cool. Let's explore the arguments one at a time. Why does each person get one vote? How does that help voting fulfill its purpose?

Carlos: People would be mad if some others got more than one vote, and if people were left out, they might not go along with the decision.

Seth: Yeah, but some people do get left out. Kids don't get to vote, not for U.S. president, anyway.

Mike: Right on. Sometimes there are rules about who gets to vote. Like being a certain age. That's another thing about voting. Think back to the arguments again, why do we have rules like this?

This dialogue illustrates only a part of the conversation. A full design conversation on voting might consume half an hour or more. But we hope this example is sufficient to show a class dealing with a challenging topic from the curriculum, to show students learning a good deal about voting, and to illustrate how the teacher learns a lot about what students do and don't know about the topic as the conversation progresses.

As the dialogue on voting reveals, as students become increasingly familiar with knowledge as design, they become able to work with the procedure without the teacher's leadership. Mark Pallota comments on how his students conduct their own design conversations:

> Once they understand the procedure well, I have my students work in small groups, perhaps with several groups each working on part of a general topic and then sharing their knowledge. When students work with knowledge as design in groups, it's important that they record their responses so that they can review the knowledge they have produced and share it with others. I like to reproduce the design conversation worksheet as a handout. This provides students with an excellent place to record their conversations and helps guide them in asking the design questions.
>
> Mark Pallota, Sixth-Grade Teacher

In concluding this section on knowledge as design, we want to say a word about how frequently you might find the procedure useful for dealing with the content you consider in your classroom. Our general thought here is that you and your students may choose to use it fairly frequently, often including a design conversation in conjunction with the reading students are doing in areas such as history, science, and health. These discussions can occur either before students read about a topic or afterward. If you hold design conversations before students read a selection, it will need to involve somewhat familiar topics, and in many cases it will be appropriate to complete the conversation after students have read the selection and gained additional information and insights. Of course, just how often you use the procedure depends on some of the same factors that you consider in planning scaffolded reading experiences—your students, the topics you deal with, and your purposes. How fre-

After students have had many experiences engaging in design conversations, they can successfully lead their own without a teacher's leadership.

quently you use knowledge as design also depends on the other discussion and thinking procedures you use in your classroom. Still, because knowledge as design is broadly applicable, easy to use, and can lead to powerful learning about a number of topics, it is certainly a candidate for frequent use.

Reflection AND *Application*

3. Choose a topic for a design conversation that primary-grade students might engage in. Remember, design conversations need to deal with topics students have some knowledge about. This could be something that is common knowledge, such as something having to do with their homes or school, or it could be a topic the class has been reading about. Once you have a topic, fill out a design conversation worksheet like that shown in Figure 8.5, giving responses that primary-grade students might make. Finally, reflect on the responses you have shown, and consider the extent to which they represent the sort of thinking you would expect from primary-grade students. To the extent that they do not, modify them to make them more authentic.

4. Choose a design conversation topic appropriate for a reading methods class, probably the class in which you are using this text, and hold the conversation with the class as a whole or with a small group. Afterward, discuss with your classmates how useful knowledge as design was in helping you hold a purposeful discussion.

Reciprocal Teaching

Reciprocal teaching, developed by Annemarie Palincsar and Ann Brown (1984), is a cooperative-learning procedure in which students and a teacher work together to improve students' understanding of complex informational texts and at the same time improve students' general ability to monitor their comprehension and to learn from such texts. The procedure has been extensively researched and has produced very positive results with first-graders (Palincsar & David, 1991), sixth- and seventh-graders (Palincsar & Brown, 1984), and even college students (Fillenworth, 1995). Studies show that students who worked with reciprocal teaching increased their group participation and use of the strategies taught, learned from the passages studied, and increased their learning when reading independently. The studies also demonstrated that the procedure could be used in various settings and that students maintained the gains they achieved.

The procedure is quite simple, straightforward, and consistent with the instructional principles we discussed in Chapter 2. For example, it includes scaffolding, puts learning in students' zone of proximal development, and follows the gradual release of responsibility model.

The procedure employs four carefully selected strategies: generating questions, clarifying issues, summarizing, and making predictions. Each of these strategies serves one or more definite purposes. Questioning focuses students' attention on main ideas and provides a check on their current understanding of what they are reading. Clarifying ensures that students are actively engaged as they are reading and helps avoid confusion. Summarizing requires students to attend to the major content of the selection and determine what is important and what is not. And predicting requires students to rehearse what they have learned thus far and approach the next section of the text with some expectations of what is to come.

Initially, reciprocal teaching is teacher-directed. At first, the teacher or some other experienced reader, such as a classroom aide, serves as the leader of the group, taking the primary role in carrying out the strategies and modeling them for others in the group. The leader's task includes modeling the strategies he wants the children to learn, monitoring students' learning and understanding, scaffolding their efforts, providing students with feedback, and tailoring the session to the students' existing level of competence. One central purpose of reciprocal teaching, however, is to get all students actively involved in using the strategies—that is, in doing the questioning, clarifying, summarizing, and predicting themselves. Thus, from the beginning, the teacher increasingly hands over responsibility to the students in the group. As soon as possible, the teacher steps out of the leadership role, and each student in the group takes his turn as group leader. It is, in fact, when students have the leadership role that they do some of their best learning. The teacher, however, continues to monitor the group as much as possible and intervenes when necessary to keep students on track and to facilitate the discussion.

Figure 8.7 shows the four steps of the procedure and very briefly illustrates the responses they might prompt for fifth-graders reading Lucy Baker's *Life in the Rainforests*.

In the formal studies of reciprocal teaching, students have usually worked with reciprocal teaching for a 20-day period, which has been sufficient to produce the gains described earlier. To give you a more concrete indication of what those gains look like, we present a transcript of a seventh-grader's work with the procedure. The following dialogue, taken from the

The session begins with the leader reading aloud a short segment of text, typically a paragraph or so. Four steps then follow:

1. *Questioning.* Once the segment has been read, the leader or other group members generate several questions prompted by the passage just read, and members of the group answer the questions. For example, after reading the opening paragraph of Baker's *Life in the Rainforests*, a student might ask, "What does a rainforest look like?" Another student might respond, "Very tall trees, lots of plants and animals, not much light under the tall tree branches."

2. *Clarifying issues.* If the passage or questions produce any problems or misunderstandings, the leader and other group members clarify matters. For example, in continuing to work with *Life in the Rainforests*, a student might point out that the only plants that can grow in the rainforest are ones that can grow upward toward the light, since the branches of the giant trees act like a sun umbrella and block the light. Other members of the group might agree but then point out that some plants, such as mushrooms, don't need light.

3. *Summarizing.* After all the questions have been answered and any misunderstandings have been clarified, the leader or other group members summarize the segment: "A rainforest is a place of giant trees, lots of rain, many different kinds of plants and animals, and with little change in temperature, day to night, season to season."

4. *Predicting.* Based on the segment just read, segments that have preceded it, and the discussion thus far, the leader or other group members make predictions about the contents of the upcoming section: "I think in the next section we will learn about some of the different kinds of things—plants, animals, and people—that live in the rainforests." The sequence of reading, questioning, clarifying, summarizing, and predicting is then repeated with subsequent sections.

FIGURE 8.7 *Four Components of Reciprocal Teaching*

work of Brown and Palincsar (1989), illustrates the student's progress by showing his performance on five different days:

IN THE CLASSROOM

Increased Questioning Ability of a Seventh-Grade Student

Day I

TEXT: *The water moccasin, somewhat longer than the copperhead, is found in the southeastern states. It lives in swampy regions. It belongs, as do also the copperhead and the rattlesnake, to a group of poisonous snakes called pit vipers. They have pits between their eyes and their nostrils which, because they are sensitive to heat, help the snakes tell when they are near a warm-blooded animal. Another name for the water moccasin is "cottonmouth." This name comes from the white lining of the snake's mouth.*

Student: What is found in the southeastern snakes, also the copperhead, rattlesnakes, vipers—they have. I'm not doing this right.

Teacher: All right. Do you want to know about the pit vipers?

Student: Yeah.

Teacher: What would be a good question about the pit vipers that starts with the word *why?*

Student: (No response)

Teacher: How about, "Why are the snakes called pit vipers?"

Student: Why do they want to know that they are called pit vipers?

Teacher: Try it again.

Student: Why do they, pit vipers in a pit?

Teacher: How about, "Why do they call the snakes pit vipers?"

Student: Why do they call the snakes pit vipers?

Teacher: There you go! Good for you.

Day 4

TEXT: *Spinner's mate is much smaller than she, and his body is dull brown. He spends most of his time sitting at one side of her web.*

Student: (No question)

Teacher: What's this paragraph about?

Student: Spinner's mate, How do spinner's mate . . .

Teacher: That's good. Keep going.

Student: How do spinner's mate is smaller than . . . How am I going to say that?

Teacher: Take your time with it. You want to ask a question about spinner's mate and what he does, beginning with the word *how.*

Student: How do they spend most of his time sitting?

Teacher: You're very close. The question would be, "How does spinner's mate spend most of his time?" Now, you ask it.

Student: How does spinner's mate spend most of his time?

Day 7

TEXT: *Perhaps you are wondering where the lava and other volcanic products come from. Deep within our earth there are pockets of molten rock called* magma. *Forced upward in part by gas pressure, this molten rock continually tries to reach the surface. Eventually—by means of cracks in the crustal rocks or some similar zone of weakness—the magma may break out of the ground. It then flows from the vent as lava, or spews skyward as dense clouds of lava particles.*

Student: How does the pressure from below push the mass of hot rock against the opening? Is that it?

Teacher: Not quite. Start your question with, "What happens when?"

Student: What happens when the pressure from below pushed the mass of hot rock against the opening?

Teacher: Good for you! Good job.

Day 11

TEXT: *One of the most interesting of the insect-eating plants is the Venus's flytrap. This plant lives in only one small area of the world—the coastal marshes of North and South Carolina. The Venus's flytrap doesn't look unusual. Its habits, however, make it truly a plant wonder.*

> **Student:** What is the most interesting of the insect-eating plants, and where do the plants live at?
>
> **Teacher:** Two excellent questions! They are both clear and important questions. Ask us one at a time now.

Day 15

TEXT: *Scientists also come to the South Pole to study the strange lights that glow overhead during the Antarctic night. (It's a cold and lonely world for the few hardy people who "winter over" the polar night.) These "southern lights" are caused by the Earth acting like a magnet on electrical particles in the air. They are clues that may help us understand the Earth's core and the upper edges of its blanket of air.*

> **Student:** Why do scientists come to the South Pole to study?
>
> **Teacher:** Excellent question! That is what this paragraph is all about.

> The thing we now realize is that it takes *time* to foster understanding, partly because students develop powerful ideas of their own that frequently interfere with what we want them to learn.
>
> —*Richard S. Prawat*
> *Educational Psychologist*

As the preceding transcript illustrates, the student progressed from being unable to phrase an appropriate question to phrasing a very clear and concise one. As the student became increasingly competent, the teacher gradually turned over responsibility for generating questions to him. On day 1, the teacher had to phrase the question for the student. On day 4, she provided substantial scaffolding to assist the student in phrasing a question. On day 7, she needed to use much less scaffolding. On day 11, when the student produced two good questions, she reminded him that the procedure called for only one. And on day 15, she simply praised the student, as he was able to produce a clear, concise, and appropriate question without her assistance.

As the transcript further shows, the leader's role is crucial. Skilled leaders can keep the discussion on track, constantly assess students' strengths and weaknesses, and provide just enough scaffolding to challenge students while ensuring that they succeed. No one, of course, is better able to do this than a skilled teacher. However, aides can certainly be trained to be competent leaders, and research has shown that peer tutors can also be trained to be competent leaders (Palincsar & Brown, 1986). Additionally, in the intermediate grades, teachers can work with an entire class by employing writing as part of the procedure, as Jim Gates does:

> To help my sixth-graders really think about what they're reading, often I will have them do some specific sorts of writing about what they are reading. For example, sometimes for the reading we do in science or social studies, I'll assign certain segments to read in the textbook each day. Before they read each segment, I'll

ask them each to write two statements about what they think they will learn. Then, as a class, we discuss their predictions. Next, they read the segment individually, write two questions about it, a summary of it, and make a note on anything that required clarification. Finally, as a whole class we discuss their questions, summaries, and clarifications.

Jim Gates, Sixth-Grade Teacher

Because reciprocal teaching is consistent with the principles of effective teaching, is strongly supported by research, and assists students in understanding and learning from challenging expository material, we recommend using it in your classroom as yet another procedure for fostering your students' critical literacy.

Reflection AND *Application*

5. Select a text that you might use in doing reciprocal teaching with a group of intermediate-grade students. We suggest that you use an expository one. Decide on a text segment to focus on, probably a paragraph or two. If the segment you choose is not at the beginning of the text, assume that the students you are working with have already read and discussed previous segments. Now do four things: Create a question that you, as the discussion leader, might pose to a small group working with the segment. Identify and then explain an issue from the segment that might need clarification. Write a brief summary of the segment. And, before you have read further in the text, make a prediction about the contents of the next segment.

6. Choose a text that students in your college class might use with reciprocal teaching, identify a segment of that text to be dealt with at one session, and complete the activities in the previous item for college students working with that segment.

Questioning the Author (QtA)

Questioning the author, the last of the four specific approaches to fostering deep understanding we discuss in the chapter, is a large-group questioning and discussion procedure developed by Isabel Beck and Margaret McKeown. It is, as Beck and McKeown explain, "an approach to text-based instruction that was designed to facilitate building understanding of text ideas" (Beck, McKeown, Hamilton, & Kucan, 1997). Beck and McKeown developed the procedures after several years of research on textbooks (Beck, McKeown, & Gromoll, 1989). They found that textbooks were often difficult for students

Research that we have been involved in over the last decade or so led us to the idea that to really help young students' reading we needed to "lift the lid off texts."

—*Margaret McKeown*
and Isabel Beck
Educational Researchers

to understand because they often assumed that students had more prior knowledge of the topics being dealt with than they actually did. As a result, the explanations of ideas and events given in the text were insufficient to allow students to construct much meaning. This shortcoming of the text-books was further compounded by the fact that students assumed the texts to be absolute authorities and thus beyond question. When students read a text and did not understand what they had read, they repeatedly saw themselves as totally responsible for their lack of understanding and failed to even consider the possibility that the text itself might be less than perfect.

Following their initial research investigating the inadequacies of text-book writing, Beck and McKeown began revising textbooks to make them more understandable; and their research showed that the revised texts were indeed more comprehensible (Beck, McKeown, Sinatra, & Loxterman, 1991; Beck, McKeown, & Worthy, 1995). However, although the revisions led to improved comprehension, they did nothing to lessen students' view of texts as absolute authorities. Moreover, Beck and McKeown could hardly revise all textbooks. These considerations led to their development of questioning the author (QtA).

Motivated by two ideas, "deposing the authority of the textbook" and "lifting the lid off texts," Beck and McKeown (1995) developed QtA. They wanted to encourage young readers to get under the surface of the material they were reading, dig into it, and engage with the ideas the texts presented; and they wanted to assist students in realizing that textbooks are simply someone's ideas written down and that readers frequently need to work hard to figure out what the author is trying to say.

Their procedure is simple and straightforward. First, the teacher ex-plains to children that texts are in fact written by ordinary people who are not perfect and who create texts that are not perfect. Consequently, readers need to continually work hard to figure out what the authors are trying to say. Once students understand this reality, QtA proceeds by having the class read a text together. The teacher stops at critical points to pose queries that invite stu-dents to explore and grapple with the meaning of what is written. The queries include initiating prompts (such as "What's the author trying to say?") to get students started in grappling with the text, follow-ups (such as "What does the author mean by that?") to encourage them to dig for deeper meaning, and follow-ups (such as "How does that connect with what the author told you?") to encourage putting ideas together. However, queries are not scripted, and teachers are encouraged to modify those suggested and to make up their own queries to fit the students and texts they are working with.

Key attributes of QtA are listed here.

- The purpose of QtA is to assist students in building understanding from text.

- Texts are prompts that constrain meaning but that frequently require the reader to interact and grapple with the information they provide.
- QtA involves whole-class discussions in which the students and their teacher read and discuss relatively small segments of text.
- QtA discussions occur "on line," that is, as students are engaged in their first reading of the text.
- Queries are prompts that teachers use to assist students in engaging with the text, grappling with its meaning, and building understanding from it.
- Queries foster discussion of the text and its meaning, rather than wide-ranging discussion of matters only tangentially related to the text.

As the list indicates and as we have noted, the key purpose of QtA is building understanding from text. As Beck and McKeown note and as we have repeatedly noted, understanding does not come from a casual reading of the text and the assumption that the author's meaning will somehow be absorbed by the reader. Instead, it comes when the reader considers, manipulates, and grapples with information gleaned from the text and then integrates it with his existing knowledge. QtA involves students in a whole-class discussion that invites and prompts this sort of activity, and it does so as students are reading the text for the first time, rather than after they have read it or during a second reading.

The last statement in the previous paragraph points up a very important characteristic of QtA, distinguishing it from many other questioning and discussion techniques. QtA takes place during the reading of the text, rather than afterward. Moreover, QtA takes place during students' first reading, rather than during rereading. This is important because the goal of QtA is to give students the opportunity to construct meaning for text as they are reading, not to be told, after the fact, what they might have experienced.

Another distinguishing characteristic of QtA is that QtA discussions focus specifically on the text. They are not wide-ranging conversations in which students are encouraged to share a wide range of opinions and ideas. Instead, the discussion focuses on clarifying, collaboratively constructing meaning for, and ultimately understanding the ideas in the text being read. QtA queries are strategically used by the teacher to direct the discussion to that end. They are general probes that have a very specific purpose—engaging students in grappling with and constructing meaning for the ideas in a text.

In the remainder of our discussion of QtA, we present a segment of a QtA session, consider queries in a bit more detail, explain the process of planning a QtA session, characterize the sorts of discussion you are trying to prompt with QtA, and suggest how you might introduce QtA into a class.

A Sample QtA Segment

The following scenario, taken from Beck et al. (1997), shows a fifth-grade so-cial studies class studying Pennsylvania history. The class had been working with QtA for some time and is quite skilled in grappling with text ideas. The class is discussing a text segment about the presidency of James Buchanan, a Pennsylvania native. The text indicated that many people believed that Buchanan liked the South better than the North because he believed that it was a person's free choice whether or not to have slaves.

IN THE CLASSROOM
QtA in the Fifth Grade

The teacher began the discussion of this segment of the text as follows:

Teacher: All right. This paragraph that Tracy just read is really full of important infor-mation. What has the author told us in this important paragraph?

Laura: Um, they um think that Buchanan liked the South better because they, he said that it is a person's choice if they want to have slaves or not, so they thought um that he liked the South better than the North.

Teacher: Okay. And what kind of problem then did this cause President Buchanan when they thought that he liked the South better? What kind of problem did that cause?

Next, Janet gave her interpretation of how Buchanan's position on slavery might have affected the voters in Pennsylvania:

Janet: Well, maybe um like less people would vote for him because like if he ran for President again, maybe less people would vote for him because like in Pennsylvania we were against slavery and we might have voted for him because he was in Pennsylvania, because he was from Pennsylvania. That may be why they voted for him, but now since we knew that he was for the South, we might not vote for him again.

At this point, the teacher summarized Janet's remarks.

Teacher: Okay, a little bit of knowledge, then, might change people's minds.

Then, another student acknowledged Janet's explanation and offered some of his own thoughts.

Jamie: I have something to add on to Janet's cause I completely agree with her, but I just want to add something on. Um, we might have voted for him because he was from Pennsylvania so we might have thought that since he was from Pennsylvania and Penn-sylvania was an antislavery state, that he was also against slavery. But it turns out he wasn't.

Finally, a third student acknowledged her classmates' thoughts and contributed her ideas to the developing interpretation.

> *Angelica:* I agree with the rest of them, except for one that um, like all of a sudden, like someone who would be in Pennsylvania you want to vote for them but then they wouldn't, they be going for the South and then you wouldn't want to vote for them after that.

The scenario illustrates several key attributes of a QtA discussion. The students are indeed grappling with meaning; they are really trying to understand the author's meaning. The students are focused on the meaning of the text. The teacher adroitly directs the discussion, but she does not dominate it. She leaves plenty of room for student input because the purpose is for the students to understand the text; if they're the ones who are going to understand the text, they're the ones who must do most of the talking and thinking. The students respond at some length. Finally, the students listen to one another and build on one another's responses as they jointly construct meaning for the text.

QtA Queries

One way to begin to understand queries is to contrast them to traditional questions, something we are more familiar with. Beck and McKeown (Beck et al., 1997) suggest three dimensions on which the two differ. First, traditional questions assess comprehension with the goal of finding out whether the students understood what they have read. Queries "assist students in grappling with text ideas" with the goal of helping them construct meaning. Second, traditional questions serve to evaluate individual student responses and foster teacher-to-student exchanges. Queries "facilitate group discussion about an author's ideas and prompt student-to-student interactions." Finally, traditional questions are generally used either before reading or after reading. Queries "are used on-line during initial reading" of the text.

> To me as a teacher, understanding means sense-making. It means the conversation in the classroom is dominated by the questions, "Does this make sense to you?" and "Why or why not?"
>
> —*Magdalene Lampert*
> *Educational Researcher*

As we have already pointed out, queries are not scripted and teachers are encouraged to adjust their queries to fit their students, the text, and the purposes in reading the text. Nevertheless, Beck and McKeown have identified a set of queries that are quite useful and illustrate the nature of successful queries. These are shown in Figure 8.8.

These, of course, are general queries. Queries for a specific text must be more specific. We have already seen specific examples of initiating and follow-up queries in the QtA segment on President Buchanan. Here is the teacher's initiating query and its lead-in: "All right. This paragraph that Tracy just read is really full of important information. What has the author told us in this important paragraph?" Here is one of the teacher's follow-up queries from this same segment: "Okay. And what kind of problem then did this

---

Initiating Queries

What is the author trying to say here?

What is the author's message?

What is the author talking about?

Follow-up Queries

So what does the author mean right here?

Did the author explain that clearly?

Does that make sense with what the author told us before?

How does that connect with what the author has told us here?

But does the author tell us why?

Why do you think the author tells us that now?

Narrative Queries

How do things look for this character now?

How does the author let you know that something has changed?

How has the author settled that?

Given what the author has already told us about this character, what do you think he [the character] is up to?

FIGURE 8.8 *Some Questioning the Author Queries*

From Beck, I. L., McKeown, M. G., Hamilton, R., & Kucon, L. (1997). *Questioning the author: An approach for enhancing student engagement with text.* Copyright © 1997 by Isabel Beck and the International Reading Association. All rights reserved.

cause President Buchanan when they thought that he liked the South better? What kind of problem did that cause?"

Narrative queries, which we haven't yet discussed, are uniquely suited to working with narratives. They are used in addition to initiating and follow-up queries. An example of a narrative query comes from a teacher whose class was using QtA as they read George Seldon's *The Cricket in Times Square* (1970). In the part of the story students have just read, Mario Bellini's pet cricket Chester ate half of a two-dollar bill. This is a problem because two dollars is a lot of money to the Bellinis. Here is the next paragraph of the story:

> *Chester Cricket sat frozen on the spot. He was caught red handed, holding the chewed-up two dollars in his front legs. Muttering with rage, Mama Bellini picked him up by his antennae, tossed him into the cricket cage and clicked the gate behind him. He half expected that she would pick him up, cage and all, and throw him onto the shuttle tracks.*

And here is the teacher's narrative query on it: "How do things look for Chester?"

As you can see from these examples, the purposes of initiating queries are to make the text information public in the classroom and to get the discussion under way, and the purposes of follow-up queries are to keep the discussion focused and to assist students in elaborating and integrating ideas. The purpose of narrative queries is to focus students' attention on characters and the roles they are playing in the story and on the way the author is crafting the plot.

Planning a QtA Lesson

There are three steps in planning a QtA lesson. The first step is to read and study the text thoroughly in order to identify the major understandings that you want students to achieve and the potential problems that they may have. For example, in reading the text on President Buchanan, the teacher might determine that one thing she wants students to understand is that President Buchanan was supported and influenced by people representing diverse views and had to somehow deal with these diverse views. She might further infer that students probably would not understand the different views on slavery advanced by different states.

The second step is to segment the text, to divide it into short sections that are read and discussed before students go on to the next section. Sometimes a segment will be quite lengthy, perhaps a page or so. At other times, a segment will be relatively short, for example, the sample discussion we presented for the Buchanan text dealt with a single paragraph: "All right. This paragraph that Tracy just read is really full of important information. What has the author told us in this important paragraph?" And at still other times, a segment might be even shorter, dealing with a single sentence, as fifth-grade teacher Rona Greene tells us:

> My fifth-graders are familiar with the QtA procedure, so when I come up with just a single sentence for them to analyze, they're not surprised. Recently, while reading R. Lawson's *Ben and Me* (1939), I ran across a sentence that was challenging enough and important enough to constitute a QtA segment. In the story, in which Benjamin Franklin has a mouse companion named Amos, who narrates the story, there comes a point at which Franklin is about to send Amos up in a kite to examine lightning. The text reads, "This question of the nature of lightning so preyed upon his mind that he was finally driven to an.act of deceit that caused the first and only rift in our long friendship." I decided that this particular sentence, which indirectly reveals the depth of the friendship between Amos and Franklin but does not directly describe it, was worth serious consideration.
>
> **Rona Greene, Fifth-Grade Teacher**

Finally, in addition to deciding what is important in a text, what the likely stumbling blocks are, and how the text will be segmented for the dis-

Teachers and educators are realizing that future adults need to be self-reliant, adaptive, lifelong learners who can reason through problem-framing and problem-solving situations collaboratively. These adults need to be able to think and act in ways which signal that they value themselves and others, know how to be responsible for themselves and others, and are respectful of themselves and others.

—*Laura Roehler and Denise Cantlon Teacher Educators*

cussion, you need to plan the actual queries to address to students. Although many queries will be modified or even discarded as the discussion proceeds, queries such as: "What has the author told us in this important paragraph?" and "How do things look for Chester?" are planned in advance.

QtA Discussion

We have already given one fairly lengthy example of a QtA discussion and said several things about the sort of discussions that QtA is designed to foster. Here, we give another example of a QtA discussion, this too from Beck et al. (1997), and conclude with a quotation emphasizing that students need to be the principal participants in QtA discussions.

The discussion here deals with the sentence from *Ben and Me* just given—"This question of the nature of lightning so preyed upon his mind that he was finally driven to an act of deceit that caused the first and only rift in our long friendship." The scenario begins with the initiating query.

IN THE CLASSROOM
A QtA Discussion

Teacher: What's the author trying to tell us about Ben and Amos?

Temika: That their friendship was breaking up.

Ms. Greene: Their friendship was breaking up? OK, let's hang on to that. What do you think, April?

April: I agree with the part that their friendship did break up, but um, I think that they got back together because when you were reading um, further, it said that he was enjoying the mouse.

Teacher: OK, so let me make sure. You say that he knows that they're friends, and something happened that made them almost not be friends? But they're still friends?

Alvis: I think that um, Amos is just, I think Amos is just lying because in the story it said if they weren't good friends, why would um, um, Ben build a um, kite for, build a kite for him so he could have fun.

Teacher: OK, so Alvis is telling us that, why would Ben go to all that trouble and build that beautiful kite if they weren't friends? A lot of people agreed that their friendship was broken up. Alex doesn't think their friendship is broken up. Can somebody help me out? What's the author want us to figure out here?

The teacher saw that April and Alvis were making sense of this sentence by bringing in supporting information from other parts of the text, and she attempted to rephrase their statements to better clarify the nature of the friendship.

The discussion continues, with two more students grappling with the meaning of the sentence:

Tammy: Um, um, deceit was an act of lying so that means, that means um, sometimes a lie broke up a friendship and, because it made a rift and um, so, and deceit was an act of lying, so their friendship must've broke up because of somebody told um, some kind of lie.

Teacher: Oh, that's interesting. Tammy said that if there were some lying going on, something to break up their friendship, because that's what Amos said, "the first and only rift in our friendship," something must've happened. How many of you agree that something had to happen?

Jamal: I disagree, cause a break in their friendship don't mean they gotta break their friendship.

Teacher: OK, so Jamal thinks that they might still be friends, even though something happened. OK? We're gonna continue 'cause the only way we're gonna find out is if we read some more.

In addition to illustrating how a teacher rephrases and clarifies ideas and keeps the discussion focused as she guides students toward full understanding of this important sentence, this excerpt shows how QtA discussions are dominated by students rather than by teachers: "Students do the work. They construct the meaning, wrestle with the ideas, and consider the ways information connects to construct meaning." Thus, "the discussion becomes an opportunity for students to formulate complete thoughts, respond to the text, react to each other's ideas, and consider new notions" (Beck et al., 1997).

Introducing QtA

Introducing QtA is a straightforward matter, but it is important to include several points in your introduction. First, tell students that the way they are going to be reading and discussing text is probably different from the way they have typically dealt with it. Next, tell them that they will be reading and discussing short sections of text at some length. They will read a segment of text and then stop and discuss what it means with their classmates. After that, explain that the reason they need to do this is that a text is simply somebody else's words written down and that sometimes, in fact in quite a few cases, understanding what the author is saying requires close attention to and a good deal of discussion of the text. Finally, note that the discussions will deal with the text and the meaning the author is trying to convey, rather than more wide-ranging matters.

That's it. With this groundwork laid, and of course after thoroughly familiarizing yourself with the QtA procedure, you are ready to begin QtA sessions.

> The literacy demands required to thrive in society have changed significantly over the last several decades.
>
> —*Larry Mikulecky*
> *Teacher Educator*

375

Questioning the Author's Impact

Beck and McKeown and their colleagues have worked with QtA for several years and have gathered several sorts of data on its efficacy. First, they implemented QtA with two teachers who at first showed the traditional pattern of teacher-initiated questions aimed mainly at retrieving information directly from the text and brief student responses that were quickly acknowledged before the next question was asked.

But with QtA, their lessons began to change. Typically, a QtA lesson showed collaborative construction of meaning. A student would offer an idea in response to a query, and the teacher and other students would build on and elaborate that idea. As an example, here is a brief excerpt from a QtA social studies lesson on international cooperation (McKeown & Beck, 1995). The class had just read a text segment about countries cooperating to share resources through world trade.

> *Teacher:* What's the author reminding us of here? Reggy?
>
> *Reggy:* That we, um, that we trade countries out of their resources and they trade us out of our resources and we cooperate, by helping each other.

Notice in the above excerpt that Reggy's response is in his own words, strongly suggesting that he is presenting his own ideas rather than simply parroting text information. Now notice in the following excerpt how the teacher handles Reggy's response by summarizing part of it and then extending the discussion by forming a question from another piece of what Reggy said.

> *Teacher:* OK, Reggy said we help each other, and that's how we cooperate. When you cooperate, you're working together to get something done. What does Reggy mean by, "we trade resources out of their country?" What's he talking about? Darleen?

Darleen responds with an explanation about how trade works.

> *Darleen:* He's talking about, when he says we're trading resources out of our country, he means that other countries, like Britain and Japan and China, we get our cotton and our resources that we have that are really popular, and we trade them for money sometimes.

Darleen's response is a fitting conclusion to our discussion of QtA because it indicates the amount of listening, thinking, and connecting that a QtA lesson can elicit. This is the sort of active engagement students need to demonstrate if they are to fully understand a text.

In Questioning the Author discussions, students dig below the surface of text by grappling with the information the author had provided to build meaning for themselves.

Reflection AND *Application*

7. Identify a narrative text that third- or fourth-graders might use with QtA. Read the text to determine the major understandings that you want students to gain and what some of the stumbling blocks are likely to be. Next, segment the text—divide it into short sections to be read and discussed before students go on to the next section. Now, take one of those segments and write an initiating query, as many follow-up queries as you think you will need, and as many narrative queries as you think you will need. Refer back to Figure 8.8 and other examples as you need to. Finally, jot down some notes about how you think your QtA discussion is likely to proceed—how long it will take to deal with the segment, how students are likely to respond to the queries, and what difficulties they may have.

   Alternatively, or in addition, you could write out a segment of a QtA discussion as we have done at several points. This is probably a more challenging and time-consuming task than just taking notes, but it is likely to give you greater understanding of QtA.

Special Needs and Special Talents

As you think about the three procedures presented in this chapter, which students do you think will benefit from them? We hope you answer, "All students." Teaching for understanding is a crucial part of the critical literacy curriculum for all students. All students—those who like school and almost always succeed, those who do not take to school and often seem uninterested in school subjects, and those who continually try but find many school tasks challenging. All of these students need to understand what they learn in school well enough to retain important information and be able to use that information in school and out of school, now and in the future. This being the case, we have only three more comments.

First, do not slight any students by denying them the opportunity to learn for understanding. All students will profit from participating in knowledge as design discussions, using reciprocal teaching, and engaging in QtA sessions.

Second, not slighting any students does not mean ignoring individual differences. In order to succeed with these understanding activities, some students will need more scaffolding and accommodation than others. Some ESL students may benefit from using their native language in QtA sessions. Similarly, some students will need assistance with activities such as summarizing; strategy instruction, which we described in Chapter 7, might be useful here.

Different students, of course, bring different stores of prior knowledge to knowledge as design discussions. Since knowledge as design demands prior knowledge of the topic being discussed, you'll want to vary the topics you use to be sure that all students have opportunities to participate in discussions of topics they are familiar with.

The situation with reciprocal teaching is similar. Even though reciprocal teaching is focused on the text, prior knowledge relevant to the text is important, and thus the texts used for reciprocal teaching need to reflect the diverse interests and knowledge bases of your students. Reciprocal teaching also requires the use of strategies—questioning, summarizing, and predicting. Some students will need instruction in these strategies; many will need a good deal of scaffolding in the discussions.

In questioning the author, as in reciprocal teaching, prior knowledge relevant to the text is crucial, and thus text selection is critical. Also, since QtA is typically a whole-class activity, there is always the danger that more verbal, outgoing students will dominate the discussion. Finding ways to encourage and support the participation of all students is vital. It helps to first establish the sort of literate environment we described in Chapter 2—one in which students feel free to speak out in class, students support one another in class discussions, and you support students' responses by acknowledging

> The prime role of our schools is the development of the full potential of each individual.
>
> —John I. Goodlad
> *Educational Policy Analyst*

partially correct responses or rephrasing a question to give a student another opportunity. Beyond that, you will want to be on the lookout for ways to draw in individuals who often do not participate. For example, students who lack confidence will gain it if you give them a lot of opportunities to answer questions that they can definitely answer; and students who lack certain sorts of background knowledge will begin to participate more when the reading they're working with taps background knowledge familiar to them. Another possibility, of course, is to use QtA with a small group rather than with the class as a whole.

Finally, recognize that these teaching for understanding techniques tend to center on verbal performances and that some students have strengths in other areas. Howard Gardner's (1991, 1993) insights on multiple intelligences can be particularly helpful here. In Gardner's view and that of many contemporary psychologists, the concept of intelligence as a single, objectively measured, unchangeable trait is misleading and unhelpful. Instead, Gardner argues for the existence of at least seven intelligences: linguistic (verbal), logical–mathematical, spatial, bodily kinesthetic, musical, interpersonal, and intrapersonal.

Although individuals are likely to be particularly strong in one or more of these intelligences, each individual possesses all seven, and most people can develop each of them to a satisfactory level. Thus, subscribing to the theory of multiple intelligences does not mean identifying individuals as requiring one particular type of instruction. Instead, it means recognizing that different students do have different strengths, and we want to give students opportunities to use all of these intelligences at various times, including when we are teaching for understanding. Listed here are some classroom activities that Thomas Armstrong (1994) considers particularly appropriate for each intelligence:

Linguistic—lectures, discussions, word games, storytelling, choral reading, journal writing

Logical–mathematical—brain teasers, problem solving, science experiments, mental calculations, number games, critical thinking

Spatial—visual presentations, art activities, imagination games, mind mapping, metaphor, visualization

Bodily kinesthetic—hands-on learning, drama, dance, sports that teach, tactile activities, relaxation exercises

Musical—superlearning, rapping, songs that teach

Interpersonal—cooperative learning, peer tutoring, community involvement, social gatherings, simulations

Intrapersonal—individualized instruction, independent study, options in course of study, self-esteem building

Of course, allowing students to make use of their multiple intelligences is not limited to teaching for understanding activities. The curriculum offers many opportunities for these varied activities; for example, they work particularly well as postreading activities in SREs. However, because teaching for understanding necessarily involves a lot of students' time and a lot of effort from them, drawing on multiple intelligences is particularly important here. For more on this powerful idea, we recommend Gardner's own writings as well as Armstrong's concise and very accessible book.

CONCLUDING REMARKS

This chapter has taken a fairly in-depth look at teaching for understanding. We began the chapter by defining *understanding* and describing some key attributes of teaching for understanding—it takes time, requires focus and coherence, involves negotiation, and is highly analytic and diagnostic. Next, we described Perkins's general framework for teaching for understanding, which suggests that we frequently teach in units that deal with generative topics, present understanding goals, require understanding performances throughout the period of the unit, and include ongoing assessment throughout the unit. Finally, we discussed and gave examples of three specific approaches that can foster deep understanding—knowledge as design, reciprocal teaching, and questioning the author.

These three approaches are by no means the only ways of fostering deep understanding. Many approaches described in other parts of the book can be used for this purpose. These include the general approach of fostering critical literacy described in Chapter 1, the Frayer method of teaching new concepts described in Chapter 5, the scaffolded reading experience described in Chapter 6, and teaching comprehension strategies and promoting independent reading as described in Chapter 7, to name only a few.

In concluding this chapter, we want to note that we consider it one of the most important chapters in the book. Teaching for understanding, fostering deep knowledge, giving students knowledge and skills that they will retain and that they can use in the world beyond school is of course a goal all teachers share. Yet we know that this goal is only sometimes achieved, and we believe that there are two quite different factors that contribute to this unfortunate fact.

First, we cannot wish understanding on students. To give students the greatest possible opportunity and capacity to learn for deep understanding, the whole of the critical literacy curriculum presented here is vital. Children who have mastered basic decoding skills, become fluent readers, amassed substantial vocabularies, received significant scaffolding as they read increasingly challenging texts and engaged in increasingly challenging activities with

Students taught for understanding can evaluate and defend ideas with careful reasoning and evidence, independently inquire into a problem using a productive research strategy, produce a high-quality piece of work, and understand the standards that indicate good performance.

—*Linda Darling-Hammond*
Teacher Educator
and Policy Analyst

them, learned comprehension strategies that they could apply independently, and been aided in becoming independent and avid readers are in the best position to learn for and with deep understanding.

Second, as we said at the beginning of the chapter, teaching and learning for understanding take time. We must give students adequate time to become engaged and competent in working with different topics. Once more, though, we want to emphasize that the time given to teaching for understanding is more than justified. The teaching for understanding activities described here are among the very best methods of promoting critical literacy in all students.

EXTENDING LEARNING

1. Arrange a meeting with a teacher who teaches at an elementary grade level that interests you, and discuss the notion of teaching for understanding generally. Ask if he or she is familiar with the term *teaching for understanding* and the general point of view it represents. If the term and the concept are familiar, ask how he or she interprets teaching for understanding, what sort of job he or she thinks schools in general are doing in assisting students to develop deep and useful understanding, and what he or she is doing to teach for understanding. Also, ask about what he or she sees as the barriers to teaching for understanding and how they might be overcome. If the teacher is not familiar with the term or the concept, explain it as fully as you can. Then discuss the matters listed here as thoroughly as possible.

2. In a separate meeting with the same teacher or in a meeting with another elementary school teacher, describe one of the three teaching for understanding procedures we have discussed—knowledge as design, reciprocal teaching, or questioning the author—and ask if he or she uses it or a similar procedure; if so, ask about how useful and effective they have found it to be. If the teacher you talk with hasn't used the first procedure you bring up, describe each of the other two, and pursue the suggested line of questioning to try to identify one that the teacher is familiar with. Finally, if the teacher does use one of the procedures, ask if you can observe the class as he or she uses it. Then observe the class, and make some notes about how the procedure works. Of course, if you have the time and opportunity to discuss and observe more than one of the three procedures, certainly do so.

3. Meet with a class or small group of elementary students and try out one of the teaching for understanding procedures—knowledge as design, reciprocal teaching, or questioning the author. This is probably the

most time-consuming of the activities we have suggested—you have to search for a class or small group, thoroughly prepare for your teaching, and then do the teaching. However, it is also one of the most beneficial because it gets you directly involved in teaching. If you do get to use one of these procedures, be sure to take some notes immediately afterward so that you have something to refer to next time you use it.

REFERENCES

Armstrong, T. (1994). *Multiple intelligences in the classroom*. Alexandria, VA: Association for Supervision and Curriculum Development. This very practical book on multiple intelligences was written by a person who has studied the topic extensively and is directed to practicing teachers.

Asfeld, S. T., Schwab, J., Gagliardi, S., & Henke, M. A. (1994). *Nutrition: The good way to health*. Unpublished manuscript. This lesson plan describes a really excellent understanding unit for first- or second-grade children.

Beck, I. L., McKeown, M. G., & Gromoll, E. W. (1989). Learning from social studies text. *Cognition and Instruction, 6*, 99–158. This study examines some of the shortcomings of social studies texts.

Beck, I. L., McKeown, M. G., Hamilton, R., & Kucan, L. (1997). *Questioning the author: An approach for enhancing student engagement with text*. Newark, DE: International Reading Association. This is the most detailed description of questioning the author available.

Beck, I. L., McKeown, M. G., Sinatra, G. M., & Loxterman, J. A. (1991). Revising social studies text from a text-processing perspective: Evidence of improved comprehensibility. *Reading Research Quarterly, 26*, 251–276. This empirical study demonstrates that social studies texts can be improved with revisions guided by cognitive psychology.

Beck, I. L., McKeown, M. G., & Worthy, J. (1995). Giving a text voice can improve students' understanding. *Reading Research Quarterly, 30*, 220–238. This empirical study shows that using more active writing and incorporating verve can increase students' understanding of text.

Brown, A. L., & Palincsar, A. M. (1989). Guided cooperative learning in individual knowledge acquisition. In L. B. Resnick (Ed.), *Knowing, learning, and instruction*. Hillsdale, NJ: Erlbaum (393–451). This is a detailed update and supplement to the 1984 Palincsar and Brown article.

Bruer, J. T. (1994). *Schools for thought*. Cambridge, MA: MIT Press. This book presents an informed layperson's views of how ideas from cognitive psychology can improve student learning.

Fillenworth, L. I. (1995). *Using reciprocal teaching to help at-risk college freshmen study and read*. Unpublished doctoral dissertation. University of Minnesota, Minneapolis. This empirical study demonstrates that at-risk college students can profit from using reciprocal teaching in studying their texts.

Gardner, H. (1991). *To open minds*. New York: Basic Books. This is Gardner's most recent general treatment of the topic. It describes the origins of the theory and developments since that time.

Gardner, H. (Ed.) (1993). *Multiple intelligences: The theory in practice*. New York: Basic Books. This book offers a collection of papers on multiple intelligences by Gardner and his colleagues.

McKeown, M. G., & Beck, I. L. (1995, Spring). Lifting the lid off text: Questioning the author. *Literacy Education Newsletter*, pp. 3-4. (Available from the University of Minnesota, Department of Curriculum and Instruction, 159 Pillsbury Drive S.E., Minneapolis, MN 55455.) This article gives a brief description of questioning the author.

Palincsar, A. M., & Brown, A. L. (1984). Reciprocal teaching of comprehension and monitoring activities. *Cognition and Instruction, 1*(2), 117–175. This is the original and most comprehensive description of reciprocal teaching.

Palinascar, A. S., & Brown, A. L. (1986). Interactive teaching to promote independent learning from text. *The Reading Teacher, 39*(8), 771–777. This is a brief, teacher-oriented article on reciprocal teaching.

Palincsar, A. M., & David, Y. M. (1991). Promoting literacy through classroom dialogue. In E. Hiebert (Ed.), *Literacy for a diverse society: Perspectives, programs, and policies*. New York: Teachers College Press. This empirical study examines the use of reciprocal teaching as a listening technique with 6-year-olds.

Perkins, D. (1992). *Smart schools: From training memories to education minds*. New York: The Free Press. The author provides a well-written, engaging, and comprehensive plan for teaching for understanding.

Perkins, D. (1994). *Knowledge as design: A handbook for critical and creative discussion across the curriculum*. Pacific Grove, CA: Critical Thinking Press and Software. This detailed description and examples of knowledge as design come with an excellent videotape showing students engaging in the procedure.

Perkins, D., & Blythe, T. (1993). Putting understanding up front. *Educational Leadership, 51*(5), 4–7. This article gives a concise description of Perkins' approach to teaching for understanding.

Prawat, R. S. (1989). Teaching for understanding: Three key attributes. *Teaching and Teacher Education, 5*, 315–328. This is a well-reasoned position paper on teaching for understanding.

Press, F. (1984, May 30). Address given at the Annual Commencement Convocation, School of Graduate Studies, Case Western Reserve University, Cleveland, OH. This is the source of the statement about the beauty in science.

Resnick, L. B. (1987). *Education and learning to think*. Washington, DC: National Academy Press. This short but thought-provoking booklet considers how and where thinking skills should be taught.

Williams, P. L., Lazer, S., Reese, C. M., & Carr, P. (1995). *NAEP 1994 U.S. history: A first look*. Washington, DC: National Center for Educational Statistics. This is the initial report on the 1994 NAEP history findings.

Williams, P. L., Reese, C. M., Campbell, J. R., Mazzeo, J., & Phillips, G. N. (1995). *1994 NAEP reading: A first look*. Washington, DC: Department of Education. This is the initial report on the 1994 NAEP reading findings.

CHILDREN'S LITERATURE

Byars, B. (1976). *The TV kid*. New York: Viking. Television is Lennie's only escape from failure, boredom, and loneliness until a snakebite jolts him into reality. Illustrated. 123 pages. Audiotape available.

Friese, K. (1990). *Rosa Parks: The movement organizes*. Boston: Silver Burdett Press. This book explores Rosa Parks's role in the civil rights movement. Illustrated. Introduction by Andrew Young. 128 pages.

Krensky, S. (1994). *Children of the wind and water*. New York: Scholastic. The author describes traditional lifestyles of children in five different tribes—the Muskogee, Dakota, Huron, Tlingit, and Nootka. Illustrated. 32 pages.

Lawson, R. (1939). *Ben and me*. New York: Little, Brown. Amos the church mouse becomes instrumental in some of Ben Franklin's inventions. Illustrated. Audiotape and videotape available. 113 pages.

Leedy, L. (1994). *The edible pyramid: Good eating every day*. New York: Holiday House. This is a children's guide to diet, nutrition, and the food pyramid. 32 pages.

Seldon, G. (1960). *The cricket in times square*. New York: Farrar, Straus. A country cricket puts his unique musical talents to use in New York's Times Square. Illustrated. Audiotape and videotape available. 132 pages.

chapter nine

Writing and Reading

*T*wega, a fifth grader, had her spiral notebook constantly with her as she read a chapter in her American history book. She frequently took time to record an event, often with a simple phrase such as this one:

1861—Civil War begins with firing on Fort Sumter

As third grader, Michael, finished Tar Beach *by Faith Ringgold, he paused for a moment and made this brief entry in his reading log.*

Cool! I'd like to fly all over the city like Cassie did. Like Superman and fix all the bad stuff.

One morning in December, second-grade teacher Maria Chavez wrote the following on the chalkboard.

Dear Class,

We have been talking about gifts lately. I just wanted to tell you that each of you is a special gift to me. Thank you for working so hard and being so nice to one another.

Love,
Ms. Chavez

CHAPTER OVERVIEW

Each of these writers is using writing for a different purpose. Twega is recording an event that she wants to fix in her memory. A test is looming and these notes will help her review for it.

Michael is exploring his feelings in his reading log. He may also decide to share his entry with his literature circle, who are also reading Tar Beach. Having the notes will help jog his memory about the story's characters and events and his response to them.

Ms. Chavez had something she wanted to communicate to her students, and she chose to do so by writing a letter to the class on the chalkboard. Ms. Chavez is modeling several things here. She is modeling the form of the letter, but she is also modeling important attitudes—she values writing, she values reading, she values her students, and she values hard work and cooperation.

As this chapter illustrates, writing is a powerful tool for learning, for understanding, and for communicating.

WRITING AND READING

Developing a classroom in which reading and writing are integral activities, which support each other and provide students with avenues to learning, understanding, and communicating, is no small task. It is, however, one of the most interesting and rewarding tasks you and your students can undertake. In this section, we discuss three concepts to consider in developing a reading–writing classroom—the reading–writing connection, a positive reading–writing environment, and informal writing in contrast to the process approaches.

The Reading–Writing Connection

Reading and writing are two sides of the same coin. Both processes involve creating meaning through print.

—Bernice Cullinan
Teacher Educator

As you know, we write for a number of different reasons and audiences, and *how* we do it—the *process*—is different for each. But no matter what the reason, the audience, or the process, what we write is usually meant to be read, either by ourselves or someone else. And quite obviously, anything we read has to have been written by someone. Writing and reading, as Bernice Cullinan (1993) has noted, are two sides of the same coin. Like speaking and listening, they are two complementary components of a communications process (Nystrand, 1986; Squire, 1984) and depend on the same cognitive structures and strategies (Langer, 1986).

In my opinion, the single most important fact that the profession did not recognize 20–30 years ago is the impetus that pupil writing gives to successful early reading.

—Dorothy Strickland
Teacher Educator

Even though this reading–writing connection might appear obvious, these two language arts have traditionally been taught as separate subjects in American classrooms. Today, however, virtually all educators agree that combining reading and writing in the classroom makes a great deal of sense, both theoretically and practically. Over 30 years ago, John Carroll (1966) suggested that reading and writing be experienced as parallel and reciprocal processes, in much the same way that their own speaking and speech that they hear are parallel and reciprocal to younger children. Today, researchers and practitioners alike continue to recommend that this notion be put into practice in the classroom (Atwell, 1987; Farr, 1993; Olson, 1996).

Throughout this chapter, we explore this reciprocal process of reading and writing, focusing on a variety of writing forms, purposes, and procedures. But before we can begin that discussion, the stage must be set. The writing classroom—what does it look, sound, and feel like?

A Positive Reading–Writing Environment

"I write because I have something important to say, and I think people need to hear it!" says Brandon, a fifth-grader. Brandon's heartfelt, if somewhat boastful, comment succinctly captures in one sentence at least three critical truths about writing that will greatly affect your own thinking about the writing opportunities you provide for students:

- Students should write for important purposes.
- What students write should be valued by themselves, by you, and by the others in your classroom community.
- Writing should function to communicate or to foster the writers' own learning, understanding, or appreciation.

If literacy is to prosper in our classrooms, we need to create an environment in which children view themselves as writers. Writers use and value the written word. Writers are people who have a need and desire to learn and sometimes to communicate what they learn to others, to inform them, entertain them, persuade them, tickle them, move them, inspire them, challenge their imaginations. Writers flourish in an atmosphere in which written words are used and valued and writers are encouraged to take risks and are supported in their attempts. This environment involves both the intellectual climate of the classroom and its physical attributes.

The Intellectual Climate

The intellectual climate of the ideal reading–writing classroom conveys this message: "We are all readers and writers. Together we are all learning to be better readers and writers." This will be reflected in the number of children seen reading and writing at any given moment and their engagement in their writing tasks. It will be reflected in the students' writing displayed throughout the room—student-made books, posters, bulletin boards. It will be reflected in the faces and voices of students meeting to read and respond to each others' writing—children who, as Charles Temple and his colleagues (Temple, Nathan, Temple, & Burris, 1993) explain, are "respectful of each other, who are in touch with their own ideas, and who are interested in each other's ideas" (p. 247).

A classroom in which students write often and for a variety of purposes is one in which they feel free to take risks. This means that students are given opportunities to write without fear of criticism. One very effective way teachers can help establish this risk-taking atmosphere is to become writers themselves. Doing so helps teachers to understand the arduous process involved in transforming thoughts into words and to appreciate what it is like to have those words evaluated. When a teacher–writer meets with a student–writer to talk about her work, there is a re-

Literacy prospers in classrooms in which children view themselves as writers, where what they write is valued by the classroom community.

spect for the student's efforts that is sometimes lacking in teachers who don't write. Listen to this dialogue between teacher–writer Norman Pite and student–writer Caroline, a middle school student:

Mr. Pite: Tell me what you've done here.

Caroline: I sort of made it so that this [part] would be on the same page and it would change the reader's mood.

Mr. Pite: Good for you.

Caroline: So it would all be sad and heavy.

Mr. Pite: Ah! That's a good idea. I like that.

Caroline: It sort of changes from sort of a sad scene to all of a sudden to a lighter scene. And . . . I'm bringing them back down, a change of mood.

Mr. Pite: Good for you. [continues reading] Umm . . . This is very clever, this is very clever. Good for you. I like this one, and I think that your idea here is good. You know what sometimes authors do, is they'll do that in a poem. They'll have a mood change like that in a single poem. (Bright, 1995, p. 37)

As this dialogue illustrates, in this risk-taking environment Caroline's efforts are received with enthusiasm and respect, and her attempt to discover new and better ways of expressing herself and communicating to others is encouraged and applauded.

Another important element in the intellectual climate of a classroom is the teacher's role as modeler. As Donald Graves (1983) reminds us, the tone of a classroom is set by what a teacher does, not by what she says. Good writing teachers don't direct students; they collaborate with students and model the problem-solving process (Dyson & Freedman 1991), *showing* children how to read and write rather than simply *telling* them how to do so (Temple et al., 1993). Writing in front of students, showing them what we are doing, and talking about what we are doing and why, provides students with concrete examples of how writers work.

The Physical Environment

The physical environment of a productive reading–writing classroom will reflect the attitude, "This is a great place to read and write!" Students need *time* to write, a *place* to do it, and *materials* to write with. Obviously, if students are to become better writers, they need to spend time writing. So the number one rule is to provide plenty of writing opportunities and plenty of time to do them in. Also as Lucy Calkins (1986) tells us, it helps to have a writing time that is stable and predictable. Establishing a sustained period for students to write daily can ensure the stability and predictability many students

> Students start out writing because you're telling them to, but the idea is to help them see the value in writing so they start to do it for themselves.
>
> —*Kathleen Tolan*
> *Sixth-Grade Teacher*

require. The writing workshop, which we describe later in the chapter, is a framework for establishing that stability.

What materials do writers need? Quality materials to read, of course—lots of them—a classroom library that is brimming with books, ideas, and connections to the world. They also need supplies—lined paper of various sizes and colors; lined paper with a space for a picture; drawing paper of all sizes; stationery and envelopes; tag board; index cards; a picture file; pencils, colored pencils, crayons, and markers; paper clips; white glue and paste; and paper punches. We also recommend at least two writing folders for each student, one for completed works and one for works in progress. Computers can be motivating and helpful, but many excellent writing classrooms exist without them.

Although writing can take place almost anywhere, some teachers find it helpful to set up a writing center that includes a table or group of desks and writing supplies close at hand. Sometimes computers are housed in the classroom writing center. Some teachers like to post a sign saying *Quiet, Please, Writers at Work* in this center and designate another location in the room as a place to discuss works in progress. However it is accomplished, the main goal is to provide a place where students feel safe and comfortable exploring ideas on paper.

IN THE CLASSROOM
Guidelines for Creating a Positive Writing Environment

- Establish a predictable writing time.
- Establish a writing center equipped with writing necessities—writing materials, dictionaries, a thesaurus, and books on the writer's craft.
- Provide opportunities to write throughout the day in all the subject areas for a variety of purposes and audiences.
- Become a writer yourself, and share with your students your writing and the struggles you experience in writing.
- Provide students with guidance and constructive feedback.
- Stock the classroom library with texts in a variety of genres—magazines, picture books, biographies, informational books, novels, beginning chapter books—that reflect a wide range of interests and readability levels.
- Read aloud quality literature—fiction, nonfiction, and poetry.
- Model writing forms and techniques.
- Guide students to write about topics that are important to them—writing that has a genuine purpose and a real audience.
- Provide opportunities for students to share their writing with their peers and receive constructive feedback from them.
- Provide direct instruction on matters of mechanics—grammar, usage, spelling, and punctuation—and the writer's craft—dialogue, characterization, voice, engaging beginnings, and so on—as the need arises.

Informal Writing and the Process Approach

As we have noted, school offers many opportunities for both informal and formal writing. In recent years, a particular approach to teaching writing—the process approach—has been widely explored, and recent evidence (National Center for Educational Statistics, 1996) indicates that students in classrooms that include more elements of the process approach indeed become better writers than those in less process oriented classrooms. We think this evidence is convincing, and we strongly endorse the process approach as a method of teaching writing. However, a good deal of the writing students do in relation to their reading is less planned, less lengthy, less polished, and less formal than that for which the process approach is appropriate. As Gail Tompkins (1996) has pointed out, effective reading teachers give students plenty of opportunities to do both process writing and informal writing. Thus, after discussing the process approach, we will describe the nature and place of less-formal writing.

The Process Approach to Writing

A person who wishes to communicate something in writing very often goes through several stages of writing before giving the final product to her reader, particularly when writing formal pieces. However, not too long ago, most writing instruction gave virtually no attention to the process of writing. Fortunately, with the release of Janet Emig's (1971) study of 12th-graders' composing process and Donald Graves's (1975) observations of 7-year-old writers, educational researchers began focusing on the process involved in writing and its implications for classroom instruction. The result of this research has been a shifting of emphasis away from the end product of writing toward the process involved in the writing.

Step into a second-grade classroom for a moment, and witness this event:

> Gabbie, wearing gray sweatpants, high-top sneakers, and a wide grin, is sitting in the "author's chair," reading her story "The Noise in the Laundry Chute." You are impressed that a second-grader could write so well. You notice, however, that Gabbie's face, her body language, and her whole demeanor are speaking even more eloquently than her words: "This is good. I like this and am proud of my story."

Gabbie didn't get to this moment of accomplishment and satisfaction in one quick leap, but went through several stages before arriving at the author's chair to read her "finished" product. First, she engaged in *prewriting* activities, which helped her generate ideas. With her teacher acting as a recorder, the whole class had brainstormed "scary moments" together on the chalkboard.

Children need to be learners-of-writing more than they need to be producers-of-good writing.

—Lucy Calkins
Teacher Educator

At the beginning of the year, I'd write something and say, "Yeah! This is fine." Now I look back and say, "No! This can be changed. This is not right." I'm a little bit more picky. If you're being your best, you have to show that in your writing. By revising and getting things perfect, that shows how good you can be.

—Melissa
Fifth-Grader

As a second prewriting activity, Gabbie did a quickwrite to let her own thoughts run free and then capture them on paper, discovering what she knew and how she felt about the frightening moments in her life. Next, her teacher had her think about the audience for her story, her purposes for writing it, and the form she would use. She decided she would write and illustrate a picture book for her younger brother and two older sisters, one that would be funny and scary at the same time.

During the next stage, *drafting*, Gabbie wrote a rough draft of her story, trying to keep her audience and purposes in mind. Gabbie went through three drafts before she felt ready to share her story with her classmates to get their feedback. When she did read her story to a small group of classmates, they responded to what she had written, giving her positive feedback on some aspects of her story and suggesting what she might think about for her next revision.

Revising the story—reviewing it in light of the comments she received from her classmates and rewriting it—was the next stage in the process. Here, Gabbie reworked her composition by adding, deleting, changing, and moving words, sentences, and even whole sections. During this stage, Gabbie's main interest was in making the story "work." Does it make sense? Is it scary *and* funny? Would her brother and sisters like it?

After Gabbie was satisfied that she had done what she could to tell the story she wanted in the way she wanted, she began *editing* the piece. Here she focused on mechanical elements such as grammar, punctuation, and spelling. This proofreading process required that Gabbie hunt word by word for errors, a different focus from the revising stage, in which she concentrated on the meaning she was creating.

The last stage of the process, *publishing*, involved a sharing of the work. At this time, Gabbie keyed her story into a word processor, printed it, cut it into sections, and pasted them in the pages of a booklet. Then she drew pictures to accompany her text. A sample of her work is shown in Figure 9.1.

The Noise in the Laundry Chute
written and illustrated by
Gabbie Hooper

Once there was a girl named Sara. Every night she heard a tap, tap, tap. She was too afraid to go across the hallway because she had to pass the laundry chute to get to her mom and dad's room.

One day Sara told her brother about the chute, but her brother said, "It's just your imagination."
"No it's not," she said.

The next night Sara sprinted past the laundry chute, but she got too tired when she got to the chute and Sara had to rest... but then... tap, tap, tap. Sara leaped up and ran to her mom and dad.

Her mother was there in their room but her dad wasn't. Her mom said, "Your dad was fixing a hole in the roof at night so you wouldn't get bothered during the day. He waited till he thought you were asleep and it made a sound like tap, tap, tap, by the chute."

FIGURE 9.1 *Gabbie's Book:* The Noise in the Laundry Chute

To me, revision is like taking off the shell of the nut and ripping out the meat. It doesn't do anything for the length of the story. It doesn't do anything for the glory of the story. It just makes it make sense. That's all that counts in revision—making sense.

—Zach
Fifth-Grader

The situation we have just described merely gives highlights of what is in reality a very complex and recursive process. Writers don't simply move lockstep from one stage to another; they repeatedly move back and forth between the processes involved in prewriting, drafting, revising, and editing, as the writing task dictates. Additionally, no two writers approach writing in exactly the same manner, and the same writer writes differently at different times. The scenario about Gabbie presented a *general characterization* of the writing process. To be sure, virtually all formal and polished writing is the product of a relatively lengthy and multifaceted process that involves thinking, drafting, and revising. However, the process itself is not always the same. Different writers, different topics, different purposes, and myriad other factors will affect the writing process.

Informal Writing

As we noted earlier, whereas formal writing represents one very important sort of writing for students to engage in, a lot of their writing in relation to their reading will not involve the process approach and thus will *not* involve prewriting, drafting, revising, editing, and publishing. Typically, a student does informal writing for her own purposes—to learn from her reading, to better understand ideas, and to explore or personally engage with what she is reading. This writing will take the form of notes, lists, diagrams, journals, summaries, and the like. Much of this writing will be a one-step process. For example, in response to her teacher's prompt "What makes you scared?", first-grader Erin writes her feelings in a journal (Figure 9.2). Third-grader Michael reads a chapter in Barbara Parks's *Junie B. Jones and a Little Monkey Business*, jots down his reaction to Junie's treatment of her new baby brother, and returns to those notes only when he is deciding how he wants to present his thoughts on Junie in his literature circle.

Sometimes, of course, informal writing will involve more than one step, as fifth-grader Twega testifies:

> I don't know why, but I can't remember very much when I read in our history book, so I take notes—lots of them—as I read. Ms. Stallman has us meet in "history circles" the day after we read a chapter to talk about what we've learned, and I don't want to sit there looking dumb with nothing to say! So I'd better be prepared. After I take these notes, I go back through them before our circle meets and underline the things I think are really important. Usually I even take my notes to the circle. After we discuss the chapter in our history circle, I sometimes make a few additions or changes in the notes. Why? Because Ms. Stallman usually tells us she is going to give us a quiz on the chapter and I want to have the right answers!!!

Twega, Fifth-Grader

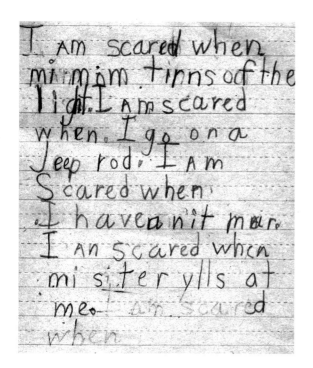

FIGURE 9.2   *Erin's Journal Entry on Feelings*

The point here is not that Erin, Michael, or Twega illustrates *the* correct way to do informal writing; instead, the point is that there are many, many ways to do informal writing. Students need to know this and be given the freedom to explore different alternatives.

Reflection AND *Application*

1. We have discussed reading and writing as being reciprocal and parallel processes or "two sides of the same coin." Explain what this idea means to you.

2. Envision a classroom of elementary school students. What are some concrete things you might do to establish these attitudes: "We are all readers and writers; together we are learning to be better readers and writers"?

3. We have just given a few examples of situations in which the process approach is appropriate and situations in which informal writing is called for. Think about your own writing experiences in elementary school. What did you write? For what audiences did you write? Did any of your writing take you through the various processes we talked

about in this section? What sorts of informal writing did you do? At this point, jot down the types of writing elementary students might do that illustrate both the process approach and informal kinds of writing.

SOME FORMS AND PURPOSES OF WRITING

As we have already discussed, in a typical elementary classroom students will be writing for a variety of different reasons and for different audiences. Some writing—such as editorials, reports, and stories—is fairly formal and will require prewriting, drafting, revising. Other types—such as writing summaries or responding to literature in a journal—are more informal and typically don't require drafting or revising. In this section, we take a look at some of the types of writing elementary students are likely to find most useful and talk about when, why, and how each type should take place. They are listed here:

- Writing to learn and understand
  - Note taking
  - Brainstorming and quickwriting
  - Semantic mapping
  - Venn diagram
  - K-W-L
  - Journals
- Writing to communicate
  - Letters
  - Biographies
  - Reports
- Imaginative writing
  - Stories
  - Poems

As you can see, we have divided the types into three broad categories. However, we want to stress that these categories only suggest what is *generally* the purpose or nature of the various types. We by no means intend to suggest a rigid category system or imply that the various types do not overlap in a number of ways. For example, a student could write a story or poem in her journal; a Venn diagram might constitute part of a report; and students could brainstorm topics for poems. These loosely defined categories can however, serve as a reminder that students can profitably undertake many sorts of writing to enrich and complement reading.

Writing to Learn and to Understand

Often, we use writing as a vehicle to learn about something or to more fully understand it. When students take this stance, they are using written language to help them wrestle with information, ideas, feelings, and intuitions. Reading done in subject matter areas such as science, social studies, and literature offers rich opportunities for this kind of writing, which fosters comprehension and personal response. In this kind of writing, students are actually "thinking on paper" or perhaps on a computer screen. In other words, they are using written language to discover, clarify, refine, expand, or reflect on meaning.

James Britton and his colleagues (1975) have noted that this type of writing is closely related to talk, and Richard Vacca and Wayne Linek (Vacca & Linek, 1992) point out that such writing can serve as a catalyst for reading and studying content area material. In fact, many of the writing-to-learn activities we discuss are often accompanied by small-group discussion centered on the topics students are writing about.

What kinds of writing can students do to help them better learn, understand, and personally respond to the information and ideas in the texts they read? To enhance their ability to "think on paper" and actively integrate new knowledge into old? To prepare them for the more formal genres such as reports and stories? Note taking, brainstorming, quickwriting, semantic mapping, using the Venn diagram and the K-W-L procedure, and journaling are the ones we discuss in this section. You will notice that we described many of these procedures in Chapter 6 when we talked about helping students comprehend the various texts they read. Here, we focus on the writing component of these endeavors.

> It's by writing about a subject we're trying to learn that we reason our way to what it means. Reasoning is a lost skill of the TV generation, with their famously short attention span. Writing can help them get it back.
>
> —*William Zinsser*
> *Writer*

Note Taking

Although note taking is perhaps the most traditional of all the activities we discuss in this section, students do not pick it up naturally. To help students learn how to take notes, Regie Routman (1991) recommends using demonstration, participation, practice, and sharing in a variety of note-taking situations. These situations include taking notes from texts, oral presentations, films, and videos. To be successful at note taking, students not only need repeated practice in the skill, but they also need to have it demonstrated to them again and again throughout the school year.

The following sample lesson is adapted from a procedure Routman and third-grade teacher Julie Beers did with a group of third-graders who were getting ready to begin research reports on animals:

IN THE CLASSROOM
Sample Lesson on Note Taking

1. Make a transparency out of the first page of the selection students will be reading, and leave the other half of the page blank. (For example, Routman and Beers made a transparency of the page on alligators and crocodiles from *Zoo Books* [Wildlife Education, Ltd., 1986].) This transparency will be used on an overhead projector to demonstrate note taking.
2. Slowly read the passage aloud, highlighting key phrases and important information by underlining them with a yellow marker. Verbalize the thought processes you go through in deciding what to highlight. Demonstrate to students how to turn these key phrases into notes by writing these key phrases on the right side of the transparency.
3. Demonstrate the process several times with additional pages from the text, inviting students to participate in choosing the notes to write down.
4. Have students form small groups. Give each group a photocopied page from the book they will read, a blank transparency, and two pens—a yellow highlighter and black marking pen for writing on transparencies.
5. Tell students to place the blank transparency over the article and underline key phrases and important points with the yellow marker (as you had done earlier as a whole class) and then write their notes on the right side of the page with the black marking pen.
6. Invite each group to come up to the overhead projector with the completed transparency. Ask members to place it over a transparency of the text they had just read, and encourage them to discuss their notes. Give feedback and guidance on their note taking and invite other students to give feedback as well.

In evaluating the effectiveness of this procedure, Routman offers the following suggestions for additional work on note taking:

- Have students work in pairs instead of groups, with one acting as scribe and the other giving suggestions and feedback.
- Allow students to take notes on their first reading of the material with their books open.
- Repeat note-taking sessions throughout the year, giving teaching demonstrations and working with various genres and contexts.

Brainstorming and Quickwriting

When brainstorming, students quickly jot down single words or short phrases that come to mind in response to a topic. For example, before a group of third-graders read Jennifer Owings Dewey's *At the Edge of the Pond*, they brainstormed words and phrases that the word *pond* brought to mind and came up with this list:

water	frogs	pollywogs	weeds	woods	forest
ducks	green	slime	mud	turtles	ducks

And before sixth-graders read *Free to Dream*, Audrey Osofsky's biography of the poet Langston Hughes, they wrote down words and phrases in response to the word *poet*. Brainstorming can be done individually, as a small-group activity, or as a whole-class activity; and it can be done before or after reading. However it is done, brainstorming generally leaves students with some raw material that they will employ as they read or write.

In contrast to brainstorming, quickwriting—a technique popularized by Peter Elbow (1973)—is a way of very quickly getting down connected sentences and phrases on a topic without stopping to correct or analyze them. Simply stated, quickwriting is merely jotting down thoughts on a topic as quickly as they come to mind. Because the students are not worrying about mechanics, structure, or communicating their ideas to someone else, they are free to generate many thoughts and ideas, and they gain confidence and fluency in writing. Below is an example of a quickwrite a seventh-grade student did in response to her teacher's request that she write down what she envisioned in a story she was reading to them (Langer, 1995, p. 62):

> Well, first I see the planet. I see any streets flooded.
> All the forest are like marshland and there are many
> insects flying everywhere. The sky is always cloudy and
> the plans look small and sickly.

Like brainstorming, quickwriting is a strategy students can use as a pre-reading or postreading activity. Quickwriting before students read a text can help them relate the reading to their lives and activate and build schemata, bringing ideas from the subconscious level to the conscious level. For example, before third- or fourth-graders read any one of Joanna Cole's Magic School Bus books, they might do a quickwrite on what they know about the topic of the book—the human body, for example. Or, as a postreading activity after reading Russell Freedman's *Eleanor Roosevelt*, sixth-graders could quickwrite on what they discovered to be the most memorable moments in this biography.

Both brainstorming and quickwriting are excellent strategies for generating ideas. Students can be invited to engage in these activities before or after they read a particular text. Both can also be very effective strategies for gathering thoughts and ideas in the beginning stages of formal writing.

Semantic Mapping, the Venn Diagram, and K-W-L

These three strategies all make use of brainstorming to some degree, but take it a step or two further by organizing the brainstormed ideas in a specific way.

As we discussed in Chapter 6, in semantic mapping (also called clustering or webbing), words generated in brainstorming are linked to a nucleus word, which reflects a main idea. This nucleus word functions in much the same way as the main idea in an outline.

Semantic maps can have one nucleus idea or several and can be used with both narrative and informational texts. Students can develop them individually or as a small- or large-group activity, and they can be used either as a prereading activity to activate prior knowledge or as a postreading activity to recall and organize pertinent information (Heimlich & Pittelman, 1986). As a prereading activity, a semantic map can activate knowledge on a particular topic before students read a selection. As a postreading activity, it can serve as a helpful prewriting technique preceding more formal writing, such as reports, stories, or biographies. Figure 9.3 shows a semantic map developed by first-graders after reading "Kate and the Zoo," a story from a basal series.

Like the semantic map, the Venn diagram is a way to organize ideas and present them graphically. However, with the Venn diagram, two or more topics or ideas are contrasted. Consisting of circles that intersect, the diagram highlights the similarities and differences between topics. The differences are indicated by words or phrases written in the nonoverlapping parts of the circles, the similarities in the space created by the intersection of the circles. Figure 9.4 shows how one group of fifth-graders used the Venn

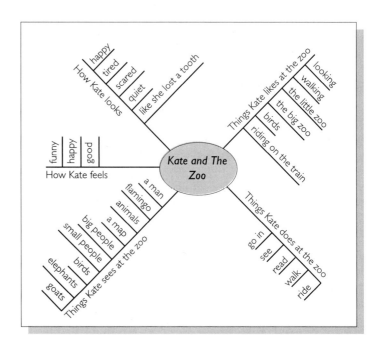

FIGURE 9.3 *Semantic Map Used with First-Graders After Reading "Kate and the Zoo"*

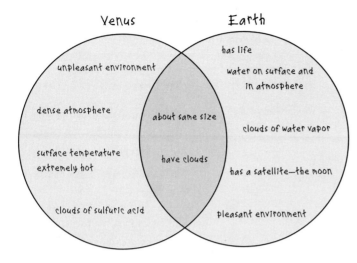

Venus

unpleasant environment

dense atmosphere

surface temperature extremely hot

clouds of sulfuric acid

about same size

have clouds

Earth

has life

water on surface and in atmosphere

clouds of water vapor

has a satellite—the moon

pleasant environment

FIGURE 9.4 *Venn Diagram Comparing and Contrasting Earth and Venus*

diagram to compare and contrast the planets Earth and Venus after reading the chapter "Members of Our Solar System" in their science text, *Science in Our World* (Hackett & Moyer, 1991).

The Venn diagram is a particularly effective device for students to use when reading informational texts in which two or more topics are being compared and contrasted. It can also be used to compare and contrast stories that have similar themes, such as *Prairie Songs* by Pam Conrad and *Sarah, Plain and Tall* by Patricia MacLachlan, or with characters in the same story, such as Prince Brat and Jemmy in Sid Fleischman's *The Whipping Boy*.

In Chapter 6, we described K-W-L as a group procedure for engaging students in the informational texts they read. However, as we illustrate here, it can also be used by individual students as a writing-to-learn tool. Figure 9.5 is an example of how K-W-L was used by a fourth-grader reading *The Magic School Bus on the Ocean Floor* by Joanna Cole.

Journals

Perhaps you have used journals yourself, either for personal reasons or as a learning tool in academic classes. If so, you're probably not alone, for journal writing is a widely recommended procedure. Chris Anson and Richard Beach (1995) view the journal as a genre in its own right and a "significant tool for learning" (p. 12). Toby Fulwiler (1988) suggests that journaling engages the writer in a vast range of cognitive activities—observing, questioning, speculating, becoming aware of oneself, digressing, synthesizing, revising, and informing. Routman (1991) describes the journal as a "nonthreatening place to explore learnings, feelings, happenings, and language through writing"

What I Know	What I would like to know	What I found out
The ocean is deep.	How deep is it?	Didn't find out!!!
The ocean has fish.	What kind of fish?	hermit crabs, sea urchins, jelly fish, squid, scallops—No! these are invertebrates—animals without backbones—not fish!!!
The ocean is salty.	Why is it salty?	Salt comes from the rocks! When the rocks are worn down by the water, the salt goes into the water.
The ocean has plants.	What kind of plants.	seaweed, plankton
Fish breathe under water.	How do fish breathe?	Fish have gills that can take oxygen from the water. Water flows into the fish's mouth then the gill, and out through the slits in the fish's sides.
The ocean has waves.	What makes the waves?	The wind!

FIGURE 9.5 *Sample K-W-L for* The Magic School Bus on the Ocean Floor

(p. 197) and of significant benefit to both teacher and student. Here we list some of the specific benefits Routman highlights:

- Promotes fluency in writing
- Promotes fluency in reading
- Encourages risk taking
- Provides opportunity for reflection
- Validates personal experiences and feelings
- Provides a safe, private place to write
- Promotes thinking and makes it visible
- Promotes development of written language conventions
- Provides a vehicle for evaluation
- Provides a personal record for students

Four types of journals—reading logs, learning logs, double-entry journals, and dialogue journals—are particularly effective for developing reading–writing connections and promoting thinking and learning.

Response journals encourage students to make personal connections with the texts they read.

Reading Logs. Reading logs, sometimes called response journals, are journals in which students record *personal responses* to the literature they read. Before students write in their journals, you will want to talk about some of the topics they might write about and model how you write responses in your own reading journal. First-grade teacher Barbara Werchadlo (Wollman-Bonilla & Werchadlo, 1995) talks about how she introduced response journals to her first-graders when she first began using them.

> During the first full week of school, I began reading aloud a chapter each day from an engaging book such as *James and the Giant Peach* by Roald Dahl. For the first two days after reading I modeled a response, expressing a few ideas by thinking aloud and then writing a sentence such as *James is very sad because his parents are gone* or, *James does not like living with Aunt Sponge and Aunt Spiker.*
>
> Beginning on the third day, children wrote their own responses to Dahl's book in journals I have prepared for them. I stapled sheets of 9 × 12" picture-story paper (paper blank on top and lined on the bottom) between sheets of manila paper, which served as a cover. I asked students to write about the story, with my prompting "What did you think about this chapter?" or "What do you think will happen?" I also invited them to illustrate their responses when they had finished writing, and most began doing so early in the year.
>
> Barbara Werchadlo, first-grade teacher

After reflecting on the outcomes of her first experience using response journals, Mrs. Werchadlo decided to provide more modeling of varied responses and prompts that were even more open-ended. She did this in order to help children view journals not as a place to simply retell or predict what might happen in a text, but rather as a place to react personally. The following is a list of possible open-ended questions:

How does the story make you feel?

Does anything puzzle you? If so, explain.

Do the characters seem real to you? Why or why not?

Are you enjoying the story? Why or why not?

Is there a word or words that you particularly like? What are they, and why do you like them?

Does anything in the story remind you of your own life?

Is anything the author says particularly meaningful to you? Why?

Figure 9.6 provides a sample entry in a fifth-grade student's reading log, written after she has read the first chapter of *Baby* by Patricia MacLachlan.

Learning Logs.   In contrast to reading logs or response journals, learning logs are generally oriented to subject matter rather than personal response and are used in content areas such as science, mathematics, and social studies. They can include a variety of entries—questions to the author, summaries of the material, explanations of problems solved, or recording of observations as in an experiment. As Stephen Koziol, Brad Minnick, and Kim Riddell (1996) observe, one important function of learning logs is to enable students to select, connect, and organize knowledge in ways that allow them to better understand what they read. They have suggested three types of questions for learning logs: questions that elicit prior knowledge, questions that encourage students to interact with the text, and questions that ask students to respond retrospectively to what they have learned. Figure 9.7 shows a question and a response for each of these three types, related to the book *Hurricane! Nature's Most Destructive Force* by Margo Sorenson.

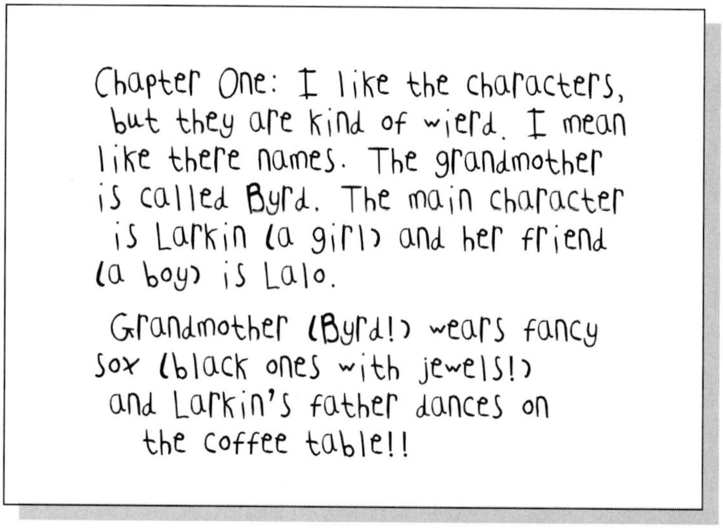

Chapter One: I like the characters, but they are kind of wierd. I mean like there names. The grandmother is called Byrd. The main character is Larkin (a girl) and her friend (a boy) is Lalo.

Grandmother (Byrd!) wears fancy sox (black ones with jewels!) and Larkin's father dances on the coffee table!!

FIGURE 9.6   *Reading Log Entry*

Anticipatory Question:

Example: What do you want to know about hurricanes?

Sample response: I'd like to know why they happen near the Atlantic ocean. You always hear about hurricanes hitting Florida, and North and South Carolina and places like that. Why not hurricanes in Kansas? Or California? California's next to an ocean, isn't it?!

Reactive Question:

Example: What didn't you understand about hurricanes?

Sample response: About global warming. Why some scientists think it's to blame for all the hurricanes in 1992. This was confusing to me. I think I need to read this section again more carefully.

Retrospective Question:

Example: What did you learn about hurricanes that meant the most to you?

Sample response: I learned I don't want to be in one! But if I am, I want to be in a good house, like the ones built by Habitat for Humanity that didn't fall down in Hurricane Andrew!

FIGURE 9.7 *Three Types of Learning Log Questions and Responses*

From Kozoil, S. M., Minnick, J. B., & Riddell, K. (1996). *Journals for active learning: A two-day workshop module for primary teachers in Bosnia.* Pittsburgh: PA: University of Pittsburgh International Institute for Studies in Education.

Double-Entry Journals. These are two-columned journals that can be used when reading any type of text. In the left column, students might write a selected passage from the text, and in the right column their comments, questions, or responses to the passage. Or, instead of writing quotations or passages from the text in the left column, the student might write about events, characters, or settings in the left column and then make personal comments on them in the right one. Figure 9.8 shows a sample page from a double-entry journal made by a student reading Patricia MacLachlan's *Baby*.

Dialogue Journals. In this type of journal, a teacher and a student, or two students, carry on a written conversation over a designated period of time. Here is a typical example from a fourth-grader. She and her teacher are

In the Story	My Response
Chapter 1 (Page 7) Mama was covered with flecks and smears of paint, and I could tell by the colors what she was working on. The Island. Mama was a walking landscape.	Ha! Grown-ups can be messy when they paint. I want to be an artist—a painter. I want to be a walking landscape. Cool!
Chapter 5 (Page 40) Sophie liked carrots and didn't like milk. <u>Beets were for spitting.</u>	I love that! <u>Peas</u> are for spitting and <u>brocolli</u>, too. Yuk!
Chapter 11 (Page 85. Ms Minifred is talking about her brother who died) "He had marked this poem, so I knew it was important to him. When I read it I felt a strange and powerful comfort—not because it made me feel better, but because it said what I felt."	I agree with Ms. Minifred. Some stories can do that too. Words put together the right way can make you <u>feel</u> something. It's true. I wonder why? Strange.

FIGURE 9.8 *Page from a Double-Entry Journal*

dialoguing about a book the teacher recommended, *The Zebra Wall* by Kevin Henkes.

Dear Mrs. G,
I'm on chapter 3 of <u>The Zebra Wall.</u> I know how A feels because I felt that way too when my mom had a baby. So much was going on. I felt kind of forgotten like A does. Do you like the way the author writes? I think he's a good writer. The way he writes is funny but kind of sad too. What do you think?

Dear Andrea,
I'm glad you're enjoying <u>The Zebra Wall.</u> Yes, I think Kevin Henkes is an excellent writer. You said it very well—he does make you laugh and feel sad at the same time. I'd never thought about it before! You are a thoughtful reader.

The dialogue journal can be used to help students become more aware of the power of language (Mode, 1989), become more comfortable writing and more willing to write (Britton et al., 1975), realize the experience of writing about familiar topics to known others (Moffett, 1968), and assist students from varied backgrounds in learning to write (Fulwiler, 1987).

The following list gives suggestions for how to respond to students' writing in a dialogue journal (Staton, 1987):

- Acknowledge students' ideas, and encourage them to continue to write about their interests.
- Support students by complimenting their behavior and schoolwork.
- Provide new information about topics, so that students will want to read your responses.
- Write less than the students do.
- Avoid nonspecific comments, such as "good idea" or "very interesting."
- Ask few questions. Instead, encourage students to ask you questions.

Before leaving the topic of journals, a word of caution: Do not overuse them. All writing forms have a time and a place. Variety is the spice of the student writer's life.

In this section we have highlighted just a few of the many ways writing can be used to help students read, understand, respond to literature, and learn subject matter, as well as to prepare them to write to communicate to an audience what they learned. Whatever the writing form students use, you will want to remind them that the primary goal is to get them to think about what they are learning, to try to make sense of the reading experience, and to discover meaning for themselves and their lives. This, of course, is what gives learning its real purpose.

Reflection AND Application

4. Think about the term *writing to learn*. What does it mean to you? Discuss your response with a classmate or classmates.

5. In addition to journal writing, five writing-to-learn activities were discussed in this section. Give an example of an appropriate reading situation for using each of these five techniques. For example, when might it be appropriate for students to take notes? To quickwrite? To use K-W-L?

6. Recount some of the benefits that you have personally gained from each of the sorts of writing described in this section, as a student or in your life more generally. If you haven't used any of the techniques, find a classmate who has, and discuss her experiences.

Writing to Communicate

While students do some writing primarily to learn and understand, they do other writing in order to communicate. When we talk about writing as communication, four interrelated factors are always involved—audience (who), purpose (why), content (what), and form (how). Read again Ms. Chavez's letter at the beginning of this chapter. Can you identify these four factors in her letter? Who is the audience? What is the purpose for this written communication? What are the content and the form? The audience is the second-graders in Ms. Chavez's class. Ms. Chavez's purpose in writing is to thank her students, both because she wanted her students to know how much she cared for them and because she wanted to reinforce their positive attitudes and actions. The content is Ms. Chavez's feelings, thoughts, and observations; and the form is a personal letter. When students write to communicate, they need to be aware of these factors. Very often, it is the audience, purpose, and content that determine the form the writing will take. Three particularly useful forms to use in conjunction with reading are letters, reports, and biographies, which we discuss here.

Before beginning this discussion, however, we want to stress how important it is for children to read the various forms they are asked to write. As Courtney Cazden (1991) notes, "Children would not learn to speak a language they do not hear; how do we expect them to learn to write forms they do not read?" (p. 420). So the first rule of thumb is to make certain that students are reading the kinds of writing you ask them to do.

Letters

Letters are a wonderful way to highlight the reading–writing connection. Students can write formal letters to request something, express thanks, issue a complaint, or express a point of view. They might be addressed to businesses, government employees, authors and illustrators, and other adults. Formal letters are likely to go through several stages—drafting, revising, and editing. Informal letters, however, may or may not require drafting and revision. Students who have had plenty of experience writing letters can often pen a friendly letter just once before sending it off. Students can write informal letters to classmates, friends, relatives, and pen pals; and in these letters they can deal with reading-related topics such as stories, story characters, and other aspects of stories that they are particularly interested in. Teacher David Carberry has his fifth-graders write letters to first-graders, a writing task his students find particularly appealing. "The kids are very aware of taking their audience and purpose into account," Carberry says.

Students can also write simulated letters to or from fictional characters or to or from real people that they encounter in reading true narratives or in-

> Writing is, in essence, a social act. Every written page postulates the existence somewhere of its own reader.
>
> —Elizabeth Tallent
> Director of the
> Creative Writing Program
> at Stanford University

formational books. For example, a sixth-grader we know once composed a simulated letter to Eleanor Roosevelt, telling her what a great role model she was.

Students can also assume the role of a character in a story and write a letter to another one of the characters. In the following letter, a student assuming the persona of Miata in Gary Soto's *The Skirt* is writing to her friend Ana:

> Dear Ana,
> What is my mother going to say when she finds out I lost my folklorico skirt? She is going to be *so* mad! You've got to help me out!
>
> > Your amiga,
> > Miata

Or two students might take on the roles of characters in stories and write letters to each other about novel situations those characters might face. For example, one student might write a letter from Arnie's perspective and another from Philip's perspective after reading Nancy Carlson's *Arnie and the New Kid*:

> Dear Philip,
> I wish they would have given me a wheelchair like yours instead of these dumb crutches. Can you believe I broke my leg falling down some steps?
> > Arnie

> Dear Arnie,
> Sorry you broke your leg, but now I can do some things faster than you. Ha! Want to come over and play some video games?
> > Philip

One effective way to teach letter writing is to model the process, composing a letter in front of students (either on an overhead transparency or on the board) and explaining the thought processes you go through. Or, you can develop a letter as a class effort—a letter to invite parents to Back-to-School Night, for example.

Posting sample letters on a bulletin board or keeping a file folder or notebook of sample letters is also helpful to students when they write them on their own. Books that feature letters, such as *Dear Mr. Henshaw* by Beverly Cleary, *Sarah, Plain and Tall* by Patricia MacLachlan, *Nettie's Trip South* by Ann Turner, and *Casey Over There* by Staton Rabin, can provide good models of this form as well.

Biographies

Biographies are another type of writing in which a primary purpose is to communicate—in this case, communicating some of the events in a person's life. Biographies are a popular genre with children because they enjoy reading about real people and because biographies often represent fairly easy reading, following as they do the basic narrative form children are familiar with. Biographies written expressly for young readers range from picture books such as *A Picture Book of Martin Luther King, Jr.*, and *A Picture Book of Helen Keller*, both by David Adler, to in-depth portraits of noteworthy figures such as *Beyond the Myth: The Story of Joan of Arc* by Polly Schoyer Brooks. Biographers take a variety of approaches in presenting their subjects, some focusing on the historical, some on the sociological, and others on the internal conflicts the person faced.

After students have become familiar with the form and content of biographies through ample reading, a good place to start writing them is with a collaborative piece on a familiar subject. This should be someone they all know, perhaps a well-known figure in the school—a secretary, custodian, cafeteria worker, or principal. Once students have had some practice writing about people they know and have built some confidence in their skill with biography, they can write library-researched biographies in conjunction with the reading they do in subject matter areas, for example, biographies of historical figures, scientists, politicians, artists, sports figures, or a favorite author.

Reports

The best children's nonfiction, like good writing for any audience, does more than present a blizzard of facts; a theme organizes the chaos and makes it meaningful.

—*Jane Resh Thomas*
Children's Author
and Reviewer

In general, reports represent a more challenging writing and thinking task than biographies or letters, primarily because they usually do not follow the chronological, narrative structure children are so familiar with and because they often require students to use several sources of information. On the other hand, we are fortunate today in that an ever-increasing number of excellent models of informational writing are becoming readily available. More and more informational books and periodicals—which include everything from why animals have tails to the mechanics of spaceflight—are being written expressly for elementary-level students. Many of these informational materials are intriguing, relevant, and expertly crafted; and they provide excellent models for students' own writing of reports. The following is a list of a few such authors and titles.

Books by Exemplary Nonfiction Children's Book Authors

Science

Aliki. *Fossils Tell of Long Ago*. Crowell, 1990. This book tells what fossils are, how they are formed, what they teach us, where to find fossils, and how to make your own "one-minute-old" fossils. 40 pages. Available in Spanish.

Margery Facklam. *Creepy, Crawly Caterpillars*. Little, Brown, 1996. With bright illustrations and crisp prose, this edition provides an up-close and personal look at thirteen different types of the fascinating caterpillar. 32 pages.

Gail Gibbons. *The Stargazers*. Holiday House, 1992. Gibbons is an expert at depicting complicated subjects in a clear and simple style. In this book, one of her many on a variety of science-related topics, she talks about stars—how we can look at them, their names, and what they teach us. Unpaged.

Sandra Markle. *Outside and Inside Spiders*. Bradbury/Simon & Schuster, 1994. In a clear and energetic style, the author tells about the life of a spider, its traits and life processes information. Fascinating photos. 40 pages. A 1995 Outstanding Science Trade Book.

Laurence Pringle. *Scorpion Man*. Macmillan, 1994. Accompanied by photographs taken by the subject of this text—Gary Polis, the "scorpion man"—Pringle describes the fascinating work of this biologist and the creatures he studies. 42 pages.

Millicent Selsam. *How to Be a Nature Detective*. HarperCollins, 1995. In this text, Selsam shows readers how anyone can be a nature detective by learning to recognize clues, especially footprints, that tell which animals have been around. 32 pages.

Seymour Simon. *Winter Across America*. Hyperion, 1994. The beauty and harshness of winter, from Alaska to the southern United States, is depicted in clear prose and stunning photographs. A 1995 Outstanding Science Trade Book. 32 pages.

Social Studies

David A. Adler. *A Picture Book of Jesse Owens*. Holiday House, 1992. One of the books in Adler's Picture Book Biographies series, this title recreates the life history of Jesse Owens, hero of the 1936 Olympic Games in Berlin. Unpaged.

James Cross Giblin. *Fireworks, Picnics, and Flags*. Clarion, 1983. This book takes a spirited look at the social history behind our national holiday and the background of its symbols. 90 pages.

Russell Freedman. *Buffalo Hunt*. Holiday House, 1988. This Newbery Award–winning author portrays the importance of the buffalo in the life of the Indians of the Great Plains. 52 pages.

Jean Fritz. *China Homecoming*. Putnam, 1985. The author gives a poignant and touching account of her return to China, the country of her birth. 143 pages.

Patricia C. McKissack and Frederick McKissack. *Christmas in the Big House, Christmas in the Quarters*. Scholastic, 1994. The author depicts the last Christmas in Virginia before the Civil War and the fears and dreams of both Blacks and whites. A 1995 Coretta Scott King Award Book and 1995 Notable Children's Trade Book. 80 pages.

Milton Meltzer. *The Amazing Potato: A Story in Which the Incas, Conquistadors, Marie Antoinette, Thomas Jefferson, Wars, Famines, Immigrants, and French Fries All Play a Part*. HarperCollins, 1993. The author spins a sprightly history of one the earth's most nutritious foods, from its cultivation by the Incas to the french fry. 116 pages.

As Shelley Harwayne (1993) so aptly states, in addition to having numerous opportunities to read the sorts of materials they are asked to write, students also need to "develop the same hunger for learning and communicating what they find out" that professional writers demonstrate (p. 23). Harwayne suggests three lessons we can learn from professional nonfiction writers that we would do well to pass on to our students:

- They take learning about their subject seriously.
- They want to claim their information as their own by offering their own slant or perspective on it.
- They know their options and their audiences.

Spending time communicating these truths to students through the reading–writing opportunities you provide will pay off in their enthusiasm for writing and the quality of their products.

As defined here, reports include a range of informational writing that generally serves two purposes—to learn about a topic and to communicate that information through written language. A report can take any form—a paragraph on table manners, a picture book on sea animals (Figure 9.9), a page or two on pandas (Figure 9.10), or, as the following scenario reveals, a multimedia research report on water pollution. In fact, as the scenario on water pollution illustrates, a report will fairly frequently include elements other than text—charts, oral reporting, and perhaps a debate. The exact form of the report will match the content of the information, the writer's purpose, and the audience.

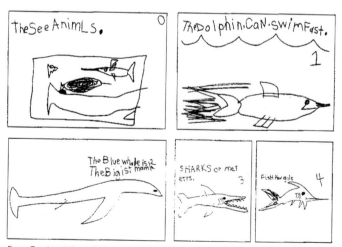

FIGURE 9.9 *Sample of a First-Grader's Picture Book on Sea Animals*

From *Teaching Writing Balance Process and Product* by Tompkins, Gail copyright © 1994. Reprinted by permission of Prentice-Hall, Inc.

What They Look Like

Giant Panda

The giant panda looks like a blown up black and white balloon that is just lying down in a pile of weeds. It looks like it doesn't weigh much, but it weighs 1,000 lbs. Now isn't that amazing!

Red Panda

The red panda looks like a deflated basketball with white spots on the bottom. Well, before I started researching I thought the red panda only weighed 8 pounds but . . . it doesn't. It weighs 80 or 90 lbs.

What They Eat

Besides eating bamboo, the panda loves honey. They stick their paws in a beehive or a honey tree and scoop out the honey for themselves. They like the honeycomb more. When they eat the honeycomb, bees sometimes get swallowed. Pandas, especially the giant panda, like cranberries or crabapples. The panda can't find these daily, like you find your breakfast. They have to walk a mile or so to find them.

How They Eat

As I told you about before, pandas like to eat honey. When they swallow bees it won't hurt, because they have a tough padding on their tongues so that a few bee stings won't hurt much.

Pandas are something like raccoons. They wash the food then feast.

FIGURE 9.10 *Elizabeth's Panda Report*

Excerpt from Harwayne, Shelley. (1993). Chutzpah and the Nonfiction Writer. *Pen in Hand: Children Become Writers*, Bernice E. Cullinan (Ed.), International Reading Association.

IN THE CLASSROOM
Four Fifth-Graders' Research Report on Water Purification

Pollution in the water supply has become a topic of widespread discussion in one Northeastern town. After an order to boil public water is issued and is covered extensively by the local media, a group of fifth-graders takes an interest in water purification. Four students—Tomas, Liz, Harrison, and Cecilia—decided to make water purification the subject of their inquiry project and prepare a presentation for the class. They name themselves the Water Purification Team.

   The four students spend a day reading different sources and talking among themselves to define the questions they will need to explore in more detail. After an initial conference with their teacher about which resources would be most useful, the students decide to begin their search with the newspaper and to seek out local sources of information. Working with the school librarian, Liz and Harrison uncover information that extends well beyond the encyclopedia, which had been the starting point for their research. A database search shows the availability of numerous books, films, free pamphlets, magazine articles, and other material. Cecilia and Tomas call the water company and talk to a spokesperson there. They also speak with a reporter who has written several articles on water supply problems for the local newspaper.

The students' research expands to include taped interviews with the water company representative and the reporter and a tour of the water plant. After reviewing all of the material gathered in their research, the students work together to outline their presentations. They divide their presentation into three parts: a description of how water purification works, using charts they drew; an explanation of how an aging piping system is causing the problems in the town's water supply; and a minidebate between Cecilia and Tomas about whether a new piping system should be funded by raising the cost of the water or by new taxes (an issue that had been raised, but not resolved, by the newspaper reporter). The presentation generates enthusiastic responses from their classmates, and the Water Purification Team considers its project a major success. (International Reading Association and National Council of Teachers of English, 1996, pp. 50–51)

Briefly, here are a few recommendations for nurturing students' enthusiasm for and adeptness with report writing:

- Use a process approach. Provide students with time, opportunities, and guidance in prewriting, drafting, revising, editing, and possibly publishing.

- Scaffold students' efforts. Give them tasks in their zone of proximal development, and then follow the gradual release of responsibility model in handing over the task to them. For example, a class of second-graders that has been studying pond life and reading informational books on the subject could write a collaborative report or a big book on frogs or the relationship between animal life and plant life in a pond. Later, students could independently create their own books on different topics they read about.

- Offer minilessons on some aspect of the form students are using. For example, you might provide a lesson on collecting data or highlight a particular text structure such as compare and contrast.

- As often as possible, encourage students to choose their own topics and genres for reporting information. This requires previous and adequate experience with a variety of genres—cartoons, posters, documentary scripts, newspaper articles—if they are to successfully choose their own form for communicating what they learn on a topic.

"Our daily classroom newspaper is a whole class shared writing activity and one of the best mini-lessons I have for helping children learn about the mechanics of writing. The students are actively engaged in constructing sentences about classroom projects and events in their lives. It's their newspaper and they know it." Barbara Brunetti

Imaginative Writing

In addition to writing to learn and writing to communicate, students deserve and will profit from opportunities to do some imaginative writing in conjunction with the literature and content area texts they read. Such writing should include not just stories and poems, but also creative and expressive forms such as play scripts, song lyrics, and riddles, as well writing that will challenge students to think imaginatively about math concepts. With all of these forms, the writer's intent is more to entertain, evoke feelings, or stimulate imaginative thinking than to inform, and the writing experience is quite different than it is with more prosaic forms.

Literature is the province of imagination, and stories, in whatever guise, are meditations on life.

—*Paula Fox*
Children's Author

Here, we suggest a few possibilities for inviting students to try writing imaginatively in conjunction with the reading they do. As always, step number one is to immerse students in the kinds of writing you are inviting them to do. Along with the reading of these various texts, you might present a minilesson on an element particular to that form—how to create a setting in a fictional piece or how to write imaginative math concepts as depicted in the following lesson.

IN THE CLASSROOM
Writing Imaginative Mathematic Scenarios and Questions

1. On a chalkboard or overhead projector, display a mathematical word problem. For example, let us say students have just read the following problem in their math book or found a similar situation described in a trade book they have read:

    > Brad saw a garage sale sign that read: Baseball cards—cheap! He fished in his pocket and found two dimes, a nickel, and five pennies. At the garage sale he discovered cards at two prices: Perfect cards = ten cents. Imperfect cards = five cents.

2. Have students read through the problem and discuss the kinds of questions they might develop out of the situation. As a whole class, work through a variety of examples. For instance,

    > What is the largest number of cards Brad could buy? The largest number of perfect cards? What is the largest number of perfect cards Brad can buy if he also buys imperfect cards? If Brad purchases one perfect card, how many imperfect cards can he buy? What did Brad buy if he spent all his money? What did Brad buy if he had a dime left?

3. As a whole-class shared writing activity, compose another mathematical situation and questions to go with it.

4. When students are ready to work on their own, have them form groups and write similar word problems and imaginative questions about these mathematical situations.

5. Have students exchange their word problems and questions with another group. Make sure students work through their own word problems and questions to confirm that they are doable before giving them to another group of students to read and answer.

Fiction

Writing fiction provides another opportunity for students to express themselves in creative ways and to explore a topic by giving their imaginations free reign. For example, after a unit on how various species adapt to their environment, Diann Stone, a teacher in Anchorage, Alaska, had her fifth- and sixth-grade students create and write about an imaginary creature. She had them select an environment with which they were familiar—in this case, their own neighborhoods—and create a creature who would dwell in that environment. Along with drawing a map of the creature's environment, students wrote a fictional report that included what this creature would look like, what it would eat, and its habits.

The "create a creature" project was the culmination of a unit on animal habitats, adaptation, and survival. Ms. Stone's students had done extensive reading and study of the subject (which included a number of field trips to

All writers know that *What if* is the phrase that ignites fiction.

—*Lois Lowry*
Newbery Award–Winning
Children's Author

wildlife habitats). Ms. Stone also had sufficiently prepared them to tackle all the cognitive tasks required in this project before they began. She also supported their efforts while they gathered their data, made their maps, created their creatures, and wrote about them. In other words, she built a sturdy scaffold to make certain that they were successful through the beginning, middle, and culmination of their efforts.

Poetry

One approach to poetry writing is to introduce a variety of poems that relate to a theme or topic your class is studying and reading about. For example, one third-grade teacher reads students a variety of "weather" poetry in conjunction with a unit they do on weather. After reading "Weather Is Full of the Nicest Sounds" by Aileen Fisher and discussing all the wonderful sounds with students, students perform it as a choral reading. Next, she invites students to try writing other types of weather poems—"Weather Is Full of the Nicest Smells" or "Weather Is Full of the Funniest Sights."

> A poem . . . begins as a lump in the throat, a sense of wrong, a homesickness, a lovesickness.
>
> —*Robert Frost*
> *Poet*

Poetry can be written in response to anything children read. For example, after reading about the Gold Rush, students could write poetry about some aspect of that particular slice of American history. Or after reading about the weather, they could write a cloud poem, as did second-grader Lucy (Figure 9.11) or a variation of the Japanese tanka on the horse as Julie did (Figure 9.12) after reading several of Marguerite Henry's horse stories.

Nimbostratus
by Lucy Hooper, second grade

Yuckey!
Nasty!
Dismal!
Nimbostratus clouds
are like a witch's huge black
hat with spiders' webs all over it.
Dismal!
Dreary!

FIGURE 9.11   *Student Poetry Sample*

HORSES
by Julie Graves, fourth grade

Horses
swift, gallant
great flowing manes
and large flying tales
beautiful!

FIGURE 9.12   *Student Poetry Sample*

Good creative writing is a marriage between great creativity and great structure. I want kids and teachers to know that a story has a beginning, a middle, and an end, and the creativity isn't just a free-for-all, a time for students to do anything they wish. Structure isn't going to stop creativity; rather, it gives creativity form.

—Jack Gantos
Children's Author

You will find wonderful examples of poetry on almost any subject imaginable to read to your students, which will inspire them to express themselves in this special form as well.

Intrinsic in each of the types of writing we have discussed in this section and the previous one is that it is meant to be read. The writer creates a letter, biography, report, story, or poem with an audience and purpose in mind—to inform, entertain, persuade, evoke feelings, and tickle or challenge the imagination. Additionally, as with any writing students do, sufficient scaffolding must be provided before students begin the writing and during the actual writing processes. Careful motivation, preparation, modeling, encouragement, coaching, and feedback are *crucial* to success.

Reflection AND Application

7. Think of a piece of writing you have done recently, and briefly answer these four questions about it: Who was the audience? What was your purpose? What was the content? What form did you use?

8. Make a list of writing you have done recently for which you used a process approach and a list of writing that did not require a process approach. Compare the lists you developed with those of a classmate or classmates.

9. Think of a piece of writing you have done for which you went through several stages before you finished the piece. Briefly describe the process you went through. Compare your process with that described on pages 390–392.

10. If you wanted to ensure that your students were successful in writing reports on a topic they had been reading about, what are some of the steps you would take to guide them to success? Be as specific as possible in your explanation.

TEACHER AND STUDENT OPPORTUNITIES AND RESPONSIBILITIES

In the previous section, we discussed the various types of writing that students are likely to do in conjunction with their reading. Here we talk about two opportunities that writing offers—using the writing workshop and publishing—and one responsibility that teachers and students share—responding to the writing students do.

The Writing Workshop

April 16, 1996

      Professor Graves suggested I visit Barbara Brunetti's first grade class at MacGregor School to observe her writing workshop. So here I am. It is Wednesday, 9:00 AM. I don't know exactly what I expected, but it is not what I'm seeing and hearing. In order to write, I guess I always thought you had to sit still and be quiet. But as I walk around the room, I overhear Chelsey and Mao Mao talking about a book they are planning to write. "We need to make the witch ugly," Mao Mao says. "Really ugly," says Chelsey. She makes a face and they giggle. Jordan is bent over his paper, writing a story about a kite. Corey, Byron, Adam, and Noah sit in a circle on the rug, reading and discussing stories they have written. Anna is pinning up her finished story on the bulletin board. Hiroto drops a finished draft in the "publishing basket." Mrs. Brunetti talks with Alexis about a piece he has written. I'm impressed how engaged these kids are in what they're doing. Even though there is movement and talking, they seem to be able to concentrate. I glance up at a colorful poster that advertises:

WE WORK ON WRITING. WE WORK HARD. WE USE QUIET VOICES.

Indeed, that is what these kids are doing. So this is what a writing workshop looks like. I wonder how Barbara created an atmosphere like this?

This journal entry records a preservice teacher's observations as she observed a writing workshop. But just what is a writing workshop? Simply stated, a writing workshop is a designated time during the school day when children write on topics of their own choosing, for their own purposes. This writing can take place several times a week or, in some classrooms, every day, and is done by students individually or collaboratively. As Charles Temple and his colleagues (1993) point out, the writing workshop provides a setting in which children's "own interest in life, coupled with their desire to express themselves" (p. 163), motivates them to write.

Over the past 20 years, educators have discovered that when students know they will have a chunk of time to write, a time in which they will be actively involved in writing for reasons that are important to them, they really develop as writers. Donald Graves (1983) suggests that it takes at least three hours a week for this habit of mind to take hold, where students are "rehearsing off stage" what they will write about (p. 223). The writing workshop—a concept developed by Nancy Atwell (1987) and a number of other teachers and researchers—is designed to provide your writers with that sort of time.

A typical writing workshop has three phases—minilessons, writing time, and sharing time. The writing workshop begins with a minilesson in which the teacher provides instruction on a specific topic important to students' being successful with the writing they are doing or are going to do. Frequently, minilessons concentrate on three areas:

1. *Procedural matters*—such as how to work in groups, using word-processing programs, or managing portfolios
2. *Literary concepts*—such as using figurative language or developing setting, character, and plot
3. *Writing skills and strategies*—such as punctuation, usage, outlining, and semantic mapping

The majority of workshop time is devoted to actual writing. During this time, students work on their works in progress, while the teacher writes herself or engages in brief conferences with as many students as possible to respond to their writing, giving guidance, encouragement, and feedback. This is also a time when groups of students might meet to collaborate on projects or to read and respond to one another's works in progress.

During the last portion of the writing workshop, the whole class gathers together to share their writing. This sharing can take on a variety of different formats—a student reading a computer printout of her piece in the author's chair, a group of students who have collaborated on a story putting on a skit, or two students displaying a poster they have created on the life cycle of a butterfly. Generally, it works best if students sign up in advance to share, with two to four students sharing on any given day.

As Figure 9.13 illustrates, the lion's share of the workshop time is spent in writing and conferencing. The other two endeavors, minilessons and sharing, support this primary endeavor.

Both teacher and student have equally important roles in the writing workshop. The teacher's role is that of facilitator, coach, and guide, someone who establishes a community of writers who interact and support one another through all the phases of the writing process. The student's role is to write and to encourage and support other writers. Coupled with the wide reading that provides students with both content and form for their writing

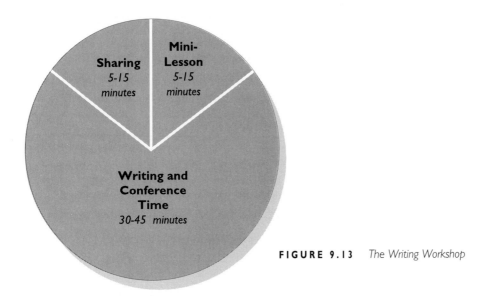

FIGURE 9.13   *The Writing Workshop*

and frequent opportunities to discuss their reading and their writing, writing workshop can be one important component of a rich and nurturing literate environment.

Publishing

There is something universal in Thomas Hine's expressed longing for "good paper and hard covers." And sometimes good paper and hard covers will be just the right format for kids' published works. However, books aren't the only publishing opportunity—charts, posters, articles, and radio or TV scripts might also be "published."

Publishing means making a work available to some "public" audience. This audience might be the writer's classmates, students in another class, the entire school, a broader audience such as a newspaper or magazine, or perhaps even an e-mail audience. Publishing highlights the importance of considering an audience while writing, and writing intended for publication is usually the result of the full writing process—brainstorming, drafting, revising, and editing. Although the larger audiences mentioned above are certainly possibilities, in many cases publishing will be accomplished by posting the work in the classroom. Wherever it goes, a lot of published work will have been produced with the aid of word processors, spell checkers, computerized dictionaries and thesauruses, and, in some cases, desktop publishing programs.

Like many journalists, I am often frustrated that my insights have, at most, a one-day shelf life, and I yearn for the relative immortality of good paper and hard covers.

—Thomas Hine
Newspaper Journalist

THE SWISS FAMILY ROBINSON
by Johann Wyss

What would you do if *you* were shipwrecked on a deserted island for *10* years? Go insane? Die? If you were lucky, survive? Who knows? In *The Swiss Family Robinson* that is exactly what happens to the Robinson family. Fritz, Ernest, Jack, Franz, and their mother and father are shipwrecked on an island for more than 10 years. Do they survive? You bet! They even had most of the conveniences of modern times. They manage to float from their ship and build a life for themselves on an island that becomes their home.

They have several homes and tons of animals including an ostrich, a falcon, and lots of farm animals. Once they have established a life on the island, they live a life of leisure and adventure.

To the end of the story: Fritz finds a girl named Jenny who had been shipwrecked for two years. Soon after finding her, they find a crew with a ship that got lost. When they have the chance to return to England, they realize how much they have come to love their island home.

Read the book to find out about their many adventures and what they decide about leaving their beloved island home!

Reviewed by Melissa Sanderson

FIGURE 9.14 *Student Review from* Just for Fun

> Children will have to be able to use technology to survive. And I'm not doing my job if I'm not preparing them to operate in this society.
>
> —*Connie Dumas*
> *Fifth-Grade Teacher*

In one of the more ambitious and sustained publishing projects we know of, Cheri Cooke's seventh-grade reading classes produce a bound volume of reviews of their favorite books each year (Cooke & Graves, 1995). They have been doing this now for five years, and each successive class of seventh-graders begs to do another volume. Figure 9.14 shows a review from one of their volumes, which they titled *Just for Fun*.

Responding to Students' Writing

To grow as readers and writers, students need to receive a variety of responses to their writing and to what their writing reveals about their reading. In Chapter 11, we will deal with assessment more generally and talk about how to evaluate students' reading–writing abilities. Here, we present a handful of suggestions on how to respond to students' writing in ways that will help them evaluate their own success at achieving their writing goals:

- Be positive. Emphasize what works in a piece first and more frequently than what doesn't—"Wow, you really got my attention with that great opening sentence!" Recall the emphasis we placed on success in Chapter 2, and realize that writing is for most of us (teachers and students alike) a place where we are very vulnerable to criticism.

- Respond to only some of what students write. Students don't need your feedback on everything they write. In many cases, they will profit from feedback from their peers. They will also profit from their own self-criticism, and in many cases they should use that self-criticism to decide what writing they want you to look at.

- Respond to only a few matters at any one time. It is simply a waste of your time and energy to respond to many things at once. Students will attend to only a limited number of comments.

- Make most of your comments on works in progress rather than on final drafts. Doing otherwise is, like making a great many comments, simply a waste of your time. Comments after a final draft is completed get very little attention.

- Frequently, give your feedback during brief conference sessions in which you and the student discuss her work in progress (Graves, 1996). A typical conference between a teacher–writer and student–writer might begin, "Tell me about your piece" or "How is it coming?" and will include the kind of teacher–student dialogue you heard between Norman Pite and Caroline earlier in the chapter, when we discussed a writing classroom's intellectual climate.

- In addition to individual conferences, give valuable feedback by observing students as they write. Asking questions or making statements can lead students to solve their own writing dilemmas.

- Deal first with content and only later with mechanics. It's not that mechanics are unimportant, but the content of students' writing is more important. This is doubly true in the present context, where our concern is with students' writing as it reflects and promotes their proficiency in reading.

- With your primary-grade writers, praise correct spelling, but encourage invented spelling. Diane Snowball (1996) suggests the following four ways to respond to students' spelling that are appropriate for their stage of development:

    I can see that you know how to spell the high-frequency words.

    I like the way you try unknown words.

    I notice you are thinking about how to spell the base word, then how to add a prefix and suffix.

    Do you know how to spell _____? This word has the same spelling pattern.

> Students need feedback from readers who genuinely strive to understand what they are trying to say and then ask questions to help them clarify their work.
>
> —*Donald Graves*
> *Teacher Educator*

If a student's goal is to have someone else read her writing, then spelling is an important means to that end, and correct spelling something to strive for.

■ Make peer response an integral and frequent part of your reading and writing program. There are 30 students and one of you. You simply can't be every place at once. Moreover, there is no better way to learn something than to teach it—which is one part of what peer reviewers are doing. Equally important, there is no better way to learn to work together—arguably the most crucial skill in our interdependent yet diverse society (Johnson, Johnson, & Holubec, 1994)—than working together. However, and this is a huge proviso, students must be taught how to be effective peer respondents. Having checklists with specific criteria listed is often useful, so students know what to be looking for. For example, if students are working on pieces that include dialogue, the criteria might be as follows:

Is the dialogue punctuated correctly?

Does the dialogue sound natural?

Is there too little dialogue? Too much?

Does the dialogue make sense?

Students need to be taught the general principles for responding to a person's writing, and they need to be taught about the specific writing elements they will be responding to—content, coherence, transitions, form, dialogue, and so on.

Finally, in addition to these suggestions, like virtually all current writers on writing, we recommend that students keep portfolios of their writing—ongoing and cumulative records and examples of their work—something we

will discuss in more detail in Chapter 11. Items to be included can be selected by both you and your students. A major strength of these portfolios is that students can "travel through their portfolios, review their writing over a period of time, and gain understanding of themselves as writers" (D'Aoust, 1996, p. 299). You and the students can use these portfolios as a tool for evaluating the writing and deciding where future efforts might be directed, sharing with parents, and determining and agreeing on grades.

Reflection AND *Application*

12. Identify a grade level at which you would like to teach, and consider for a moment the minilesson component of the writing workshop. Name some topics you might choose to cover early in the year, some you might choose to cover in the middle of the year, and some you might choose to cover late in the year. Now consider what surprises you might find in your students' writing and how these would affect your plan.

13. Get together with at least two other classmates, and make a list of the sorts of publishing opportunities you might make available to second-grade students, fourth-grade students, and sixth-grade students.

14. We listed about eight suggestions for responding to students' writing. Rank these in order from those that you think are most important to those you think are least important, and ask a classmate to do the same. Then get together and discuss the similarities and differences in your rankings, particularly trying to understand any large differences and what those differences suggest about your views of writing instruction.

Special Needs and Special Talents

With writing, as with any other curricular area we have discussed, one of the most effective ways to meet the needs of different students is to differentiate the curriculum. For example, let us say that after a class of fourth-graders has completed a unit in which students have been reading self-selected books on the theme of courage, you want them to respond to what they read by writing on the topic. Students who struggle with writing can enjoy success by dictating "courage stories" to an adult, who then transcribes them for the student. Students who are skilled in writing in a language other than English might write in that language in this situation. Verbally talented students can be challenged to write a researched biography on a courageous person whom they admire.

Modifying writing tasks to address needs and talents is another approach. The form illustrated in Figure 9.15, which is based on suggestions by Susan Winebrenner (1992), can be used a guide and reminder as you individualize writing activities. Of course, it is neither possible nor desirable to individualize writing activities all of the time, but it is something you can do some of the time and the individual success it fosters is certainly worth the effort.

Student's name	Purpose of the activity	Activities student will be engaged in as an alternative to the regular class activities
Jason DeWitt	Synthesize, recall, and apply information in science chapter on the water cycle	Develop a way to teach the water cycle to a group of first- and second-graders—perhaps a picture book
Jennifer Wong	Synthesize, recall, and apply information in science chapter on the water cycle	Research and write about a question the chapter brought to mind or left unanswered. Perhaps an "I search" paper.
Eric Sanders	Synthesize, recall, and apply information in science chapter on the water cycle	Listen to tape of chapter, then tell important information learned to aide, who writes what Eric dictates. Eric then reads back what he "wrote."

FIGURE 9.15 *Sample Guide for Individualizing Writing Activities*

Students who find writing a challenge, who speak and write in a dialect other than standard English, or whose native language is not English may also profit from your observing the following practices, some of which were suggested by Robin Scarcella (1996), director of the ESL program at the University of California at Irvine, and some of which are our own:

- Show respect for students' home languages and cultures.
- Keep directions simple, and check to be sure students understand them.
- Have a model of the completed writing task available.
- Demonstrate or model the writing activity.
- Guide students through the activity.
- Make sure students have the writing supplies they need readily available.
- Ensure that your feedback is both comprehensible and constructive.
- Teach students to use a simple word processor.

Finally, in some situations, students should be allowed to write in their own dialects. However, as educator Lisa Delpit (1988) has eloquently argued, students of color need and deserve to become adept at writing in standard English, and teachers need to assist them in doing so. Two questions can guide both you and your students with regard to whether or not dialect is appropriate and effective in a piece of writing: What is the purpose for writing? And who is the audience?

Some approaches to writing are especially appropriate for very skillful writers. One activity we have found particularly useful and well received by skillful developing writers is creating narratives or expository pieces related to their reading. Here are some possibilities (Graves & Graves, 1994):

- Select a scene from a book, and rewrite it to show what might happen if a character did something differently. For example, in the scene from Katherine Paterson's novel *The Great Gilly Hopkins* in which Gilly first meets William Ernest, students might develop the scene showing an assertive instead of passive William Ernest.
- Write a scene from the perspective of another character. For example, in *The Great Gilly Hopkins*, any one of the scenes that include Gilly and William Ernest might be written from William Ernest's viewpoint instead of Gilly's.
- Write an alternative ending to a story.
- Write a sequel to a story.
- Present the events of a text in newspaper format.
- Rewrite a contemporary story (such as *Willie Jerome* by Alice Faye Duncan, which tells about a young trumpet player and the effect his music has on his sister) as a fairy tale. "Once upon a time there was a boy named Willie Jerome. No one in the Kingdom of Brooklyn liked his music. No one but his sister."

Of course, less-skilled writers can also profit from some of these activities, but remember that less-skilled writers will need sufficient scaffolding to be successful with them.

Another activity particularly suited to gifted writers is participating in writing contests. Submitting writing to contests can be highly motivating, as it provides students with an authentic goal and audience. And even though it is the competitive element that motivates students to work their hardest at achieving writing excellence, students can be very supportive of one another, generous with praise and constructive in their feedback. Teacher Margo Sorenson tells us, "When one of my students wins a competition, it's as if they all had won." Magazines, organizations, and state and county fairs all sponsor writing competitions. A listing of writing contests can be found in the *Children's Writer's and Illustrator's Market* (Buening, 1996) in the section titled Young Writers and Illustrators.

CONCLUDING REMARKS

The value of establishing a curriculum and developing an environment for students to grow as writers in concert with their reading has been the overriding theme of this chapter. That means providing a classroom atmosphere, both physical and intellectual, that is safe and nurturing as well as inviting, fun, and challenging. It means providing opportunities to write for real purposes and for real audiences, purposes that include writing to learn for one's self and writing to communicate with someone else. It means providing students with opportunities to improve their writing and thinking skills through all sorts of writing—informal writing, such as brainstorming, quickwriting, and journaling as well as formal writing, such as reports and storybooks that require the process approach. It means giving students every benefit possible—providing daily time to write, publishing their works, and giving them constructive feedback. In short, your reading–writing environment and curriculum will help and inspire students to write more often and more effectively. It will encourage them to use writing both as a thinking tool to learn more about themselves and their world and as a communicative tool to share their knowledge, feelings, and insights with others.

EXTENDING LEARNING

1. Get together with several classmates, and develop a set of interview questions that you can use with teachers to learn how they use writing in conjunction with reading in their classrooms. Limit yourselves to five or six questions that can be answered rather briefly. For example, you might ask how often their students write in conjunction with the reading they're doing. Once the questionnaire is developed, try it out first on one teacher and modify it as necessary. Then, each person in the group can interview two teachers and record their answers. Finally, get together with your classmates, share the results of your interviews, and discuss to what extent the writing you learned about is consistent with the principles and techniques recommended in this chapter. After your group meeting, you might consider presenting the results of your project to your university class.

2. This activity parallels the previous one. In this case, however, you interview students rather than teachers. Again, limit yourselves to five or six questions that can be rather briefly answered. Since you are working with children and want to be certain they understand your interview questions, trying your questions out on several students is essential. Also, it is quite likely that you will need to revise them as a result of the

trial. For the actual interview, it may work best to talk with students in groups of four or so. As you did after interviewing the teachers, get together with your classmates afterward, and discuss how the writing that students describe is and is not consistent with the principles and techniques recommended in this chapter. If you interview students of the teachers you previously worked with, it may be informative to compare the students' and teachers' perceptions of the writing. As before, you may wish to present your results to your university class.

3. Observe the reading and language arts periods of an elementary class for at least one week and for two weeks if possible, and keep a detailed record of the writing the students do. Then, as a writing-to-learn activity for yourself, write a description of the class and the teacher, the writing you observed in the one- or two-week period, and the extent to which the writing you observed is and is not like that recommended in this chapter. Next, write an evaluative statement on the quality of the writing activities you observed and the extent to which they seem to support and extend the reading experiences students had during the period. Finally, if you believe that what you observed could be modified to better support and extend students' reading, briefly describe the modifications you would suggest.

REFERENCES

Anson, C. M., & Beach, R. (1995). *Journals in the classroom: Writing to learn*. Norwood, MA: Christopher-Gordon. Although aimed at English classes, this well-documented discussion of the purposes and uses of journals can be useful for middle school and upper elementary as well.

Atwell, N. (1987). *In the middle: Writing, reading, and learning with adolescents*. Portsmouth, NH: Heinemann. This book documents and discusses how to teach adolescents by connecting reading and writing through reading and writing workshops.

Bright, R. (1995). *Writing instruction in the intermediate grades: What is said, what is done, what is understood*. Newark, DE: International Reading Association. The author offers useful insights into the interrelationships between students' writing, their thinking about their writing processes, and the language of instruction.

Britton, J. N., Burgess, T., Martin, N., McLeod, A., & Rosen, H. (1975). *The development of writing abilities*. New York: Macmillan. This very important report describes the written language of British 11- to 18-year-olds and gives recommendations for practice.

Buening, A. P. (1996). *Children's writer's and illustrator's market*. Cincinnati: Writer's Digest Books. This book provides information on publishing fiction, nonfiction, illustrations, and photos for children of all ages.

Calkins, L. M. (1986). *The art of teaching writing*. Portsmouth, NH: Heinemann. The author discusses the essentials in teaching writing, how children develop as writers, how to repond to and evaluate students' writing, and the various writing modes.

Carroll, J. B. (1966). Some neglected relationships in reading and language. *Elementary English, 43,*

577–582. This is one of the earliest considerations of the relationship between reading and the other language arts.

Cazden, C. B. (1991). Contemporary issues and future directions: Active learners and active teachers. In J. Flood, J. M. Jensen, D. Lapp, & J. R. Squire (Eds.), *Handbook of research on teaching the English language arts* (pp. 418–422). This is a thoughtful analysis of the roles of active teaching and active learning in the classroom.

Cooke, C. L., & Graves, M. F. (1995). Writing for an audience—for fun. *Middle School Journal, 26*(3), 31–37. The authors give a detailed look at the whys and hows of a student publishing project.

Cullinan, B. (1993). *Pen in hand: Children become writers.* Newark, DE: International Reading Association. Five chapters, each by a different author, discuss aspects of helping children become better writers.

D'Aoust, C. (1996). Portfolio assessment. In *Practical ideas for teaching writing as a process at the elementary and middle school levels* (rev. ed., pp. 298–299). Sacramento: California Department of Education. This article describes classroom portfolios, their purposes, and how teachers can and do use them as assessment tools.

Delpit, L. D. (1988). The silenced dialogue: Power and pedagogy in educating other people's children. *Harvard Educational Review, 58*, 280–298. In this powerful article, a Black educator describes the linguistic skills students of color need to develop.

Dyson, A. H., & Freedman, S. W. (1991). Writing. In J. Flood, J. M. Jensen, D. Lapp, & J. R. Squire (Eds.), *Handbook of research on teaching the English language arts* (pp. 754–774). The authors present a succinct discussion of the uses and processes of writing and developing students' writing in the classroom.

Elbow, P. (1973). *Writing without teachers.* Oxford, UK: Oxford University Press. In this book, the author proposes a model of informal writing, particularly freewriting, and how to use writing to foster learning.

Emig, J. (1971). *The composing process of twelfth graders.* Urbana, IL: National Council of Teachers of English. This detailed study of how students actually write has been a major influence in promoting the process approach.

Farr, R. (1993). Writing in response to reading: A process approach to literary assessment. In B. E. Cullinan (Ed.), *Pen in hand: Children become writers* (pp. 64–79). Newark, DE: International Reading Association. The author discusses ways in which individual teachers developed writing-in-response-to-reading assessment to match their instructional objectives.

Fulwiler, T. (Ed.). (1988). *The journal book.* Portsmouth, NH: Boynton/Cook. This book discusses the value of using journals in the classroom to improve student learning across the disciplines.

Graves, D. H. (1975). An examination of the writing processes of seven year old children. *Research in the teaching of English, 9*, 227–241. This article describes an investigation of the writing processes of 7-year-olds.

Graves, D. H. (1983). *Writing: Teachers and children at work.* Portsmouth, NH: Heinemann. This book emphasizes what teachers can do to foster children's writing fluency, children's development in the writing process, and issues of recording and reporting student progress.

Graves, D. H. (1996, April). Spot the lifetime writers. *Instructor*, p. 27. This article describes the traits of lifetime writers and suggests how teachers can help nurture these same traits in their students.

Graves, M. F., & Graves, B. B. (1994). *The scaffolded reading experience: Designs for student success.* Norwood, MA: Christopher-Gordon. This books presents the theoretical base for the scaffolded reading experience and, with many concrete examples, describes how to implement the framework.

Harwayne, S. (1993). Chuzpah and the nonfiction writer. In B. E. Cullinan (Ed.), *Pen in hand: Children become writers* (pp. 19–35). Newark, DE: International Reading Association. The author takes an inspiring look at how teachers can help students improve their nonfiction writing by adopting the stances and strategies of professional writers.

Heimlich, J. E., & Pittelman, S. D. (1986). *Semantic mapping: Classroom applications.* Newark, DE: International Reading Association. This brief text gives many practical examples of how to use semantic mapping in the classroom.

International Reading Association and the National Council of Teachers of English. (1996). *Standards for the English language arts*. Newark, DE, and Urbana, IL: Author. This publication details the 12 interrelated standards and guidelines for implementing them.

Johnson, D. W., Johnson, R. T., & Holubec E. J. (1994). *The new circles of learning: Cooperation in the classroom and school*. Alexandria, VA: Association for Supervision and Curriculum Development. This is the latest version of a readable, thorough, and common-sense book on cooperative learning.

Koziol, S. M., Minnick, J. B., & Riddell, K. (1996). *Journals for active learning: A two-day workshop module for primary teachers in Bosnia*. Pittsburgh, PA: University of Pittsburgh International Institute for Studies in Education. This monograph presents theory, background, and practical suggestions for using journals in primary classrooms.

Langer, J. (1986). *Children reading and writing*. Norwood, NJ: Ablex. This report examines the basic cognitive activities children engage in when reading and writing.

Mode, B. A. (1989). Dialogue journal writing. *The Reading Teacher, 42*, 568–571. The author describes dialogue journal writing as a practical means for empowering both teachers and students in grades 1–6.

Moffett, J. (1968). *Teaching the universe of discourse*. Boston: Houghton Mifflin. This is one of the first and most influential textbooks to describe a student-centered approach to language arts.

National Center for Educational Statistics. (1996). Can students benefit from process writing? *NAEP Facts, 13*(3), 1–6. This is one of a series of short, interpretative reports about NAEP results put out by the U.S. Department of Education.

Nystrand, M. (1986). *The structure of written communication*. New York: Academic Press. The author discusses the interactivity of language and the reciprocity principle as they relate to writing.

Olson, C. B. (1996). Strategies for interacting with text. In C. B. Olson (Ed.), *Practical ideas for teaching writing as a process at the elementary and middle school levels*. (rev. ed., pp. 231–235). Sacramento: California Department of Education. This article describes a variety of ways of responding to text, many of which involve writing.

Routman, R. (1991). *Invitations: Changing as teachers and learners K–12*. Portsmouth, NH: Heinemann. Written for practicing teachers, this text encourages teachers to try whole-language techniques and strategies.

Scarcella, R. (1996). English learners and writing: Responding to linguistic diversity. In C. B. Olson (Ed.), *Practical ideas for teaching writing as a process at the elementary school and middle school levels* (pp. 97–103). Sacramento, CA: California State Department of Education. This article gives a short and practical set of suggestions for working with linguistically diverse students.

Snowball, D. (1996, August). Spelling strategies: Starting points for spelling. *Instructor*, pp. 36–37. This article pinpoints four strategies to get children off to a good start with spelling in the classroom.

Squire, J. (1984). Composing and comprehending: Two sides of the same process. In J. M. Jensen (Ed.), *Composing and comprehending*. Urbana, IL: National Conference on Research in English. This is a well-known essay on the reading–writing relationship.

Staton, J. (1987). The power of responding in dialog journals. In T. Fulwiler (Ed.), *The journal book* (pp. 47–63). Portsmouth, NH: Boynton/Cook. In this chapter, the author discusses dialog journals as powerful tools for student response.

Temple, C., Nathan, R., Temple, F., & Burris, N. A. (1993). *The beginnings of writing* (3rd ed.). Boston: Allyn & Bacon. This book gives a description of children's early literacy learning and how teachers can best nurture developing readers and writers.

Tompkins, G. E. (1996). Becoming an effective teacher of reading. *WSRA Journal, 13*(2), 1–7. The author notes a very balanced set of suggestions for becoming an effective reading teacher.

Vacca, R., & Linek, W. M. (1992). Writing to learn. In J. W. Irwin & M. A. Doyle, (Eds.), *Reading/writing connections: Learning from research* (pp. 145–159). Newark, DE: International

Reading Association. The authors present research and practical ideas on how to encourage students to think on paper.

Winebrenner, S. (1992, September). Meeting the needs of your high-ability students. *Instructor*, 60–63. In four scenarios, the author describes strategies teachers can use to address the needs of high ability students.

Wollman-Bonnilla, J. E., & Werchadlo, B. (1995). Literature response journals in a first-grade classroom. *Language Arts*, *72*(8), 562–570. This article shows how response journals motivate first-graders to express in writing a range of responses to literature.

CHILDREN'S LITERATURE

Adler, D. A. (1989). *A Picture book of Helen Keller.* New York: Holiday House. This is an illustrated biography of a blind and deaf girl who courageously overcame her handicaps. Unpaged.

Adler, D. A. (1990). *A Picture book of Martin Luther King, Jr.* New York: Holiday House. This is an illustrated biography of the American civil rights leader who, through his example of nonviolent protest, helped Blacks in obtaining equal rights. Audiotape available. Unpaged.

Brooks, P. S. (1990). *Beyond the myth: The story of Joan of Arc.* Boston: J. B. Lippincott. This nonfiction book portrays the life of the 15th-century French martyr within the social, political, and religious context of the times. 176 pages.

Carlson, N. (1990). *Arnie and the new kid.* New York: Puffin. In this picture book, Arnie begins to better understand the new kid in a wheelchair after he falls himself and becomes temporarily disabled. Unpaged.

Cleary, B. (1983). *Dear Mr. Henshaw.* New York: Morrow. In this Newbery Medal book, 10-year-old Leigh writes letters to his favorite author that help him cope with his parents' divorce, a new school, and finding his place in the world. 134 pages. Audiotape and filmstrip available.

Cole, J. (1989). *Magic school bus inside the human body.* New York: Scholastic. In an adventure, Ms. Frizzle takes her class, via the magic bus, inside the human body to take a look at how body parts work. 40 pages. Spanish audiotape available.

Cole, J. (1992). *Magic school bus on the ocean floor.* New York: Scholastic. Ms. Frizzle takes her class to the ocean floor aboard the magic school bus, where they learn firsthand the mysteries of underwater life. 40 pages. Spanish audiotape available.

Conrad, P. (1985). *Prairie songs.* New York: Harper & Row. The Nebraska prairie in pioneer days is the setting for this novel about Louisa, whose life changes when a new doctor arrives with his beautiful, but tragically frail, wife. 167 pages.

Dahl, R. (1961). *James and the giant peach.* New York: Scholastic. Young James experiences madcap adventures as he enters a peach as big as a house and encounters new friends. 128 pages. Audiotape available.

Dewey, J. O. (1987). *At the edge of the pond.* Boston: Little, Brown. This lyric text about the ecology of pond life is divided into six chapters, each of which describes a different aspect of pond life. 44 pages.

Fisher, A. (1965). "Weather is full of the nicest sounds." In A. McGovern (Ed.), *Arrow book of poetry* (p. 58). New York: Scholastic. Poem highlighting words that connote the many and varied sounds of weather.

Fleischman, S. (1986). *The whipping boy.* New York: Greenwillow. In this Newbery Medal book, Prince Brat and his whipping boy, Jemmy, run away from the palace, end up trading identities, and have many adventures together. 90 pages. Audiotape available.

Freedman, R. (1993). *Eleanor Roosevelt: A life of discovery.* New York: Clarion. This photobiography explores the life of the first wife of a president to carve out an influential career of her own. 198 pages.

Hackett, J. K., & Moyer, R. H. (1991). Members of the solar system. In *Science in your world*. New York: Macmillan/McGraw Hill. This is a section from a chapter in a fifth-grade science text.

Henkes, K. (1988). *The zebra wall*. New York: Greenwillow. In this short novel, 10-year-old Adine not only has to adjust to a new baby in the family, the first boy among girls, but to her divorced and unconventional aunt who comes to live with them. 147 pages. Audiotape available.

Hirschfield, A. (1986). *Happily may I walk: American Indians and Alaska natives today*. New York: Scribner. This nonfiction book describes many aspects of contemporary Native American life—government, religion, culture, economic issues, organizations, and writers and journalists. 152 pages.

Lowery, L. (1996). *Wilma Mankiller*. From the On My Own biography series, this biography tells how Wilma Mankiller found strength in her Cherokee heritage and how she became chief of the Cherokee nation. 56 pages.

MacLachlan, P. (1985). *Sarah, plain and tall*. New York: HarperCollins. This Newbery Medal novel tells the story of mail-order bride Sarah from Maine and the family who longs to have her stay with them on the prairie. 91 pages. Spanish text, audiotape, and videotape available.

MacLachlan, P. (1993). *Baby*. New York: Delacorte. This exquisitely crafted short novel portrays a family learning to deal with the death of their own infant son after a baby girl is left on their doorstep for them to care for. 132 pages.

Osofsky, A. (1996). *Free to dream: The making of a poet, Langston Hughes*. New York: Lothrop, Lee, & Shepard. This is a biography of the Harlem poet who gave a voice to the Black experience in America. 112 pages.

Parks, B. (1993). *Junie B. Jones and a little monkey business*. New York: Random House. Excitement is created in Junie's kindergarten when Junie misunderstands her grandmother and reports that her new baby brother is a monkey. 68 pages.

Paterson, K. (1978). *The great Gilly Hopkins*. New York: Crowell. This novel portrays feisty 11-year-old Gilly, a foster child who, in her longing to be reunited with her birth mother, schemes against all who try to befriend her. 152 pages. Spanish text and audiotape available.

Rabin, S. (1994). *Casey over there*. San Diego: Harcourt Brace & Company. Seven-year-old Aubrey and his brother Casey, who is sent to fight in France during World War I, communicate their loneliness and love through letter writing. 34 pages.

Ringgold, F. (1991). *Tar beach*. New York: Crown. Eight-year-old Cassie Louise Lightfoot enjoys family outings on their Harlem apartment-building rooftop and imagines flying over the city, righting wrongs along the way. 32 pages. Available as a big book.

Sorenson, M. (1997). *Hurricane! Nature's most destructive force*. Logan, IA: Perfection Learning. Engaging text, photos, tables, maps, and illustrations explain this devastating weather phenomenon. 56 pages.

Soto, G. (1992). *The skirt*. New York: Delacorte. When fourth-grader Miata accidentally leaves her folklorico skirt on the bus, she tries desperately to get it back before her parents find out. 74 pages.

Spinelli, J. (1991). *Fourth grade rats*. New York: Scholastic. Suds's best friend tries to convince him that you have got to be a tough guy in fourth grade, but Suds learns otherwise—the hard way. 84 pages.

Turner, A. (1987). *Nettie's trip south*. New York: Macmillan. Based on the actual diary of the author's great-grandmother, this picture book tells of the cruel realities a 10-year-old girl encounters when she visits Richmond, Virginia, and witnesses a slave auction. 32 pages.

Wildlife Education, Ltd. (1986). *Zoo Books 2: Alligators and crocodiles*. San Diego: Author. This series of books depicts a variety of zoo animals.

chapter ten

Literacy Instruction for Non-Native Speakers of English

by Elizabeth B. Bernhardt and Michael L. Kamil

Scene One: A Teacher's Lounge

Ms. Q.:   *I don't know what to do about Yanni. All he does is smile at me. I have no idea of whether he understands what I'm saying or not. At least the kids don't ignore him, so I guess he'll get along.*

Ms. P.:   *You're lucky. One of my children comes in every morning crying and hanging onto his older brother. I keep asking Laril to have his parents come in, but he just says, "Busy. Busy." I really wish there was someone who knew how to work with him. I just don't know enough to really help him.*

Scene Two: An Academic Conference

Presenter: *Our study of science teachers and their beliefs about how young children's scientific literacy should be assessed included children of different racial and socioeconomic backgrounds. Thirty percent of the children in our participant-teachers' classrooms were Latino, 20% African American, and 50% white.*

Teacher from the Audience: *In the Latino population, could you tell me the distribution of language proficiency within the group?*

CHAPTER OVERVIEW

Presenter: We were only looking at the teachers' perceptions.

Teacher: Yes, I understand that, but since the study was conducted in California, could you give me the distribution of students who are bilingual, who have limited English proficiency, and English-only students?

Presenter: Unfortunately, we can't. We were only looking at the teachers' beliefs about science instruction, and it just happened that some of the children were Latino.

Scene Three: An Inservice Class

Classroom Teacher: I work with seventh graders who read and write at the third grade level. Some of them are Hispanic.

University Teacher: So how many of your Hispanic students can read in Spanish?

Classroom Teacher: I'm afraid I can't tell you exactly. I know some of them do, but I don't know just who.

LEARNING TO READ ENGLISH AS A SECOND LANGUAGE IN THE UNITED STATES

Here, we first provide several perspectives on second-language reading instruction and then briefly describe the historical and contemporary American landscape within which today's second-language learners must learn to read English.

Perspectives on Second-Language Reading Instruction

The 21st century promises that ever-increasing numbers of students from diverse language backgrounds will enter the public school system.

—*Dale Lange*
Teacher Educator

We began our chapter with several scenes rather than just one to suggest the varied forces at work in classrooms when children are not native users of the classroom language. We need to be concerned about a variety of issues that influence the language learning of these children. We also need to think about our own perceptions of our language and those who use it. Do we believe that we speak with an accent, or is it just people from other places that do? Is our grammar always perfect? And we need to think about our perception of people who may not use language as skillfully as native English speakers do. Are we disturbed by their accents and imperfect grammar?

It is important to understand the extent to which children who speak English as a second language populate almost all American classrooms—not just ones in certain geographic areas. Although states such as Florida and California, or cities such as New York and Chicago, come immediately to mind when we think of ethnic and linguistic diversity, the teachers depicted in the opening scenarios represent typical situations for millions of children and challenges for thousands of teachers (Scarcella, 1990). How do entire teaching staffs in schools effectively serve the children who come through their doors not speaking English? How do classroom teachers work with staff specialists in English as a second language without making the children feel different and excluded from the native English speakers in class?

In a world where probably more people speak two languages than speak one, language learning and language teaching are vital to the everyday lives of millions.

—*Vivian Cook*
Linguist

These are critical questions, but an exclusive focus on teachers would be unwise. We also need to ask what the research community has to contribute. How has the research community come to understand the issues involving children who speak different languages? What information do we have about these children to help us make wise decisions? Has the research community really understood the complexities of what teachers and children face when they do not hold a linguistic base in common?

And what about individual classrooms? What do teachers need to know about the language and cultural backgrounds of the array of children

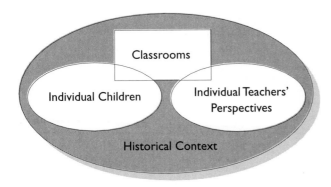

FIGURE 10.1 *The Interplay Between Factors That Affect Second-Language Reading Instruction*

with whom they will interact over the span of their teaching careers? How can teachers become effective diagnosticians when they perhaps do not know the structure of the language that children bring with them to school? Which strategies can teachers use, given the restricted conditions under which they have to work?

Figure 10.1 displays relationships between the forces that shape what we do in classrooms in which some students are not native speakers of English.

The American Landscape

More than 6% of the children in public and private schools in the United States are classified as Limited English Proficient (Scarcella, 1990). According to data collected by the National Clearinghouse on Bilingual Education (1995), 66% of these children are in the elementary grades, 18% are in middle school, and 14% in high school. The vast majority of these children—almost 75% of them—speak Spanish at home. The remainder of them speak an array of languages such as Vietnamese, Hmong, Cantonese, Cambodian, and Korean, as well as a number of Native American languages (Henderson, 1994). Although many of them live in states such as California and Texas, a significant number of non-native speakers live throughout most of the United States.

On the one hand, these figures portray an America that somehow seems different from the image of sameness portrayed in many social studies textbooks. On the other hand, we might ask how different this distribution of ethnic and linguistic diversity really is. Is it really so different from the diversity in the United States in the early years of the century? It is important to remember that the first great wave of immigration took place a century ago. Clearly, elementary school teachers have had to confront the challenges of linguistic diversity for many years. Have the lives of teachers really had to change that much? A look at the history of linguistic diversity in the United States provides some perspective and suggests that teaching linguistically diverse students is something that many American teachers have successfully accomplished.

American classrooms are products of the social and political history of the United States (Spring, 1990). Our classrooms are in many ways microcosms of our society. In their classrooms, teachers get to see firsthand both the good and the ills that exist in society. They see children who are ready and willing to learn and who are excited by learning, no matter what their intellectual level or linguistic background is. They also see children who are not supported in their learning, either by circumstances at home or by those in society. Such is the situation for many non-native speakers of English. The society at large does not support them in their attempts both to maintain their ethnic identities and to become successful at school. The former requires use of their home language; the latter requires the use of English. The apparently opposing forces of the home language and English have been at issue since the birth of the United States.

The works of American founders such as Benjamin Franklin, John Adams, and Noah Webster reveal great concern for language and for useful literacy skills. The founders argued strongly for skills exclusively in the English language (Simpson, 1986). A 1789 paper by Webster underlined the view by arguing that, having won independence, Americans needed to "embrace any scheme that shall tend, in its future operation, to reconcile the people of America to each other" (p. 36). The key scheme for Webster was a common language.

In the century and a half that American schools at all similar to those of today have existed, issues of language have continued to be in play. As suggested in our discussion of the history of reading instruction in Chapter 2, between 1800 and 1850 public education was focused on developing social responsibility. As Daniel and Laurel Tanner, authors of *The History of the School Curriculum* (1990), put it, "there was no theoretical framework for curriculum development beyond the objectives of the meeting of student and societal needs and realizing the promise of democracy" (p. 66). During this period, public schools seldom had to deal with students who did not speak English. For the most part, children who did not speak English went to parochial schools that were not part of the public system.

By about 1900, a critical force was molding the American nation—massive European immigration. This turn-of-the-century phenomenon signaled many changes in society: a turn from an agricultural, rural society to an industrial, urban one; a need for social services; and the arrival of the human

In countries forged from speakers of many languages, it is important to plan which language or languages are going to be used officially in education, the legislatures, and the courts, and those whose languages are not used may be at a serious social and political disadvantage.

—*Elaine Chaika*
Sociolinguist

Around 1900, a critical force molding the American nation was massive European immigration.

capital necessary to build a middle class. These forces were seen as potentially disruptive to the national unity that the founders had counted on. Language differences represented this threat to the common core. A political movement called Americanization became the catchword for unity.

Americanization was not an educational movement, but a civic movement. It was sponsored by groups who "had little in common with one another except a felt need for closer social unity" (Higham, 1988, p. 236). The first group that supported Americanization was social workers. The social work perspective on the problem was to provide new immigrants with a feeling of "home" by acknowledging the value of their home languages and cultures, yet also by empowering them with a knowledge of the language and culture of wider communication, namely English. For example, Chicago's Hull House—the pioneering social service settlement established by Jane Addams at the turn of the century—provided both English language teaching and native language literacy instruction, often in Italian and German. Such efforts stand as tributes to social workers, who were committed to furthering ethnic pride and American unity through social services.

At the same time, patriotic hereditary societies, groups such as the Know-Nothings, were also concerned about the immigrants and their knowl-

> Even a meager knowledge of English may mean an opportunity to work in a factory versus non-employment. Or it may mean a question of life or death when a sharp command must be understood in order to avoid the danger of a descending crane.
>
> —*Jane Addams*
> *Social Worker and*
> *Nobel Laureate*

edge of English. These groups, populated by persons of northern European stock and of long-established families, were not, however, motivated by a desire to assist the immigrants. They feared that the nation would not hold together because of the increased number of immigrants who did not speak English (Higham, 1988). School boards, major corporations such as Ford Motors, and the U.S. Chamber of Commerce all supported Americanization. The position is clearly shown in this pronouncement from one prominent proponent of Americanization, Theodore Roosevelt:

> We must have but one flag. We must also have but one language. We cannot tolerate any attempt to oppose or supplant the language and culture that has come down to us from builders of the Republic with the language and culture of any European culture. Whatever may have been our judgment in normal times, we are convinced that today our most dangerous enemy is the foreign language press. (1968, p. 129)

With victory in World War I and the economic depression that followed, the fervor and the resources spent on Americanization efforts declined. In fact, what resources were left were frequently dedicated to keeping immigrants out of the United States. The 1921 Quota Act, for example, which seriously restricted southern European and Russian immigration, was essentially an English literacy law. Intelligence tests for immigrants were administered in English (Leibowitz, 1984). Those who could not "pass" the tests in English were declared "feeble-minded" and not permitted to enter the country. Commenting on such laws, Jane Addams noted (1938) that the 1921 Quota Act was as cruel a law as the 16th-century laws enacted to expel Jews and Moors from Spain.

The attitudes and events just outlined should seem eerily familiar. Americans of the late 20th century have had to contend with this same issue—the role of non-English-speakers' native languages within an English-speaking dominant culture. Since the 1960s, developments involving non-native speakers have been largely the result of massive immigration, much like that of the beginning of the century.

The wave of immigration in the latter half of the 20th century began in the wake of the Vietnam War. Beginning in about 1960, America experienced the pressure of enormous numbers of political refugees from Southeast Asia. This influence has continued to the present time. From every corner of the globe and speaking literally hundreds of languages, people continue to flock to America, seeking a better life.

Some of these immigrants arrive legally; others arrive illegally. Social service agencies push for increased resources for these groups, particularly for children who must be schooled. Political groups push also, crying out

I'm afraid my child is at a disadvantage because the teacher spends so much time helping these kids who don't speak English.

—Paula Brooks
Parent

against the potential harm of linguistic diversity and establishing action groups such as the English Only movement (Tollefson, 1995). Thus, social and political forces continue their battles. But one issue remains constant: Teachers still must teach, and children still must come to school.

No other single issue at play in American classrooms is so ripe with social and political history and controversy. America has always been concerned about unity. Many Americans view linguistic unity—meaning that everyone speaks English—as the major element in national unity. However, we want to emphasize that linguistic diversity does not mean national disunity. Data indicate that very few persons in the United States are monolingual in a language other than English. In fact, the most recent census data indicate that less than 1% of Americans are non-English-speakers and that this population is learning English faster than many previous generations of foreign-born Americans (National Clearinghouse for Bilingual Education, 1995). It has always been the case in American history that immigrant families became English-dominant within two generations. These recent data show that today we are achieving linguistic unity in even less time, even though the country currently includes greater ethnic diversity than ever before.

All in all, the American landscape of the past 200 years reflects both many changes and many continuing patterns. Yet, whatever political position is espoused and however non-native speakers are perceived at a particular time, it is important that teachers see children as individuals—not as representatives of societal issues. We need to ensure that adult biases do not interfere with the learning of children.

Reflection AND Application

1. We mentioned the American founders and wrote about their perspectives on language. Imagine that you were a speaker of German in Pennsylvania or of Italian in Virginia. What kinds of conversations do you suppose took place about language in the 18th century?

2. Imagine you were a social worker in inner-city Chicago around 1900. Would you have supported efforts to help children both learn English and maintain their home language? What might you have said to the parents of non-English-speaking students? Now examine your thinking about *current* efforts to make English the only language spoken in schools. How have times and attitudes changed?

3. Listen to the television or read print media carefully. What kinds of attitudes toward non-native speakers of English do you find in news-oriented print or popular television broadcasts?

SOME CHALLENGES OF READING
IN A SECOND LANGUAGE

If today's immigrant families become English-dominant in less than two generations, why is there anything to be concerned about? We know that the children before us will more than likely become speakers of English. Isn't it a simple case of "waiting" until this happens? The answer is no! Research indicates that it takes a non-native speaker between six and eight years to reach the oral skill level of his English-speaking peers (Collier, 1987). Waiting six to eight years to begin reading instruction would mean that many second-language children would be adolescents before we started them on literacy learning. This would be educationally and morally absurd. We know that all children need to begin literacy learning as early as possible in order to become effective literacy users. What then does every teacher need to understand about what having a first oral language means in relation to learning a second language and learning to read in that language? We will discuss this first in terms of the challenges faced by learners, then in terms of the challenges faced by teachers, and finally in terms of the light that research can shed on these challenges.

Before we do so, however, we will introduce some linguistic terms and concepts. Some are probably familiar to you and some probably are not, but at this point it is crucial that you become familiar with all of those listed here:

Syntax refers to the ways in which words combine to form sentences. The syntax of an English sentence is most often a subject followed by a verb followed by an object, as in *I see the man*. An unacceptable combination in English would be *I the man I see* because the syntax of English requires the verb to follow the subject in most cases.

Morphology refers to ways that words are built through adding parts. *Man*, for example, is an individual word and one morpheme. We can add other morphemes such as *-ly* to form *manly*, a new word that contains two morphemes. Different languages have different morphological systems for word building.

Inflections are special types of morphemes. The addition of *-s* on many words indicates plural in English. We add *-ed* to regular verbs to indicate past tense and *-er* to indicate the comparative. Inflections do not change the type of word they are attached to (verbs remain verbs and nouns remain nouns).

Sentence structure refers to the relationships between words in a sentence. In the most common type of English sentences, for example, the subject is the doer of the action indicated by the verb, as in *John threw the ball*.

The *lexicon* of a language is the body of words that make up the language. As we have pointed out previously, there are hundreds of thousands of words in the English lexicon. As we have also pointed out, the English lexicon is made up of a very small set of frequently used words and a very large set of infrequently used words.

Orthography refers to writing systems. English, Spanish, French, German, and Finnish all use Roman letters and hence have a Roman orthography. Russian uses a different alphabet, the Cyrillic alphabet, and hence has Cyrillic orthography.

Challenges Faced by Second-Language Learners

As we pointed out in Chapters 3 and 4, the oral language that children bring to school is a terrific starting point for literacy learning. As we explained, English-speaking children have internalized an extraordinary amount of language by the time they come to school—about 75% of all the syntax and morphology they will ever acquire. Effective literacy teaching is rooted in understanding how children use what they already know about oral language as they learn to deal with printed language.

Like their English-speaking classmates, second-language children come to American schools with an extraordinary amount of language. They too possess nearly all of the structure and morphology they will need to become fluent speakers. The difference, though, is that they are on the road to becoming fluent speakers of a language that is not typically used for either instruction or assessment in U.S. schools. It is not that non-English-speaking children come to school with a language deficit. They come with a lack of the particular language that is used in schools they will be attending—English. This presents several significant challenges.

There is a surface-level mismatch between the child's language and the language of the school. Children who speak a language other than English will approach learning to read with the best strategy they have—to match the oral language they know with the written language they see. This, however, presents an enormous challenge for second-language learners: *The oral language students know and the written language they must learn will have only a moderate amount of overlap.*

In addition to this surface-level mismatch, there are less obvious and in some ways deeper differences between English-speaking children raised in the United States and some non-English-speaking children raised in other settings. As we pointed out in Chapters 3 and 4, most children who have grown up in the United States have internalized a number of concepts relevant to learning to read. These concepts, of course, may or may not be well developed, and some children certainly have more extensive and richer preschool literacy experiences than other children. Nevertheless, regardless of their background, an English-language print experience surrounds virtually all students who grow up in the United States. They generally know that print signals a relationship to meaning.

The situation is quite different with some students who were not raised in the United States. Some children come from cultures that are not literate. Print, reading, and the many experiences that surround print and reading have never been part of their world. These children must learn what print actually is and how it functions. This brings us to a second challenge: *The rich and varied schemata that children internalize from growing up in a literate culture are yet to be developed.*

Like their English-speaking classmates, second-language children will exhibit different degrees of skills, intelligences, and motivations. As with all children in our classrooms, we see the array of talents that they demonstrate each day. We often assume that the more verbal children are the more able learners, and that the very social children are the more cooperative and interested learners. However, second-language children frequently come from cultures that do not value a great deal of verbal behavior from children, perceiving it to be rude. Moreover, and perhaps more important, second-language children frequently cannot express what they do in fact know. This brings us to a third challenge, really a pair of them: *The verbal abilities of children may not match what they actually know, and children may be reticent to express themselves verbally in class.*

> I could understand the question, but I just couldn't come up with an answer until I had some time. By the time I could speak, the teacher was already on the next point.
>
> —Kimie Kosako
> Student

Challenges Faced by Teachers

Like children who must learn to read in a second language, teachers who strive to assist second-language students in becoming competent readers face significant challenges. How can we bridge the gap between students who have five or six years of oral language development that is directly relevant to the literacy task at hand and students who have five or six years of oral language development that is only indirectly relevant to the literacy task at hand? Three particularly important challenges confront us here.

First, the extra processing steps necessary for second-language children make the instructional task doubly difficult. In many cases, children have the concepts necessary to understanding a text, but they use sounds and words that do not match the print. *We as teachers must prepare students to succeed at this difficult matching task by building their oral English skills.*

Second, as Figure 10.2 illustrates, speakers of different languages will have varying amounts of processing to do as they move from the language they know to the language they are learning. The Spanish-speaking child needs to go from the Spanish *gato* to English *cat*, two words that show some distinct print overlap. But what of the child who has to go from Vietnamese *mäo* to *cat*? The task for the Vietnamese-speaking child is considerably more difficult, since none of the letters overlap with those of the English word. *We as teachers must prepare for success both those students whose language overlaps a lot with English and those whose language overlaps very little with English.*

As daunting as these instructional issues are, they pale in comparison with the third challenge—the potential mismatch between children's conceptual understanding and their verbal abilities in English. Figure 10.3 illustrates this mismatch. As shown in the figure, Juan clearly learned a lot from the field trip, and he appears to understand the teacher's question, but he is unable to verbalize his understanding. As a result, the teacher mistakenly believes that he learned nothing from the trip and thus grossly underestimates his understanding. Most unfortunate, this inaccurate assessment is quite likely to influence her future work with Juan. Her developing schema for Juan is that he does not understand, and she is very likely to interpret much of his future actions in light of this schema. *We as teachers must work to build students' conceptual understanding and also realize that they may sometimes be unable to verbalize the conceptual understanding they actually possess.*

Spanish: **gato** ➡ English: **cat**   Vietnamese: **mäo** ➡ English: **cat**

In a language with much overlap, less effort is required to transform the concept and first language representation into the second language. The Spanish speaker has the advantage over the Vietnamese speaker in the example above for learning the English word *cat*.

FIGURE 10.2   *Differential Amounts of Overlap in Languages*

443

FIGURE 10.3 *Mismatch Between What a Student Knows and What He Says in Response to a Teacher's Question*

What Light Does Research Shed on These Challenges?

Second-language reading research is one of the oldest strands of reading research. In the modern era, prompted by the huge increase in learners of English as a second language, much of this research has focused on how best to help non-native speakers of English develop a functional use of literacy skills in English.

There are, of course, many important dimensions of reading in a second language to learn about from research. Here, we focus on several of the most immediate ones: the importance of language knowledge, the importance of literacy in the first language, cross-language differences, and cross-cultural influences.

The Importance of Language Knowledge

There is no question that, when doing tasks in a second language, the more the learner knows about the structure and lexicon of the language, the better. Research has indicated that at least 30% of the process of second-language reading involves grammatical and lexical knowledge (Bernhardt & Kamil, 1995; Brisbois, 1996; Hulstijn, 1991). This finding suggests that facilitating language development is crucial. Simply put, the more English words that children know and the more English sentence structures they learn, the better off they will be.

It is critical, however, to place this finding in the context of the following: Second-language acquisition is developmental in nature. That is, learning a second language is more like learning a first language than different from it. Neither direct instruction of forms before developmental readiness nor teaching forms out of context will lead to functional proficiency in a second language any more than it does in a first language. ESL teacher James Garcia stresses the importance of recognizing this developmental sequence:

> Whenever I am working with second-language children, I remind myself that they will follow certain sequences in their learning of English, regardless of what I do. For example, verbs with -ing forms will appear early in their spoken language; inflections, such as the third-person singular -s, will appear quite late, if they ever appear. Similarly, learning to deal with forming negatives is a process of first learning the negation words and attaching them externally to sentences; internal negation develops over time. The development of question forms and the creation of relative clauses also proceed over time. They are not "not there" one day and then "there" the next, no matter how much instruction I provide.
>
> James Garcia, ESL Teacher

In order for this developmental growth to occur, the learner must experience many examples of language use. How can the learner know what is more sophisticated unless he hears it or sees it? In like manner, the influence of peers—the desire to be part of the group—is enormous. This desire compels the learner to take on the linguistic characteristics present in the environment. The more rapidly these dynamics take hold, the higher the second-language literacy achievement. Bilingual teacher Margaret Thayer suggests one powerful way to foster interactions between second-language students and native English speakers—establishing a buddy system:

> One of the most successful things we have done in our classroom is to set up a buddy system in which we deliberately pair our English-language students with our second-language students. We do this at the beginning of the year or whenever a non-native speaker enters the class, and from that time on, the two stu-

dents do many things together. They work as a pair doing in-class assignments, talk about what they have read, and work together on homework. Of course, in many cases, the English-language student serves more often as the tutor and the second-language student as the learner. But whenever possible, we try to get the second-language student in the teacher's role. Often, for example, the second-language student teaches his English-speaking buddy some things about his language or culture. And, in many cases, the pairing doesn't end at the school. Buddies often visit each other's homes, share holidays, and pal around together. As I said, the buddy system has been a real success. Also, it does not take up a lot of the teacher's time, always an important consideration when you have lots of kids who need your assistance.

Margaret Thayer, Bilingual Teacher

The Importance of Literacy in the First Language

Unquestionably, there is a strong relationship between literacy skills in a first language and literacy skills in a second. Research indicates that about 20% of the process of reading in a second language is predictable on the basis of the level of first-language literacy (Bernhardt & Kamil, 1995; Brisbois, 1996; Hulstijn, 1991). In other words, the more knowledge of reading and literacy a student has in his first language, the better off he will be in a second. Even when children are literate in a language that has little or no structural or orthographic overlap with English, the mere fact that they are already literate really helps them. Why is this the case?

Attaining literacy means having developed a set of strategies for coping with written materials. Literate children understand already that print represents meaning. They understand that there are purposes for reading. They have already begun to develop many of the proficiencies described throughout this book.

The most challenged second-language learner is one who has no first-language literacy. This type of learner is in double jeopardy—he has to learn the language, and he has to learn what literacy is about.

Cross-Language Influences

How a person processes a second language is influenced by the processing from the first language (Bernhardt, 1991). English, for example, tends toward subject–verb–object word order, as in *The boy sees the dog*. Other languages, such as German, have more flexible word order; it is the inflectional system that indicates who is seeing what. While *man* and *dog* in German may stay in the same place, the inflectional system might indicate that the man is being seen by the dog: *Der Mann sieht den Hund; Den Hund sieht der Mann; Der Hund sieht den Mann;* and *Den Mann sieht der Hund*. These sentences are all possibilities in German. As a different example, languages such as Chinese that are subject–object–verb languages will represent the word order as *The man the dog sees,* and so forth.

Because of the linguistic transfer from language to language, readers will assume that the word order they are used to will be used in the language they are learning to read. The comprehension challenges that such cross-language influences present are daunting.

Cross-Cultural Influences

There is no question that second-language readers employ background knowledge. This is consistent with what you have learned throughout this book about all learners. Unfortunately, in some cases the background knowledge a second-language learner brings to a text is absolutely irrelevant, and in other cases it is simply inconsistent with the knowledge assumed by the text. Such situations, of course, create serious challenges for second-language learners.

One study forcefully demonstrating this influence of background knowledge was conducted by Margaret Steffenson and her colleagues (Steffenson, Joag-Dev, & Anderson, 1979). Readers were asked to read passages about weddings—from their own culture and another culture. Even though they had no language problems, the readers recalled the passages in a way that was consistent with the way in which weddings are conducted in their own culture. They took the language at hand and reconfigured it in a way that made sense within their own framework. This is an absolutely critical issue in the second-language literacy process. Learners will both read and write within the framework that is most familiar to them—their linguistic and cultural framework. They will need to learn to break with these patterns in order to develop literacy abilities in English. Sixth-grade teacher Susan Chen comments on being alert to cross-cultural differences:

> If you want to get across concepts such as *above/below* or *over there*, use your body.
>
> —*Rosa Quintana*
> *Multiage Grades 1–2 Teacher*

I'm always on the lookout for concepts and ideas that my Hmong students are likely to interpret somewhat differently than my Anglo students or points at which my Hmong students are likely to have had somewhat different experiences that they can share with other students. For example, whenever we talk about U.S. holidays such as Martin Luther King, Jr. Day or Labor Day, I make it a point to ask my Hmong students to talk about some of their holidays and what they celebrate. Or, if we are talking about farms and most of my students are thinking of the huge farms that exist in California and the Midwest today, I ask my Hmong students to describe the small family farms that they have known or have learned about from their parents and other grown-ups. This leaves both my Anglo students and my Hmong students knowing more than they would have without the other group's contributions. It also avoids confusion, such as that which develops when both groups are considering farms but one group is thinking of huge corporate farms and the other group is thinking of small plots of land.

Susan Chen, Sixth-Grade Teacher

447

4. Imagine you are in a foreign country and you see the following words: *Ristaurante, Panaderia, Krakenhaus,* ресторан, 割烹店 . In which country or countries would you feel the most comfortable? What theory or perspective would predict your comfort level?

5. Imagine that someone you're talking to says the following: "Yesterday no home go. Brother here." Based on some of the things you have learned about language structure in this section, what could you hypothesize about the structure of this person's native language?

INSTRUCTIONAL PRINCIPLES

Although language minority students often enter our schools bilingual and bicultural and are therefore intellectually gifted, many of them fail in our schools.

—Robin Scarcella
Teacher Educator

We now turn to practical application of the information we have discussed in the earlier sections of the chapter. Your own situation will of course be different from those we have described. You will almost certainly have children in your classroom who speak languages other than those we have used for examples. You may have a class in which only one language other than English is spoken, or you may have a class in which several different languages are spoken. You may have only one or two non-native speakers in your classroom, or you may have many. Whatever your specific situation, the following guidelines and principles will lead you to ask appropriate questions and work toward effective classroom instruction.

As a cardinal rule, note that it is important that you remember everything you know about first-language reading when you are teaching reading to speakers of other languages. Most of the principles and practices will work as they do for children who speak English as natives. Some of them, of course, will have to be adapted. But very few will have to be discarded altogether. In the next two sections of the chapter, we present two sets of instructional suggestions, the first from Lisa Delpit and the second our own.

Delpit's Principles for Working with Poor Urban Children

Lisa Delpit (1995) has presented ten principles for working with poor urban children. Many children who do not speak English as a native language are urban and poor; many are not. However, most of what Delpit says applies to children who are learning a second language, even if they are not poor or urban. In fact, it is reasonable to suggest that these principles apply to all children. Let us examine them one by one.

Do Not Teach Less Content, but Recognize Children's Strengths and, If Anything, Teach More

It is simply not the case that children know less simply because they do not speak English. We have to be constantly on guard against presuming that a child is not intelligent when he is simply revealing that he is not proficient in English. Our opening scenarios illustrate teachers coping with such problems and feelings. When you are working with students who do not read or speak English fluently, realize that in the majority of cases they are competent students who simply do not have fully developed English language skills. This will prompt you to design instruction to give them the skills they need, rather than write them off as incompetent.

Whatever Methodology or Instructional Program You Use, Demand Critical Thinking

This is certainly an extension of the first point. Often, we fall into the trap of thinking that students who are from lower socioeconomic classes or who speak a different language are not as bright as other students. Consequently, we often reason that they cannot handle critical thinking. No judgment could be more debilitating to students' growth. The goal of critical literacy and the critical literacy curriculum that we outlined in Chapter 1 and have discussed throughout this book are just as appropriate for second-language learners as they are for any other students. For example, the goal of deep understanding and the approaches to teaching for deep understanding that we described in Chapter 8—such as knowledge as design and questioning the author—are absolutely crucial to second-language learners.

Ensure Access to the Basic Skills, Conventions, and Strategies Essential to Success in U.S. Education

We often "dumb down" the curriculum for children who do not meet the traditional standards. Further, we may begin teaching non-native speakers with less emphasis on skills than middle-class children typically receive. This will not work! We are not suggesting that you teach only basic skills. As we just noted, critical literacy is the goal. But do remember that, although not all children come to school with the same skills, all students need to master the building blocks that lead to critical literacy. As a teacher, you want to be certain that your students acquire whatever skills they need to be successful in school and in later life, something Timothy Hayden, a third-grade teacher, makes a conscious effort to do:

One thing I really try to work on with my Puerto Rican students is mastery of basic skills, such as standard usage and spelling, while still giving them plenty of chances to do critical thinking. This is a tough decision to make because I know that in many cases my kids know more than their English skills show, and so in some sense I'm slowing them down to work on the basics. Yet I also know that if they can't read when they leave school, or use poor grammar or spelling when they're looking for a job, they won't get very far. That's why I feel that I have to balance attention to basics with attention to higher-level stuff.

Timothy Hayden, Third-Grade Teacher

Empower Students to Challenge Racist Views of Their Competence and Worthiness

My main concern is that every new student not only begins to learn English, but also feels a part of our classroom community.

—John Hom
Sixth-Grade Teacher

Racism and classism often extend to children who are non-native speakers of English. You must support your second-language students' egos and help them build the sort of self-worth that will lead them to persevere when they encounter challenges. As we discussed in Chapter 2, all students need the support and skills that will enable them to meet challenges, be successful, and realize that success is something under their control. Creating an "I can do it!" attitude in your second-language students and conveying to them that you as their teacher hold an "I can help you do it!" attitude are crucial. Providing reading experiences such as the kind sixth-grade teacher Ann Beecher does in the following activity will promote positive attitudes:

IN THE CLASSROOM

Using the Shared Reading Experience in a Sixth-Grade ESL Class

Ann Beecher teaches sixth grade in a public school in a Los Angeles suburb. The majority of the students in her ESL class speak Spanish as their primary language, with a sprinkling of students speaking a variety of other languages. Ms. Beecher has found that the shared reading experience—students and teacher reading aloud together—is a highly effective technique for developing confidence and building on students' skills in reading and speaking English. "My ESL students are often reticent to risk being wrong or making mistakes when it comes to speaking or reading in English," Ms. Beecher says. "So I need to think of ways to create a safe environment that will support their learning. One of those ways is the shared reading experience. It's a risk-free way for them to use oral language." Here are the steps Ms. Beecher usually follows in preparing a shared reading experience:

- Choose a selection. Ms. Beecher most frequently uses poetry, perhaps a poem from Shel Silverstein's *Falling Up* (1996) or a poem from their literature text. "One of the class favorites is 'The Shark' by John Ciardi. They enjoy reciting the colorful words

Ciardi uses to describe the shark, such as 'gulper, ripper, snatcher, grabber.'" Ms. Beecher occasionally uses a very short piece of prose, also something from their literature text. "The key is choosing something that will engage students, something that they will really enjoy and can relate to," Ms. Beecher says. "One of the values of using the shared reading experience is that the students are reading 'at grade' materials. This is a big boost to their confidence. It gives them a real sense of accomplishment."

- Set up an overhead projector, and make copies of the selection for each student.
- Prepare and motivate students for the selection. "This usually takes very little effort," Ms. Beecher says. "When the kids see the overhead projector, they know it means we're going to read something together. It's one of their favorite things we do. Like singing or reciting jazz chants, they enjoy the rhythm of the language and the community experience of speaking the same words together."
- With expression and enthusiasm, read through the selection once or twice, then invite students to read along in unison.
- Focus on a particular reading skill or strategy. "If we are reading rhyming poetry, usually I will circle the rhyming words on the overhead and have students do the same on their copies. I will talk about certain words and check for students' understanding. Also, sometimes when I first read the piece through, I will stop occasionally and have students predict what will happen next."
- Follow-up for this postreading endeavor might include any number of activities—art (illustrating the shark *gulping, ripping, snatching, grabbing,* for example), writing, or evaluating: "How did we do? Did you like the piece? Why? What did you like about it? Is there anything we should do differently next time? What's your favorite new word you learned?"

Recognize and Build on Strengths

The importance of building on students' strengths is such a truism, repeated so often, that it often does not have a great deal of meaning for many of us. How, indeed, does one "build on a strength"? If you do not go beyond what a student already knows and can do, you may run the risk of boring that child and losing him for the real tasks of learning that are to follow. Building on strength means that you should *begin* with what a child can do best and work toward those things that a child does not know or does not do well. Again, many of the principles from Chapter 2 and elsewhere in the book are very applicable. Ensure that students take on challenges they can meet and experience a steady diet of success by scaffolding their efforts as they move from the known to the new. Then gradually release responsibility to the students themselves as their competence and confidence grow. For some students, this will mean a lot of scaffolding and a very gradual handing over of responsibility. Others may readily accept challenges and thrive on them. Here, Taiwanese-American Ed Chi, a very strong student who is currently a Ph.D. candidate at the University of Minnesota, talks about his success in meeting the challenge of an immersion class:

I think that the greatest school challenge I had was being totally immersed in an English-speaking environment, but I also think that this immersion was essential for me to really develop my English skills. In school, I received ESL instruction for only about an hour a day. The rest of the time, I functioned in much the same way as any other students in our elementary school. This total immersion enabled me to learn to think in English instead of translating everything from Chinese to English.

However, I think the value of immersion must be carefully balanced with concern for the student's self-esteem, because the differences between someone who is just learning English and all the other kids becomes very pronounced in an immersion situation. I have some friends for whom immersion was just too much of a challenge.

Ed Chi, Ph.D. Candidate

Use Familiar Metaphors and Experiences from the Children's World

Once again, this is simply a matter of what good teachers do instinctively. We know the importance of background knowledge. As Delpit suggests, instead of insisting that all children have the same background knowledge at the beginning, deal with the students' knowledge and background and use that as the basis of teaching. For example, if you are teaching about the destructive power of tornadoes and have Vietnamese children in your class, you can use their knowledge of the awesome power of typhoons as a bridge to their understanding the power of tornadoes.

Create a Sense of Family and Caring

ESL teacher Lillian Colon-Vila knows how crucial it is that all students feel that they are a valuable part of the class and will be supported in their efforts by both the teacher and by the other students in the class:

To welcome my ESL students, I always begin the semester by telling a story. It's usually a simple one to welcome them to the United States and particularly to my classroom. Since I use the students' names and their native countries, I invent the stories on the spur of the moment. I use puppets, pictures, flash cards, or the chalkboard to draw pictures as I go along.

I make it a point to share my own first day of school, too—how I stuttered, mispronounced the teacher's name, and wished for the floor to swallow me. The students laugh and relate to my experience. The iceberg between us breaks and I can begin to teach.

Lillian Colon-Vila, ESL Multigrade Teacher

In the terminology we used earlier in the book, your classroom must be a literate environment for all students. Delpit uses the example of a teacher telling students they are "Ms. X's students" with the result that the students believe that someone really cares about them. As a result, they are willing to work harder so they will not disappoint Ms. X. Another way to create a sense of caring, particularly useful with primary-grade children, is to remember and celebrate children's birthdays—posting announcements of birthdays on the board and perhaps having treats. Of course, doing this is worthwhile with all students, but for those who may feel a little distance between themselves and school, it can be extra valuable.

Monitor and Assess Needs, and Then Address Them with a Wealth of Diverse Strategies

Effective teaching cannot be done without careful assessment and evaluation of what students know and learn. Teachers need to be vigilant to discontinue teaching techniques that prove inappropriate for some students. Students can often benefit from a different teaching strategy when the initially attempted one did not work. Such choices require careful reasoning based on data gathered in assessing the students. As we emphasize in Chapter 11, assessment does not simply mean formal assessment. You will need to use a wide range of techniques to gauge students' strengths and weakness and then create ways to build on their strengths. These techniques are likely to include the use of formal tests, but they will also include talking to students, carefully observing them as they work at school tasks, and seeking insights from parents and others in your students' home communities. Figure 10.4 illustrates how a drawing can show a student's understanding of a story.

> You'll see kids first trying their language skills with one another while they play or interact in cooperative groups. That's where you can begin to grasp how much they know.
>
> —Donna Clovis
> K–5 ESL Teacher

FIGURE 10.4 *Maria's Drawing of* Island of the Blue Dolphins *by Scott O'Dell (1960) Reveals Her Understanding of the Story*

One specific technique that builds on students' strengths as readers while at the same time providing an opportunity to assess their reading skills is to have students use puppets while they read. Read what Ann Beecher has to say about the value of puppets:

> I often use puppets as a device for helping my ESL students feel less self-conscious when they read aloud. The students will put a puppet on their finger or hand and pretend that it is the puppet who is speaking, not them. This puts the focus on the puppet, not the student. Sometimes students will even assume the puppet's persona and talk in a high, squeaky voice or a deep, slow voice, depending on the puppet and how the student imagines that character speaking. Although I have both hand and finger puppets available, my sixth-graders seem to like the finger puppets best, especially our fly puppet that looks incredibly like a real fly. Puppets are fantastic "ice breakers" and provide a "crutch" or "support" to students who are reticent or shy about reading aloud.
>
> Ann Beecher, Sixth-Grade Teacher

Books That Present Hispanic Children and Family Life

Isabel Schon (1995) has identified a number of noteworthy fiction and nonfiction trade books that present a nonstereotyped view of the Latino families experiencing life, celebrating special occasions, or dealing with difficult situations. Mary H. Cordier and Maria A. Pérez-Stable (1996) also provide an extensive listing of trade books that affirm the heritages and lifestyles of Hispanic Americans. We list a few of these recommended titles here. More can be found in the bibliographies themselves.

Alma Flor Ada. *My Name Is Maria Isabel.* Atheneum, 1993. Maria, a student recently arrived from Puerto Rico and named after her two grandmothers, gets her name changed to Mary because there are already two Marias in her new class. She does, however, courageously find a way to communicate her unhappiness about this to her teacher. 64 pages.

Rudolfo Anaya. *The Farolitos of Christmas.* Hyperion, 1995. Set in New Mexico in 1944, this Christmas story tells of Luz's anticipation of making *luminarias* with her grandfather. However, when he becomes too ill, Luz's uses her own ingenuity to create little lanterns, *farolitos*, out of paper bags, sand, and candles. 32 pages.

Robert Baden. *And Sunday Makes Seven.* Whitman, 1990. In this traditional tale from Costa Rica, Carlos is rewarded by 12 witches for adding to their song about the days of the week. To appreciate this tale, students will need to know the days of the week and numbers one to seven in Spanish. 36 pages.

Larry Dane Brimner. *A Migrant Family.* Lerner, 1992. This photo-essay, which describes the living conditions of a migrant family through the eyes of a 12-year-old boy and his family, provides a candid overview of many of the issues that surround migrant workers. 40 pages.

Maria Cristina Brusca. *On the Pampas.* Holt, 1991. This story depicts a young girl's summer on her grandparents' ranch in Argentina, which includes caring for the horses and cattle, spending time with the gauchos, enjoying big family dinners, and learning to dance the *zamba*. 32 pages.

Honor and Respect Children's Home Cultures

It would be difficult to imagine anything seemingly easier than the application of this principle, but unfortunately, honor and respect are too often lacking in classrooms. Knowledge that has been gained in children's home culture constitutes a strength that can be brought into the classroom and used as the basis for learning to read about all manner of ideas and topics. Besides, changing children's cultural orientations and allegiances is not really an option. Children come to school having spent a huge amount of time within their cultures and their families, and once they begin school, they will continue to spend far more time at home than in the classroom. You cannot win against such odds. It is just not possible to instill in children a totally different culture in a few hours a day—it may even be impossible to do so in a lifetime. Unlike the goals of the Americanization movement that we discussed earlier in the chapter, your goal must be to support students' attempts to

Matt Christopher. *Centerfield Ballhawk.* Little, Brown, 1992. Nine-year-old Jose Mendez's greatest wish is to play baseball. He struggles through mishaps, such as hitting a ball through a neighbor's car window, and competition with his older sister who shines at softball, to finally prove himself as an excellent outfielder. 59 pages.

Arthur Dorros. *Radio Man/Don Radio: A Story in English and Spanish.* HarperCollins, 1993. While traveling with his family from place to place harvesting fruits and cabbages, Diego keeps in contact with his cousins and friends through call-in radio programs. 40 pages.

Tony Johnston. *Lorenzo, the Naughty Parrot.* Harcourt, 1992. Lorenzo, a naughty parrot, is in the center of all the action and excitement that happen to a family in Mexico in this short chapter book. 30 pages.

Pat Mora. *A Birthday Basket for Tia.* Simon & Schuster, 1992. As her great-aunt's 90th birthday approaches, Cecilia wonders what present she can give her *tia.* She decides to fill a basket with things that remind her of her aunt—a ball

they play with, a mixing bowl they use to make *bizcochos,* a flower pot, and their favorite book. The story ends with a wonderful family celebration. 32 pages.

Gary Soto. *Crazy Weekend.* Scholastic, 1993. While visiting their photographer uncle in Fresno, two seventh-graders from East Los Angeles, Hector and Mando, find themselves in for an exciting weekend when, while on an aerial photo shoot, Uncle Julio inadvertently foils a robbery in progress. 144 pages.

Gary Soto. *Local News.* Harcourt, 1993. With humor, understanding, and an easy-going style, Soto gives his readers 13 memorable stories depicting the lives of Mexican-American children and their families living in California's Central Valley. 148 pages.

Jane Resh Thomas. *Lights on the River.* Hyperion, 1994. This poignant story of the plight of migrant workers is viewed through the eyes of Teresa, a young Hispanic girl, who travels with her family from field to field, following the crops in order to earn enough money to sustain them throughout the year. 32 pages.

Creating an "I can do it!" attitude in second-language learners and conveying to them that you as their teacher hold an "I can help you do it!" attitude are crucial.

maintain their cultural identities and to support their becoming successful in the mainstream culture represented by the school. One small step toward doing this might be taken during the birthday celebrations we mentioned. Inviting second-language students to share their birthday traditions with the class gives status to those traditions and adds to other students' stores of knowledge about different cultures.

Another and more significant step toward demonstrating and fostering respect for children's home cultures is to provide students with literature that accurately and fairly represents a variety of cultures, as does the Hispanic literature listed in the bibliography on pages 454–455.

Foster a Sense of Children's Connection to Community— to Something Greater Than Themselves

The purpose of learning in school is to be able to do something beyond school. Of course, given the nature of our society, students have to do well in school to do well beyond it. Delpit encourages educators to teach students that they owe a debt to the community, that they should give something back as they become adult community members. In doing this, it is helpful to present students with role models, local members of their linguistic and cultural communities who have succeeded in school and have gone on to become productive members of their communities. Here are some thoughts of Latino educator Felipe Golez on the role models in his family:

> My parents had primary school educations, thick accents, and were uncomfortable speaking English but spoke it anyway for survival purposes. I admired their always-working-too-many-jobs tenacity and their never-in-sync-with-the-dominant-culture ability to persevere. They rarely exhibited the domineering expectations of other surrounding parents, but would willingly give me their last dollar if I asked for it, so I never asked. When my older sister went off to college, I proudly took over the family scribe tasks: balancing checkbooks and writing important letters. She was actually my main academic model, her face always buried in a book when she wasn't knocking people senseless in organized sports. At her urging I filled out the forms to enter the University of California, Santa Barbara, through an economic opportunity program.
>
> Felipe Golez, Teacher Educator

As we have said, Delpit's ten principles are clearly applicable to all students, but they are particularly applicable to second-language students. All children need and deserve the instruction and support that Delpit suggests. Children who come to school having to master a new language and quite possibly a new culture especially deserve them.

Reflection AND Application

6. Think about attitudes toward non-native speakers of English that you have observed. Have you encountered attitudes that might negatively influence the ways in which teachers interact with students? How might you guard against those attitudes negatively affecting your classroom style?

7. Consider your own family traditions. Can you think of any holiday celebrations you and your family observe that are not widely observed? Do you think they are any less valuable because they are not more widely observed? How might they be useful when you are teaching students?

8. Reflect on the purpose of schooling. What is it that you want your students to do when they finish school? What is it that you think "society" expects of students who finish school? What are some of the ways in which you can get students to "connect" to the values of society? What are your own experiences in this area? How might you use your experiences to help others? What are some of the negative influences you will have to overcome?

Ten Techniques for Working with Second-Language Children in Typical Classrooms

In this section, we have combined Delpit's principles with the linguistic concepts, research findings, and historical context of language teaching described earlier in this chapter (as well as the general principles of teaching reading described throughout the book) to suggest some specific techniques you can use for teaching students to read in English when they speak a different first language. We have placed these techniques in an order reflecting their utility; thus, you should probably attempt to implement these principles in the order given. If you do this, you will probably have a good deal more success than if you simply select one or another from the list.

Take Advantage of the 20% Rule

Remember that, although languages are different, there is considerable transfer between them. As indicated in the first part of this chapter, research suggests that the overlap between languages can be as much as 20%. Thus, your task in teaching literacy in a second language is far easier than if there was little or no overlap. You do not have to start at the beginning with second-

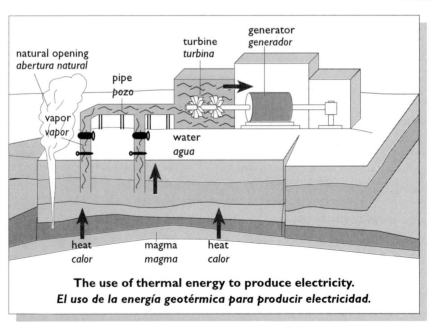

The use of thermal energy to produce electricity.
El uso de la energía geotérmica para producir electricidad.

FIGURE 10.5 *Graphic Display of Overlap Between Spanish and English Vocabulary*

From *Ciencias* by Mallision, Mallision, Smallwood, & Valentino. Copyright © 1985 by Silver Burdett Ginn, Simon & Schuster Elementary. Used by permission.

language students; rather, you can consider that you are almost one fifth of the way to being successful.

Figure 10.5 shows the 20% rule in action. In this graphic display of geothermal energy, there are 16 Spanish words used. Two of the words—*natural* and *vapor*—are identical to the equivalent terms in English. Another seven words—*turbina, generador, uso, energía, geotérmica, producir,* and *electricidad*—are almost identical and certainly recognizable. This simple example illustrates the overlap between English and Spanish and reminds us that children do possess substantial information that they can draw on for reading second-language texs.

Of course, as we all know, there is never a free lunch, and this rule holds true for the 20% dividend. The percentage will be different for each language. In some languages the overlap may be greater than 20%, and in others, less. Figure 10.6 shows some of the features that English, Spanish,

	English	Spanish	Vietnamese	Chinese
Phonolgy				
Tones			X	X
Phonetic	X	X		
Orthography				
Roman	X	X	X	
Character				X
Morphology				
Inflections	X	X		
Plural markings	X	X		
Articles	X	X		
Word classes	X	X		
Syntax				
Signaled by inflection				
Signaled by word order	X	X	X	
SVO	X			
VO		X		
Signaled by semantics				X
Tense				
Signaled by morphology	X	X		
Signaled by modifier			X	
Lexicon				
Monosyllabic			X	
Polysyllabic	X	X		X

FIGURE 10.6 *Some Linguistic Features Found in Four Languages*

Vietnamese, and Chinese have in common, and some of the ways in which these languages differ. The figure suggests the sorts of things to look for in deciding where to spend your time in instruction. For example, if the child's native language overlaps with English a great deal in orthography, that is one skill you will not have to worry about immediately. You can spend your time doing other reading-related activities.

Give Second-Language Students Plenty of Time

It is important to remember that children who do not speak English as a native language will, in all likelihood, not be as automatic as native speakers at completing any English language task, including, of course, reading. Figure 10.7 provides an example of the very different amounts of time it would take students reading at three different rates to complete a typical intermediate-grade book, in this case Gary Soto's *The Skirt*. The instructional implication of this suggestion is straightforward: Provide second-language students with extra time to complete the linguistic tasks you ask them to do. Following this simple suggestion can minimize what is perhaps the greatest difficulty teachers face in multilanguage classrooms. The question, of course, is how you can provide this extra time, and we have several suggestions. Students who need the time can be given opportunities to complete their work as part of free-choice activities. Or they might be allowed to take home work that isn't completed during class. Or you might give students questions you will ask ahead of time during reading lessons, being sure to give *all* students sufficient time to do the reading and thinking necessary to answer them. Still another option is to shorten some of the selections students are asked to read by summarizing parts of them. The following activity, for example, includes a summary of the first half of Pegi Deiz Shea's *The Whispering Cloth*:

Student	Reading Rate (words per minute)	Chapter One (1,000 words)	Whole Book (8,000 words)
Anita	50	20 minutes	2 hours, 40 mins
Carlos	150	7 minutes	53 minutes
Maria	250	4 minutes	32 minutes

FIGURE 10.7 *Times Required for Three Students, with Varying Reading Rates, to Read Gary Soto's* The Skirt

IN THE CLASSROOM
Summarizing Part of a Selection

The Whispering Cloth: A Refugee's Story is a touching story of a young Hmong girl, Mai, who learns to create embroidered tapestries—*pándau,* in the Hmong language—while in a refugee camp in Thailand. The book is beautifully illustrated with both watercolors and reproductions of the *pándau* Mai created. Although the book is not a long read for students who read fluently, for students beginning to read English, it constitutes a formidable task. Summarizing the first half of the book would simplify that task considerably, particularly for Hmong students, coming as they do from a culture that does not have a written language.

Preparation:
Introduce the book in a fashion that you and your students will be comfortable with. You might tell children that it is the story of a young Hmong girl in a refugee camp in Thailand, show children the location of the refugee camp and the Hmongs' homeland in northern Laos, and briefly discuss the situation that led to the Hmong's being in the refugee camp. Then, explain to children what embroidery or *pándau* is, show a sample of embroidery (actual Hmong *pándau,* if possible), and explain that *pándau* plays an important part in the story. You might also tell children that the main characters in the story are Mai and her grandmother, who is simply called Grandma. Finally, tell children you are going to summarize the first half of the book for those who would like it summarized and that they can either listen to your summary or begin reading on their own. After children have made their choices, perhaps with some guidance from you, you can gather around you those who want to hear the summary and read or paraphrase a summary like this one:

> As The Whispering Cloth *opens, we learn that Mai lives in a refugee camp with her grandmother and that Mai can remember little of her life outside of the camp. She knows, though, that many people leave the refugee camp and some of them go to America, and it seems that she would like to go there too. Partly to give her something to do and partly to provide the family with some income, Grandma teaches Mai to make* pándau. *Mai learns very quickly and is soon very good at making this beautiful "flowery cloth." One day, Mai begins to work on a* pándau *in which she tells a story that is filling her head with thoughts.*

As you read the rest of the book, you will see pictures of the *pándau* that Mai stitched. Now read the rest of the book to see the *pándau* and what it meant to Mai and her Grandma, and what they decided to do with it.

Use the Rosetta Stone Technique

We have all heard about the wonder of the Rosetta stone. This tremendous discovery, shown in Figure 10.8, contains the same text in Egyptian hieroglyphic, Egyptian demotic script, and several ancient Greek languages. The

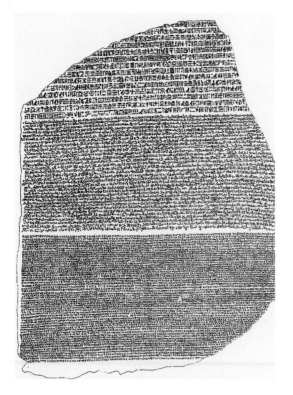

FIGURE 10.8 *The Rosetta Stone—Showing Greek, Demotic, and Hieroglyphic Scripts*

discovery of the Rosetta Stone allowed linguists to decipher Egyptian hieroglyphic, which they did not know how to read, based on their knowledge of ancient Greek, which they could read.

One useful vocabulary technique for working with a class of students who have different language backgrounds is based on this notion. If you make a chart of everyday English words in one column, your students who speak other languages can contribute the equivalent words from each of their languages in other columns. Alternatively, your non-native speakers might periodically bring in a word from their native language, put it on the chart, and solicit the equivalent English word and words from other languages represented in your class. Or, as you encounter words in a content lesson, you can use them as the entries in the "Rosetta" chart, and have students add the words from their languages.

Whatever the specific source of words you put on the chart, be certain to practice pronouncing both non-English and English words with the non-native speakers, as well as with the entire class. In this way, all students will be able to do well at some parts of the task. Also, not only will your students for whom English is a native language begin to learn some vocabulary in another language, they will also begin to appreciate the difficulties other students are having. And they will be able to see that non-native speakers know a great deal that they do not know.

Figure 10.9 shows one example of such a chart. In this instance, Diane Lane, a teacher in a midwestern suburban school, selected the words from the unit on farm animals the children were studying in class. She then asked children's parents to provide the words in those languages that were represented in the classroom. As can be seen from the chart, the languages were Greek, Spanish, and Ukrainian. Note also that in addition to writing the words in the native orthographies, Greek parents have used the English alphabet to write them. Situations like this, in which students and their parents work together in gaining proficiency in English, are terrific learning events.

As the lessons change, the words to be learned will, of course, also change. However, the dialogue with parents, older siblings, relatives, or other members of the language community should continue. You might also

English	Spanish	Greek (Greek alphabet)	Greek (Roman alphabet)	Ukranian (Cyrillic alphabet)
good	bueno	καλο	kalo	добрий
day	día	ιμερα	imera	день
chicken	pollo	κοτα	kota	курка
horse	caballo	αιοδο	alogo	кінь
sheep	oveja	αρνι	arni	овечка
cows	vacas	αγελαδεσ	agelades	корови
pig	puerco	γουρουνι	gourouni	свиньі
goat	cabra	κατικι	kachiki	цал
ducks	patos	ραριεσ	papies	ьутки

FIGURE 10.9 *The Rosetta Stone Technique— A Cross-Language Chart for a Class Unit on Farm Animals*

encourage students to create their own pictorial charts using the Rosetta stone technique, as shown in Figure 10.10.

One important caution in using the Rosetta stone technique is that words in isolation can often have multiple meanings. In the chart from Ms. Lane's class, for example, the word *ducks* could mean an animal or the action of quickly bending down. You may have to give your translators more information than just the single words. For example, you might tell them that most of the words name farm animals.

One extension of the Rosetta stone technique is to make charts featuring holidays celebrated in the various languages and cultures represented in your classroom. In this case, each holiday might be the subject of a different chart, with the name of the holiday and some of its traditions in the native language listed in one column and then translations of the name of the holiday and its traditions into English and the other languages of your classroom shown in the other columns. Figure 10.11 shows a chart for the Mexican holiday Cinco de Mayo, with words in English and Spanish. Of course, discussions of the Mexican independence day are likely to lead to discussions of other independence days, including the American Fourth of July; thus children from different cultures will learn more about one another's languages and traditions.

Finally, charts like these can often be a focus of instruction and should be displayed prominently. Children will be able to refer to the chart to remember the words and the ideas they represent during writing, reading, and discussion.

FIGURE 10.10 *A Student-Made "Rosetta Stone"*

Words and Phrases to Celebrate Cinco de Mayo

Spanish	English
Cinco de Mayo	Fifth of May
1862	1862
fiesta	big party
amigos	friends
Comida: carne, pescado, tortillas, enchiladas, tacos	Food: meat, fish, tortillas, enchiladas, tacos
piñata	piñata
música	music
los mariachis	mariachi band
maracas	maracas
baile	dance
canta	sing
divertido	good time

FIGURE 10.11 *Cinco de Mayo Chart Showing Spanish and English Words Associated with the Holiday*

Involve Parents, Siblings, and Other Speakers of the Children's Languages

Often, parents, siblings, or other relatives can help in translating between the native language and English, or vice versa. Sometimes all it takes is a bridge between languages to get children started. Translating the first page or so of a text they are reading or making a graphic organizer of what students are going to read, such as that shown in Figure 10.12, can be extremely helpful for young learners. Moreover, such a bridge can work both ways. As students become more proficient in English, many times they assume a role of translator for parents who are not quite as proficient. This will give students a reason for wanting to learn more English and may encourage the parents to learn more English as well. In addition, as students become increasingly competent in English, they will be motivated to become still more competent.

Try to find someone in the community who can and is willing to come into the classroom. He or she can ask the LEP student questions for you so that you can show interest in who the child is.

—*Marta Weiss*
Director of Elementary ESL Programs

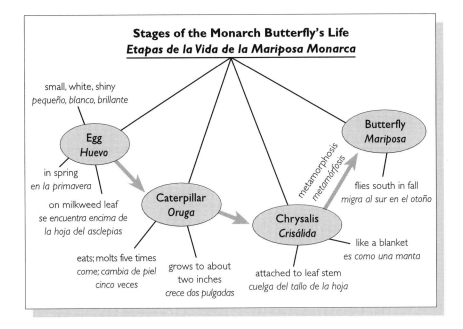

FIGURE 10.12 *Graphic Organizer in English and Spanish for a Section of Gail Gibbons's* Monarch Butterfly

Siblings can sometimes be particularly helpful in the classroom. Older brothers or sisters who may be reluctant to participate in their own class because they are not as proficient as their first-language classmates may work extremely well with their younger brothers or sisters. An added bonus here is that, when tutoring these younger students, the older siblings may very well realize that they know more English than they thought and consequently be encouraged to attempt to read when they would have otherwise been reluctant to do so.

Use All the Available People Resources

As we have pointed out several times, tutoring can be a useful technique in a host of literacy learning contexts. For learning to read in a second language, it may have particular benefits. Of course, one great benefit will accrue if you are fortunate enough to have older students who speak the same languages as your students and are somewhat more proficient in reading English than they are. Again, sometimes the older students may realize that they know more English than they thought and be encouraged to attempt more challenging reading tasks themselves. They may also be motivated to learn more because they begin to realize what they do not know yet or because they wish to do a better job in helping the younger students.

Of course, students who are the same age as the tutees but have somewhat more advanced English reading skills can also serve as classroom tutors. And as is the case with cross-age tutors, peer tutors are likely to benefit from the teaching they do. As we have noted before, the research strongly demonstrates that students tutoring other students is a true "win–win" situation in which both tutor and tutee benefit markedly (Cohen, Kulic, & Kulic, 1982). Finally, students are not the only people resources that may be of help in your classroom. Aides, volunteers, college students preparing to be teachers, and sometimes even administrators and maintenance personnel can perform a variety of helpful tasks with non-native speakers.

Give Students Freedom to Choose the Language in Which to Respond

Research tells us that students who are given a choice often demonstrate greater abilities when they can respond in the language in which they feel most comfortable. This is particularly true, of course, when the text is in English and the students are not fluent in English.

Although this is a very easy thing for you as an instructor to do, it can pay big dividends. In addition to demonstrating better understanding when using the language of their choice, students may also be able to remember more of what they have learned in the language with which they are more comfortable. Also, students' language preference may vary for different reading materials. For example, a reading passage about a student's native country might be best responded to in the student's native language. In reading a passage about American history, however, a student might choose to use English. The key is to allow the student to choose the appropriate language in which to respond.

One thing that concerns some teachers about this technique is that they feel they will not be able to understand and assess what the students wrote or said. However, even if you cannot understand the language the student chooses, all is not lost. The easiest way to handle the situation is to have the student respond in his native language and *then* have him do the translation into English. Note the terrific practice this gives the student. He is in effect using the language-experience approach—writing down his own words and then translating them. Note also that allowing students the time to do this is one way of providing the extra time we have recommended. Alternatively, if the student cannot read what he wrote back to you or translate it into English later, you might obtain the assistance of a sibling, parent, or other speaker of the language to do the translating.

In addition to giving students the opportunity to respond in the language they choose, you can sometimes give them the opportunity to read in

When a bilingual individual confronts a monolingual test, developed by monolingual individuals, and standardized and normed on a monolingual population, both the test taker and the test are asked to do something they cannot.

—*Guadalupe Valdes and Richard Figueroa*
Researchers

the language of their choice. Bilingual books, a growing set of children's books in which the same book contains both English and another language, make providing this option very convenient.

Books Available in Bilingual Formats

Barbara Elleman, former editor of *Book Links*, recommends the following sampling of bilingual picture books to use with children across grade levels. (Additionally, Yvone Freeman and Carolina Cervantes (1991) have compiled an annotated bibliography of over 300 children's books written in Spanish, which you might find helpful.)

George Ancona. *The Piñata Maker / El Penatero*. Harcourt, 1994. With full-color photos and text in both Spanish and English, this book provides a glimpse into the art of piñata making. 40 pages.

Excerpt from *The Piñata Maker / El Penatero*:

When the glue is dry, he pastes metallic paper to the point of each cone, the *pico*, so they will glitter.

Cuando se seca el engrudo, pega papel metalico a la punta de cada cono, o al pico, para que reluzcan.

Fred Burstein. *The Dancer / La Bailarina*. Bradbury, 1993. As a father accompanies his daughter to her ballet lesson, the sights they encounter—a horse, a flower, a fish, and more—are given in English, Spanish, and Japanese. 32 pages.

Lulu Delacre. *Vejigante Masquerader*. Scholastic, 1993. Carnival time in Puerto Rico is the setting for this bilingual story about a boy's difficulties in getting a costume for the celebration. 40 pages.

Lois Ehlert. *Moon Rope / Un Lazo a la Luna*. Harcourt, 1992. In this adaptation of a Peruvian folktale, Fox and Mole try to climb to the moon on a rope woven of grass. 32 pages.

Carmen Lomas Garza. *Family Pictures / Cuadros de Familia*. Children's Book Press, 1990. The author-artist depicts family scenes, including fiestas, holidays, and religious activities, from her childhood days in Kingsville, Texas. 32 pages.

Nancy Abraham Hall and Jull Syverson-Stork. *Los Pollitos Dicen / The Baby Chicks Sing: Traditional Games, Nursery Rhymes, and Songs from Spanish-Speaking Countries*. Little, Brown, 1994. The artwork of Kay Chorao adds a lighthearted touch to the attractive collection of games and songs. 32 pages.

Juan Ramon Jimenez. *Platero y Yo / Platero and I*. Clarion, 1994. Short vignettes, evocatively illustrated with woodcuts, tell of the rambles of a man and his donkey around the countryside in Andalusia, Spain. 42 pages.

Pat Mora. *Listen to the Desert / Oye al Desierto*. Clarion, 1994. In this informational book, author and artist portray the sounds and sights of the desert. 32 pages.

Lynn Reiser. *Margaret and Margarita / Margarita y Margaret*. Greenwillow, 1993. English and Spanish cleverly interact with each other in this story of two little girls' encounter in the park. 32 pages.

Eileen Roe. *Con Mi Hermano / With My Brother*. Bradbury, 1991. A Latino boy admires his brother and wants to be like him when he gets older. 32 pages.

Harriet Rohmer. *Uncle Nacho's Hat / El Sombrero del Tio Nacho*. Children's Book Press, 1989. In this amusing Nicaraguan folktale, a young girl shows her uncle how to rid himself of an old habit. 32 pages.

Realize That Most of Your Students Can and Do Read and Comprehend

Since there is a great deal of transfer between languages, it is probably the case that students who do not speak English fluently can often do far more than many teachers suspect. As we have already noted, many children have some literacy abilities in their native language. These abilities allow children to develop their own strategies for learning to read in a second language, particularly when the second language is similar to their native language in its orthography, sound system, or other linguistic features. Realizing your students' likely potential is of course in keeping with Delpit's first principle—recognizing your students' strengths. Again, be careful never to underestimate the cognitive abilities of children who do not speak English as their native language.

Use Informational Texts as a Significant Part of Instruction

Informational texts are not often used in our schools for reading instruction, and this can have serious consequences. In one metropolitan school district, for example, over 60% of the students tested—a number of whom were second-language students—failed to pass a test of basic competency in reading informational text (Drew & Smith, 1996).

We strongly recommend that you do use informational texts with second-language students for two reasons: First, students can read informational texts to find out things that they can use in their lives outside of the classroom. This may be a greater motivation to learn to read in English than anything else you can do. It will give students a reason for working as hard as they can to understand texts in English. The task can be as simple as reading a recipe for making chocolate chip cookies or as complex as reading a science article on hibernation. The child who develops skill in reading informational texts and can use it to help others at home may win his family's appreciation, which in turn contributes to his self-respect.

Second, it is possible to find informational texts dealing with topics about which second-language students have background knowledge and that do not demand knowledge of American culture or English. Knowing basic facts about common animals, for example, is independent of the language and culture in which those facts were learned. Conversely, stories written for American children often assume a good deal of cultural knowledge that your non-native speakers may not have.

When giving second-language students informational texts, it is important not to require them to learn large bodies of new knowledge in English.

And be sure to provide second-language students with sufficient instructional assistance when they are expected to learn from informational English texts. In other words, provide students with plenty of scaffolding. Requiring students to learn large amounts of new information from English texts without sufficient scaffolding is simply an invitation to failure.

Also remember that it is often not necessary for students to read an entire informational selection, as it typically is with narratives. If you locate the critical information in a text and have students read only what is relevant to the task at hand, the reading task will be considerably simplified, enabling students to complete the reading in a reasonable amount of time.

In addition to the teaching suggestions and descriptions of informational books provided throughout this book, Evelyn Freeman and Diane Person's *Using Nonfiction Trade Books in the Elementary Classroom* (1992) provides a number of useful teaching ideas and bibliographies of informational books.

Remember That Variety Is the Spice of Instruction

Another way to lessen the burden on the students who are not yet fully proficient in English is to give them opportunities to use some of the multiple intelligences that Howard Gardner (1993) has described and that we briefly described in Chapter 8. For example, drama, which we discuss in some detail in Chapter 6, is often an effective means for getting students to develop oral language skills, and those oral skills will be useful bridges to comprehending written text. Art and music, which we also consider in Chapter 6, are also useful. Not only will you find that students can develop their literacy skills by using these diverse modes of expression, but you may often be able to better understand their intended meaning when they use them.

For example, if a child is allowed to draw a picture to illustrate a written assignment, you may be able to determine what the student meant to write, even if it is not clear from his text. This information will help you determine what the child needs to know about the language. You will not have to assume, for example, that the child did not know how to write, read, or understand *any* of the content of the lesson.

> In a democratic society, the idea that every person can learn is axiomatic. Furthermore, every person can make a significant contribution to the well-being of society. Every person can gain the satisfaction of learning to use his or her talents productively.
>
> —*Ralph Tyler*
> *Curriculum and*
> *Assessment Expert*

Learn a Second Language Spoken in Your Classroom

The experience of learning a language that is spoken in your classroom is extremely valuable for several reasons. First, it will help you in communicating with your students and their parents. Second, it will send students the message that you care about them and the knowledge and experiences they bring to school. Third, learning another language is probably the most powerful way to really appreciate the task students face in learning another language. In Chapter 9, we talked about the value of teachers being practicing writers so that they could better understand the writing processes of their students. The situation is similar here. Finally, learning another language will give you a real sense of the structural similarities and differences among languages. As we noted earlier in this chapter, languages overlap to varying degrees in their sound systems, orthographies, and other linguistic features. Learning another language will allow you to experience this firsthand.

Learning a language does not have to be a matter of obtaining formal instruction. It can be as simple as listening to one of the commercially available taped lessons in another language, buying a dictionary in order to be able to understand the vocabulary of another language, or trying to converse with speakers of that language in informal settings. (Of course, a most enjoyable option when learning a second language is traveling in countries where it is spoken.) Any of these approaches will pay dividends as you attempt to address the linguistic challenges in your class.

One last point in this regard. It is not enough that you learn to speak a language, although that will help a great deal. It is important that you attempt to learn to read it as well, since that is the task your students have to accomplish.

Reflection AND Application

9. Think about reading activities that are not specific to a particular language. For example, using a table of contents in a book is the same, regardless of the language used. What other reading tasks are similar across different languages?

10. Create your own "Rosetta stone" chart, with words or phrases that you know in English and in one or two other languages. For example, you might already know that *mesa* is the Spanish word for *table*. If you cannot construct much of a chart by yourself, get together with classmates who speak other languages and create a chart together.

11. Find several different texts written in languages you do not speak. Try reading them to see whether you can comprehend any of them. It is likely you will comprehend some of at least one of them. Try writing what you comprehended in the language you just read. Now try it in English. Which was more successful? Why? Could you have found a language that allowed you to comprehend more? If you could, how might that language allow you to comprehend more?

CONCLUDING REMARKS

In this chapter, we have outlined some of the history of second-language learning in this country, noted some of the linguistic challenges that second-language learners and teachers face, and described a number of instructional approaches for dealing with second-language learners. In concluding the chapter, we want to return to the three scenarios we presented at the outset. In the first, Ms. Q. and Ms. P. had students who reacted in different ways to the classroom. We hope that the information and techniques we have offered here provide some insights into where the starting points can be found to work with such students. Problems similar to those of Yanni can be approached in ways that do not require highly specialized expertise in the language of the students.

In the second scenario, we attempted to show that the problems of second-language learners cannot be solved by assuming that all non-native speakers of English have the same abilities. A range of student abilities is often masked by category labels. We cannot forget that the focus of our efforts needs to be on the individual students and their success in our classrooms—even though that may be a difficult and challenging task.

Finally, we presented a scene that is, unfortunately, all too common. We cannot ever assume that students are not literate because they cannot read or write in English. They may well be literate in another language, and it is *that* literacy on which we should build and expand.

With second-language children just as with all children, it is not merely low-level literacy or the rudiments of literacy that we must assist students in reaching. The goal is critical literacy in English—the ability to use the English language as a vehicle for thinking, for problem solving, and for communicating—in other words, the ability to use English in a way that makes possible full and productive participation in our society.

The task of assisting non-English-speaking children in reaching the goal of critical literacy is difficult. Yet it is a task we can accomplish and the one we must aim for, and we believe that the ultimate rewards for our society will be among the greatest we could imagine.

> *All* students are a significant part of every nation's future; they all deserve the collective energies and talents of all resources the schools can offer.
>
> —*Eleanor Wall Thonis*
> *School Psychologist*

EXTENDING LEARNING

I. The World Wide Web is becoming an increasingly powerful educational tool. One excellent use you can make of it is finding resources for teaching second-language students. Here are some Web addresses to get you started. Because the Web is huge and changes so rapidly, we

471

have given only a few addresses, but these will give you an idea of what is available. And of course, what is available is growing very rapidly.

Center for Study of Books in Spanish for Children and Adolescents / para el Estudio de Libros Infantiles y Juveniles en Espanol

http://www.csusm.edu/public_html/yin/intro_eng.html

This site provides information on more than 2,000 recommended books in Spanish for children and adolescents. Bibliographic information, grade level, subject headings, and a brief description of each book are given in both English and Spanish. Updated monthly.

Hong Kong University of Science and Technology Language Center Web Page of Recommended ESL Sites

http://lcsu2.ust.hk/~sac/uweb.htm

This site has many links to resources for second-language learning. There are links to writing resources as well as links to individual language-learning resources.

Hello India

http://www.helloindia.com/india/

This site provides a wealth of information about India, often with attractive graphics. A kids' page, for example, contains elaborately illustrated Indian folktales. A calendar page lists Indian festivals and holidays and describes some of the events that take place on these days. And a music page contains Indian music you can download.

The World Wide Web Virtual Library: Languages

http://www.willamette.edu/~tjones/languages/
WWW_Virtual_Library_Language.html

This site has links to many resources for different languages (dictionaries, online texts in those languages, and a host of reference materials about language and linguistics). There are also links to other pages that deal with computer software for language learning.

The English as a Second Language Section in Yahoo

http://www.yahoo.com/Education/Languages/
English_as_a_Second_Language/

This address leads you to dozens of sites on English as a second language. For example, there is an online magazine for ESL teachers, listings of ESL games and lessons, and an open forum in which ESL teachers can share classroom activities and lesson plans.

2. As we suggested earlier, it is definitely worthwhile taking the time to begin to learn a second language. You might simply pick up some audiotapes to listen to and practice in your spare time. Many people find it useful to listen to language learning tapes while driving. Alternatively, you might enroll in a course at your university. In addition, many other organizations provide language instruction.

3. Visit a school that has second-language students. You might volunteer to work with some students whose first language is not English. If you cannot find such a school, many social service agencies, religious organizations, and other nonprofit groups have programs that target reading for second-language students. Volunteering to work in these settings, or even simply observing, will allow you to see how the principles in this chapter play out in real life.

4. Throughout this chapter we have tried to provide you with both a social and political overview and a technical, research-based overview of issues surrounding second-language children in classrooms. We hope we have inspired you to learn more about the many issues related to this complex topic. Consider reading one of the following books in order to help you get broader perspectives on all of these concerns:

    Power and Inequality in Language Education, edited by James Tollefson, contains essays from persons familiar with trying to educate individual children in the midst of political firestorms.

    Teaching Language Minority Students in the Multicultural Classroom, by Robin Scarcella, is a practice-oriented book that includes sections on parents, which you might find particularly useful.

    Reading, by Catherine Wallace, is a general book about reading, but it includes major sections devoted to second-language populations.

REFERENCES

Addams, J. (1938). *Twenty years at Hull House, with autobiographical notes.* New York: New American Library. This book chronicles Addams's experience as a social worker in Chicago during the first part of the 20th century.

Bernhardt, E. B. (1991). *Reading development in a second language.* Norwood, NJ: Ablex. This is a comprehensive synthesis of research and theory behind second-language reading, focused mostly on adult readers.

Bernhardt, E. B., & Kamil, M. (1995). Interpreting relationships between L1 and L2 reading: Consolidating the linguistic threshold and the linguistic interdependence hypotheses. *Applied Linguistics, 16,* 15–34. This research study looks at the contributions of grammatical knowledge and first-language literacy to second-language reading achievement.

Brisbois, J. (1995). Connections between first- and second-language reading. *Journal of Reading Be-*

havior, 27, 565–584. This research study investigates the contributions of grammatical and vocabulary knowledge as well as second-language writing ability to second-language reading.

Cohen, P., Kulic, J., & Kulic, C. L. (1982). Educational outcomes of tutoring: A meta-analysis of findings. *American Educational Research Journal, 19*, 237–248. This reanalysis of a number of studies of tutoring makes a very convincing case for the effectiveness of tutoring.

Collier, V. (1987). Age and rate of acquisition of second language for academic purposes. *TESOL Quarterly, 21*, 617–641. This empirical study indicates the length of time it takes to develop substantial second-language skills.

Cordier, M. H., & Pérez-Stable, M. A. (1996, March). Que vivan estos libros buenos! *Book Links*, pp. 25–31. This annotated bibliography lists picture books, middle-grade fiction, information books, folklore and legends, poetry, music, art, and anthologies representing the Hispanic culture.

Delpit, L. (1995, December). *Other people's children.* Paper presented to the National Reading Conference, New Orleans. The author surveys principles of working with students who are not from mainstream culture.

Drew, P. D., & Smith, M. M. (1996, June 9). For schools, tests act as mirrors. *Minneapolis Star Tribune*, pp. A1, A18, A19. This newspaper article describes the current state of literacy in Minnesota.

Elleman, B. (1994, July). Reading bilingually. *Book Links*, pp. 6–7. This annotated listing of bilingual picture books suggests how to link them with related books.

Freeman, Y. S., & Cervantes, C. (1991). Literature books en Español for whole language. In K. S. Goodman & Y. M. Goodman (Eds.), *Occasional papers: Program in language and literacy*, University of Arizona. The authors discuss the benefits of using books written in Spanish in the whole-language classroom and includes an annotated bibliography of more than 300 titles.

Freeman, E. B., & Person, D. G. (1992). *Using nonfiction trade books in the elementary classroom.* Urbana, IL: National Council of Teachers of English. This collection of articles about using nonfiction trade books gives many suggestions of specific books.

Gardner, H. (1993). *Multiple intelligences: The theory in practice.* New York: Basic Books. This is a collection of papers on multiple intelligences by Gardner and his colleagues.

Henderson, A. (1994). *Summary of bilingual education SEA program survey of states' LEP persons and available educational resources: 1992–1994.* Arlington, VA: Development Associates, Inc. This brief fact sheet provides information on limited English populations in the United States.

Higham, J. (1988). *Strangers in the land: Patterns of American nativism, 1860–1925.* New Brunswick, NJ: Rutgers University Press. This social history of the United States stretches from the Civil War to just prior to the Great Depression.

Hulstijn, J. (1991). How is reading in a second language related to reading in a first language? *AILA Review, 8*, 5–15. This research study discusses the relationships between first- and second-language reading among younger readers.

Leibowitz, A. H. (1984). The official character of language in the United States: Literacy requirements for immigration, citizenship, and entrance into American life. *Aztlan, 15*, 25–70. This article reviews language policy development and legislation in the United States.

National Clearinghouse for Bilingual Education. *AskNCBE.* January 20, 1995. This fact sheet discusses limited English populations in the United States.

Roosevelt, T. (1968). Children of the crucible. In *Annals of America, 14*, 129–131. Encyclopaedia Britannica. Chicago: William Benton. This is a reprint of an important speech.

Scarcella, R. (1990). *Teaching language minority students in the multicultural classroom.* Englewood Cliffs, NJ: Prentice Hall. This is a practice-oriented book for teachers who have a number of different language minority children in their classrooms.

Schon, I. (1995). Latinos/as and families: Books to enhance reading togetherness. *The Reading Teacher, 48*, 636–638. This annotated bibliography lists 18 noteworthy trade books illustrating Latino family life.

Simpson, D. (1986). *The politics of American English, 1776–1850*. New York: Oxford University Press. This book gives a review of policy and legislation involving language issues in the early history of the United States.

Spring, J. (1990). *The American school, 1642–1990*. New York: Longman. The author offers a comprehensive social history of American schools.

Steffenson, M. S., Joag-Dev, C., & Anderson, R. C. (1979). A cross-cultural perspective on reading comprehension. *Reading Research Quarterly, 15*, 10–29. This is a classic research study of the role of cultural factors in reading.

Tanner, D., & Tanner, L. (1990). *History of the school curriculum*. New York: Macmillan. This is a comprehensive history of the U.S. school curriculum.

Tollefson, J. W. (1995). Introduction: Language policy, power, and inequality. In J. W. Tollefson (Ed.), *Power and inequality in language education*. Cambridge, UK: Cambridge University Press. This text introduces a work focused on the social dimensions of second-language reading.

Wallace, C. (1992). *Reading*. Oxford, UK: Oxford University Press. This practice-oriented book for all teachers of reading emphasizes second-language lessons.

Webster, N. (1789). *Dissertations on the English language*. Boston: I. Thomas & Co. This is a collection of classic commentaries on the role of English in American life.

CHILDREN'S LITERATURE

Gibbons, G. (1989). *Monarch butterfly*. New York: Holiday House. This book describes the life cycle, body parts, and behavior of the monarch butterfly. 32 pages.

Graves, B. (1997). *The whooping crane*. Des Moines, IA: Perfection Learning. While on an airplane ride from Texas to Maryland, a young girl sits next to a biologist transporting a whooping crane chick to the Patuxent Wildlife Research Center and learns about this endangered species. 64 pages.

O'Dell, S. (1960). *Island of the blue dolphins*. Boston: Houghton Mifflin. By using her wits and the resources at hand, a young Indian girl survives alone on an island for several years. Newbery Medal winner. 154 pages. Audiotape and videotape available. Spanish text also available.

Shea, P. D. (1995). *The whispering cloth: A refugee's story*. Honesdale, PA: Boyd Mills Press. A young Hmong girl in a Thai refugee camp creates a *pándau* (embroidered tapestry) that tells her own story. Includes glossary. Illustrated by A. Riggio. With reproductions of *pándau* by Y. Yang. 32 pages.

Silverstein, S. (1996). *Falling up*. New York: Scholastic. This book contains over 100 poems and drawings by this favorite author. 171 pages.

Soto, G. (1992). *The skirt*. New York: Delacorte. When Miata leaves the skirt she is to wear for the Folklorico dance performance on the school bus, she must use all her wits to get it back before her parents find out. Illustrated by Eric Velasquez. Audiotape available. 74 pages.

chapter eleven

Classroom Assessment

by Robert Calfee

The Test

10:00 o'clock, Friday morning, early May. Ms. Aiken tinkles a small bell. "Put away your books, sharpen your pencils. Time for the reading test. Put your name at the top, fill every circle. No talking." Some groans, but by 10:15, the 32 students hunch in silence over test packets, bubbling answers. Ms. Aiken roams the classroom, patting a shoulder, cautioning a student with roving eyes, reminding students to recheck their answers, warning when five minutes are left. "11:05, Time is up. Pass in your tests—Robert, right now!" The test is finished.

The Project

One month before, early April. Ms. Aiken's students return from lunch for science. "Today is the A-team report on Mars. Eduardo, you're in charge. Bring up your group to tell us about your project." Eduardo and his three classmates tape sheets of butcher paper on the front wall with the headings: "Place in the Solar System," "Physical Characteristics," "Building a Habitat." Each sheet is a collage made up of graphics, photos, a note from the World Wide Web. For forty minutes, the group describes the red planet. Then, they add their sheets to a huge "Planets" display being prepared for parents' night.

CHAPTER OVERVIEW

The Report Card

Fast forward to June, only two more weeks of school! Mid-afternoon, students are gone, and Ms. Aiken prepares for the end-of-school-year parent conferences. Phillippa's mother enters the room with her daughter. They greet Ms. Aiken. Phillippa retrieves her portfolio, and the gangly 11-year-old begins her report. "When I started this year, I really wanted to concentrate on history. I don't know why, it just seemed interesting. I'm African American, and there's lots of prejudice, so I wanted to study about civil rights." For ten minutes, Phillippa discusses her year's work, noting strengths and limits. "I really worked hard this year, and I'm really happy with the paper I did on Coretta Scott King. It's only three pages long, and I had some problems with spelling and punctuation. But I fixed everything, and the computer art work was really good." Ms. Aiken draws the mother into the conversation, and then offers her own evaluation. Phillippa is making solid progress. The report card will contain no surprises.

OUR PERSPECTIVE ON ASSESSMENT

The three anecdotes in the opening scenario span the range of methods available to the classroom teacher for appraising student learning. At one end of the continuum are the standardized tests familiar to all of us; at the other end are strategies like "kid-watching," less obvious to students but essential in the teacher's repertoire. Figure 11.1 compares assessment designed for instruction with assessment designed for practice.

Here we discuss parts of the assessment continuum that deserve particular emphasis, three themes underlying our approach, and the importance of balance in assessment.

Our Emphasis

For three reasons, this chapter emphasizes the left side of the assessment spectrum. First, the teacher's role in standardized tests is often limited to management and reporting. Administrators select the tests, manuals tell how to give

Assessment Designed for Instruction	Assessment Designed for Accountability
Purpose and Source	
Designed by teachers for classroom decisions	Designed by experts for policy makers
Combines several sources of information	Stand-alone, single indicator
Strong link to curriculum and instruction	Independent of curriculum and instruction
Criteria	
Valid for guiding instruction	Predictive validity to other tests
Profile reliability—strengths and weaknesses	Total test reliability—one score
Sensitive to changes in performance	Stable over time and situations
Pragmatics	
Judgmental, quick turnaround, flexible	Objective, cost and time efficient, standardized
Performance-based "real" task	Multiple-choice "school" task
Administer continuously as needed	Once, sometimes twice, per year

FIGURE 11.1 *Comparison Between Assessment Designed for Instruction and Designed for Accountability*

them, and publishers score them and return results and interpretations. Reading series often include worksheets and end-of-unit tests that resemble the standardized versions, but neither demands much input from the teacher.

The second reason for focusing on teacher-based assessment is that this type of assessment requires substantial knowledge and skill; it requires professional judgment. You may remember teachers who relied on routines, who prepared their lessons long ago and stayed with the material year after year. This approach can't prepare today's students for a changing world and doesn't mesh with the view of reading and writing presented in this book.

This leads to the third reason—assessment of critical literacy cannot be "standardized." Although prepackaged tests provide a gross index of reading and writing achievement, it is the classroom teacher who can best monitor students' ability to use language to think and communicate. Knowing that a student is at the 50th percentile on reading comprehension doesn't tell you what the student can and can't do. Picking the right answer from a multiple-choice question is less important than being able to explain the shift in the relationship between Charlotte (a spider) and Wilbur (a pig) from the beginning to the end of E. B. White's *Charlotte's Web*.

> Assessment is fundamental to the improvement of education. It provides measures of success for student learning, for educators' leadership, and for evaluation of instructional programs.
>
> —*Scott Paris*
> *Developmental Psychologist*

Three Themes

Three themes run through this chapter. First is the notion of *assessment as inquiry*. It is easy to build a test that fails students; it is tougher to discover what students know and can do. Developing this sensitivity requires the teacher to act as a researcher, creating situations that support success and provide a starting point for instruction.

A second theme centers on *development*. As an elementary teacher, you will deal with children from kindergarten through sixth grade, from 4-year-olds to 13-year-olds, from preschoolers to adolescents! You may have your sights set on a particular grade or age, but even if you succeed in being hired to work at the level of your choice (and many times new teachers don't have a say), developmental levels within any class are likely to span two or more years. Students are not identical peas in a pod, and assessment must adapt to individual differences.

The third theme is the *measurement of progress*. Teacher-based assessment often builds on observation, qualitative information, stories, and pictures. As September moves toward June, however, someone must judge learning and achievement; someone must come up with a "bottom

line," a number, a score, or a grade. How much has the student grown? How well can the student perform various tasks expected at a particular grade level? Surveys show that elementary teachers don't like to grade students. They have a "success orientation" and prefer to "accentuate the positive." But parents and other clients need and deserve information about progress and accomplishment. If teachers don't supply the information, then someone else will—probably using standardized tests.

To be sure, teacher-based assessment demands subjective judgment, which can be difficult. Yet professional judgments are often subjective. We rely on expert raters in many fields of human endeavor. In the Olympics, for instance, measurement is objective in some events (races, javelin throw, high jumps, and pole vaults). Other events, however, are more complex (gymnastics, diving, and figure skating) and depend on expert ratings. Judges raise their cards, and the audience learns how the participant has done. The ratings depend on their expertise; the judges can justify their ratings, and the explanations are consistent. The judges clearly talk with one another! In countries such as Great Britain, where classroom teachers are primarily responsible for appraising student achievement, they also rely on frequent professional interactions to ensure consistency. We think that we can trust teachers to assess student learning—indeed, for the kind of learning described in this book, we must!

Balanced Assessment

Figure 11.1 laid out the spectrum of assessment strategies: more objective or subjective, more formal or informal, more prepackaged or based on teacher judgment. In your role as a classroom teacher, the practical question is how to achieve a balance that makes effective use of this full range.

Some educators question whether standardized tests can have any meaningful role in today's schools (Johnston, 1990; Mitchell, 1992; Wiggins, 1993). But though these tests have limitations, they also have strengths. Problems arise when they are misused or overused. Public information about student achievement too frequently depends entirely on what students do in an hour or two on multiple-choice items that tap knowledge and skills quite unlike their regular classwork. Imagine the plight of a 7-year-old used to working on "real" problems with adequate time and resources and able to ask questions when confused. Suddenly one morning the teacher tells the class, "Put away your books, sharpen your pencil, be quiet, no questions." Then the test begins. Let's hope that no one needs to go to the bathroom.

Teachers often prepare their students for testing—sometimes that effort constitutes almost the total reading program! But standardized testing measures only part of what students need to know and be able to do, and testing conditions can hinder students' ability to demonstrate their competence. Moreover, students often lack motivation to do well because their performance has no consequences for them. The same holds true for teachers and schools. Test scores are printed in the local newspapers, but rarely is a school or teacher rewarded or punished based on the results. The bottom line is that test scores offer a limited picture of how students handle the literacy tasks described in this book.

At one time, parents and the community depended on teachers to learn about and report on student achievement. By the 1950s, the factory model of schooling was in full swing in the United States, a trend that had started after the Civil War. Schools had become assembly lines: Teachers were workers following instructions, administrators managed and enforced quality controls, and efficiency was the watchword. Students were considered raw material to be shaped to a prescribed pattern. A few schools, mostly for the elite, offered a different experience. By and large, however, student achievement was treated as a "product." Behavioral principles matched the model, and standardized tests provided a scientific methodology. The system seemed to work. Many students dropped out, but they found jobs on farms and in industries.

> Any use of power. . . involves moral questions and consequences, and testers have extraordinary and often unilateral power.
>
> —*Grant Wiggins*
> *Assessment Expert*

The world of the 1980s was a different place. Students had changed, jobs had changed, and society had changed. Research on learning and teaching gave us new understanding about promoting effective language and literacy instruction. In the words of a wise farmer, "Don't grade—grow." Principles from cognitive psychology offered the foundation for an instructional revolution, complementing rather than replacing behavioral methods. Fourth-grade teacher Mia Lorenz talks about the teacher's role in the new curriculum:

I'm pleased to see the new curriculum emphasizing *problem-based learning*, where my role is to confront students with genuine puzzlements and to support them as they struggle with questions and solutions. Many of the questions I ask my students begin with the words *why* and *how*, rather than *what* or *who*.

- Why are there so many stories like *The Three Little Pigs*, and where do they come from?
- What makes Grimm's fairy tales different from African folktales?
- Why do some stories seem better than others?
- How can you make your own story really interesting?
- Why is it that sometimes a final consonant is single and other times double, as in *sit* and *mitt*?
- Why do we have capital letters and commas?

Such questions can't really be answered by looking at the "back of the book," nor does it make sense to ask students to pick the one best answer. Rather, students best show skill and knowledge by applying what they have learned in real tasks, working together in small groups to take advantage of "group intelligence."

Mia Lorenz, Fourth-Grade Teacher

481

Critical literacy challenges the image of the traditional classroom. The curriculum is no longer a preplanned scope-and-sequence chart. Instruction is no longer transmission of knowledge from teacher to students. Assessment is no longer choosing the one best answer to a simple question. Performance is viewed as complex and interactive. The final product is one indicator, but process is also important. Both group and individual contributions must be assessed. By comparison, the task confronting Olympic judges seems a piece of cake!

This chapter will explore both sides of the assessment picture, suggesting how you can use a full range of methods to see how well your students are reading and writing and how to make sound instructional decisions during the school year. Genuine balance requires the classroom teacher to move across the spectrum from multiple-choice tests to portfolios.

TEST-BASED STRATEGIES

Suppose you could scan hundreds of elementary classrooms with a gadget that buzzed whenever it detected *reading test*. What would you find? When does it happen? What does it look like? Why do people do it? In the United States, the picture is pretty clear. First, you would see a lot of testing embedded within the basal reading systems described in Chapter 2. All systems provide worksheets and end-of-unit tests for *formative* appraisal of student progress. Second, if you showed up in May, you would find most school districts administering the annual standardized test of reading achievement for *summative* assessment. These tests are scored during the summer, and the results are reported in the local newspaper in the fall. Formative assessment refers to focused and ongoing evaluations, like the scores on pop quizzes. Summative assessments appear at the end of a course of study, when assessing student mastery is the aim and when the final grade is to be given. The purpose of formative assessment is to guide instruction, while the purpose of summative assessment is to evaluate achievement (Bloom, Hastings, & Madaus, 1971; Bloom, Madaus, & Hastings, 1981). This section describes these types of tests, discusses how to use the information they provide, and suggests how to prepare your students for the task.

Basal Reader Tests

Although, as we noted in Chapter 2, basal readers currently are in flux, all are planned around the scope-and-sequence chart, a road map of specific objectives laid out in a predefined order (Chambliss & Calfee, in press). The text is divided into *units* (several stories lasting a month or so) and *lessons* (one or two stories that actually last a week). Each lesson includes several *objectives*. Objectives, the basic building blocks in basals, range from fine-grained tasks (the vowel *a* with silent *e*) to broad goals (character analysis) and deal with matters such as decoding, vocabulary, and comprehension. For each objective there is a sequence of instruction, practice, and testing.

Basal lessons frequently follow a standard format, beginning with vocabulary. The teacher is told, "Write the following words on the board: *changes, autumn,* and *seasons.* Ask students to pronounce each word, tell what it means, and use it in a sentence." The teacher next leads a discussion to prepare students for the reading, and then guides them as they read the story. In the primary grades, each student reads aloud a sentence or two; older students read the story silently before the lesson. The teacher asks questions from the manual to check story understanding. As the week progresses, students practice objectives by completing worksheet assignments.

Assessment activities are woven throughout these activities—responses to teacher questions, skill in oral reading, and worksheet performance. The teacher has numerous opportunities to judge student performance and understanding. Many teachers regard oral reading fluency and skill in answering questions as important indicators (Cazden, 1988). The student who struggles with a new sentence may be in trouble. So too the student who shrugs her shoulders when asked, "What was the cat's name?" Teachers seldom record this information, but they keep mental notes.

Basal systems offer several other indicators of student performance. Workbooks and worksheets solve practical problems, including—unfortunately—keeping students busy. They also offer practice on testlike activities; each worksheet covers one objective and is easily scored by classroom aides or parents. Students struggling with print often make mistakes and fall behind in their worksheets.

Basals also include end-of-unit tests to measure student progress. These tests, usually given every four to six weeks, closely resemble standardized tests. They use the multiple-choice format, are administered to the entire class, and are scored according to the manual. The results can significantly affect decisions about student placement and progress. Assignment to ability groups can mean that some students are considerably ahead of or behind the "middle" of the class. All students go through the same materials (at least as much of it as they get to), but the pacing and activities depend on group assignment. *Low* groups spend time on remedial worksheets, and *high* groups on enrichment exercises. *Low* groups fall steadily behind in content coverage; by the end of sixth grade, they may be doing fourth-grade work, which is poor preparation for middle school. Of course, students in low groups are often placed in special education programs or classes.

Assuming that you are a teacher who strives to foster critical literacy, what can these assessment materials offer you? By themselves, they are of questionable validity for judging a student's ability to think and communi-

In elementary and secondary education, a decision that will have a major impact on a test taker should not automatically be made on the basis of a single test score.

—*Joint Statement of the American Psychological Association, American Educational Research Association, and National Council for Measurement in Education*

cate. But standardized tests are gatekeepers, and students need to learn how to deal with them. Our recommendation is that you introduce worksheets to students not only as "things to do" but also as "problems to be solved." We agree with sixth-grade teacher Peter Stall's approach:

> As much as we may want to, we just can't get away from the "assessment work-sheet." So why not approach it in a positive way, to empower students and help them with both skills and attitudes? Often, before my struggling remedial students approach the end-of-unit tests in the basal that our district requires, I ask them questions like these: "What does the person who made this page want you to do?" "Do you see any traps and tricks? Where are they?" "Look at question 5. How could you help someone having difficulty understand that problem?" Obviously, these assessment worksheets were not designed for this problem-solving purpose, but the possibility is there, and I take advantage of it when I can.
>
> Peter Stall, Sixth-Grade Teacher

As you will see later in the chapter, we recommend approaching assessment activities and worksheets in much the same spirit that Mr. Stall does.

Standardized Tests

You are well educated, and so you know about tests. You have been there—college admissions, teacher certification, driver's license, CPR approval. In the modern world, the multiple-choice test is a fact of life. These instruments will stay around because they are cheap, they are efficient, they give a simple bottom line, and they are "scientific" (Airaisan, 1994; Baumann, 1988; Nitko, 1996; Popham, 1995; Stiggins, 1994).

Standardized tests fall into two categories, as shown in Figure 11.2—those that use criterion-referenced scoring and those that use norm-referenced scoring. *Criterion-referenced tests* include many of the basal assessments described earlier. The principle guiding these tests is that the student must meet a preset performance level. The class takes a 10-item test on vowels; students who are correct on 9 items have "mastered" the objective.

Criterion-referenced tests became popular in the 1960s for management of objectives-based curricula. Many basal systems still include criterion-referenced tests that direct the teacher to assign particular students additional practice on specific objectives. In recent years, curriculum developers have begun to favor *domains*, or collections of related objectives. The concept of mastery has also undergone change. Answering 9 of 10 multiple-choice questions may mean a lot or a little, depending on the questions. Most students need to learn more about the vowel domain than a short test can measure.

Norm-Referenced Scoring	Criterion-Referenced Scoring
Performance Is Compared with Others' Performance	**Performance Is Compared to an Absolute Standard**
■ Once the test is developed, it is tried out on a norm group, and then each student's performance is described by how she ranks with the group.	■ The test is developed with a goal in mind (students must read at a rate of 150 words per minute), or a standard is assigned after the test is constructed (80% of the answers must be correct).
Scores Represent a Norm Group	**Scores Represent a Standard**
■ Percentile—the percentage of students falling below a score; if a student scores in the 60th percentile, then she outperforms 60% of the students in the norm group.	■ Pass-Fail—the score either meets or exceeds the preset value.
■ Grade-level equivalent (GLE)—the average performance of students at a given grade is used to convert a score into a comparative indicator; if a student scores at the average level for all students leaving third grade, he is given a GLE of 3.9, meaning "end of third grade."	■ Mastery of learning objective—often linked to a curriculum sequence, where students by a given grade level are expected to achieve a specific outcome; for instance, by the end of kindergarten, the students should know all letter names, numbers 1–10, colors, and "common" words.
■ Grading on the curve—the common practice of assigning grades based on the distribution within a particular class on a particular test; the teacher decides that the top 15% of the scores will receive A, and so on.	■ Advanced, proficient, basic—this variation on pass-fail, similar to regular grades but not on a curve, is used by many state and federal assessment programs.

FIGURE 11.2 *Norm-Referenced and Criterion-Referenced Scoring*

Norm-referenced tests measure the individual's standing relative to others—"grading on the curve" (Nitko, 1996, Ch. 18). *Percentile scores* show how many other students rank above or below a particular individual. Someone at the 50th percentile falls right in the middle; a person at the 99th percentile does better than 99% of everyone in the test pool. *Scale scores* are statistical refinements of percentile scores. Another variation on the percentile is the *grade-level equivalent,* or GLE. The third-grader who scores 3.8 at the end of the year is doing about as expected; a score of 3.0, on the other hand, means that the student reads like an entering third grader, and so is in trouble. Although assessment experts have pointed out that GLEs can be misinterpreted (Nitko, 1996, Ch. 18), teachers often favor the GLE because it makes sense to them. Most problems with GLEs have to do with extreme scores; an entering third-grader with a score of 8.0 can't really handle Dickens's *Tale of Two Cities*. She may be able to read most of the words in the novel, but she is unlikely to get much out of it and certainly will not understand the nuances of the narrative.

Normative scores seem precise, but need to be taken with several grains of salt. Publishers design tests in *levels* that fit students within a limited range of performance. You can find "wide-range" tests (Wilkinson, 1995), but these typically cover limited domains. More often, publishers select an item pool appropriate for "most students" at a particular grade level, try out the test on a large sample of students at that level, and keep those items that yield a "spread" of individual differences. Then they apply statistical methods to convert the total score (the number of correct answers) to percentiles, grade-level equivalents, and other normative indexes. The system works for students in the middle range, assuming they know how to play the game of taking the test, but is less valid for students at the extremes. Nor can the scores be trusted to correctly assess students who lack testing strategies or are unfamiliar with the middle-class cultural and linguistic traditions that underlie standardized tests.

To understand this point, let's look at a typical reading test. It includes two subtests—vocabulary and comprehension—each with about 40 items. Each item offers four choices, so a student who chooses at random will be correct 25% of the time, entirely by chance. Practically speaking, a student scores in the cellar until she has 10 to 12 correct answers. Suppose a young child worries too much about tough items or runs out of energy and therefore does not mark the last four questions. This student is at a disadvantage no matter how well she can read. Or suppose a third-grader who is really reading at the second-grade level is given a third-grade test. Discouraged by the difficult material, she may receive a lower percentile score than she would if she took a second-grade test. A similar problem arises for students at the top. To score in the highest ranks at a given grade level, a student cannot make *any* mistakes. The student with a score of 38/40 may be at the 90th percentile, while a score of 39/40 places another student at the 97th percentile. The percentiles look quite different, but the two students' reading skills are probably quite similar.

What can you do as a teacher? Publishers offer sound advice in the test manuals, although it may be buried in technical detail. For instance, you should not trust incomplete or extreme scores. If a student does not finish the test, the scores will not be trustworthy; think about giving another form of the test. If a student scores at the bottom *or* top of the distribution, then the margin for error is large; think about administering a more appropriate level of the test. The advice is sound, although not always practical.

How can you use standardized test scores? First, recognize their strengths. They are *reliable* (Nitko, 1996, Ch. 4). This word implies a degree of consistency that is important to testing experts and administrators, who are likely to challenge whether your classroom assessments are equally trustworthy. Standardized tests are reliable in that they rank students in much the same way, no matter how you slice the scores. Suppose you line up the scores of a group of students from top to bottom on one version of a standardized reading test, and then line them up on another version of the same test. The students' rankings will not change very much. Or suppose you compare students' rankings on the vocabulary and comprehension subtests. Again, the rankings will be much the same. Whatever it is that standardized tests measure, they measure it consistently.

Second, standardized tests are *predictive*. Reading tests administered in first grade correlate with scores throughout a student's entire academic career. An entering kindergartner's knowledge of the alphabet is one of the best predictors of reading achievement in the later grades. Does this mean that we can markedly improve students' reading achievement simply by teaching the alphabet? No, although teaching the alphabet makes good sense for a variety of other reasons.

The problem is that predictability is not the same as *validity*. Here is where standardized tests have serious limits. A test is valid if interpretations and decisions stand up against other evidence. Prediction is one criterion for validity—the student was at the 10th percentile in first grade and is still doing poorly in sixth grade. The first- and sixth-grade tests tell the same story. But the picture isn't that simple. First, other evidence may show that the student has skills and knowledge not tapped by the standardized test. Students with poor decoding skills may do quite well on oral language tasks, especially in the early grades. What about the fifth-grader who helps others write on a computer but fails multiple-choice tasks?

Figure 11.3 shows part of a simulated class record for the *Terra Nova* test, an innovative assessment system developed by the California Test Bureau (1996). What should you do with your printout of test scores? As noted above, the printout may arrive on your desk after school has started, and you may be busy with other matters. But we do have a few words of advice.

First, use the numbers as one piece of information for gauging students' achievement level. Some tests advise the teacher to select reading materials based on a student's standardized score. But a student who scores at a grade level of 2.6 may understand and prefer a book at a 3.0 readability level. Grade levels and readability indexes offer clues about whether students can handle a book on their own. But test scores and readability indexes are subject to error of measurement. Interest matters a lot; children's schemata have a huge effect. A student struggles with a third-grade book on butterflies, then zooms through a third-grade book on dinosaurs. You can often "open" a book for stu-

> The more important and less reversible the decision about an individual made from an assessment, the higher the reliability should be.
>
> —*Anthony Nitko*
> *Educational Psychologist*
> *and Psychometrician*

dents, especially in the early grades, by simply reading some of it aloud. And whatever grade level you teach at, you can make books accessible by providing students with well-planned SREs such as those we described in Chapter 6.

Second, look at the big picture. Test reports can be overwhelming: multiple scores on multiple subtests on dozens of students. In Figure 11.3, for instance, the summary at the bottom of the printout shows that, at the

Terra Nova

TEACHER: JONES
GRADE 6

Record Sheet

Purpose:
The class record sheet serves as a permanent record of test results for students in a class or other specified group. It is most often kept in the classroom for easy access by the teacher. It also provides summary data or average scores, for the group as a whole. The report lists up to six scores, chosen by the local test coordinator, for each test section and total score. The results may be used to evaluate individual and group achievement compared to the nation, determine overall performance and identify areas of strength and weakness.

Students	Scores	Reading		Lang		Math		Total Score
Abby, Karen DOB: 2/26/83 Codes: ABCDEFGHIJKLMNOPQRST. ....12222221. Form: A Level 16	**NP** **NS** **GE** **NCE** **SS**	68 6 9.1 60 758		36 4 4.7 42 723		67 6 8.4 60 758		59 5 7.7 55 748
Arnold, Stephen A DOB: 6/21/83 Codes: ABCDEFGHIJKLMNOPQRST. ....12122221. Form: A Level 16	**NP** **NS** **GE** **NCE** **SS**	57 5 7.8 52 743		41 5 5.2 45 728		91 8 12.+ 82 797		45 5 6.4 47 735
Brown, Susan J. DOB: 8/22/83 Codes: ABCDEFGHIJKLMNOPQRST. ....12222221. Form: A Level 16	**NP** **NS** **GE** **NCE** **SS**	55 5 7.7 53 741		18 3 3.3 31 699		70 6 9.7 61 765		49 5 7.1 49 736
Chong, Louisa A DOB: 8/07/83 Codes: ABCDEFGHIJKLMNOPQRST. ....22222222. Form: A Level 16	**NP** **NS** **GE** **NCE** **SS**	89 7 11.7 77 786		71 6 9.5 60 758		75 6 9.6 64 766		79 7 10.1 67 767
Class Summary Nu,mber of Students = 26	**MDNP** **MNS** **GME** **MNCE** **MSS**	60.0 6.0 8.8 55.0 750		37.2 4.5 5.1 43.8 724		68.2 6.8 8.8 60.4 759		52.0 5.3 7.3 51.8 742

NP: NATIONAL PERCENTILE		**MDNP:** MEDIAN NATIONAL PERCENTILE	
NS: NATIONAL STANINE		**MNS:** MEDIAN NATIONAL STANINE	
GE: GRADE EQUIVALENT		**GME:** GRADE MEAN EQUIVALENT	
NCE: NORMAL CURVE EQUIVALENT		**MNCE:** MEAN NORMAL CURVE EQUIVALENT	
SS: SCALE SCORE		**MSS:** MEAN SCALE SCORE	

FIGURE 11.3 *Simulated Class Record from the* Terra Nova *Test*

From CTB/McGraw Hill, *Terra Nova.* Reprinted by permission of McGraw-Hill Companies, Inc.

end of sixth grade, the students' reading scores averaged a GME (grade mean equivalent, another name for GLE) of 8.8, almost two grade equivalents ahead of expectation, placing the class at the 60th percentile level (MDNP) when compared with national norms—very good news! Language performance, in contrast, was at a GME of 5.1 and a percentile rank of 37, meaning that the students were well below the 50th percentile—bad news. Susan Brown does reasonably well in reading, but has a very low language score, whereas Louisa Chong excels in both domains. Skimming a printout for the highlights can yield worthwhile information.

Third, look for profiles and puzzlements, using the indicators that make most sense to you. Big differences between subtests often warrant attention; higher scores are probably more indicative of students' ability, because it's easy to fail even if you have the necessary skills but tough to succeed if you lack the skills. In Figure 11.3, for instance, both Karen Abby and Susan Brown score much better on reading than language, suggesting that they have potential but haven't learned what is needed to handle the language objectives. Also, think about surprises—students who do much better or worse than your judgment suggests. Are you surprised that Louisa Chong scores at the 89th percentile in reading? Perhaps she needs to be challenged more than you thought.

Finally, look over the range and distribution of scores. You can't teach the "average" student, since the average student is merely a statistical abstraction. Think instead about the scatter of scores and the "shape" of the class. Does it look like the bell-shaped curve, or is it fairly flat? Are there "lumps" of students? Again, distrust extreme scores, but think about them. If the students in your class differ a lot from one another, then you will need to take extra effort to ensure that all of them succeed at the reading tasks they undertake.

Rubric-Based Tests

The multiple-choice format has long dominated standardized assessment, but the past several years have seen some important changes. In the 1970s, several states developed standardized writing tests. Students had an hour to write to a prompt, such as this one: "What do you think is good and bad about school uniforms?" But someone had to grade the compositions—quite a task, compared to scoring a multiple-choice test. The test is considered standardized because the task was very specific and involved limited time and resources. Students couldn't ask for help, and they couldn't go to the bathroom.

But how can such efforts be scored? This is where *rubrics* come in. A rubric is a scoring guide—something like assigning a letter grade but without the letters—which describes the meaning of each level on the scale. Figure 11.4 shows a rubric for evaluating primary-grade writing. Later in the chap-

> Test reports can be overwhelming. The teacher's task is that of the artist . . . , to find some use for scientific measuring instruments . . . , but dare not let them shift his attention from the whole picture to the elements.
>
> —*D. E. Scates*
> *Educational Researcher*

Exceptional	Sparkles! Vocabulary uses descriptive words. Creates suspense or surprise. Aware of audience. Strong personal voice. Emotion transmitted. Clincher at end.
Commendable	Clear beginning, middle, and end. Strong story sense. Mostly conventional spelling. Passage flows. Supporting detail.
Adequate	Listing of events. Phonetic spelling. Catalogue of facts. Train of thought, sense of beginning and end, but lost in details.
Some Evidence	Complete thought. Coherent but weak. Inventive spelling.
Little Evidence	Minimal fluency. Off topic. No story line or train of thought. Repetitive.
Minimal Evidence	No meaning in print; random letters with pictures.

FIGURE 11.4 *Rubric for Evaluating Primary-Grade Writing*

ter, we will present a rubric for evaluating fourth-grade reading. The best systems include *benchmarks*, samples of work illustrating each level on the scale, along with an explanation of why the sample work received a particular grade. Rubrics are now widely used, and most of the major test publishers now incorporate some type of performance assessment either as an integral part of the system or as an option. For instance, the *Terra Nova* assessment mentioned earlier contains both multiple-choice and open-ended items. The latter tasks require students to write about topics in literature, social studies, science, and even math.

An aside—some educators are worried about assessing reading by asking students to write. Doesn't this mean that we are testing *both* reading and writing? The answer is yes, but it doesn't matter. Until we develop a probe that allows us to observe a person's internal thoughts, we have to rely on indirect measures. Like writing assignments, multiple-choice tests also are not pure measures of reading itself; as we shall see later, they require strategies, motivation, and background knowledge. You might ask a student to discuss a passage with you, to determine her comprehension of it; this method can have advantages over writing, but it can be impractical with a class of 35 students. Writing is likely to be used increasingly for the assessment of reading comprehension, as well as other curriculum domains.

You should look for different features when assessing writing skills and when assessing reading comprehension. If a student's book report on Colin Powell has spelling, grammar, and organization problems but shows an understanding of what the biography is about, then the reading score should be high and the writing score should be low. To be sure, writing can be so terribly incomprehensible that no evaluation of reading skill can be made, and in such cases alternative methods are necessary.

Preparing Students for Taking Standardized Tests

Now let's look at the other side of the equation. How can you help your students do their best? What can you do to genuinely prepare your students for standardized tests, while also ensuring that they receive an authentic education? This question concerns validity. "Teaching to the test" may improve scores, but the scores no longer mean what they are supposed to mean. When your car runs low on gas, you can fiddle with the gas gauge to make it point to full, but you will eventually run out of gas anyway.

The challenge is to ensure that students can demonstrate their knowledge and skill on standardized tests, without falling back on meaningless practice on worksheets and the like. Our first word of advice is to *educate*, to focus on the important outcomes emphasized throughout this book. There is no substitute for genuine learning.

The second word of advice is to help students see the test as a problem to be solved strategically and thoughtfully. Testing can be a shock. *First Grade Takes a Test* by Miriam Cohen delightfully describes young children's thoughts on their first encounter with a test; Figure 11.5 provides an excerpt. The moral of the story is plain: The children are suddenly alone, the task is distressing, the activity is not connected with classroom routines, and for them, the results are meaningless.

What does strategic preparation look like? Probably the most important outcome from kindergarten through graduate school is to provide students with the big picture. Here, we consider three facets of that picture.

The first facet is figuring out what the question is. Why am I taking this test? What will happen if I fail? Who will find out how I did? On your driving test, you have some idea of the *purpose* and *audience*. You take the test

FIGURE 11.5 *Excerpt from* First Grade Takes a Test *by Miriam Cohen*

From *First Grade Takes a Test* by Miriam Cohen. Illustrated by Lillian Hoban. Text copyright © 1980 by Miriam Cohen. Illustration copyright © by Lillian Hoban. By permission of Greenwillow Books, a division of William Morrow & Company, Inc.

so you can get a driver's license. Your test will be checked by a computer program that accepts only one right answer for each question. If you fail, you study more and retake the test.

Ask fourth-graders similar questions about tests, and you will be amazed at their answers. They seldom understand the purpose of most tests. They don't know the rules of the game: "Is it all right to guess?" They fear the worst from failure, whatever that means. Sometimes test scores are used to retain students. Publishers caution against this practice, but it happens. Most often, however, standardized test scores don't affect individual students. When the scores finally arrive, the fall semester has already begun, students are in class, and teachers are busy. The printouts go to the principal's office, generally unnoticed until the pile gets too high.

And so preparation for test taking begins by uncovering students' perceptions about purpose and audience, and setting these straight. This doesn't mean a cavalier attitude of "It doesn't affect me," but rather an understanding that "It affects all of us!" It means offering clarity and honesty about a test's purposes and potential outcomes.

Another big-picture concern centers around *test instructions*, sometimes a hindrance rather than a help. Standardized tests "script" the teacher: "Read the following instructions." You can't repeat instructions. You can't explain them. You can't answer questions. You can't reassure students. But you *can* familiarize yourself with the instructions, and decide how to prepare the students in advance for the test. This doesn't mean rehearsing the instructions with students, but it does mean helping students learn to listen carefully and actively. It means providing them with experience in following instructions (such as by playing the game Simon Says as demonstrated in the following scenario) and in checking understanding. Most standardized tests provide practice sets; it's generally more helpful to use them for discussing the procedures for taking the test rather than for practice itself.

> "How'm I doing?" Good schools not only tell their students how they are doing, but get them into the habit of asking the question for themselves.
>
> —*Ted Sizer*
> *Educational Reformer*

IN THE CLASSROOM
Using Simon Says to Practice Test-Taking Instructions

The day that students are to take the district's benchmark reading tests is fast approaching. To help prepare his second-graders to follow the kinds of directions given on the tests, George Westbelle engages his students in several short games of Simon Says in the weeks prior to the test day. With a sheet of paper and a pencil placed on each student's desk, Mr. Westbelle gives his second-graders a series of prompts:

Mr. W.: Simon says, "Pick up your pencil."

Mr. W.: Simon says, "Write your name on the top of your paper."

Mr. W.: Write your name on the bottom of your paper.

(Some students write their names on the bottom.)

Mr. W.:   Oops! Simon didn't say!

Mr. W.:   Simon says, "Turn your paper over."

Mr. W.:   Write your name on the back of your paper.

(Some students start to do this.)

Mr. W.:   Oops! Simon didn't say!

Mr. Westbelle keeps these sessions short and sweet, focusing on the kinds of actions the students will be involved with in their test taking. "One word of warning," Mr. Westbelle cautions. "If you play the game too close to the actual test day, you may find that students expect you to say 'Simon says' before each of the directions on the test!"

Preparing students to deal with test instructions also requires "talking it through." Here is where worksheets can help. Construct a page with directions, a short reading passage, and some items like those on the test, similar to the page shown in Figure 11.6. The sample items should give students an opportunity to practice particular test-taking strategies. Using standard instructions, tell students that they have a certain amount of time to finish the page; you might give two minutes for a page like the one shown. Then ask students to give their answers. Tally them, and then discuss the experience. What was easy? What was hard? What was confusing? What did it feel like? Your students will begin to develop their own test-taking strategies. And as they see themselves improving, they will become more comfortable and competent when taking the real thing.

The third big-picture item highlights *time* and *stress*. Even with unlimited time, students have only so much energy. Most tests do not penalize incorrect choices, and so the best advice is to finish the test. If uncertain, pick the best-looking answer and go to the next item. Older students can check items when uncertain, and return to these if they have time. But don't skip and don't fret.

To manage stress, you first must be aware of it. Look at second-graders during a test; note wrinkled brows, fingers tight around pencils, bodies hunched over the desk. It's painful, but the students seldom realize their agony. They can learn to monitor stress. Here again, talking it out is important. Once aware, what can you do about stress? Ask your students for their ideas; they will surprise you with their answers. Put your pencil down, relax your shoulders, think pleasant thoughts. You lose a minute, but a fresh mind is worth it.

Additionally, remember Ben Franklin's adage: "We must indeed all hang together, or, most assuredly, we shall hang separately!" Competition may be the goal in high school—who will be valedictorian, receive the high-

---

THINK ABOUT IT! Taking a reading comprehension test is a tough job. You should always **study the questions** before you try to pick an answer. What do you need to know? Do you need to read the passage? Do the question and the answers raise any alarms? Think about these things while you take this test.

It is easy to make butter. First you need a jar and some *heavy* cream. Fill the jar part way with cream. Then shake it for about 20 minutes. Soon the cream will start to get lumpy. Stop when most of the cream turns into *lumps*. You will find that the lumps are butter.

Take the lumps out of the jar and wash them with cold water. Mix a little salt with the lumps and pat them together. Leave the butter in a cool place over night. In the morning the butter will be hard and ready to eat.

Mark the word that rhymes with *lumps:* • cream • leaves • bumps • butter [You don't have to read anything in the passage to answer this question. Why not?]	Mark the word that means the same as *heavy:* • large • thick • strong • bulky [Answering this question depends completely on carefully studying the passage. Why?]
What does the passage tell you to do after you have finished making the butter? • put the lumps on toast in the morning • throw away the lumps • shake the lumps for 20 minutes • salt the lumps and put them in a cool place [You have to read the passage, which tells you exactly what to do.]	If you forget to refrigerate the butter after you have made it, then • mix it with some more salt • eat it as soon as you can • it will be soft and not good to eat • melt it in a pan and then cool it down [The passage doesn't really answer this question, but gives you a clue about the right answer. What do you think it is?]

FIGURE 11.6 *A Brief Practice Test*

est SAT scores, and so on. But in the elementary grades, testing can be a community event. Listen to what fourth-grade teacher William Settlemeyer says on the matter:

I like to try to build team spirit around the test event for my fourth-graders. Seldom do standardized tests have competitive consequences for individual students in the elementary grades. In fact, the better the class does as a whole, the better the school looks! That's what I try to sell.

How does this idea translate into practice? First of all, I make it clear to students that they are not really competing with one another. I encourage them to do their personal best. That's what really counts. That's what they should strive for. Second, I encourage my students to support one another before the test—"Hey, good luck! I know you will do great"—and after the test—"I bet you aced that puppy!" Third, I involve parents. I advise them to talk with their sons and daughters in the days before the test, make sure they get a good night's sleep and a solid breakfast on the day of the test, and talk with them about the test once it is over.

William Settlemeyer, Fourth-Grade Teacher

What has this advice to do with reading assessment? We haven't stressed content or skills. In fact, reading tests are only partly about reading. To excel on a sixth-grade science test, students should bone up on electricity, astronomy, geology, and so on. Success on a sixth-grade math test is more likely if students have worked with fractions. But studying *The Diary of Anne Frank* does not guarantee that students will do well on a sixth-grade reading test. And though learning Latin and Greek prefixes may help on a reading test, don't count on it.

That is why we recommend a strategic approach to reading tests. You can help your students by emphasizing fluent decoding and techniques for

In the elementary grades, testing can be a community event where students are encouraged to do their personal best and support one another before the test. "The better the class does as a whole, the better the school looks!"

searching a passage for specific information. But the most effective preparation is to back away from the details, find out what is being asked, and consciously think about how to approach the task. Such preparation helps with all sorts of tests, from reading readiness to college admission.

All of this advice requires a sensitivity to developmental level. It makes little sense to assess children younger than age 6 with group-administered methods. By second grade, most students can handle the strain and stress of testing, but they really benefit from strategic preparation. By the upper-elementary grades, students need to be confident about managing the test situation. In the middle and high school years, prospects for college and jobs increasingly depend on this ability.

Finally, what should *you* do when the test is finished? Don't wait for the results. Districts rely on publishers for scoring and reporting, which means that your students will not learn the results of a May test until September. Handle the experience immediately. Talk with your students. How did they do? How did they feel? Celebrate the event! Let students know you're proud of their efforts! Knowing you did your best is important in its own right.

Reflection AND *Application*

1. You are serving on a school committee to review standardized tests for the district. The committee is looking at six tests, and you can pick one of the following three assignments: review a teacher manual and instructions, student test materials, or a technical manual (reliability, validity, and other technical features). Which assignment would you prefer, and why?

2. It is March, and your district requires that third-graders take a standardized reading test in May. As a third-grade teacher, how would you prepare your students for this assessment? You have decided to begin test preparation in April, and so have a month to plan. You want to keep test preparation to a minimum, except as it meshes with your curriculum. What will be your strategies and timeline?

3. Your school places great emphasis on standardized test scores. All students in grades 1–6 will be tested in three weeks. Students in your fifth–sixth combination class have talked about testing for the past week. From their memories of previous grades, they are planning a skit to help first-graders with the tests. The first-grade teacher is enthusiastic about the idea. The principal calls you in; he has heard about the plan and wants to know what is going on. Why are you wasting time on this skit when your students should be practicing for the test? How will you explain this activity?

TEACHER-BASED STRATEGIES

Here, we move from standardized tests to classroom assessment, from administrators to teachers. What should the elementary classroom teacher assess in reading and writing? What do you need to know, week by week, and why? What about students? What feedback do they need, and when? What about parents? What should they learn during the parent–teacher conference? What about other teachers? The principal?

Classroom assessment has changed dramatically in recent years, part of a larger movement described as *performance-based assessment, portfolios,* or *exhibitions* (Harp, 1991; Hart, 1994; Herman, Aschbacher, & Winters, 1992; O'Malley & Pierce, 1996; Phye, 1996; Wiggins, 1993). This list shows several features that distinguish these methods:

- *Production* is more important than *recognition;* students must show that they can actually do something, rather than just picking the right answer.
- *Projects* are more important than *items,* a preference for depth over breadth and an emphasis on validity rather than reliability.
- *Informed judgment* is more important than *mechanized scoring.* The teacher replaces the ever-popular Scantron machine in the assessment process.

> Assessment has come to represent a new ethos, an empowerment in which assessments are designed and implemented to serve the needs of students and teachers.
>
> —*Gary Phye*
> *Psychologist*

The Case of Ms. K.

We presented standardized tests in an expository style. To describe classroom assessment, we will open with a scenario showing how curriculum, instruction, and assessment can blend together:

IN THE CLASSROOM
Assessment and Achievement in Ms. K.'s Class

Ms. K.'s 30 third- and fourth-graders vary in background, interests, and achievement levels. Several youngsters are labeled as learning disabled, others are on "free lunch" (the family is poor), and the eight fourth-graders were candidates for retention.

In September and early October, Ms. K. organizes each week around "little lessons," each based on a short text or a familiar topic. For example, to find out what students know about the concepts of character and plot, Ms. K. plans a "movie review," in which students talk about their favorite summer movies. To find out what students know about informational text, Ms. K. arranges a "news report," in which students discuss several newspaper articles.

Small groups present reports on current events. By mid-October, her logbook contains entries about each student: proficiencies, predilections, and problems in reading and writing. Students are also compiling personal journals, doing "free writing" (Monday) and assigned topics (Wednesday and Thursday). Work samples (individual and group) are posted on the walls.

For the post-Halloween parent conferences, Ms. K. prepares a one-page summary for each student, reviewing areas of competence and need and drawing on her journal notes and student journals regarding these subjects: literature, science, social studies, citizenship, art/music, physical education. Where are reading and writing? Ms. K.'s response is short and simple: "We work on reading and writing all day long."

Suddenly it's April. Ms. K. gathers the class:

"We don't have much time left," she tells her students. "Time for our 'big' project. This spring it's *Roots,* your family history, your own *book* to keep!"

The *Roots* project is Ms. K.'s culminating assignment. It lasts almost six weeks. The project is a genuine product, but also provides summative assessment of student achievement.

The project proceeds in several phases. The students first view selections from the *Roots* television series, which is available on videocassettes. Next, students discuss the story line and prepare "book reports," prologues to their own books. For Ms. K., the exercise is an opportunity to assess students' proficiency in the concepts of character, plot, setting, and theme.

In the second phase, students analyze autobiographies and biographies—from the autobiographically based Little House on the Prairie books by Laura Ingalls Wilder to several trade book biographies of Martin Luther King, Jr. They then review their family's past, making notes and collecting data. A wall chart displays interviews, Bibles and genealogies, letters, and photo albums. The work is both individual and collaborative; Ms. K. notes in her journal contributions of specific students and group effectiveness.

In the final phase, students create individual books, some with the aid of a word processor, some not. These are lengthy pieces, 20 pages or more (handwritten or computer print-out). Each includes a title page, table of contents, dedication ("To my parents, without whom this report would not be possible"), thematic overview (the *Roots* story), research on the student's family, and a "forward to the future" piece in which youngsters imagine themselves at high school graduation in the year 2005. Lots of writing, artwork, graphics, and other artifacts are included.

Visiting the classroom in May, you note several things. First, every student has completed the *Roots* project with distinction. These are quality pieces. Second, this is no mere homework assignment—students show pride in their accomplishments, which they plan to "keep forever." They are eager to explain how they approached the project and what they learned as a result. Third, students display a strong sense of audience. They are the primary audience, which is why they will keep the books forever. But they also comment on how proud their parents and relatives are of the work, and they obviously see any classroom visitor as an audience. Finally—and this is very important—they express a sense of fulfillment.

What Does This Case Mean?

So much for the *Roots* project—what does it say about assessment? The linkages between student learning, curriculum, and instruction appear seamless. A conversation with Ms. K. offers some insights. *Roots* was an experiment. She had assigned projects before, but usually they were much more pre-planned. She admits that the activity went far beyond what she had originally intended, both in time and effort. She had expected much of all her students, but was genuinely surprised by their accomplishments. In planning and carrying out the assessment, she has played the role of a "researcher": She developed a design, tried some innovative methods, collected data, and thought about the results. We will return to this idea of a teacher as a researcher in the next section, but first a few thoughts about the findings from this particular example.

This case conveys several themes: Assessment is *integrative*. The *Roots* project yields a wealth of information about reading and writing, as well as research skills. The portrait covers the entire curriculum, formal (literacy, literature, social studies, art) and informal (initiative, cooperation, persistence). The casual observer may experience a collage, but the teacher sees distinctive elements.

Assessment builds upon *a meaningful task*. The students aren't taking a test; they are working on a project, solving a problem, doing something that matters. Motivation stimulates achievement. It is easy to establish conditions where students do poorly; creating a situation in which students strive to do their best is more difficult.

Assessment emphasizes *top-level competence* as well as skills. For Ms. K., the most critical achievements are "top-down": understanding of overall passage structure, an awareness of audience, a sense of thematic coherence. Her notes also cover the "microskills" of spelling, grammar, neatness, and even aesthetics. Although the final products are all polished, students differ in the guidance they need to make revisions and complete the job. Ms. K. has noted these differences, which she shares with students and parents.

Assessment is *purposeful* for all involved. Ms. K. describes each task, from the year's beginning to its end, in ways that make sense to both students and parents. She explains her September assessments: "I'm going to be checking what each of you can do and where you need help." She connects each lesson with an upcoming job: "We are studying dinosaurs, and you need to divide long words like *tyrannosaurus* into syllables. The key is to look for vowels." By the time they begin the *Roots* project, students have learned that classroom activities have a purpose, which motivates them and leads them to do their best.

Assessment emphasizes *explanation*, students' capacity to describe what they are doing and why and how they are doing it. Many years ago in math class, we had to show our work; right answers with wrong reasons did

> Good assessment should emulate good teaching practices and reinforce good instruction.
> —*Educational Testing Service*

not count. Ms. K. adheres to the same principle. She encourages group activities in planning, reviewing, and presenting because it promotes genuine discussion. Ms. K. teaches students labels to help them communicate with one another. An interesting story requires character development. It needs to include a *problem* that is *resolved* during several *episodes*. In creating stories of their past, present, and future, students use these labels to explain their own efforts and to help one another.

Assessment is *scaffolded*. Just as you can and should scaffold students' reading of individual selections, you can and should scaffold their efforts on larger projects such as this one. Every student produces an exceptional book, but some require more support than others in moving ahead with the project, in their approach to the task, in their ability to sustain the effort, and in their willingness to assist and to seek out assistance. Ms. K. makes sure that support is available from her and from others. And her notes include information about these facets of student performance.

Finally, assessment is guided by *developmental standards*. Ms. K.'s guideposts are as clear in her mind as a scope-and-sequence chart. Her assessments are not numbers, but they refer to growth and to relative strengths and weaknesses. Here are her summary comments for one student, Sam:

> Sam's oral language skills are exceptional, and he works hard on topics that interest him: science, computers, and games. He has made great progress in his writing and spelling, but still lacks fluency with mechanics. Unless he is really excited about a project, he is sloppy with the details. He is better with exposition than narrative. Stories bore him, but his report on rockets shows that he is capable of top-flight work. He is sometimes immature for a fourth-grader and does not listen well. He is impatient with "boring" tasks like documenting or summarizing.
>
> This year, however, he has learned a lot about himself and about the importance of working on assignments that don't have immediate payoff, but offer rewards in the long run. He stayed with his *Roots* biography, even though he became distracted halfway through. At the beginning of the year, he would have dropped it or done a sloppy job. He came to me and explained that he was stuck and wanted to start over. He had lost a page of notes and didn't want to redo them. I asked him to spend a day thinking over his choices and talking about them with his project buddy. Sam returned the following morning—he had written down his choices, and explained why he had decided to stay with his plan. That is one sign of his growth.

Ms. K. prepares a similar paragraph for each student, which she attaches to the district's report card. She finds that parents value these comments as highly as the official grades. They are also pleased with the *Roots* project, which they see as a trustworthy indicator of their child's achievement.

Some Answers to Our Opening Questions

What does this case say about the questions that began this section? Actually, it says quite a bit. Here, we answer these questions one by one.

First, What Does the Teacher Need to Know, Week by Week, and Why?

Ms. K. responds to this question throughout the school year. At year's beginning, her assessments are formative. They are also frequent, focused, and individual. She assigns minitasks that inform her about students' skills and interests. By midyear, she switches to bigger questions, giving students more responsibility for their own learning and for assessing themselves. By year's end, her assessments have become summative. She looks at the quality of the projects, but attends to process as well as product, to the way that students handle problems as well as the solutions that they manage to come up with, to collaborative contributions as well as individual accomplishments.

What About Students?

What feedback do they need, and when? Ms. K. brings students into the feedback loop early and often, explicitly but gently, individually and as a whole class. She begins the year by telling students what she expects of them by year's end. She makes it clear that reading and writing are high on her list, along with skills in speaking and in attentive listening. By late fall, she spends several sessions with individual students, reviewing what she sees as strengths and areas for improvement. She does not keep detailed records, but relies instead on student work and brief journal notes. At midyear, students are appraising their own work. When they finish *Roots*, they have become their own toughest critics.

What About Parents?

Ms. K. relies on three methods to connect parents with their children's achievements. The first is through homework. She assigns homework regularly; weekly newsletters explain assignments and suggest how parents can help their students. She tailors assignments to individual needs; every student receives the same basic assignment, but she jots notes for each student's parents with specific suggestions and requests. The parent whose child is handling basic spelling and punctuation, but seldom experiments with unfamiliar words, might receive this note: "For the dinosaurs report, have Pete concentrate on different *words*—he has a rich vocabulary but doesn't use it much in writing. Encourage him to use some wild-and-crazy adjectives." The second connection is through the quarterly conference. The student conducts the event, describing her goals for the quarter, displaying the collection of work, discussing successes and shortcomings, and laying out goals for the next quarter. The final connection is the back-to-school night at year's end, where the projects are the centerpiece.

A Final Word on the Scenario

Numerous features in this scenario support the literacy outcomes described in earlier chapters. Ms. K. has a substantial impact on her students. She relies on intuition and experience, but can explain her methods if asked. She relies very little on standardized tests, but knows how to prepare her students for them. She understands assessment concepts such as reliability and validity, but has her own way of interpreting them. Her experience, conviction, and success with students allow her to practice her "art" in her own special style. The next section will tell the story behind this story.

Reflection AND Application

4. It is spring, you have moved to a new neighborhood and are looking for a job. You are invited by the personnel director to visit several schools. The district has a reputation for emphasizing thematic projects and reading–writing portfolios. One item on your list is the district's assessment policy. As you visit classrooms and talk with the teachers and principals, what do you look for in the classrooms and ask from potential colleagues about the role of projects and portfolios in assessing student achievement?

5. You and a colleague want to replace the report card with a narrative report based on a final project. You have collected several examples, and although it will take work, you are convinced it's worth a try. You have five minutes to explain your plans to the school board, enough time to make three points. What will they be? How will your answer depend on the grade you teach?

ASSESSMENT AS INQUIRY

This part of the chapter, building on our previously mentioned concept of the teacher as a practical researcher, describes how the teacher assesses students' development of critical literacy through a process of professional inquiry. The idea has a long history (Calfee & Hiebert, 1991; Cronbach, 1960;

Paris et al., 1992). In 1960, Lee Cronbach described assessment methods based on careful observations, multiple methods and measures, and integrated information. His list mirrors the methods found in research textbooks. Research begins with a question that leads to design and methods. Then comes the task of collecting and analyzing evidence. Next is interpretation—how to make sense of the findings. Finally comes the job of acting on the results. The process, shown in Figure 11.7, is nonlinear, interactive, and cyclic. It is more a set of processes than a sequence of stages, more a roller coaster than an elevator. The arrows are bidirectional, pointing both ways. We will discuss each element in the following sections, linking Ms. K.'s classroom to new cases along the way. You will see how, in a curriculum of critical literacy, assessment becomes an integral part of instruction.

> If a teacher doesn't talk to anyone else about [assessment], I don't think it helps you reflect. When teachers talk with each other about kids' strengths and weaknesses, there's a mixture of different kinds of thinking. It helps us look at kids and figure out how to help them grow.
>
> —Greta Maday
> Kindergarten Teacher

Framing the Problem: What's the Question?

At the beginning of each school year, the primary question confronting the classroom teacher seems simple enough: What do the students already know? Likewise at year's end: What have the students learned? Along the way, questions become more dynamic: How are students responding to various instructional activities? The foundation for these questions is the curriculum—the course of study. For Ms. K., the curriculum meant much more

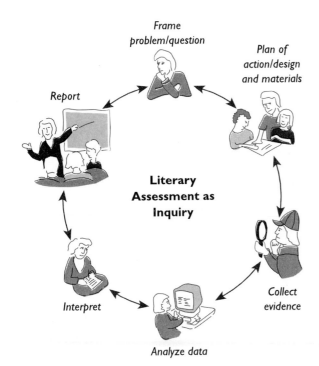

FIGURE 11.7 *Literacy Assessment as a Process of Inquiry*

than "getting through the book." She began by reviewing goals for the school year. Having taught several grades, she had a good idea of what students needed to know and do in order to handle the demands of fourth grade. She was also familiar with the *learning standards* that the school district had prepared, statements describing student performance at certain mileposts, including the middle-elementary grades. Figure 11.8 shows samples from the *New Standards* program used by many districts as a model. Ms. K. was not exactly sure when or how the district would decide to test these standards, but in her view it was the classroom teacher's responsibility to interpret the goals in light of her situation. She saw the standards as a minimum and placed greatest emphasis on understanding and communication.

The student reads at least twenty-five books. . . . The quality and complexity of materials to be read are illustrated in the sample reading list . . . [and] should include traditional and contemporary literature . . .

The student reads and comprehends at least four books . . . about one issue . . . by a single author . . . or in one genre and produces evidence of reading that:
- makes and supports . . . assertions about the text;
- supports assertions with . . . evidence;
- draws texts together to compare and contrast . . . ;
- makes perceptive and well-developed connections;
- evaluates writing strategies and . . . the author's craft.

The student reads aloud, accurately (in the range of 85–90%), familiar material of the quality and complexity illustrated in the sample reading list, and in a way that makes meaning clear to listeners by:
- self-correcting when subsequent reading indicates an earlier miscue;
- using a range of cueing systems, e.g., phonics and context clues . . . ;
- reading with a rhythm, flow, and meter that sounds like everyday speech.

The student produces [four types of writing]:
- . . . a report [that] engages the reader . . . develops a controlling idea . . . creates an organizing structure . . .
- . . . a response to literature [that] advances and supports a judgment . . . demonstrates an understanding . . . provides closure . . .
- . . . a narrative account [that] . . . establishes a situation, plot, point of view, setting, and conflict . . . creates organizing structure . . .
- . . . a narrative procedure [that] . . . provides a guide to action . . . makes use of appropriate writing strategies . . .

FIGURE 11.8 *Elementary School Performance Description—English Language Arts*

Her thoughts about the final summative outcomes shaped all other assessment questions for Ms. K. She knew her entering third-graders varied considerably, and so her first questions centered around the students. Her specific questions are models for every teacher: What will this class be like? What are their past experiences? What do they know? What can they do? What do they like? How do they get along together? Some questions are linked to curriculum outcomes: Where is each student in relation to year-end standards? Other questions relate to immediate instructional plans: What activities will help this (probably) diverse collection of

Arranging tasks and observing students is a good way to assess their strengths and weaknesses.

youngsters attain the goals? Finally, some questions address program effectiveness: How will I find out what works and what doesn't work throughout the year?

As a teacher, you need to frame these questions in practical language. Classroom assessment is *applied action research* (Hiebert & Calfee, 1992; Patterson, Santa, & Smith, 1993). Although the strategies and methods for action research are similar to those for basic research, you don't have the luxuries of unlimited time and resources available to basic researchers, and so questions must be focused and timely. For example, one set of questions centers around *guiding instruction*, for individual students and for the class as a whole. If September's activities suggest a lack of interest and capability in writing, what about assigning small-scale writing activities around holiday topics? Interest should be high; will this actually support skill learning? Three students enter your class midyear, all recently arrived from Cambodia and with limited English proficiency; how can you learn about these children? You probably don't need to administer a lengthy diagnostic test. What tasks and observations can you arrange to tell you what they can do and under what conditions they can do it?

Designing a Plan of Action

Designs and questions often weave together, as shown in the previous section. A design is a refinement on the question, a more detailed plan for arranging conditions and deciding what to assess. You often begin with hypotheses or "hunches," and then move to creating different situations to explore these guesses, as Sophia Furakawa does in the following scenario. Considering various alternatives is important; you can fool yourself by favoring a particular answer and then setting up a situation to prove it.

IN THE CLASSROOM
Vocabulary Assessment in the Third Grade

It is the beginning of the school year, and Ms. Furakawa, a second-year teacher, is planning to assess her third-graders' vocabulary skills. She knows that in order to comprehend texts and compose readable compositions, students need to be proficient in vocabulary—not a simple accumulation of words but a mastery of concepts, of collections of ideas, of words as keys to communication. She has noticed that her third-graders often seem to lack the words to express their ideas. Many are wary of "fancy" language and fall back on informal and commonplace terms. For example, her students will make statements such as this: "Like, what I think about the atmosphere, is that it's about air and clouds and storms and stuff like that."

Ms. Furakawa begins her assessment with this question: What do the students *really* know? Her first hunch is that her students are using whatever words they know, but she then decides that this is unlikely—they must know more words than they actually use! When she asks the other third-grade teacher for advice, he recommends the vocabulary section of the Nelson-Denny reading test (Brown, 1985) for a quick vocabulary check. She administers the test and makes some preliminary observations during class discussions.

Next, she decides to look a bit more closely at a few students who appear to have particular problems. For example, Sam scores at a grade level of 1.2 on the Nelson-Denny vocabulary test, two grades below expectation. Her initial observations are that Sam seldom volunteers during classroom discussions, often shrugging his shoulders. She decides to explore an alternative hypothesis: Sam actually has a rather substantial vocabulary (most 9-year-olds do), but his storehouse of words is poorly tapped in typical school situations such as tests and formal talk.

The *design* problem in this case is for Ms. Furakawa to imagine other ways to explore Sam's vocabulary. He may lack the range and depth of concepts expected in third grade. He clearly needs to learn how to express himself more effectively. But just what does this mean, and how might Ms. Furakawa help him? Designing an assessment usually means planning "mini-experiments" for observing performance under different conditions:

- When does Sam use familiar words?
- When does he have trouble with such words?
- How does he handle unfamiliar words, including "school" words such as *define, mean the same, main idea, character?*
- How does he explain the meaning of a word?
- What does he say about how he works on vocabulary tests?

■ How does he respond in different situations? With support from peers? With support from the teacher? With clues such as passage context and dictionary or glossary definitions?

This design begins with easy tasks, moves to tougher ones, and then adds support. All of us fail under some conditions. A "clean" assessment investigates student performance when conditions are optimal. If Sam fails to use the word *atmosphere* correctly under some conditions but succeeds under others, then he must have some grasp of the word. By observing his performance under different conditions, Ms. Furakawa will better understand Sam's capacities and can better plan instruction for Sam—and her other students.

Sam is only one student, and you cannot ignore the rest of the children. You will be collecting information on the fly, switching your attention for a few moments to Sam, then to Deborah and a few other key students, taking advantage of naturally occurring variations in classroom situations. On occasion, you may direct a specific question to Sam to check out a hunch or assign him a particular task to see how he does. You cannot give huge amounts of individual attention to every student—nor do you need to. What you learn from studying Sam is likely to teach you a lot about other students that you will encounter along the way.

Planning an assessment design is a matter of making choices. Should you work with *groups* or *individuals*? Group testing brings to mind paper-and-pencil tasks, but there are other choices. Individual assessment offers greater latitude, but is costly and raises problems in class management. Is the assessment *oral* or *written*? Does the task require *production* or *recognition*? The student writes a sentence about petroleum or picks the correct answer (oil) from four choices. The first task requires more effort from both student and teacher, but offers more information.

Time is an important consideration in assessment design. Most schools begin in September and end in June. You have nine months to make something happen. What will be your assessment plan during this time and for these students? Ms. K. relied on the concept of the *differentiated school year*, as do many other teachers, such as fifth-grade teacher Loreen McFay:

> The first week or two of the school year is a time to learn about my students—their abilities, interests, strengths, and limits. I do this through formal testing when appropriate, but mostly through observations and conversations. Next comes "teaching for testing," short lessons I create to find out what students can do with instructional support. For example, I read a short, familiar story and pose comprehension questions. Or I'll have the class create a collaborative fantasy such as "Our Favorite Summer" or "The Creature Who Came to School." I use these activities to find out which students contribute ideas, what words and ideas come to the fore, and what the class knows about constructing a story.

In most other countries, [assessments] include essay examinations and performances in areas like debating and the arts.
—Linda Darling-Hammond
Educational Researcher

507

The fall holidays—Halloween and Thanksgiving—offer opportunities to teach strategies and skills in attractive situations by incorporating art, music, and cooking. December is my time for instruction in areas where I think my students need additional work. In January, I reassess skills and knowledge following the winter break. This sets the stage for thematic projects, where assessment is embedded in weeks of work. In May, my agenda moves from assessment that guides my instruction to assessment to measure how well students are doing. At this time, I need to prepare my fifth-graders for standardized tests, along with my own summative assessments. Whatever the time of year, however, assessment is always in the background of my thinking.

Loreen McFay, Fifth-Grade Teacher

Time considerations should also reflect a developmental dimension. As a kindergarten teacher, your September focus is quite different than that of the teacher with a combined fourth–fifth grade. Kindergarten classes allow time to study individual children and their interests. What do they know about letters, sounds, words, sentences, books? Year-end goals also have a greater margin of tolerance in the early grades. Your major task is to move 5-year-olds from a wide variety of entry levels toward the demands of first grade.

As a teacher of upper-grade students, your choices are more limited. You must quickly learn how close your students are to handling middle school demands. You can't spend September casually engaging students about their interests and backgrounds. With a combination of fourth- and fifth-graders, you are likely to have a larger class and greater diversity than your kindergarten colleague. Your plan of action requires focus and efficiency. The basic strategy is the same—explore conditions under which a student succeeds or fails, but assume that success is possible. Motivation is especially critical in the later grades. A youngster with five years of failure has learned that she cannot learn. Assessment means convincing students that they can succeed. Both skill and will are important, both for arranging conditions and for deciding what evidence to obtain.

Collecting Evidence

The collection process is very practical. Because of its importance, we will discuss it at length. At the beginning of the chapter, we noted the importance of ranging across the continuum of assessment options, from informal tasks to formal methods. Here we focus on the midrange methods that provide the most informative strategies for collecting data: observing, discussing and questioning, interviewing, and collecting student work samples in portfolios. As noted earlier, these strategies overlap with good teaching practice, and instruction and assessment often intertwine.

Observing

The best information about student learning comes from looking and listening—kid watching (Goodman, Goodman, & Hood, 1989; for more information on informal assessment, see Johnson, Kress, & Pikulski, 1987, and Johnston, 1992). This is easier said than done. If you don't know how to look and listen, it is hard to attend simultaneously to instruction and observation. The classroom seems a blooming, buzzing confusion. How can you make sense of the activities? What can you look for? How can you find out what's happening? To gain skill in this task, you need to spend some time observing others, using questions like these to guide you:

- *Who are the students?* How many are there? How are groups organized? Which students stand out, and why?
- *Who are the adults?* How many are there? What is their status and role? Who are they working with?
- *What is going on?* What is each group doing—reading, writing, talking, completing worksheets, whatever?
- *Who is instructing, and how?* Is it a teacher, aide, or tutor? Is the instructor talking, asking questions, managing, facilitating, observing?
- *What is the instructional content?* What is the subject matter? What skills and activities seem central? What is the focus? What materials and supports are present?
- *How are the students responding?* Are they attentive? Productive? Interested and engaged? What is their level of performance? Of social interaction?

The answers to these questions will allow you to understand the classroom and to share that understanding with others—parents, other teachers, and the principal. As teacher, you confront two additional hurdles: First, you can't monitor all six facets for all students. What do you do? The answer is to center yourself—select facets and students critical for a particular purpose, and put everything else in the background. A clear purpose allows you to "zoom in." In addition, you can set the stage for your research. By organizing groups and assignments for students and helpers, you can focus on how a particular student handles different situations with varying amounts of support. How does Sam handle vocabulary in whole-class activities and small groups? With

> I learn about kids by observing them in order to help them with their work. Observing makes me more precise, and it makes teaching harder and more interesting because it demands more of me and makes me ask more questions of myself.
>
> —Mark Lillebo
> Second-Grade Teacher

The best information about student learning comes from looking and listening— kid watching.

and without a helping hand? On topics of more or less interest? When he is talking or writing? Data collection is often done on the fly; but by focusing for a while on a single student like Sam and his vocabulary difficulties, the job becomes possible. And, as we noted earlier, what you learn about Sam will probably tell you something about other students as well.

Second, it is hard to look while you are teaching. You can remedy this problem in two ways. First, *practice* observing. Study your class while they are taught by someone else: a colleague, a student teacher, the principal! Even brief looks can give you a different perspective on students, a chance to see how individuals respond to the ebb and flow. "David never seems to join the discussion. I placed him at the front on the reading rug so I could watch him. Now I see that he is totally distracted by the posters that I tacked underneath the chalkboard! I should move David or the posters."

Another way to find time for observation is to build it into your teaching. Organizing group activities and individual assignments in the right way can give you an opportunity to look at learning. It is tempting to use these occasions to work with students with special needs, or to respond to homework papers. But sometimes, rather than talk, you should *stop, look,* and *listen.* Also, becoming generally more familiar with kids and classrooms will enable you to gain more from your observations. The bibliography on page 511 describes books that may be helpful in this regard.

Discussion and Questioning

Every new teacher looks forward to active student discussions and is frustrated by lack of participation. Often it seems that students either say nothing or go completely wild. One thing you can do to foster meaningful discussion is to use the knowledge as design approach we described in Chapter 8. Using knowledge as design gives students a scaffold for their discussion and an opportunity to think deeply about a topic and voice a variety of opinions while still keeping the discussion on track.

You can also study successful questioners and their methods. How did Socrates, the philosopher of ancient Greece, manage it? He would pose one question, and his students would go on for hours. Modern versions of Socrates appear in unlikely places: television talk shows (Oprah Winfrey) and newspaper columns (Dr. Ruth and Ann Landers). In these exchanges, rich dialogues depend on three elements: *why* the questioner is asking the question, *what kind* of question is asked, and *how* the questioner handles the situation (Dillon, 1988).

Why are you asking the question? Outside of school, a question is usually a genuine effort by one person to learn something from someone else. Students can be startled when classroom discussion takes this turn, and they

Books That Invite You into the Elementary Classroom and the World of Kids

The following list samples the many books that can help you develop a schema for modern classroom settings, the plots that can develop there, and the roles of the main characters—teachers and students. Many of the authors are former teachers, and all, of course, have once been students themselves. All provide a sense of authentic classroom experiences and the feelings and perceptions of children within a classroom setting.

Miriam Cohen. *When Will I Read?* Greenwillow, 1977. Impatient to begin reading, a first-grader doesn't realize there is more to reading than just books. 32 pages.

Barthe DeClements. *Sixth Grade Can Really Kill You.* Viking, 1985. After being sent to special education classes because of her behavior, "Bad Helen" meets a sympathetic teacher who helps her with her reading problem and to fulfill her dream of going to junior high. 146 pages.

Patricia Reilly Giff. *The Beast in Ms. Rooney's Room.* Dell, 1984. One of the titles in the Polk Street School series, this entry tells of Richard "Beast" Best's adjustment to his second year in second grade and how he helps his class win a banner. 76 pages.

Bonnie Graves. *Mystery of the Tooth Gremlin.* Hyperion, 1997. When Jesse loses his first tooth at school only to have it snatched away by the "Tooth Gremlin," Maxine has this reluctant reader reading mysteries to try to solve the Gremlin's identity. 64 pages.

Kevin Henkes. *Lilly's Purple Plastic Purse.* Greenwillow, 1996. Lilly (a mouse) adores school, especially her beloved teacher, Mr. Slinger. However, she runs into difficulty when she brings her purple plastic purse to school and can't resist showing it off to everyone. 32 pages.

Joanna Hurwitz. *Class President.* Morrow, 1990. Julio discovers his leadership abilities as his fifth-grade class prepares to hold an election for class president. 96 pages.

Suzy Kline. *Song Lee in Room 2B.* Viking, 1993. Worried about having to speak in class, Song Lee brings in a large cardboard cherry blossom tree to stand behind while she gives her oral report on Korea. 56 pages.

Gordon Korman. *Radio Fifth Grade.* Scholastic, 1989. Benjy, Mark, and Ellen-Louise coproduce Kidsview, the fifth grade's zany radio show, with hilarious results when Menace Venice bullies them into letting him become a regular guest. 179 pages.

P. J. Peterson. *The Sub.* Dutton, 1993. Savvy teacher Mrs. Walters plays along when two best friends switch identities when the regular teacher is out sick. 86 pages.

Todd Strasser. *Help! I'm Trapped in My Teacher's Body.* Scholastic, 1993. To his horror, 12-year-old Jake Sherman finds himself turned into his weirdo teacher, Mr. Dirksen. But the results are hilarious. 115 pages.

may feel reluctant to respond. They have learned that school questions have a right answer, and the teacher knows what it is. But "real" questions seldom have one right answer.

What kind of question should you ask? Actually, it's better to consider what kind of answer you are seeking. Questions that lead to yes or no an-

Student self-evaluation is important. I remember this conversation with a student: "Anna, you've been in second grade for three months. What have you learned about reading?" "I'm better!" "Prove it to me," I said, with a grin.

—Joseph Gomez
Third-Grade Teacher

swers don't yield much dialogue unless asking why is a natural follow-up; this also holds true for questions that call for specific answers. Broad questions can be quite simple. While reading a story, for instance, a natural question at critical episodes is "What do you think will happen next?" Also, starting with broad questions and then exploring what turns up can often promote discussion. We consider this *funnel approach* in the next section of this chapter.

How can you extend children's answers to your questions to more fully reveal their competencies? Again, keep it simple. "Gee, that sounds interesting—say more." Several boys in a Hawaiian classroom, after reading about volcanoes in the science book, are building a soda–vinegar model. The teacher asks, "Do you *really* think that if you dig deep enough you'll find melted rock?" The boys mull it over, and decide "Naw—can't be!" The teacher continues, "You know, all of Oahu [their island] was once a volcano." Similar disbelief registers on their faces, but then one boy mentions that his father had told him that the lava rocks in their yard were from old volcanoes. For the teacher, it becomes clear that the students "understood" the text at one level, but had not connected it with their personal experience.

Interviewing

Sometimes, you need to spend time with individual students. Not an on-the-fly, casual conversation, nor a formal assessment, but a 3–5 minute session centered on a particular problem with a particular student. The *funnel approach*, which we illustrate in the following scenario, provides an efficient strategy for collecting both broad and focused information during an interview:

IN THE CLASSROOM
The Funnel Approach

The basic idea of the funnel approach is to begin with general questions and move toward specific queries. For example, second-grader Martha had problems with story comprehension and couldn't seem to identify with characters. After reading *Nate the Great*, a simple detective story that tells how Nate finds his friend Annie's lost picture, Martha showed little empathy for the situation. Here are Martha's teacher's funnel questions:

Teacher: Martha, tell me what you remember about Nate's story. What did you like most?

Martha: I dunno. I guess I like the way Nate helped Annie find her picture.

Teacher: Why do you think that Nate was an important character?

Martha: (Shrugs)

Teacher: Do you need more time to think about why Nate was an important character?

Martha: (Nods, and is quiet for a minute.) He found it. Annie's picture, I mean.

Teacher: Yes, he did, indeed! You said that Annie is also a character. Tell me how Nate and Annie are the same and different as characters.

Martha: Hmmm. Well, Nate is a boy, and Annie's a girl. That's different. Hmmm. Same . . . uh . . . let me think . . . they both like pancakes!

Teacher: How do you think Nate feels when Annie calls him on the phone and tells him about her missing picture?

Martha: Happy, because he likes to solve mysteries and call himself "Nate the Great!"

Teacher: How do you think Annie feels? Sad? Angry? Disappointed?

Martha: Sad and mad, 'cause I think she really liked that picture.

Notice how the teacher starts with a broad question. This is designed to reconnect Martha to an earlier discussion about the story. Then the teacher probes further about her understanding of the differences between Nate and Annie as characters. The point is to learn whether Martha understands the characters' feelings. *Why* questions delve into a student's reasoning and explore her capacity to reflect. Whatever Martha's answers, the teacher will learn something from this exchange, even though she has only jotted a brief note in her logbook.

Student Work Samples: Performances and Portfolios

During a typical school day, students produce a lot of paperwork. Some products (for example, worksheets) are for practice, the work of a moment and seldom worth keeping. Today's assessment methods emphasize performance and "showing your work." Students now assemble *portfolios* for writing and mathematics, science and social studies (Farr & Tone, 1994; Tierney, Carter, & Desai, 1991). These collections, like Ms. K.'s *Roots* project, are major activities representing significant time investment, engaging the creative impulse, and reflecting meaningful personal investment.

Work samples assess both *product* and *process.* A writing portfolio can show the student's progression from early ruminations about a writing assignment through an outline to the first draft, and then on to the stages of review, revision, and final polishing and publication, as illustrated in Figure 11.9. The final result can be judged as a product, but the process reveals student learning and can help improve instruction.

Portfolios often include captions, brief notes by the teacher that reflect on the work, pointing out both strengths and areas for improvement. Teachers sometimes use Post-its for these captions rather than mark up the origi-

[A teacher's] responsibility involves reflectiveness, and reflection requires record keeping and time.

—*Peter Johnston*
Literacy Educator

The series of portfolio entries here illustrate a sixth-grader's efforts as she and her classmates work to improve the "locker" situation.

DEVELOP: The big problem for us sixth-graders is that we have to share a locker with another student. We talked with our teacher, and she said we ought to write a letter to the principal asking for more lockers. But we also need to think about the principal's problems. I talked with other students, and we brainstormed a letter for the principal.

[Portfolio includes brainstorming results.]

DRAFT: Sixth-graders need privacy, and it's hard on us when we have to share a locker with someone else. The school really needs to make sure that every one of us has our own locker. This will cost money, and the halls are already crowded. But if we ask parents for help, we can probably find a way to solve the problem. Our class would like to meet with you to talk about lockers.

[This is a synopsis of a two-page draft, all of which is included in the portfolio.]

REVIEW: I asked other students about the letter, and they suggested a couple of things. One was to ask a few parents to write a letter saying that they were willing to help. Another was that it will take a while to do anything, and are we expecting changes before we go on to middle school.

REVISE: Some of us have talked with our parents, and they are willing to help. Three of them have written letters promising to meet with you and with our group. We also know that putting in new lockers will take a while. It's March, and we will soon be leaving for middle school. But we think that better lockers will be good for everyone, and so we are willing to help solve the locker problem even if it won't make things better for us.

[This is one of several notes on revising that are in the portfolio.]

FIGURE 11.9 *Portfolio Entries from a Sixth-Grade Student*

POLISH: We looked over the revision for spelling and grammar errors, and other ways to improve the final version.

[The portfolio contains several drafts, making it possible to see how successful students were in revising.]

PUBLISH:

Dear Ms. S,

Our sixth grade class is worried about the locker problems at the school. As you know, students have to share lockers, which causes lots of problems. We don't have enough room for our books and supplies. We don't have any privacy. And we get into arguments with one another.

Getting more lockers will cost money, and we know that the school needs lots of things. The halls are crowded, but we think that there is some room at the end of north hall, and one student went to a school that had three lockers in a stack instead of two.

We have talked with our parents, and three of them have promised to meet with you and us to talk about how to fix the locker problem. We have their letters to show you.

It will take a while to put in new lockers, and since we are graduating in March, it won't help us. But better lockers will help everyone. We have talked with the seventh graders, and they agree. Will you meet with our class and our parents to see what we can do?

Sincerely,

The 1997 Sixth Grade Class

[The letter, prepared on a computer and signed by all of the students, was delivered to the principal's office by a delegation. The portfolio includes a photograph of the principal receiving the letter from the students.]

nal. That way the student can receive feedback and instructional support, without her paper being marred. Also, students can add their own Post-it captions, thus connecting themselves to the assessment loop.

Teacher-Made Tests

Although this section has emphasized performance assessments, you will also want to rely on old-fashioned tests when appropriate. Nitko (1996) and Stiggins (1994) both describe procedures for the development of various types of teacher-made tests, ranging from multiple-choice instruments to portfolios. For children in the early grades, informal reading inventories (Farr & Carey, 1986) and running records (Clay, 1993; Goodman et al., 1989) offer a useful middle ground between standardized methods and completely open-ended approaches.

In both of these approaches, students read aloud passages of increasing difficulty until they reach a frustration level (too many misreadings or too much time). The teacher records the student's oral reading errors and hesitations, both to indicate level of performance, but also to diagnose the strategies and error patterns. The emphasis in these methods is on oral reading fluency, but it also makes sense to ask the student to talk about her understanding of the passage, and even to talk about her word-attack strategies. These methods require a good deal of time, and so you will be able to use them only sparingly, often as supplements to your ongoing observations and to check the results from other, more formal tests, such as the WRAT (Wilkinson, 1995), the Nelson-Denny (Brown, 1985), or the Woodcock-Johnson (American Guidance Service, 1987).

Analyzing and Summarizing the Data

It is late September. You know something about your class, partly from the previous teacher and spring testing, partly from observations and journal notes. You need to combine this information into a consistent and understandable portrait, partly for upcoming parent conferences, but also for deciding how to fine-tune your instructional plans for the fall. You will face numerous tasks like this throughout the year. The school day has limited hours, and you must choose how to spend them. Students differ, and you must decide how to meet individual needs, how to organize students, and how to plan activities. You need to think about what you know.

Analysis and summarization are not a sudden shift in the assessment process. You don't stop collecting evidence and begin analysis; the process is ongoing and interactive. Throughout September, you have formed individual portraits. But now you need to shift emphasis, to think about where the class as a whole is now and how to shape the road ahead. It is time to assemble the evidence so you can decide what it means and how to use it, for your own purposes and for feedback to others.

Teachers use a variety of strategies to handle these tasks. Some rely on basal management systems, while others keep narrative journals. The Teacher Logbook, shown in Figure 11.10, is a middle-of-the-road method for

The Teacher Logbook

Section I: Student Summary

Fall Entry Level

Student	Reading/Writing/Language			Math . . .
	Vocab	Narrative	Expos Skills	
Able, J.				
. . .				
Zeno, K.				

Section II: Journal Notes

Week of _____

Section III: Curriculum/Plan Record

Plans for Fall Qtr

Sept:	Activities	Vocab	Narr	Expos Skills
	Update			
Dec:	Activities	Vocab	Narr	Expos Skills
	Update			

FIGURE 11.10
The Teacher Logbook

From Calfee, R. C. & Perfumo, P. A national survey of writing portfolio practice: What we learned and what it means. In R. C. Calfee and P. Perfumo (Eds.), *Writing Portfolios in the Classroom: Policy and Practice, Promise and Peril.* Mahwah, NJ: Erlbaum.

merging the evidence (Calfee & Perfumo, 1993). The logbook is not something you buy, but an idea for organizing your inquiries. It contains three segments: *evidence* about student performance, *judgments* of student achievement, and a *curriculum-planning record*.

You begin work with the logbook by establishing a small number of curriculum outcomes: What do your students need to know by year's end, and how will you judge the quality of their accomplishments? Story comprehension and composition, for example, are built around four critical outcomes (Lukens, 1995): character, plot, setting, and theme. For kindergartners, understanding the moral of a simple fable is a reasonable goal. By third grade, students should be able to identify thematic issues in works such as E. B. White's *Charlotte's Web* and express the personal meaning of such stories. Sixth-graders should be able to use thematic elements in their compositions, and appreciate the themes that link related stories. Like *Charlotte's Web*, Katherine Paterson's *Bridge to Terabithia* tells how two characters begin at odds with one another, but then develop a deep friendship that ends in tragedy. In *Bridge to Terabithia*, the characters are two adolescents, a boy and a girl, and the tragedy is sudden and unpredictable. The competent sixth-grader will understand the parallels and can relate the theme—the abiding importance of genuine friendship—to experiences in the real world.

The logbook builds on such curriculum strands; the analysis task is to locate each student on each strand. For example, in Ms. K.'s combined third and fourth grade, one student may be struggling with the task of describing Wilbur and Charlotte at the beginning and end of *Charlotte's Web*, while another is able to relate the meaning of these changes to her own personal experience and to use her understanding in composing a personal narrative about the development of her friendship with her new stepbrother.

You work on the logbook from back to front. Your first task, before school begins, is to review your curriculum plans, especially those for the fall quarter. You need to learn something about your class and about end-of-grade expectations. You need to learn your options for materials and activities; a change in the textbook series, a new collection of trade books, a conference with the librarian—these will all influence your curriculum plans.

The *curriculum-planning* section at the end of the logbook provides a place for you to record these reflections. It is at the back because it is *your* section; it is for your analysis and reflection, not day-by-day but long-term, not set in stone but constantly changing. It is not a collection of daily lesson plans for the principal, but a background for the analysis: Where is the class headed, and where are they located at present?

The middle of the logbook provides journal space to record *evidence* about student performance: observations, informal assessments of student activities and projects, and questions requiring further thought and action. The notes may cover student portfolio entries and formal assessments. These are brief jottings, notes based on student discussions, pointers to other information, ponderings about individual students. Before school starts, you enter information from the previous year. During September, a time of ongoing and intense formative assessment, pages fill quickly.

Like Ms. K., many teachers keep written notes, but seldom do they view these as "research." In fact, journal notes offer a valuable record for reflection and action. An empty student sheet warns that the student has slipped from sight. A long list of books read but no evidence of written work is a reminder to encourage the student to put her thoughts on paper. The logbook is a memory jogger.

Finally, *student summaries* at the beginning of the logbook are for official analysis and summative assessment. The class list runs down the left column, curriculum strands along the top. Although this section ends the process, you open it first for parent conferences, to review student progress, and to discuss students and the class with colleagues and the principal. The entries are your estimate of student performance levels in each strand. The entries summarize your judgments of individual student performance, based on your interpretation of test scores, observations, and interviews. You enter a question mark when uncertain. Samantha shows little interest in writing; her journal contains a few brief sentences, most obtained under duress: "Satrdy we went to Grat Amrica. I went on the Wav." But you heard her talk with a friend about her day at the amusement park, and she shared a great deal more information. She clearly has greater command of language than appears in her written work. Analysis will lead back to action. How can you find conditions that elicit the best that she can do? She prefers talking to writing and is impatient with the mechanics of writing. But for now, you enter a question mark under expository writing, a puzzlement to discuss with her parents.

Analysis combines information from many sources. Edward scores at a 4.0 grade level on standardized tests, reads voraciously, and completes assigned writing tasks. His papers are longer than average, the mechanical details precise. But in both writing and in-class discussions, he reacts to thematic issues like a first-grader, still at a mundane level. He chooses short, simple books for free reading, and races through them at breakneck speed. He retains the literal information but shows little depth of understanding. Reading seems a retreat into himself. He is small for his age and young for his cohort, and has few friends. Perhaps he needs a better audience for sharing his ideas. Your analysis combines current performance with context and thoughts about instructional decisions. Figure 11.11 presents several entries from Ms. K.'s logbook.

Here are three out of the many entries that fill Ms. K.'s Teacher Logbook—one from the student summary section, one from the journal notes section, and one from the curriculum plan/record section.

Section I: Student Summary

		Reading/Writing/Language	
	Vocab	Narrative	Expos Skills
Matthews, K.	++	++	−

Section II: Journal Notes—Week of Dec. 15

Karen M. is an avid reader, as long as a book fits her interests. She is absorbed by stories—Snow Goose and Shadows are tough going, but when she found them in the library, she wouldn't let them go. Her oral report was excellent. She has written very little in her personal journal though. Her skills are way above average, but she hesitates to write unless it is perfect. Nonfiction writing is not her thing, and she has no idea how to prepare a report.

Section III: Plans/Record

This class needs work on exposition. Girls are especially lacking. Check with Thelma [the librarian] on any recent acquisitions. Orr's nature books have great graphics—can connect with science.

FIGURE 11.11 *Some Entries from Ms. K.'s Teacher Logbook*

Interpretation: Making Sense of the Results

Interpretation gives meaning to evidence and shapes generalizations that lead to action. Interpretation goes beyond concrete data to broader meanings. Inquiry is not linear; interpretation is embedded in the questions, the design, and the evidence. Interpretation requires reflection and expression, time and occasion to ponder the evidence. Pondering means consulting with colleagues and seeking opportunities for professional interactions.

Interpretation faces two challenges—achieving consistency and persuasiveness, or *reliability* and *validity*. As we noted earlier in the chapter, reliability asks whether the evidence is dependable, while validity asks whether the evidence can answer your question. Standardized tests determine reliability and validity by statistics. Teacher-based assessment handles the issues by argument and debate. In the following scenario, you will see a first-year teacher learning how to give meaning to evidence and shape generalizations that lead to action:

IN THE CLASSROOM

Interpreting Evidence in the Sixth Grade

Jennifer Coombs, a new sixth-grade teacher, has been assigned at the last minute to a school in a low-income urban neighborhood. The previous teacher, Mr. Milton, has taken a health leave. His notes and the principal's comments suggest that the students have limited experience and poor language skills. Working from lesson plans left by Mr. Milton, Ms. Coombs begins her first class. The morning goes fine. After lunch, she begins social studies with a discussion of the Constitution:

> *Ms. Coombs:* Today we're going to study the U.S. Constitution. Who can tell me something about the Constitution?
>
> *Students:* [Silence]
>
> *Ms. Coombs:* What about the federal government? The government in Washington?
>
> *Students:* [Again, silence; clearly a problem]
>
> *Ms. Coombs:* [Writes on the board: *President, Congress,* and *Supreme Court.*] Who can tell me about these words? [Still no response. Ms. Coombs reluctantly abandons the discussion and starts the lecture.] Well, our nation recently celebrated its two-hundredth anniversary . . .

What do these data mean? Several alternatives are consistent with the evidence but call for different courses of action:

- The students are not used to open-ended questions in school and don't understand strategies like brainstorming.
- They feel uneasy with a new teacher and uneasy about seeming foolish.
- They know something about how government works, but don't know the official vocabulary.
- They really don't know much about the government and have a limited vocabulary.

How is Ms. Coombs to match the slim evidence with one of these possible interpretations? As we noted earlier, inquiry is not a straight-line process. Validating an interpretation often calls for experimentation—for changing conditions and collecting new data:

IN THE CLASSROOM
Collecting More Evidence

Ms. Coombs decides to check whether students lack discussion strategies and are uneasy with open-ended questions. She plans a discussion for the following day around the topic of weather. The Constitution may be unfamiliar, but students surely know something about weather:

> **Ms. Coombs:** Today, let's talk about the *weather*. What comes to mind when you think about this topic?
>
> **Students:** [Silence]

Ms. Coombs realizes this evidence suggests that something is at work other than lack of knowledge, and she makes a strategic move by offering some "starters." Pointing toward the window, she asks:

> **Ms. Coombs:** What is it like today?
>
> **Student:** Cloudy?
>
> **Ms. Coombs:** Right! What was it like yesterday?
>
> **Student:** Cold.
>
> **Ms. Coombs:** OK. These are weather words! What about some others?

By lesson's end, Ms. Coombs has collected considerable evidence about conditions that engage this particular group of students in discussion. Now she has new ideas about how to approach abstract topics like the U.S. government. If her interpretation had rested solely on the first lesson, she might have decided to teach basic skills. Now she is more inclined to focus neither on government nor skills, but on developing some sense of classroom community.

Assessments like these may appear subjective. How can teachers assure critics about the trustworthiness of complex judgments? One answer is to *triangulate*, using multiple sources of evidence. You might gather one piece of evidence from students' oral reading, another from class discussion, and still another from their writing. Triangulation provides evidence of consistency, the keystone of reliability (Fetterman, 1989). Another answer depends on professional interaction. In Great Britain, teachers employ what they term *moderation* as a basis for establishing validity (Harlen, 1994). Teacher teams review samples of student work. They evaluate the samples and defend their interpretations as a group. With moderation, interpretation becomes a collaborative activity.

Jennifer is still learning about interpretation. It is early in her first year as a teacher. She has had little chance to triangulate and is too busy to consult with colleagues, who are as busy as she is. But she is on the right path—not a bad beginning for the first week of school. Ms. K., who employed the same principles in the *Roots* project, would be proud of her.

Reporting and Decision Making

Now to the final stage of the inquiry process. The teacher has evidence about student achievement and is satisfied with consistency and substance. What should be done next? Inquiry-based assessment serves little purpose unless it leads to actions like reports and decisions. This is where the inquiry cycle comes full circle.

Reports generally take the form of either *grades* or determinations of whether or not students have met *standards* (Nitko, 1996, Ch. 14). Grading relies on competitive ratings (norm-referenced; grading on the curve) or preset limits (criterion-referenced; 90-plus means an A). These tactics can frustrate teachers and students by their arbitrariness. Teachers view student achievement as a complex mix of effort and accomplishment. Joan's end-of-year compositions weren't as polished as Susan's, but Joan entered fourth grade barely able to finish a complete sentence, while Susan already viewed herself as an author. It is difficult to reflect these dimensions in a single letter or number, and so teachers often prefer brief narratives—when they can find the time to write them.

Standards-based assessment is a new variation on criterion-referenced testing. Standards begin with descriptions like those shown earlier in Figure 11.4 about what students should be able to do in a particular area at a particular grade level, along with rubrics that describe how well they need to do it. Figure 11.12 shows the rubrics for two reading standards developed for fourth-graders. When working with rubrics, your job as a teacher is to rate student performance against these guidelines. As you can see, the rubrics are broad and subjective, and they require considerable judgment. In the inquiry model, teachers work together as professional teams to interpret performance standards at the local school, placing the mandated requirements within their context. Many states set standards at selected mileposts (for example, third and eighth grade), which allows the local school to distinguish between *progress* and *accomplishment*.

Here is how this distinction works. Entering kindergartners differ greatly, and although parents need to be reassured that their children have made progress in language, literacy, and communication skills, students are likely to still differ considerably at the end of the year. First-graders will also differ, but by the end of the year they should all have attained a reasonable degree of fluency in oral reading. Second-graders may sometimes be judged by their spelling, but as long as they are learning to write, spelling can take a

Grading means abstracting a great deal of information into a single symbol to ease communication.

—*Rich Stiggins*
Assessment Specialist

Standard	Level of Proficiency		
	Exemplary	*Proficient*	*Developing*
Making Sense of a Story	Thoroughly understands complex stories	Understands most stories including some complex ones	Limited and literal understanding of simple stories
	Connects personal experiences to characters and themes	Some connections with personal experiences to characters and situations	Extracts meaning but with little personal connection
	Multiple perspectives across stories	Different perspectives on a story	Describes events, people, and places factually
Using Tools and Strategies in Reading	Masterful use of several strategies to deepen understanding	Uses various strategies to understand story	Limited range of strategies
	Sophisticated analyses of plot and theme	Uses rereading and rethinking to support understanding	Some use of rereading to support understanding

FIGURE 11.12 *Sample Rubrics for Intermediate-Grade Literacy Standards*

back seat. Third-grade graduates face a different challenge; they are expected to handle demanding textbooks in the content areas (science, social studies, and mathematics) and to write fairly extensive compositions—book reports and research reports. Moreover, they are expected to complete these assignments with less guidance than they received in the earlier grades. In the third-grade standards, accordingly, accomplishment matters more than progress. If the student has made reasonable progress in the first four years of school but cannot handle the demands of fourth grade, then he or she will encounter problems, and the third-grade report needs to make this clear for the student, the parents, and the teachers. During the four years from kindergarten entry to third grade graduation, the primary team's job is help children move from where they begin to where they need to be, reporting along the way students' progress toward the goal.

A similar transition occurs at the end of fifth or sixth grade, when students move from a single-teacher classroom to separate classes for different subjects. As long as students are together in the same class for most of the school day, the teacher can help them make connections, to see how reading and writing skills need to be adapted to different tasks. With separate classes, students must deal with different teaching styles as well as different content. The social studies and science teachers are specialists in their disciplines, and they may be neither willing nor able to help the student with reading and writing assignments. Assessment at the end of the one-teacher stage of a student's school life should ensure that she has the skills and knowledge needed to take on this new challenge.

Decisions mean creating alternatives and making choices. In the earlier scenario involving the topic of the Constitution, the teacher decided to take time to teach discussion based on everyday topics *before* turning to discussion of more demanding content. But textbooks cover enormous amounts of content, and talking about the weather may mean slighting the Louisiana Purchase. Teachers, especially in the later grades, feel enormous pressure to "finish the book." Our recommendation here, consistent with the approach of teaching for understanding we presented in Chapter 8, is to use assessment to help you decide when to slow down to solve a problem. Taking time to set the stage can be particularly important at the beginning of the year. By establishing procedures for class discussion and small-group work, and by teaching some essential skills and strategies needed for effective individual work, you can then move ahead at a more rapid pace, assured that most students will stay with you.

You must also decide how much to invest in individual students. Concept mapping will increase the flow of discussion, but a few students may still hold back. You could search for other topics of interest to this handful, but at what cost for the class as a whole? At some point, students must take individual responsibility. You can ensure that every student has a chance to get started, and you can keep the curriculum flexible by offering options along the way. You can foster responsibility by teaching self-assessment. Ms. K. exemplified both of these practices. She was directive early in the school year, pressing students on particular tasks, and then she moved back, giving students more opportunities for individual achievement and greater accountability.

A final set of decisions centers on program evaluation. Some materials work better than others. Student textbooks are often lengthy and filled with more information than students can absorb, and you should think about the coverage issue raised above; if you can't cover everything equally well, what are the priorities? The way you introduce a topic or a project can make a difference. By making notes about what works and what doesn't, you can refine your instructional program from year to year. Ms. K. spent almost six weeks on the *Roots* project—the longest investment of time she has spent on a single project during her teaching career. But as she looked back on the results at year's end, she decided that next year she would plan a similar activity, laying the groundwork more carefully and informing the parents more fully of her plans.

Last year, on the last day of first grade, Courtney handed me a small book. "First. I didn't know how to read. Soon anofe [enough] you tout [taught] me." I had my report card.

—*Linda Pils*
First-Grade Teacher

525

Each of the actions described above requires *reporting* (how to say it) and *deciding* (what to do about it) for students, for parents, and for you and your colleagues. The task is never complete, because students and problems change. Next year's questions are unlikely to be the same as this year's, and the answers will certainly be different. Assessment as inquiry takes time and effort, especially at the beginning of a teaching career. But it becomes easier with time, and it pays off!

Reflection AND Application

This matrix sets the stage for the following questions:

	K–2	3–4	5–7
September			
December			
March			
May			

6. As you move through the matrix, how do the six stages of inquiry-based assessment apply to each situation? What are their relative importance for different age groups and at different times of year? Jot down your thoughts on a copy of the matrix, and then discuss them with a classmate.

7. You and two other teachers have discussed the inquiry model and are planning for the coming school year. You meet to finalize arrangements, and one partner raises concerns. What about students with special needs? Your school has a full-inclusion policy, and he will have two students with learning disabilities in his fourth-grade class. What about combination grades? He is a new teacher and may have a three–four combination class. What about mobility? He may have to deal with midyear entrants. As the experienced team member, how would you handle these issues from an assessment perspective? How would your advice change for dealing with younger or older students?

8. Following on the previous question, the other partner, also newer to teaching than you, has better news. She will have two top-of-the-line computers in her classroom. She will also have an aide because her class is three students over the limit specified in the contract. Finally, she has visited most of the families on her class list (she has incredible energy), and several parents have volunteered to help in the classroom.

But she is worried about the class size and the wide range of student differences (she knows that she will have a three–four combination). What are your recommendations about how she can take advantage of her resources to handle the assessment tasks throughout the year? How would your advice change for younger or older students?

CONCLUDING REMARKS

Assessing reading, writing, and language is a tough job requiring professional judgment. Effective assessment means using information from a broad range of strategies, from standardized tests to classroom portfolios. External tests become increasingly important in the later grades, but are no substitute for the teacher's ongoing inquiries into student growth and accomplishment. Asking the right questions is the key to discovering useful answers. This chapter has emphasized the interrelatedness of curriculum, instruction, and assessment. The examples have highlighted the academic side of the assessment process. But it's important to keep the human element in mind. We mentioned earlier that elementary teachers have a success orientation; they want success for every student!

The inquiry approach begins with a clear view of what success means, assurance that these goals are clear to all involved, instructional strategies that support all students in meeting the goals, and candid feedback to students about their weaknesses as well as their strengths. This is really the most caring method, even if sometimes it means giving a student some bad news. But the long-term chances of genuine success are higher for all involved when we are candid with students, their parents, school administrators, and of course ourselves. The ultimate aim of literacy assessment is to gain the information you need to lead each student to the highest possible level of critical literacy.

> Teaching for understanding is what we are supposed to be doing. Test results get a lot of attention, and sometimes assessment takes away from learning time. But how else do you know that students are learning?
>
> —*Betsy Tsai*
> *Third-Grade Teacher*

EXTENDING LEARNING

There is no substitute for involving yourself directly in assessment activities and the inquiry process. The three following exercises are designed to "get you into it."

I. Visit a school or district office, and talk about testing policies and practices with the people in charge. What tests are used? At what grades? Why? What happens to the results? After you have located the information, study a couple of standardized tests and printouts of their results with a class or two. Think about what you can learn from these documents. Once you have digested the information, discuss your impressions with a principal, a teacher, and a couple of upper-grade students.

2. Find a student, and informally assess her reading and writing knowledge and skills. You will find several assessment models in the annotated bibliography, but the simplest approach is to find a few short passages of text, read them yourself to think about what it would mean to understand them, and compose an effective summary of the material. Your assessment should cover performance: How well can the student read, respond, and write? Equally important are think-aloud questions that ask the student to describe how she is approaching the task and attitudinal questions about motivation and efficacy.

3. Locate two teachers who vary in experiences and assignments, and ask them about their assessment policies. Plan a brief interview format to explore various facets of their inquiry process. How do they plan the assessment year? What methods do they use to measure student progress and accomplishment? How do they use standardized test results? How do they communicate with students? Parents? Teachers? Whom do they rely on for consultation? How do they handle assessment of special students? Once you have finished these interviews, think about what you have learned—if a new teacher approached you in a few years asking about this topic, how would you prepare for the discussion?

REFERENCES

Airaisan, P. (1994). *Classroom assessment.* New York: McGraw-Hill. This book provides classroom teachers with background and practical applications of traditional assessment methods.

American Guidance Service. (1987). *Woodcock-Johnson reading mastery test.* Cinole Pines, MN: Author. This is one of the most frequently used instruments for individual assessment of students who may be in need of special instruction.

Baumann, J. F. (1988). *Reading assessment: An instructional decision-making perspective.* Columbus, OH: Merrill. This book offers a wide variety of practical examples for applying many of the principles described in this chapter.

Bloom, B. S., Hastings, J. T., & Madaus, G. F. (1971). *Handbook of formative and summative evaluation of student learning.* New York: McGraw-Hill. This is the foundation for criterion-referenced assessment.

Bloom, B. S., Madaus, G. F., & Hastings, J. T. (1981). *Evaluation to improve learning.* New York: McGraw-Hill. This is a companion volume to the previous item. It deals more directly with ongoing formative assessment.

Brown, J. I. (1985). *Nelson-Denny reading achievement test.* Chicago, IL: Riverside Press. This group-administered multiple-choice test is widely used by classroom teachers and reading specialists for a quick assessment of reading vocabulary and comprehension.

Calfee, R. C., & Hiebert, E. H. (1991). Classroom assessment of reading. In R. Barr, M. Kamil, P. Mosenthal, & P. D. Pearson (Eds.), *Handbook of research on reading* (2nd ed., pp. 281–309). New York: Longman. This technical chapter describes the teacher's role as an applied researcher in the assessment of reading.

Calfee, R. C., & Perfumo, P. (1993). Student portfolios: Opportunities for a revolution in assessment. *Journal of Reading, 36,* 532–537. This article describes results from a survey of teachers using classroom portfolios for reading assessment.

California Test Bureau. (1996). *Terra nova.* Monterey, CA: Author. This is one of several innovative standardized testing systems that incorporate both multiple-choice and open-ended items.

Cazden, C. (1988). *Classroom discourse.* Portsmouth, NH: Heinemann. The author describes the discussion patterns of teachers and students in the elementary grades.

Chambliss, M. C., & Calfee, R. C. (in press). *Today's textbooks, tomorrow's minds.* London: Blackwell. This book describes the important roles of textbooks in schools.

Clay, M. (1993). *An observation study of early literacy achievement.* Portsmouth, NH: Heinemann. This book reports findings of reading acquisition in the primary grades, but is also useful as a model of a variety of classroom-based assessment methods.

Cronbach, L. J. (1960). *Essentials of psychological testing* (3rd ed.). New York: Harper & Row. This is a classic volume on formal and informal testing methods.

Dillon, J. T. (1988). *Questioning and teaching: A manual of practice.* New York: Teachers College Press. Only a few books are available on the use of questions in teaching, and this is probably the best.

Farr, R., & Carey, R. F. (1986). *Reading: What can be measured?* (2nd ed.). Newark, DE: International Reading Association. This informative review of testing concepts and issues is also useful as a resource book.

Farr, R., & Tone, B. (1994). *Portfolios and performance assessment.* San Antonio: Harcourt Brace. This work goes beyond the previous citation by discussing innovative methods for gauging reading achievement at the classroom level.

Fetterman, D. M. (1989). *Ethnography step by step.* Newbury Park, CA: Sage. This slim volume has lots of practical advice for how to look and listen carefully to understand what is happening in complex situations.

Goodman, K. S., Goodman, Y. M., & Hood, W. J. (1989). *The whole language evaluation book.* Portsmouth NH: Heinemann. The basic book reflecting whole-language approaches to student assessment.

Harlen, W. (Ed.). (1994). *Enhancing quality in assessment.* London: Paul Chapman Publishing. This book describes assessment practices in Great Britain, including the process of moderation.

Harp, B. (1991). *Assessment and evaluation in whole language programs.* Norwood, MA: Christopher-Gordon. This book complements Goodman et al. with several classroom-level case studies.

Hart, D. (1994). *Authentic assessment: A handbook for educators.* Menlo Park, CA: Addison-Wesley. This book gives examples of innovative assessment practices from a variety of sources and covering a variety of subject matters.

Herman, J. L., Aschbacher, P. R., & Winters, L. (1992). *A practical guide to alternative assessment.* Alexandria, VA: Association for Supervision and Curriculum Development. This is one of the best brief books describing the strengths and limits of nonstandardized testing methods.

Hiebert, F., & Calfee, R. C. (1992). Assessment of literacy: From standardized tests to performances and portfolios. In A. E. Farstrup & S. J. Samuels (Eds.), *What research says about reading instruction* (pp. 70–100). Newark, DE: International Reading Association. Designed for teachers, this chapter describes the "inquiring teacher's" role in assessment of literacy achievement.

Johnson, M. S., Kress, R. A., & Pikulski, J. J. (1987). *Informal reading inventories.* Newark, DE: International Reading Association. The authors describe methods for classroom assessment of reading, using a technique that goes back more than 50 years.

Johnston, P. H. (1983). *Reading comprehension assessment: A cognitive basis.* Newark, DE: International Reading Association. This is one of the first accounts of social–cognitive alternatives to standardized testing of reading achievement.

Johnston, P. H. (1990). Steps toward a more naturalistic approach to the assessment of the reading process. In J. Algina & S. Legg (Eds.), *Cognitive assessment of language and mathematics outcomes* (pp. 92–143). Norwood, NJ: Ablex. The author points out limitations of standardized tests and describes methods for teacher-based "on-the-fly" appraisal of reading.

Johnston, P. H. (1992). *Constructive evaluation of literate activity.* New York: Longman. This is a rich source of information on constructive and informal approaches to assessment.

Lukens, R. J. (1995). *A critical handbook of children's literature* (5th ed.). New York: HarperCollins. This is a brief, well-written, and practical paperback for teachers who want to understand how to connect students with the pleasures of good children's stories.

Mitchell, R. (1992). *Testing for learning: How new approaches to evaluation can improve American schools.* New York: Free Press. The author presents a well-reasoned discussion of alternative assessments.

Nitko, A. J. (1996). *Educational assessment of students* (2nd ed.). Englewood Cliffs, NJ: Merrill. This is a standard assessment textbook used in college courses.

O'Malley, J. M., & Pierce, L. V. (1996). *Authentic assessment for English language learners: Practical approaches for teachers.* New York: Addison-Wesley. The emphasis here is on "real reading and writing" as opposed to standardized tests. The book covers the early grades and includes many concrete illustrations. Although intended primarily for ESL students, much of the book is applicable to all students.

Paris, S. G., Calfee, R. C., Filby, N., Hiebert, E. H., Pearson, P. D., Valencia, S. W., & Wolf, K. P. (1992). A framework for authentic literacy assessment. *The Reading Teacher, 46,* 88–98. In practical language, the authors lay out a way of thinking about literacy instruction and assessment for students who vary widely in their cultural and linguistic backgrounds.

Patterson, L., Santa, C. M., & Smith, K. (1993). *Teachers as researchers: Reflection and action.* Newark, DE: International Reading Association. This is an important document for the inquiring teacher.

Phye, G. D. (1996). (Ed.). *Handbook of classroom assessment.* Orlando, FL: Academic Press. This is an up-to-date review of contemporary issues and techniques in teacher-based assessment.

Popham, W. J. (1995). *Classroom assessment: What teachers need to know.* Boston: Allyn & Bacon. Another standard textbook for college courses, this book is not as comprehensive as Nitko, but more readable.

Stiggins, R. J. (1994). *Student-centered classroom assessment.* New York: Merrill. This book is designed to be especially teacher-friendly in acquainting practitioners with the challenges of a broad spectrum of assessment tasks.

Tierney, R. J., Carter, M. A., & Desai, L. E. (1991). *Portfolio assessment in the reading–writing classroom.* Norwood MA: Christopher-Gordon. This was one of the first works to describe the practicalities of classroom portfolios.

Wiggins, G. P. (1993). *Assessing student performance.* San Francisco: Jossey-Bass. The author presents a major attack on the effects of standardized tests on classroom practice and offers compelling examples of assesment techniques that are more engaging and informative.

Wilkinson, G. S. (1995). *Wide range achievement test 3.* Wilmington, DE: Jastak Associates. This individually administered test is designed, as the title suggests, to cover a wide range of achievement levels, which makes it especially useful when you aren't sure about a student's capability.

CHILDREN'S LITERATURE

Butterfield, M. (1995). *Richard Orr's nature cross-sections*. New York: Dorling Kindersley. Description and detailed illustrations show the "insides and underneaths" of a wide range of natural settings. 130 pages. Illustrated.

Cohen, M. (1983). *First grade takes a test*. New York: Dell. Not a typical piece of literature, this little book tells a worthwhile story for children and adults about the challenges of standardized tests. 32 pages. Illustrated.

Eco, U., & Carmi, E. (1989). *The three astronauts*. London: Stecker & Warburg. This is an outstanding example of contemporary children's literature—a moving story that celebrates the pursuit of peace in a diverse universe. 36 pages. Illustrated.

Gallico, P. (1940). *The snow goose*. New York: Knopf. In this tale from the early years of World War II, a hunchbacked artist and a shy village girl join forces to rescue Allied soldiers stranded on the beach at Dunkirk. 40 pages. Illustrated.

Haseley, D. (1991). *Shadows*. New York: Farrar, Straus, & Giroux. A *New York Times* review recommends this book as "strong and appealing . . . , tightly written and fast moving . . . , perfect for reluctant readers as well as those who love good books." 74 pages. Illustrated.

Haskins, J. (1992). *Colin Powell: A biography*. New York: Scholastic. This is a well-written biography of the famous general and chairman of the Joint Chiefs of Staff. 101 pages.

Landau, E. (1991). *Colin Powell, four-star general*. New York: F. Watts. This book examines the life and accomplishments of Colin Powell. 63 pages.

London, J. (1993). *The race: A Karuk coyote tale about how fire came to the people*. San Francisco: Chronicle Books. The origin of fire may not seem a mystery to today's children, enveloped as they are in a world of automobiles, electric lights, and computers, but this book brings the mystery to life in an engaging way. 32 pages. Illustrated.

Paterson, K. (1977). *Bridge to Terabithia*. New York: Crowell. This is a tale of an enchanted place that a boy and girl create from their emerging friendship. The story ends tragically, but the author's skill in handling this tension earned a Newbery Award. 128 pages. Illustrated.

Seuss, Dr. (T. S. Geisel & A. S. Geisel). (1990). *Oh, the places you'll go*. New York: Random House. The Seuss stories have the remarkable power to connect rhyme with theme, to engage both children and adults. They provide an excellent opportunity for finding out what a young student can do with a complex text. 44 pages. Illustrated.

Sharmat, M. W. (1972). *Nate the great*. New York: Dell. When Annie's newly painted picture of her dog Fang is missing, she calls on Nate to help her find it. 64 pages.

White, E. B. (1952). *Charlotte's web*. New York: Harper. A widely recognized classic of children's literature, this story of an empathic spider and a runty pig appeals to a wide array of readers. The Newbery Honor story offers many opportunities for assessing students' understanding of thematic issues. 184 pages.

chapter twelve

Classroom
Portraits

The day finally arrives when you get your teaching assignment. You are both excited and apprehensive. All that you have learned about children and how you can most effectively help them become competent, lifelong readers will be put into motion. So how do you take the bits and pieces you have learned over years of study and practice and transform these, amalgamate them into an exciting and workable reading program for your students?

As you know, or will soon discover, as you plan your reading program, there are certain factors already in place that will influence it—the school district and the school to which you have been assigned, its philosophy, policies, expectations, curriculum; the

CHAPTER OVERVIEW

resources at your disposal—number and kind of computers, number of library volumes, audiovisual material; resource staff and teacher aides; your classroom, its size, shape, character; and most of all, the students—their needs, interests, and abilities. These sorts of considerations combined with your own philosophy, knowledge, and experience will help you to mold and shape your own reading program, from the general contours of the year's broad goals to the smallest details of individual lessons. What might those broad contours and small details look like? In this chapter, we present one possibility for three different situations—first grade, a third-fourth combination class, and a fifth-sixth combination class.

A DAY IN THE LIFE OF JENNA LEBLANC AND HER FIRST-GRADE STUDENTS

Jenna LeBlanc is a first-year teacher in a first-grade class at Edgebrook Elementary school on the outskirts of Washington, D.C. Her student teaching had been with older children, so she was not quite prepared for the squirmy nature of 6- and 7-year-olds! Now, in mid-October, however, she believes she would never want to teach another grade. She says, "I have really seen these children emerge as readers and writers. I keep a portfolio on each child and included in it are samples of their writing since the beginning of the school year. It's exciting to look back at these and see the progress—and to know I had something to do with it. While it took me a little while to understand how much nurturing, hands-on activities, and structure young children need, I now can't imagine teaching any other grade level."

Jenna teaches 20 children of varied backgrounds and abilities. Most of her students come from working-class families that represent a wide range of cultures. Several of her students have parents who recently immigrated to the United States. Among her students there are eight different languages spoken at home.

Jenna tells us that, of her 20 students, three were already reading first-grade-level texts when they entered her classroom. Most of the others were not able to read conventionally and possessed quite a range of knowledge about print. Some children, for example, knew all the alphabet and some initial consonant sounds, while others had difficulty naming more than a handful of letters. All were eager to learn.

None of her students has problems communicating in English. But there is a considerable range in their knowledge of English vocabulary. "One of my goals is to help *all* of the children grow in their knowledge about the world and the labels for things in it," Jenna says. She frequently reads to her children from narrative and informational books—and enjoys the lively discussions that evolve from these readings. She sees this as one avenue for getting her children, as she puts it, "ready for the world and, of course, second grade!"

Jenna's school district uses a basal reading series that includes an anthology of children's literature and informational texts. Many of the selections are written by well-known children's authors and are grouped by theme. Within a particular theme, such as The World We Share with Animals, there might be a range of genres including predictable texts, narratives, poems, and information texts. Every child has a copy of the anthology. The basal series also has about 200 "little books," which we described in Chapter 4. These little books range from 6 to 25 pages each. Each little book is a complete text. The 200 little books span a continuum of reading difficulty, from books with very predictable texts to ones with well-developed stories. As we discussed in Chapter 4, these little books are leveled readers. That is, the vocabulary in the little books is "controlled." Little books provide practice in reading words with the phonics features under study. Jenna has six copies of each of the 200 little books.

In one corner of Jenna's classroom is the library. This inviting place contains an old sofa, pillows, a rug, a few plants, and, most of all, numerous books, magazines, and other reading materials. Many books are displayed with their covers showing, as the children are drawn to those rather than to ones with only their spines showing. There is a magazine rack and a low table on which books can be displayed with the covers showing. Jenna frequently displays books that relate to the theme that is the focus in the basal reading anthology. She checks out books from the school library and brings in books from her personal library to add to her theme collection. In choosing books, she tries to include a wide range of reading levels to match the wide range of reading experience among her students.

"Children do best when they feel secure," Jenna reports. "That's why routines and a daily schedule that become familiar to the children are very important. I begin each day with a morning message, a calendar activity, and a return of books checked out the previous day. When there is time, I invite children to share or read from books they had checked out the day before."

In addition to a vast selection of interesting reading materials, a classroom library should provide comfortable, inviting places to read.

Twice a week Jenna's students participate in a schoolwide buddy reading program. Every child in the school is paired with a buddy. The buddy may be a younger or an older child at the school, a community volunteer, or a teacher. The buddy may provide individual tutoring of the child, mentoring, or simply reading to or listening to the child read. Buddy assignments are made at the beginning of the school year. Most last for the whole year. At the beginning of the school year, Jenna did some assessments. She decided who might benefit the most from the intensive tutoring provided by adult tutors—either a teacher or a community volunteer. The community volunteers are trained tutors who provide individualized tutoring of the child in an adaptation of a program called Book Buddies (Invernizzi, Juel, & Rosemary, 1996).

The three children in Jenna's class who are reading at a first-grade level each have a kindergarten buddy. They frequently share a book they have recently read with their buddy. This buddy reading occurs in the classroom of the kindergarten teacher. It lasts for about 20 minutes. Then the first-grade children return to Jenna's room, where they select books to read the next time they see their buddies.

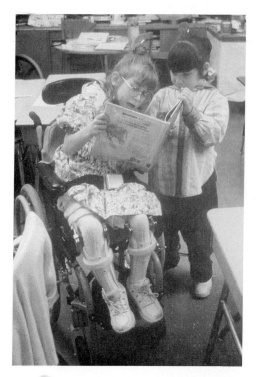

Students enjoy selecting and sharing books with younger or older reading buddies.

Five children are tutored by community volunteers in the school library. One child is tutored by the speech teacher in her classroom. These sessions last about 40 minutes. The volunteers and the teacher pick up and return the children to Jenna's room. The other 11 children remain in Jenna's classroom and are paired with third-grade children. The third-grade child usually reads to the first-grade child for part of the time, and then the younger child reads to the older one. These sessions last about 20 minutes, and when the third-grade children leave, the first-grade children have free-reading time. Each of Jenna's students has a plastic bag filled with little books and other reading materials, which they like to share with their older or younger buddies.

After buddy reading, the whole class regroups. Usually, Jenna spends about a half hour to 45 minutes in a whole-class, theme-related activity. So far this year, Jenna has followed the themes suggested in her basal teaching manual. She is, however, getting some ideas for other themes and may soon try out one of her own. The next 60 to 90 minutes are spent in center activities—reading, writing, and word study. Finally, her whole class regroups for about 15 minutes to recap what they have been doing in the centers.

Let's join Jenna for her morning reading and language arts period. This is a day when buddy reading occurs.

8:30–8:50	Morning message, calendar, book check-in
8:50–9:30	Buddy reading and free reading
9:30–10:15	Theme-related whole-class activity
10:15–11:30	Centers
11:30–11:45	Whole-class sharing of center activities
11:45	Lunch

8:30–8:50—Morning Message, Calendar, Book Check-in

As children enter the classroom, they pass a bulletin board that has a chart on it with each of their names printed on an individual library pocket. Jenna got the library pockets from the librarian. Each book in the class library has a check-out pocket and a card in it with the name of the book on it. When the children leave at the end of the school day, they check out one or two books by putting the library card from the back of the book into the pocket with their name on it on the bulletin board. When they first arrive the next morning, they remove the card from the bulletin board library pocket, place it back into the book they took home, and return the book to the class library.

After checking in their books and putting their personal items in their cubbies, the children gather on a rug in front of the chalkboard and large calendar. Jenna first goes over the calendar and has them locate the date and day. The amount of time spent on this activity varies from day to day. They talk about the season, the weather, birthdays, and other special events.

Everyday Jenna prints a morning news message on the chalkboard. Jenna asks for volunteers who would like to tell what special things are happening at home, in their lives, or in the world. She writes what is said on the chalkboard under the heading *Morning News*. If there is time, she then has children share information about the books they checked out and read at home.

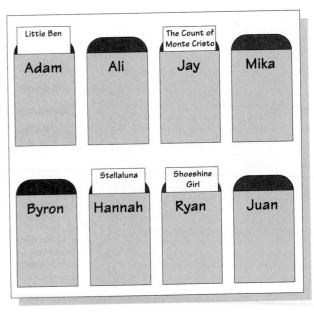

The morning message is an important literacy event in a first-grader's day.

8:50–9:30—Buddy Reading and Free Reading

At 8:50, five community volunteers, the speech teacher, and the third-grade children appear at the door. Jenna watches the three children in her room who are the kindergarten buddies walk down the hall to that classroom. Buddy reading and tutoring begin.

Jenna loves this time. She likes to walk around and see how grown-up both the first-grade and the third-grade children appear when they work with their buddies. When needed, she is there to pitch in and help. She also enjoys the time when a buddy is absent and she has a chance to interact one-on-one with a student.

9:30–10:15—Theme-Related Whole-Class Activity

Jenna likes to start her theme-related work with a whole-class activity that develops the children's knowledge about the theme. The theme for the next few weeks

Students benefit immensely by one-on-one reading experiences, either with an older student, the teacher, or an adult volunteer.

is "animals who share the world with us." This is the first day of this theme unit. In prior conversations with us, she emphasized that she likes "to start with what children know." We see that is the case, as Jenna begins the session today by engaging the children in a discussion about animals they have seen. She makes a language chart on a large sheet of butcher paper. After a child says something, she records the child's name next to what he says. As she records their words, she often makes comments about them—such as why she used a capital letter. Here's part of the language chart:

Jamal	I saw a horse with a policeman on it in DC!
Malt	I have a gerbil at home.
Kara	My dog Nick is black and white.
Tyron	I saw a black and white zebra at the zoo.
Cynara	There are lots of deer in the woods and I saw some.

Jenna steers the discussion to where the different animals were seen—to the environments in which different animals live. She brings out a large piece of butcher paper on which the class will start a wall chart. The paper is divided into sections with the several headings printed across the top, with room to add additional ones, as shown in Figure 12.1.

In the Water	On a Farm	In the Woods	In Our Homes	In the Jungle			
fish	horses	deer	dogs	monkeys			
	cows	raccoons	cats	giraffe			
		wolf					
		snake					
		owl					

FIGURE 12.1 *Wall Chart on Animals*

Jenna starts by asking the children where the animals they have mentioned live, and she records their responses under the appropriate categories. There is some discussion about where zebras might live if they weren't in a zoo and where horses normally would be found. "Is a zebra a horse?" Joey asks. "That's a very good question," Jenna says. "It's a question we might be able to answer after we do some research." So they won't forget the question, Jenna writes it on a large pad. As the children read about animals during the next two weeks, they will add their names, pictures, and facts about them to the wall chart.

Next, Jenna brings out a big book copy of *Hoot Howl Hiss* by Michelle Koch. "The author," she tells the children, "lives on the east coast in New Jersey, but she decided to write this book when she was on a vacation hiking out west. She ran across an animal called a marmot on her hike. Have any of you seen a marmot?" None have. She shares with them a picture of one and tells them a little about them and where marmots live.

Jenna points to the illustrations on the cover. "Michelle Koch is not only the author, she is also the illustrator of the book," she tells the children. "The watercolor illustrations of animals are painted a lot like you paint in our class! Can you name any of the animals you see on the cover and tell where you might find them?" Jenna points to the title words as she asks which animal says *hoot*, which one *howls*, and which one goes *hiss*. They add the words *wolf*, *snake*, and *owl* to their *In the Woods* chart. Jenna particularly emphasizes the sounds in the word *snake* as she prints the word on the chart. Jenna tells the children that when they are in the writing center, they will draw some of these animals, write about them, and paste their creations on the wall chart.

Jenna had told us that next year she wants to try to actually create some of the environments in parts of the classroom by making construction paper trees, drawing backgrounds of ponds, and so forth. She also told us that during the next few weeks the class will write class books about each environment. They will create an *In the Woods* book, for instance, which will contain their drawings and statements about animals that live in the woods. She mentioned that these class-made books are often the most popular books in the classroom library center.

Jenna asks the children to think about where each animal mentioned in the book lives as she begins to read, "Deep in the woods, owls . . . hoot . . ." She pauses before *hoot*, and several children correctly anticipate it. *Hoot Howl Hiss* is a short book with a very predictable structure. The illustrations help the children identify the animal words. When she finishes reading the book, Jenna asks the children about the sounds various animals make, as well as where they live. "What quacks, roars, growls?" she asks. "Where might you be if you heard a growl?"

Of course the children can't help but make these noises themselves. Jenna encourages the fun by saying, "Let's all roar like a lion . . . , quack like a duck . . . , growl like a bear . . . , hiss like a snake."

10:15–11:30—Centers

There are three centers in Jenna's classroom: a reading center, a writing center, and a word-study center. Jenna generally works in direct instruction with children in the word-study center. She groups children who need similar word-level instruction there. She randomly divides the rest of her class into groups that rotate through the reading and writing centers. Most days the children rotate through all three centers. If children finish a center activity before it is time for the next rotation, they are free to return to their desks and read from their anthologies, little books, or books from the library.

The reading center is the classroom library. In that center, the children can either read to a buddy or read independently. Sometimes they have assignments; sometimes they do free reading.

During the animal unit, they will find lots of books about animals prominently displayed on the low table in the reading center. "*Hoot Howl Hiss* is in your reading books, so you each have a copy of it," Jenna tells her first-graders. "You may want to take the book to the library and buddy read it. As you read, it might be fun to make sounds like the animals!" Next, she holds up a copy of *World Water Watch* by Michelle Koch. She encourages the children to look at it and compare the illustrations to those in *Hoot Howl Hiss*. Jenna briefly introduces the book by saying that it describes the dangers faced by various water animals such as sea turtles, seals, and whales. It's easy to see that some children can't wait to get their hands on the book. "It's really quite amazing what a personal introduction to a book does to spark interest in it!" Jenna told us later.

In the writing center, the children are going to draw and write. They can draw a picture of an animal, write its name, and then paste it onto the wall chart. Before they paste it, they need to discuss with one other child which environment the animal lives in and whether its name is correctly spelled. The children are encouraged to check the spellings and animal habitats by looking at books in the library center. Jenna tells us that she encourages the children to use invented spelling in free writing, but when the time comes to make the writing public, she wants the words correctly spelled. She says that she doesn't want the children to reread incorrect spellings on a permanent basis—and she intends to make use of the wall chart throughout the unit.

Each group that comes to the word-study center will participate in different phonics instruction. The particular focus of the phonics instruction depends on the needs of students. One group of children is working on initial consonants, another on the consonant digraphs *ch* and *wh*, and a third group on short vowels. The basic format for each group, however, is the same. Jenna begins each group by having the children chorally read *Hoot Howl Hiss*. The focus then shifts to a word or two in that story that contains the phonics feature that is under study. The consonant digraph group, for example, will focus on the words *chirp* and *whistle*.

After locating words with the phonic features in *Hoot Howl Hiss*, Jenna extends the phonics instruction to other words. This extension often involves three activities:

1. Sorting picture or word cards (as described in Chapter 4)
2. Reading a "little book" that contains several words with the phonics features
3. Writing a dictated sentence with words that contain the target spelling pattern

Jenna asks children in the first rotation of the word-study group to bring their anthologies and their personal word banks (which were discussed in Chapter 4) to the word-study center. After they chorally read the story together, she has them focus on the three *h* words on the cover. She says each word and has them point to the letter in it that said /h/. She gives each child a word card with the word *hoot* printed on it. She knew that would be a favorite word. Jenna asks them to dig through their word banks and locate other *h* words. Then each child reads his or her list of *h* words to a child sitting nearby. She does the same thing with the word *lion*.

Next, Jenna introduces a consonant combination that is new to the group—*qu*. She has the children locate the word *quack* on the page that says "ducks quack." She says, "Point to the word *quack*. Point to the letters that say

/kw/. Qu says /kw/. Cover up the letters that say *ack*. What do you have left? Let's say it, /kw/. Now lets add the *ack*, /kw—ack/." Children add the word cards *lion*, *quack*, and *hoot* to their word banks.

To develop phonemic awareness of initial consonant sounds, Jenna has the children do a group picture sort on a pocket chart. She has the children help her sort picture cards based on initial consonant sounds. She calls out the name of a picture, and they help her place it under the word card headings *hoot*, *lion*, and *quack*. She holds up a drawing of a hen and says "Hen, hoot—hen, lion—hen, quack." The children agree that the hen picture belongs under *hoot*. Then, she takes out a drawing of a leg and says, "Hen, leg—lion, leg—quack, leg." The group continues in this manner with pictures of a queen, quilt, horse, hat, and pictures representing other words from *Hoot Howl Hiss*.

To provide reading practice with the newly introduced initial consonant combination *qu*, Jenna uses a little book entitled *Quack!* by Matthew Benjamin (1996). She gives each child a copy. "Can you read the word on the cover?" she asks. "The ducks are a good clue!" She has the children point to the letters that say /kw/ in *quack*. She tells the children that *Quack!* is about a mother duck and her three ducklings. Joey spontaneously declares, "Ducks live in water!"

Jenna reads the story as the children follow along, finger-pointing to the words as she says them. Then they all read it aloud together. After this rereading, Jenna asks them to go through the book on a word hunt. They are to find all the words that start with *qu* and read them to the child sitting next to them. There are lots of shouts of "Quack!" and "Quick!" and "Quiet!" as they locate these words in the story.

To end this word-study session, Jenna reads simple sentences and has the children write them. She will later examine what each child writes to see which children might need some extra help. She is particularly interested in their spelling of the initial consonants. She hands out a piece of lined paper and tells them to write as best they can: *Ducks quack. Lions roar. I hoot.* Here's what a few children wrote:

Wu	Dks quak. Lins r. I ht.
Kara	Duks quak. Lions rar. I hut.
Dustin	DS QUK LN RR I HT
Jamal	Duks quack. Lions ror. I hoot.

11:30–11:45—Whole-Class Sharing of Center Activities

The class gathers back on the rug in front of the calendar. Children bring with them any books they would like to share. Jenna begins by asking them to quack like a duck. Then, she turns to the *In the Water* portion of the wall chart and asks if anyone put a duck up there. Several hands go up and she has each child go over and point to his or her duck. She then asks for other children who had animals that live in the water to come up and identify their picture. There's a sea turtle and a whale among the group. Jenna does the same thing for the other categories.

With only a few minutes remaining until lunch, not everyone who has a book to share gets a chance to do so. But there's always tomorrow, and Jenna will make sure that any student who didn't get a turn today will get one tomorrow! Additionally, Jenna looks forward to the afternoon, where she and her students' will be able to put their budding literacy skills to use in other curricular areas—science, math, social studies, art, and music.

A DAY IN THE LIFE OF DOLORES PUENTE AND HER THIRD- AND FOURTH-GRADE STUDENTS

Dolores Puente has been teaching for five years at Lincoln Elementary School, a K–6 school in a suburb of Los Angeles. Lincoln's students are primarily from middle- to lower-income families. About half of the students in Ms. Puente's combination third–fourth grade are of European American descent; the other half are of Hispanic, Asian, and African American descent. When we asked how she would describe her reading program, Ms. Puente smiled. "I guess you'd say it's a combination whole language, literature-based, and direct instruction—if that's possible! Although our district has just bought a new basal reading series, I still plan to do a lot with literature— I always have, and I plan to continue. I have an overall plan for teaching the literacy skills that appear in our curriculum. But I make a big effort to teach certain skills when my students find they need them in order to reach a particular goal. For example, if they are involved in projects that involve library research, I'll create lessons to help them with note taking. But I can tell you this, no matter what we're involved in—social studies, science, art—reading and writing instruction is an integral part of our day, beginning with the morning meeting and continuing to the afternoon wrap-up."

Dolores Puente is a teacher who, like Jenna LeBlanc, realizes that teaching reading and writing cannot and should not be limited to one specified time slot in the day. Although Ms. Puente does set aside a specific amount of time each day for what she officially designates as reading—a time in which students are actively engaged in reading activities aimed directly at improving the reading skills, strategies, and behaviors that we have discussed in previous chapters—this is only the beginning of literacy learning in her classroom. Because she and her students use language throughout the school day—and beyond, for that matter—there are literacy opportunities from the moment students step into the classroom to the moment they leave.

Let's join Ms. Puente for a day with her third- and fourth-graders. The day is Monday, January 11. She has written the following schedule on the chalkboard.

9:00	Journal writing
9:05	Sustained silent reading
9:15	Morning meeting
9:25	News reports
9:30	Reading, language arts, social studies, music, and art
10:30	Recess

10:45	Language arts: response journals
11:45	Lunch
12:15	Read-aloud time
12:35	Mathematics
1:25	Physical education
2:15	Science and health
2:50	Wrap-up
3:00	School day ends

9:00—Journal Writing

As students arrive, they take out their journals and write their entry for the day. Ms. Puente, who believes in modeling the behavior she expects of her students, writes in her journal as well. Here is her entry for January 11.

> Today we begin our unit on courage. I've been excited about this unit ever since I wrote the idea on my school calendar back in August. And I'm even more excited now because of the successful unit we had in the fall that revolved around the concept of thankfulness. What I had written on the yearly calendar was "courage"—the unifying theme for January–February. Courage to my way of thinking is a concept worth spending some time on, and January–February seems the perfect time to do it—since Martin Luther King Jr.'s birthday is in January and February is both Black history month and a month to remember and honor past presidents. I'm looking forward to seeing how the kids will respond to this idea and what we will learn together.

As you can see from Ms. Puente's journal entry, much thought and planning occurred well before this day arrived. The idea for building activities around the central concept of courage had sprouted many months earlier. In fact, she had written it on her yearly planner back in August. Shortly after the winter holiday, Ms. Puente formulated a general goal for her literacy activities:

> To learn more about the concept of courage as displayed in the lives of people past and present from a variety of cultures as it is expressed in literature, music, art, science, and in the community, school, and families.

After formulating a general goal, she started to do some brainstorming as the second step in planning the unit's activities. She thought about her curriculum and how she could incorporate literacy activities and the theme of courage in a variety of subject areas:

Reading, Language Arts, and Social Studies:

Read and write biographies. Biography as a literary form or genre. Discuss various genres. Present opportunities for listening and viewing, also—tapes and films, a guest speaker. Choral reading and dramatics? Time lines? Graphic display showing what parts of the world courageous people have come from. Work on strategies of summarizing and determining what is important. Figurative language—simile and metaphor?

Science:

We will be reading about the plant and animal kingdoms. Think about where courage might come in here—can plants be courageous? Animals? (Food for thought!) Present some biographies of courageous scientists, particularly those representing diverse cultures. George Washington Carver? East Indian physicist Subrahmanyan Chandrasekhar? Others? Work on strategies for gleaning information from informational books.

Mathematics:

Students are working individually, but we will work as a class on word problems. This takes courage! Peer tutoring a success. Doing a lot more of it this month. Bring in biographies of mathematicians. How about engineer Mary Ross? This Cherokee woman helped launch Sally Ride into space! Continue working on strategies for solving story problems. Have students write story problems. Make books containing story problems? Put story problems on computer?

Music:

Songs about courage. Have students share contemporary songs that talk about courage. Bring in biographies of courageous musicians. What about Stevie Wonder and Ray Charles? Discuss when and why composers might write songs that instill or celebrate courage. Gospel music is very illustrative of this theme. Learn a gospel song which illustrates aspects of courage (ask Danika for suggestion).

Physical Education:

We will be learning how to play volleyball. For many students this takes a lot of courage. Discuss courage for doing sports. Biographies of courageous sports figures. How about Native

American long-distance runner Billy Mills? Have students read rules, directions, and daily reminders written on board. Use context cues. How about a "courage" box or "good sportsperson" box for students to write about evidence of courage or good sportsmanship?

Health:

We will be reading about diseases in the health text. People who have diseases need courage as well as the people who are trying to find cures. Read about Ryan White and his battle with AIDS? Biographies of physicians and researchers. What about Constance Tom Noguchi, who works on sickle cell anemia? Work on summarizing strategy and other strategies for gleaning information from chapters in textbooks.

Art:

How is courage expressed in art? Visit art museum to view selected paintings illustrating this theme? Create a classroom mural depicting our most courageous heroes? Are artists themselves courageous? What about Hopi potter Al Qoyawayma, who switched from being a successful engineer to pursue his culture's ancient art? Children's book illustrator Filipino Jose Aruego. Chinese artist Maya Lin who designed the Vietnam War Memorial. Does it take courage to pursue your artistic dreams? Let students pursue individual art projects if they are so inspired. Pottery? Sculpture? Weaving? Jewelry making? (Senator Ben Nighthorse Campbell is also a Native American jewelry maker. Students could write to him to find out more about his art.)

After this brainstorming, Ms. Puente plotted her ideas on her monthly calendars, outlining her general plans for the weeks to come. Once she had her general plans outlined, she then focused on the individual weeks and days, making more detailed plans, ordering books and films, and lining up field trips and guest speakers.

Her overall plan is shown in Figure 12.2. Figure 12.3 shows Ms. Puente's weekly plans in a bit more detail. By looking at Ms. Puente's plans, it is obvious that she has more ideas than it will be possible to implement. However, the activities that best fit her students and their mutual goals will come into focus as the days progress and her plan becomes more precise and detailed. Also, the ongoing needs and interests of her students will influence her choices of which activities to implement—plans for Tuesday will need to be altered to reflect what occurred on Monday. Ms. Puente's plans are guidelines that she knows will be shaped and reshaped day by day, minute by minute.

	Week I	Week 2
Morning Meeting	Intro concept of courage, courage unit, and news reports on courage	Daily concerns Preview of week News reports
Reading and Language Arts Social Studies Music Art	Review skimming Begin "determining what is important" strategy Silent and oral reading Discuss biographies (culturally diverse) Figurative language Response journals Courage in gospel music: Learn Black National Anthem Film on Harriet Tubman	Practice "determining what is important" w/ bios Review focusing; start silent reading in bios Discuss vocab work Response journals Read aloud Maya Lin bio and "The Wall" by Eve Bunting Students plan memorial sculpture or other project Make time lines representing people in bios Research major event of time periods represented
Reading Aloud	Martin Luther King, Jr. biography	MLK
Math	Independent and peer tutoring Group word problems Mystery word: *product*	Writing word problems Mary Ross bio Mystery word: *mathematician*
P.E. (Display bios of sports figures throughout unit)	Volleyball Context cues in directions, rules, etc.; "Courage" box	Volleyball Students write and read evaluation of group progress
Science or Health	Plant and animal kingdoms Strategies for gleaning info from informational books Ask question: Do plants and animals display courage? George W. Carver bio	Plant and animal kingdoms Strategies for remembering info (graphic organizers) Answer question: Do plants and animals display courage? Bio of monkey lady (get name)
Wrap-up	Discuss concerns and highlights of day	Discuss concerns and highlights of day

FIGURE 12.2 *Five-Week Plan for a Unit on Courage*

Week 3	Week 4	Week 5
Daily concerns Preview of week News reports	Concerns; preview of week Reports on courage of presidents	Concerns; preview of week Reports on courage of presidents
Finish reading bios Motivate, explain, and model bio writing Strategy (a writing strategy to be determined) Students do prewriting for bios Guest speaker: Native American Gary Cavanaugh Students interview him for possible bio Begin courage mural Native American songs and drumming	Continue adding to time lines Students write rough drafts of bios Students read bios aloud to groups Critique groups; revise bios Continue mural and individual projects Individual conferences to hear students read bios Final draft of bio due Monday Listen to Asian guest musician	Make books or produce radio shows of bios Finish mural projects and time lines Read and perform bios to other classes and at nursing home Trip to art museum to view portraits Perform songs and dances Invite parents and others to class Compare and contrast Native American and Asian music
MLK and Comanche chief Quanah Parker	Quanah Parker	Quanah Parker
Students find bios of mathematicians, especially those from other cultures Mystery word: *dividend*	Independent skills work and peer tutoring Einstein bio Mystery word: *base*	Work w/ other numeric bases Bio of An Wang Compose and read chart of possible careers in math
Dance Read Billy Mills bio Learn Native American dance	Dance Learn Asian dance Read diagrams	Dance Review Native American and Asian dances
Diseases Review approaches to chapter reading Read chapter using reading guide Group work	Diseases Reread chapter to complete chart Group work Read aloud bio on Constance Tom Noguichi	Review science and health units Evaluations and reports
Discuss concerns and highlights of day	Discuss concerns and highlights of day	Make drums for dances and songs

	Monday	Tuesday
Morning Meeting	Semantic map on courage Explain and model news reports on courage Read and discuss daily schedule	Read and discuss daily concerns and schedule Explain and model second example of courage for news report
Reading and Language Arts Social Studies Music Art	Intro bios as a genre Read snippets from bios to motivate Review skimming strategy Students skim at least three books to select bio to read SSR	Motivate, explain, and model "determining what's important" strategy Group work practicing strategies w/ bios Evaluate skills work and group functioning
Recess		
Reading and Language Arts Social Studies Music Art	Motivate, explain, and model response journals Distribute journals Silent reading bios Write responses in journals	Intro MLK and his colorful language—simile and metaphor Read excerpts Students write and illustrate own examples
Read Aloud	MLK—*I Have a Dream* Ch 1	Ch 2
Math (Mystery word for week: *product*)	Group work—Review steps to solve story problems (see Collier and Redmond article) Mystery word clue 1 Independent work	Answer math question from previous day Mystery word clue 2 Skills group—long division
P.E.—Volleyball	Review context cues while reading conduct reminders	Introduce "Courage" or "Sportsmanship" box
Science or Health	Review info vs. fiction Review features of info books Pose courage theme—students skim and begin reading in trade books Plant and animal kingdoms	Meet with groups that want to do extra projects Groups meet to share what they learned yesterday
Wrap-up	As needed	As needed

FIGURE 12.3 *Week One of Unit on Courage*

Wednesday	Thursday	Friday
Daily concerns and schedule Form news report groups and review report model	Daily concerns and schedule Have one member from each group present news report in one category	Daily concerns and schedule Have one member from each group present news report in one category
Skills group on blending	Reading guide for practicing "determining what is important" w/ bios Evaluate activity and discuss as a class	See film on Harriet Tubman Discuss courage Make chart a slave — brave smart — Harriet Tubman — spiritual
Students share responses from journals Silent reading in bios Write in journals	Courage as expressed in music Listen to recording of Black National Anthem; read lyrics; look for courage and examples of metaphor and simile; sing anthem	SSR in bios; meet individually with students Students and teacher make portfolio entries
Ch 3	Ch 4	Ch 5
Whole class—word problems Skill group—word problems Math word clue 3	Student write story problems Skills group—long division Math word clue 4	Solve student story problems Skills group? Reveal mystery word Treat—new math game for class
Review rules—use context cues	"Sportsmanship" box	Read "Sportsmanship" entries Choose sport
Film strip on classifying plants and animals Group reading and recording in journals	Read from George Washington Carver bio	Whole class shares journal responses Classify plants and animals as a whole-class activity Make chart
As needed	As needed	As needed

Let's return now to January 11, and see how Ms. Puente incorporates reading activities into every aspect of her students' day. After students finish writing in their journals, they begin sustained silent reading.

9:05—Sustained Silent Reading

Each morning students read silently from material of their choosing. While the students are reading this morning, Ms. Puente is reading also—an article from *The Reading Teacher*.

9:15—Morning Meeting

The morning meeting is a time to discuss daily concerns and to read and discuss the schedule for the day. Today, before the schedule is even discussed, Ms. Puente puts the outline for a "courage map" on the chalkboard and has students brainstorm to suggest examples of three related concepts—courageous people, courageous deeds, and other words for *courage*.

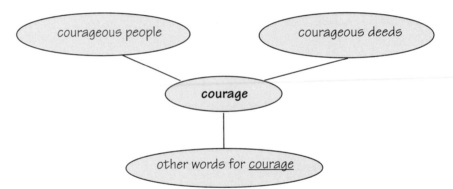

After students have given their responses, Ms. Puente explains that they will be focusing on the concept of courage for the next several weeks, thinking about how courage relates to many things they learn about and do, in school and out. "By the end of the time, we'll all probably have a different view of this concept," she tells them.

Ms. Puente asks a volunteer to transfer the responses she has written on the board onto a chart. The chart will be kept on display and new ideas added to it as the month progresses.

9:25—News Reports

Ms. Puente has allocated this portion of the day to current events. Ms. Puente's class has been working on giving news reports, which involves answering these questions: Who? What? When? Where? Why? How? Today,

Ms. Puente will also use this time to introduce the courage theme, completing the semantic map she has outlined on the board in order to motivate students and get them thinking about the concept of courage.

Ms. Puente begins by telling students she is going to read a newspaper article that she thinks illustrates the concept and asks students to listen to see whether they agree with her. The article focuses on a single mother of five who is getting her college degree. After reading the article, Ms. Puente tells students why *she* thinks the woman shows courage and then encourages students to give their opinions.

Next, Ms. Puente displays the news report chart and shows students how she would complete it, sharing with them her thought processes as she does so.

News Report Chart

What is the report about?   A woman getting her college degree.

Who is the report about?   Janet Crow, single mother of five.

Where did the event take place?   State University, Middletown, U.S.A.

When did the event take place?   December 23.

How does this event show courage?   I think it takes courage to go back to school when you're older because there may not be many people your age at school and it's probably been a long time since you've had to study and take tests. Also, Janet had to give up some things for herself and her kids. She was taking a chance that getting a college education would allow her to get a better job so her kids might have more opportunities. I think that takes courage.

Ms. Puente explains to students that their news reports for the next several weeks will focus on courage. They can select articles from newspapers or magazines to read to the class, or they can write up a short report from TV or radio news. They can also report courageous events that take place in school or at home. As a class, they will do two things to help remember the people and events they report—complete a What, Who, Where, When, and How chart and record all courageous events reported on a large sheet of butcher paper on a Courage All Over the World chart.

Courage All Over the World

Family: On Feb. 9, Billy's little brother took three steps by himself.

School: On Feb. 11, Marta read a paragraph aloud in English.

City: On Feb. 3, Byron Slone. . . .

State:

Country:

World:

9:30—Reading, Language Arts, Social Studies, Music, and Art

After the morning meeting and news reports, Ms. Puente begins the reading, language arts, social studies, music, and art block of activities, which usually runs from 9:30 to 11:45, with a 15-minute recess in the middle. Today, though, Ms. Puente is not following her usual time schedule. The activities for the morning meeting and news reports demanded extra time. Also, since the activities Ms. Puente has planned for reading and language arts require a sustained block of time, music and art will not be included in this time block today. However, if you look at her weekly planner, music activities are slated for later in the week. For their reading activity this morning, Ms. Puente and her students will discuss biographies as a special genre, review skimming as a reading strategy for selecting a biography to read in depth, and read silently for 15 minutes. Beginning tomorrow, Ms. Puente will also work with a selected group of students who need help with various skills. Language arts endeavors revolve around journal writing and social studies activities and include investigating courage as displayed in real people's lives. All of these subjects are interrelated. This interrelatedness mirrors the real world.

9:45—Reading: Motivating and Suggesting Strategies

To motivate her students, Ms. Puente has spent some time selecting biographies (with the help of librarians as well as several bibliographies) that reflect her students' linguistic and cultural backgrounds, interests, and abilities. Because one of her goals is to expose students to individuals of many different cultures, her selection of biographies also reflects this.

On the chalkboard ledge and table, she has displayed numerous trade biographies of culturally diverse individuals. These books range from picture books to lengthy chapter books.

Ms. Puente begins by telling students that all the books on display have one thing in common—each of them focuses on the life and deeds of a single individual. After that, she has students think about and discuss why a book might have been written about these people and writes students' suggestions on the board.

Next, she reads a paragraph or two from several of the biographies that she has preselected and that she knows will pique her students' interests. After reading, she reminds students that these books are called biographies—written accounts of a person's life. She writes *biography* on the board and talks about how biographies differ from other types of books. She asks students to tell about biographies they have read, note if they liked them, and explain why. She asks, "Why do you think people are interested in writing about and reading about other people's lives?" but doesn't ask for a response at this time. She tells students to keep that question in mind as they explore the contents of "these wonderful biographies."

Ms. Puente explains to students that during the next five weeks they will be reading and writing biographies and will get to choose which biographies they want to read and whom they want to write a biography about. She discusses with them what they might expect to gain from biographies, why biographies are interesting and informative, and how the ideas revealed in biographies might be useful in their own lives.

To help students decide which biography they want to read, Ms. Puente suggests that a good strategy to use is skimming. She models the strategy with several of the biographies—reading the title and the table of contents, scanning the chapters from beginning to end, commenting on il-

Teachers can make a number of biographies available and invites students to skim these to select one to read in depth.

lustrations and photographs, and maybe reading a few passages aloud. Then she models the thinking she went through in trying to decide whether or not *Beyond the Myth: The Story of Joan of Arc* by Polly Schoyer Brooks was the biography she wanted to read:

> Hmm. This might be an interesting book. I like reading about heroic women. But I see that Joan of Arc lived in the 15th century, and I think I'd like to read about someone a little more modern. Also, it's kind of long and has a lot of words I don't know. I like learning new words, but it may take me too long to read if I have to stop and look up a lot of words in the dictionary, and I wouldn't want to skip too many words. I think this is a book Tara would like—and I'm going to recommend it to her—but I think I'll see what some of the other books are like.

Ms. Puente then models skimming and considers a few more books before letting students choose their own books to skim. Finally, she tells students to skim at least three books and then choose one of those to read. They will have until recess to skim and get started on their reading. Some of these books include *A Picture Book of Jesse Owens* by David Adler, *Beyond the Myth: The Story of Joan of Arc* by Polly Schoyer Brooks, *Chingis Khan* by Demi, *Hiawatha: Messenger of Peace* by Dennis Fradin, *Teammates* by Peter Golenbock, *The Last Princess: The Story of Princess Ka'iulani of Hawai'i* by Fay Stanley, *Diego* by Jeannette Winter, and *Fight in the Fields* by Margo Sorenson.

10:45—Language Arts: Response Journals

The next activity, writing in and sharing response journals—which Ms. Puente has labeled in her plans under the subject language arts is a continuation of the previous reading activity and is one the students are familiar with, having kept reading journals of various sorts since the beginning of the school year. It is also an activity students will be involved in daily until they finish reading their selected biographies.

Ms. Puente's students have made dual entries in their journals before, but since they will be doing something slightly different in these journals, she spends a little time motivating, explaining, and modeling the procedure.

"You know," Ms. Puente tells her students, "when I was reading through biographies to bring to class, I kept reading things that made me stop and think, 'Wow, that's neat,' or 'I know how she feels. I felt that way myself.' Things like that. I'll show you what I mean."

After that, Ms. Puente reads a sentence or two from a biography about mathematician and computer genius An Wang, to illustrate her point, and then writes the following on the board:

Response Journal

Idea from Biography   My Response

Page 8. Wang's new word processor   I love you, Wang!
made it easy to see your words
and to correct your mistakes.

As Ms. Puente explains to her students, "When I read that Wang had invented the word processor, it really hit me how this man had made my job so much easier and more enjoyable. I really feel grateful to him."

Ms. Puente proceeds to describe several other types of responses she had—questions brought to mind, ideas that prompted her to make connections with her own experiences, strong feelings she had in response to certain events or ideas—and writes these on the board. After sufficient explanation and modeling, Ms. Puente tells students she wants them to use their journals similarly while reading in their biographies—to write a quotation, idea, word, or whatever, on the left side of the journal page and their response to the quote, idea, word, or whatever, next to it on the right side of the page. This kind of activity encourages the generative learning we discussed in Chapter 8.

Next, Ms. Puente distributes the journals, but before students begin reading and writing in them, she makes certain that they are clear on the purpose and procedure for this activity. She assigns reading buddies to students who might need extra help with reading and writing. Buddies go to special locations designated to be conference areas—places where students are free to interact with each other without disturbing other students.

While students are reading silently and writing in their journals, Ms. Puente is reading a biography and writing in her journal. Her classroom aide (who is

Writing personal responses in journals requires that students think about the ideas in a text and express their ideas in writing.

available every day from 10:30 to 12:00) circulates among students to offer advice and encourage students to keep on task.

Before students leave for lunch, Ms. Puente asks if any of them have something they would like to share from their journals. If so, a few students read from their journals; if not, Ms. Puente shares something from hers.

11:45—Lunch

12:15—Read-Aloud Time

This routine fosters quiet and rest after an active play period. It also provides students with an opportunity to hear good literature skillfully read. When Ms. Puente's students come in from lunch, they can sit wherever they feel most comfortable, at their desks with their heads down, on the rug, in the bean bag chairs—as long as they are quiet and polite and don't interfere with others. If there is disruption of the calm that Ms. Puente insists on for read-aloud time, then students forgo their right to choose where to sit, and Ms. Puente chooses for them.

Today, Ms. Puente begins reading aloud from *I Have a Dream; The Life of Martin Luther King, Jr.,* by Margaret Davidson. To preserve the atmosphere of calm that prevails at this time of day, she begins reading with only a brief introduction in which she talks about courage and how students will see many examples of courage as they listen to the biography. Before she begins reading the first chapter, she encourages them to think about and remember one example of King's courage that is illustrated in the chapter.

For the next 15 minutes, Ms. Puente reads the first chapter. At the end of the reading, she asks students if they noticed any illustrations of courage. But instead of discussing their ideas, she asks them to keep their thoughts private, think about them, and maybe share them later with a friend or parent.

12:35—Mathematics

Most of Ms. Puente's students typically work on math skills independently while she instructs a group of students on specific concepts and procedures. Which students are in the group and what is being taught changes as necessity dictates. While Ms. Puente is working with a small group on skills, students spend ten minutes of their independent work time tutoring and ten minutes being tutored. Highly skilled students are tutored by upper-grade students, high school volunteers, and computers. Each student, no matter what his or her ability, has a tutoring responsibility. Ms. Puente has had good results with this approach, finding that even the most reluctant students can learn if they are expected to teach someone else.

Before students begin independent work, tutoring work, and small-group instruction on a specific skill, Ms. Puente will conduct a 15-minute whole-class lesson, which includes two topics: reviewing how to solve story problems and presenting the new "mystery" math word for the week.

From prior lessons, Ms. Puente's students already know that math is a language that requires an approach different from the language in a story or informational book. Today's lesson is a review of the steps used to solve story problems. Ms. Puente took the problem from one that had come up in the previous week when students were running laps in the gym and trying to keep track of their progress.

At the beginning of the lesson, Ms. Puente writes this problem on the board: The gym floor is $100' \times 50'$. How far did Matt run if he ran 10 lengths of the gym?

"Does this problem sound familiar?" she asks her students.

The students are well aware of what Ms. Puente is talking about. The week before, they had been keeping track of how many times they ran across the gym, but didn't calculate how *far* they had run.

Ms. Puente refers her class to the questions for solving word problems on the chart shown here (Collier & Redmond, 1974), and together they come up with this equation: $100' \times 10' = 1,000'$.

Questions to Ask When Solving Story Problems

What situation is described?

Can I describe the situation with a drawing, diagram, or mathematical sentence?

What am I trying to find out?

Do I need to combine, separate, or compare?

Are all the data given necessary?

Are the data complete?

Do I know what to do to determine the answer?

How will I know if the answer I get is reasonable?

Ms. Puente challenges students with these questions: "Did Matt run more than a mile or less than a mile? How much more than a mile or less than a mile? Try and find out, and we'll discuss the answers tomorrow."

Before students begin their tutoring and group sessions, Ms. Puente shows them the first clue for the "mystery" math word for the week—$A \times B = C$. Students are not to say the word out loud, but put their written guesses with their name and the date on them in the mystery word box. Each day, Ms. Puente reports how many have correctly guessed the word and gives a new clue. At the end of the week, she reveals the mystery word, and if 90% of the class has guessed it, the class gets a special reward. The mystery word this week is *product*.

1:25—Physical Education

For the next few weeks, Ms. Puente's students will be learning how to play volleyball. Besides actually playing the game, they will need to learn volleyball rules and review etiquette for traveling to and from the gym. Both activities will require some reading. Since the class has recently completed a unit on using context cues to figure out unknown words, she decides to reinforce this skill in reading these rules, which are rich in context cues. The concept *courage* will also be reinforced as an attribute of those who participate in sports. To encourage sportsmanlike behavior and to provide a concrete way for students to use writing skills, Ms. Puente has developed a Sports Person of the Day box. The procedure is similar to that used for a suggestion box: Students write the name of someone they think demonstrated good sportsmanlike behavior or courage. On the paper, students answer these questions: Who did the sportsmanlike or courageous behavior? What was it? When was it done? Why is it sportsmanlike or courageous? Ms. Puente will introduce this idea on Tuesday or Wednesday.

Before students go to the gym to play volleyball, Ms. Puente writes these sentences on the board:

> When we walk to the gym, we need to remember that other classes are working. If we are noisy, we might d_____b them. Let's try to remember to walk q_____y.

Ms. Puente encourages her students to use context cues to figure out the unknown words. She asks students who can guess what the unknown words are to raise their hands and tells them she will know if they had the right words if they do as the sentences tell them on their walk to the gym.

After students return from the gym, Ms. Puente praises their excellent behavior and then discusses the missing words in the sentences on the board, encouraging students to explain just how they used context to determine the words and which clues in the sentences enabled them to figure out the unknown words.

2:15—Science and Health

Last week Ms. Puente began motivating students for their unit of study on the plant and animal kingdoms. She decided that reading and research in these topics would best be accomplished through both group and individual work. When planning goals and activities for the unit, she also made provisions for those with special needs and interests. Additionally, the books Ms. Puente selected for the unit reflect the varied reading abilities of her students. She wants to be sure that all students succeed with the reading they do.

To begin, Ms. Puente reviews the special features of informational books, reminding students that informational books are written and organized differently from picture books and chapter books because their main purpose is to provide the reader with information, whereas stories are primarily meant to entertain. To illustrate what she means about communicating information being the main goal of informational books, she reads a few book titles aloud and asks students to tell what sort of information they think the book will disclose. Next, she explains that informational books often have a number of special features. Some of these include a table of contents, headings and subheadings, introductory paragraphs and summaries, graphs, illustrations, labels, charts, maps, indexes, and glossaries. Ms. Puente points out these features in several books she has preselected for this purpose.

After Ms. Puente has reviewed these features, she asks students why the author might have included them. After a brief discussion, Ms. Puente offers students the bottom line: "The author includes these features to make information more memorable and understandable for readers. They're put there for us—the readers. That's why we want to take advantage of these things when we read."

Next, Ms. Puente divides the class into two groups—those who have decided they want to learn more about plants and those who want to learn more about animals. Each student is to select at least three books to skim. Paying at-

Some students enjoy working on projects in a small group rather than individually.

tention to the various features of the books—table of contents, headings and subheadings, introductory paragraphs and summaries, graphs, illustrations, labels, charts, maps, indexes, glossaries—students are to record in their informational books journal one piece of information they find interesting about each book. (These journals are binders that students have kept from the beginning of the year to jot down various responses while reading informational books.) The next day they will meet again with their groups to share what they found. To tie in the courage theme, Ms. Puente also asks students to think about the question of whether or not plants or animals are capable of courage. They will discuss this idea as they get further into their study of the plant and animal kingdoms.

Students gather with their groups and select and skim their books, recording the title and one piece of information from each in their journals. Since students have differing interests and abilities and work at varying rates, Ms. Puente has provided for these individual needs:

- Students who need special assistance, for example ESL or visually challenged students, will be assigned to reading partners.

- Additional activities will challenge students who are particularly talented in various areas. Students can create a graph, either on graph paper or on the computer, indicating the number and kind of features found in the various books on their selected topic; or write glossaries for those books without them and include student glossary pages in the books for other readers to use; or draw additional illustrations, charts, or maps for the various books.

- These projects are optional and ongoing, with students working on them at their own pace. Ms. Puente will meet with students interested in pursuing these projects to explain how to do them. Any student in the class has the option of working on these projects. Students can work on them individually or in groups. Also, students might choose to work on these projects at other times of the day when their other work is completed.

2:50—Wrap-Up

Although days are busy and sometimes a bit hectic, Ms. Puente strives to include time at the end of each day to bring closure to the day's activities. The daily wrap-up usually includes some sort of review and discussion of the special delights or problems the day held.

About 10 or 15 minutes before the end of the day, one of Ms. Puente's students plays the class theme song on the xylophone—a simple melody the class composed at the beginning of the year. This tune gives students a sense of order and belonging—they expect it, they know what it means, and it is *their* class song. By the time the song is completed, students are in their seats and ready to review the schedule for the day, which is written on the chalkboard. Together they read and briefly talk about each subject or activity, with a student in charge of leading the discussion. During this time, students ask questions, share something they enjoyed or learned, or bring up problems they had. Problems that can't be resolved easily are tabled until there is a better time for resolution, perhaps at the next day's morning meeting time.

3:00—School Day Ends

After the students have gone, and while the day's events are still fresh in her mind, Ms. Puente begins planning for the next day. Ms. Puente knows this planning can't take place without first reviewing the day's activities and reflecting on what worked, what didn't work, and why. Quickly, she makes a few entries in her teacher's logbook. On Jenny's page she writes *Used context cues to figure out several unknown words she ran across in her reading,* and on Terrell's page, *Pleased to see Terrell become extremely absorbed in Margo Sorenson's* Fight in the Fields, *a hi-lo adventure biography about Cesar Chavez. Ask him about it.* She jots down comments for a few other students and glances briefly at some of her yearly goals. Next, as she looks at what she had planned for Tuesday, she realizes she will have to make some changes. In math, some students had a difficult time solving the word problem. Instead of taking whole-group time for another problem, she decides she will group the students who need a bit more instruction for a minilesson. Other students then will have more time to work independently and to do their tutoring. Since her parent volunteer comes on Tuesdays from 12:25 to 1:25, the volunteer can monitor these students while Ms. Puente works with the group that needs some more assistance on word problems. She jots down her plans, makes a few additional comments in her Logbook, and walks to the teachers' lounge to get a well-deserved cup of coffee.

A DAY IN THE LIFE OF DAVID CARBERRY
AND HIS FIFTH- AND SIXTH-GRADE STUDENTS

David Carberry has been teaching fifth and sixth grade at Oak Grove Intermediate School for ten years. Oak Grove, which includes grades 4–6, is located in a southern suburb of Minneapolis. Most of the children at Oak Grove come from middle-income families, the majority of which are European Americans, with a sprinkling of Asian Americans, Native Americans, and African Americans.

David works in a team with three other teachers, which is fairly typical of many upper-elementary classrooms. Before the school year begins, the team meets to make program decisions and to discuss matters such as scheduling or curricular responsibilities. The four classrooms in David's team are made up of approximately 15 fifth-grade students and 15 sixth-grade students each. When the sixth-graders move on to junior high school, 15 fifth-grade students take their place, so students are with the same homeroom teacher for two years.

In addition to being a teacher, David is a Ph.D. candidate and an advisee of one of us. He has read most of the manuscript for this book, and in describing his program he frequently refers to topics from the book.

When we asked David to describe the literacy program he and his colleagues have developed, this is what he had to say:

> The literacy program we have developed over the years reflects the unique challenge we face as upper-elementary teachers. Differences in reading ability are extreme in students in grades 5 and 6. For example, one of my students, 11-year-old Kelly, reads at an 11th-grade level and devours John Grisham novels during her free reading period. Tommy, also 11 years old, struggles with anything beyond second-grade materials. He finds it difficult to read even short, episodic stories. This disparity presents a critical question for me and my teammates: How do we meet the needs of students, given such a huge range of ability? Given that current thinking in elementary instruction is to move away from ability grouping of students towards whole-group and flexible group instruction, meeting the needs of the students becomes even more challenging. My team has developed a plan we think best meets the needs of our students.

On the following pages, David describes in his own words his team's plan for organizing the fifth–sixth grade curriculum to emphasize reading and writing instruction throughout the school day.

Our Daily Schedule

There are four important features in our organization of time, curriculum content, space, and students. First is the concept of the homeroom, second is scheduling large blocks of times for students to be in one place with one teacher, third is centering instruction around a broad theme, and fourth is selecting reading comprehension strategies and procedures to teach throughout the year that are flexible and broadly applicable. Here is what our typical schedule looks like:

9:00–11:00	Homeroom
9:00	Sustained silent reading, journal writing
9:20	Morning meeting
9:30	Language arts: reading, writing, listening, and speaking
11:00	Mathematics
12:00	Lunch and recess
12:30	Physical education and music
1:30	Themes: social studies, science, art, and health
3:00	Homeroom and school logs

As the schedule shows, each homeroom stays intact for two hours in the beginning of each day. For example, fifth- and sixth-grade students in my homeroom stay with me from 9:00 to 11:00.

Large blocks of time have a number of advantages. To begin with, the students have less downtime between classes. They spend less time moving from room to room. Lengthier time periods also allow for greater depth and breadth of instruction. We have greater opportunities to go into detail on a given topic, or we can use the extended time to develop connections to other curricular areas. Another advantage of large time blocks is greater flexibility for everyone involved, making it easier to schedule special education services, computer lab time, and guest speakers.

After homeroom, students separate into grade-level groups for mathematics, music, and physical education. Heterogeneous groups made up from each of the four classrooms within our team comprise the classes for instruction in social studies, science, art, and health.

Every district has a list of goals and objectives or learning outcomes. At the beginning, during, and following the school year, my colleagues and I sit down and figure out what to teach. Our team looks for connections within all the language arts and within broad themes as well. As a starting point, we choose a broad theme. We rarely use the term *schema*, but theoretically speaking, we are trying to connect all the students' learning experiences to developing rich schemata. The theme we choose is determined by a number of factors, including appropriateness of topic, access to resources, our own talents and failings, and district outcomes.

Typically, we choose three themes over the course of the year. Last year our three themes were challenges, perceptions, and the future. This fall, we chose to organize our teaching units around the theme of the sea. We chose the sea for rather mundane reasons: The basal text we are using begins with the same theme, and one of our members has just received pretty extensive training in teaching oceanography. Typically, basal texts include a number of cross-curricular connections that are written into the manual, which can save a good deal of time.

Although each day has a particular focus for instruction, I have found it useful to teach content that will serve the students in a variety of settings throughout the school year. Over the years, I have become more and more convinced that the teaching of comprehension strategies makes for more powerful readers. I choose strategies that are flexible and widely applicable. I will ask the students to use them in their content area classes and when using self-selected materials, as well as in my class. A number of helpful comprehension strategies are noted in Chapter 7. My suggestion to a beginning teacher, or any teacher, is to develop a small number of them (perhaps three) throughout the year. I have found periodically returning to a strategy to be particularly helpful to students.

At the beginning of the year, I note several strategies I think would be helpful for my students. One of my favorites is teaching students to create story maps (see Chapter 6). Although the use of story maps is presented as a teacher-led procedure in this book, I teach students to make their own story maps and in this way give them a tool that they can use independently to improve their understanding of any selection they are reading. My first goal is to teach the strategy in such a way that all students will learn, regardless of their reading level. This is particularly difficult, given the broad range of abilities in my classroom. For this reason, I choose content that is familiar to all students and that they do not need to read. For example, I may ask them to recall the story "Little Red Riding Hood" as a text to use in doing their first story mapping. I let students know that they will be learning a strategy designed to help them understand what they are reading and that they will be using it throughout the school year and beyond. Then I model the activity in a large-group setting. I begin by working with students to compose a "T" graphic similar to this one:

Important events	Mapping questions
Red begins her journey to Grandmother's house.	Where is Red Riding Hood going?
Red encounters a wolf.	Who does Red meet along the trail?
The Hunter slays the wolf, releasing Grandma.	How does the story end?

I ask the students to assist me in completing the map. Thus, since students do not have to read a text to construct the map, they can learn to map regardless of their reading proficiency. After creating their first simple map, I use a read-aloud for the next one; again, my interest is minimizing the effect of reading ability as a critical factor in acquiring the strategy. I've found storybooks to be an excellent vehicle for this, as they are nonthreatening to the listener—short, full of illustrations, and appealing. Or, instead of using storybooks, I read a basal selection aloud.

Following whole-group instruction, small groups work with picture books in cooperative groups. One member of the group is responsible for an oral reading. The group as a whole is responsible for developing a story map. Each group checks with me for feedback, and following my okay (signified by a scrawled set of initials), groups may exchange their story maps with other groups working through different books. Now the students have learned a strategy that may be applied to a variety of texts; have had an opportunity to integrate reading, writing, listening and speaking; and have provided curriculum for a real audience (other groups). Figure 12.4 shows one student's map for *The True Story of the Three Little Pigs* by Jon Scieszka.

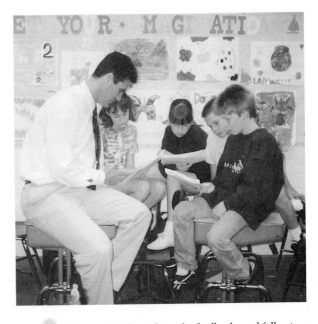

Of course, it takes a great deal of time to introduce a comprehension strategy such as creating story maps. Even so, the time is well spent. Having learned the strategy, students have a tool to attack just about any narrative.

Two aspects of our team approach are particularly important to our literature-

"Each group checks with me for feedback, and following my okay, groups exchange their story maps with other groups working on different books." David Carberry

Name: *Silipanh, L.*

Title of Book: *The True Story of the Three Little Pigs*

Author of Book: *Jon Scieszka*

On the left side of the page, list important events in the story (choose between 8 and 12). On the right side, write a question for each event, to create a **story map.** Story maps help readers understand what they are reading.

1. The wolf was sick and wanted a cup of sugar.	1. Why did the wolf go to the pigs' houses?
2. The wolf sneezed and blew down the first pig's house.	2. What happened when the wolf got to the first pig's house?
3. The wolf ate the first pig.	3. What happened after the wolf blew down the first pig's house?
4. The wolf sneezed and blew down the second pig's house.	4. What happened when the wolf got to the second pig's house?
5. The wolf ate the second pig.	5. What happened after the wolf blew down the pig's house?
6. The wolf went to the third pig's house and sneezed, but nothing happened.	6. What happened when the wolf got to the third pig's house?
7. The police came and thought the wolf was trying to blow down the pig's house.	7. What did the police think when they saw the wolf at the pig's house?
8. The police took the wolf to jail.	8. What happened to the wolf?

FIGURE 12.4 *A Sample Story Map*

based orientation and our use of a language arts block. The language arts block provides time for focusing on and interrelating all of the language arts. My team chooses to use the concept of a language arts block to illustrate the interconnectedness of reading, writing, listening, and speaking. I think the concept of interconnectedness is perhaps the most significant gift the literature-based movement has provided educators. Indeed, finding ways to connect the language arts is a helpful criterion for determining what should be taught in the upper—or more accurately—*any* elementary classroom.

The literature-based orientation trumpets a call for integration of content and flexibility in instruction. I'm always looking for opportunities to connect reading with the other language arts. Another important aspect of literature-based instruction is its advocacy of both flexible grouping and student self-selection of reading materials. In my classroom, we use a "book wheel" (like the one shown in Figure 12.5) to meet individual needs and interests. The students use this graphic organizer to ensure that they respond to a variety of genres. The students may read individually or in self-selected groups. They respond to the texts in a variety of ways, sometimes determined by the instructor and sometimes determined by the students. The book wheel is designed to encourage broad reading and the meeting of individual needs.

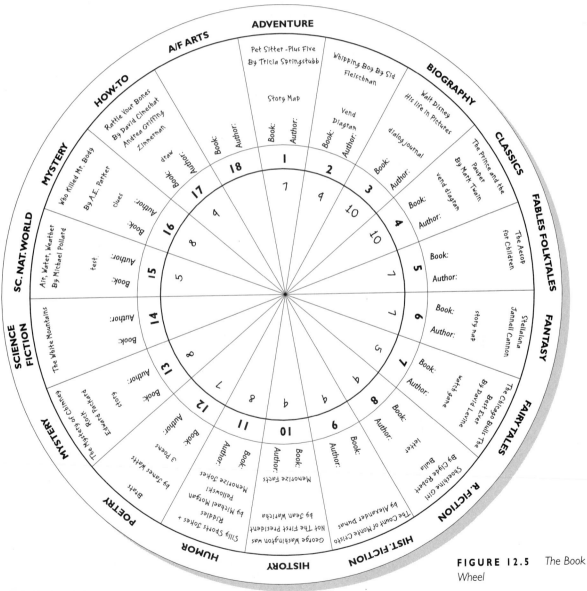

FIGURE 12.5 *The Book Wheel*

A literature-based approach is particularly attractive to fifth- and sixth-grade students. Meeting to discuss what they read in literature circles, which were described in Chapter 7, helps students develop rich, engaging schemata. The students really get into a piece of writing when they are sharing the experience with others. I find it easy to model and be enthusiastic about appropriate literature circle behaviors as I am able to relate my own experiences in a book club. Literature circles and other literature-based approaches encourage deep understanding of texts. The circles have an advantage over whole-group instruction in that participants find it difficult to check out of the discussion. Students who are eye-to-eye and knee-to-knee and responsible for developing meaning have a greater chance of experiencing the "aha" phenomenon—gaining a perspective that they hadn't considered before. An additional advantage to literature-based approaches is that students are able to self-select their groups. The teacher, for example, may select four texts, which all relate to a broad general theme. Each text differs in length, type of characters, and so forth. Emily may be ready for Ellen Raskin's *The Westing Game*, a complex, Newbery Award–winning story, while James may prefer a book made up of short, easy-to-read episodic stories, such as Donald Sobol's *Encyclopedia Brown Takes the Cake*. Student choice increases the likelihood that students will choose an engaging book at their level of reading competence.

The following is a brief description of our daily routine:

9:00—Sustained Silent Reading, Journal Writing

Homeroom begins with one of two different activities—sustained silent reading or journal writing. I find it helpful to have a preplanned activity for students when they first enter the classroom each morning. Like adults, 11- and 12-year-olds enjoy the predictability of events that they can count on. Having a structured activity ready for the students helps them warm up for school and sets a healthy working culture for the classroom.

Even though students appreciate knowing what is expected of them at the beginning of their school day, they appreciate some variety as well. I typically use two different begin-the-day activities, sustained silent reading and journal writing, which I alternate throughout the school year.

Sustained Silent Reading. Sustained silent reading (SSR, which was discussed in Chapter 7) is an important part of any elementary-level reading curriculum. I've found it helpful to ask the students to have their books out and ready to read the moment class begins. SSR is a terrific way to begin the school day. The students are relaxed and ready to learn following the SSR session. I think it is good practice to feature sustained reading of student-selected texts as a primary feature of the classroom, rather than an adjunct to the "real work" of the day. If students are asked to do silent reading only when their other assignments are done, this almost guarantees that the least-successful students will get the least amount of time to read independently and the least opportunity to develop fluent, success-oriented reading practice. My students are especially interested in sustained quiet reading time, as this gives them time to complete their book wheel, which is part of the independent reading program I require.

Journal Writing. I have tried all sorts of journal writing, both structured and nonstructured. I have responded at length to students' writing and have enjoyed it, although it is terrifically time consuming. However, having students write to a real audience is powerfully motivating. Lately, I have found it particularly productive to have students share their writing thoughts with two or three others. I may suggest a topic for a journal entry, or the students may choose their own. The small group that develops as a result of this journaling activity is asked to respond to what each member of the group writes. Conversations between students develop in print, similar to what happens in dialogue journals (which were discussed in Chapter 9). I like to introduce this activity by modeling my own journal writing and students' responses, sharing these on an overhead projector. See Figure 12.6 for two student journal entries. These students were reading *Matilda*, by Roald Dahl.

4/14	Kaj—So far I think this book is very interest, but it is kind of hard to believe that a four year old could read books like <u>Oliver Twist</u>, <u>Kim</u>, & <u>Animal Farm</u> & actually understand what she is reading. J. R.
	I think that your right Justin, because it is amazing that she read books that thick and that fast. It also is amazing that she understands the books that she is reading when she goes to the library every afternoon. K. L.
4/15	Kaj—I think it is hilarious how Matilda put glue in her Dad's hat, it was also pretty good how she put the parrot up the chimney & her parents thought it was a ghost. I'm surprised when she didn't cry when her father tore the pages out of the library book. J. R.
	Justin—I think that you are right it is pretty hilarious, you were also right that the book is different than the movie that I saw. I like the part where Matilda slams the door on her dad. K. L.

FIGURE 12.6 *Entries in a Dialog Journal*

Working in small groups not only provides students with a real audience, but also allows me to give feedback quickly and efficiently. To give this feedback, I ask each group of three or four students to come up to my desk, where I respond orally to their writing.

9:20—Morning Meeting

Just about every teacher I know sets aside time during the beginning of the day to do the routine chores that are part of every classroom. Here, we talk about the day's schedule, important dates, current events, and the like. The time required for our morning meeting varies day by day. It is common practice in my classroom to use this time to assign ad hoc student committees designed to solve problems. For instance, we may have a party coming up. Following a list of guidelines, a student committee is formed to submit their written recommendations as to treats, activities, and the like. A committee may be responsible for cleaning and putting fresh water in the iguana cage or figuring out a way to get homework to absent students. In almost all cases, students are asked to submit a written plan, which I will review. These authentic language arts experiences allow students to have an impact on their world and really work well with fifth- and sixth-graders.

9:30—Language Arts: Reading, Writing, Listening, and Speaking

What might a typical day of instruction look like in the language arts, considering that the students have acquired the story-mapping comprehension strategy and we are investigating the sea as a theme?

Because of the purpose I have in mind—having students explore another aspect of our sea theme—a selection in the basal appeals to me. The selection is taken from *Call It Courage*, Armstrong Perry's Newbery Medal–winning story about a shipwrecked boy searching for courage. Purpose and selection, of course, are two of the three factors of the scaffolded reading experience (which was described in Chapter 6). The third is taking into account the readers. So, next, I consider how to make the selection accessible for all my students: What sort of scaffold will I build for them to ensure their success in reading this piece?

I begin developing a reading scaffold by thinking of my prereading activities, asking myself what sort of background knowledge will be required for the students to understand the story. One advantage of using a story out of a basal text (which is usually highly illustrated) is that all students have access to a powerful cue—illustration. Illustrations are one way to tap into the students' existing schemata. I ask them to look at the pictures and to write predictions of what they expect will happen in the story. The illustration for

Call It Courage shows the character Mafatu on a beach, apparently making something out of bamboo. He appears to be alone, but for a seagull and a dog. Students might predict that he is alone on an island and that he is intent on building a shelter, which they will later find to be the case. Analyzing illustrations is also a helpful way to introduce semantic mapping to further activate background knowledge. Besides activating background knowledge, mapping serves an additional purpose. Inevitably, important vocabulary will surface; or you, as the instructor, can make it surface. My colleagues and I have found that the key in vocabulary instruction is picking out several critical terms or concepts (three is a good number) and giving the students repeated exposure to them, using a variety of techniques. Students need to hear and use critical vocabulary in a variety of contexts.

At this point in the instruction, the students have activated their background knowledge through illustrations and a semantic map. And since they have had previous experience creating a story map as a comprehension strategy, they are ready to go. Right? Perhaps not. I have to ask myself whether all of my students will be able to successfully read the text, given its length and difficulty. If the answer is no, I need to provide additional scaffolding. I have found that reading the text aloud is the easiest way to make it more accessible. A read-aloud provides additional scaffolding and shortens the amount students will be responsible for. Finally, I often provide written instructions—whether on the board or in a handout—including a checking-for-understanding feature. The assignment might read like this:

> I am interested in whether you can apply story mapping as a strategy for your reading of the selection taken from Call It Courage. Remember, comprehension strategies are designed to help you understand what you read. Note important events, and the question that goes along with each. Look over pages 232–236, and pick out three events. Then, write out one appropriate question about each of the three events, and come see me with your questions. When we meet, we'll talk about those questions and about your choosing the dozen most important events of the story and developing an appropriate question for each of them.

Notice that the entire class is engaged in this activity, and individual accountability and opportunities for teacher feedback are built in as well. Following the activity, the students discuss their choices in small groups and try to come up with a common core of 12 important events. Again, there is an implicit appeal here for integrating language arts—students are reading, writing, speaking, and listening. Furthermore, now that students have demonstrated facility in creating story maps, each is able to use this strategy with his own content. Students are able to use the procedure to take notes, to test others, and to generate discussion questions.

As part of creating story maps, students meet in small groups and try to come up with the most important events in a story.

11:00—Mathematics

As I said earlier, our team is made up of four classrooms, each serving two grade levels. My teammates and I are always looking for ways to connect with our theme. For instance, it might be interesting to have students examine the composition of seawater as an illustration of the use of percentages. The most likely connections are to be found between math and science. For example, I know through team meetings that the science teacher will be using whales to illustrate content in a unit on oceanography. I have an opportunity to illustrate mathematics in an engaging way, which will enrich their understanding of our theme by having my students create cutout re-creations of whales. In doing so, the students work from a pattern, grid out an image, and convert their numbers, using the concept of scale in creating life-size paper or chalk models. Students are taught how to estimate distance in an interesting context. In a variety of ways, my students will develop a better sense of number and demonstrate facility in the use of ratios and estimation, while further developing a rich and engaging schema that will serve them in other content areas.

12:00—Lunch and Recess

The themes here are eating and playing!

12:30—Physical Education and Music

Our district uses specialists to teach these two content areas. The students alternate classes each day. I can't always integrate physical education and music with common themes, as these teachers have their own scope and sequence. Integration requires meeting with these teachers to plan our curricular content together, which, although it is a challenge, I occasionally do with music. For example, a music teacher developed a score for a play that my classroom was working on.

1:30—Themes: Social Studies, Science, Art, and Health

As I mentioned earlier, my team—Nancy Eller, Troy Miller, and Suzy Neet— uses a thematic approach to interrelate our classes. Our goal is to find a way to connect the disciplines of science, social studies, art, and health, given available curricular materials, district outcomes, and teacher expertise. Nancy's area of expertise is social studies, Troy's is science, and Suzy's is health.

Social Studies.   Nancy has a pretty good background in ancient civilizations. For the present unit, she's going to focus on the Roman Empire's movement throughout the Mediterranean. She will be able to focus in part on trade routes, commerce, and the transmission of Greco-Roman culture throughout the Mediterranean. (Social studies requires a good deal of expository reading by the students, which is particularly difficult. It would be appropriate for all team members to use a comprehension procedure—for instance, K-W-L, which was discussed in Chapter 6—in the language arts setting.)

Science.   Troy has decided to do a unit on oceanography. The content fits with our district outcomes in that he will explore relationships between a marine environment and all sorts of creatures. There are a bunch of opportunities to connect with mathematics, including graphing the ocean floor via echo sounding and determining the speed of sound in various environments.

Art.   I'm responsible for art instruction. Our art instruction includes teaching students to use lines in a variety of ways. Students are asked to use contour drawing and abstract and impressionist techniques to represent the world. I've found that still photographs of marine creatures taken from various periodicals serve as good prompts for drawing. In the past, my classroom has drawn huge murals made up of both living and nonliving things in an ocean environment as a culminating activity.

Health.   Connecting health to other content areas has always been a stretch for our team. Suzy has agreed to do health the past several years. Sometimes she is able to make connections, but in this case the topic of the sea fails to inspire her. As her colleagues are at a loss to make thematic connections between health and the sea, she will be out of the loop this time around. She will likely have greater success when we pursue other themes, perhaps challenges, for example.

In trying to find connections between theme and subject areas, we have learned something that Sean Walmsley (1996, p. 54) stresses: "Don't try to integrate every subject area into every theme." Sometimes there are important connections, and sometimes not. We try to concentrate on connections that really make sense. Walmsley offers some other tips about theme teaching that I'd like to pass along:

- When you teach a theme, tuck the skills inside it.
- Balance teacher-generated and student-generated themes.
- Avoid cutesy treatment of themes.
- Draw themes from a variety of arenas—concepts, content areas, current events, people, the calendar.
- Make sure your themes are the right size.
- Approach year-long and schoolwide themes with caution.
- Bump up your own knowledge of the themes you're preparing.
- Teach a theme twice (to a different group of students) to recoup your investment in it.
- Borrow theme ideas from others.

Although writing thematic units can be hard work and time consuming, we have found the process of planning together to be fruitful and stimulating and the results rewarding.

3:00—Homeroom and School Logs

All of our students have school logs. At the end of each day, I ask students to write down what happened over the course of the day. The purpose of the activity is to give them an opportunity to reflect on learning, to have a written record to communicate to parents, and to note any assignments or other tasks that will be due. This can be difficult unless you really make it a vital part of your classroom culture.

AFTERWORD

These classroom portraits of Jenna LeBlanc, Dolores Puente, and David Carberry illustrate, of course, only three of the many possible ways literacy instruction might be implemented in similar elementary school classrooms. You, of course, will develop a unique program of your own to fit the needs and interests of the particular group of students and the school and community in which you teach.

There is a song from a Broadway musical with lines that go something like "Bit by bit, putting it together, we can make a work of art." Although, the lyricist is alluding to a musical production, in many ways a teacher, along with his or her students, plays every role in the ongoing production of classroom instruction—playwright, producer, actor, audience, and critic. What they produce together, with the help of many stagehands and with hard work, energy, commitment, laughter, and sometimes tears, is a work of art whose value is measured by the degree to which the lives of those who had a hand in its creation are enriched and empowered.

We wish you a great deal of success and satisfaction as you pursue a career that we believe is second to none in its potential to have an impact on individual lives, which in turn in will affect the lives of others. We close with the words of the great French novelist Gustave Flaubert, which were written in the mid–19th century but are still true as we near the end of the 20th century and will be even truer in the 21st century:

Read in order to live.

With all best wishes,

Michael Graves
Connie Juel
Bonnie Graves

REFERENCES

Collier, C. C., & Redmond, L. A. (1974). Are you teaching kids to read mathematics? *The Reading Teacher*, 5, 804–808. This article discusses the importance of helping students read mathematics more efficiently and effectively.

Invernizzi, M., Juel, C., & Rosemary, C. A. (1996). A community volunteer tutorial that works. *The Reading Teacher*, 50, 304–311. This article describes a one-on-one tutorial program that promotes the literacy development of young children and involves a wide range of community volunteers.

Walmsley, S. A. (1996, August). Ten ways to improve your theme teaching. *The Instructor*, pp. 54–60. This article discusses how to choose themes and to create and manage theme teaching.

CHILDREN'S LITERATURE

Adler, D. A. (1992). *A picture book of Jesse Owens.* New York: Holiday House. This book describes Owen's life, from his birth as the son of sharecroppers, through his career as a track star and the disappointments that followed, to his death in 1980. 32 pages.

Benjamin, M. (1996). *Quack!* Needham Heights, MA: Silver Burdett Ginn. Three little baby ducks search for their mother in this Silver Burdett Ginn readable. 8 pages.

Brooks, P. S. (1990). *Beyond the myth: The story of Joan of Arc.* Boston: J. B. Lippincott. This nonfiction book portrays the life of the 15th-century French girl within the social, political, and religious context of the time in which she lived and died a martyr's death. 176 pages.

Dahl, R. (1988). *Matilda.* New York: Viking. Matilda uses her mental powers to rid her school of the evil, child-hating Miss Trunchbull and restore her beloved teacher Miss Honey to financial security. 240 pages.

Davidson, M. (1986). *I have a dream: The story of Martin Luther King, Jr.* New York: Scholastic. The life of Martin Luther King, Jr., from his childhood to his role as leader of the civil rights movement, is portrayed here. 128 pages.

Demi. (1991). *Chingis Khan.* New York: Holt. This book shows the legendary Mongol leader and military genius at the height of his power as master of the largest empire ever created in the lifetime of one man, while also revealing his emotions and weaknesses. 54 pages.

Fradin, D. B. (1992). *Hiawatha: Messenger of peace.* New York: Margaret McElderry. Illustrated with photographs, this biography details the life of the peacemaker Hiawatha, who helped create the Iroquois federation of five tribes in what is now New York. 40 pages.

Golenbock, P. (1990). *Teammates.* San Diego: Harcourt. This moving story brings to life a dramatic moment in sports history—Pee Wee Reese standing up for his Dodger teammate, Jackie Robinson, the first African American to play on a major league baseball team. 32 pages.

Koch, M. (1993). *Hoot howl hiss.* New York: Greenwillow. This story depicts sounds that animals make in the woods, by the pond, in the jungle, at the farm, and in the mountains. 32 pages.

Raskin, E. (1979). *The Westing game.* New York: Dutton. Sixteen game players, heirs to Sam Westing's fabulous fortune, are all suspected of his murder. 185 pages.

Scieszka, J. (1989). *The true story of the three little pigs.* New York: Viking. The wolf gives his version of what really happened in his encounters with the three little pigs. 32 pages.

Sobol, D. J. (1983). *Encyclopedia Brown takes the cake!* New York: Four Winds. Encyclopedia Brown solves a number of food-related mysteries. The cases and solutions are interspersed with recipes that the reader will want to try. This is one of many titles featuring this popular ten-year-old sleuth. 121 pages.

Sorenson, M. (1998). *Fight in the fields.* Des Moines, IA: Perfection Learning. Two teens time-travel back to 1966, joining Cesar Chavez and the grape boycott. They work to keep a new migrant worker from using violence against the angry growers and jeopardizing Chavez's vision for the union. 80 pages.

Sperry, A. (1960). *Call it courage.* New York: Macmillan. This is the story of Mafutu, a young island boy who overcomes his fear of the sea and proves his courage to himself and his tribe. 95 pages. Audiotape and Spanish text available.

Stanley, F. (1991). *The last princess: The story of Princess Ka'iulani of Hawai'i.* New York: Four Winds. This sympathetic portrait of Princess Ka'iulani describes her fight against the powerful U.S. government, which toppled the monarchy and annexed Hawaii in 1898. 40 pages.

Winter, J. (1991). *Diego.* New York: Knopf. In simple text, in both Spanish and English, this picture book focuses on Mexico's renowned artist and mural painter, Diego Rivera, from his childhood to early adulthood. 32 pages. Videotape available.

name index

subject index

Illiterate, 26
Imaginative writing, 413–416
Imaging, 292, 296–297
Immersion classes, 451–452
Immigrants, 436–437, 438, 439
Important information, determining
    what is, 294–295, 303
Independent reading, 292
    defined, 312, 313
    encouraging, 312–331
    establishing and maintaining a
        program, 318–319
    framework to promote reader
        response, 324–328
    literature response groups, 320–324
    providing time for, 313–314,
        318–319, 328
Inert knowledge, 61
Inferences, making, 292, 293, 294
Inferential questions, 280
Inflections, 440
Information
    background, shared, 136–137
    determining what is important,
        294–295, 303
    graphic, 292, 295
Informational texts, 8, 9
    using with second language students,
        468
Initial consonant sounds, 113
Intellectual climate, 387–389
Intelligences, 379–380
Interactive model, 11–14
    bottom-up and top-down models,
        11–12
    modular processing and, 14
    oral reading and, 13
    schema theory and, 11–12
Interest groups, 49
International Association for the Evalua-
    tion of Education (IEA), 19–20
Interviewing students, 512

Jamaica and Brianna (Havill), 3
Journals, 114–115, 325, 562
    dialogue, 403–405, 571
    double-entry, 403
    response, 401, 556–557
    types of, 401
    writing, 399–406, 545–547, 571
Junie B. Jones (Park), 45–46, 392

Kindergarten, 89, 94, 111, 113, 114, 118
    typical day in, 120–126
Kite, The (Lobel), 295
Knowledge
    active use of, 61
    attitudes and inclinations, 26, 28
    background, 234, 240, 447
    declarative, 25, 28, 29
    emerging, 87–106
    inert, 61
    language, 445–446
    metacognitive, 16, 18
    about print, 26–27, 30, 442, 446
    prior, 3, 4, 16, 234, 242, 292, 293, 378
    procedural, 25–26, 29
    retention of, 61

schemata and, 6–8, 11, 234, 240, 294
    self-, 16
    shared, 136–137
    strategy, 16
    task, 16
    text-specific, 240–242
    of text structures, 7–8, 88–90
    using for understanding, 61, 340
    of word structures, 90–95
    of the world and its conventions, 6–7
Knowledge as design, 352–362, 510
    categories of questions, 356
    closure, 357
    continued work with, 357–362
    leading a design conversation,
        355–362, 359–360
    principles of, 352
    topics for, 354–355, 358
Known concepts, learning new words
    that represent, 190, 193–194
Know-Nothings, 437–438
Known words
    clarifying and enriching the meanings
        of, 190, 196–199
    learning to read, 189, 193
K-W-L, 271–273, 397–399

Language arts, 554, 572
Language experience, 158–159
Language-experience activities, 115–116
Language-experience approach, 115–116
Latin word roots, 205, 207
Learning
    active, 52–53
    cooperative, 652
    discovery, 53
    social, 62
    writing and, 394, 395–403
    zone of proximal development, 56–57
Learning logs, 402
Learning standards, 504
Learning to Read: The Great Debate
    (Chall), 151
Learning web, 23
Lessons, 482–483
Letter cards, 172
Letter puppets, 101
Letters, 143
Letters, writing, 406–408
Letter-sound activities, 112
Letter-sound correspondences, 160–180
Leveled books, 160
Lexicon of a language, 441
Life in the Rainforests (Baker), 363–366
Limited English Proficient, 435. *See also*
    Second language students
Linguistic diversity, 439
Linguistic terms and concepts, 440–441
Linguistic unity, 439
Listening, easier than reading, 136–137
Listening comprehension, 118
Listening opportunities, 118–120
Literacy
    books to foster, 92
    critical, 21–23
    definition of, 21
    emerging, reading instruction for, 92,
        107–128, 440

environment for, 45, 48
    in the first language, 446
    fostering, 45
    present-day, 21–23
    program, 564
    see also Critical literacy; Critical
        literacy curriculum
Literate environment, 45–48, 75, 95,
    107–108, 188, 387
Literature, connecting to life, 44–45
Literature-based approaches, 67, 68, 69,
    70, 71, 72, 73, 149–150
Literature circles, 321–323
Literature response groups, 49, 320–324
Literature Works, 160
Long-vowel patterns, 174–175

Mailboxes, 118
Main idea, 343
Mamma Bear (Sun), 9–10
Maps, 296
    semantic, 196, 197, 277, 298,
        397–399
    story, 268–270, 566–567, 573
Massachusetts, 63–64
Metacognition, 16–18, 297, 312
Metacognitive knowledge, 16
    in the classroom, 18
Mitten (Tresselt), 84–85, 86
Modeling, 45–46, 115, 203, 209, 303
    cognitive, 59–60
    diction, 213–217
    letter-writing, 407
    as a writer, 388
Modular processing, 14
Morning meeting, 537, 552, 572
Morphemes, 141–142
Morphology, 440
Motivation
    fostering, 40–48, 555
    reading purpose and, 228
    to use comprehension strategies, 302,
        311
Motivational activities, 239
Multicultural books, 93
Multiple-choice format, 489–490
Multisyllabic words, 145, 171–178,
    176–177
Music
    books that invite connections, 260
    to develop oral language skills, 469
    responding to selections through, 258,
        259
Myths, 93

Narrative texts
    comprehension of, 28, 231, 265–270
    guided reading for, 249
    purpose of, 270
    structure of, 7, 88, 231
National Assessment of Educational
    Progress (NAEP), 19–20, 26, 340
Nelson-Denny reading test, 506
New concepts
    learning new words that represent,
        190, 195–196
    using the Frayer method to teach, 196
New England Primer, 64